HUMAN SEXUALITY

Human Sexuality

Zella Luria
Tufts University

Susan Friedman

Mitchel D. Rose

JOHN WILEY & SONS

New York Chichester Brisbane Toronto Singapore

To Salva, to Harris, and to Karen

Cover and frontispiece art: Henri Matisse, Dance I,
1931–1932, 11'8½" × 42'1",
oil on canvas, The Musée d'Art Moderne
de la Ville de Paris. © by SPADEM 1986.

Cover and interior design: Kevin J. Murphy
Production Manager: Jan M. Lavin
Production Supervisor: David S. Smith
Copy Editors: Jane Hanley
Susan Giniger
Photo Editor: Dana Dolan
Photo Researcher: Maura Grant
Illustration Supervisor: John Balbalis
Positional Drawings: Robert Reynolds

Library of Congress Cataloging in Publication Data:

Luria, Zella, 1924–
  Human sexuality.

  Includes index.
  1. Sex instruction. 2. Hygiene, Sexual.
I. Friedman, Susan, 1947–   . II. Rose, Mitchel D.,
1945–   . III. Title. [DNLM: 1. Psychosexual
Development. 2. Sex. 3. Sex Behavior. 4. Sex
Disorders. 5. Sex Offenses. 6. Venereal Diseases.
HQ 21 L967h]

HQ35.2.L87 1987   613.9'5   86-22629
ISBN 0-471-88653-X

Printed in the United States of America

10 9 8 7 6 5 4 3 2 1

Preface

This book is the product of an ideal collaboration among Zella Luria, a developmental psychologist, Susan Friedman, a professional writer, and Mitchel D. Rose, a physiological psychologist now in private clinical practice.

We have had two major goals in presenting our version of human sexuality. First, we have wanted to help you, the reader, evaluate the credibility and accuracy of what we or anyone else offers as the facts of life. Because we think this evaluative process is so important, we have devoted an entire chapter, early in the book, to the methods of research in human sexuality, Chapter 2. Where material in this book has come from scientific investigations, we encourage you to accept, question, or—most importantly—to refute it, depending on its accuracy and credibility. Where material is opinion or advice, we make that clear and invite you to accept or reject it.

Our second goal is to help you to negotiate your anxieties over sexual matters. We assume that all readers (and writers and instructors) of sexual information will react with strong feelings to some of the topics in this book. At best, those feelings can be channeled usefully—and never extinguished—if you will explore the sexual perspectives of many other minds: minds of the other sex, from across the world, throughout history, among those in different stages of development or of different sexual tastes. We encourage you to see that your feelings about sexual matters often do not lead to firm, fixed, comfortable conclusions.

In pursuing these goals, we have organized the book as follows to cover the major areas in human sexuality:

- The foundations of sexuality in history, culture, and their attendant values.
- The physical bases of human sexual functions, as well as contraceptive methods to intercept reproduction.
- Life-span development of sexuality.
- Widespread personal problems in human sexuality and, where available, solutions.
- The social and cultural devices for dealing with the social problems that

sexuality poses, as viewed from the standpoint of the individual, the society, and the law.

We have included a number of features that we hope will be useful to our readers. They are rooted in our experience of team-teaching human sexuality courses.

- Up-to-dateness: the book is up to date on common sexually transmitted diseases—chlamydia, herpes, AIDS—and includes the latest work on the changing nature of the family. Chapter 4, "Gender Roles," includes the latest government information.

- Special and current coverage on the relationship between biological factors and gender.

- Extended attention to the data base for the relation between early and later gender roles and sexuality.

- Historical and anthropological coverage of human sexuality, as an introduction to the book, to help teachers show how sexual values are embedded in history and culture. We pay special attention to modern contrasts, such as between China and Sweden.

- A lifespan focus: two chapters are devoted to sexual development through the lifespan. New work on children of school age, the middle aged and those over 80 is discussed.

- Researchers in sexuality: two interviews, one with Sherry Ortner, an anthropologist, and one with Julian Davidson, a physiologist, are included in which these distinguished researchers talk about their current work and how they first came to do research.

- An Afterword that we hope will challenge you: based on one week's newspaper articles on sexual topics, the Afterword asks you how you would assess the information, now that you have taken a course in human sexuality. How will you use what you have learned?

- Interdisciplinary focus: we have sought to deal with issues in the theory and practice of human sexuality from psychology, biology, sociology, and health sciences. Lawyers, physicians, epidemiologists, physiologists, endocrinologists, demographers, and economists all have helped us. Their traces are visible in the interdisciplinary range of this book.

We are indebted to many people who shared with us their knowledge and their research. Zella Luria owes a special debt to the Rockefeller Foundation for their hospitality in August, 1982, at the Villa Serballoni in Bellagio, Italy; to Stanford University's psychology department, especially Eleanor Maccoby and Carol Jacklin; and to Stanford's Center for Research on Women, and Marilyn Yalom in particular, for access to research on sexuality in fields outside of psychology. A special thanks also to Julian Davidson who invited Zella into his course on the physiology of sex. We also thank the many reviewers and respondents who read and criticized the manuscript and who helped us to focus it. Any errors that remain are ours alone, and not those of our generous colleagues. We thank the people who put up with long conversations about disagreements. In the end, we have had to make judgment calls about where we saw the evidence pointing most strongly. We thank:

Susan Baker

Grace Baruch

Frank Beach

Kathleen Camara-Ryan

Ruth Clifford

John Conklin

Julian W. Davidson

Carol Dweck

Joseph DeBold

Deirdre English

David Finkelhor

Maria Luisa Flaherty, M.D.

Michael Fleming

Estelle Freedman

Harris Friedberg

Richard Green, M.D.

Susan Griffin

Eleanor W. Herzog

Candace Howes

Martha Kirkpatrick, M.D.

Elissa Koff

Morris Lipton, M.D.

S.E. Luria, M.D.

Thelma McCormack

Robert Meade

Heino Meyer-Bahlburg

Stephan Morse, Esq.

Sherry Ortner

Joseph Pleck

Seymour Reichlin, M.D.

Jeffrey Z. Rubin

Marilyn Safir

Linda Sagor, M.D.

S. Bruce Schearer

Arlene Skolnick

Walter Swap

David Swinney

Barrie Thorne

Catherine Triantifilou, Esq.

Louise Tyrer, M.D.

Harriet Whitehead

Beatrice Whiting

and the librarians at Stanford University Medical School, Tufts University, and the Massachusetts Institute of Technology

Zella Luria
Susan Friedman
Mitchel D. Rose

Academic Advisors

Paul Abramson, Ph.D.
University of California, Los Angeles

Lynda Anderson, Ph.D.
University of North Carolina at
Chapel Hill

Wayne Anderson
University of Missouri, Columbia

Joseph L. Audah
Ohio University, Belmont

Dale Beckman
Arapahoe Community College

Philip A. Belcastro
Borough of Manhattan Community
College

M. Betsy Bergen
Kansas State University

Paul Bishop, Ph.D.
Northern Kentucky University

Ruth Blanche
Montclair State College

Iver Bogen
University of Minnesota

Robert Bowen
UW-Stevens Point

Betty C. Boyle
Pasadena City College

F. Robert Brush
Purdue University

Dr. T. Jean Byrne
Kent State University

Paul Cambeil
Hofstra University

Chwee Lye Chng, Ph.D.
North Texas State University

Sarah Cirese
The Marin Community Colleges

Mona Coates, Ph.D.
Orange Coast College

Eva E. Conrad
San Bernadino Valley College

Dr. Joseph F. DeBold
Tufts University

John DeLamater
University of Wisconsin, Madison

Judy Drolet
Southern Illinois University

Karen G. Duffy
State University of New York,
Geneseo

Garland M. Embrey
WLA College

Gene Ezell
University of Tennessee
at Chattanooga

Frederick P. Gault, Ph.D.
Western Michigan University

Carol Gay
Fitchburg State College

Dr. Thomas A. Gentry
California State College, Stanislaus

Alberta S. Gilinsky
University of Bridgeport

Ronald Goldstein, Ph.D.
Bucks County Community College

Michael Gonzales, Ph.D.
University of California, Irvine

Judith B. Greenberg
San Diego State University

Marshall S. Haith
Ramapo College of New Jersey

Curtis P. Hinckley
University of Lowell

Dr. Wayne B. Holder
California State University

Betty M. Hubbard
University of Central Arkansas

Karen Huffman
Palomar College

Paul A. Huizenga
Grand Valley State College

Frederick G. Humphrey
University of Connecticut

Jeanne A. Jacobsen
University of South Dakota

Louis H. Janda
Old Dominion University

Luther T. Jansen
Tacoma Community College

Don Jensen
University of Colorado

Richard A. Kaye
Kingsborough Community College

Bonnie Kellogg
California State University,
Long Beach

Mark Kittleson
Youngstown State University

Marvin A. Klavons
Highland Park Community College

David M. Klein
University of Notre Dame

Edward W. Klink, M.D.
Northern Illinois State University

Beverly J. Kukowski
Drake University

Eugene E. Levitt, Ph.D.
Indiana University School of Medicine

Elizabeth M. Lion
Indiana University

Jim W. Lochner
Weber State College

Dr. Joseph LoPiccolo
Texas A&M University

Norma L. McCoy
San Francisco State University

Joseph A. McFalls, Jr.
Temple University

Stephen Maltz
Chabot College

Mary Mautz
Ohio University, Athens

Ron Mazur
University of Massachusetts
at Amherst

Naomi Beth McCormick
State University of New York-
Plattsburgh

Helen Mountain
Lakewood Community College

Dan Murphy
Creighton University

Monroe Pastermack
Diablo Valley College

Valerie Pinhas
Nassau Community College

Ollie Pocs
Illinois State University

Stephen A. Poffel
University of Idaho

Elizabeth Powell
St. Louis Community College,
Meramec

Phyllis J. Priest
Southwestern Community College

Laura Rubinson
University of Illinois

Contents in Brief

CONTENTS

PART II
SEX AND GENDER

PART III
THE BIOLOGICAL PERSPECTIVE

PART IV
SEXUAL DEVELOPMENT AND ORIENTATION

PART V
SEXUAL PROBLEMS AND SOLUTIONS

PART VI
SOCIAL AND CULTURAL ISSUES

Special
Features

Chapter 20

PART I
INTRODUCTION

ROBERT DELAUNAY, "PLAN FOR THE AIR PAVILLION: HELIX AND RHYTHM." COURTESY NATIONAL MUSEUM OF MODERN ART, PARIS.

Chapter 1

Sexual Values across Cultures

SEX AND SEXUALITY

By the time that most people in our society reach adolescence, they know pretty well what **sex** is. It is the coming together of two people—or two dogs, or other animals—to copulate and perhaps to produce offspring. Except for the simplest forms of life—bacteria or viruses—all living organisms reproduce sexually. Each offspring begins with the fusion of two **germ cells**, one from a male and one from a female, into a single cell that grows and develops into a new individual. Even in plants like pears or oaks, in which each flower has both male and female germ cells, each fertile seed is the sum of a male and a female germ cell. Sex is everywhere in the living world. Its function is essential to life.

Children are never exact copies of their parents. They are unique mixtures of their mother's and father's features, for each germ cell—the father's **sperm** and the mother's **ovum**—contributes one copy of each of the thousands of **genes** that determine each individual's physical functions and features. To each child, parents contribute an assortment of the genes they inherited from their own parents. Exactly which assortment is decided by chance—the reason that each of us is unique. Heredity is thus a true and equal participation by both sexes in the creation of offspring. The more diverse the individuals within a species, the greater the species' chances of surviving to reproduce offspring should natural forces threaten their survival. Natural evolution, driven by diversity, is driven by sexual reproduction. The human species is subject to another kind of evolution—**cultural evolution**. Although sex itself has probably changed very little since human history began (fewer than 100 centuries ago), sexuality *has* changed. Over time, people's ideas and values about sexuality have changed as human **cultures** have changed. Many concepts, rules, and laws about sexual practices mark changes and developments in human history.

People in different societies attach different meanings and values to aspects of sexual behavior. Contrast the display of women's bodies by the Bedouin and the modern Israeli woman.

What, then, about sexuality? We human beings are unique in our brain's ability to think about sex, to color it with values and feelings, to shade it with symbolic and personal learning, to plan for it, to long for it, to regret it. The human ability to think and dream about love, kissing, "having sex" is certainly driven by biology—by the chemicals in the body that stimulate sexual desire. But human consciousness gives us the power to make of our sexual feelings and drives ideas, fantasies, poetry, shared wishes and beliefs. In human life, biological forces work in concert with cultural forces—and sex blossoms into sexuality. **Sexuality** is the totality of our human ideas about sexual relations, our sexual values, the meaning of sex, how we practice it, and even how we control or limit it.

In our society today, sexuality is both a personal and a shared, communicative experience. Sexual experience often is meaningful *because* two people unite and share something intense and intimate. People repeat aspects of sexual experience in fantasy, as they have sexual daydreams, or masturbate. In our modern world, when sexuality always is experienced as impersonal, loneliness and isolation often intensify. When sexuality is part of a relationship between caring people, it can vanquish loneliness and isolation. Sexuality is a special form of communication, with meanings that transcend the physical acts performed.

SEXUAL VALUES AND SOCIAL RULES

Some aspects of sexual behavior vary little from one society to another. People everywhere know about masturbation, sexual intercourse, ejaculation, pregnancy. But people in different societies attach different meanings and values to particular aspects of sexual behavior. As a result, in different societies people commit particular sexual acts at different rates, in different ways, and with different meanings. For example, one society may encourage pregnancy before marriage (to prove a couple's fertility), and another may condemn unwed mothers. One society may allow open and public cross-dressing, but another may restrict it to secret, private circumstances.

It is important to remember that sexual behavior and sexual values are not the same things. Thus while a particular sexual *behavior* may be value-neutral, the sexual *values* attached to it may be intensely positive or negative. Sexual behavior is biologically driven, although subject to cultural forces; sexual values are entirely cultural. All societies regulate sexual behavior, although social control is only as effective as people's acceptance of these regulations. **Sexual values** are those social rules that people internalize, those rules with important, socially shared, personal meaning.[1]

CHARACTERISTICS OF SEXUAL VALUES

We can make some generalizations about sexual values in virtually all cultures.

1 Sexual values tend to act as *regulators* of sexual behavior (if people internalize them).

---

[1]Sociologists use the term **norm** to mean a social standard or rule. We use the term *value* to mean any social standard that people internalize, and we use *internalize* to mean not just compliant acts but the attitudes consistent with that compliance.

2 Sexual values also tend to be *conservative* in that they conserve what already exists (or is believed to exist), rather than tending toward the untried or the unconventional.

3 Sexual values also tend to *favor reproduction of the species* and some form of the *family* to care for the young.

4 Sexual values in complex societies tend to *vary among the subgroups* within the societies, and changes in these subgroups can lead to changes in sexual values.

In our own society, the Judeo-Christian premium on reproduction fostered social rules that favor reproduction: biblical exhortations to "be fruitful and multiply" and condemnations of birth control or **onanism** (ejaculating outside of a woman's vagina). Similarly, sexual values favoring the traditional family are reflected in rules against divorce, extramarital affairs, and illegitimacy.

The **incest** taboo may be a universal sexual norm. Virtually all societies forbid sexual intercourse between parents and their children, and this taboo probably strengthens the family by keeping out strong sexual tensions. By sending people outside of the family to mate, the taboo also conforms to the biological principle of genetic diversity. The only formal exceptions to the taboo are allowed among people of special rank and family relationship such as royalty among the Incas, the ancient Egyptians, and the African Azande. Sibling unions are permitted in only one or two cultures studied by anthropologists, and these are also restricted to people of special social status (Ford and Beach, 1951). But people do violate rules encouraging heterosexual intercourse and the incest taboo, although societies vary greatly in the degree to which they punish these rule violations (Ford and Beach, 1951; Kinsey et al., 1953).

If we are tempted to see heterosexuality and the incest taboo as biological imperatives, we should look further. Human inventiveness has woven these "imperatives" into remarkably varied tapestries. Human explanations for these sexual events show that sexual values are the product of culture and not simply of biological evolution. They are handed down from one generation to another by agents of socialization, as part of cultural evolution.

RELIGIOUS VALUES AND SEXUAL MORALITY

Religious values often support particular sexual values. In some societies, in fact, they are inseparable. Such is the case in countries with a state religion, such as Spain, or England, or Israel; it is also the case in homogeneous religious communities, as among the Amish, or Catholic nuns, or Hasidic Jews. As Nathaniel Hawthorne (1804–1864) said about the stern New England Puritans, they were "a people amongst whom religion and law were almost identical" (*Scarlet Letter*, p. 52). Similarly, in some officially atheistic societies, the state promulgates sexual values. In the People's Republic of China, for example, it is the state that decrees rules about sexual modesty, courtship, age at marriage, and family planning. The Chinese sexual ethic is quite restrictive, and, because the state wants to limit population increase, the degree of social control is extensive. Pornographic and religious videotapes are forbidden. Public displays of affection between adults are few, and the ideal number of children in a family is one. In 1982, the age of marriage for women was moved from the sanctioned 28 or 29 to 21, an enormous liberalization. Neighborhood committees in Chinese cities not only provide contraceptives to married couples but rebuke those who have more than the acceptable number of children. Social control is less strict on farms where people marry earlier and have more children (Butterfield, 1982).

SEXUALITY IN HISTORICAL PERSPECTIVE

Historically, religions have varied enormously in their sexual standards. In Buddhism sex is, at best, a distraction from the path to inner spiritual perfection. In many non-Christian cults, sex preserves social structures through ritualized initiation practices. Many religions worship feminine fruitfulness and thereby exalt sex.

Mesopotamia and Egypt

Between 3000 B.C. and 300 B.C., the civilizations within the areas now called Egypt and Iraq—then called Mesopotamia—included the Egyptians, Assyrians, Babylonians, Sumerians, and Persians. These peoples were polytheistic, believing in many different gods, many of whom were believed to influence sexuality and fertility in some way. Many religious festivals were merged with harvest and fertility festivals. On the New Year, for example, priests and priestesses engaged in a symbolic act of sexual intercourse to ensure fertility for all. Just as the Old Testament contains a story of creation and a story of a great flood, so too do the ancient Mesopotamian and Egyptian religions. These stories contain references to the need for humans to be fertile and to reproduce themselves—to "be fruitful and multiply," as Genesis says. In sexual intercourse, the culturally prescribed position was man on top, woman below—a mirroring of their social positions. Many of these peoples worshipped a powerful female goddess, a Great Mother, who was called by various names—Astarte, Cybele, Isis—and who held power over life and fertility or their opposites, death and sterility, famine and want. Through processes mysterious to humans, the Great Mother sometimes withheld life, and so she was feared and placated.

The great, fertilizing River Nile flooded its banks each year in Egypt, ensuring that life would continue. From the records of their civilization, we learn that the early Egyptians were monogamous and concerned with the stability of the family unit. Girls married early in their teens, boys at 15 or so—soon after they reached sexual maturity. The culturally prescribed position for sexual intercourse was woman on top, man below. Papyri tell us that the Egyptians used contraceptives, most of them not especially effective, but a clue that sexual intercourse for purposes other than producing children was culturally sanctioned. Among royal families, marriage between brothers and sisters was sanctioned. Cleopatra, for example, married her two brothers. Historians are in disagreement over whether these marriages were incestuous, that is, whether they involved sexual relations between relatives.

The Early Hebrews

Unlike their neighbors, the Hebrews were monotheistic—believing in a single God—and ascribed no sexual traits to their God. Old Testament Hebrews exalted feminine chastity. God, they believed, wished humans to engage in sexual intercourse in order to multiply their numbers on earth and, in so doing, spread righteousness everywhere. Sexual acts that did not legitimately lead to procreation—masturbation, contraception, celibacy, premarital sex—were prohibited. Although intercourse outside of marriage was forbidden to both sexes, women were more severely punished for transgressing than were men. Marriages were arranged, and love was not a factor in choosing a mate. Marriages were for producing children, and sex within marriage was a joyful and sinless pleasure and duty. Adultery was a serious offense, a violation of a man's rights to his property, his property being his wife. Women were believed to have stronger sexual appetites than men—think of all the temptresses that populate the Old Testament—and women's sexuality was considered a danger to all. It was Eve, of course, who cast humans from paradise by luring Adam from God's way. Women were considered dangerous and sexually impure during certain periods, including after childbirth, during and for two weeks following menstruation.

The Greeks and Romans

One idealized sexual relationship among the early Greeks was that between an older man and an adolescent boy, in which the man taught the boy about masculinity. The relationship was not just sexual, but intellectual and emotional as well. By early adulthood, boys were expected to marry women and to form heterosexual ties. Although little historical evidence survives about the physical relations among women, Sappho, a poet from the Isle of Lesbos, wrote lyrics that survive today about the erotic love between women. From the name of her island, we get the word **lesbian**, for female homosexual. The Greeks also idealized physical beauty. Olympic athletes, for instance, participated in the games without clothing. Some Greek myths describe gods and goddesses whose power over fertility of the earth and its inhabitants resembles those of the Mesopotamians and Egyptians. In Greek cults, priests and priestesses performed sexual rites to placate powerful gods, to celebrate bounty, and to ensure fertility on earth.

The Romans disapproved of public nudity and often punished homosexual acts. Marriages were formed as economic connections between families, not as love matches. Girls could marry at 12, boys at 14, and fathers could betrothe—promise in marriage—their children virtually from birth. Rome was a large and sophisticated city, within which many people engaged in many different forms of sexual behavior. Prostitutes were easy to find. As in most large cities, Rome was fairly tolerant of the religious and sexual diversity within it.

The ancient Greeks idealized the sexual relationship between an older and a younger man, in which the older taught the younger about masculinity.

Christianity and Western Sexual Morality

Christianity has been an important force in attaching guilt to sexual acts and thoughts. The official and formalized standards of Western sexual morality essentially go back to the proclamations of early Christian saints, St. Paul in the first century after Christ and St. Augustine in the fourth century. As Augustine put it:

> *I feel that nothing so casts down the manly mind from its heights as the fondling of women and those bodily contacts which belong to the married state* (Soliloquies).

This morality informs Western legal tradition, art, and literature. Its first tenet is that sexual behavior is tinged with original sin: because Adam and Eve disobeyed God, woman would forever after bear children in pain. The second tenet is that all people are born sinners. The third is that sexual intercourse is not sinful if it is performed by husband and wife for the purpose of begetting children within a marriage sanctified by the Church (or, in a few countries since the French and American revolutions, a marriage sanctioned by the state). Finally, therefore, all other sexual practices are sinful, including heterosexual intercourse outside of marriage, homosexual acts, or masturbation. Some of these have been dealt with more harshly than others by the law as well as by the Church, in actual practice.

But early Christian sexual morality since has been violated often. At certain royal courts, for example (those of Charles II of England or Louis XIV of France), as well as among the peasantry, the violations of official moral codes were massive. But rarely did these violations take the form of anything we might label a sexual rebellion. Reformers did not call for free love to replace the codes of the Church. Sexual rebellion would come later, in our century.

IN ONE ERA, WOMEN ARE PRESUMED TO HAVE STRONGER SEXUAL APPETITE THAN MEN, AND IN ANOTHER ERA, IT IS JUST THE REVERSE.

In Britain and the American Colonies

Although all societies seem to recognize a kind of motivation that we can call "sexual appetite," even a quick look shows how ideas about sexual appetite have changed from era to era and from one society to another. Thus in one era, women are presumed to have stronger sexual appetite than men, and in another era, it is just the reverse. In England and America in the sixteenth and seventeenth centuries, it was widely believed that women had greater sexual appetites than men. Marriage manuals of the period advised the husband "to ensure his wife's faithfulness by seeing that her libidinous [sexual] urgings were never aroused" (Vann, in Degler, 1980, p. 250). The idea that women were sexually avid may have fueled the persecution of witches.

The English heritage of the American colonists is often described as being severely repressive of sexuality, and "Puritanism" has come to be synonymous with sexual repression. But, in fact, the Christian ideal of abstinence from sex probably had been muted significantly by the Puritan era. New England church records are dotted with marriages consecrated *after* a pregnancy had occurred. Little, if any, stigma was attached to these pregnancies or to the sexual desire that created them. To the Puritans, it was not improper for unmarried couples to entertain each other in bed; petting (called "bundling") and premarital intercourse were not necessarily condemned. Stigma came if a union was not sanctified by a church marriage, however.

By the late 1700s, marriage in England and America, for propertied families at least, was idealized as a marriage of companions. For example, John Adams and his wife, Abigail, had a long correspondence, in which they addressed each other as "Dear Friend." Hawthorne would consider this period one during which "every successive mother has transmitted to her child a fainter bloom, a more delicate and briefer beauty, and a slighter physical frame, if not a character of less force and solidity, than her own" (p. 52). At this time, too, romantic love was emerging as a cultural ideal and was replacing older ideas about women's strong sexual appetites. By 1780, popular novels reflected and contributed to this idealization. One consequence was that young people were less likely to be forced into marriages purely for considerations of property. Romantic love was making marriage a new kind of relationship.

By the nineteenth century, people were likely to think of men and women as equally interested in and capable of sexual responsiveness. Women were understood to desire orgasm. As a popular treatise on birth control from 1832 warned women, "The male system is exhausted in a far greater degree than the female by gratification" (C. Knowlton, cited in Degler, 1980, p. 252). Marriage manuals and medical books warned against practices such as **coitus interruptus** (in which the man withdraws his penis from the woman's vagina before he ejaculates), because these robbed a woman of sexual pleasure by ending intercourse before she was ready. The advice books tell us that the experts of the early nineteenth century saw both male and female sexuality quite positively and that striving for sexual pleasure was seen as legitimate and healthy. Although some theories of the period about the relationship of orgasm, menstruation, and conception were incorrect, much of the American literature of the first 40 years of the nineteenth century implies the legitimacy of sexuality.

The Victorian Legacy

Between about 1840 and 1860, a new literature emerges that denies and diminishes the idea of women's interest in sex. These are the sexual values that we label "Victorian." The new values seemed to describe what women were like, but in reality they told what women were *supposed* to be like. One English physician, William Acton (1813–1875), produced in 1857 a book that some people consider the epitome of Victorian sexual views. Acton asserts, for example, that well brought-up children will never entertain any "sexual impression" on mind or body. He considered masturbation—usually attributed to males—to have these unhealthy consequences:

The frame is stunted and weak, the muscles undeveloped, the eye is sunken and heavy, the complexion is sallow, pasty or covered with spots of acne, the hands are damp and cold, and the skin moist. The boy shuns the society of others, creeps about alone, joins with repugnance in the amusements of his schoolfellows. He cannot look any one in the face, and becomes careless in dress and uncleanly in person. His intellect has become sluggish and enfeebled, and if his evil habits are persisted in, he may end in becoming a drivelling idiot.

Most women were "modest," Acton's word for sexual unavailability regardless of cause. Acton saw such "modesty" as dampening male sexuality and thereby saving a husband from "spending" his semen.

Acton's prescriptions fitted into a picture of "true womanhood" that was widely circulated and probably widely believed within the emerging middle class. "True" women were pure, pious, submissive, domestic, and plainly morally superior to men. Women occupied the moral haven of the domestic sphere; men occupied the rough, not-so-moral sphere of the competitive world. Catherine Beecher, the sister of Harriet Beecher Stowe and author of a popular book on the home, told the nineteenth-century American reader that the housewife was the head of the "Christian family state" (Strasser, 1982, p. 185). As Americans settled westward, the separate spheres of the sexes were preserved as a mark of propriety and civilization. Thus even though the journey west subjected women to chores once performed by men (such as hauling water or shooting firearms) and to grueling physical hardships, frontier women resisted changing their manner of dress to one that might be more suitable to the realities of their hard lives.

In their steadfast clinging to ribbons and bows, to starched white aprons and petticoats, the women suggest that the frontier, in a profound manner, threatened their sense of social role and sexual identity (Schlissel, 1982, p. 85).

Sexual values were such that femininity was a self-conscious, refined, and sexually noble condition. Women were to be maternal but not sexual, passionate about beauty but not about joys of the flesh.

From their moral sphere, nineteenth-century British and American women effectively changed society. They increased the value and importance of children, and they changed the image and the reality of women's sexuality in marriage. It was not uncommon for women to die in childbirth or from miscarriage; many children also died of illness or accident. In the group of people between the ages of 10 and 35 in the mid-1800s, many more females than males died. Women spoke out, arguing that fewer pregnancies, longer nursing periods uninterrupted by another pregnancy, and fewer babies to care for would improve the lives of children, mothers, and families as a whole. It was an age of uncertain birth control; the alternative was to curb sexual behavior. Therefore what have been called "purity movements" arose among members of both sexes. These effectively curbed male sexuality. Thus for a variety of reasons, not the least of which were many women's—and their husbands'—wishes for a healthier and less stressful family life, ideas about the sexual appetites of both sexes changed profoundly during the late nineteenth century.

The Purity Reformers

An historian at the University of Pennsylvania, Caroll Smith-Rosenberg, has analyzed (1978) the books on sex and marriage that Americans were reading between the 1830s and 1880s and the purity movements aimed at curbing men's sexual behavior. Male evangelical reformers who praised male sexual continence flourished between the 1830s and 1860s. Women writers and reformers in the next 20 years agitated against frequent marital intercourse and early marriage. Women were to decide on the timing and frequency of sex, issues that were seen as related to women's desire for children. A man's sexual needs were to come after the needs of children. Although sex in marriage, even during the flower of Victorianism, was probably not exactly what the purity reformers wished for, there were real changes in sexual behavior. In the cities and on the frontier, the birth rate went down, and pregnancies were spaced further apart. By 1900, the death rate among males had surpassed that among females; it has stayed there ever since in this country (Degler, 1980).

Two Revolutionary Theories of Sexuality

In western Europe in the second half of the nineteenth century, two thinkers emerged whose theories of sexual development, while very different in scope, rocked the pillars of the scientific, religious, and artistic establishments of their day—and our own.

Charles Darwin and the Theory of Evolution   In 1859, an English naturalist, Charles Darwin (1809–1882), published a book that changed many people's views of the nature of life. In his *Origin of Species,* Darwin traced in the record of fossils how groups of breeding animals arose and then disappeared or were selected by the accident of their adaptation to their particular environment. Darwin saw natural selection as a blind force, unlike humans' willed selection of culturally valued traits. Darwin saw how sexual reproduction produced the genetic diversity of biological characteristics that allowed for the selection of the few favorable variations and the destruction of the many unfavorable variations.

To those who believed in an eternal natural morality, Darwin's work was a challenge. Those who held a religious view of how human uniqueness arose saw a challenge in the fossil evidence. To Darwin, the uniqueness of humans or any other animals arose from evolutionary forces. Since Darwin's time, some people have been able to reconcile their religious views with his theory, but others even today remain staunchly opposed to this powerful theory of sex and evolution.

Sigmund Freud and the Psychoanalytic Theory of Sexuality   The Viennese physician, Sigmund Freud (1856–1939), knew of Darwin's work and incorporated some of its principles into his own revolutionary theory of sexuality. To Freud, sexual and aggressive drives lie at the core of men's and women's motives. Like Darwin, he stressed the centrality of sex and the struggle for survival. Freud saw culture and sexual morality as the outer—and necessary—covers by which civilization restrains these central impulses. Freud's theory feeds more relativist views of sexuality and sees cultural controls as difficult but necessary acquisitions for modulating powerful, biologically driven sexuality. For Freud, silent, unacknowledged sexual wishes lie beneath human controls. They drive us powerfully, inexorably, and soundlessly.

Decadence and Disillusion

During the early 1850s, England, France, and Sardinia fought against Russia in the Crimean War. The lasting effect of this war was a deep, widespread disillusionment over the sickening waste of human life. In England, France, Vienna, Italy, and later in the United States, a spirit of cynicism, decadence, and world-weariness crept into art, literature, politics, and sexual values. Many people, especially the young, wanted to experiment with sensual pleasures—drugs, "free love," new kinds of poetry and decorative designs. Among the avant-garde, the wish was strong to go beyond convention and to extend the limits of experience. Just as the art and poetry, music and theater of the period broke through to new forms, moral values changed also. As Victoria's reign ended, a spirit of pleasure as good was replacing older ideas of absolute right and wrong. In a civilization that had proved itself *un*civilized, young people in many countries were ready to act out in sexual morality a variant on the Golden Rule: nothing is forbidden so long as no one gets hurt.

By the end of World War I, the old moral order was among the 5 million dead. This war was the first large-scale war *not* conducted for religious or humanitarian principles. It came to be viewed as a hypocritical operation between governments for power. The disillusion was all the greater because people had hoped that *this,* the "Great War," would be the war to end all wars. Instead, it made people feel that many social—and sexual—values were shallow. The broad challenge to traditional morality continued in the form of short skirts that showed women's legs; mass magazines in Germany and France that exhibited nudity; theater and novels that advocated free love.

The Crimean War and World War I, 75 years and three generations apart, destroyed the sexual ethic of the early saints as surely as they destroyed lives and property. The deep shift in sexual morality took the form of rebellion against an ancient Christian principle. This principle held that whatever gives pleasure is sinful, because it distracts from the only legitimate goal of life on earth: the preparation for an afterlife in heaven. Slowly, incompletely, and with conflict, the principle of sex as pleasure has reshaped the old religious principle. The law and churches have moved slowly in accepting sex as pleasure. Today, society is divided. Some groups support a broad, not fully legal, sexual freedom. Others support a not fully legal sexual restrictiveness. Religious denominations are represented in both camps.

LEARNING SEXUAL VALUES

When we are young, we learn our culture's sexual values from **agents of socialization**: parents and other relatives, teachers, religious or political leaders, and others who are authorities to us on social values. Agents of socialization may also be objects: texts or other books, billboards, television programs, and so forth. We learn sexual values about sexual play ("Do that in private, dear.") and nakedness ("Zip your fly!") and sexual intercourse ("Tell her you love her.") and pregnancy ("Don't get caught."). We learn what is "normal" (heterosexual intercourse) and what is not (sex with close relatives). We learn what society will tolerate (private homosexual relations between consenting adults) and what it will not (rape, for instance).

Much of the point of this chapter has been to show how society regulates and gives meaning to sexuality. For some people, sexual regulations are easy to accept, while for others, they induce feelings of constraint, conflict, or confusion. Young adults, sometimes caught between their parents' and peers' views, may feel conflict as they grapple with their own system of sexual values. Many parents went through similar conflicts when they were younger. Just as the social and economic roles of men and women, the risks of pregnancy, and the stability of marriage were issues that influenced adults in the nineteenth century, so do they in somewhat different form influence young adults today.

SEXUAL VALUES IN VARIOUS CULTURES

When we compare our sexual values with those of others, we learn as much about our own unexamined assumptions as we do about alien cultures. Most people are **culture-bound.** They believe that the way things are in *their* culture is the "right" and "natural" way. But as we saw earlier, few sexual norms represent biological necessities. The only exceptions probably are the norms favoring heterosexual intercourse and forbidding incest, and even these are violated often.

People in every culture engage in sexual activity, but they vary in just what they view as sexual. For example, we consider a family meal a symbol of togetherness. But in a culture where food is considered erotic, a sexually mature brother and sister may not eat together without committing "alimentary incest" (Davenport, 1976, p. 118). Extreme obesity was considered very erotic in the women of the old Hawaiian aristocracy. In Polynesia, it is sexual for a man and a woman to exchange betel nuts and pepper, but it is not sexual for brothers and sisters to do so. All cultures regulate sexual behavior—or try to—according to norms of family, property, inheritance, and marriage. Sexual rules are not random. They make perfect sense within a society.

Much of what we know about the cross-cultural meanings of sex comes from the work of male anthropologists, but as more women join the professional ranks, new evidence and new views of sexuality emerge. We are beginning to understand the sexual lives of women from other cultures, an area of understanding that has remained nearly hidden until quite recently. One young anthropologist, for instance, has published the life story of a frankly lusty woman of the !Kung, a hunter-gatherer society (Shostak, 1981). We do not know yet, however, how cultural variations in the meaning of sex actually come to be. Some are probably historical in origin. For example, in the U.S. Trust Territories of the Pacific, the people of Yap Island strongly *de*value sex. They believe that intercourse makes people weak and susceptible to illness. Sexual intercourse is taboo during pregnancy and for several years afterward. Mothers, they believe, should not be weakened by intercourse when their children need them. These rules make some sense in the context of Yapese history. Contact with Europeans early in this century brought the Yapese gonorrhea (a sexually transmitted disease) and other illnesses to which they had no immunity. Untreated gonorrhea caused sterility; the other illnesses left misery and poor health in their wake. The culture's solution: avoid sexual intercourse. The Yapese population decreased. Only after World War II did antibiotics and other treatments improve the general level of health.

Some sexual values may justify a particular balance of power between the sexes. Some value systems handle the issue of inheritance when a child's paternity is not certain. Some make sense out of other problems a culture may face, and therefore similar beliefs may crop up independently in several cultures. Some almost identical beliefs have grown up in South America and in New Guinea, for example. Sometimes views shared by several cultures point to a common cultural origin. But about the origin of certain shared beliefs, anthropologists can only speculate.

SEXUALITY IN CROSS-CULTURAL PERSPECTIVE: SEXUAL RITES—FEMALE CIRCUMCISION

When immigrants enter their new country, they carry with them the customs and values of their native culture. In some cases, these values clash with those of their new country severely enough so that the immigrants risk legal prosecution or deportation. In France, poor laborers have come from Africa to find jobs, and they have brought with them the custom of *excision,* or female circumcision (a custom practiced in about 40 countries, mostly in West and East Africa and the Arabian Peninsula). (See Figure 5.3, page 132, for the structures in the female external genitals.) Excision may consist of a simple nicking of the clitoral hood, but it may also be as extensive as the removal of all the external genitals. Performed by a child's relative or by a professional (and in some cases botched), the practice has angered some western Europeans, especially those who have seen the damage done to improperly excised children. The practice is outlawed in Scandinavia and Kenya. In France, the parents of a Malian baby who died after an excision were tried on charges of criminal negligence. Although England has no law against it, the Royal College of Obstetricians has called excision "barbaric, futile, and illogical."

Yet to those who defend the custom, the Westerners are culture-bound and ignorant. A Malian workers' group in Paris has protested that the French government must "guarantee our rights to live according to our customs," and a delegation from Upper Volta marched out of a world conference of the U.N. Decade for Women in 1980 rather than debate the rite of excision.

The Westerner may consider the removal of a female's organs of sexual pleasure brutal and the epitome of degrading attitudes toward women. Yet to the African or Middle Easterner, the ancient practice (which did not originate in Islam, contrary to widespread belief) fully feminizes a girl by removing the "male" clitoris and makes her ready for sexual life. It is presumed to dampen a woman's excessive sexual desire, although it is not believed to interfere with her sexual pleasure in marriage. Circumcision is also valued purely as a family custom. It protects a woman's modesty and chastity and ensures her value as a wife. The uncircumcised woman, in some places, is unlikely to attract a husband, a severe consequence in sexually segregated societies where women are defined by their roles as wife and mother. Said one Egyptian woman:

For example, many cultures believe that menstrual blood pollutes or weakens men. In these cultures, menstruating women are isolated; rules govern the avoidance of women's blood or even symbols of women's blood. Men in some of these cultures scratch and bleed from the penis to expel the "remnants" of "female blood." Yet we still do not know *why* some cultures find women dangerous and others do not (Bamberger, 1974).

We are circumcised and insist on circumcising our daughters so that there is no mixing between a male and a female. The woman must be truly female, and the man must be male. Every woman must be circumcised in order not to be oversexed and constantly in a state of excitement. . . . This is our custom; our boys and girls must get circumcised. We don't want our girls to be like men. Men derive pleasure only from circumcised women. . . . It is shameful not to be circumcised. We are not foreigners; only foreigners do not get circumcised (Assaad, 1980, pp.12, 13).

Based on "A Sexual Rite on Trial," *Newsweek,* November 1, 1982, p. 55; and Assaad, M. B. "Female Circumcision in Egypt: Social Implications, Current Research and Prospects for Change," *Studies in Family Planning,* January 1980, pp. 3–16.

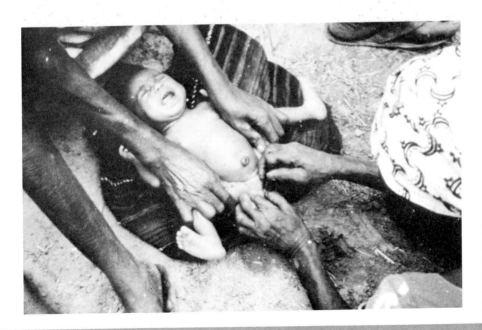

In Upper Volta, a baby girl is placed on a ceremonial cloth and circumcised. Her clitoris, labia minora, and part of her labia majora are excised with a scalpel.

Sexual Intercourse

Sexual intercourse is common to all cultures and subject to many rules. Even though the values surrounding intercourse vary enormously, it remains among the dominant forms of sexual behavior in virtually all cultures.

THE PROPER CIRCUMSTANCES   Most cultures have sexual norms governing the circumstances within which intercourse can occur. Humans are extremely inventive on this topic. Some cultures perform intercourse in the family dwelling; others perform it outside. Some couples require complete privacy; others perform in the presence of children who share their sleeping quarters. Even in our society, wedded to sexual privacy, some couples have intercourse in front of pornographers, sex researchers, friends, or even theater audiences. The variations are many: lights on, lights off; clothes on, clothes off; during menstruation, never during menstruation; during pregnancy and right afterward, never during those times; always before athletic events, never before athletic events. Intercourse may be forbidden

The !Kung are a hunter-gatherer society, and we—in our very different society—are just beginning to understand their sexual lives.

during periods of mourning for close relatives; for the ill, wounded, or deformed; before hunting, fishing, farming, or combat; for medical, social, legal, religious, ceremonial, and occupational reasons. The norm for most societies, however, seems to be intercourse at night for young people, except during forbidden periods (Ford and Beach, 1951).

THE PROPER PARTNER   Cultures also make social rules about who may have intercourse with whom. According to the *Kama Sutra*, the world's oldest sex manual, a man is forbidden intercourse with: a woman of higher caste, a woman too dark or too fair, a woman who publicly shows affection for a man, a woman who is a friend, a lunatic, or a leper. In Judeo-Christian law, one of the Ten Commandments forbids a man to have intercourse with a married woman. Virtually every society has a written or traditional code that regulates acceptable partners for intercourse.

HOW OFTEN   Frequencies of intercourse vary widely within and among societies. The Dani of New Guinea, as we will see, have very low rates of intercourse. Cayapa Indian men of Ecuador may brag that they have intercourse as often as twice a week when they are in their twenties, yet the young Aranda of Australia may have intercourse three to five times every night. During the 1930s and 1940s in the United States, some young men reported an average of more than 3 acts of intercourse every day with their wives.

FOR HOW LONG   How long intercourse lasts also varies. In the Balinese culture of Oceania, people believe that prolonged intercourse deforms children, and so they avoid it. The Kinsey survey (1948) in the United States determined that intercourse usually ended when the man ejaculated. About three-quarters of all men reached orgasm within two minutes, and a "not inconsiderable number" reached orgasm within one minute after intercourse began.

Usually the duration of intercourse is socially rather than biologically shaped. For example, most lower-class men studied in the 1930s and 1940s did not want intercourse to last any longer than two minutes. But more upper-class men did want longer intercourse and therefore more often achieved it. In our culture, the "sexual revolution" of the 1960s ushered in the expectation that in intercourse,

TABLE 1.1
Premarital Intercourse Across Cultures

Male coital behavior	Percent of cultures showing the pattern
Universal or almost so; almost all males engage in premarital coitus.	60
Not uncommon for males to engage in premarital coitus	18
Occasional; some males engage in premarital coitus but this is not common or typical.	10
Uncommon; males rarely or never engage in premarital coitus.	12
Female coital behavior	
Universal or almost so; almost all females engage in premarital coitus.	49
Not uncommon for females to engage in premarital coitus.	17
Occasional; some females engage in premarital coitus but this is not typical or common.	14
Uncommon; females rarely or never engage in premarital coitus.	20

TABLE 1.1

A survey of 186 cultures showed these patterns of premarital intercourse among men and women.

longer is better, and sex manuals and therapies began to reflect this attitude. In a more recent survey, however, some women complained that long intercourse made them feel less aroused and more uncomfortable. There may be limits to the longer-is-better trend in this country (Hite, 1976).

THE NUMBER OF POSITIONS HUMANS CHOOSE FOR INTERCOURSE REVEALS US TO BE THE MOST INVENTIVE OF ANIMALS.

FAVORED POSITIONS   The number of positions humans choose for intercourse reveals us to be the most inventive of animals. Most animals copulate in one position. Even the other primates cannot touch us for variety of positions. The *Kama Sutra* lists over 35 positions, each named poetically: "the Bamboo Cleft," "the Lotus," and "the Union of the Elephant with His Mates." Despite the variety, in practice people from each culture favor one or two positions (Gebhard, 1971) and substitute others for expediency or for special physical conditions like pregnancy or obesity. In our culture the most common position is probably the woman lying on her back (supine) and the man lying on top of her. Even in the United States, intercourse in positions besides this one has been illegal in some states. People do, of course, use other positions. The woman on top of the man is also popular in this culture. In some cultures, the most common position is to lie side by side, and sometimes even the proper side for each sex is prescribed by convention.

Sexual Behavior and Gender Roles in Other Cultures

Anthropologists have compiled excellent information on the habits and conventions of other cultures in their **ethnographies** (literally, "writings about nations"). By going to live with another group and recording what they see and hear about its customs, anthropologists can see patterns of behavior both unique and shared. One of the greatest anthropologists of this century was Margaret Mead. She conducted three early studies of gender roles in other cultures.

MARGARET MEAD'S SEX AND TEMPERAMENT   Even before her classic, *Sex and Temperament in Three Primitive Societies* (1935), was published, social scientists knew that societies varied widely in defining the behaviors considered feminine and masculine. Margaret Mead's fieldwork in New Guinea verified it. She found two societies that minimized the differences between the sexes. Mead observed that among the Arapesh, males and females showed a gentleness and nurturance toward others that would, by our values, seem feminine. In contrast, she observed among the Mundugumor that both males and females seemed, by our values, personally and sexually masculine, aggressive, and minimally nurturant. In a third society, the Tshambuli, Mead found gender roles that, by our standards, would seem inverted, with males being quiet, dependent, and sexually undemanding, and females assertive, impersonal, and sexually aggressive. Thus Mead found these three cultures making gender distinctions, but distinctions very different from those that prevail in Western societies. Anthropologists still find great variety in the definition of gender roles and especially in the relation of gender roles to sexual behavior, marriage, and the productive adult life. Despite criticism of

Mead's work on adolescence in Samoa (Freeman, 1983), no one has challenged her work on gender roles.

More recent studies than Margaret Mead's of other cultures' sexual behavior and values show that they extend from strict and repressive to lenient and permissive. Below we take examples along the whole continuum: a repressive northern European culture and a permissive Scandinavian culture; primitive cultures that range from the very permissive to the sexually indifferent. In all, it is important to remember that these accounts describe the dominant gender roles rather than the inevitable, tolerated exceptions.

Inis Beag: Sexual Repression

The Irish island of Inis Beag has about 350 inhabitants. Between 1958 and 1966, when they were studied, the people were mostly poor and engaged in agriculture (Messenger, 1971). Late marriage and abstinence were the rule, with men marrying at about age 36, women at about 25. The people did not accept love as a reason for marriage. The average family had seven children. The people of Inis Beag were devout Catholics, although the folk cultures mixed Catholicism and older, pagan beliefs. Fear of the evil eye, of damnation, and of gossip were important forms of social control.

> FOR A WOMAN TO HAVE AN ORGASM WAS CONSIDERED "DEVIANT" AND WAS RARE, ALTHOUGH FEMALE TOURISTS HAD BEEN KNOWN TO SHOW THIS "STRANGE" BEHAVIOR.

On Inis Beag, men were believed to have more sexual appetite than women, because the men consumed more potatoes. Women "endured" sex as a marital "duty," and intercourse involved little foreplay. For a woman to have an orgasm was considered "deviant" and was rare, although female tourists had been known to show this "strange" behavior.

The men believed (incorrectly) that intercourse wears them down, and they refrained from sex before any job requiring hard work. Menstruating women were considered dangerous to men. Nudity, urination, and defecation were considered shameful and intensely private. There was no tradition of sexual jokes: at most the people attempted weak sexual puns. Children were sexually segregated in school, play, and church, and sexual segregation pervaded adult life as well.

An important religious theme was the exercise of self-control over passion. Aspects of sexuality such as nudity, masturbation, body touching, sexual slang, or references to sexual states such as pregnancy or menstruation were sources of embarrassment, gossip, and censure. Inis Beag was a culture of sexual repression and wide presumed differences in the sexual appetites of men and women.

The Bala: Intermediate Sexual Freedom

Different from Inis Beag are the standards, meanings, and attitudes toward sexual behavior among the African Bala. A. P. Merriam (1971) studied a Bala village of 240 permanent residents between 1959 and 1960. Because the Bala are more sexually permissive than the people of Inis Beag, and because they attach less shame to sexual behavior, it was probably easier for anthropologists to learn about Bala sexual behavior and to recognize subtleties in their sexual attitudes. For instance, the sexual folklore and songs of the Bala provide subtle distinctions about discrepancies between rules and behavior, but because the people of Inis Beag talked reluctantly about sex informally with anthropologists, their folk sources were less available for analysis.

Most Bala villagers were engaged in agriculture and fishing, but the village also contained about 25 storekeepers, their families and several transients. Like the people of Inis Beag, the Bala sharply differentiate gender roles. There are female occupations and male occupations, and people who publicly cross these boundaries are considered strange. Women are considered men's subordinates, although people are aware that a man's authority may diminish after many years of marriage.

The Bala approve of nakedness among groups of the same sex and disapprove of it in mixed groups. However, the Bala accept transgressions of this rule far more readily than people of Inis Beag accept discrepancies between rules and behavior. For instance, everyone in the Bala culture knows that young boys have looked at the elaborate design-markings on women's bodies. But it is still considered improper for boys to look at naked women or girls. The Bala accept nakedness for intercourse of husband and wife, but the Bala are modest about nakedness, urination, and defecation.

Unlike the culture of Inis Beag, the Bala tolerate children masturbating, and group masturbation among boys is widely acknowledged. A little girl masturbates with her fingers and later with a plant root. But masturbation, like nudity, is not for mixed-sex groups.

Male circumcision takes place when boys are between 7 and 12 years old, although the circumcision rite does not seem to be accompanied by sexual education. Girls' body markings, made of scar tissue, have sexual significance, but they do not form part of a rite of passage to adulthood, as boys' circumcision does. Fondling of the scars is part of sexual foreplay to intercourse, a good example of how cultures can determine cues for sexual arousal.

The desirable woman is described as having breasts "bigger than your hand" and a graceful walk. Males are the aggressors in courtship, but the Bala know that women cooperate in being "caught." Ideally, marriage partners are physically alike: fat marries fat, tall marries tall, and so on. Premarital sex is the rule, and virginity at marriage is not an issue. Girls engage in sex play even before they reach puberty. The Bala value intercourse because it brings both children and pleasure. Although males are said to initiate intercourse (as their god has decreed), women are said to enjoy it also, although women are supposed to be modest about expressing that enjoyment. (These beliefs are closer to our own than to those of Inis Beag.)

Bala foreplay involves mutual caressing of the whole body. Kissing is not universal, although some people do kiss. They kiss breasts and, more rarely, penises; vulvas are not kissed. The preferred position in intercourse is for the man to lie on the right side and the woman on the left. Some couples have intercourse with the man atop the woman, but other positions are considered odd and are not used.

Adultery with a married person is considered a serious transgression, although adultery by either sex is considered inevitable if a spouse is absent for a long time.

In such a situation, the adultery is not considered harmful if no child results from the relationship. Even so, a double standard does prevail in the rules about adultery: adultery by a woman but not by a man is grounds for divorce. Information gathered from a small number of Bala men show that adultery by men accounts for about 10 percent of sexual intercourse.

What we see quite clearly from Merriam's work among the Bala is how a society can have, on the one hand, strict rules about approved sexual behavior but, on the other hand, make allowances for deviations from those rules.

Mangaia: Extreme Sexual Permissiveness

A very different set of rules about sexual behavior and gender roles exists among the Polynesian culture of Mangaia, a culture that is sexually very permissive but that nonetheless has rather strict standards of public friendship and intimacy. Mangaia is in the South Pacific, at the southernmost part of the Cook Islands in central Polynesia. D. S. Marshall, the anthropologist who studied the Mangaians between 1951 and 1958 (Marshall, 1971), found a culture of sexual permissiveness and freedom, one at the opposite end of an imaginary continuum from Inis Beag's repression.

Boys and girls are separated after age 3 or 4, and it is considered immodest for older children to mingle with those of the other sex. Young, uncircumcised boys can acceptably go about naked. Sexual jokes in single-sex groups are widely enjoyed and give much-appreciated spice to life. Privately, great sexual freedom is allowed and encouraged. It is assumed that young children will masturbate, a practice that is accepted if the children masturbate privately. Public expressions of sexual interest among young people—smiling at one another, giving gifts, or holding hands—are considered immodest and impolite. Privately and informally, however, the young adults engage in varied and intense sexual intercourse that the adults close their eyes to.

THE MANGAIANS STRESS PHYSICAL PLEASURE IN SEXUAL INTERCOURSE, PLEASURE THAT MAY BE FOLLOWED BY AFFECTION BETWEEN PARTNERS.

The Mangaians stress physical pleasure in sexual intercourse, pleasure that may be followed by affection between partners. The reverse, with affection preceding pleasure, they consider unlikely and a strange notion. Children of about 8 learn from one another where babies come from, and boys of 13 or 14 are taught techniques of sexual pleasure by older women. Older women also instruct girls of the same age about sexual techniques. Thereafter boys and girls have intercourse with many different partners, and the emphasis in foreplay is to make "every part of the body move." Thus hip movement is sexually arousing as are the "wet" sounds of intercourse. For a woman to be sexually passive is considered unerotic, inconsistent with her training, and therefore deviant.

Couples use many different positions for intercourse. Orgasm is universal for both sexes. When told that some western women do not regularly have orgasms in intercourse, Mangaians responded with great concern about the probable injury to the women's health. Mangaian boys know that the girls judge and compare them as sexual partners, and boys are taught to avoid ejaculating until a woman has climaxed two or three times and to reach orgasm simultaneously with the woman's final orgasm. Boys in their teens and twenties have intercourse several times every night. In their thirties and forties, men may begin to "miss" some nights, especially if they are married. Erection problems among young men are relatively rare and, given the importance of sexual expression, difficult for the men to accept.

The rite of passage to adulthood for boys is **superincision,** a more extreme operation than circumcision. In superincision, not only is the foreskin removed, but the length of the penis is also cut. This painful wound is cured by a series of medicinal and dietary rituals. Part of the rite of passage includes sexual instruction by an older woman in how to find a "good girl" and in how to have intercourse. The superincision rite ends when an older woman removes the scabs from the boy's wounds during the process of intercourse.

Mangaian language has rich descriptions of sexual anatomy and functioning. The culture rewards sexual talk, interest in sexual organs, and frequent intercourse. Invitations to have sex are delivered by go-betweens or by "night-crawling," a process by which a boy enters a girl's house after everyone is asleep, has intercourse with her, and leaves before dawn. The girl's entire family "sleeps" through the visit. Parents want their daughters to know many men and believe (incorrectly) that pregnancy results from repeated intercourse with one man. They encourage their daughters, therefore, to experiment with many partners. Marriage comes after young people have had much sexual experience, but it is based not only on sexual compatibility. Kinship rules, personality, property arrangements, and a pair's work characteristics also determine marriage arrangements. Until recently, illegitimacy was no stigma, and about half of marriages were between couples with babies or expecting them. The biological father is not necessarily the betrothed, because marriage, unlike sex, may exclude some partners for reasons of class, kinship, or property.

Homosexuality is said not to occur in Mangaia. Some men prefer the work and habits of women, and some women prefer the work and habits of men, but these people are heterosexual. Mangaia is thus a culture that segregates the sexes quite early, according to its formal rules, but that later allows and encourages frequent, intense, and admittedly pleasurable sexual expression. When we turn to another group of cultures, those of East Bay, we find early segregation of the sexes but a very different pattern of sexual development.

East Bay and Some Other New Guinea Cultures: Heterosexual Values, Homosexual Behavior

A Melanesian culture called "East Bay" is like Mangaia in that it early segregates the sexes, but it is unlike most cultures in the training its members believe necessary for adult sexuality, a belief it shares with some neighboring New Guinea cultures.

Until the children can talk, East Bay adults let them masturbate. But after that, boys are teased and girls scolded for any sex play in public. Boys and girls are not to touch each other publicly. Girls stay close to their mothers and sisters, working at home and in the garden. The sexual segregation of work helps to keep physical contact between the sexes to a minimum. However, young children are told frankly about sex and go about naked until adolescence.

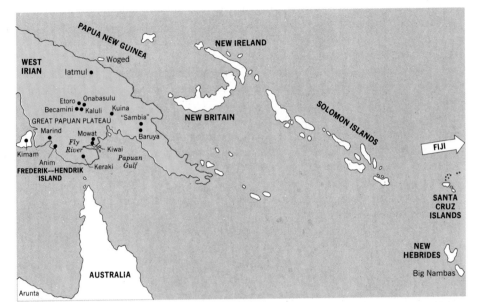

FIGURE 1.1

In many New Guinea cultures, like East Bay, tribal peoples believe that males need homosexual experience to become fully masculine and heterosexual.

In early adolescence, the boy goes through a ceremony that changes his status and moves into a house where only men may live. Now masturbation in private and homosexual acts are considered the normal sexual outlets. Any two male adolescents, no matter how closely related, may engage in mutual masturbation and anal intercourse so long as they do it privately. Another homosexual relationship is openly accepted, that between an older man and an adolescent boy. A father may help choose a boy's partner, although he may not be his son's sexual partner. An early homosexual relationship is considered normal and necessary for healthy masculine development.

SEMEN-EATING CULTURES AND MASCULINE POWER   Many New Guinea cultures, like East Bay, share a set of beliefs about how society works, beliefs based, in turn, on beliefs about gender and age, and bolstered by sexual practices that are very different from those publicly espoused in most of the West. In these cultures, men are reputed to be superior to both women and children because they possess rituals and magic known only to men. Part of a boy's initiation into adulthood is to learn about men's rituals and magic at a safe distance from women. The myths about how men came to possess magical instruments and secrets tend to share common themes in these cultures: once women controlled the secrets, the magical flutes and ritual drums, but the men stole them and stole their strength as well. Now that the men are more powerful, the women must never be allowed to recapture the secrets, the source of power (Bamberger, 1974; Herdt, 1981; Whitehead, 1982).

But this power carries great responsibility: men must use it to assure the community's health and fertility. A fertile, virile man has semen and no female blood. Girls manage to develop into sexual adults without outside interference, but boys must be isolated from women and administered special substances only by men in order to mature sexually, to have semen but no female blood. The Etoro of New Guinea believe, for example, that:

semen does not occur naturally in boys and must be planted in them . . . . A youth is continually inseminated from about age 10 until he reaches his early to mid-twenties. This period is also marked by rapid growth in stature, increased physical strength and endurance, the sprouting of facial and body hair, and the development of masculine skills and characteristics such as hunting ability and courageousness in war. These empirically observable changes are uniformly regarded as the direct results of insemination (Kelly, 1976, p. 45).

Boys are inseminated by performing **fellatio** (oral intercourse) with a partner who is already fully mature. They learn that their health, physical growth, and their own production of semen depend on the inseminations. The semen-eating cultures explain the homosexual acts and the isolation of the men's house as being consistent with men having more power than women and as ways of avoiding females and female blood, which hamper development. Only by homosexual acts, they believe, can a boy be made into a man who is strong, powerful, and fertile. Only men can create men out of boys. Many New Guinea cultures hold to this sexual-substance theory for producing healthy men (Whitehead, 1982), and they have many words for the growth of men, for their attractiveness, and for their intellectual characteristics. But they have no word for the concept "homosexual," as we know it (Lindenbaum, 1982).

Boys live in men's houses from as early as age 8 to as late as age 28, depending on the culture (Harriet Whitehead, personal communication, 1982). When they are fully mature, they go through a ceremony marking their new status. They are now considered fit for marriage, and they rejoin the society of women. Marriage and children soon follow. Marriages are usually arranged by families, but sexual pleasure is so highly valued that partners may veto their families' choices if they find the other incompatible.

In East Bay, the newlyweds move into the house of the groom's father and live there until the first pregnancy. Both are heterosexually virgin. Men who are discovered to have violated the rule of heterosexual virginity are more harshly dealt with than are the women. As long as a woman keeps a good reputation, she is assumed to be a virgin. Because of the long period of sexual segregation, husband and wife have virtually no social experience with people their own age of the other sex. The first few years of marriage may be difficult, but couples seem to manage. Sex is frequent, very satisfying, with elaborate foreplay. Heterosexual intercourse is considered more satisfying than homosexual relations, and homosexual techniques are not used between the sexes. Husbands may have extramarital affairs, some with young boys. A wife may not have sex with anyone but her husband. Once women have had several children, they are said to have less sexual interest than men, and men take concubines. The concubines do not live in the family home. Concubines, who have fewer rights than wives do, are generally accepted by the wives.

No adult men are exclusively homosexual. Unlike Inis Beag's, the sexual segregation accompanies frank sexual talk with children and comfortable nudity. Sex is not considered debilitating or sinful. Men and women expect, and get, pleasure from intercourse. When told that homosexuality is not an accepted phase of western men's sexual development, East Bay men have asked, "But what do your older men do?" (Davenport, 1965; Money and Ehrhardt, 1972).

The Dani: Sexual Indifference

Another New Guinea culture, that of the Dani, seems to defy the view of human nature that says that sex will command a good amount of human energy, either in its expression (as in Mangaia) or in its suppression (as in Inis Beag). The Grand Valley Dani of West New Guinea seem exceptionally unconcerned about sex. Studied for 30 months by the anthropologist Karl G. Heider (1976), the Dani men, said Heider—himself skeptical about the existence of a healthy society with low sexual interest—have "an extraordinarily low level of sexuality." Heider only observed Dani women and rarely discussed sexual matters with them.

Heider's evidence is impressive. He observed that men and women seem invariably to observe four to six years of sexual abstinence after the birth of a child, a period during which men do not have other means of sexual expression (such as adultery or masturbation). Although this period is extremely long for previously active adults to abstain without external justification or sanctions, Heider found no evidence of either adultery or masturbation. No Dani seemed upset, unhappy, or stressed by this abstinence.

Even at other times, sexual activity seems low. The Dani birth rate is barely at replacement level, apparently only because of infrequent intercourse and not because of contraception, abortion, or the killing of unwanted infants. Homosexuality seems absent, and intercourse outside of marriage seems rare. Married couples do not begin intercourse until two years after their wedding and only after they have established a common residence. Weddings take place only every four to six years, after the irregular Pig Feast. The only obvious interest in sex appears in the art and music of teenage boys and girls, who are said to understand the risqué nature of their sexual references. Postmarital sex (that after separation, divorce, or a partner's death) is also rare.

Why this sexual indifference? It is not due to a harsh environment. The Dani live in a remarkably fine climate, have a decent diet, are free of native diseases, and are, as Heider said, "healthy, vigorous, strong people." Nearby peoples show more typical levels of sexual interest. There is similarly no evidence that the Dani suffer from any biological deficiency. Low androgen, for example, might reduce sexual motivation, but it also diminishes fertility, and the Dani's fertility seems in line with their sexual activity. Severe androgen deficiency would also deprive men of secondary sexual characteristics such as beard growth, but they do not suffer from this.

We are left with the hypothesis that Dani culture is responsible for their sexual indifference. Heider believes that their sexual attitude is in line with their generally low-key, unemotional style. Overt anger and fights are rare, they show little hatred of enemies, and battles are short and not terribly intense or exciting. The Dani are not especially accomplished either. Dani adults seem not to invest much energy in anything, although they are not physically lazy. Dani child-rearing practices reflect their low energy. Infants seem free of stress or of much stimulation of any kind. Toilet training and education are relaxed.

Sweden: Permissiveness with Equality

Like us, Sweden is highly industrialized and modern. However, as late as 1950, more than half of all Swedes lived outside of cities. Even then Sweden had a tradition of permissiveness about premarital sex, an outgrowth of its rural tradition. Courtship in Sweden had included sex before marriage, and in fact marriage often followed a pregnancy, proof of fertility. A farmer could not risk having a barren wife (infertility being presumed, not correctly, to be solely a woman's affliction.) A man needed a family to work the soil or run a shop.

Sweden is unlike the United States in certain ways. It is racially uniform, and nearly everyone is officially Lutheran. (Religious minorities are quite small.) The government, regardless of which party is in power, is committed to an economy somewhere between capitalism and socialism. It is also committed to ending the double standard and to use social welfare to help create equality between men and women. Officially, Sweden is a feminist nation (U.N. Report, *The Status of Women in Sweden*, 1968).

Sexual life in Sweden is much like ours as far as behavior goes, but the context and some of the meanings of sex differ from ours. From preschool on, all children receive sex education. Preschoolers learn the differences between the sexes and where babies come from. They also learn a bit about contraception. Older children receive more detailed and more sophisticated messages. The ultimate goal of sex education is to teach not only the facts about sexuality but also the responsibilities and intimate personal relationships that go with sexual behavior. The message is that sexual behavior can give pleasure but that it also requires people to avoid causing others pain. Sex education also contains information on sexual minorities: homosexuals, sadists, and the like.

Sexual laws protect children and other dependent people from sexual acts of those in a position to dominate them (Linner, 1967). Rape and sex with minors and close relatives are forbidden by law. Consensual sex among adults is not illegal, and there is probably more public tolerance of consensual sex between adults in Sweden than in the United States. That tolerance applies not only to heterosexual intercourse, but also to homosexuality and uncommon forms of sexual behavior.

Among Swedish teenagers, the first experience of sexual intercourse comes when they are, on the average, 16 years old, a bit younger than it was a generation or so ago. School nurses give contraceptive advice because so many teenagers are sexually active. A recent survey (Lewin, 1982) in the city of Uppsala, Sweden showed that 63 percent of sexually active tenth graders used reliable contraception. In 1975, about half of Sweden's 15,000 teenage pregnancies ended in births, the other half in legal abortions. More than three-quarters of the teenaged mothers married within a year or two, most to the baby's father. Mothers who do not marry receive government support of many kinds, including housing and child care. The government view is to foster the healthy development of children in families of any kind. Many Swedish cities have walk-in advice clinics to help young people with sexual and emotional problems.

SWEDISH LAWS ABOUT SEXUAL BEHAVIOR SAY SEVERAL THINGS ABOUT SEXUAL VALUES: SEX IS NATURAL AND EQUALLY SO FOR BOTH SEXES; SEX IN AN INTIMATE RELATIONSHIP MUST BE RESPONSIBLE; PREGNANCIES SHOULD BE WANTED, AND IF NOT, PEOPLE SHOULD USE CONTRACEPTION.

Swedish laws about sexual behavior say several things about sexual values: sex is natural and equally so for both sexes; sex in an intimate relationship must be responsible; pregnancies should be wanted, and if not, people should use contraception. Furthermore, the laws state that illegitimate children have the same rights as those born to married people, and single parents deserve social support. The laws create a permissive atmosphere and reduce anxiety and secrecy about sex. Swedish culture has traditionally been relaxed about nudity and premarital sex. The family, for instance, wears no clothes in a Swedish sauna. Sweden's homogeneity has allowed it to develop an excellent sex education program in all schools, and although there is frequent debate over what the program should contain, there is no debate about whether sex education is necessary.

Life on the surface, then, seems very much like American life, but the experience of the Swedish teenager is probably different in important respects from that of the American teenager. Swedish parents are more likely to know about their children's premarital sexual encounters. Teenagers are more likely to know more about sexuality, especially contraception. Abortion is available and subsidized by the national health service for the first 18 weeks of pregnancy (abortion in the United States is available for the first 24 weeks of pregnancy, but public funding is not always available). In Sweden, the secrecy and riskiness surrounding early sexuality in the United States are replaced by social support from families, schools, and medical networks (Sundstrom, 1976).

The sexual values prevalent in Sweden clearly differ from those in much of the United States. Differences in sexual values derive in part from differences in history, in part from differences in contemporary cultures. Even within a society like the United States, subcultures with different histories hold different sexual values.

SEXUAL ETHICS

The historical shift in sexual values that took place between about 1850 and 1920 was a shift from one sexual ethic to another. Speaking in broad terms, the old order was absolutist in that people tended to believe in the existence of right and wrong absolutes. The answers that people provide to their questions about sexual values depend on broader systems of values—religious, political, economic, or the like—and can be classified as partaking of the ethics of relativism, hedonism, or absolutism.

People who subscribe to an **absolutist ethic** believe that right and wrong are absolutes. The original Jewish and Christian positions were, for example, absolutist. An absolute value system is appealing because it proposes clear guidelines for correct action. Absolute rules do not change from one day to another. Making absolute judgments may seem easy, but carrying them out may be harder. The absolutist is helped, however, by the certainty of the judgment of right and wrong.

When people say that there is not always a definite right or wrong answer, that sometimes the best one can do is to come up with a "least bad" or an "acceptable given the circumstances" answer, they are arguing from a **relativistic** position. This situationist ethic requires that people evaluate the probable consequences of their actions for themselves and for others in a given situation. This position may create conflict because each situation requires thinking anew. Actions are taken on the strengths of their probable, not their certain, consequences.

Relativists believe that what is right today may be less right or even wrong tomorrow (Fletcher, 1966).

Finally, value systems may be **hedonistic** if they hold that pleasure is the greatest good. Hedonists do not necessarily equate pleasure with irresponsibility. In fact, for the hedonist, responsibility consists in choosing actions that will give the greatest pleasure to the greatest number and that will minimize hurt. Responsible hedonists therefore have to evaluate the pleasure and pain to all others touched by their social actions.

FORMAL AND INFORMAL SEXUAL STANDARDS

Sociologist Ira L. Reiss (1967) has suggested a way of analyzing and comparing the sexual values of different cultures, both past and present. He maintains that each culture has a **formal standard** for sexual behavior that is an idealization of how people *ought to* behave. The religious principles of the early saints are an example of a formal standard for sexual behavior. Each culture usually also has an **informal standard** that more closely resembles how people *do* behave. Reiss further suggests that sexual standards may be the same or different for the two sexes and that a culture's standards may be relatively permissive or strict during any given historical period. The shift in sexual morality after World War I, for example, was a shift from the strict to the permissive.

Informal standards tend to draw the line at how far people can transgress. They mark what a particular subculture will tolerate rather than what it idealizes. Thus informal standards may accept masturbation and divorce and pornography even as formal standards condemn them. We find interesting combinations of formal and informal standards: Christian congregations made up entirely of homosexuals, including clergy; a nude beach on one side of a fence and a beach where nudity is illegal on the other side; prostitution flourishing in certain districts even though it is illegal. Other examples from our pluralistic society abound: the Roman Catholic couple that uses birth-control pills; the prominent man who dresses as a woman. An interesting historical example shows the difference between formal and informal sexual standards. In a fine piece of detective work, Stanford University historian Carl Degler (1974) showed that at least some educated American women rejected some of the formal values of the Victorian period.

Degler found the papers of a Stanford physician, Dr. Clelia Duel Mosher (1863–1940), a remarkable woman who conducted a study by questionnaire of the health and sexual "habits" of married, college-educated women. Forty-five women answered her questions. Most were born before 1870, more than half before the Civil War. These middle- and upper-class women reported that they felt sexual desire quite independently of their husbands' interest. More than three-quarters of the women had had an orgasm at least once. More than one-third had orgasm usually or always during sexual intercourse. In spite of the common sexual ignorance of unmarried women, these educated wives had discovered sexual pleasure with their husbands.

SINGLE AND DOUBLE STANDARDS

Sexual standards may be different for men and women. A **single standard** means that the same rules apply for judging the sexual behavior of both sexes. It is egalitarian in that men and women are judged equally. A **double standard** means that sexual rules differ for the two sexes. In most western cultures, the rules typically have been more liberal for men than for women. In all periods of history, men could have sex without stigma, but women could not. Women who violated this standard have been stigmatized as "promiscuous" or "easy." Men, by contrast, may actually be admired for "having a fling" or "sowing their oats."

In practice, single and double standards may be strict or permissive. A strict single standard means that both men and women must observe the rules of chastity. In our society, young white people with strong religious faith and who are active in their churches are more likely to adhere to a strict single standard and to abstain from sex outside of marriage than are agnostics. A permissive single standard, in contrast, might mean that both sexes could have intercourse if the partners cared for one another. A permissive double standard allows relatively unrestricted sexual intercouse for males but intercourse for females only under special conditions, such as when they are engaged to be married. (Such a standard is often considered transitional, moving toward a single standard.) A strict double standard restricts only females from sex outside of marriage. We have used sexual intercourse as the example here of sexual behavior, but standards—single or double, permissive or restrictive—can apply, at least in principle, to other behaviors as well (such as oral or extramarital sex).

SHAME AND GUILT

In any society, sexual standards will feel oppressive and wrong to some people. American teenagers, for example, may feel chafed by pressures to postpone sexual intercourse. Yet teenagers from a culture that insists marriage *follow* a successful pregnancy may feel just as pressured by that standard. When our sexual behavior diverges from what *we* personally feel is right, we feel sexual guilt. When our sexual behavior diverges from what *other* people feel is right, we may feel shame or fear if we are found out. Some societies tend to use shame, and others use guilt to regulate behavior. (No culture is monolithic; the labels we use apply only to some of the people, some of the time.) Japan, like many Eastern cultures, is a shame culture. There people learn the need for "face." Shame cultures invite their members to escape into settings where there are no judges of the shame. Guilt-ridden people, in contrast, carry their conflicts inside. Only new values will work for them. The United States, like many Western cultures, is a guilt culture. Both guilt and shame are painful reminders of the price members of society pay for social standards.

We can illustrate the difference between shame and guilt as follows. A person may engage in homosexual acts but feel that they are wrong. That person is likely to feel guilty. Likewise, homosexuals who feel that homosexual acts are acceptable may feel shame (but not necessarily guilt) if their parents find out that they engage in homosexual acts. Only when you break a rule that you believe in do you feel guilty for it. Shame and guilt are both so unpleasant that many people confuse one with the other. Sometimes shame and guilt get covered over with anxiety. Then people lose track of *what* is bothering them. What began as a conflict about sex can end up as diffuse anxiety. At that point, trying to figure out one's values becomes a psychological necessity.

Although societies differ greatly in the degree to which their rules control members by guilt or shame, these can be important means of social control. For our purposes, guilt and shame are important because they mark the gap between what society wants and what people actually do, and they mark sometimes painful conflicts within individuals.

SUMMARY

1 Sex is the biologically essential union of two individuals to reproduce off-spring. Sexuality is the totality of human ideas about sexual relations, values, practices, and even controls over sexual behavior.

2 Sexual values and sexual behavior are not the same things. Sexual values are social rules that people internalize. They have important, socially shared meaning.

3 Sexual values regulate sexual behavior. They tend to be conservative, to favor reproduction of the species, some form of the family, and to vary among subgroups.

4 In ancient cultures, sexual and religious values often were linked. Some ancient cults worshipped fertility gods and goddesses and ascribed sexual characteristics to their gods. The ancient Greeks idealized certain sexual relationships, such as that between adolescent boys and older men. The early Hebrews believed in a single God, valued the family, and strongly regulated sexuality.

5 Religious values often support sexual values. Christianity has been an important force in attaching guilt to sexual behavior.

6 In England and America in the sixteenth and seventeenth centuries, women were thought to have greater sexual appetites than men. By the end of the eighteenth century in this country, marriage was idealized as a relationship of companions. Romantic love also emerged as an ideal for marriage.

7 Between 1840 and 1860, women's sexuality was supposed to make them morally superior to men and moderators of their husbands' sexuality. Purity movements to regulate male sexuality arose among both sexes.

8 Darwin's theory of evolution and Freud's psychoanalytic theory both appeared in the second half of the nineteenth century in Europe. Both were revolutionary, and both envisioned sexual behavior to be at the core of human history and development.

9 A shift in sexual morality followed the disillusionment created by the Crimean and First World Wars. A belief in the value of pleasure replaced or coexisted with the ancient religious principle of pleasure as sinful.

10 All cultures consider sexual behavior necessary and have some form of marriage and family. All cultures regulate sexual behavior in some way. Cultures vary greatly in norms governing the proper circumstances for intercourse, the proper partner, frequency and duration, and positions.

11 Margaret Mead's classic work on three New Guinea cultures and their gender roles established cross-cultural research as an important tool for social scientists interested in sex and gender.

12 Inis Beag is a repressive, Christian culture, in which men are believed to have more sexual appetite than women, women do not have orgasm during intercourse, and references to sexual matters are very inhibited.

13 The Bala of Africa sharply differentiate gender roles but accept transgressions against sexual standards more readily than the people of Inis Beag. Intercourse is valued and enjoyed by both sexes.

14 In the sexually permissive society of Mangaia, the formal standard is modesty in public and intense, pleasurable, and varied heterosexual intercourse in private. Orgasm is universal for both sexes.

15 In East Bay and some other New Guinea cultures, homosexual relations are considered necessary for the attainment of (heterosexual) manhood. As husbands, adults are heterosexual in identity and behavior.

16 The Dani are a New Guinea culture of little sexual interest or activity. Nothing in their environment, diet, or health explains this apparent violation of the human tendency to invest great energy in sexuality.

17 In Sweden, sexual behavior seems rather like that in our society, but its context and meaning differ from ours. Sex education, contraceptives, social support of unwed mothers, freedom from sexual guilt, and social support are available to young people.

18 A sexual ethic may be relativistic—requiring people to evaluate the probable consequences of their actions for themselves and others in each situation. It may be absolutist—requiring people to carry out decisions based on a belief in absolutes of right and wrong. A sexual ethic may be hedonistic—positing pleasure for the greatest number and pain for the fewest as the greatest good.

19 Societies may have a formal sexual standard, which is an idealization of what sexual behavior ought to be like, and an informal standard, which more closely resembles how people actually behave.

20 Sexual standards may vary by sex. A single standard means that the same rules apply for judging the sexual behavior of both sexes. A double standard means that sexual rules differ for the sexes, typically being more liberal for males than females in the West.

21 Shame and guilt are the painful feelings that societies may use to regulate sexual (and other) behavior in their members. Some cultures tend to use shame; others, guilt.

KEY TERMS

sex
germ cells
sperm
ovum
genes
cultural evolution
sexuality
sexual values
norms
onanism
incest
lesbian
coitus interruptus

agents of socialization
culture-bound
ethnography
superincision
fellatio
absolutist ethic
relativistic ethic
hedonistic ethic
formal standard
informal standard
single standard
double standard

SUGGESTED READINGS

Butterfield, F. *China: Alive in the Bitter Sea.* New York: Quadrangle/New York Times Book Co., 1982. The second part of this excellent look at China is about love, marriage, and sexuality generally. The author is a New York *Times* journalist who speaks Chinese and who lived in Peking. The book is well written and full of surprises.

Filene, P. G. *Him/Her/Self: Sex Roles in Modern America.* New York: Mentor, 1976. Really a history of gender roles from 1890 to 1974, Filene's book shows how history changes gender roles.

Mead, M. *Sex and Temperament in Three Primitive Societies.* New York: Morrow, 1935. Mead's book convinced generations of social scientists that the cross-cultural view was the best one for understanding values. This book is a classic and good reading.

Sarrel, L. J. and Sarrel, P. M. *Sexual Unfolding: Sexual Development and Sex Therapies in Late Adolescence.* Boston: Little, Brown, 1979. The Sarrels run the sex education program at Yale. The first part of their book provides a careful, non-dogmatic framework for readers to make judgments about their own sexual values and choices.

Dr. Sherry Ortner's work in the last ten years has concerned how biological sex and gender roles are culturally connected. Her early work suggested that in many cultures, women were seen as connected with a mysterious Nature and men with a knowable Culture. Women's realm was childbirth and childcare, and men's was the political realm. More recently, Dr. Ortner has worked with anthropologist Harriet Whitehead to see how cultures' gender roles are tied to prestige systems among men.

QUESTION   How did you and Harriet Whitehead come to edit *Sexual Meanings?* What led you to an interest in what you call the sex/gender system?

ORTNER   Harriet and I were undergraduate majors together and then graduate students together. We don't think identically, but we share a world view. We thought lots of people were working on how cultures put sex and gender together in symbolic terms. We knew the work of Jane Collier and Michelle Rosaldo (Stanford anthropologists) and we decided, well, there's a process going on out there. Let's see if we can collect it. We also began kicking ideas around theoretically. We were trying to figure out what the significance of the social context was. Then we decided that we could understand a lot if we understood the male prestige system. We were feeling our way around to begin with, criticizing one another's ideas.

QUESTION   You have lectured on the differences in the way in which various cultures put together things like sex, marriage, parenting, and the like. I wonder if you could tell us a little bit about that.

ORTNER   The argument I make is that in our culture there is a very tight linkage between marriage, sex, reproduction, and parent–child bonding. In principle, each is at least partly independent, but that's not our culture's view. Marriage entails sex, sex entails reproduction, reproduction entails close parent-child bonding. For an alternative view, I looked at Polynesian culture. The Polynesians link these very loosely, if at all. For them, sex is not necessarily exclusively tied to marriage. There's a lot of premarital sex and extramarital sex, and this is considered normal. As in our culture, on the other hand, marriage is linked to biological reproduction. A child should be born in marriage. But in fact there is a fairly high rate of illegitimacy there and greater tolerance for it.

Finally, reproduction in Polynesia is not tightly linked to parent-child bonding. Instead, there's a good deal of adoption and fostering of children. Children switch their parents too, and on the whole, in spite of our values on parent-child bonds, the Polynesians are reported to have generally good parent-child relations, whether they're between

*Sherry Ortner is Professor of Anthropology at the University of Michigan.

natural parent and child or adopted parent and child. The relationship is described as easygoing, affectionate, and not full of heavy psychological burdens.

I'm speaking generally here. I have not done psychological research to establish that everybody is just fine, but it looks that way from the descriptions we have available.

QUESTION   Do you see any changes in the linkages over time in our society?

ORTNER   Well, clearly things are changing. Almost all of these links are loosening up to some degree in our cultural thinking. Sex before marriage is virtually the norm by now. Contraception is also considered normal, and sex is not so tightly tied to reproduction in people's minds. Even the links between marriage and reproduction are loosening up, so that it is becoming more acceptable to have or to adopt a child without being married. But we are still a long way from being like Polynesians. These changes in our cultural thinking have provoked very strong and hostile reactions in many quarters.

QUESTION   Why are these cultural issues important?

ORTNER   They're important because they shape people's reactions to other people, and also they influence how we think about ourselves. For example, if we think of women as largely determined by their sexual and reproductive capacities—and this has been our standard cultural view—then we are unlikely to think they will succeed in intellectual or artistic work or in social leadership and so forth. This generates what we call "sexism" on the one hand—prejudices about what women should or shouldn't do—and also inhibitions in women themselves, doubts about their own capacities to succeed in these activities. So these symbolic associations or linkages are actually the underpinnings of our attitudes and values.

QUESTION   But what produces those symbolic associations in the first place? Why does one culture adopt one set of views about what's linked with what, and another culture adopts another set of views?

ORTNER   This can't be answered in terms of any single cause, like purely economic factors, or purely historical factors. But Harriet Whitehead and I have found that a culture's views about sex, gender, and reproduction are very closely tied to the ways in which men gain status and prestige in that culture. We have looked at the links between gender beliefs and men's status arrangements in other cultures, and we hope to continue with these investigations, also moving into our own culture on this question.

QUESTION   Your major field of work has to do with the Sherpas in the Himalayas. How did you come to work with them?

ORTNER   That's a very hard question for me to answer. I have three or four
         stories I tell myself without knowing which one is true. I knew I was
         interested in religion. I also knew I didn't want to work with very
         primitive societies. High culture, peasants, and up; that interests me.
         Christianity and Islam, that wasn't for me. That just left Buddhism.
         And I wanted a remote, far off place.

QUESTION Did you really walk 10 days to get to the Sherpa village?

ORTNER   Yes. The first trip was exactly that. Now you can fly in and walk only
         three days. Also, the first time we had absolutely no contacts. We
         just showed up.

QUESTION Can you just do that? Decide you're interested in a culture and just
          appear?

ORTNER   You can't do that with the American Indians or with societies that
         have councils where you have to get approval. But you can with the
         Sherpas, because the Sherpas are very open. I still remember being a
         naive first-time fieldworker, but by now I'm one of the senior people
         that has worked there.

QUESTION Do you mind if I ask how you became an anthropologist?

ORTNER   I majored in anthropology as an undergraduate at Bryn Mawr. I saw
         anthropology in the catalogue, and I thought it was about insects.
         Someone told me that it was the study of tribal peoples. I was inter-
         ested before I took my first course. I didn't do especially well in
         anthropology, but I liked it. I scraped through and decided to go to
         graduate school because it was easy to get in at that time and because
         I liked being in school. So I did go to graduate school (at the Uni-
         versity of Chicago) and I came out the other end as an anthropologist.

QUESTION I'd like to ask you a really personal question. How do you manage
          what a lot of people call a normal life when you take off for Nepal to
          study the Sherpa monasteries? What happens to husband and children?

ORTNER   In my case I had my child *after* my last field project. I don't think
         I'll take my 5-year-old into the field. It's too risky to her health to
         take her to Nepal. Husbands? Some want to be left home. Some want
         to go along. My three trips were done three ways. One way was with
         a husband who was also doing research there. Another way was when
         I was single. The third way was with my present husband, who ac-
         companied me but was not doing a project. It was different each time,
         and a lot of that difference related to the changes in my marital status.
         But it also changed as a function of my age, and from the fact that
         when I went back, I had more money. It's a different experience every
         time. I'm not a big materialist, but it was wonderful to have some
         money to give people jobs, and to be more hospitable, to make work
         a little bit easier. However you do it, fieldwork is an amazing expe-
         rience—exhausting and exhilarating.

Frank Stella, "Abra Variation I." Collection, The Museum of Modern Art, New York.

Chapter 2

Studying Sexuality

How do findings about sexual behavior come into existence? Why should we believe them? Why do researchers follow one path of inquiry rather than another, and why are their findings so often narrowly focused rather than general and sweeping? After all, it is a lot more interesting to see the whole picture than just a few brushstrokes.

THE NATURE OF RESEARCH

Why can't a psychologist research a broad and interesting question like "What does the average American couple do in bed?" In fact, researchers do try to keep the big question in mind ("How do people behave sexually?") as they break it down into more manageable questions. These questions might revolve around people's sexual behavior during adolescence, or after divorce, or perhaps around the sequence of experiences in their sexual biographies. Researchers sometimes frame questions that elicit what the behavior actually means to people. For example, young people have different feelings about intercourse from long-married people, and an artful survey would get at that difference. Thus researchers have to decide of whom to ask their questions, how to ask them, how to code their answers, and what comparisons to make. Comparisons of answers from different groups of people—males and females, educated and uneducated, young and old, religious and not religious, rural and urban, and so forth—can provide information on the meanings of different sexual acts to different groups of people.

Why can't a researcher simply observe what the average American couple does in bed? First of all, that kind of observation would take too much time. Second, it would be very difficult to find enough of the right couples to arrive at the "average." Third, people would wonder if the presence of a researcher had changed the couples' behavior.

Researchers sometimes ask specific questions, such as, "Do women and men find erotic images sexually arousing?" Questions like that lend themselves to experimental test. Researchers can test whether erotic and unerotic material do *different* things physically to men and women. The researchers vary the material presented, erotic or unerotic. The nature of the material controlled and systematically varied by the researchers is called the **independent variable.** The researchers then measure some aspect of their subjects' behavior, in this case, an indicator of arousal. The measure of arousal is called the **dependent variable.** It depends on the nature of the independent variable. People do not get sexually aroused by travel films of boating on the Danube River, after all, but a film of intercourse between a man and a woman has been shown to produce genital responses in both males and females. Knowing this, the researchers use the film of the Danube as a **control condition** to assure that people are not getting sexually aroused just by being in an experiment or in a sex laboratory. It assures them that a lovemaking sequence has something special that arouses people, that it qualifies as erotic, just as the researchers had suspected.

The Questions Determine the Research Design

The nature of a researcher's questions determines the design of the research. Common sense tells us that asking about gender roles in New Guinea requires a different kind of research from asking about sexual attitudes among Victorian women. Harriet Whitehead (1982) and Gilbert Herdt (1981) are two anthropologists who lived among and observed different semen-eating tribes in New Guinea to learn their ideas of masculinity and femininity (as we saw in Chapter 1). Theirs was a **cross-cultural**, or **ethnographic method**. Carl Degler, a Stanford University historian, learned about sexual attitudes among some educated Victorian women from digging in the university's archives and finding the papers of a female physician who had conducted a survey on women's "sexual habits." Degler's was the **historical**, or **archival method**.

Studying behavior is trickier than gathering valid data about blood samples. Biochemists have agreed-upon rules for hormonal assays, and people are not usually self-conscious about blood samples. Few people believe that they should be able to control their hormones. But studying sexual behavior can be touchy indeed. Most people do believe that they can control their sexual behavior, and therefore any inquiries expose them to others' judgments. Thus people are not always eager to discuss their personal and private lives with a stranger. How can researchers make sure that people will answer their questions? How can they know if the answers they get are true? What if the people who answer are a self-selected population of braggarts? Once upon a time researchers worried about people understating their sexual experiences because there were more sexual taboos than there are today. But today many of us are so sophisticated that we think nothing of reading the most intimate details about behavior in newspapers and mass magazines. It was not always so. The first sex researchers had a tough battle to fight.

Researchers still face the problem of getting people to talk honestly to them. Surveys among college students are relatively easy to conduct. Students believe in research, want to talk about their sexual lives, and tend to be truthful to scientific researchers. Surveys off campus are harder to conduct. One technique for getting large numbers of people to respond is to embed sexual questions in more neutral questions. Some Gallup International Polls in Sweden and France have used this strategy. Another successful survey strategy is to explain the purpose and the need for information on some important topic. Surveyors interviewing about rape within marriage and sexual abuse have used this approach. Still another possibility is to mail a short questionnaire to a sample of people and then follow up repeatedly to get their answers. Answers to questionnaires inserted in magazines will reflect the characteristics of their particular readers: the relatively affluent and sexually liberal, mostly male *Playboy* readers, for example, or the well-educated, mostly white readers of *Psychology Today*. These samples do not represent the characteristics of the adult population as a whole; they represent only people like the respondents. Some surveys make little or no attempt to be representative. Their goals are more descriptive or literary; they sometimes can reveal effectively what certain acts mean to the people who participate. The two Hite reports on sexuality (1976, on females; 1981, on males), in which the author chose whom to quote from among the questionnaires mailed to her, are examples of unrepresentative surveys full of fascinating quoted responses. What people say about sex is almost always interesting, but drawbacks of unrepresentative studies are that probably no one could replicate their results, and the results from the population sampled apply only to people like the respondents. To conclude that the same percentage of the total population would say that they do what *Playboy* readers say they do, for example, would be a mistake. The conclusion would be wrong.

Replicability, or **reliability,** the ability of one researcher to repeat a line of inquiry and to arrive at the same or highly similar results, is an important criterion for studies of behavior. Replicability means that other researchers can duplicate the findings, either with the same method used or with another method. When more than one method reveals the same results, the results are considered very strong and are said to have **convergent validity. Validity** means that research has tested what it purported to test, that it did not test one aspect of sexual behavior—an attitude, say—and represent it as another—an act. Replicability and objectivity usually go hand in hand. The **scientific method** hinges on asking questions and obtaining data in an objective fashion such that others can repeat the methods and reach comparable results—or refute them. The scientific method is aimed at generating new knowledge and refuting findings that cannot be reproduced.

Let us turn to the various methods of studying sexual behavior: surveys, including interviews and questionnaires; observational methods, including participant observation; experimental and clinical methods; and cross-cultural and field studies. Before we begin, we should emphasize that the criteria for good research are the same for all methods: good research aims to be valid, replicable, and objective.

THE SURVEY METHOD

A sex **survey** gives a static picture of some aspect of sexual behavior within a certain group of people. It may describe how that aspect of behavior breaks down by social class, age, religion, ethnic origin, marital status, or the like. Thus a survey may reveal the percentage of females and males between 18 and 35 who are married and have children or the percentage of the same group who have ever had a homosexual encounter to orgasm, or both. Most surveys elicit answers from people at only one time, but occasionally surveys elicit answers from the same people at several different times and thereby track any changes that may have occurred in the behavior under study, as when researchers study the sexual experience of the same group of couples during the first and fourth year of marriage (Udry and Morris, 1971). Such a study is called **longitudinal.** When groups are followed over time, they are called **panels.** Studies of panels allow researchers to make strong, solid inferences about people's lives because they can compare a person's earlier and later sexual behavior.

THE INFORMATION SURVEYS GENERATE

Surveys produce certain kinds of answers because they ask certain kinds of questions. Most often they produce answers about **frequencies** ("How often do you ...?") and **incidence** ("Have you ever ...?") of kinds of behavior. These are **descriptive statistics.** For example, an excellent survey was conducted in 1976 by Melvin Zelnik and John Kantner (1977) at Johns Hopkins School of Public Health. They wanted to know how many teenage women, excluding those who lived in college dormitories, practiced birth control. They found that nearly 30 percent of women between the ages of 15 and 19 who were having intercourse used some form of birth control every time they had intercourse, but that 35 percent used no contraception at all. By 1979, the news had changed: the young women's regular use of contraception went up to 34 percent, and the number of women who used no contraception at all dropped to 27 percent (Zelnik and Kantner, 1980). (For some ideas about how to evaluate surveys that appear in the popular media, see "Sexuality in Perspective: Should You Believe What You Read?") Zelnik and Kantner are two researchers we will meet again. Their surveys always begin by telling their readers how their current sample was drawn, what group it represents, and how alike or different the sample is from one they studied a few years past. They say, for example, that they have comparable data from samples of 15- to 19-year-old women in 1971, 1976, and 1979 who lived in households (but not institutions or dormitories) in cities and their nearby suburbs.

Surveys also may lead to comparisons *between* groups. Let us say that we see a big difference in percentages of people who engage in oral-genital sex, which we happen to be studying. We see this difference between two groups, perhaps young as compared to old. We need to determine whether the difference represents a chance happening or something we could find again if we ran the study many times over. If our statistic tells us that the big difference we see is likely to happen by chance only one time in twenty or less often, we can conclude that the difference corresponds to a true difference in the behavior of the two groups.

These kinds of statistics are called **inferential statistics.** They let researchers draw inferences from their otherwise descriptive statistics. In the Zelnik and Kantner study that we mentioned above, the sample of never-married, 15- to 19-year-old women was truly representative of women of that age who lived in metropolitan-area households. In 1971, half of the 936 subjects had had intercourse by age 16.4 years. In 1979, the age was 16.2 years for another sample of about the same size. (Those ages are both part of the study's descriptive statistics.) The inferential statistics tell us that the difference probably was not due to chance, that it corresponded to a true change in the time of first sexual intercourse. The inferred conclusion: age of first intercourse for women went down between 1971 and 1979. A similar comparison of 1976 and 1979 data showed no decrease in age at first intercourse. The change occurred some time between 1971 and 1976.

Samples of Populations

What do we mean when we say that a sample was "truly representative"? A survey poses one or more questions about a particular **population,** all those in some group of people: all college students, all urban adults over 18, all married couples, etc. But because it is impossible to reach every member of a large population, researchers choose a **sample,** or subset, of that population. They make sure that the sample is representative of the population in either of two ways. They may take a **random sample.** If they were investigating college students in the United States, they might take every 100th or 1000th name from a huge list of U.S. college students. Alternatively, if they want a sample of all Americans, they may take a **stratified sample** or a **quota sample,** a selection of people that matches the demographic characteristics of the total population by having, for instance, the right proportions of males and females, age groups, socioeconomic statuses, religious memberships, and ethnic origins. Researchers go to the trouble of finding representative samples because what they learn from any sample only tells them about people like those sampled. Representative samples of college students tell them about the total population of college students.

Choosing their subject population only starts things going. Researchers also have to find people to participate. Inevitably, some people refuse, and new subjects have to be substituted. Researchers tend to pitch their requests to these treasured first respondents very carefully, in order to lose as few as possible. They know that once they have to substitute for more than about one in five respondents, the randomness or representativeness of their sample begins to be threatened. When so many people turn down survey researchers, the researchers may end up with the right demographic characteristics, but they may find that their subjects have been selected for some other variable related to the research. Recent research on people who refuse or delay responding suggests that those who refuse are older and poorer than early responders (Fitzgerald and Fuller, 1982). Age and class are related to sexual behavior, as we know from other research. In the history of sex research, large-scale, truly representative studies could only be conducted once people perceived the research as completely responsible. This point probably was reached relatively recently, between 1953, when the second survey report (on women) was published by Alfred Kinsey and his colleagues, and 1966, the date of publication of the observational studies by William Masters and Virginia Johnson.

Interviews and Questionnaires

Researchers sometimes want to ask many survey questions of their subjects, and so they choose to interview them or to administer a questionnaire. Kinsey and his colleagues conducted surveys (fully described in the following section) with up to 350 questions. When researchers pose that many questions, they can choose either to **interview** their subjects or to give them a **questionnaire** to complete. Both strategies have risks and rewards. Kinsey chose to interview his subjects so that they would not misunderstand any questions and so that he could pace the questioning to catch contradictions and to undercut lies. Interviewing of this kind takes a lot of time for training, for coding to assure consistency, and for administering. But it minimizes the number of people who fail to answer all the questions.

Questionnaires are like interviews, but the respondent reads the questions and writes answers. That saves costly interviewing time. Questions must be unambiguous and clear, and only people who can read can answer them. If the questions are not clear, the researcher may not have any way of knowing that a respondent does not understand a question. Careful researchers pretest an independent group (not used in the sample) to learn whether respondents may misunderstand or misread any questions. Some questionnaire surveys are so long—the Hite reports on sexuality, for example—that one suspects that the respondents are very verbal people selected for their need to tell their views. How many people willingly stay through over 300 multiple-choice items plus essay questions? Questionnaires have the advantage of being standardized, however, so that all respondents receive the same questions. There are no human interviewers exerting subtle influences on particular items on a questionnaire by means of tone of voice, gestures, pacing, or the like. Some European researchers (e.g., Gondonneau et al., 1972) use a mixture of techniques. They might interview subjects on a fairly neutral topic and follow the interview with personal questions or a questionnaire.

The Kinsey Survey

Alfred Kinsey and his colleagues at Indiana University's Institute for Sex Research administered their interviews to 18,000 people. Kinsey, a famous insect biologist, and Wardell Pomeroy, a young psychologist, each collected 8000 of the interviews. They spoke to males and females, homosexuals and heterosexuals, old and young, whites and blacks (the data on blacks were not published until recently, and then only as tables [Gebhard and Johnson, 1979], because of dissatisfaction with the representativeness of the sample). All of their respondents were volunteers. Because Kinsey knew that a problem inherent in volunteer samples was **skewing** (displacing true frequencies up or down), he tried to correct for that tendency by interviewing whole groups, whom he solicited by offering lectures in exchange for interviews. Thus the entire Rotary Club or an entire department at a university or all the people in a prison would be interviewed. Kinsey then compared the "true" volunteers to the groups.

KINSEY ORIGINALLY bEGAN COLLECTING dATA bECAUSE HE WAS TEACHING A COURSE ON MARRIAGE ANd COULd NOT find AdEQUATE INFORMATION ON SEX IN MARRIAGE.

Kinsey originally began collecting data because he was teaching a course on marriage and could not find adequate information on sex in marriage. Having earlier in his career specialized in studying insects, he applied the techniques he had learned in that field to human behavior, with results that set a high standard both for sample size and details of behavior studied. His findings remain important today, fully 35 years after he began publishing them. Before Kinsey began work, in the late 1930s, most studies of sexual behavior had relied on small samples, often of college students (a very special population), and had focused on common forms of sexual behavior. Kinsey, by contrast, inquired unjudgmentally into the ages at which people had had uncommon or tabooed sexual experiences (sex with blood relatives, for instance) as well as common experiences. Kinsey did not survey sexual attitudes or values so much as forms of behavior that could be quantified.

The Kinsey reports were published in two large chunks, a volume on males in 1948 and a volume on females in 1953. Both were best sellers, much to Kinsey's amazement. Although they were roundly criticized by some of the clergy and by members of the psychiatric establishment, among others, the method and the findings survived scrutiny.

Some of the shocking findings from the Kinsey surveys thus included the amount of premarital sex women engaged in; the amount of oral sex, especially among college-educated, married people; the lack of guilt women felt about premarital intercourse; and the amount of extramarital sex people admitted to. Other findings from the Kinsey surveys:

1 The number and variety of sexual activities for both sexes were greater than people would have predicted in the 1940s and 1950s. (See Figures 2.1, 2.2, 2.3, and 2.4.)

2 Since puberty, about one in four males had experienced orgasm in the presence of another male.

FIGURE 2.1

Means and medians from active samples that represent the number of ejaculations per week, by males' ages (based on Kinsey et al., 1948). Means are mathematical averages, and medians are midpoints between top and bottom statistical halves of samples.

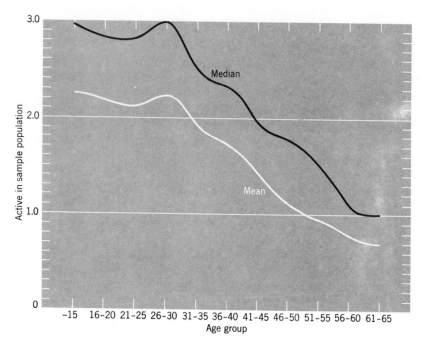

FIGURE 2.2

Onset of adolescence and sexual response in males and females. Ejaculation is evidence of sexual response in males, and orgasm is evidence in females (from Kinsey et al., 1953).

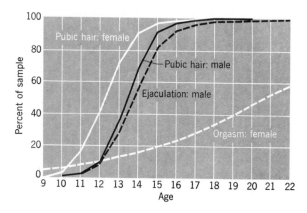

FIGURE 2.3

Cumulative incidence of orgasm in females (from masturbation, intercourse, or any other source), according to the females' ages and marital status (from Kinsey et al., 1953).

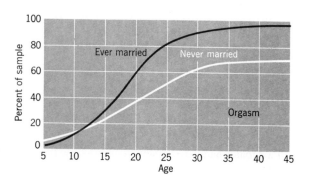

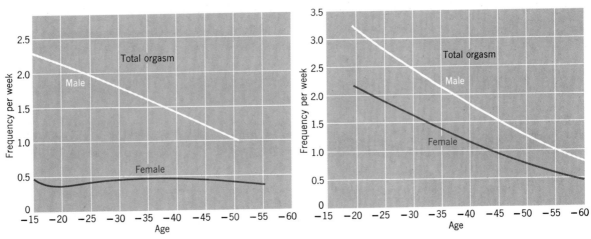

FIGURE 2.4

Number of orgasms per week for males and females (from masturbation, intercourse, or any other source), according to their ages and marital status. The curve for singles is on the left; the curve for married people is on the right (from Kinsey et al., 1953).

3 For males, educational level was inversely related to the likelihood of premarital intercourse. The more education men had, the less likely they were to have had premarital intercourse. Thus grade-school or high-school graduates were likelier to have had premarital intercourse than college graduates. College graduates who did have premarital intercourse were older at their first time than the less educated men and to have used their experience with petting and with fantasizing during masturbation for elaborate foreplay.[1] For females, the imminence of marriage was directly related to particular sexual behaviors. **Orgasm** during petting and premarital intercourse, if they happened, did so in the year or two before a female married. Religious women and those born before 1900 were much less likely than less devout women or those born after 1900 to have had premarital intercourse or orgasms in petting.

4 The **median age** of ejaculation (the age at which 50 percent had experienced it) for males was 13 to 14. For females, the median age of orgasm was 20. Ninety percent of males had ejaculated by age 15. Their first ejaculation was likely to be solitary—by **masturbation** (68 percent) or spontaneous emission (13 percent). Females' first orgasm was likely to be social—by marital intercourse (30 percent), during petting (18 percent), during premarital intercourse (8 percent), or homosexual contact (3 percent).

5 A woman who had experienced orgasm before she was married was likelier than one who had not to experience orgasm in her first year of marriage. After 20 years of marriage, 90 percent of women had had orgasms.

No study since Kinsey's has covered the same breadth of sexual behaviors (we have considered here only a few of those researched), the large number of male and female subjects, along with the care in trying to form a representative sample out of fairly educated volunteers, and the checking for memory and truthfulness. For these reasons, many contemporary sex researchers prefer to compare their findings with Kinsey's, even though the sample is not truly representative.

---

[1]"Foreplay" means the sexual activities that lead to intercourse. In contrast, "making out," "necking," "petting," and that marvel of vagueness, "fooling around," do not imply that intercourse necessarily follows.

TABLE 2.1

Frequency in Percents of Precoital Techniques, Reported by Education Level of Male Partner, All Ages[a]

Sexual Behavior	Frequency in Percent (All Ages)		
	Lowest Educational Level		Highest Educational Level
Kiss, Lip, M[b], frequent	88	–	98
Kiss, Deep, M, frequent	41	–	77
Breast, manual, M, frequent	79	–	96
Breast, oral, manual, M, frequent	33	–	82
Female genitals, manual, PM[c] frequent	80	–	91
Female genitals, manual, M, frequent	75	–	90
Male genitals, manual, PM, frequent	66	–	75
Male genitals, manual, M, frequent	57	–	75
Male genitals, oral, PM (ever)	22	–	39
Male genitals, oral, M (ever)	7	–	43
Female genitals, oral, PM (ever)	9	–	18
Female genitals, oral, M (ever)	4	–	45

[a] *Based on Kinsey et al, 1948, Table 93, p. 368.*
[b] *M = Marital*
[c] *PM = Premarital*

RECENT SURVEYS

Kinsey set a high standard for gathering evidence on sexual behavior. Others since Kinsey have conducted generally more limited surveys. Some of the patterns Kinsey found have changed, and some have remained stable over time. As we look at the more recent survey findings, we can also evaluate the method of the surveys.

MASTURBATION   In an excellent interview study of a representative sample of unmarried, West German city dwellers between the ages of 20 and 21, reports from males indicated that when they were between the ages of 13 and 16, they had been twice as likely as females to have masturbated. Males also masturbated more often than females (Schmidt and Sigusch, 1971). According to the reports of young German women, by age 16 they had reached the cumulative incidence of masturbating that the women in Kinsey's sample had reached by age 25. More women reported masturbating and masturbating earlier than in Kinsey's day. Morton Hunt, a science writer and journalist, in a Playboy Foundation study (1974) of adult Americans, duplicated the German results in the United States. Although Hunt's report is not based on a representative sample (too many people refused to participate), the results on masturbation fit the pattern found in studies with better samples. Even in an enormous but unrepresentative sample of over 65,000 men and nearly 15,000 women in the United States who responded to a 133-item questionnaire in the early 1982 issues of *Playboy,* women reported masturbating one-third as often as their male counterparts (the median frequency was 44 times a year compared to 140 times a year). The males and females were very experienced sexually. Even so, the rates for masturbation were not alike.

As we say in the chapter on sexual values, whether people ever perform a given sexual act and the frequency with which they perform that sexual act depend in large part on people's attitudes and sexual values. People's sexual values also affect how they respond to the questions of a researcher. So many people, in both France and the United States, refused to answer survey questions about masturbation that we conclude that many people are ashamed of masturbating. Even in representative samples, one in six French men and women simply refused to answer (Gondonneau et al., 1972), as did one in five in the United States (Wilson, 1975). As Kinsey knew, even when people answer, they are likely to underreport their experience with forms of sexual behavior they consider taboo. Such underreporting of masturbation occurs among sexually active teenagers, too (Sorenson, 1973).

PREMARITAL INTERCOURSE   Kinsey found that many males had had intercourse before marriage. The rate for those whose education ended with grade school was 98 percent; with high-school, 84 percent; and with college, 67 percent. Half of all females who married had had premarital intercourse, and most had no regrets about it. Half of these females had had intercourse with their fiancé only; 41 percent had had intercourse with at least one man other than their fiancé.

We know from the Zelnik and Kantner studies of teenagers living in metropolitan-area households that between 1971 and 1979, the proportion of females between 15 and 19 who had had sexual intercourse outside of marriage rose from 30 percent to 50 percent. The 1979 figure for males between 17 and 21 is 70 percent. The average age at first intercourse by unmarried women is 16. Between 1971 and 1976, the average age went down about two to three months. Depending on age, about one or two in ten "sexually active" women have had intercourse only once. About half of all these experienced women have had one partner only, usually a man two to three years older than they are.

A sound, large-scale study of Michigan high-school students found that by age 17, females were as likely as males to have had intercourse. However, college-bound daughters from professional families were less likely than daughters from blue-collar families to have had premarital intercourse (Vener and Stewart, 1974). Another excellent sample of 14- to 17-year-olds from Illinois found the same class effect (Miller and Simon, 1974). The patterns for the two sexes seem to be growing more alike. In the West German study cited above, for example, by age 13, half of the young men and women had had at least one date. By 14, most had kissed. By 15, half had had a steady relationship, had been in love, and had breast petted. By 16, half had experienced genital petting, and one-third had had intercourse. By 17, half had had intercourse (Schmidt and Sigusch, 1973). The research results are consistent: social sex for men and women is *converging*. It is not exactly the same for men and women, but it is far less different than it was in Kinsey's day—at least as assessed by surveys.

SEX IN MARRIAGE   Most sexual encounters happen in the marriage bed. Married couples are simply more physically available to each other for long periods of time than unmarried couples. They do not have to orchestrate dates or other opportunities. Nevertheless, folklore has it that the familiarity and predictability of marriage somehow diminish the sexual urge. In fact, Kinsey found that married couples at age 20 started having intercourse about three times a week but declined to roughly half that frequency 20 years later. Today sex in marriage is more frequent (Hunt, 1974). A demonstrable increase happened between 1965 and 1970, when two successive National Fertility samples (in which demographers track the relationship among women's age, their plans for having children, and intercourse) showed that for women of virtually all ages, but especially young women, intercourse rates went up (Westoff, 1974).

No matter where it's studied, the rate of intercourse declines over the course of most marriages. Work and careers interfere, and there is nothing like an infant to put a damper on its parents' sexual expression, as one British study amply demonstrated (James, 1981). But husbands' sexual interest also seems to wane. As the Kinsey findings showed, women had more orgasms and were increasingly interested in sex as their marriage progressed. Yet the frequency with which the couple had sex declined. The inescapable conclusion to Kinsey was that the more sexually interested partner started out as the male but then became the female.

As for orgasm among married women, figures since Kinsey (at least for samples as broad as his) are difficult to find. The most nearly comparable are from the far-from-representative study by Morton Hunt (1974). That study reports a substantial increase over Kinsey's figures in the incidence and frequency of orgasm among newly married women. Hunt's results are believable because they jibe with smaller, more valid studies. German studies of premarital sex reveal a much higher incidence of female orgasm in intercourse today than in Kinsey's day.

EXTRAMARITAL SEX   Marriage partners in our culture are expected not to engage in sexual relations outside of marriage. The **formal standard** is for both partners in a marriage to be monogamous, but in the past the standard has been applied more loosely to males than females. Kinsey knew that his subjects were probably underreporting the incidence of extramarital sex because it was tabooed. He found that extramarital sex happened irregularly for both sexes. One-half of males and one-quarter of females admitted to extramarital sex. Males of higher educational and economic levels had less and later experience with extramarital sex than other males. Women at all educational levels had had little extramarital sex. Younger women and those active in their church were especially unlikely to have had extramarital sex. Kinsey found that husbands and wives usually did not know about their mate's infidelity, but those who knew reacted in ways that said something significant about the double standard. Men were twice as likely as women to ascribe their divorce to their partner's extramarital affair. Once again we see the sexual standard applied more harshly to women than to men.

Most recent studies of extramarital sex rely on volunteers, but volunteers may distort estimates of incidence and frequency of tabooed or uncommon behavior. Thus we conservatively conclude from many studies that extramarital sex is probably starting earlier among young married couples. A 1970 French study with a representative sample showed more young people of both sexes admitting to extramarital sex than in the Kinsey sample (Gondonneau et al., 1972). In an interesting *Redbook* magazine study, volunteers reported that 25 percent of all wives between 20 and 25, and 38 percent of wives between 35 and 39 had had extramarital intercourse. Working wives had a higher incidence than wives who stayed at home; of course, women who work ouside their houses have more chances to meet men (Tavris and Sadd, 1975). Women in Kinsey's sample often had only their husband's friends and colleagues as candidates for extramarital affairs. To-day's *Redbook* readers, by age 25, had accumulated an incidence of extramarital affairs found by Kinsey among women age 45. But remember that the representativeness of the *Redbook* study for all women is dubious. Although 10,000 questionnaires were counted, most *Redbook* readers are young, educated, white, and affluent.

One enlightening study on extramarital sex used the survey method to uncover factors among married women that might make some likelier than others to have affairs (Bell, Turner, and Rosen, 1975). Questionnaires were distributed by a group of sociologists. A sample created in this fashion is not representative (and is likely to resemble the *Redbook* sample). The questionnaires revealed three factors that individually or collectively went with higher rates of extramarital sex for women. The three factors: unhappiness with their marriage, liberal sexual preferences (such as for oral or anal sex), and liberal styles of living. Among this mostly young group of women, about one in four had had extramarital affairs, an incidence that agrees with the *Redbook* survey. Thus from two not so representative studies emerges a picture of the incidence of extramarital sex among young women and what might motivate them. Since Kinsey's time, the rate of extramarital sex by women is probably up. Although both young and middle-aged women resort to extramarital affairs if they are unhappy with their marriages, among young women, the added factors of liberal sexual preferences and styles of behaving increases the likelihood of extramarital sex.

Women today are likelier to work outside their home than they were in Kinsey's day. They are likelier to have more education. They have seen more divorces among their peers and are less ashamed of divorce than women of Kinsey's day. An affair is likelier today in the period between a couple's separation and divorce. But there are no studies that separate out affairs during that period from those in the rest of a woman's life.

Opinion Surveys: Sex on Campus

College students traditionally have differed from others their age in their choices of sexual behavior. They have started having intercourse and have married later—and still do, on average. But they are having intercourse earlier now than they did in Kinsey's time. In the late 1950s, depending on the school that was studied, between 7 and 39 percent of college women and over 50 percent but less than 75 percent of college men had had intercourse (Ehrmann, 1959). During the 1960s and 1970s, variations by school still held true. The best estimates are that between two-thirds and three-quarters of college women have intercourse before or during college. Many are sexually experienced when they reach college, and many live with a man during college. At one eastern state university with permissive dormitory rules, nearly half of all seniors of both sexes had lived with someone of the other sex (Peterman et al., 1974). Studies of students living together reveal that many college students accept the practice, especially those at schools with equal numbers of both sexes, coed dorms, unrestricted visiting, and off-campus housing (Macklin, 1976). Under these conditions, one-quarter to one-third of students live together for some period of time. In the early 1970s, about one-third of students' parents knew about their sexual arrangements (Arafat and Yorburg, 1973).

> College students overestimate others' experience with intercourse before marriage, and they overestimate how many college women want to have intercourse before they get married.

College students tend to underestimate how different they are from others who are older and less educated. They overestimate others' experience with intercourse before marriage, and they overestimate how many college women want to have intercourse before they get married (Jackson and Potkay, 1973). As late as July 1969, when attitudes on sex had liberalized among college students, the Gallup Poll found in a representative national sample that 80 percent of people thought it was wrong for men and women to have sexual relations before they were married. People under 30 were least likely to think it was wrong. Women at all ages were more conservative than men. The college educated were the most liberal group of all (Alston and Tucker, 1973). As a whole, people in the United States think that young people have a healthier attitude toward sex than their elders had when they were young (Wilson, 1975): an attitude that is tolerant of sexuality without explicitly endorsing it.

During the 1970s, research showed college men and women were having more sexual experiences that were more alike than those reported by earlier researchers. At the University of North Carolina, for example, unmarried men and women had an equal incidence of sex (Bauman and Wilson, 1974). The similarity in

Feiffer

THINKING ABOUT SEX.

THE MORE I READ ABOUT IT IN SEX MAGAZINES THE LESS APPEALING IT IS.

THE MORE I SEE IT IN X-RATED FILMS THE LESS EROTIC IT IS.

THE MORE I LEARN ABOUT IT IN SEX MANUALS THE MORE INTIMIDATING IT IS.

I WISH SCHOOLS WOULD TEACH SEX IGNORANCE COURSES.

THEN I COULD ENJOY IT LIKE MY FATHER.

patterns between the sexes marked an important shift in gender roles: although college men are having intercourse more than their counterparts of the 1940s did, they have fewer partners, and they are offering these partners more companionship and commitment (Finger, 1975). A 1975 sample of a southern state university showed premarital sex in virtually equal incidence for men and women students (Robinson and Jedlicka, 1982). In practice, if not always in people's attitudes, the double standard for nonmarital sex seems to be diminishing.

Figures for the late 1970s from New England campuses show that 35 percent of male students arrive sexually experienced, and 70 to 80 percent leave that way. Some 10 to 15 percent have intercourse only once, the number that in the past might have gone to a prostitute to shed their virginity. In this study, only 2 percent went to a prostitute. The story for women was more subtle. About 25 to 30 percent—not very different from their male counterparts—were sexually experienced when they arrived at school, but their sexual experience during college depended on the kind of school they were attending. In schools where large numbers of women go on to graduate work, about 70 percent graduate with sexual experience. But in schools where three-quarters of women marry within two years of graduating, 95 percent graduate with experience in intercourse, just as Kinsey would have predicted (Sarrel, cited in Eisenberg and Eisenberg, 1977). Thus men and women who plan graduate careers are more likely than those whose schooling ends with college to delay intercourse, given all of the demands that social sex makes on time and energy. Even so, the vast majority of men and women finish college sexually experienced. However, the issue of virginity is not dead on campus. Its social context has changed. Virginity remains important to many students, especially religious students. In a midwestern university there was little change in the incidence of males' virginity in the fifteen years between 1963 and 1978. During the same period, the incidence of virginity among female students went from 75% to 38% (Sherwin and Corbett, 1985). But in all, many more students than in Kinsey's day are having intercourse, because of changes in gender roles and sexual attitudes as well as reliable methods of contraception and legal abortion.

Kinsey's remain the most famous and important of the surveys on sexual behavior, although researchers since Kinsey have contributed important information to the field. Some of that information confirms Kinsey's findings; some of it charts genuinely new trends: increased convergence in social premarital sex by men and women, specifically, intercourse, oral, and extramarital sex; increased masturbation among women, although they still begin masturbating at a later age than men and masturbate less often than men do (Hunt, 1974). Surveys have told us what sexual acts people are performing as adolescents and adults. From that information, we can infer a growing convergence in the behavior of males and females. But surveys are certainly not the only research tool available to the researcher. They answer some, not all, questions about sexuality.

THE OBSERVATIONAL METHOD

Early in the development of any field of knowledge, researchers must simply look at behavior to find out what it consists of. Later they refine the kind of research questions they might ask in a survey or an experiment. William Masters and

Virginia Johnson's famous work used the **observational method.** They developed and refined techniques for observing and describing how people respond when they are sexually aroused (1966). (We will detail these findings in Chapter 7.) Kinsey asked people to report their sexual experience; Masters and Johnson asked to be shown. They developed instruments for seeing how the vagina changes with excitement, for measuring the circumference of the penis at rest and in erection. They put together a technology for repeatedly observing and recording the cycle of sexual responses in subject after subject. Their volunteers masturbated alone and with a partner and had intercourse in the laboratory. Masters and Johnson have observed homosexual as well as heterosexual responses (Masters and Johnson, 1979). Selecting subjects for sexual observation can pose problems simply because the people who will allow observation may be unlike people who will not allow it. Masters and Johnson's volunteers included prostitutes, Ph.D.s, and M.D.s— certainly not the average cross-section of people. But they had to start somewhere, and this was the sample of people they could recruit.

In spite of jokes about Masters and Johnson in soft-pornographic magazines, they did not participate in the sexual behavior they were observing. But when two other researchers wanted to learn about swingers, a special group with its own rules about who may swing and how to say yes or no to a sexual invitation, they (Constantine and Constantine, 1973) had to adopt the method of **participant observation.** In such a case, the very presence of anyone—researcher or partici-pant—influences the other people present. Yet observers who did not seem to

William Masters and Virginia Johnson

participate would alter absolutely the character of a group of swingers. Participant observation is the one way to study groups suspicious of outsiders. Participant observation of such groups differs from other kinds of observation in that other researchers have trouble subjecting the findings to test in another such group, a common method of verifying observational work. Some participant observers reveal their purpose and identity when they believe that their role as researchers is jeopardized by participating—when a group member solicits sex with them, for instance.

The Cross-Cultural Method

Anthropologists who go to live among a group of people and observe them engage in one form of observational research. Called the **cross-cultural method,** this kind of research is often difficult to replicate, and the observer inevitably affects the people under study, whether those effects are subtle or gross. Thanks to videotape and voice recordings, in the last decade or so anthropologists have been able to "freeze" their data and bring them home to share with skeptical colleagues. Of course, anthropologists learn useful things about a culture besides what they capture on tape or reliably coded behavioral observation.

Sociologists conduct a similar kind of research when they observe how various groups of people behave in their natural situations. Sociologists are the anthropologists of their culture. Like anthropologists, they conduct **field studies.** Thus anthropologists study the Hopi or the Swedes, and sociologists study, in their own culture, the teenagers of a town or the behavior of crowds, or homosexuals, or medical workers. One field study, for example, took place in men's public toilets, an excellent place to study the largely unspoken soliciting and granting of homosexual favors between men. (See "Sexuality in Perspective: Observing the Tearoom Trade.")

EXPERIMENTAL METHODS

In research using the **experimental method,** researchers try to isolate the biological or environmental factors that they think may determine a particular behavior. They therefore try to test if their subjects' behavior changes when such a factor is present but not when it is absent. Experimenters try to define the crucial factor(s) sharply and to prevent any extraneous factors from intruding, no mean feat. We can illustrate the advantages of experimental methods with an example. Kinsey had asked his survey subjects whether they were aroused by seeing sexually explicit pictures. He found that women said they were less responsive to such **erotica** than men said they were. But it later turned out that the wording of the question had led men and women to answer differently. Thus the answers were suspect (Gebhard, 1973).

Whan a West German team investigated the effects of erotica on college students' levels of psychological arousal, sexual behavior, and emotions in a laboratory experiment, they came up with some interesting new results. Schmidt and Sigusch (Schmidt and Sigusch, 1973; Schmidt, 1975) wanted to know whether there were any differences in the way that males and females responded to erotica and if so, what those differences might be. They brought volunteer college students into the laboratory and exposed them to erotic slides, films, or stories. Shortly after-

SEXUALITY IN PERSPECTIVE:
OBSERVING THE TEAROOM TRADE

The more thoroughly forbidden an act is, the harder it is to learn about. That is why one sociologist, Laud Humphreys, studied homosexual activity and in the process violated people's privacy without their consent. Yes, he turned up valuable knowledge, but how should the value of that knowledge be measured? Yes, his study was useful, but could he have conducted it in another way? Participant observation can raise troubling issues of ethics.

Humphreys observed the "tearoom trade." **Tearooms** are men's toilets in subways, parks, recreation areas, and the like where men, the "trade," meet to have fast, impersonal sex (usually fellatio). Humphreys watched the homosexual acts and, at the same time, looked through the roof of the toilets to warn pairs about roving police cars. (But he also took down the license plate numbers of the "trade" and later, after tracing the men's identities, called on them to answer his "survey.") Embedded in the "survey" were questions on sexuality. The men remained unaware of the true criterion for their inclusion in the "survey."

Humphreys found that most of the "trade" were self-designated heterosexuals, married, some with wives who were uninterested in sex or fearful of pregnancy. Their tearoom acts ostensibly conferred no homosexual identity on these men. Many seemed to lead lives of quiet desperation. Humphreys wrote about them with obvious care and sensitivity. But at each step in his research, he violated their right to privacy. They were observed, tracked, and interviewed without any awareness of what they were contributing to.

The research caused a storm of controversy. Humphreys' university department was far from unanimous about his ethics in research. It is doubtful whether a university oversight committee would grant permission for such a research project today. Yet Humphreys' research broke the link between homosexual act and homosexual identity as no research had done before. His story has been confirmed by others, although none has captured the richness of the stories told by the tearoom trade in their own homes. The ethical dilemma was magnified the minute that Humphreys began acting as lookout, license-plate detective, *and* survey researcher. So long as people study the real life of socially stigmatized minorities, they must be acutely sensitive to ethical issues. No one has the right to expose a research subject to harm.

Based on Laud Humphreys, *Tearoom Trade: Impersonal Sex in Public Places.* Chicago: Aldine, 1970.

ward, the students filled out questionnaires about their mental and physical responses, their reactions to the erotic materials, and their emotional state. They then left the laboratory with another questionnaire about their emotional state and their sexual behavior on the day *after* they had seen the erotic material. Contrary to what Kinsey had found, the experimenters found no differences between the sexes in the five areas they assessed:

1 Sexual stimulation: both women and men found all three types of erotica "moderately stimulating." On the average, men rated their own arousal slightly higher than women did theirs, but the area of overlap was great.

2 Physiological reactions to the erotica: both sexes reported feeling them and in proportions that showed no statistically significant differences (males, 80 to 91 percent; females, 70 to 83 percent).

3 Masturbation: defined as any activity used to heighten arousal, the experimenters found that about 20 percent of women and men masturbated during the erotic presentations.

4 Sexual behavior: for both sexes, it remained stable over the next 24 hours. Small increases may have occurred for a minority of subjects in masturbation, petting, number of orgasms, sexual fantasies, talking about sex, sexual tension, and sexual desire. Only women significantly increased the amount of intercourse they had in the next 24 hours.

5 Emotional arousal: both sexes felt positive and negative emotions and in similar patterns, although women expressed more shock and disgust, indicating that they either felt more conflicted about their feelings of arousal than men did or their arousal did not alter their view of erotica. This difference probably stemmed from cultural conditioning. A day after exposure, most subjects of both sexes were no longer emotionally aroused.

Thus both sexes may be physically aroused by all types of erotic material. The experimental design clearly had advantages over the survey method in investigating the matter of arousal, because the experiment allowed for multiple measures of arousal for the exact same erotic material.

Researchers can study the question of sex differences in arousal in even more interesting ways. They can find out whether women and men are equally accurate in labeling their body's level of arousal. In one study, experimenters showed neutral movies (as a control condition) and erotic movies (an experimental condition) to both male and female subjects and measured their physical responses to arousal (blood flow to the genitals). After finding that both sexes were more aroused by erotic than by neutral movies, the experimenters gave subjects questionnaires to find out how closely the subjective measure of their arousal corresponded to the physiological measures the experimenters had taken. They found that males' subjective assessments corresponded more closely to the physiological assessments of their level of arousal. Sexually inexperienced females have a particularly low correspondence between vaginal blood congestion, the physiological measure of arousal, and subjective judgment of arousal (Geer et al., 1974). This experiment leads us to suspect that because men can see their erections, they can connect their genital with their subjective reactions. Women may take longer to learn the connection between genital changes and the subjective feelings of arousal, because their genital responses are less visible.

Experimental methods have their limits. Researchers must not harm their subjects. They must also formulate their question very precisely and set up controlled conditions for the test. Experiments allow researchers to compare subjects to themselves (in the erotica experiment, a subject's response to the neutral stimuli could be compared to her response to the erotic stimuli). This use of a subject as her own control is a powerful source of information. Controls also let experimenters rule out certain faulty interpretations of their results. For example, if we wanted to test a new contraceptive, we would need to match the demographic characteristics of the couples using Contraceptives A and B. But we would also have to separate the couples according to a very important criterion: whether their goal in using contraception was to delay or to terminate childbearing. Usually, the former group (the Delay condition) has less success using contraceptives than the latter group (the Terminate condition) does. If we failed to control for these conditions—if one group consisted mostly of delayers and another mostly terminaters—we might conclude that the wrong contraceptive was superior. If we do control for the different goals and still find that A is better than B, we are safe in our conclusion.

Men and women respond to erotic materials in many of the same ways.

Experimental methods are therefore excellent for testing hypotheses. A method that often suggests hypotheses for experimental test is the clinical method. We will turn to that now.

CLINICAL METHODS

Clinical methods are used to generate hypotheses. They provide descriptions of unusual samples of people. Often they describe how a particular course of treatment affected one or more patients. The early clinical studies of Sigmund Freud (1856–1939) are well known instances in which he tried to cure patients of emotional difficulties by using techniques (hypnosis and, later, psychoanalysis) that he evolved over his working lifetime. Havelock Ellis (1859–1939), a contemporary of Freud, was an astute clinical observer. He produced descriptions of clinical cases involving sexuality as well as a theory of their source. Both men wrote many, many case studies. The enduring value of their clinical contributions lies in these investigators' willingness to examine the origins and the variability of human sexual behavior. Such attitudes were far from the norm in the late Victorian period when they worked.

More recently, a clinical study appeared that allowed a psychologist to submit a theory about sexual fantasy to test. Since Kinsey, it has been theorized that sexual fantasies based on visual stimuli are more readily evoked in males than in females. John Money and Anke Ehrhardt (1972) proposed that males respond to visual images by fantasy and erection. They also proposed that young women are far less likely to turn such visual stimulation into sexual fantasy. Part of the difficulty in investigating the question of arousal by visual stimuli has been that groups of boys, but not of girls, share sexually stimulating magazines like *Playboy, Penthouse,* and *Hustler*—from about the age of nine on. In short, the same sex differences in exposure to visual erotica that affected the arousal question discussed above affects the study of sex differences in visual fantasy. Clearly, researchers cannot expose groups of boys and girls to equal amounts of erotica while they grow up in order to test for later differences. But two adult women were found (Luria, 1982) who *had* grown up with pornography since they were preschoolers, their father having been a distributor of pornography. Like the boys' groups, they had looked at the pornography together. (Unlike the boys, they never felt they were breaking any rules in doing so.) Did these women incorporate the visual imagery of the pornography into their sexual lives? One did; one did not. From this interview study, we know that a woman can incorporate visual imagery into her sexual fantasies but that not all women will do so. With only two cases, it would be absurd to draw conclusions about women in general. But studying the two women is enough to support the conclusion that males are not the *only* people who will incorporate pornographic imagery into their sexual fantasies.

As you would expect, clinical studies almost never are conducted on random samples. Typically they are done on people who show some special clinical characteristics, and the very specialness of their condition evokes hypotheses from clinicians. Clinical studies have rules, of course. Interviews can be standardized, for instance. Some clinical studies do test hypotheses rather than just generate them. For example, psychologists might compare groups with sexual problems by dividing them in half and instructing only one group in how to fantasize.

SEXUALITY IN PERSPECTIVE: SHOULD YOU BELIEVE WHAT YOU READ?

The old rule for consumers, "Let the buyer beware," holds true for consumers of information as well as used cars. If you have ever been jolted awake by the morning newspaper telling you that "A study has found that all college students do thus-and-such while making love," you know the worry that comes from knowing that *you* have never done thus-and-such (or the relief from knowing that *of course* you do thus-and-such). What is the best way to evaluate the information? Be wary. Adopt a "show-me" attitude. Ask questions.

To what population does the sample apply? The newspaper may brag that it applies to "all college students," but does it really? See whether the respondents are of one or both sexes, from colleges all over the country or just parts of it, from all social classes and races, from the same age group. Students should not all be fraternity members or 18-year-old males or southerners, if the sample is to represent all college students. One interesting book on teenagers appeared that had sampled 90 percent of its subjects in southern California and 10 percent in the Northeast (Hass, 1979). The author said that he found the two groups not to be different. That may be so, but how do we as readers know? He did not tell how his sample was drawn or how many people turned him down. His sample was not representative, although readers could cull from it information on clusters of responses: the differences in attitudes between, say, sexually experienced and inexperienced high school students.

Do the questions asked appear verbatim? It's very helpful if they do. (Hass does include his questions.) Then you can see exactly what was asked. Did the respondents understand the questions and all agree on their meaning? Not all social groups describe sexual acts in the same ways. After all, you may have been thus-and-suching for years and never have known it. Are the answers clear enough so that coders can judge when answers mean the same or different things?

Does the study assure respondents of anonymity so that they'll answer honestly? Not everyone likes to admit publicly to performing thus-and-such. Are the questions phrased judgmentally? You can imagine the differences in responses to a question worded, "Have you ever cheated on your wife/husband?" and one worded, "Have you ever had a sexual relationship outside your marriage?"

So the next time you hear about what "everyone" is doing, dig in and find out who everyone is and what everyone really said. *Caveat emptor:* let the buyer beware.

(Some clinical studies have elaborate experimental designs.) In fact, such studies show that learning how to fantasize can help some women increase their sexual pleasure.

Generally speaking, no matter whether researchers use the survey method, observational, experimental, or clinical methods, their questions shape the design of their research, and that shape influences content. Furthermore, no matter the design, the criteria for good research do not vary. Good research is valid, replicable, and objective. Above all, it provides answers to a question worth asking.

SUMMARY

1 Researchers follow delimited lines of inquiry so that they can subject their questions to test by some scientifically acceptable method.

2 The nature of the questions researchers ask often determines the design of the study.

3 Good research is valid and replicable. The scientific method hinges on asking questions and gathering data objectively, so that others can repeat the methods and reach comparable results on comparable samples. The scientific method allows researchers to challenge any study that cannot be replicated or the results of which can be refuted.

4 Surveys show how a particular behavior breaks down for certain groups of people. Surveys produce answers about incidences and frequencies of behavior. Surveys are helpful for people who must make judgments about unfamiliar patterns of behavior. Survey results are, however, static and may tell little about the meaning to people of the behavior surveyed.

5 Descriptive statistics produce answers about frequencies of kinds of behavior. Inferential statistics are those from which researchers draw inferences about group differences.

6 A representative sample—whether random or probability—provides answers that truly represent behavior of the total population in question. Unrepresentative samples, such as those conducted by some popular magazines among their readers, do not represent the total population, only groups like the magazine's particular readers.

7 Surveys may be conducted by interview, by questionnaire, or by a combination of these.

8 Alfred Kinsey and his colleagues produced the most famous and perhaps the most influential survey of Americans' sexual behavior in the 1940s and early 1950s by questioning 18,000 subjects. Their findings shocked the nation with greater than expected frequencies of premarital sex by women, oral sex by everyone, and homosexual encounters by males.

9 More recent surveys than Kinsey's indicate that more women are masturbating and are doing so earlier than in Kinsey's day; that solitary sex followed by social sex is still the pattern for males, with just the opposite still being the pattern for females; that females are having premarital intercourse younger than in Kinsey's day; that sex in marriage still declines in frequency over

time; that women who had orgasm before marriage are likelier than others to have it after marriage; that wives who work outside the home are likelier than housewives to have extramarital sex; that college students have intercourse later and marry later than others their age; and that the pattern of companionate sex is being found among males as well as females.

10 Masters and Johnson devised techniques for standardizing the observation of sexual response in the laboratory. Other researchers have worked as participant-observers among groups that would otherwise be suspicious of observation of their sexual behavior.

11 Anthropologists use the cross-cultural method to study behavior in other cultural settings. They have found that all cultures regulate sexual behavior in some way.

12 In research done by experimental methods, researchers isolate factors they think may determine a particular behavior and then try to account for their subjects' behavior and prevent extraneous factors from intruding. Experiments are good for testing hypotheses. They require researchers to formulate their questions carefully and to observe an ethical standard of conduct toward their subjects.

13 Clinical methods of study, carried out among other special groups of people, often patients with some problems, typically are better for generating than for testing hypotheses.

KEY TERMS

independent variable
dependent variable
control condition
cross-cultural (ethnographic)
   method
historical (archival) method
replicability (reliability)
convergent validity
validity
scientific method
survey
longitudinal study
panels
frequencies
incidence
descriptive statistics
inferential statistics
population
sample

random sample
stratified (quota) sample
interview
questionnaire
skewing
orgasm
masturbation
median age
formal standard
observational method
participant observation
cross-cultural method
culture-bound
field studies
tearoom
experimental method
erotica
clinical method

SUGGESTED READINGS

Green, R. and Wiener, J. (eds). *Methodology in Sex Research*. Rockville, MD: U.S. Dept. of Health and Human Services (Publication #ADM 80-766), 1980. This volume, edited by a psychiatric researcher and a government official who long supported sex research, may be unique in its focus on methods.

Robinson, P. *The Modernization of Sex.* New York: Harper & Row, 1976. A Stanford historian reviews the people who have done the central empirical work on human sexuality. He looks for their more personal contributions, the values and views beneath the work.

Tanfer, K. and Horn, M. C. "Contraceptive Use, Pregnancy, and Fertility Patterns among Single American Women in their 20s." *Family Planning Perspectives* (January/February 1985) *17,* no. 1, pp. 10–18. An updated survey of contraception and pregnancy among single women. Like surveyors Zelnik and Kantner, the authors are explicit about how their sample was drawn.

PART II
SEX AND GENDER

Chapter 3

Gender Identity and Biology

When your parents conceived you, they did not know which sex you were. When you were born, someone examined you and said, "It's a girl" or "It's a boy." "It's a girl," of course, meant that you had female genitals. "It's a boy" meant that you had male genitals. (For more on sexual anatomy, see Chapters 5 and 6.) But "It's a girl" or "It's a boy" described something important besides the structure of your genitals.

Knowing your sex also answered endless questions and set in motion a lifelong list of expectations. Now you could be named. Now people would know which gifts were appropriate: "girl things" or "boy things." Even the most egalitarian parents would not be able to ignore all the social meanings that people attached to your biological sex. The *interpretation* of your physical appearance by others would prove nearly as important as your biological sex itself. For you were not merely one *sex* or the other. You were also adding on elements of *gender*, masculine or feminine, with all of their psychological and social meanings.

Strictly speaking, **sex** is one's biological maleness or femaleness, and **gender** is one's masculinity or femininity. Sex is binary, and people arrive "packaged" as males or females. Gender has far more possibilities and variations. Males may be "men's men" or more or less feminine in mannerism, and females may be tomboyish or more or less feminine or masculine. Once you were born into this social world, your maleness or femaleness shaped people's reactions to you and, ultimately, your reaction to yourself. At some point, most probably in your first two

Sexually, people are either male or female, but shadings of gender—masculinity or femininity—are far more subtle and varied.

or three years of life, you came to understand that there exist such things as boys and girls and that you were one or the other. From this understanding ultimately grew your private, subjective, deeply held sense of your femaleness or maleness that psychologists call your **core gender identity.** As young children learn about the two sexes, their early impressions can be very imprecise, even comical.

> *As a kid, I thought that people told boys from girls by the length of their hair. Girls had long hair, and boys had short hair. I must have been in third grade before I figured out that was wrong (22-year-old male senior).*

> *Once my little brother stayed at my aunt and uncle's house and took a bath with their daughter. In the tub, he and she compared genitals. My brother seemed confused about why his cousin didn't have a penis. My aunt said, "Boys have a penis, and girls have a vagina." To which my brother replied, "That's not true. Girls have penises, too. I know because my mother has one!" (21-year-old female junior).*

The private conviction that one has about one's own maleness or femaleness, one's gender identity, takes hold early and tenaciously and is very resistant to change. Every once in a while, you may hear or read about someone whose physical sex conflicts with his or her gender identity. These people with apparently reversed gender identities, or **transsexuals,** demonstrate that biological sex and gender are not always perfectly matched. (We will talk more about the puzzle of the transsexual later in this chapter.) Gender identity is a complex construction, the psychological house on the biological foundation.[1]

SEXUAL DEVELOPMENT: THE BIOLOGICAL FOUNDATION

Biologists call the structural and functional differences between the sexes, **sexual dimorphism.** These differences are inherited. Your sexual characteristics are the products of chemical messages located in your genes and your hormones.

HEREDITY

You inherit your biological sex. Whether you were born with the body of a male or a female was determined at the instant that a sperm, from your father, joined your mother's egg. At that instant of your conception, you became a **zygote,** consisting of one cell. Like all human cells, you contained 23 pairs of chromosomes, half of each pair from each parent—23 chromosomes from the sperm and another 23 from the egg. When they united, the pairs lined up. **Chromosomes** are the physical structures that carry the instructions for chemical processes of development through your entire lifetime. They instruct your cells to give you

---

[1]A few words about "identities" are in order here. We all partake of many sorts of identities: work identities, social identities, religious identities, and so on. In this book, we use the term **gender identity** to describe a person's inner conviction of his maleness or her femaleness. **Sexual identity,** in contrast, describes a person's heterosexual, homosexual, or bisexual orientation. The vast majority of homosexual males, for example, are *not* confused about their maleness.

blue or brown eyes, curly or straight hair, male or female genitals, and many other characteristics. The instructions are carried in your **genes,** chemicals that are arranged linearly on the chromosomes. Genes work by organizing proteins that function in the body's cells. Human chromosomes contain over 20,000 genes, but not all genes function in all cells.

Human sex thus is inherited through chromosomes. Of our 23 pairs of chromosomes, 22 are the same in both sexes. These are called **autosomes.** But one pair, the **sex chromosomes,** differentiates males from females. The sex chromosome pair in females is two similar X-shaped chromosomes. In males, the pair consists of one X-shaped and the other, smaller and of different shape, called the Y chromosome. Human eggs always contribute an X chromosome. Human sperm contribute *either* an X *or* a Y chromosome, and for this reason, a father always determines his children's sex. Females carry an XX pair of sex chromosomes, and males carry an XY pair. The genetic identification of the normal human male and female are, respectively, 46,XY and 46,XX. Two X chromosomes are nec-

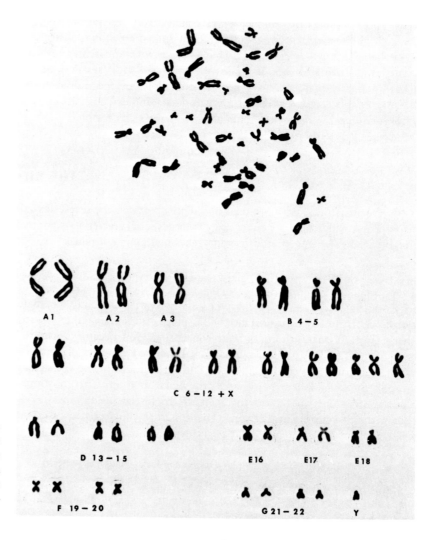

FIGURE 3.1

Karyotyping. When the 23 pairs of human chromosomes are sorted into groups of similar size and shape, missing or extra pieces become obvious. The sex chromosomes here are male—XY.

essary for complete genetic instructions for building the female's internal reproductive organs. (Oddly enough, a baby can *appear* female at birth with only one X chromosome. We will talk about such errors of development later in this chapter because, although they are rare, these errors help us to define the boundaries between sex and gender, biology and psychology.) The X chromosome, which everyone has, is longer and bears more genes than the Y chromosome. The X chromosome contains many genes for sexual and nonsexual development.

Sex-Linked Disorders   Because males have only one X chromosome, they are vulnerable to whatever genes that X carries. Females, with two Xs, are protected from certain defects like color blindness and hemophilia. These defects will show up in females who have two defective genes, but they will show up in males who have only one defective gene. The reason why males are more vulnerable to such genetic defects is fairly simple: the defective genes are **recessive**. Recessive genes will not show up if there is another, **dominant** gene on the matching chromosome. If a male or a female has *one* copy of the normal gene for color vision and blood clotting, that person will be normal. Males, with only one X, have only one throw of the dice for the X they get. Females, with their two Xs, have two throws of the dice. Thus males, because they bear only one X chromosome, are more vulnerable to these recessive **sex-linked disorders** than females are.

The normal human male is genetically a 46,XY. The Y chromosome is necessary for the complete determination of both internal and external male sex organs. The genes on the Y chromosome give the first chemical signals, long before birth, for forming rudimentary sexual structures in the male. Once these structures form, a whole series of events determines further sexual development. The sex chromosomes do not exclusively govern sexual development—other genes and other chemicals play a part—but the sex chromosomes do ultimately determine a baby's sex. Conversely, the other chromosomes also contribute to sexual development both before and after birth.

The First Six Weeks of Development

For the first six weeks after conception, the developing human **embryo** is about the size of a pea, complete with the beginnings of a heart, brain, spinal column, and limbs. Embryos of both sexes look the same—and more like tiny seahorses than humans—and the chromosomes' instructions are apparently the same at this stage for both sexes. At the fifth week, all embryos develop a pair of early **indifferent gonads**, or sexual glands, with cells on the outside, or **cortex**, capable of becoming the female's **ovaries** (egg-producing glands) and cells in the center, or **medulla**, capable of becoming the male's **testes** (sperm-producing glands).

If a Y chromosome is present to instruct the embryo, the medulla cells later (at seven weeks) will grow into primitive testes. Further **prenatal** (before birth) development of male sexual characteristics will depend on chemical secretions from these testes. In the absence of a Y chromosome, the outer cells of the gonad will grow into an ovary, although not until the fourth month of pregnancy. The cells of the primitive gonad that do not multiply will remain undeveloped and visible only under a microscope. Unlike the male's early sexual development, the female's early sexual development does not depend on her ovaries.

THE SECOND SIX WEEKS OF DEVELOPMENT

Between the seventh and twelfth weeks of pregnancy, the embryo continues to differentiate and to develop: beating heart, eyes and ears, large head, hands, feet, and webbed toes! At the seventh week, the embryo is the size of a coffee bean and if it carries a Y, it will now have primitive testes. All embryos at this stage contain primitive forms of *both* sexes' reproductive ducts. The **Mullerian ducts** can later differentiate into the female's uterus, fallopian tubes (that connect uterus to ovaries), and the innermost part of the vagina. The **Wolffian ducts** can differentiate into the male's semen-producing and delivering pathways, comprised of the vasa deferentia, seminal vesicles, and ejaculatory ducts. In the absence of particular hormones during the time for duct development, the Mullerian ducts will develop. This is the case in normal female development. But the hormones produced by the male testis will determine first that the Mullerian ducts will regress and, second, that the Wolffian ducts will develop. Both sexes still look alike to the naked eye. Figure 3.2 shows the first, early similarities between the sexes and the later differentiation into male and female genitals.

HORMONES   The environment in which a gene operates is important for biological structures and functions. Genes can operate to turn on hormones. Hormones then alter the environment of structures already formed and ultimately change these structures as well. **Hormones** are chemical messengers that turn on or turn off activities in various parts of the body. Hormones before birth and at **puberty** (the maturation of the sexual organs at adolescence) provide environments, themselves genetically programmed, that determine crucial steps in the creation of observable sex differences. The prenatal development of a penis rather than a clitoris, for example, depends on the presence of a hormone. The development of breasts at puberty also depends on the presence of hormones.

In embryos with XY chromosomes, primitive testes develop after the first seven weeks. Those testes produce two types of hormones. One is called the **Mullerian inhibiting substance (MIS)**. It is named for what it does rather than for what it is for one excellent reason: it has not yet been fully identified chemically. The second hormone is an **androgen**. Androgens are a class of hormones. Embryos with XX chromosomes produce neither of these hormones. Their Mullerian duct system develops without androgens. The male, Wolffian duct system, in contrast,

TABLE 3.1

Homologous and Analogous Reproductive Organs[a]

Homologous organs		Analogous organs	
Female	Male	Female	Male
Clitoris	Glans of penis	Ovaries	Testes
Labia majora	Scrotum		
Labia minora	Underside of shaft of penis		
Skene's glands	Prostate		
Bartholin's glands	Cowper's glands		

[a]Homologous organs develop from the same tissue in the embryo. Analogous organs function similarly but develop from different precursors.

FIGURE 3.2

Differentiation of the internal and external genitals from shared structures. Left: differentiation in the female. Right: differentiation in the male (after Money and Ehrhardt, 1972).

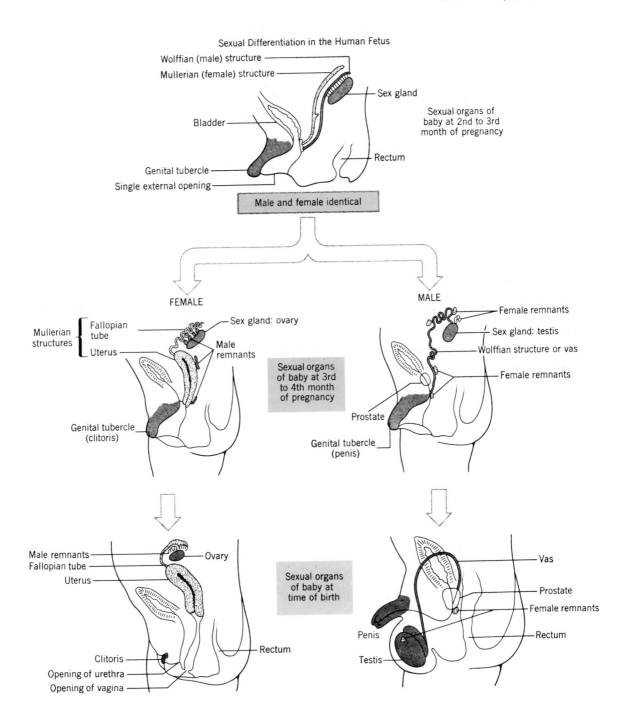

Sexual Differentiation in the Human Fetus

Wolffian (male) structure

Mullerian (female) structure

Sex gland

Sexual organs of baby at 2nd to 3rd month of pregnancy

Bladder

Rectum

Genital tubercle

Single external opening

Male and female identical

FEMALE

MALE

Mullerian structures

Fallopian tube

Sex gland: ovary

Uterus

Male remnants

Sexual organs of baby at 3rd to 4th month of pregnancy

Female remnants

Sex gland: testis

Wolffian structure or vas

Female remnants

Genital tubercle (clitoris)

Prostate

Genital tubercle (penis)

Male remnants

Ovary

Fallopian tube

Uterus

Sexual organs of baby at time of birth

Vas

Prostate

Female remnants

Rectum

Penis

Clitoris

Testis

Opening of urethra

Opening of vagina

Rectum

does require the testes to secrete androgen to stimulate its growth. In sum, the kind of duct system that comprises the internal reproductive tract is determined by the presence (in males) or the absence (in females) of two critical hormones.

From Twelve Weeks until Birth

At seven weeks after conception, both XX and XY embryos have the same external genitals. About half an inch long, embryos now have rudimentary genitals that consist of a bump called a **genital tubercle** and a crevice below it called a **urogenital slit.** Beside the slit are folds of tissue called **urethral folds,** and next to these are **labio-scrotal swellings.** At the top of Figure 3.3, you can see this early structure of the external genitals. For this undifferentiated, "unisex" configuration to become male or female depends on whether the hormone androgen is present or absent.

The genital tubercle will become a penis if androgen is present; it will become a clitoris if androgen is absent. Because they develop from structurally similar tissue, we call organs like the penis and the clitoris **homologous.** The urethral

FIGURE 3.3

Differentiation of the external genitals. Top: undifferentiated state of early fetal development. Middle: differentiation begins at the third to fourth month of pregnancy. The most noticeable difference pictured is the greater fusion of the male's urethral fold. Bottom: completed differentiation of the external genitals at birth.

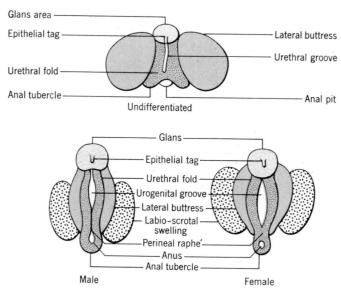

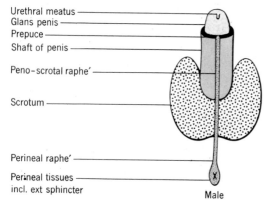
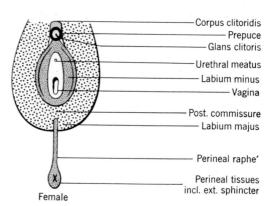

folds will fuse around the shaft of the penis if androgen is present. If androgen is absent, they will remain separated as the **labia minora** (small, inner folds of skin around the opening of the vagina). The labio-scrotal swelling will fuse and become a scrotum if androgen is present; it remains separated as the female's **labia majora** if androgen is absent. Thus the presence or absence of androgen during a critical period, in the third to fourth month of pregnancy, determines whether the baby's external genitals will look male or female.

For complete male genitals to develop, androgen must be produced and turned into a specific chemical form. At this critical period, if androgen is introduced (either from inside or outside the embryo), external male genitals will develop—*even for XX embryos*. If androgen is absent or cannot be used by the target site in the developing embryo, female genitals will develop. Usually the embryo's hormones "match" its chromosomes: XXs have female internal and external genitals; XYs have male internal and external genitals. But in some cases, XYs have a genetic condition that blinds the body to androgen, and so a baby who looks like a female will develop. Likewise, XXs may be bathed in androgen given to their mothers or produced, through a fluke of nature, by their own body. The result is a male-looking baby.

After the twelfth week of development, the embryo has acquired most of its basic structures and enters the phase of growth and maturation when it is called a **fetus.** (We are called "embryos" during the first 12 weeks of prenatal development, the period of most concentrated differentiation. Then we are called "fetuses" until we are born.) The fetus will go from one inch long to 20 times that by the time of birth. Hormones will continue to influence sexual differentiation. By 20 weeks, the fetal ovaries appear, the upper vagina differentiates, and a full-length vaginal canal is formed. Some time after the seventh month, the male fetus's testes descend from the abdomen into the scrotum. If they do not, the boy will have **undescended testicles,** a condition that may cure itself by puberty or that can be treated by surgery or hormones. Testes must descend in order for sperm to be fertile, for the temperature inside the body is too warm.

Hormones affect the fetus's brain as well as its genitals. In one area, the brain of the female differs from that of the male. Because of the prenatal differentiation of the **hypothalamus,** when puberty arrives, females (46,XX) will begin their menstrual cycles. (Details of the menstrual cycle appear in Chapter 9.) But in males (46,XYs), androgens that affect the hypothalamus before birth will suppress hormonal cycling. The male's hypothalamus governs a relatively constant production of sex hormones. (In lower animals, scientists can add androgens at a critical period when pathways in the hypothalamus are being formed. They can actually suppress a female rat's estrus, or sexual cycling, forever. [Goy, 1973; Bermant and Davidson, 1974]). In human females, androgen at a critical period in fetal development delays but does not eradicate cycling.

Thus males and females differentiate from tissues that both sexes have early in development. From this early, "indifferent" embryo, programmed by our genes and by hormones, we become male or female. Yet at birth, the two sexes are remarkably similar. Some of the differences are listed below. They are more matters of quantity than quality. Only very slight differences in size exist, and these appear only in the averages of large numbers of babies. Boys are born about 30 grams heavier on average than girls and about one-half to one centimeter longer. Newborn females have more mature bone development than boys. On average, girls are four to six weeks more advanced in such development than boys.

SEXUALITY IN PERSPECTIVE: SEX DIFFERENCES IN THE BRAIN

Because some sex differences have been found in scores on cognitive tests (i.e., mathematics, spatial, and language tests), some researchers have wondered whether the sexes differ in the development of cerebral functions. Because some sex differences appear at or near puberty, and because brain plasticity seems greater before than after puberty, theorists have tried to figure out how sex and pubertal development might together influence cerebral function.

Neuroscientists use two basic methods to study cerebral function. The first is the *lesion* method, an old and respected technique. If a part of the brain in one hemisphere is injured (lesioned) in a set of animals and the animals lose some function (i.e., vision), then we conclude that control of visual function is, at least in part, localized in the injured hemisphere. Ethical concerns do not allow us to lesion humans, but accidents of wartime and auto traffic (unfortunately) produce human lesions for study of localization of psychological functions.

A newer, clever technique to study cerebral localization was developed by Doreen Kimura, a Canadian physiological psychologist. She reasoned that if one heard two auditory messages (numbers, words) in the two ears simultaneously but independently and if one ear repeatedly "heard" its message first, then we could conclude that the hemisphere to which that ear "talked" was dominant over the "slower" ear.

Because the left ear connects faster to the brain's right hemisphere and the right ear to the left hemisphere of the brain, the "faster hemisphere" is called "lateralized," "advantaged" or "dominant." Speech processing produces evidence of left hemisphere lateralization for almost all of us (except a minority of left handers). (Lesion *and* dichotic listening data are consistent with such lateralization.)

Data on sex differences in lateralization never show the brain's hemispheres to be used one way by all people of one sex and another way for the other sex. When psychologists say that girls are more lateralized for verbal processing, they mean that girls' dichotic listening scores show, on average, more discrepancy between processing of messages to the two ears than do boys' average discrepancy scores. When one sex, on average, has a significantly greater left or right cerebral advantage in processing some types of material, we speak of a sex difference in lateralization or cerebral dominance.

At the California Institute of Technology, Roger Sperry, the Nobel Prize neurobiologist, and his colleague Jerre Levy proposed a theory of sex differences based on spatial lateralization. Adult males on spatial and language tests show more lateralization than females; hence males are more lateralized overall, according to the theory. An earlier theory had found earlier female lateralization of verbal functions determining greater female than male lateralization. Clearly, the two theories do not agree (Buffery and Gray, 1971; Levy-Agresti and Sperry, 1968). Other theories connecting age at puberty and lateralization have been proposed only to be disproved (Rierdan and Koff, 1984; Waber, 1976; 1977).

The Levy and Sperry view is more widely held (even if tentatively) today than is any other view. Levy and Sperry described the left hemisphere as being specialized in verbal, analytic, and sequential processing. Although girls are often found to be superior to boys in many verbal tasks, girls do not score better on the average than boys do in the latter two types of tasks. Why does left lateralization not confer advantages in *all* the left-localized abilities? No convincing answer has yet appeared (Maccoby and Jacklin, 1974).

Summaries of dichotic listening and split-viewing studies understate the number of factors or variables in such experimentation. Results are neither as consistent nor as clear cut as verbal summaries. Some investigators who use these very methods remind us that the methods may have more to do with cognitive *strategies* than with brain function, more to do with attention than perceptual processing (Bryden, 1978; Caplan et al., 1985).

On the average, boys and men do better on spatial and mathematical tasks, girls and women on verbal tasks. But there are many individual exceptions, and psychologists are still investigating whether the observed differences stem from sex differences in the brain.

Until they are at least seven months old, males and females produce hormones at different ratios. Androgens predominate over estrogens, another class of hormones, in males, estrogens over androgens in females. (Both sexes produce both classes of hormones.)

PUBERTY

Before birth, it is our **primary sexual characteristics** that develop: our internal and external genitals. But not until puberty, when we become able to reproduce, do our **secondary sexual characteristics** develop. Puberty consists of a series of biological events that further differentiate the two sexes. Under the influence of the hormones, the sexual organs grow larger and more mature. Puberty typically happens over a period of several years called **adolescence.** Adolescence is a sociological and psychological term for the mental and social growth of the child into a young adult (and we will describe that more fully in Chapter 12). Here we will describe the physical changes of puberty.

The series of physical changes called puberty typically starts about two years earlier in girls than in boys, although the normal age span is wide. Girls usually see the first changes when they are somewhere between 12 and 16. First pubic hair emerges, and then their nipples swell. Girls grow several inches in height. Later they notice hair coming in under their arms, a slight coarsening of other body hair, more breast development, and still later they will have their first menstrual period, although eggs may not be released regularly until several cycles have passed. The uterus and pelvis grow larger, and the vaginal walls thicken. Fatty deposits on breasts, hips, buttocks, and elsewhere plus the wider pelvis make women look more rounded than men. Males typically gain muscle mass at puberty. They also have a growth spurt and develop pubic and underarm hair. Their voice deepens, sometimes after a period of unpredictable squeaks and squawks. Penis and testicles enlarge and lengthen, and facial hair coarsens first into fuzz on the upper lips and sideburns and then into a beard. Boys have erections more often, as their androgen levels mount. Boys may experience their first ejaculations as **wet dreams,** or nocturnal emissions. Live sperm begin to be produced and appear in the seminal fluid.

HORMONES   Puberty is when the sexual programs begun before birth get played out. It is when the sexually differentiated brain triggers, via releasing hormones,

FIGURE 3.4

Average ages for the physical changes of puberty. Age ranges appear in parentheses. Figures here are from West Germany; North American figures are a few months earlier (Tanner, 1962).

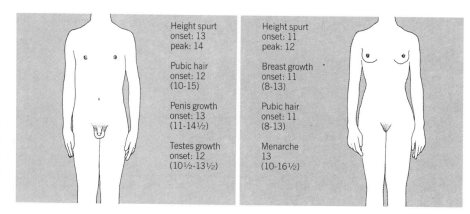

Height spurt
onset: 13
peak: 14

Pubic hair
onset: 12
(10-15)

Penis growth
onset: 13
(11-14½)

Testes growth
onset: 12
(10½-13½)

Height spurt
onset: 11
peak: 12

Breast growth
onset: 11
(8-13)

Pubic hair
onset: 11
(8-13)

Menarche
13
(10-16½)

the growth and maturation appropriate to both sexes. The hypothalamus triggers the nearby **pituitary gland** to release **luteinizing hormone (LH)** or **follicle-stimulating hormone (FSH).** Males produce these hormones rather continuously; females produce them cyclically (the average cycle is 28 days). In females, the two hormones stimulate the ovaries and a structure the ovaries cyclically produce around an ovum, called the **follicle,** to release an ovum, or egg. From the follicle comes a new endocrine organ, the **corpus luteum,** which produces the hormone progesterone. The release of the egg into the uterus is the first step in the fertilization process. In males, the two pituitary hormones stimulate the testes to

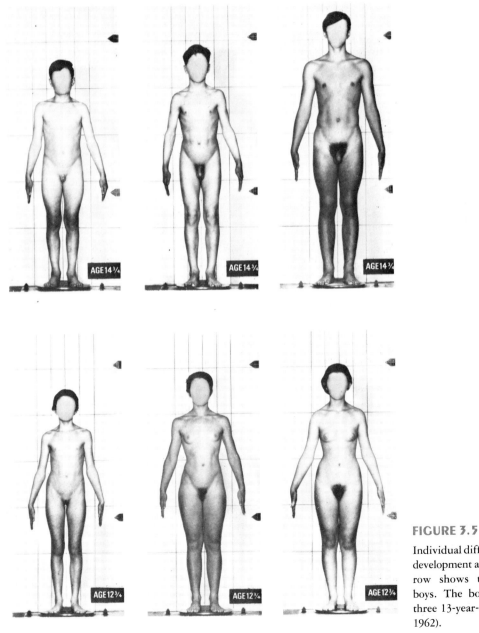

FIGURE 3.5

Individual differences in rates of development at puberty. The top row shows three 15-year-old boys. The bottom row shows three 13-year-old girls (Tanner, 1962).

manufacture sperm and the hormone testosterone, an androgen. The pituitary also produces **somatotropin**, a growth hormone, that triggers both sexes' typical growth spurt. Girls usually grow ahead of boys—with the awkward consequences that most of us can remember about sixth- or seventh-grade socializing. But estrogen slows girls' growth before boys' growth, and adult women are therefore, on the average, shorter than adult men.

A problem common to adolescents is the very suddenness of all their physical changes. Their bodies may feel awkward and uncoordinated.

I was a terrific basketball player until I turned 14. During that one school year, I grew six inches, and I lost my physical coordination. I never really got it back either (18-year-old freshman male).

I was in seventh grade when I started to grow like I was going to go right through the roof. I ate from morning to night. A "glass" of milk meant a quart. My dad and I used to wrestle on the playroom floor, and I broke his arm. It was like I didn't know what my body could do. It was scary (18-year-old freshman male).

Some boys temporarily develop small breasts in response to hormone secretions, which can be horrendously embarrassing (some newborn males have the same problem, of which they remain blissfully unaware). Acne, which is clogged oil glands of the face, chest, and back, may bother both sexes, although it now can be treated medically with some success.

Puberty thus lays down more of the biological foundation of sex and gender. If all biological development has gone according to plan, the result is a chromosomal, genital, and hormonal female or male. Happily, most of the time that is just what happens.

GENDER IDENTITY: A DEVELOPMENTAL SEQUENCE

As we have seen, sex and gender are not identical, although they are linked. Now that we have traced the development of sex, let us turn to the development of gender: to how we actually get to *feel like* males and females who value being male or female.

In our culture, children learn that they are boys or girls by the time that they are somewhere between the ages of 18 and 36 months. This age is a period of rapid development of language and cognition when children in our culture learn to label things as for boys or for girls. At this age, they are classifying what they observe in this physical and social world. Their **gender identity**—the deep, personal sense of one's maleness or femaleness—is nurtured by other people's belief that children are one sex or the other. The sex they are assigned at birth is generally consistent with their earlier biological development. When a toddler learns its gender assignment and firmly believes that she is a girl or that he is a boy, the toddler's core gender identity has formed.

The lists below show the eight steps in the development of gender identity as described by John Money of Johns Hopkins University in Baltimore and Anke Ehrhardt at the College of Physicians and Surgeons in New York (1972).

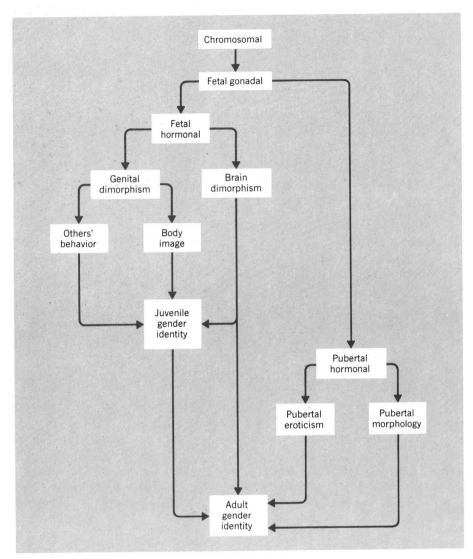

FIGURE 3.6

First come the steps in the development of childhood (core) gender identity. At adolescence come the steps in the development of adult gender identity (after Money and Ehrhardt, 1972).

Influences on How Children Form
Core Gender Identity

1 Chromosomes: whether one is 46,XX or 46,XY or some other unusual combination.

2 Fetal gonads: whether one developed ovaries or testes before birth.

3 Fetal hormones: whether androgen and MIS were present or absent before birth.

4 Structural dimorphism: whether one's internal and external genitals are male or female and one's hypothalamus is programmed for hormonal cycling (female) or steady production (male).

5 Image: whether one sees one's body as male or female and whether others do.

With puberty come three other developments that affect adult gender identity.

Influences on How Adolescents Form Adult Gender Identity

6 Pubertal hormones: whether one secretes primarily male or female hormones.

7 Pubertal morphology: whether one develops male or female secondary sexual characteristics.

8 Pubertal eroticism: whether one is sexually attracted to the other or the same sex.

The sexual events of puberty generally reinforce the gender identity formed during childhood. The young boy begins to feel like a young man; the young girl begins to feel like a young woman. Even homosexuals, who are attracted to members of their own sex (step 8), do not typically change their core gender identity, just their sexual orientation. "Pubertal eroticism" is a psychologist's term for the dominant sexual fantasies that many people begin to have during puberty. Most men in our society fantasize about and have sexual experiences with women; most women fantasize about and have sex with men.

These fantasies and sexual experiences are viewed as an expression of one's gender identity. (Many sexually inexperienced men and women decide that they are homosexual because of the nature of their fantasies alone. Their decision may be premature. In fact, no one knows much about how such fantasy in most people relates to the other indicators of gender identity.) In sum, gender identity ordinarily forms in two broadly complementary stages: core gender identity during early childhood and adult gender identity during adolescence. (We will have more to say about gender identity in Chapter 12.)

How one publicly expresses one's gender identity is called one's **gender role.** It is the pattern of behavior considered usual for one's sex. Gender identity is one's personal conviction about oneself; gender role is its social, public enactment. Gender identity is very stable over time in almost all people. Gender role changes more, both with age and with cultural currents. (We explore gender role in Chapter 4.)

ERRORS OF DEVELOPMENT

The great majority of us are unambiguously male or female, and we slip into our gender identity very easily. But at any one of the critical steps before birth (as we will see below), sexual differentiation can go awry. Depending on when and what in fetal development goes wrong, a child's sexual development at birth may already be profoundly altered. To tamper with developing humans in order to learn more about the course of sexual differentiation would be grossly unethical, but in the spontaneous errors that nature produces and in some inadvertent human errors, we can begin to identify certain crucial elements in the differentiation of sex and, perhaps, of gender. These errors in development are, luckily, quite infrequent, but they help us to tackle the riddle of how biology and psychology together produce gender identity.

Sex-Chromosome Errors

Errors of development may occur in the chromosomes. Some of these errors render those affected sterile; some affect aspects of adult appearance like height and build. Others affect neither one's reproductive ability nor one's physique.

Turner's and Klinefelter's Syndromes   One of the earliest possible errors in biological development may occur in the sex chromosomes. Normal females, you will recall, are 46,XX, and normal males are 46,XY. In a chromosome error that befalls one in 2500 live baby girls, **Turner's syndrome,** they have only one X chromosome and are therefore 45,X0. (Some girls with Turner's syndrome lack only part of the second X or lack the second X only in some cells. No fetus

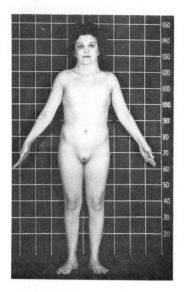

FIGURE 3.7

Turner's syndrome. Girls with Turner's syndrome are short, have short necks, and develop breasts when estrogen is prescribed for them at puberty.

survives as a 45, Y0. The genetic information on the X chromosome is essential to life.) To look at, their external genitals are those of a normal girl, but internally they have no functional uterus, just a streak of ovarian tissue. But because they have an X chromosome, they have been feminized. Because they lack the second X, the full differentiation of the gonads and the uterus is incomplete. Yet because they look like girls, they are raised and feel like girls: they quite unambiguously assume a feminine gender identity.

As they get older, girls with Turner's syndrome show certain distinctive physical traits: they are short and have short necks. Only when they receive estrogen treatments will they develop breasts and menstruate. But they are sterile, because they lack functional ovaries and uterus. The degree and kind of their physical symptoms depend on how much and which arm of the second X chromosome is missing (some, for example, have fallopian tubes, and others do not). Interestingly enough, and for reasons that are not entirely clear, girls with Turner's syndrome seem to act in more feminine, more gender-**stereotyped** ways than other girls their age. As young girls, they are unlikely to be interested in athletics and are more likely to be interested in self-adornment. As teenagers, they fantasize about marriage and motherhood even more than do other girls their age. We do not know whether studies of Turner's syndrome teenagers today might find them agreeing with many of their peers that women can combine both work and family. But we do know, thanks to Turner's syndrome females, that fantasies of marriage and children, that is, traditionally feminine fantasies, do not depend for their existence on female reproductive organs or the hormones they produce (see Figure 3.7).

Extra sex chromosomes also affect prenatal development. In about 1 in 500 births of male infants, an extra X chromosome is present, in addition to the usual XY. The infant is therefore 47, XXY, a condition called **Klinefelter's syndrome.** These boys are born with normal looking genitals, but as they develop, their genitals do not get larger. They gradually shrink and atrophy, and the results are sterility and a delay of puberty. Some clinicians suggest that many Klinefelter's boys are mentally retarded, but others maintain that they fall within the normal range of intelligence. At puberty, Klinefelter's boys are less interested in sex than others their age, a symptom that may be corrected in therapy with the male hormone, testosterone.

Klinefelter's boys are assigned and reared as males, and have a male gender identity. Although the changes they undergo at puberty are unusual, some clinicians have treated adolescents for behavior and personality problems without the boy, his family, or the clinician raising any questions about this unusual secondary sexual development. Both counseling and hormones seem to help boys with Klinefelter's syndrome.

The XYY Male   Some men have an extra Y chromosome and are therefore 47,XYY. The men with this rare chromosomal anomaly tend to be tall, probably because of the extra Y. Because many XYY men were found in prison populations, some researchers suggested that XYY men were prone to violence. One early study had shown that seven out of a group of 197 Scottish prisoners convicted of violent crimes had the extra Y (Jacobs et al., 1965). That rate was far higher than might be expected. Did the extra Y contribute in some way to the men's violent natures?

Several investigations helped to provide the answers. First, when XYY males are carefully compared—on economic and social factors—to chromosomally normal males, their rates of aggressive behavior are similar (Borgaonkar and Shah, 1974). Second, a group of researchers (Witkin et al., 1976) went to Denmark, because the Danes keep a register for national service of all men 19 or older. The researchers looked for tall men from the register of those born in Copenhagen during the mid-1940s. They found over 4000 men who met the criteria. The researchers tested them for educational background and intelligence. Only 12 tall, XYY men were found, of whom five—40 percent—had criminal records. Of the chromosomally normal men, only 9 percent had criminal records. But the riddle was solved. The XYY men, on the average, had slightly lower IQ scores and were arrested more often than XY men. The crimes committed by XYYs were most often crimes of property and not crimes of violence, and they were caught more often because they did foolish things like climbing back into an apartment they'd already been caught burglarizing. The XYY criminals were easier to catch because they were less likely to adopt wise strategies. Their incidence of violent crimes was about what would be predicted for the general population (Witkin et al., 1976).

Hermaphroditism: An Error of Fetal Gonadal Formation

Very rarely, a fetus develops with the gonads of both sexes. These are called **true hermaphrodites.** Mysteriously, some 46,XX fetuses develop testes and, later, ovaries. In some cases, a small piece of a Y chromosome has attached to another chromosome, but that small piece is enough to direct the production of testes without suppressing ovaries (Wachtel et al., 1976). The appearance of the genitals varies: some infants have a testis on one side and an ovary on the other; some have a testis and an ovary on each side; some have an **ovatestis,** an organ containing ovarian and testicular tissue; some have an ovatestis on one side and a testis or an ovary on the other. With such a confusing biological legacy, one might expect true hermaphrodites to be very confused about their gender identity. But they are not.

Most true hermaphrodites have masculinized external genitals, and so these XXs are assigned and reared as boys. As children, they consider themselves as boys. Most of these boys at puberty begin to develop breasts, but they react to them as horrible mistakes. They do *not* react to them by shifting their gender identity. Furthermore, over a quarter of them ovulate and half menstruate internally, but they feel like males. About four out of five true hermaphrodites choose medical treatment to remove the female internal organs (Federman, 1967). From a reproductive view, such a choice is a loss. As females, these children would be fertile. As males, they will be sterile. But psychologically, it would be absurd to tell a teenage boy that he must turn into a girl.

In contrast, some true hermaphrodites are assigned and raised as girls because their external genitals look more feminine than masculine. Some, for example, have an undescended testicle and a small, incompletely fused penis with **hypospadias,** a urethral opening near or at the root rather than the tip of the penis. In cases where the testis is internal and where the penis looks like a clitoris, the child may be assigned as a girl. These girls feel like girls. They want breasts, they want to menstruate, and their gender identity is securely feminine. Once

FIGURE 3.8

Androgen insensitivity. This completely androgen-insensitive female is 46,XY. Her external genitals (bottom photo) are female, but her chromosomes are male. She develops breasts and feminine contours because her testes produce estrogen.

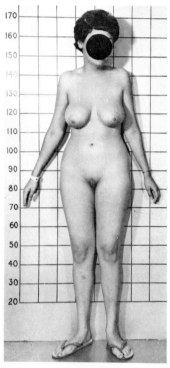

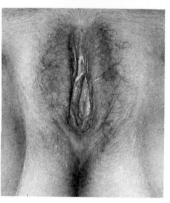

assigned a sex, true hermaphrodites are treated with surgery and hormone therapy that support their chosen gender identity. For gender identity to develop smoothly, the external genitals must be plausibly related to a child's sex of assignment. Not only must a child find the genitals plausible, but others—especially other children—must as well. True hermaphrodites are fascinating not as medical curiosities but as examples of how strongly gender identity relies on choices made by parents for their child, and not simply on chromosomes or reproductive organs.

Fetal Hormone Errors

Before birth, hormones can sometimes cause inconsistencies between a fetus's genitals and sex chromosomes. Hormone errors can produce a variety of sexual and gender problems—problems of physical appearance and function and problems of psychological adjustment. We describe some hormone errors, because they shed light on the differences between the biological and psychological aspects of sexual development.

Androgen Insensitivity   Some people with XY chromosomes prenatally develop normal testes but lack the ability to use the androgen their bodies produce. Their genes lack the instructions for building androgen receptors, and because of this lack of receptors their external genitals are female rather than male. Thus at birth, they look like girls. They are raised as, and they think of themselves as girls. At puberty, the testes in their abdomen produce enough estrogen so that breasts and feminine contours develop. (See Figure 3-8.) But these 46,XY **androgen-insensitive** women never menstruate, because they have neither uterus nor ovaries. (MIS has defeminized their internal ducts; but androgen has not been able to masculinize them.) When they seek medical help either because they have not menstruated or because the hard lumps in their groin embarrass them when they dance with a partner, they learn of the problem for the first time. The lumps are testes and must be removed because they are at high risk for cancer. Because part of the differentiation of the internal ducts in females produces the upper vagina, androgen-insensitive women ultimately may choose to have the short vagina surgically corrected. Although these androgen-insensitive females are sterile, they are women, and they have a firmly feminine gender identity. They fantasize about male sexual partners, about getting married, and about having babies. They make good adoptive mothers.

Adrenogenital Syndrome: Fetal Androgen When Not Needed   Some fetuses of both sexes are subject to too much androgen because they have inherited a pair of recessive genes (which are not on the sex chromosomes). The effect is an error in the production of the hormone **cortisone.** This error leads to an excessive production of androgen. For male fetuses, the effect on the genitals is not serious. But female fetuses are born with masculine-looking external genitals. These babies are called **pseudo-hermaphrodites,** because they have gonads (ovaries), and these are inconsistent with their external, masculinized genitals (see Figure 3.9). Today, **adrenogenital females** (as they are also called) are surgically feminized at birth and given cortisone therapy, which delays puberty a bit for girls but allows them to bear children. The cortisone also corrects the serious problems that adrenogenital children of both sexes would otherwise have: problems of fluid balance, blood pressure, and the immune system.

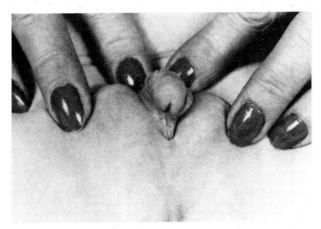

FIGURE 3.9
Some females are born with masculine-looking external genitals, although they have ovaries. These females, called pseudo-hermaphrodites, are surgically feminized at birth.

Females with adrenogenital syndrome raise intriguing points about gender identity, for these are normal XXs who have gone through part of the male hormonal program. In the past, some of these children chose to be males after being assigned as males. If they are raised as female, as today all are, they are females who adopt female roles, have babies, and have pretty much the same sexual preferences as other females. But when girls treated early for the syndrome were compared to their nonandrogenized sisters (to control for heredity, but not for age) or to nonandrogenized girls of similar age, race, social class, and intelligence, psychologists found that the androgenized girls were more likely to think of themselves and to be thought of by others as tomboys and to prefer playing with boys rather than girls (Ehrhardt and Baker, 1974). Adrenogenital females are no more aggressive than their sisters or the nonadrenogenital controls. But as a group, the androgenized girls chose boys' toys and games over dolls and chose slacks over dresses, choices less frequently made by the nonandrogenized girls. The androgenized girls were less interested in taking care of babies, fantasized less about pregnancy and motherhood, and placed more emphasis on careers than the other groups did, although none was sexually oriented toward females. In fact, the androgenized girls were far less content with the traditional feminine role than their nonandrogenized counterparts (Money and Ehrhardt, 1972). It would be a mistake to assume that fetal androgens alone determine gender identity or sexual preference. It would also be a mistake to think that only androgenized girls are tomboys or unhappy with the restrictions on women. There are far more tomboys and career-minded women than there are females with adrenogenital syndrome. In fact, it is precisely because so many women do accept these attitudes and behaviors that androgenized women easily can identify themselves as feminine.

Some of these women used to remain androgenized well into adulthood. (The cortisone treatment for the syndrome dates only from 1950.) These late cortisone-treated women show the same tomboyishness and other preferences as the fetally androgenized women, but they appear significantly more masculine—consistent with their having been exposed to male hormones much longer, that is, through and beyond puberty. Some have an overdeveloped clitoris. Before cortisone therapy, many could experience visible clitoral erection because of their own androgen production, an experience they shared with men, not women. Not only were their bodies different from those of nonandrogenized women, but their sexual lives were as well. (See Figure 3.10.)

FIGURE 3.10

Adrenogenital syndrome. Both of these individuals are 46,XX and were born with similar degrees of masculinized external genitals. Both were treated early, the 14-year-old on the left assigned as a girl, the 15-year-old on the right assigned as a boy (from Money and Ehrhardt, 1972).

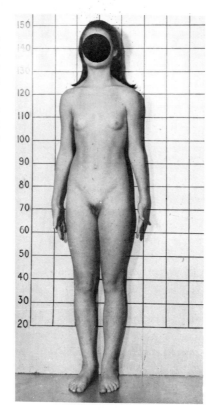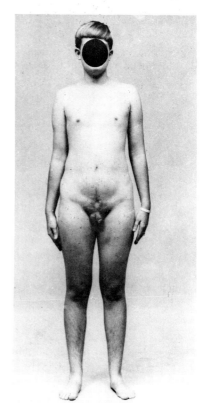

Almost half of the androgenized women who started cortisone therapy late in life reported having dreams and fantasies of both male and female sexual partners. In fact, **bisexuality** was more common among these women than among nonandrogenized and only fetally androgenized women. No women in the masculinized group were exclusively lesbian, however. As a group, they reported having greater interest in sexual activity before their hormone therapy, and in fact the cortisone is believed to reduce sexual motivation because it reduces production of androgens (Ehrhardt, Evers, and Money, 1968). Some of the women who had late hormone treatment have married, had babies, and nursed them. The same females who, as children, showed no interest in babies and who may have doubted their abilities to be mothers turned out to be fine mothers. A real baby creates much of the stimulation that elicits loving care from mothers (and fathers), even those who never fantasized becoming parents.

A group of men who lack some, but not all, androgen receptors have a story to tell that complements the story of the androgenized girls. Just as these girls were found to be *more* active at sports than nonandrogenized girls, so the partially androgenized men were *less* active at sports than other men. They did not choose to participate in the usual competitive games males play. Whether this choice reflects an intrinsic lack of interest in sports or competition or concern about exposure of a markedly small penis (called a **hypophallus**) in a locker room is not yet known. Although this finding on sports activity suggests that androgen may affect some kinds of behavior, there is another message: despite their lack of interest in sports or competition, these males are making it as men without team play, locker room experiences, and the like. They are attracted to women, marrying, and working at traditionally male jobs, and in so doing offer another proof that gender roles have wide enough outer limits to provide room for many different choices **partially androgen-insensitive** of behavior. Their work does not require a specific amount of androgen. These men have a consistent self-image and presentation of themselves as male (Money and Ogunro, 1974). (For a case of a different kind of hormone error but similar issues of gender identity, see "Sexuality in Perspective: Kallmann's Syndrome.")

Boys with Prenatal Estrogen or Progesterone: Do They Feminize?   What is the gender identity of male (46,XY) fetuses subject to greater than normal amounts of the female hormones estrogen and progesterone? (Both the ovaries and testes produce estrogens. Males produce progesterone on the chemical path to producing both androgens and estrogens. The balance of both estrogens and progesterone to androgens is greater in females than in males.) Work with animals suggests that estrogens and progesterone interfere with androgens. In a case involving humans, doctors treated severely diabetic pregnant women who might otherwise have lost their babies through miscarriage. The women received estrogen and progesterone, and these probably increased the ratio of estrogen and progesterone to androgen in their male fetuses. The boys, who were studied at age six or at puberty, looked like normal males and felt masculine. There were no problems of gender identity among them. Yet compared to boys their age who were born to diabetic mothers but who had not received estrogen or progesterone during pregnancy, the hormone-treated boys were less involved in contact sports and less coordinated at throwing a ball. But the hormone-treated mothers had more serious diabetes than the other mothers did, and it is entirely possible that sicker mothers discourage competitive and rough-and-tumble play in their sons more than healthier mothers do (Yalom et al., 1973). In a more recent study (Kester et al., 1980) men who had been exposed to a variety of female hormones as fetuses were studied between the ages of 18 and 30. (Some had been exposed to estrogen in the form of **DES**, or **diethylstilbestrol**, a synthetic estrogen; some to DES and natural progesterone; some to natural progesterone alone; and some to synthetic progesterone.) As in all "natural" experiments, the hormone groups were not all perfectly matched. However, the gross findings were that DES exposure was associated with quite conventional boyhoods, and progesterone and synthetic progesterone exposure with lowered sex drive compared to controls. The incidence of homosexuality did not vary significantly among the different groups of hormone-treated men.

Another group of young men, studied when they were between 16 and 19 years old, had been exposed as fetuses to large doses of progesterone to treat their mothers' **toxemia** (a serious disease of pregnancy, characterized by high blood pressure, swelling, and protein in the urine). These young men, compared to others their age not exposed to progesterone, were less physically active and less heterosexually active. But here, too, it is important to take into account the effects of the inhibitions that (formerly sick) mothers might place on their children (Zussman, Zussman, and Dalton, 1975).

To rule out such complications, psychologists have used computer data banks to compare samples of boys who are genuinely well matched. Some normal boys not hormonally treated before birth were compared to boys aged 9 to 14 who had been given synthetic progesterone before birth. When many factors, such as social class, age, race, and mothers' experience with vaginal bleeding during pregnancy

SEXUALITY IN PERSPECTIVE: KALLMANN'S SYNDROME

In the course of normal development, a child deeply and firmly comes to understand that she is feminine or that he is masculine. This understanding is profoundly important to a person's entire identity and self-image. But some errors of sexual development prevent people from achieving a clear sense of self or gender. A young man who suffered from the effects of Kallmann's syndrome describes just this problem. In **Kallmann's syndrome,** the hypothalamus at puberty fails to trigger the release of male hormones, and normal adult male sexual characteristics fail to develop. The testes remain as small as a child's.

Because in effect he never reached puberty, the young man could not feel like a fully sexual male. Although he had received hormone replacement therapy and psychotherapy as a teenager, he twice had considered suicide. He waited until he was 30 to have surgery to correct the cosmetic error. Surgeons implanted artificial, inert, but realistic-feeling testes. Only after the implant surgery did he feel like a real man. As he said afterward, the surgery cured him of feeling "that I was somehow excluded from being human" (Money and Sollod, 1978). Two days after his operation, he tried to explain the "magic":

I think it really hits a lot of pretty unconscious stuff. . . . It's deeper than I imagined. . . . It's more in the realm of magic—it's really magic (p. 92).

Ten months after the surgery, we see his identity firming, his sense of himself healing:

Sexually, I am more confident. . . . I have developed a deep relationship. . . . I am a sexier person in general. My physical appearance is better. I am proud of my appearance. . . .

What I am mystified about is how this surgery could have such a profound impact. It must operate on an unconscious level, for, before the operation, I consciously thought of myself as a male. I could function sexually and my penis was normal size. I was certainly lusty enough (pp. 92, 93).

But perhaps most expressive of all:

I no longer feel like an outcast but now feel like a normal member of the human race. . . . For myself, I experience my sexual drive as coming from my body. Before the operation, my lust was not experienced as coming from my body but actually was for me an invention of my mind . . . Sexuality now seems to be a natural part of living, coming from the make-up of the body, instead of a mental creation (p. 93).

Psychologists are far from understanding how body image develops and is maintained. Not all men with Kallmann's syndrome see themselves as this man did.

Based on John Money and Robert Sollod, "Body Image, Plastic Surgery (Prosthetic Testes) and Kallmann's Syndrome," *British Journal of Medical Psychology* (1978), 51, pp. 92–94.

were held constant for both groups, and when only the administering of the hormones was the difference, no differences in the masculine behavior of the two groups appeared. One possible interpretation of the results is that masculine, rough-and-tumble play only diminishes after exposure to much larger doses of prenatal estrogen and progesterone than those given to the boys in the computer sample. A likelier explanation is that the earlier study had less well-matched groups of boys. It is too early to conclude that prenatal estrogen and progesterone decrease a boy's interest in roughhousing (Meyer-Bahlburg, Grisanti, and Ehrhardt, 1977).

In sum, given the uncertainties in the studies, the tentative conclusions are that: studies with good control groups and low hormone doses (such as the Meyer-Bahlburg et al. study) show no effects of prenatal female hormones on the behavior of males; studies with wider-ranging hormone doses (such as the Yalom, Zussman, and Kester studies) seem to suggest that progesterone in higher doses may interfere with rough-and-tumble play and interest in heterosexuality at puberty. Appropriately, researchers are keeping open the question of the feminizing effects of hormones (Kester, 1984).

Thus what we see in cases of hormonal errors (especially those concerning internally produced hormones) reinforces the contention that gender identity is not the simple outcome of biological programming. The sex of assignment and rearing surely play an important role. John Money, whom we have already mentioned, contends that we can help to create a male or a female gender identity if a child is assigned (or, in some cases, medically *re*assigned) and reared as that gender while still very young. Money argues that there is a critical period for the creation of gender identity, between the ages of 18 and 36 months, after which gender identity is fixed. He believes that this normal development mechanism applies to cases where abnormal but repaired genitals are plausible to the child and its peers as fitting the sex of reassignment. The argument for the assignment of sex by age three is based on clinical experience. Later reassignment of sex was found to be associated with poor psychological outcomes (Money, Hampson, and Hampson, 1957). Money and his colleagues do *not* suggest that parents can tell their daughters that they are male or their sons that they are female. Money believes that gender identity requires consistent environmental support from family and peers as well as surgical and hormonal support in cases of reassignment. But Milton Diamond, of the University of Hawaii, argues (1982) that gender identity is affected far more by biology than Money suggests. Diamond's position is that genes and hormones in early development and again at puberty set outer limits on behavior, on physical structure, and also on motivation. Thus although genes do not produce fixed, unchanging outcomes, the range of these outcomes is not infinitely wide. Diamond views the heredity-environment interaction as biased toward the biological. Bear these competing arguments in mind as you read about the identical twins of two different sexes.

The Case of the Identical Twins

In 1963, identical twin boys were born. They were normal in all respects. **Identical twins** are always of the same sex because they are the result of the division of the single-celled, fertilized egg into two identical cells, each of which develops to maturity. Identical twins have identical genes and chromosomes. When the twins were 7 months old, they were circumcised. But on one twin, the doctor cut an artery, and part of the penis was lost. On the advice of doctors at Johns

Hopkins, the parents agreed to reassign the affected twin to be a girl. This difficult decision was made because the best that surgeons could do would be to restore the boy's ability to urinate standing up. They could not restore full male sexual functioning. When the twins were 17 months old, the parents decided to go ahead with the gender reassignment. (Recall that 18 to 36 months is considered by John Money to be the critical period for the formation of gender identity.) When the twins were between 17 and 21 months old, the parents changed the affected twin's name, clothing, and hairstyle. The first surgery to feminize the genitals was then done (surgery to correct her vagina would be needed after she reached puberty). The psychologists at Johns Hopkins Medical School gave the parents support and guidance. It was decided that the twins would not be told what had happened. If the twin knew about her sex reassignment, the solidity of her gender identity would be endangered (Money, 1975; Money and Ehrhardt, 1972).

By age 4, the little girl preferred dresses to slacks and was proud of her long hair. By age 4½, her mother reported:

One thing that really amazes me is that she is so feminine. I've never seen a little girl so neat and tidy as she can be when she wants to be. . . . She is very proud of herself, when she puts on a new dress, or I set her hair. She just loves to have her hair set; she could sit under the drier all day long to have her hair set. She just loves it (Money and Ehrhardt, 1972, pp. 119–120).

The parents' teaching was clearly taking hold. Indeed, the descriptions are of a very traditional feminine rearing. For example, the mother was stricter about sexual immodesty in the little girl than in the boy. When the girl took off her panties in the yard, she was spanked and told that "nice little girls didn't do that." But when the boy "took a leak . . . in the front yard," the mother said nothing, laughed, and told the father about it. The mother carefully explained sexual reproduction and the value of each sex's role to the children. She discouraged the girl's tomboyishness. The girl, who was described as the dominant twin and the leader until the gender reassignment, was at age 3 described by her mother as "bossy." The boy was protective toward his sister.

The daughter was encouraged to help her mother and liked to do so. The boy did not help. The daughter preferred and got dolls and similar toys; the son, cars, garages, and tools. When the twins were 5 years and 9 months old, their mother reported:

I found that my son, he chose very masculine things like a fireman or a policeman or something like that. He wanted to do what Daddy does, work where Daddy does, and carry a lunch kit, and drive a car. And she didn't want any of those things. I asked her, and she said she wanted to be a doctor or a teacher. And I asked her, well, did she have plans that maybe some day she'd get married, like Mommy? She'll get married some day—she wasn't too worried about that. She didn't think about that too much, but she wants to be a doctor. But none of the things that she ever wanted to be were like a policeman or a fireman, and that sort of thing never appealed to her. So I felt that in a way that's a good sign . . . I think, it's nice if your boy wants to be a policeman or a fireman

*or something and the girl wants to do girl things like a doctor, or teaching,
or something like that, and I've tried to show them that it's very good
. . . (Money and Tucker, 1975).*

Until a few years ago, psychologists were concluding that from two boys
perfectly matched genetically and hormonally during their first year and a half,
reassignment and child rearing had shaped one child with a thoroughly masculine
and one with a thoroughly feminine gender identity and role. But then some less
happy news began to drift in. At 13, the female twin seemed beset by trouble.
Her gait and her looks were masculine. When she tried to make friends, school-
mates teased and called her "cavewoman." She has had trouble finding a supportive
peer group, and she has few friends. She believes that boys have a better life than
girls and wants to become a mechanic. Doctors said that she is having a hard
time as a girl (Diamond, 1982). The reassignment has not been as easy as people
once hoped and believed. What we do not know is, first, how much she might
know about her masculine beginnings. The question can never be posed directly.
Second, given her great unhappiness, her few friends, and her reticence about
matters sexual, what will be her sexual orientation, her gender role, or her gender
identity as an adult?

Given the facts, what can we conclude about this case? If the female twin does
not know about her sex reassignment, Milton Diamond's argument that the
prenatal male hormones are working to masculinize her is a credible one. If she
does know, the clinical rules have been violated, and her problems may well stem
from her knowledge. In that case, John Money's argument that gender identity
is flexible in very young children remains credible. This tantalizing case shows
how much more than academic is the question of the early roots of gender identity.
The case also illustrates the problems facing clinicians in assessing a baby for sex
reassignment. Complicating issues still further are the few cases in which children
who have not yet reached puberty are sexually reassigned, apparently successfully,
and who move with their entire family to a new place so that the children may
take on a new public gender identity (Lev-Ran, 1974; Julius Richmond, personal
communication). These sex reassignments, managed by psychiatrists, have been
undertaken when the children were well beyond the age of three, the outer limit
of the so-called "critical period" for forming core gender identity (Money, Hampson, and Hampson, 1957).

TENTATIVE CONCLUSIONS   We can draw some conclusions from what we know now
about prenatal hormones. If the fetus is exposed to *no* androgen in the critical
periods of development, as in normal female development, Turner's syndrome,
and full androgen insensitivity, the baby has female external genitals and a female
gender identity. If the fetus *is* exposed to androgen, as are normal males, it will
be assigned as male. But if its genitals look even somewhat male, the XX baby
might be assigned *either* sex. For example, adrenogenital syndrome XXs used to
be able to choose surgery and hormone treatment that would make them look
more fully masculine or feminine. (Today, as we have said, all are feminized as
infants.) Depending on their early sex assignment and rearing, some chose to be
female and some male.

Why did some choose to be boys and some choose to be girls? Some chose, of
course, because of assignment, rearing, and the appearance of their genitals. But
perhaps some of the flexibility is due also to the wide variations in both the

amount and time of prenatal exposure to the hormones (Money and Ehrhardt, 1972). When it comes to the question of the effects of androgen on the brain, we simply have no solid data on humans, and the data on other animals are still inadequate to answer the complex human questions. Female monkeys exposed during varied prenatal periods to androgen, both those with *and* without a visibly enlarged clitoris, show more childhood rough-and-tumble play. These females still produce hormones cyclically at puberty, like normal females, although they reach puberty a bit late. They are also capable of mating and rearing young (Goy and Phoenix, 1971). The human female responds to prenatal androgen somewhat like the monkey: androgenized before birth by adrenogenital syndrome, she will reach puberty late, will cycle, and will rear young. Prenatal hormone programming is likely to be more subtle than even our current experiments suggest. Our knowledge is limited not only by uncertainty about hormone action on the prenatal brain but also by the inadequacy of the behavioral measures we can use with even rough comparability across species.

THE GUEVODOCES

A group of people from a small town in the Dominican Republic illustrates again how critical is the male hormone androgen in development. In late 1974, a Cornell Medical School team found 24 girls-turned-boys among 13 families in a remote farming village. At birth the babies were considered girls from the appearance of their external genitals. Although they did not look totally feminine, they looked feminine enough to be assigned as females. At puberty, however, their voices deepened, their testes descended, the "clitorises" lengthened, and some of them ejaculated live sperm. On examination, it was found that the girls' chromosomes were 46,XY, those of a normal male. But they had inherited recessive genes that interfered with their conversion of prenatal androgen from one form of the hormone to another. This condition is named after the missing enzyme, *5 alpha-reductase deficiency.* Before birth, the form of androgen they had was adequate to masculinize their internal genitals but not adequate to masculinize their external genitals. At puberty, it was adequate. The most remarkable aspect of the case of these **guevodoces,** as they were called in the community—*guevo* meaning penis, *doce* meaning twelve, thus "penis at twelve"—is that the "girls" readily shifted their gender roles and identities to become men (Imperato-McGinley et al., 1974). The ease with which they shifted gender seems to violate the idea that late sex assignment works only in cases of early gender ambivalence (that is, where doctors and parents cannot decide which sex a baby is).

But as with the identical twins, new and apparently contradictory evidence is coming in on the guevodoces. At the age of seven, some of these "girls" showed signs of discomfort with their femaleness. In this culture, until age 7, boys and girls play together. At seven, girls' activities take on an adult cast. Their lives become versions of their mothers'. Some of the guevodoces didn't like doing girls' things and found the boys' freer lives more appealing. They also thought that their genitals were different from those of girls (Baker, 1980). Thus it is not simply that at adolescence the girls became boys. The process was more gradual, although the change in publicly expressed feelings about gender did come well after the age of three.

As adults, most of the guevodoces seem to function well as men. They marry and become fathers, just as other men in their society do. One man has a wife and a mistress. Yet another man goes alone into the fields at night and dresses in women's clothing. From studies in our own society, we know that males who dress in women's clothing may do so because of discomfort about gender. Dressing in the clothes of the other sex reflects a tension about aspects of gender.

Why has this late shift in gender apparently been so easy for the guevodoces? No one can know for sure, but one possibility is that in this Latin American culture, the feminine role is so onerous and restrictive that the masculine role is far more attractive. Another factor is probably the guevodoces' feelings at seven that their genitals were not like normal girls'. Thus the remarkable case of the guevodoces now seems not an outstanding case that breaks all the rules, but another in a series of gender and sex anomalies in which prenatal exposure to androgen was strong enough to alter not only internal genitals and some parts of the external genitals, but also some aspects of motivation and behavior. In the culture that devalues women and devalues most of all a childless woman, sex reassignment at puberty for guevodoces has many advantages.

A final twist in this interesting tale, and one that leads to the conclusion that the guevodoce's genital form is identifiably different from the normal young girl's: a variant form of the gene that operates in the guevodoces also occurs among some people of New Guinea. But in New Guinea, some tribes raise these children not as girls, but as intersexes—people of sexual form intermediate between the two sexes. In other tribes in New Guinea where this genetic disorder occurs, the culture "shifts" the girls into boys all at once, when they reach puberty. They are rapidly resocialized, quickly taught the steps by which boys normally are initiated into manhood. According to the medical researcher who reported on these tribes, the reassignment is a marvel of "cultural invention" (Gajduszek, 1964).

Thus androgen may play a guiding role in establishing gender identity. If it is not present, a female and a feminine gender role readily follow a female sex of assignment and rearing. If it is present, other questions arise. We must know when—during the formation of internal genitals, external genitals, or brain differentiation—and in what form the androgen was present. But culture guides gender identity, too. The guevodoces and the New Guinea tribes remind us that we need to understand the role of socialization. The cases of unusual sexual development tell us about the central role that hormones play in establishing ranges of possibilities for behavior. They also tell us that hormones alone do not settle the issue of human gender identity.

TRANSSEXUALISM

We have been describing how gender identity develops in males and females. But some people break away from the commonplace course of such development. **Transsexuals** are people who feel as if they are trapped in the body of the wrong sex. A female transsexual is horrified by her breasts; a male transsexual is horrified by his beard and genital growth. Puberty seems a cruel, public violation of their private sense of self. Is transsexualism a reversal of core gender identity? Clinicians treat it as such, but its origin remains a mystery. It probably has more than one cause. Transsexuals' chromosomes and hormone levels are normal for their biological sex. Clinicians often find that transsexuals have very rigid ideas about what men and women "should" do. They wish to dress, live as, and be the other sex.

FIGURE 3.11

Male-to-female transsexual. Top: Dr. Richard Raskin and bottom: Dr. Renée Richards, after sex-change surgery. In a court case, a judge ruled that Dr. Richards could legally play in women's tennis matches.

They seek all the trappings of the other sex, for life in their biologically given sex feels sad, wrong, even perverse. (Donald Laub, personal communication, 1983).

In her autobiography, Renée Richards—who was born as a man—describes how as a teenager she tried to make herself look like a woman and how she hated the physical evidence of her biological maleness:

> *. . . I hated my genitals; my penis and testicles seemed ugly and abnormal. I recoiled at the cumbersome, embarrassingly external complex of fleshy parts flopping between my legs. (Richards and Ames, 1983, p. 56).*

The autobiography (1983) of Renée Richards reveals that from her early childhood, she enjoyed dressing in her sister's clothes. But unlike many young transsexuals, most of her friends were boys, and she was a first-rate competitive tennis player (first as a male and then, after surgery, as a female). Before her sex-change surgery, Renée fantasized herself a woman. Her first sexual encounter (with a male homosexual) as Renée came while she was looking for a night-club job that involved cross-dressing. As Dr. Richard Raskin, an ophthalmologist, he married. But his gender problems ultimately grew so overwhelming that he sought sex-change surgery.

The early clinical work with transsexuals turned up histories in which these elements appeared:

1 As children, they already considered their biological sex to be in conflict with their felt sex.

2 As children, they dressed in the clothes of the other sex (called **cross-dressing**).

3 They avoided playmates of their own sex and preferred playmates of the other sex.

4 At puberty and afterward, they felt disgusted by their "contradictory" external sexual traits: breasts or penis.

5 As adults, they did not consider themselves homosexual because they fantasized that they were of the other sex when they had sexual encounters with people of their own biological sex.

6 Depressed, often suicidal, they thought that they would be cured by sex-change surgery.

Today clinicians do not find so uniform a set of histories (Green, 1973; Laub and Gandy, 1973) among transsexuals as they once did. In fact, the great uniformity of the earlier histories was a product of an effective grapevine among transsexuals within the homosexual community about the "right" answers to get by psychiatrists' questions to those seeking sex-change surgery. The surgery is very complicated, only partially satisfactory, and very difficult to come by in good hospitals. Psychiatrists screen out the vast majority of candidates for sex-change surgery.

What could cause people to hold such rigid gender beliefs and to wish so strongly to change their bodies? UCLA researchers Peter Bentler and Virginia Prince reasoned that transsexuals who had had surgery would have no motive for lying, and so they asked a group of postsurgical transsexuals about their sexual experiences before surgery. Their research turned up three equally frequently used routes to transsexualism for male-to-female transsexuals. The first is the route of effeminate homosexuality. Most often the homosexual candidate for sex-change surgery is an effeminate male who is having a hard time in the gay community. The second route is heterosexual **transvestism,** or cross-dressing. (Transvestism is a form of gender discomfort found usually in men. They find relief from this discomfort by dressing in women's clothing. Most transvestites are heterosexual in orientation.) For those on the second route, transsexualism seems to resolve problems that develop when a marriage crumbles under the strains imposed by a man's cross-dressing. The third route is the one that comes closest to the "classical" view of transsexualism, the asexual, where any sexual experience is felt to be anomalous because of uncertainty about maleness or femaleness. Most transsexuals' alienation from their gender roles probably occurs after the age of three. One does hear of cases of early dissatisfaction with gender, but most cases seem

FIGURE 3.12

Genitals of a male-to-female transsexual after sex-change surgery (left). Genitals of a female-to-male transsexual after sex-change surgery (right).

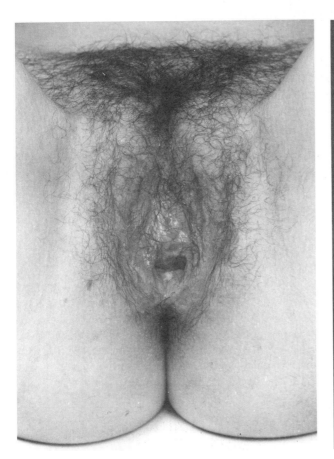
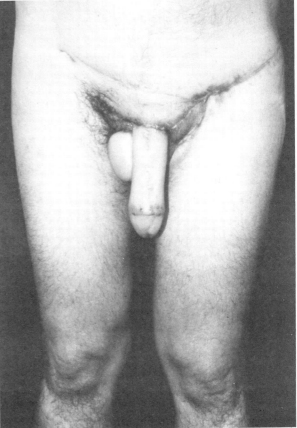

FIGURE 3.13

Pathway to transsexualism. The specific steps taken by a large sample of female-to-male transsexuals appear here. Filled circles represent mean ages; dotted lines represent age ranges (from Pauly, 1974).

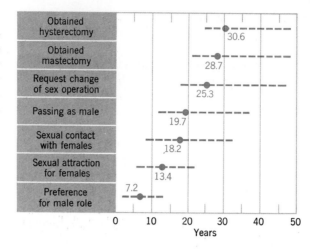

to begin after the presumed "critical period" for gender identity, 18 to 36 months of age (Donald Laub, personal communication). *Transvestia,* a journal that provides information on transvestism, supports those transsexuals for whom cross-dressing relieves gender problems. Cross-dressing is, of course, a far less drastic solution than sexual surgery. Sex change is rarely a simple route to happiness for anyone (Bentler and Prince, 1976).

Female-to-male transsexuals are very masculine girls whose tomboyishness has been extreme or very long lasting. There are many fewer female-to-male transsexuals than male-to-female transsexuals. They already differ from lesbians at puberty. Unlike lesbians, transsexuals experience the changes of puberty as violations of themselves. They often bind their breasts and make few compromises with the biological changes of puberty. Most female-to-male transsexuals have tried dating boys; half of one group had had sexual intercourse (a proportion that holds for lesbians, too). Female transsexuals tend to prefer sexual partners who are decidedly feminine women with no homosexual experience. Many female transsexuals want sex-change surgery to legitimate a close relationship of this kind (Pauly, 1974). About half marry their female partners after surgery. Female-to-male transsexuals typically make faithful husbands.

Surgery may not be the only treatment for the transsexual. Most transsexuals want to be made physically like the other sex, but a handful of cases have accepted some other "cure" than surgery. One 17-year-old transsexual agreed to try a form of behavior modification therapy in which he was slowly retrained in male behavior because surgery for a minor was impossible. It is rare that transsexuals agree to undergo behavior modification. They like their behavior, not their bodies. But the fact that behavior modification ever "works" makes many clinicians wish still more to dissuade transsexuals from costly, mutilating surgery. If the past is any guide to the future, however, these efforts will not succeed: most transsexuals want surgery, for surgery provides a transsexual a way out of a "failed career" in one gender role and entry into a new career. Surgery provides a new chance (Feinbloom, 1976).

EARLY TREATMENT
OF GENDER IDENTITY PROBLEMS

Some clinicians now try to correct the cross-gender patterns of feminine boys who want to be or believe that they are girls. These boys dress up in female clothing, avoid rough play with boys, prefer girls' toys, and have few skills with which to enjoy playing with boys. They tend to be isolated from other boys and sometimes from both sexes once they begin grade school. Early work on such children suggests that about half of them, with treatment that consists only of support, grow up to be feminine homosexuals, transvestites, or transsexuals (Green and Money, 1969; Green, 1976; Lebovitz, 1972; Zuger, 1970). Some people have questioned the ethics of even this minimal clinical intervention, because it implies that a prescribed set of gender roles is required for everyone. (See Chapter 14, "Homosexuality," for Green's 1986 follow-up of feminine boys in adulthood.)

Many clinicians who do therapy with feminine boys want them ultimately to be successfully integrated into any community, gay or straight. The isolation of some transvestites and transsexuals can be awesome. Much more is involved in working with them than helping them change their sexual behavior. Many transsexuals need skills to negotiate any form of closeness to others. To isolated people, that kind of negotiation is terribly difficult. Most people take for granted their ability to form intimate relationships and do not appreciate how much experience and learning went into that skill.

Intervention usually takes two forms, social learning therapy and behavior modification. Social learning therapy describes a male therapist who consciously acts as a **role model** for a boy and shows him what masculine behavior looks like. Behavior modification consists of rewarding and teaching masculine behaviors and gestures, teaching a boy athletic skills, and dissuading him (with the cooperation of his parents) from feminine behavior. (Some of the behavior might seem trivial, like how to hold yourself or stand up out of a chair, but acts like these can be strong gender advertisements.) Parents may be unaware of the ways in which they support a son's feminine behavior, and so they may be told to discard a feminine pet name, for instance, or to stop praising a boy for dressing like a girl or curling his long hair. All rewards for feminine behaviors are stopped. Younger boys are steered toward forming friendships with boys their age; older boys are steered toward dating (Bates et al., 1975; Bentler, 1968). Clinicians generally try to increase a boy's social contacts so that he later can belong to some group or community. No long-range outcome data on any sizable sample and untreated control subjects have yet appeared to tell how the intervention works.

Masculine girls are less often brought to therapists. Even extreme tomboyism, as we have said, is accepted by girls' groups more than feminine behavior is by boys' groups. Tomboyish girls maintain ties to other girls and learn what girls teach one another. Although female-to-male transsexuals recall adolescence as a crisis of gender identity, these girls were rarely as isolated from their gender group as were untreated feminine boys. Perhaps the smallness of girls' groups makes it possible for tomboys to have at least a single good friend, but the largeness of boys' groups may mean that feminine boys must be acceptable to more boys. That task is harder. Some parents do seek help for girls who insist that they *really are* boys, or that they have male genitals inside their body, or will never develop breasts. Psychiatrists have begun to study persistent tomboys longitudinally (over time) but do not find them so much at risk for developing severe problems as the feminine boys are. Because they are generally not isolated from girls' groups, after puberty they go out with boys and girls their age. Thus they navigate puberty quite well. They begin to use makeup and to date on the same schedule as other girls (Green et al., 1982). The isolation of feminine, cross-dressing boys and the acceptance of masculine girls tells a great deal about the difference between male and female gender groups and the roles they teach.

In the next chapter, we will turn from the topic of gender identity, with all of its complexities, to the related topic of gender roles, with all of *their* complexities.

SUMMARY

1 One's genitals at birth confirm one's biological sex—boy or girl—and start the process of acquisition of one's gender—masculine or feminine.

2 By the age of three, one has developed a deeply held sense of oneself as a male or a female, a sense that psychologists call one's core gender identity. At puberty come events that affect adult gender identity.

3 All humans have 23 pairs of chromosomes in their cells. One pair is the sex chromosomes. The genes are arranged on the chromosomes and carry the chemical instructions of heredity.

4 Human sex is inherited via the sex chromosomes. The mother always contributes an X chromosome. The father contributes an X or a Y. Normal females are 46,XX; normal males are 46,XY.

5 In the first six weeks of development, human embryos of both sexes look alike and develop primitive genitals that are not yet male or female. In the second six weeks of development, sexually differentiated internal genitals form.

6 The presence or absence of hormones will determine the course of sexual differentiation before birth. XY embryos develop testes that produce androgen and MIS. XX embryos produce neither hormone.

7 After 12 weeks, the fetus's external genitals develop. If androgen is present, male genitals will develop. If it is not present, female genitals will develop.

8 Hormones also affect the hypothalamus. Fetal androgens will suppress the later cyclical production of hormones in males. Females, however, are programmed to produce hormones cyclically at puberty.

9 Primary sexual characteristics develop before birth. Secondary sexual characteristics such as breasts, pubic and facial hair, menstruation and ejaculation, and the growth of the genitals all develop at puberty. Puberty is governed by hypothalamic hormones that stimulate the gonads into reproductive maturity and that stimulate growth spurts.

10 Errors of development, in which a person's chromosomal sex may be inconsistent with his or her gender, illustrate some important elements in the formation of sex and gender. Hermaphroditism is an error in the prenatal formation of gonads, such that gonadal tissue of both sexes is present. Pseudo-hermaphrodites have gonads inconsistent with the appearance of their genitals. Chromosomal errors include Turner's syndrome (45,XO) and Klinefelter's syndrome (47,XXY). Genetic errors produce androgen insensitivity, adrenogenital syndrome, and 5 alpha-reductase deficiency, all of which involve fetal hormonal errors.

11 The effects of hormonal errors indicate that gender identity relies on biological programming and on the sex of assignment and rearing.

12 A crucial issue in gender identity is the exact role of androgen and other sex hormones, prenatally and at puberty, in the formation of gender identity.

13 Transsexuals break out of the usual gender role *and* gender identity. Many feel that they are trapped in the body of the wrong sex, consider the changes of puberty a violation of their private sense of their gender, and want sex-change surgery.

14 Because of the painful social isolation of feminine boys, clinicians may try to intervene and shape their behavior to make it less feminine. The clinician's goal is to help the young man fit into a community of peers, be that community homosexual or heterosexual. Masculine girls are less likely than feminine boys to be socially isolated and terribly unhappy. Their adjustment may be easier, because girls' groups are less likely to reject a tomboy than boys' groups are to reject a feminine boy. As a consequence, these girls may have friends their age and the support of a reference group.

KEY TERMS

labia
clitoris
urethra
vagina
penis
scrotum
sex
gender
core gender identity
gender identity
sexual identity
transsexual
sexual dimorphism

medulla
testes
prenatal
Mullerian ducts
Wolffian ducts
hormones
puberty
Mullerian inhibiting substance
   (MIS)
androgens
genital tubercle
urogenital slit
urethral folds

zygote

chromosome

gene

autosome

sex chromosome

dominant gene

recessive gene

sex-linked disorders

embryo

indifferent gonads

cortex

ovaries

luteinizing hormone (LH)

follicle-stimulating hormone (FSH)

follicle

corpus luteum

somatotropin

brain hemisphere

gender role

Kallmann's syndrome

Turner's syndrome

stereotype

Klinefelter's syndrome

true hermaphrodite

ovatestis

hypospadias

androgen insensitivity

labio-scrotal swellings

homologous organs

labia minora

labia majora

fetus

undescended testicles

hypothalamus

primary sexual characteristics

secondary sexual characteristics

adolescence

wet dreams

pituitary gland

partial androgen insensitivity

cortisone

pseudo-hermaphrodites

adrenogenital females

bisexuality

hypophallus

diethylstilbestrol (DES)

toxemia

identical twins

guevodoces

transsexual

cross-dressing

transvestism

role model

SUGGESTED READINGS

Feinbloom, D. *Transvestites and Transsexuals: Mixed Views.* New York: Dell (Delacorte Press), 1976. Through a description of a transvestite club, the author illuminates transvestism, transsexualism, and unhappiness with gender. Her thesis is that once people feel that they have failed at the "career" of a gender role, they seek a new career. Her documentation is intriguing.

Jones, R. E. *Human Reproduction and Sexual Behavior.* Englewood Cliffs, NJ: Prentice-Hall, 1984. For the student with some biology, this book can be useful. Chapters 5 and 6 deal with the topics of our chapter.

Money, J. and Ehrhardt, A. A. *Man and Woman: Boy and Girl.* Baltimore: Johns Hopkins University Press, 1972. A classic, this book is full of interesting facts on the biology of sex in humans and other animals. Clinical material and the discussion of gender identity show the uniqueness of human identity issues.

Money, J. and Tucker, P. *Sexual Signatures.* Boston: Little, Brown, 1975. This book is a popular form of the Money and Ehrhardt book with an emphasis on the material about humans.

Morris, J. *Conundrum.* New York: Harcourt Brace Jovanovich, 1974. A fascinating biography of how James Morris, famed journalist, became Jan Morris. The transsexual phenomenon is presented in a very human form by as believable a source as one is likely to find on the subject.

Chapter 4

Gender Roles

All cultures make social definitions about the differences between females and males. Furthermore, people everywhere believe that *their* culture's definitions reflect the laws of nature. Thus we may believe that men are assertive and unemotional or women unassertive and emotional because they are "made" that way. Societies attach a whole host of obligations and expectations to their gender labels. To be masculine, we believe, a man "should" wear trousers and ignore physical discomforts. To be feminine, a woman "should" wear skirts and be interested in children. Thus, starting from "male" and "female," terms with clear biological referents (such as penis and vagina), people develop two different lists of adjectives to describe "masculine" and "feminine."

If we plotted babies' scores on any measure of continuous behavior such as activity level, we would find that the curves representing the scores for boys and girls overlap. But people may learn to consider male and female behavior as more or less similar than they really are (Brown, 1965). In so doing, people effectively amplify in social terms the weak biological differences between the sexes. This amplification is at least as influential as the biological differences in determining how the sexes will behave. (See Figure 4.1.) In fact, people do not act in such sharply different ways. Gender is not a simple either/or matter, of one sex being passive and one active, one logical and one emotional. The sexes are not really opposites at all. Some masculine males are more sensitive and helpful than some females; some feminine females are more mechanically skilled and aggressive than some males. The distribution of traits studied by psychologists show more overlapping between the sexes than segregation.

Every person holds a deep, inner feeling about his or her gender. This feeling develops early in life, usually before the age of three. Psychologists call this inner conviction—this "I know I'm a girl" or "Hey, I'm a boy" feeling—a person's **gender identity.** How people, male or female, publicly express their gender identity is called their **gender role.** Many of us find some aspects of the expected gender role easy to play, other aspects hard or disagreeable. We cherish some aspects and dislike others. Here are four people's thoughts about aspects of the gender roles that they feel expected to play:

Why is it that I'm only considered masculine if I make the first move sexually with a girl? I would like to see what it's like to be on the receiving end for once (19-year-old male college sophomore).

FIGURE 4.1

This curve represents the degree of overlap between males and females in any particular biologically given characteristic. Social pressures may cause weak biological differences, present at birth, to intensify or weaken in the course of development.

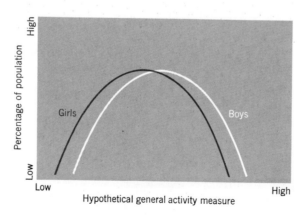

I hate having to wait for men to take the initiative. But if I go ahead and call a guy or, heaven forbid, come on to a guy sexually, I worry about whether he'll think I'm too pushy and masculine (19-year-old female college junior).

I love my job, and I'm good at it. Babies don't really interest me, but I'm getting a lot of pressure from my husband's parents to produce a grandchild. I worry I'm too masculine, and that makes me feel guilty (31-year-old female lawyer).

The aunt who raised us as kids believes in my being fruitful. But my wife and I are content to be aunt and uncle to my sister's children. First my aunt worked on me, and then she worked on my wife. My aunt thinks that eventually we'll feel desperate about our "fruitlessness," as she calls it. But I doubt it (28-year-old male college professor).

As these thoughts suggest, many aspects of gender roles have a bearing on sexual matters. To understand human sexuality, we must understand gender roles. In this chapter, we will explore how we as individuals are molded by our society's definitions of gender differences and gender roles.

LEARNING GENDER ROLES: A DEVELOPMENTAL SEQUENCE

Children get information on how "proper" girls and boys behave from several sources. Parents are one important source. Other children, teachers and texts, and even television also reinforce gender differences. Although not all parents agree on the content of gender roles, and some allow their children more latitude than others, even nontraditional, nonsexist parents cannot totally avoid exposing their daughters and sons to what other girls and boys know and believe. Children themselves, with their limited information and cognitive abilities, may enforce narrow definitions of gender, sometimes more fiercely than parents. Because sex comes in two packages, male and female, children may think that sex-related feelings and acts come in the same two packages. Even adults hear the two sexes spoken of as "opposite" sexes when in reality they are closely related structurally.

Stereotypes About Gender

Young children find it difficult to sort several classes of events or people at the same time, and so it is not surprising that their ideas about male and female show early **stereotyping.** Stereotyping is the quality of possessing an oversimplified, preconceived idea about all individuals in a given group of people. It leads to treating individuals as if they had all of the group's characteristics rather than their own personal characteristics. Stereotypes applied to groups other than one's own are often derogatory.

The stereotype of the masculine role emphasizes competence and dominance, doing, competing and striving. It minimizes expressions of feelings and ambivalence. Males are supposed to control their feelings, except anger, which they may express. They must not act afraid. It has long been a compliment to tell a man that he is "the strong, silent type." A result of the masculine stereotype is that many males have friendships full of horsing around, doing things together, with affection conveyed *indirectly,* through jokes, insults, punches, a clap on the shoulder.

The female role, in contrast, emphasizes the qualities of expressiveness, caring for others, and attending to cues from other people. Perhaps above all, females are taught the world around to seek acceptance by others (Whiting and Edwards, 1973). Thus they focus on people rather than on things. They control their negative feelings and express their positive ones. In one study, parents read to preschoolers from books without words (Greif et al., 1981). Mothers explained emotions equally to girls and to boys. Fathers, however, explained emotions twice as often to girls as to boys.

Children tend to generalize as they acquire language and form ideas about descriptive categories. Early learning is heavy on binary categories: "Who is the good guy, and who is the bad guy?" "I'm big, and you're little." "This one is pretty, and that one is ugly." It would be surprising if children did not extend this tendency to see dichotomies from sex, which *is* binary, to gender, which is not (Luria, 1979). Children certainly do this, but we should be cautious about speculating that ideas about gender role are acquired *and* fixed early, as are ideas about gender identity. Psychologists know that simple sorts of realities over time can diminish this tendency to form dichotomies. For example, children who grow up with siblings of the other sex believe fewer stereotypes about the sexes than do only children (Heise and Roberts, 1970).

STEREOTYPES AbOUT GENDER FORM VERY EARLY. TWO-ANd-ONE-HAlÍ-YEAR-OLd GIRLS ALREADY THINK THAT bOYS FIGHT ANd NEVER CRY; TWO-ANd-ONE-HAlF-YEAR-OLd bOYS THINK THAT GIRLS "LIKE TO CLEAN HOUSE" ANd "NEVER FIGHT."

Stereotypes about gender form very early. Two-and-one-half-year-old girls already think that boys fight and never cry; two-and-one-half-year-old boys think that girls "like to clean house" and "never fight." Two- and three-year-old boys and girls believe that boys break rules, hit, and like to help their fathers and that girls don't hit and do like to help their mothers (Kuhn, Nash, and Brucken, 1972). Beliefs about gender stereotypes seem to proceed in an orderly fashion, with some beliefs expressed as early as age 2, some as late as age 7 (for instance, that girls are emotional), and some in between (Reis and Wright, 1982; Williams et al., 1975). The process is a continuous one, and it takes the form of a series of potential constraints and limits on children's behavior.

Children are susceptible to learning stereotypes in part because they have a limited ability to understand the difference between what is (as they see it) and what might be. The ability to imagine "what if?" comes fairly late in childhood. Kindergartners, for example, when exposed to a curriculum designed to show them that existing gender roles could be changed, simply could not grasp the basic idea. But older children, those 10 and 14, could understand the difference. Girls' views changed readily; 14-year-old boys were the most resistant to change.

Perhaps boys of that age already have learned to avoid things feminine and therefore resist the notion that boys might adopt less stereotypic gender roles and grant girls the same freedom that boys have, as in choosing occupations (Guttentag and Bray, 1976; Guttentag and Longfellow, 1977).

We know that by 24 months, children do well at identifying other people's gender. They can identify boy and girl and "mommy" and "daddy" as fitting pictures of males and females. But they cannot yet consistently use pronouns like "she" or "he." They know the gender associated with certain items of clothing and common articles like toys, tools, and appliances. By 30 to 36 months, children quite perfectly label their own and others' gender. By age 3, children's gender identities are essentially well in place. When objects are labeled "for boys" by an experimenter, boys prefer them. When the same objects are labeled "for girls," girls prefer them (Thompson, 1975). Thus the 24-month-old is already smart about gender, but it may take the child another year to use that knowledge to guide preferences.

I knew that our 20-month-old son had not mastered all the sex differences when he heartily thanked his father with, "Good girl, Dada!" (26-year-old mother).

As my two-and-one-half-year-old was trying to learn the differences between males and females, she would ask very loudly in public places whether someone was "Man?" or "Lady?" People reacted as if she was cute when she got it right, but it was awfully embarrassing when she didn't. In a shoe store one afternoon, she bellowed, "Lady?" at a 13- or 14-year-old boy who had a head of carefully arranged Michael Jackson curls. He cringed (27-year-old mother).

Parents

One of the very earliest sources of children's learning about gender is their parents. Some evidence suggests that parents—and fathers especially—treat their sons and daughters differently. Parents talk and smile more to their firstborn daughters than their sons (Thoman et al., 1972). They see their sons as sturdier and less in need of protection than their daughters (Robson, 1967). Parents of firstborn, one-day-old babies label sons on questionnaires as stronger, bigger, hardier, more alert, easier going, and larger featured than do parents of firstborn, one-day-old daughters. They see their girls as weaker, smaller and smaller featured, more fragile, less alert, and less easygoing than the parents of the boys see them. Fathers tend to perceive these characteristics even more strongly than mothers do. Parents (at least in this sample) engage in this kind of labeling despite the lack of any observable difference in the babies' weight, length, or response to stimulation (Rubin, Provenzano, and Luria, 1974). Strangers who see a one-day-old baby whose sex they know are far less likely than parents to stereotype that baby (Luria, 1979).

In one study of nursery-school children and their parents, fathers—but not mothers—steered their children toward toys conventionally associated with the child's gender (Jacklin et al., 1984). Observations of children for their first six years of life, at home, at school, and in the laboratory, showed that parents do not stereotype their children. Mothers and fathers doled out essentially equal amounts of love and restrictions to their sons and their daughters. Fathers, however, offered their children more gender-stereotyped toys and played more roughly with their sons than their daughters (Maccoby and Jacklin, reported in Turkington, 1984).

Children and Their Peers

All of the psychological theories about how children develop gender identity and roles agree on several points:

1 Children learn the name for their gender early in life.
2 They attach value to their own gender.
3 They identify others as being of the same or of different gender.
4 They remember and imitate people of their own gender more than people of different gender.

Some psychologists interested in social learning theorize that children adopt gender roles because they see that people are rewarded for behavior "appropriate" to their gender—"What a good girl you are for helping Mommy clean up!"—and punished for "inappropriate" behavior—"Big boys don't cry, Johnny" (Kagan and Moss, 1967; Mischel, 1966). According to modern social learning theory, rewards and punishments to others—as well as to themselves—teach children gender rules.

Lawrence Kohlberg, a Harvard psychologist, has theorized that children know more about gender than just behavior they have seen rewarded or punished. He believes that children search out information about their gender much as they search out information about physical reality. Information about what boys or girls do and like becomes its own reward for children, because they attach value to their own gender label. Kohlberg's cognitive-developmental theory (1966) is intriguing, because if children socialize themselves, some of the peculiar ideas preschoolers have about gender grow more understandable.

School and Textbooks

As children, most of us segregate ourselves in same-sex groups, and do so even more strictly as we grow older. As we get older, we have increasingly less chance to compare our stereotypic views with the reality of the other sex. Children, especially in grade school, feel enormous pressures from others their age to act in ways considered appropriate to their sex. Once in grade school, children are pressured to give up behavior that does not conform to the stereotype. Boys who do not want to get involved in sports are pressured by other boys to hide this kind of "sissy" behavior, and they cannot—as they could until about age seven— take refuge among the girls. (Grade-school boys probably experience stronger pressures of this sort than girls do [Luria and Herzog, 1985]). Part of this pressure is internal in that children compare themselves to others who are like them; these others form a **reference group**—a group against whom one judges oneself. Other boys are significant to a boy, other girls to a girl. Said one elementary-school teacher:

> *During recesses in the schoolyard, I can see how an eight-year-old boy watches every move of a ten-year-old boy or an eight-year-old girl tags after a twelve-year-old girl. The younger ones idolize the older kids. The imitation borders on hero worship.*

Thus it seems that children themselves, by their own social comparison, by peer pressure (especially among boys), and by overgeneralizing, learn and enforce stereotypes about gender.

Teachers also have been blamed for perpetuating stereotypes. Of course, teachers share gender stereotypes with the rest of society. Textbooks until quite recently have been stereotyped: children lived in a house with a mother at home and a father who went off to work. Families contained one son and one daughter, both solid and good children. The son was active and wore trousers. The daughter was passive and wore a skirt. They lived in a one-family house surrounded by a lawn (Saario et al., 1973; Weitzman and Rizzo, 1980). Many textbooks have changed to reflect more accurately the activities of men and women and children.

Television

Another voice that speaks loudly and long to many children (and adults) comes from the television. Although television writers seem to be trying to introduce fewer stereotypes in gender roles into the current crop of comedies and dramas, the world of television is largely **sex stereotyped** in that the gender roles portrayed there are highly standardized and distort reality. On the television screen, there are three times as many male characters as female characters. In reality, there are slightly more boys than girls until age five and then increasingly fewer males to females over the entire life span. Female television characters are mothers, mistresses, or adornments to more powerful male characters. Female characters are nearly all young and attractive helpmates who do little; male characters have a wider span of ages, are not necessarily attractive, and actively do things. Television also vastly underrepresents the number of blue-collar workers—about 60 percent of the workforce in reality but only about 6 to 10 percent on television—and distorts the picture of society so that it seems to be teeming with male doctors, lawyers, and athletes. Television shows the elderly, when they appear at all, as sexually defunct, silly old codgers (Gerbner and Signorielli, 1982).

EARLY DIFFERENCES IN BEHAVIOR

Psychologists have also found differences in the behavior of the sexes after the age of two (differences before two generally are not reliable), but it is important to realize that these are *average* differences. In one study, 20-month-olds were tested at home by familiar examiners and played more freely with toys typed for their own sex than for the other sex. The toys that they owned were also typed largely for their own sex, with one exception: girls had more boy toys than boys had girl toys. Out of 24 children, only one had a "favorite" toy that was not sex-typed. Adults choose many toys for children, of course, but that fact alone cannot explain why 7 out of 11 boys who saw an adult rocking a doll actually threw the doll away. No girl in the study ever expressed such negative feelings toward any of the male-stereotyped toys or objects (Fein et al., 1975). Psychologists are hard put to account for such early toy preferences. (See "Sexuality in Research: Boy Toys and Girl Toys.") In another study, the investigators looked at newly formed groups of infants, toddlers, and preschoolers to find out who excludes whom and who successfully initiates interaction. It was found that infants do not discriminate against infants of the other sex but that toddlers and preschoolers do discriminate. After only one year in school, toddlers and preschoolers initiate play more often and more successfully with children of their own sex (Howes, Rubinstein, and Eldredge, 1983).

Although nursery-schoolers sometimes separate by sex when they play, their separation is not as pronounced as older children's. Developmental psychologists Carol Jacklin and Eleanor Maccoby (1978) devised a study of 33-month-old children that raises intriguing questions about how and why the sexes separate. Pairs of children played together, and the pairs were either of the same or cross sex. All children wore clothing that gave no indication of their sex. The observers who coded the children's play did not know which sex the children were. The results showed that same-sex pairs played more peacefully and steadily together than cross-sex pairs did. Perhaps their styles of handling disagreements, or similarities in temperament, or some other, unidentified elements made the same-sex play more integrative.

Before grade school, children are already tending toward gender-segregated play. They tend to prefer playmates of their own sex. On average, girls play in smaller groups—very often in pairs—less roughly than boys do, and less often in games with multiple roles (Lever, 1976; 1978). Girls in their (smaller) groups also fight less than boys in their (larger) groups. Boys' larger groups may help them to learn how to deal with organized hierarchies better than with subtle interpersonal cues. Girls' small groups may help to make them better than boys at identifying others' nonverbal messages and in sending such nonverbal messages themselves (Hall, 1980).

*From third to sixth grade, five of us girls called ourselves "The Group."
We always played together. Our games weren't very competitive, and we
spent a lot of time talking about our teachers and boys we "liked." "The
Group" fell apart when we went to junior high school, but I am still
best friends with one of the girls (21-year-old female junior).*

Girls tend to express concern for their playmates and to settle disputes tactfully.
One observer has inferred that the game seems less important to girls than the
feelings of the players (Lever, 1976). Many girls form a special bond with one
friend, and in this "best" friendship, they track one another's feelings, moves,
and thoughts. When feelings grow unmanageable, best friends may part. Boys
may need groups; girls seem to need one special friend.

Girls seem to use adults more than boys do as resources in performing tasks.
Preschool boys do few "girls'" activities; girls are freer to do "boys'" things
(Maccoby, 1976; Maccoby and Jacklin, 1974). The different names for crossing
gender lines in play tells the story. "Sissy," for example, is a name no one relishes;
boys will try to avoid acting in any fashion that might call down upon them that
punitive name. "Tomboy" is not punitive for girls before puberty. Adults generally have more trouble managing groups of boys than girls, perhaps because
boys are expected to test limits. They are also more likely than girls to break
rules; even unaggressive boys will break rules in league with aggressive boys.
Rule-breaking can grow positively contagious among boys. Girls certainly break
rules as well, but they do not often get involved in the same cycles of contagion.
It is possible that the excitement of breaking rules—"Will we get caught this
time or not?"—feeds into boys' sexual excitement. By the fourth or fifth grade,
for example, many boys have had plenty of practice with "bad words." Adults
have a hard time controlling this play. The boys may have limited notions of
what certain bad words mean, but they *know* that they're secret because adults
forbid them. One such game is "Mad Libs," in which incomplete sentences are
filled in. Here is one sentence, supposedly about the Constitution: "The _____
[shit] was ratified in _____ [Cuntville] in 1788" (Luria, 1983). The flushed,

As children get older, the pressure will intensify on them to
play exclusively with children of
their own sex.

giddy, furtive excitement on boys' faces leaves no doubt that they find these games exciting. Through the games, boys share "dirty," forbidden things and lay the foundation for their later sharing of soft and hard pornography.

Gender segregation is especially pronounced in grade school groups, less pronounced in informal neighborhood and family groups. By the age of seven, some public schools boys have devised an ideology about why they avoid girls. As investigators in Michigan and California schools learned, children confer on certain unfortunate girls—those who are poor or badly dressed—the title of "cootie queen." ("Cooties" actually are the eggs of lice.) The negative value of girls is emphatically communicated in the demeaning phrase (Thorne and Luria, 1986).

SEXUALITY IN RESEARCH:
BOY TOYS AND GIRL TOYS

Is it all right for little boys to play with "girl things" like dolls and cooking sets? Is it all right for little girls to play with "boy things" like toy trucks and footballs? Will toys usually associated with the other sex interfere with a boy's masculine development or a girl's feminine development? Will a boy who plays with "girl toys" develop into a homosexual? Because these are some of the issues that worry parents, psychologists have sought answers. Said Michael Lewis, a researcher in child development at the Rutgers Medical School-University of Medicine and Dentistry of New Jersey, parents feel strongly about what is appropriate behavior for boys and girls. Parents may let boys play with humanlike figures, but they get worried when boys play with frilly dolls. Parents let girls play with baseballs, but they discourage them from playing football.

To learn whether playing with "boy" or "girl" toys affects children's later development, Lewis has been following a group of 150 children longitudinally, from birth to (most recently) the age of nine. When 128 of the children were two years old, they were videotaped playing with toys that independent raters had judged to be "sex-role appropriate." At the same time, the children's mothers took a standardized psychological test to determine whether their beliefs about sex roles were traditional or androgynous. Four years later, when the six-year-old children had entered first grade, their teachers rated their adjustment and included such factors as language ability, considerateness, introversion, creativity, participation in class discussions, and adaptability to classroom routines. The number of females and male friends each child had was tabulated also.

From all of these data, Lewis found that the mothers were split between

Even when they play the same games, boys and girls usually do not mix. When fourth-graders who routinely fielded both girls' and boys' kickball teams were asked why they did not join forces, they answered, "Don't you know, boys don't play with girls," or "Boys play with boys; girls play with girls." They seemed to consider adults who ask such questions rather foolish (Luria and Herzog, 1985). Fourth-grade boys avoid behaviors modeled by fourth-grade girls more than girls avoid behaviors modeled by boys. Girls are willing to take on behaviors modeled by their peers without regard to their sex (Bussey and Perry, 1982). After all, what is the harm in being a "tomboy"? Early social differences like these make the sexes behave increasingly differently as time goes on (Block, 1976; Maccoby and Jacklin, 1974).

traditional (56 percent) and nontraditional, or androgynous (39 percent), orientations to sex roles. How well a child had adjusted to first grade was *not* related simply to whether a mother believed in traditional or untraditional sex roles. But the children's adjustment *did* relate quite markedly to how well their behavior fit with their mothers' sex-role orientation. Said Dr. Lewis, when children's toy play *matched* their mothers' sex-role expectations, the children were rated by their teachers as better adjusted than children whose toy play *violated* their mothers' expectations. In families where mothers held traditional beliefs about sex roles, if a boy played with girls' toys or a girl played with boys' toys, the child was likely to end up less well adjusted, according to teachers' ratings.

What then does the professional answer to parents who want to know whether it is "all right" for children to play with toys of the other sex? It's perfectly fine, Lewis believes, *if* it doesn't matter to the parents. But if it does bother the parents, "then don't buy your child the kinds of toys you don't like."

Finally, what about the worry of some parents—often unexpressed—that if their son plays with girls' toys, he might develop homosexual tendencies? There is no ground for worry, says Lewis, "[H]omosexuality has nothing to do with gender identity. There was, and is, no evidence that if your little boy plays with little-girl toys, he'll be a homosexual."

Based on G. Collins, "New Studies on 'Girl Toys' and 'Boy Toys'," New York *Times,* February 13, 1984.

In grade school, girls generally are better students, have somewhat better verbal skills, and are more oriented toward adults than boys are. If they are good athletes, some girls at this age can play with boys. But boys cannot otherwise freely play with girls at school without risking censure or ridicule from other boys. In grade school, boys are more attentive to their peers and less interested in teachers than girls are, and boys are also more often disciplinary problems than girls are (Dweck and Goetz, 1978). Boys also get more practice at organized, competitive, hierarchical games than girls do (Lever, 1976, 1978). Sports metaphors help to shape boys' ideas about mastery. The earlier preferences and segregation of the two sexes intensify as they proceed through grade school.

In short, *average* differences in behavior between boys and girls show up even before grade school. Boys and girls form gender-segregated play groups. Boys' groups are larger and more aggressive than girls' groups, and in them boys learn about sports, competition, and hierarchies. Girls, in their smaller play groups, pay closer attention to adults and to interpersonal messages than boys do. Girls learn that they may do certain "boy" things—play Little League ball, for instance, or wear jeans—but boys learn that they do "girl" things—like playing with dolls or jacks, or wearing jewelry—at the risk of being called a sissy.

GENDER ROLE AT PUBERTY

The events of **puberty** further differentiate the two sexes, both physically and socially. Their expectations for themselves as well as others' expectations for them now diverge sharply. Parents may now start exerting pressures to make a child conform to the "proper" gender role. The tomboy may not have been as pressed to change as the "sissy" was at age seven or eight. But by age 12, the tomboy is much less acceptable to her parents than she had been.

Teenaged girls are more concerned on average with their popularity and social skills than boys are. Even in junior high school, girls are worried about how to balance a job and a family, about which strategies to pursue to get both (Tittle, 1981). The boys are beginning to worry about a livelihood and are more concerned with learning work-related skills and becoming competent than girls are (Douvan and Adelson, 1966; Offer, 1969; Offer and Offer, 1975). Most boys grow serious about success and achievement; the girls grow conflicted, wondering whether they will be accepted by others. Consequently, the two sexes' strategies for achieving differ. While many young women worry about their looks, grow self-conscious, and turn to close friendships and success in their relationships with others, boys move toward the occupational goals they have chosen for themselves. Boys at adolescence may be serious about athletics, and in high school may be more concerned with cars and basketball coaches than with girls (Offer and Offer, 1975; Rosenberg and Simmons, 1975; Simmons et al., 1979). But even as early adolescents, boys usually aim for achievement and success.

Adolescence is also when we see larger differences develop in the two sexes' spatial and mathematical abilities. Traditionally, males have tended on average to perform and express themselves better than females in these cognitive areas (Maccoby and Jacklin, 1974; Block, 1976). Recent studies of spatial and mathematical abilities still show significant differences between the sexes, but the differences are smaller than those that appeared in older studies (Rosenthal and Rubin, 1982). (See "Sexuality in Perspective: Sex Differences in the Brain," in

DOONESBURY

by Garry Trudeau

Garry Trudeau exaggerates to show how ambivalent some men are towards changes in gender roles.

Chapter 3.) Perhaps the new routes through adolescence and adulthood—more girls are studying mathematics, for example—will change traditional patterns of sex differences. Some of the new paths girls are taking are making them feel better intellectually and sexually (Offer, 1981).

GENDER ROLE IN ADULTHOOD

As we have seen, teenaged girls traditionally have worried about their social skills. Boys traditionally have worried about their work skills. These qualities are quite consistent with the adult gender roles of the two sexes, for although she may work outside her home, a woman long has been expected to derive much of her identity from her role as wife and mother; and although he may be a husband and father, a man has been expected to derive more of his identity from his work. For this reason, many women, especially those who marry fairly young, choose career or job goals that will mesh with those of whomever they marry (Angrist, 1969). In contrast, men use strategies of their own devising and pursue them without respect to women.

THE CHANGING AMERICAN FAMILY

Erik Erikson has offered an influential theory of human development that sees people coping and changing throughout their entire lives. Working within Erikson's framework on development, researchers of work and family identities suggest that women are taking many different routes to base identities. The newest, least-traveled route is that of career-oriented women who bear children after their career is established. That means choosing to work and postponing having children until perhaps well after the age of 30. (When we talk about "choosing" to work, we are talking largely about middle-class women. Poor, immigrant, divorced, and widowed women, of whom there have always been many, have been contending with juggling two roles for a long time [Filene, 1974.] But many modern, middle-class wives feel that they have no choice but to work, given the high cost of maintaining a home and family.) Work identities are thus formed earlier in such women, just as they are in their husbands (Daniels and Weingarten, 1983). Women who marry late or choose not to marry, who get advanced degrees and training, and the like, are adopting strategies more like those of males.

Census data show that the stereotypical American family—a father-breadwinner plus a mother-housewife and (at least) two school-age children—now describes only a minority, one family in seven. Government figures also say that by 1990, 85 percent of all women will be working without interruption from age 35 on (Terleckyj and Levy, 1981). The implications of this development for women, for families, and for people's stereotypes can only be guessed at now. Although many women in earlier generations worked, they worked in their homes, part of the pattern of the rural family. Today, in a predominantly urban labor force, women leave their homes to work. The guilt that many working mothers feel today as they try to satisfy the demands of work and family is partly a vestige of the view that mothers should not work outside the home, that they should stay at home to be mothers and wives.

As the percentages of working women increase, and as gender segregation in jobs declines, guilt may decrease, and the women-are-nurses, men-are-doctors stereotypes also may decrease. Many fathers today share in child care, especially when their children are very young. When couples have one or more children and both work at home and in the workforce, they often feel overloaded (Rapoport and Rapoport, 1971). Some research suggests that husbands who help with child care describe themselves as happier than men who do not help (Staines and Pleck, 1983). But these may be a self-selected sample of husbands, or they may be the first to show that sharing the investment in work and family adds to life's satisfactions. It is too early yet to know for certain which is the truth of the matter.

Middle age typically brings men to their peak of productivity and earnings in their jobs, at which point their careers tend to reach a plateau. Men also grow closer to their families at this time. Older men may share responsibilities at home more readily than younger men do, and old age seems an easier adjustment for these men than for those whose interests remain outside their home. Middle-aged women typically are finding their places in the workforce and are turning away from the family as their primary or only focus. Many women at middle age see the "empty nest," the home emptied once the grown children have dispersed, as their freedom rather than as a source of grief (Rubin, 1979). Many women also feel freed by **menopause**—the end of menstrual cycling—from anxieties about conceiving children (Neugarten, 1968). Women begin to be widowed in their mid-50s, and fully half are widows at age 65. At that age, some women may be forced to assume the roles that previously belonged to their husbands.

> *When my husband entered his last illness, I felt almost panicky. Although I had paid the household bills and kept things running day to day, he had always handled our long-range finances. I didn't know how or where to begin. My son-in-law helped some, and so did a few close friends of the family. But I have been alone in ways that I never thought about (67-year-old widow).*

It is also true that as the cumulative numbers of divorced men and women increase with the years, living as a single adult or a single parent may pressure a person to adopt aspects of the missing mate's role.

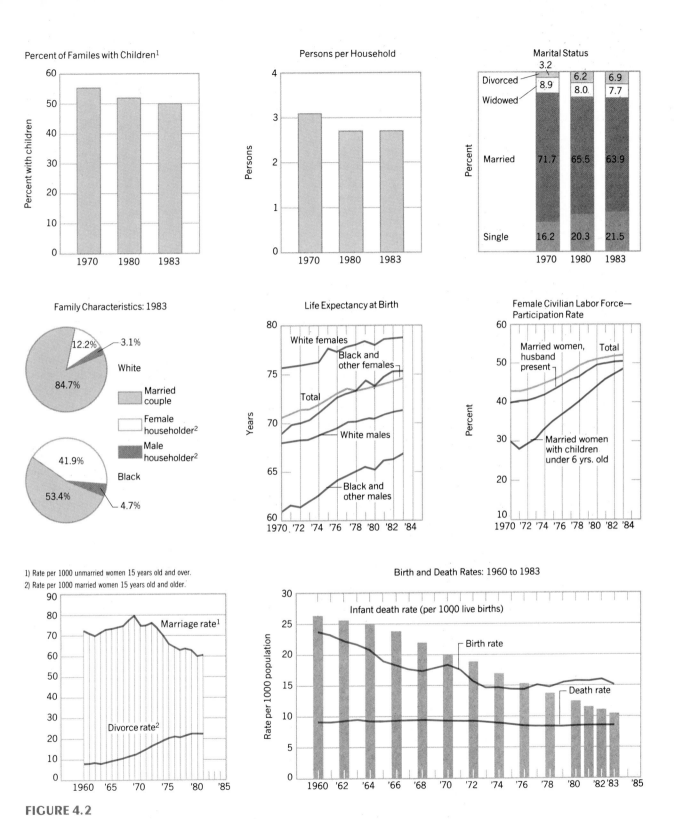

FIGURE 4.2

The changing American family. Today, fewer American families include children, the average family size has dropped, and more married women are in the paid labor force. The number of single and divorced has grown, as the number of marrieds has dropped. Life expectancy has risen, as infant death rates have fallen slightly and birth rates have risen slightly (Source: U.S. Bureau of the Census).

SEXUALITY IN PERSPECTIVE:
ANDROGYNY: MASCULINITY AND FEMININITY COMBINED

Sandra Bem, first at Stanford and now at Cornell, and a pair of social psychologists at the University of Texas, Janet Spence and Robert Helmreich, developed similar strategies but different measures of gender roles. They found some self-descriptions that virtually only females endorsed, some exclusively chosen by males, and some that both sexes endorsed. They labeled these traits feminine, masculine, and neutral, respectively. Both research groups assumed that people with masculine *and* feminine characteristics would be *androgynous* and more flexible about taking on the gender role that would be effective in a particular situation, rather than sticking by stereotypic gender responses.

The Texas group has concentrated on characterizing different sorts of groups. They have found, for example, that lesbians and women athletes are either highly androgynous or masculine on their measure. High androgyny on their test goes along with high self-esteem. (Spence and Helmreich are validating their test with other self-report measures.)

Sandra Bem has used her androgyny scale to categorize subjects in experiments. She compares androgynous people with those who are more traditionally masculine or feminine in situations that call for the ability to step out of a traditional gender role. The experimental situations may call for nonconforming behavior, as when a male subject is in a situation where he can comfort a baby or an animal. Generally, females who score high on androgyny can be nonconforming, assertive, and independent. Males who score high on androgyny can be comforting and empathic to others.

Work on androgyny, however it is measured, has had important effects on how social scientists treat gender roles. First, it showed that the characteristics of a single person can be a happy mix of the masculine and the feminine. Thus psychological tests that characterize a person as masculine *or* feminine no longer hold water. Second, androgyny research showed that many people who function quite well socially describe themselves as *neither* masculine *nor* feminine.

Bem argues, frankly politically, that gender schemas of any sort limit people's choices. She proposes "not that the individual be androgynous, but that society be aschematic" (Bem, 1981, p. 363). Bem and her husband have tried to put their ideas into practice in raising their own two children. Asked how they managed to raise their children this way despite the gender schema of the larger society, Bem will answer that they taught their children everything about *sex* and nothing about *gender*. When the children brought home statements about behaviors that went only with a given gender, the parents made them test the statements against what they already knew. ("How could having a penis make someone less understanding?" "Do a uterus and vagina make it harder to understand science?") Bem maintains that all parents educate their children about certain cultural truths. Just as parents might intervene to prevent their children from being racist, Bem believes, they should prevent their children from becoming sexist as well.

Based on S. L. Bem, "Gender Schema Theory: a Cognitive Account of Sex Typing," *Psychological Review* (1981), 88, pp. 354–364.

We have been talking about "scripts" for sexual roles. The idea of **sexual scripts** originated with John Gagnon and William Simon (1970), who proposed that childhood sexuality differs in an important way from adolescent and adult sexuality. They also proposed that sexual behavior may express and serve motives that are not purely sexual. Gagnon and Simon argue that children's understanding of their own sexual behavior is limited because it is not yet incorporated into a peer context that is sexual. Orgasms may occur as children slide down the bannister, ride a horse, or even rub their genitals. But not until they are teenagers will they have a framework for their sexual behavior. Parents also teach their children as *manners* rules that will only later be sexual: "Nice girls don't walk around the house in panties," or "We close the door to the bathroom." Only after adolescence will these experiences fit into a frankly sexual context.

The sexual changes of puberty trigger a whole new understanding of sexual behavior. Earlier training about modesty, sexual exploration, and behaving with the other sex takes on new meaning. Now the peer group attaches meanings and values to new and old events, rendering them fully sexual. When this adolescent sexual activity appears, it is, according to Gagnon and Simon, scripted, because it follows social conventions and prescribed sequences. Adolescents learn how to be sexual: what one does, when one does it, with whom one does it, and what it means. The two sexes learn different scripts, and the segregation of the peer groups of boys and girls widens the gap between their scripts.

The part of Gagnon and Simon's theory with the most supporting evidence is about the sequence of masturbation and social sex play. Within a few years after puberty, most boys in our culture have had an orgasm, usually when they are alone masturbating or in a wet dream. Young men masturbate at the highest

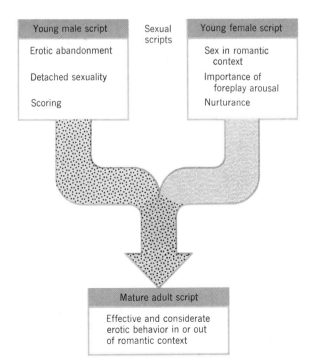

FIGURE 4.3

Sexual scripts for adolescents, as proposed by Gagnon and Simon. Over time, members of the two sexes integrate elements of the two scripts into a mature sexuality.

rates they ever will during their adolescence. They therefore understand how they react sexually to the sequence from erection to orgasm before they get involved in sexual relationships. Boys have trouble imagining what early social sex is like for a young woman who has heard about orgasm but has no idea what that feels like. Girls usually have their first orgasm later than boys and in a social context. They may add solitary masturbation to their sexual repertory after they have done some sexual exploring with a boy. Girls tend to feel anxiety about granting boys sexual access to them. Boys feel anxiety about secret masturbation and forbidden fantasies about their sexual performance. Thus boys typically proceed from solitary to social sex, and girls move in the opposite direction. The male's script is low on the interpersonal qualities that comprise the whole of the female's script. He treats early social sex as a manipulation of genitals, like masturbation. She must learn from early social sex how to focus on genitals and how to value the interpersonal and the romantic. The anxiety that accompanies their practice of the new sexual script heightens its significance for most young men and women.

Dating becomes a way of learning about sex. Boys teach girls how to abandon themselves to sensual pleasure and to put aside manners and tidiness. Boys teach their partners not to carry on continuous conversations during sex. As we have already seen, the male role teaches boys to value performance and domination, the female role to value responsiveness and emotional expression. Males follow a sexual script in which they first dominate; females at first nurture and support. She makes the male happy and so feels close, giving, even protective. Gagnon and Simon call this a woman's "social service" orientation. As couples grow closer, they share and compromise elements of the two sexual scripts they brought to the relationship and produce a combined script of adult sexuality in which each, ideally, acts out considerate, effective erotic behavior both in and out of romantic settings.

DO GENDER STEREOTYPES AFFECT SEXUAL EXPERIENCE?

During adolescence, as we have just seen, male gender stereotypes focus on "being the best," on achievement, and on attaining public signs of success. When sexual myths join gender stereotypes, adolescent males' myths about potency grow exaggerated. Stereotypes about sexual performance—about "scoring"—converge with metaphors of success on a baseball field. In the stereotyped vision, real men are ever-ready to perform sexually, ever-ready to initiate sex, and ever-arousable on demand. Sexual contacts move quickly to erection, intercourse, and orgasm. During adolescence, female gender stereotypes focus on the value of close friendships with other girls, on succeeding in relationships with others, and on looking good. Certain sexual myths grow attached to those values: that love and intercourse go together; that sex is more important to males than females; that males initiate and girls respond. Many adolescent girls value personal relationships so deeply that they believe good sex will follow good relationships (a sequence the adolescent male's imagination may reverse).

Gender stereotypes affect sexual functioning, too, although there is no *simple,* one-to-one relation among sex stereotypes, sexual myths, and pleasurable (or unpleasurable) sexual functioning. It is true that adolescent girls' concerns for being well liked can prevent them from asserting their sexual wishes. Sexual interaction is more than servicing a partner (Kaplan, 1974, 1978). But it is also true that, as some researchers have found, men who function well sexually tend to be more "masculine"—assertive, vigorous, not passive, interested in novelty and variety—than dysfunctional men and that women who function well sexually tend to be more androgynous—having higher scores on measures of *both* femininity and masculinity—than dysfunctional women (Derogatis and Meyer, 1979). Trust and experimentation may be good teachers. Trust within a relationship undoes some of the sexual myths that women believe. One researcher found that a girl's trust in her father as she grew up related to her ability to reach orgasm, for she was then more likely to be able to trust her sexual partners (Fisher, 1973). People who have sought and received help for sexual problems—help that includes increasing their trust—typically emerge with fewer sex stereotypes (Clement and Pfafflin, 1980).

People, in short, are flexible. They can—and do—change their behavior and their views about sex. Along with the social changes in family life and work, which we have discussed, some stereotypic behavior also seems to be changing. Although some of the old fantasies remain, both boys and girls may know that as adults they will be working. Many children who grow up in single-parent households see their parent dating and acting as a sexual person. Young women may be less guarded about granting men sexual access, and more young women report now that they masturbate, so that they focus on genital sex as boys have done. In fact, male groups may tend to approve less of purely exploitative sex and to approve more of companionate relationships between men and women. Whatever the relation of sexual functioning to sex stereotyping, it is not a simple one.

SUMMARY

1 Cultures make social definitions about gender differences and attach many obligations and expectations to their gender labels. These social definitions amplify the weak biological differences between the sexes.

2 Children ordinarily acquire their gender identity in their first three years of life. The public, social expression of gender identity is called a gender role.

3 Children's ideas about male and female show early stereotyping. The stereotype of the masculine role emphasizes competence, dominance, competition, and striving. The stereotype of the feminine role emphasizes expressiveness, caring for others, and niceness. Females are also taught to seek acceptance by others. Children are susceptible to adopting stereotypes because their ability to understand what might be (as opposed to what is) is limited.

4 Parents, and fathers especially, teach their children about gender differences. Children themselves perpetuate stereotypes about gender, and peer groups in grade school may exert strong pressures on children to conform to the stereotype for their gender. Teachers and textbooks may reinforce gender roles. Television programs present a world of sharply stereotyped images of males and females.

5 Behavior differences between boys and girls show up on the average as early as age two. Children tend to prefer playmates of their own sex. Girls play in smaller groups than boys do. Girls often feel freer to do "boy" things than boys to do "girl" things. Boys' groups may help them learn how to act in organized hierarchies, how to compete, and how to attend to their peers. Girls' groups may help them to tune into nonverbal messages, to use adults as resources, and to be better students than boys are.

6 Puberty further differentiates the sexes, both socially and physically. Parents and peers may renew pressure on a child to conform to the "proper" gender role.

7 Teenaged girls worry more about their popularity than boys do. They worry, too, about how they are to balance the responsibilities of family and work. Teenaged boys worry about developing work-related skills. Teenaged girls often accommodate themselves to males' goals; males are freer to act independently when it comes to achievement.

8 Adult males are busy forming their work-related identity. Career-oriented women may do the same, postponing child-rearing until after the age of 30. Most mothers work outside the home, and have to juggle the responsibilities of family and job. The long-term effects of so many women working on gender stereotypes will be interesting to chart.

9 By late adulthood, as the situations of males and females grow more similar, gender differences may soften.

10 Stereotypes about gender probably affect people's ideas of themselves as sexual beings.

11 The masculine "script" for sexuality stresses performance and winning in a kind of sexual game. Men are pressured to achieve and "score" in the eyes of their peers and may worry about how well they perform as sexual athletes. The feminine "script" is a romantic one, in which males are to be "sensitive" and females are to be wooed.

12 The idea of sexual scripts originated with John Gagnon and William Simon. At adolescence, sexuality is incorporated into a sexual context among peers and is "scripted." The two sexes learn different sexual scripts, with males low on interpersonal qualities and high on genital focus and with females high on social qualities but low on solitary genital experience. Each sex must learn some of the other's script as they form relationships.

KEY TERMS

gender identity	puberty
gender role	menopause
stereotyping	androgyny
reference group	sexual scripts
sex stereotyping	

SUGGESTED READINGS

Liss, M. B. *Social and Cognitive Skills: Sex Roles and Children's Play.* New York: Academic Press, 1983. A fine series of reviews on how play influences the development of skills in girls and boys.

Ortner, S. B. and Whitehead, H. *Sexual Meanings: the Cultural Construction of Gender and Sexuality.* New York: Cambridge University Press, 1981. A collection of articles by anthropologists that describe how gender works in Samoa, Andalusia, and other cultures. Part II of the book and the introduction are gems for anyone interested in culture, gender, and sexuality.

PART III
THE BIOLOGICAL PERSPECTIVE

Pablo Picasso, "Girl Before a Mirror." Collection, The Museum of Modern Art, New York.

Chapter 5

Female Sexual Anatomy

EXTERNAL GENITALS
    Vulva
    Mons
    Outer Lips
    Inner Lips
    Clitoris
    Urinary Opening
    Vaginal Opening
INTERNAL GENITALS

Vagina
Cervix
Uterus
Fallopian Tubes
Ovaries

BREASTS
    Breast Self-examination
    Internal Examination

In this chapter, we will describe parts of female anatomy locally involved in sexual functioning and reproduction. We will describe the female genitals and the breasts.

Cultural influences have caused many women to feel ashamed of their genitals—parents tell their young daughters that it is "not nice" to touch themselves "down there." This is a culture in which one scientific term for a woman's external genitals is "pudendum," which derives from the Latin word meaning shame. Advertisers urge women to buy products that will "freshen" and "cleanse" their genitals, as if genitals are otherwise dirty and smelly. Many women, in turn, believe that they must perfume and scrub their genitals into acceptability. Yet except when disease or infection are present, regular bathing with soap and water is enough to keep the external genitals clean. The internal genitals do not even need that; all women come equipped with the self-cleaning model. Even after a heavy menstrual flow, the vagina cleans itself quickly. For women without clear medical problems, douches and sprays are unnecessary and may leave the genitals irritated and prone to infection.

Both sexes, of course, have genitals, a term that derives from the Latin word meaning "to beget." The female genitals include, on the external surface of the body, the mons, inner and outer labia, clitoris, and the separate openings to the bladder and vagina (see Figure 5.1). The internal female genitals include the vagina, uterus, fallopian tubes, ovaries, and the muscles and surrounding structures (see Figure 5.2). With one's finger or with a special instrument called a **speculum** to hold the vagina open, one can see the vagina, cervix, and bottom of the uterus, but the other internal genitals are not ordinarily visible. By kneeling over a mirror, a woman can see her external genitals. Many women do not know what their genitals actually look like. In fact, many boys know many slang terms—often derogatory—for female genitals. But many girls know *no* names for their genitals. Valuing their body parts—genitals included—and naming them are important in the sexual education of women.

Men as well as women may worry that they look ugly or abnormal in some way. As a male psychotherapist said,

Almost half my women patients think that their breasts are too small, and almost half think that theirs are too big. On the other hand, no man ever thinks that his penis is too big. It's a funny business, people and sex. We use our bodies to feed our insecurities.

Many women do not know what their genitals actually look like. Examining themselves in a mirror can help to dispel ignorance and misconceptions.

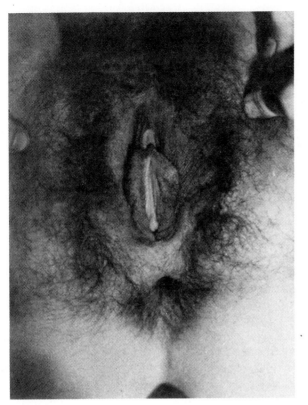

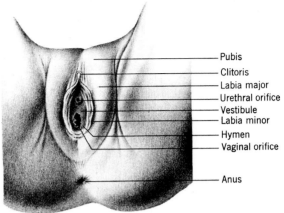

Pubis
Clitoris
Labia major
Urethral orifice
Vestibule
Labia minor
Hymen
Vaginal orifice

Anus

FIGURE 5.1

The external female genitals include mons, inner and outer labia (lips), clitoris, and separate openings to bladder and vagina.

As we describe female sexual anatomy, we will show that there are large individual variations in what is normal. These variations include, but certainly are not limited to, breasts of two different sizes, extra nipples, inner labia that protrude beyond the outer labia, very sparse and very thick pubic hair, labia of many different shapes and sizes, and on and on.

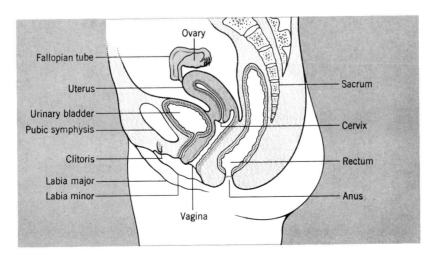

Ovary
Fallopian tube
Uterus
Urinary bladder
Pubic symphysis
Clitoris
Labia major
Labia minor
Vagina

Sacrum
Cervix
Rectum
Anus

FIGURE 5.2

Female genitals when they are not sexually aroused, a midline view.

EXTERNAL GENITALS

The external genitals of the female include the mons, clitoris, inner and outer labia, vaginal, and urethral openings. We will use the all-inclusive term **vulva** for these body parts.

Vulva

"Vulva" is a good, neutral, all-inclusive term for the external genitals. It is not derogatory, as are informal terms like "snatch" or "beaver"; it is not so formal as "pudendum."

Mons

The triangular "mound of Venus," or **mons veneris,** is named after the Roman goddess of love. This area is at the base of the abdomen and, after puberty, is rounded with fat and covered with pubic hair.

> *The first time I undressed in front of Richard, he looked at me and said, "You have nice hair." I was flattered (22-year-old female senior).*

> *My pubic hair is kind of flat when I wash, and then it frizzes up over time. He'll say to me, "Your cute permanent is showing" (24-year-old female law student).*

Under the skin, the mons is lined with fatty tissue and a rich supply of nerve endings and blood vessels that make the area sensitive to touch and pressure. Many women find stimulation of the mons erotically pleasing. The pubic hair may hold scents from the natural secretions of the vagina during sexual arousal, and these scents may also be erotic.

Outer Lips

The outer lips or **labia majora,** of the vulva are the two pads of skin that go

FIGURE 5.3

Underlying structures of the vulva. Small drawing shows structures in relation to pelvis and spine.

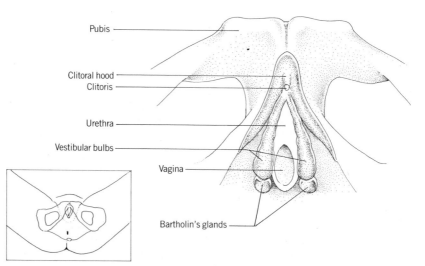

Pubis

Clitoral hood
Clitoris

Urethra

Vestibular bulbs

Vagina

Bartholin's glands

from the mons, between the thighs, to the entrance of the vagina. On their outer surface, the labia majora are covered with pubic hair.

By some point during my teens, a lot of dark pubic hair had covered my crotch. I felt sad that I'd never see my lips again (22-year-old college senior).

On their inner surface, the labia majora are hairless and to the fingertip feel like the skin inside one's mouth. The skin of the outer lips, especially on the inner surface, may be darker than the skin of the thighs. Like the mons, the outer lips are richly supplied with fatty tissue, nerves, and blood vessels and are sensitive to touch.

Inner Lips

The two smaller lips of the vulva, the **labia minora,** extend from the hood covering the clitoris to the area near the vaginal opening. They are smooth, hairless, and darker than the skin of the thighs. The inner lips may look like two flower petals or leaves, and there are enormous individual variations in their shapes and size. The appearance of the inner labia may change over time as well, with age, pregnancy, or sexual arousal. In some women, one or both of the inner labia protrude beyond the outer labia. Perfectly normal variations include labia that are smoothly rounded or irregularly edged; symmetrical or asymmetrical; narrow or broad; loose flaps or taut bands. The inner lips have many nerve endings and blood vessels as well as glands for producing sweat and oil. During sexual arousal, the **Bartholin's glands,** located within the inner labia near the vaginal opening, may produce a few drops of fluid to lubricate the labia. It was once believed that these glands lubricated the vagina during sexual arousal, but they do not. (If they should become clogged or swollen, a woman should be checked by a doctor. Symptoms may include pain, itching, irritation, or the formation of a hard, pimple-like lump.)

Clitoris

Where the inner lips meet, toward the mons, is the **clitoris,** an organ whose only

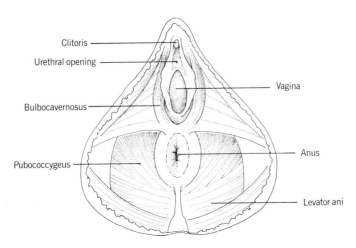

Clitoris

Urethral opening

Vagina

Bulbocavernosus

Pubococcygeus

Anus

Levator ani

FIGURE 5.4

Underlying muscles of the vulva.

function, so far as we know, is to provide sexual pleasure. A surprisingly large number of men and women do not know where the clitoris really is. (See Figure 5.1.) Some think that it is much closer to the vagina than it actually is or that it is in the vagina. Said two students:

I confess to not knowing exactly where the clitoris is. I think it's at the opening of the vagina (18-year-old freshman).

But the clitoris is not at the opening of the vagina; it is farther forward, toward the mons, almost at the beginning of the genital slit.

I've tried to find a woman's clitoris with my fingers, but it always seems to disappear off to one side or the other (19-year-old freshman).

Men may be embarrassed to ask a woman about her clitoris or to confess their ignorance of it. A woman, in turn, may either assume that men know about female anatomy or feel embarrassed about showing her genitals so plainly. Continuous with the inner lips is the **clitoral hood,** which covers the clitoris. The clitoral hood feels fleshy and is probably why the student quoted found the clitoris always disappearing to one side. If the hood is gently moved aside, the head (**clitoral glans**) and **clitoral shaft** are visible. The glans of the clitoris is rounded and smooth and powerfully sensitive to stimulation. It is so sensitive, in fact, that most women find direct stimulation irritating. The clitoris, and especially the glans, is very richly supplied with both blood and nerves.

I masturbate by rubbing the sides of my clitoris. That's what I like my boyfriend to do, too. It if gets rubbed directly, head on, it turns me right off (20-year-old junior).

I didn't find my clitoris until I was 22. I figure I lost all those years fumbling (27-year-old graduate student).

During sexual arousal, the clitoris grows **tumescent** (engorged) as it fills with blood, although it does not erect away from the body. A tumescent clitoris may be easier for a man (or a woman, of course) to find than a resting one. The clitoral shaft contains two spongy bodies of tissue that branch up into the pelvis. Secretions from under the clitoral hood may combine with bacteria to form a pungent, whitish substance called **smegma** (from the Greek word for cheese), which some

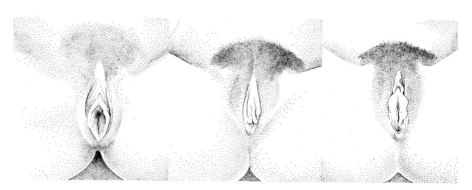

FIGURE 5.5

There are many normal variations on how the vulva looks.

people think smells like fish or strong cheese. Gentle washing with soap and water is ordinarily adequate to remove smegma.

Although the clitoris and the penis are **homologous organs** in that they develop before birth from structurally similar tissue, the clitoris is not a small penis (and the penis is not a large clitoris). The clitoris functions *only* for sexual pleasure. Unlike the penis, it does not pass urine, and it plays no direct role in reproduction. As with the other parts of the external genitals, the appearance, size, and exact position of the clitoris in relation to the other genitals vary somewhat among females. Women vary in how the clitoris is positioned and in the degree of clitoral stimulation they like during sexual intercourse. Women vary also in how they like to stimulate their clitoris or be stimulated by a lover's hand or mouth. As a woman gains sexual experience and comes to know her body, she can adjust her position during intercourse to regulate the amount of stimulation her clitoris receives at any time. For some women, clitoral stimulation feels so intense that they choose positions that modulate their arousal.

Urinary Opening

You mean I've got two holes down there? (20-year-old college junior)

Like this student, many people do not know that urine travels from kidneys, to bladder, and then along a duct called the **urethra** to the urethral opening. It is a rather small opening about halfway between the clitoris and the vagina. Thus, urine does not leave the body through the clitoris, and it does not leave through the vagina. Unlike males, in whom urine and sperm leave through the same opening in the tip of the penis, females have a separate urinary opening. (Some men avoid oral stimulation of a woman's genitals because they are afraid that she might urinate at the height of sexual excitement. The clitoris, center of sexual excitement, and the urinary opening are separate and independent structures. Sexual excitement does not cause urination. In fact, it typically inhibits it.)

Vaginal Opening

The opening to the vagina, called the **introitus**, lies between the inner labia. It may or may not be covered by a thin membrane called a **hymen.** (Slang for the hymen is "cherry" or "maidenhead.") A hymen ordinarily has one or more openings; these allow the passage of secretions and menstrual flow or the insertion of tampons and fingers. Rupturing the hymen, contrary to popular myth, is not

Annular hymen   Septate hymen   Cribriform hymen   Parous introitus

FIGURE 5.6

The hymen. There are several normal variations on the appearance of the hymen, the membrane over the vaginal opening.

very painful. If it occurs when the female is quite sexually aroused or caught up in an active sport or the like, she may not even feel it. Blood loss, if there is any, is slight. First intercourse may not rupture the hymen, only stretch it. Women who worry that rupturing the hymen will be painful can practice stretching it to the side gradually with their fingers, or they can have a doctor clip it in a very minor surgical procedure. As with the other external genitals, the hymen varies greatly in form and appearance from one female to another. Its purpose is not clear.

Some girls are born with no hymen or with one that is fragmentary. Thus a physical examination is not a reliable way of telling whether a female has had sexual experience. Even so, it has long been traditional in many cultures for a bride's virginity to be "certified" either by an examination to make sure she had an intact hymen or by the presence of blood on the sheets from the marital bed. (Hymen, in fact, was the name of the god of marriage in Greek mythology.) Here, for example, is the account of an Egyptian woman:

> *My wedding night was great. My husband deflowered me with his finger wrapped up with a hanky. I knew all about it from my grandmother. My mother-in-law, my mother, and my aunt were present with me in the room. They received the blood in a handkerchief, which they passed on to my brothers. My brothers showed the stained handkerchief to a crowd amid beating of drums and great jubilation (Assaad, 1980, p. 13).*

INTERNAL GENITALS

The internal genitals consist of the vagina, uterus, fallopian tubes, ovaries, and the structures that surround and support them.

Vagina

Today young children seem able to understand that women have vaginas and clitorises and men have penises. They can enjoy their bodies in ways that seem to disappear as they grow older and more inhibited:

> *We were entertaining some senior colleagues of ours one summer afternoon. The adults were sitting in chairs in the sun when my two-year-old daughter came flying outside stark naked and asked delightedly, at the top of her voice, "Okay, who wants to see my 'gina?" (34-year-old clinical psychologist, male).*

Just inside the vaginal opening extends a passageway with soft, flexible sides. This is the **vagina**, a thin muscular tube, and it leads from the internal organs of reproduction to the outside of the body. It is into this "tube" that the penis is inserted during (vaginal) intercourse, and through this tube a baby is delivered into the world. The vagina slants slightly backward. To the touch, it feels smooth and warm. Its walls are extremely elastic and, rather like an elasticized glove, will expand to contain a fully erect penis during intercourse or a fully developed infant. The vaginal canal is about 3 to 5 inches long in its resting state, although during sexual arousal it enlarges. The elasticity of the vagina means that sexual pleasure and responsiveness do *not* depend on the size of the vagina. Bigger—or smaller—is not necessarily better.

The inner surface of the vagina, like the inside of one's cheeks, is a mucous membrane. It has a rich blood supply but, especially in the upper two-thirds, relatively few nerve endings. Thus the innermost parts of the vagina are not very sensitive to touch. This insensitivity is the reason why women do not feel a properly inserted tampon or diaphragm; it is adaptive in that it reduces the discomfort of childbirth. Many men mistakenly believe that women experience the vagina the way men fantasize it: as the center of sexual feeling. Probably part of the wish for a large penis reflects the belief behind the fantasy.

> *I like my husband to put his fingers in my vagina sometimes when he is stimulating me. But it has to be in addition to stroking my clitoris. I can't get turned on just by his touching my vagina alone (24-year-old female medical student).*

The environment within the vagina is ordinarily slightly acidic and, except in the presence of infection or disease, perfectly clean.

Cervix

The **cervix** is the neck of the uterus and projects down into the vagina. To the finger, it feels like the tip of your nose: cartilaginous and slightly bumpy. The cervix has a small opening (the cervical **os,**) into the uterus, through which menstrual fluid or a man's ejaculate can pass. The cells of the cervix secrete clear or pale-colored mucus that varies in consistency and amount according to a woman's menstrual cycle, age, and whether she is pregnant. Except during childbirth, the combination of the small opening and the cervical mucus offers the uterus some protection from infection. During childbirth, the cervical opening widens (to 3 or 4 inches) to allow the passage of the baby and closes again after birth. This opening and closing makes the cervix of a female who has delivered a baby vaginally look slightly different (often more puckered) from the cervix of a female who has not.

Uterus

The size and shape of a pear, a muscular organ that can expand to house a fully developed infant, the **uterus,** or womb, is a remarkable organ. It is made of three layers of contractile tissue. The bottom of the uterus is called the cervix; the top is called the **fundus.** The uterus is held in place by strong ligaments and may tilt forward, backward, or perpendicularly to the vagina. Some women are even born with a double uterus. It used to be thought that a backward-tilting uterus impaired fertility, but this belief has been disconfirmed. Some women with a double uterus have also borne children successfully. (See Figure 5.7 on uterine tilting.)

The inner lining of this hollow organ, the **endometrium,** is partially shed during every menstrual cycle and then renews itself. This build-up and shedding are controlled by hormones (for more on menstruation, see Chapter 9). If a female conceives, the fertilized egg attaches itself to the endometrium for nourishment

FIGURE 5.7

Positions of the uterus. A normal uterus may tilt forwards, backwards, or be perpendicular to the vagina.

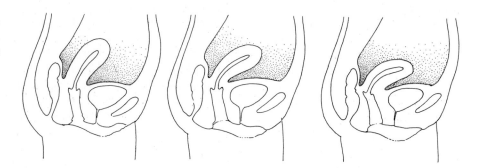

and remains attached until it is born. Muscles surround this inner layer in a basketweave that expands during pregnancy. These smooth muscles contract rhythmically during childbirth and during orgasm. Some women can feel these muscles cramping during their menstrual periods as well.

Fallopian Tubes

The **fallopian tubes** are two ducts that run from the sides of the uterus to the two ovaries. They are about 4 inches long and tiny in diameter. They take their name from Fallopius, a sixteenth-century Italian anatomist, who discovered them. The end of the fallopian tubes near the ovaries is funnel-shaped and ends in many fringed extensions, called **fimbriae.** This end floats in the peritoneal (or lower body) cavity, with the fimbriae curving around the ovaries. Medical researchers still do not know what force first attracts the ovary's discharged egg to the fallopian tubes, but once the egg arrives from the ovary, the fimbriae wave it into the tube. Tiny hairlike **cilia,** which line the tubes, propel the egg toward the uterus. If sperm are present, fertilization usually takes place in the fallopian tube.

Most fertilized eggs drift into the uterus and attach to the uterine lining. A few, however, attach themselves to the inside of the fallopian tubes. But because the tubes cannot expand to accommodate a developing embryo, these **tubal pregnancies** end after two or three months, because the tube ruptures, causing sharp pain and bleeding.[1] Often the affected fallopian tube must be surgically removed. (Another form of surgery performed on the fallopian tubes is a **tubal ligation,** a fairly uncomplicated sterilization procedure in which the tubes are severed so that eggs cannot be reached by sperm and fertilized.) Rarely, fertilized eggs implant in the body cavity. More rarely still, a live birth by Caesarean section can follow such implantation. But the number of escapees from the trip down the fallopian tubes and into the uterus is very small.

Ovaries

The **ovaries** are the two egg- (or ova-) producing organs of the female. About the size and shape of an almond in its shell, each ovary contains up to 200,000

---

[1]**Ectopic pregnancies** are those in which a fertilized egg implants somewhere besides the lining of the uterus—fallopian tube, exterior of the uterus or ovary, or elsewhere in a woman's lower body cavity. Tubal pregnancies therefore are one kind of ectopic pregnancy.

immature eggs when a baby girl is born. The eggs, like the ovaries themselves, develop in the baby before birth. The ovaries do not only produce eggs, however. They are the female gonads, the central reproductive organ. (We will have more to say about the ovaries when we turn to physiology, reproduction, and pregnancy in Chapters 7, 8, and 9.) The ovaries produce the sex hormones estrogen and progesterone, without which reproduction and menstrual cycling could not occur. The immature eggs reside in **follicles** in the ovaries, and several follicles may ripen during each menstrual cycle. A ripened follicle moves to the surface of the ovary and bursts open, releasing the mature egg in a process called **ovulation.** The ovary on one side of the body ordinarily alternates with the ovary on the other side in releasing an egg. Usually only a single egg matures fully and is released from one ovary each cycle. For this reason, most human births are singletons. If more than one egg is released and fertilized, **fraternal twins** may result.

BREASTS

The breasts are not genitals, but they are certainly important both erotically and reproductively. Not all cultures attach erotic value to breasts; in some cultures, the breasts are functional objects for nourishing infants and have no more or less allure than any other nonsexual part of the body. But in our culture, the breasts, which are **secondary sex characteristics** in that they develop at puberty, may signify qualities of attractiveness and femininity. Many men find breasts highly arousing.

My husband's caressing of my breasts is an important part of our love-making. When I was nursing our daughter, though, I just didn't like having him touch them. I felt that they belonged to her. It was a stressful time. Sex was not so good then (26-year-old female graduate student).

In high school, my friends and I would compare notes on how guys felt us up. I never said much because my breasts never gave me much of a charge. To me, feeling up was just an announcement of the agenda. But my present boyfriend really knows how to turn me on. He tells me how I look, and he does something to my nipples with his tongue. Now I know about breasts turning you on (20-year-old sophomore).

Breasts are certainly the topic of endless sexual jokes and double entendres. One has only to watch a bosomy movie star walk onstage during a TV talk show to hear the snickers of the audience and see the clowning of the host, to perceive the cultural attitudes attached to breasts.

This loading of qualities onto one part of the sexual anatomy has two contradictory effects. Dirty jokes and snickering laughter seem to reduce women to their breasts alone. But the other effect is to idealize the breasts. Idealized breasts may be large and voluptuous, or they may be small and fashionably elegant. As a consequence, many women worry that their breasts are too small—"How can I be womanly and sexy enough with these little things?"—or too big—"How could a cow like me be attractive?" Many women believe that all men require big breasts on a woman for turning on. In truth, some men find small breasts thrilling;

FIGURE 5.8

Breasts come in lots of different shapes and sizes.

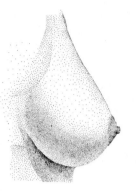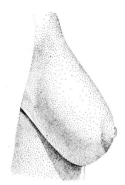

others get excited by large breasts; and some look elsewhere for turn-ons. For both sexes, erogenous zones are distributed not only on the body but also in the personality as well.

Real breasts, as opposed to idealized ones, may be conical or pendulous or flabby or noticeably asymmetrical (see Figure 5.8). During pregnancy and breast-feeding, the breasts swell. After pregnancy and breast-feeding, they return to their previous size, though they may be less firm. Normal women (and men) may even have more than two nipples. Breast size and shape are determined by the amount of fatty tissue in the breast and attachment to the underlying muscles. Fat distribution is largely an inherited characteristic, and so, barring large weight changes, breast size does not change, especially not by means of the many advertised exercise devices or "bust developer" lotions. A surgeon can change breast size, however, either by removing tissue or by inserting pads of silicone gel under the skin.

NO MATTER THE SIZE OF THE BREASTS, THEIR INTERNAL STRUCTURE VARIES LITTLE FROM ONE WOMAN TO ANOTHER.

No matter the size of the breasts, their internal structure varies little from one woman to another (see Figure 5.9). Each breast contains 15 to 20 lobes of **mammary, or milk, glands,** each of which is connected to the nipple by a **milk duct.** After childbirth, the glands respond to hormonal signals and begin to produce milk, which the baby sucks from the nipple. The **nipple** has many nerve endings and is often, therefore, a source of pleasurable sensations during lovemaking,

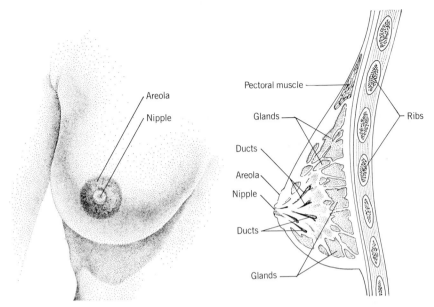

FIGURE 5.9

Underlying structures of the breasts.

Areola

Nipple

Pectoral muscle

Glands

Ducts

Areola

Nipple

Ducts

Glands

Ribs

masturbation, or breast-feeding. Not all women's nipples are sensitive, however. The nipple is made up of smooth muscle. When this muscle, which extends under the dark skin of the nipple and surrounding **areola,** contracts, the nipple stands erect. Cold or arousal may make the nipple erect. Breast size affects neither the number of nerve endings nor the number of milk glands in the breasts, and so large breasts are not necessarily more sensitive or better milk-producers than smaller breasts. Some women have **inverted nipples,** in which the nipple turns inward rather than outward from the areola. Inverted nipples are normal physical variations, and although many women worry about them, inverted nipples almost never interfere with actual functioning. Women whose nipples turn in can get sexually aroused and can breast-feed. Sexual arousal itself tends to make the nipples stand erect and therefore turn outward; the sucking of a baby has the same effect.

Breast Self-Examination

The breasts develop in response to sex hormones secreted at puberty. They continue to respond to the cyclical production of these hormones and may feel tender, lumpy, or puffy at certain times during the menstrual cycle or pregnancy. It is important that a woman learn what her breasts normally feel like so that she can notify her doctor if she finds anything unusual in her breasts. Most lumps are harmless, but the presence of the occasional tumor has to be ruled out. Therefore, women should examine their breasts at about the same point in each menstrual cycle (or each month, for women who do not menstruate), perhaps right after menstruation or at mid-cycle (see Figure 5.10).

Lying flat on her back, a woman places one hand under her neck. With the other, free hand, she slowly probes the entire breast and nipple, quadrant by quadrant, feeling for any mass that might be suspicious. She should repeat the

FIGURE 5.10

Breast self-examination. Women should examine their breasts for lumps at the same time each month. After a shower, when the skin is wet and slippery, is a good time to probe the breasts with the fingers, moving methodically from one segment to another.

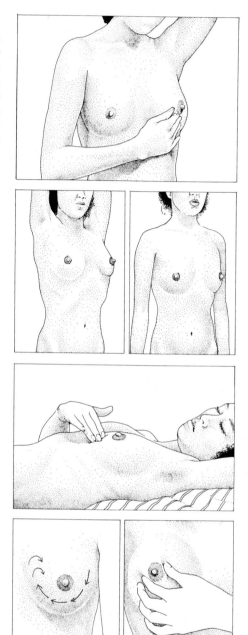

examination on the other breast and squeeze each nipple gently to see if there is a secretion. A good look in the mirror at the naked breasts, side view and front view, can reveal any changes in shape or outline. Unusual lumps are also fairly easy to feel when the skin is wet and slippery during a shower or bath. A woman should tell her doctor about any changes at once—and not wait until her scheduled yearly examination.

INTERNAL EXAMINATION

While we are on the subject of examinations, we should mention the **pelvic,** or **internal, examination** that every adult woman should have at least once a year. Many women dread these examinations and feel embarrassed or ashamed to be examined. Many women dread that the **gynecologist** (a doctor who specializes in treating female anatomy) or other doctor will find something wrong with them or that somehow the examination will reveal facts of their private sexual behavior. Masturbation, sexual intercourse, and other forms of sexual behavior do not "show." Routine examinations are important for detecting and preventing problems.

A century ago, modesty conventions required physicians to conduct internal examinations while their patients were dressed.

SEXUALITY IN PERSPECTIVE:
GYNECOLOGICAL EXAMINATION: VOTE WITH YOUR FEET

Many women in our culture feel embarrassment or shame at the prospect of a doctor examining their genitals. Few situations tax a woman's dignity more than lying naked on a table, her legs bent outward like a frog's, her feet in metal stirrups, and her genitals exposed to a stranger's scrutiny. But routine examinations are very important, and so in choosing a doctor, women should try to find someone who is sensitive to these kinds of feelings—as many doctors are today.

Ideally, the doctor learned in medical school how to conduct an examination without embarrassing the patient, how to put her at her ease, how to avoid making the examination in any way a sexual encounter. Doctors should be sensitive to the special needs of young girls, who often are more afraid of pain during an internal examination than of sexual feelings, and of adolescents, who are easily embarrassed and self-conscious.

Only when girls become sexually active should they begin coming for routine examinations and Pap smears as well as contraceptive advice. Before that, healthy girls need gynecological examinations only when some problem warrants. The exceptions are daughters who were exposed as fetuses to **diethylstilbestrol**, or **DES**, a form of estrogen their mothers took to prevent miscarriage, and which in rare cases produces genital malignancies in their children. Like adolescents, older women have the right to shop for a sensitive, forthcoming, and helpful physician. No woman need subject herself to an incompetent, insensitive, or inept examiner. No woman need feel bound by moral opinions with which she disagrees: if she wants contraception or sexual counseling or an abortion, she should not be forced to go without by a physician's moral code. The converse also holds true, of course.

One fact of life is that sexually active females need routine gynecological examinations. Another fact of life is that all women should be encouraged to find a doctor to examine them whom they trust and like. In the matter of examinations, vote with your feet.

Adapted in part from C. A. Cowell, M.D. "The Gynecologic Examination of Infants, Children, and Young Adolescents," in *The Pediatric Clinics of North America* (May 1981) *28*, no. 2, Carol A. Cowell, M.D. (Ed.), Philadelphia: Saunders, 1981, pp. 247–266.

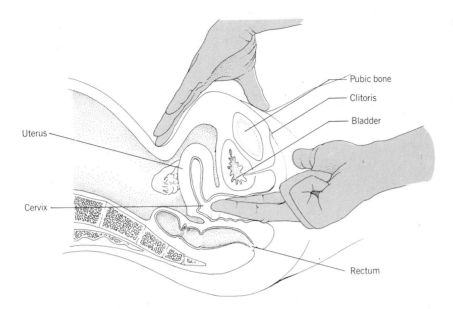

Uterus

Cervix

Pubic bone

Clitoris

Bladder

Rectum

FIGURE 5.11

Pelvic examination. Once past adolescence, women need regular—and painless—check ups of their internal and external reproductive organs, bladder, and rectum. It helps to be examined by a trusted physician.

Gynecological examinations are not painful. A woman should be encouraged to shop around in the medical community until she finds a practitioner with whom she feels comfortable.

In the routine examination, the medical practitioner will take a urine specimen, blood pressure, and weight, examine the breasts by hand, and will look at the external genitals—without any sexual stimulation of any kind. Then the gynecologist will examine the vagina and rectum, feeling through the abdominal wall for the uterus and ovaries. While the vaginal walls are held apart painlessly with a speculum, a painless swab, a **Pap test,** is taken as a check for cancer of the cervix and other abnormalities. (See Figure 5.11.) Some women's health centers train women to examine their own genitals. For an investment of 20 to 30 minutes, a woman can do a lot to keep herself healthy.

SUMMARY

1   The vulva includes all the external genitals of the female: mons, inner and outer lips, opening for urine, and vaginal introitus.

2   The mons is the triangular area at the base of the abdomen, covered with pubic hair, that has many nerve endings and is therefore sensitive to touch and pressure.

3   The outer lips, or labia majora, which may or may not be symmetrical, are sensitive, fleshy pads of skin that have pubic hair on their external surface but not on their internal surface. They enclose the inner lips.

4   The inner lips, or labia minora, are two hairless, dark-colored, sensitive flaps of tissue that extend, at the front, from the clitoral hood to near the vaginal opening.

5 The clitoris functions to provide sexual stimulation and is therefore extremely sensitive. Protected by a clitoral hood, the glans of the clitoris may be so sensitive that direct stimulation is irritating. The clitoris is unlike the penis in that it does not pass urine or ejaculate.

6 Females have a separate urinary opening, leading outside the body from the urethra and bladder.

7 The vaginal opening, or introitus, may or may not be partially covered by a membrane called the hymen. There are many normal forms to the hymen. Contrary to cultural beliefs, the absence of a hymen has no necessary bearing on a woman's sexual innocence.

8 The internal genitals consist of the vagina, uterus, fallopian tubes, ovaries, and their supporting structures.

9 The vagina is a passageway with elastic walls that expand or contract to accommodate a fully erect penis, a tampon, a fully developed baby. It is relatively insensitive, especially in the upper two-thirds, because it has few nerve endings.

10 The cervix is the neck of the uterus. It protrudes downward into the vagina and has a small opening, the os, through which ejaculate and menstrual fluid can pass.

11 The uterus is a muscular organ that houses the developing fetus during pregnancy. During each menstrual cycle, the uterine lining is shed.

12 The two fallopian tubes lead from the sides of the uterus to the egg-producing glands. It is in the fallopian tubes that eggs are normally fertilized.

13 The two ovaries are the egg-producing, female gonads. They also produce sex hormones. Each contains thousands of eggs, only one of which (or less usually, more than one) ripens and leaves one ovary each month. The ovaries alternate in releasing eggs.

14 The breasts have erotic significance in this culture as well as functional significance in producing milk for babies. Although many women are dissatisfied with the size of their breasts, size affects neither sexual responsiveness nor the ability to produce milk.

15 Women should examine their breasts monthly for unusual masses or secretions and should have a pelvic examination once a year from a medical practitioner they trust.

KEY TERMS

speculum	clitoral glans
vulva	clitoral shaft
mons veneris	tumescence
labia majora	smegma
labia minora	homologous organs
Bartholin's glands	urethra
clitoris	introitus
clitoral hood	hymen

vagina
cervix
cervical os
uterus
fundus
endometrium
fallopian tubes
fimbriae
cilia
tubal pregnancy
ectopic pregnancy
tubal ligation
ovary

ovarian follicle
ovulation
fraternal twins
secondary sex characteristics
mammary (milk) glands
milk duct
nipple
areola
inverted nipples
pelvic (internal) examination
gynecologist
Pap test
diethylstilbestrol (DES)

SUGGESTED READINGS

Boston Women's Health Book Collective. *The New Our Bodies, Our Selves.* New York: Simon and Schuster, 1984. An excellent book about women's bodies. This successful and appealing volume is explicit about health matters of concern to women, from diet to menstruation, infertility to homosexuality. It is a good source for simplified and humanized anatomy.

————. *Ourselves and Our Children: a Book by and for Parents.* New York: Random House, 1978. This volume talks about parenthood and childhood in helpful, informative, uncondescending, and explicit terms.

Jones, Richard E. *Human Reproduction and Sexual Behavior.* Englewood Cliffs, NJ: Prentice-Hall, 1984. For readers with some biology background, Chapter 3 is a good explanation of female sexual anatomy and the hormones controlling sexual cycling and development.

Chapter 6

Male Sexual Anatomy

A male's reproductive anatomy is deceptive. Although male sexual anatomy *looks* to be mostly external, in fact much of it is internal. Most boys grow familiar with their penis—an external organ—early in life, because they handle it when they urinate. As boys they are familiar with the pleasure they get from stimulating their penis, and they are familiar with the way it grows erect when they are aroused. A boy's penis may grow erect when he is excited or feels some urinary urgency. Nature has arranged the penis so that erections are a repeated, daily presence. Few young women are as familiar with their external **genitals,** or reproductive organs, as young men are with theirs, although men may know somewhat less about their internal structures.

I have always thought that males are pretty complicated looking on the outside and that females are pretty complicated on the inside (20-year-old male college sophomore).

GENITALS

A male's genitals consist of the penis, which functions both for reproduction and for elimination of body waste, and the scrotum, which contains the gonads and sperm-delivering ducts (see Figure 6.1).

PENIS

The **penis** is the organ in the male that eliminates urine, ejaculates, and is very sensitive to erotic stimulation. For many men, their penis is the focus of strong emotions as well. They admire or worry about "his" size and general appearance. They wonder whether he will perform when called upon. They may give their penis a familiar name—"Peter," "John," or "Dick" are common—and think of it as a trusty friend or vile traitor. In D. H. Lawrence's *Lady Chatterley's Lover,*

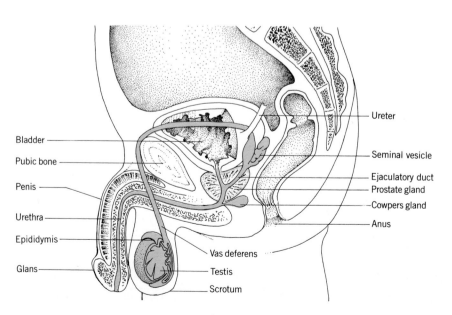

FIGURE 6.1

Male sexual anatomy, side view. The route along which sperm are produced and delivered appears in color.

the hero's penis actually assumes a central role. It is fondly named, dallied with lovingly, and draped with flowers. It enters Lady Chatterley's body as a tender boy, an ardent man, a wondering explorer.

Don't ask me how I got this way, but I'm really fond of my penis. I take good care of it, and it takes good care of me (21-year-old college junior).

The strong negative feelings sometimes associated with penises show in the slang names for penis that people call each other. To call someone a "prick," a "dick," or a "schmuck" is to imply nastiness, crassness, and general uncouth.

Urine and sperm come out of the **urethral opening,** or **meatus,** on the tip of the penis. The tip, which is very sensitive to touch and pressure, is called the **glans.** In newborn boys and other uncircumcised males, the glans is covered by a **foreskin.** The foreskin attaches behind the ridge at the bottom of the glans called the **corona.** Many males find the corona very sensitive to stimulation, and it is richly supplied with nerve endings. The **frenum,** a triangular spot on the underside of the penis where the foreskin is attached, is also highly sensitive in many males. The glans has more nerve endings than the **shaft** of the penis or the **root,** the part that attaches to the abdominal wall.

Although the entire penis is sensitive to erotic stimulation, some parts are more sensitive than others, as most males discover when they masturbate. They may be inhibited about telling a sexual partner just which parts of their penis are or are not responsive to stimulation. Surveys (Pietropinto and Simenauer, 1977; Hite, 1976; 1981) tell us that about one-third of males (and two-thirds of females) have trouble telling their sexual partner what turns them on. Boys who masturbate regularly may become quite expert about their body's response. As a 22-year-old psychology student once said:

I was a loner as a kid. When I discovered masturbation, I thought I'd invented it. It was great but scary. I had no close friends among the boys because I wasn't into basketball, so I spent a lot of time masturbating. My folks kept trying to get me out of the house. Finally, they got me to a psychiatrist who floored me when he told me how great he thought masturbation was. He told me how he discovered it too. I didn't feel like a freak after that.

The penis consists of three parallel columns of spongy tissue, of nerve endings, blood vessels, but—contrary to popular belief—neither bone nor muscle (see Figure 6.2). Lengthwise, through the penis, runs the **urethra,** the passageway leading out of the body for urine and sperm. Two columns of this tissue, the **corpora cavernosa,** (singular: **corpus cavernosum**) or **cavernous bodies,** extend along the top of the penis. Their ends attach to the pubic bone. The corpora cavernosa have many small spaces that fill with blood during arousal. When the penis is not erect, the corpora cavernosa are largely empty of blood. Thus it is blood flow alone that makes the penis stiffen and stand erect. A third, smaller **corpus spongiosum,** or **spongy body,** runs below the two cavernous bodies. The corpus spongiosum feels like a definite ridge along the underside of the erect penis.

The skin of the penis is usually without hair and stretches tautly over the erect penis. It is looser and folded on the flaccid penis. In most uncircumcised males,

FIGURE 6.2

The penis and its internal structures appear here in cross section.

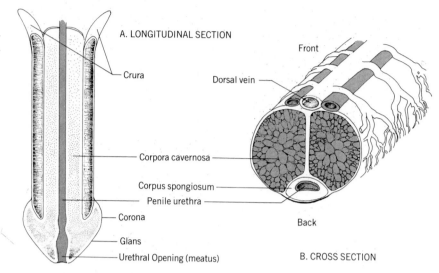

A. LONGITUDINAL SECTION

Crura

Front

Dorsal vein

Corpora cavernosa

Corpus spongiosum

Penile urethra

Corona

Back

Glans

Urethral Opening (meatus)

B. CROSS SECTION

the foreskin pulls back easily from the glans. If it does not, the male can be **circumcised** (have his foreskin surgically removed) or, in some cases, shown how to loosen the foreskin by gradually stretching it. Small glands behind the corona and inside the foreskin secrete **smegma,** a pungent, cheese-like substance. Because smegma, which is a good medium for bacterial growth, collects more readily under the foreskin than on a circumcised glans, cleanliness is one common reason for seeking circumcision. Uncircumcised males can, of course, keep themselves clean by pulling back the foreskin and washing away the smegma with soap and water. Other reasons for circumcising males are religious or cultural. For Jews and Moslems, ritual circumcision of the infant commemorates the convenant between God and Abraham. Many African and Middle Eastern cultures consider the foreskin feminine, and circumcision is thought to masculinize a boy fully. In many tribal cultures, circumcision marks sexual maturity at puberty and is performed during a **rite of passage** on adolescents. Some people favor circumcision because they believe it makes the penis cleaner, healthier, and more sensitive to stimulation in that the entire glans is exposed. Sensitivity, in fact, is not changed by circumcision. Until recently, circumcision was believed to cut down on the incidence of cancer of the penis and of cervical cancer in female partners. But the cause probably lies elsewhere. In contrast, some people argue that routine circumcision dulls sensitivity of the glans (by overstimulation), may contribute to premature ejaculation (also by overstimulation), and is unnecessary for hygiene. In truth, circumcision seems to affect neither sexual responsiveness (Masters and Johnson, 1966) nor physical health. The American College of Pediatricians, which used to recommend routine circumcision of baby boys, no longer makes that recommendation.

Is Bigger Better?   Circumcised and uncircumcised penises look different, and, in fact, there are wide normal variations in appearance from one male's genitals to another's (See Figure 6.3). Many males believe that bigger is better; they may feel anxious about whether they measure up. Among our culture's harmful sexual myths are two that relate to penis size. The first is that "real" men have large

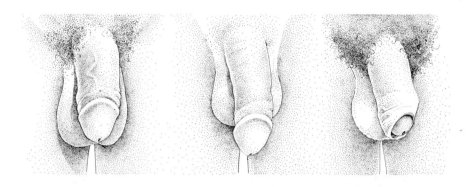

FIGURE 6.3

There are many normal variations on the appearance of penis
and scrotum.

THERE ARE wide NORMAL VARIATIONS IN APPEARANCE from ONE MALE'S
GENITALS TO ANOTHER'S.

penises, that these enormous organs drive women mad with ecstasy, and that men
with such endowments never tire. Like battering rams, like swords, like iron and
steel, they can thrust powerfully and forever. The second myth is that black men
are endowed with larger penises than white men (and therefore that black men
are sexier and, in an extension of this line of thought that is especially racist and
dangerous, want to ravish all women, including white women). In reality, skin
pigment has no bearing on penis size.

The locker room and the bedroom can become sites of high anxiety for a male
who worries that his penis is too small, or funny looking, or oddly made.

*In high school, one boy in our clique was nicknamed "J-Bone." Appar-
ently, his penis curved like the letter J. Try explaining that to your
mother when she asks where your friend got his nickname (22-year-old
male college senior).*

Although flaccid penises range in size between about 2½ and 4 inches, erect
penises vary less in size and average about 6 inches long. That means that smaller
flaccid penises grow more when erect than larger flaccid penises do. Furthermore,
the female's vagina is elastic and comfortably shapes itself around a small or large
penis with equal ease.

*My penis is 8 inches long when it's fully erect. I once had my girlfriend
measure it (20-year-old college sophomore).*

There is a condition in which the flaccid penis is less than ¾ of an inch long,
congenital microphallus, that requires medical attention. The very small penis
may indicate that the boy lacks hormone receptors not only in his penis but
elsewhere in his body as well. Early treatment consists of applying topical androgens that test whether the hormone receptors are present and whether the hormones of adolescence are likely or unlikely to enlarge the penis. The condition is
relatively rare. Therefore, for the vast majority of males, anxiety about penis size

FIGURE 6.4

Flaccid (unaroused) and erect penis sizes. The white columns show the length and circumference of the flaccid penises of 2310 white Americans. The filled columns show the length and circumference of their erect penises. The men all measured themselves to the nearest half inch (Gebhard and Johnson, 1979).

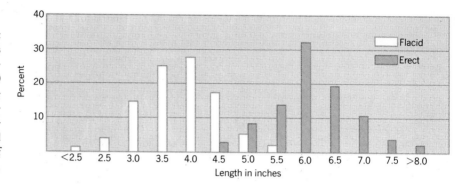

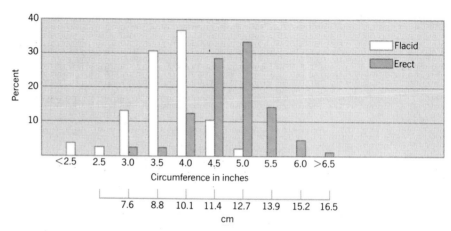

has more psychological than physiological truth (see Figure 6.4). (See "Sexuality in Perspective: Worries about Penis Size.") Just as the claims of advertisers that their creams and lotions will increase the size of a woman's breasts are fraudulent, so are the claims that creams and lotions can increase the size of anyone's penis (except by temporary arousal to erection through massaging). (See Figure 6.5).

Many males also worry that their penis is funny colored: the normal penis is darker than the surrounding skin, often redder or browner, and quite red during

FIGURE 6.5

Erection of the penis. These are pictures of the same penis, shown at the same scale, when the penis is not erect (left) and erect (right).

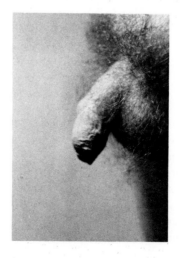
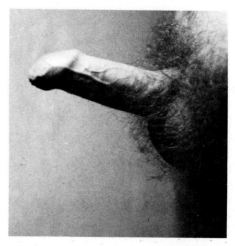

arousal (when it is engorged with blood). They worry that it has a funny shape: normal penises may curve in one direction or the other, look chubby or slim, long or short.

> *When I was in my thirties, I had a suit custom-made by an expensive tailor. I had to go for several fittings. As he was fitting the trousers, the tailor asked me, "Which side do you dress on, sir?" He had to tell me that he wanted to know on which side my penis hangs on. I loved that quaint expression (51-year-old salesman).*

Males may worry that their testicles are uneven. But one testicle hangs lower than the other in nearly all men, because the spermatic cord (about which more

SEXUALITY IN PERSPECTIVE: WORRIES ABOUT PENIS SIZE

Even fame and wealth cannot always protect a man from worrying that his penis is too small. F. Scott Fitzgerald, the important American writer, had been told by his wife, Zelda, that his penis was too small ever to satisfy a woman sexually. This destructive—and false—accusation so worried Fitzgerald that he asked his friend, novelist Ernest Hemingway, for help. Here Hemingway recounts the scene in a Paris café:

> *In the time after Zelda had what was then called her first nervous break-down and we happened to be in Paris at the same time, Scott asked me to have lunch with him at Michaud's restaurant on the corner of the rue Jacob and the rue des Saints-Pères. He said he had something very important to ask me that meant more than anything in the world to him and that I must answer absolutely truly. I said that I would do the best that I could. When he would ask me to tell him something absolutely truly, which is very difficult to do, and I would try it, what I said would make him angry, often not when I said it but afterwards, and sometimes long afterwards when he had brooded on it.*
>
> *When we were eating the cherry tart and had a last carafe of wine he said, "You know I never slept with anyone except Zelda."*
>
> *"No, I didn't."*
>
> *"I thought I had told you."*
>
> *"No. You told me a lot of things but not that."*
>
> *"That is what I have to ask you about."*
>
> *"Good. Go on."*
>
> *"Zelda said that the way I was built I could never make any woman happy and that was what upset her originally. She said it was a matter*

later), from which the testicle is suspended, is longer on one side than the other.

What is the criterion for normal? At least one physician's answer is, "If it works, it's normal."

Bodies are only approximately symmetrical. Lots of small asymmetries in development occur that are of no importance.

SCROTUM

The loose pouch that attaches to the abdominal wall and lies behind the penis is the **scrotum**. Typically covered lightly with hair and darker in color than the surrounding skin, the scrotum is part of the male's external genitals. It consists of two layers: the skin visible to the eye and the inner layer of muscle, or **tunica dartos**. These smooth muscles contract during arousal, strenuous exercise, or

---

of measurements. I have never felt the same since she said that and I have to know truly."

"Come out to the office," I said.

"Where is the office?"

"Le water [the toilet]," I said.

We came back into the room and sat down at the table.

"You're perfectly fine," I said. "You are O.K. There's nothing wrong with you. You look at yourself from above and you look foreshortened. Go over to the Louvre and look at the people in the statues and then go home and look at yourself in the mirror in profile."

"Those statues may not be accurate."

"They are pretty good. Most people would settle for them."

"But why would she say it?"

"To put you out of business. That's the oldest way in the world of putting people out of business. Scott, you asked me to tell you the truth and I can tell you a lot more but this is the absolute truth and all you need. You could have gone to see a doctor."

"I didn't want to. I wanted you to tell me truly."

"Now do you believe me?"

"I don't know," he said.

Hemingway did not judge his vulnerable friend harshly and did his best to reassure Fitzgerald about his penis size. Many other men need the same reassurance in this "matter of measurements."

Excerpted from "A Matter of Measurements," in Ernest Hemingway, *A Moveable Feast.* New York: Scribner, 1964, pp. 189–191.

exposure to cold; they expand during exposure to heat. These movements in response to variations in temperature help protect the sperm (which are produced in structures within the scrotum) from growing too warm or too cool to survive. The scrotum has sweat glands that also help regulate its temperature. Sperm do best in an environment of constant temperature about two degrees cooler than body temperature. Some people believe that very hot baths or tight jockstraps will kill enough sperm to provide a reliable means of preventing a pregnancy, but unfortunately they are wrong: not enough sperm are likely to be disabled that way for reliable contraception. Conversely, a male who is having fertility problems and who might have only a marginal number of healthy sperm is usually advised by physicians to avoid heating his testicles to the point that *any* sperm are endangered. The medical advice is usually to wear loose underwear and trousers and to avoid scalding baths. Some animals that produce sperm and store it internally have evolved an elaborate, internal "air conditioning" system to lower the temperature for their sperm. The method humans have evolved is a bit like keeping perishable foods in a cold box outside the window of a house. It may be cruder, but it works.

TESTES

The scrotum contains the male's two sperm-producing glands, his **testes** (see Figure 6.6). The testes descend from the abdominal cavity into the scrotum before or soon after birth. If they do not, the male may have **undescended testicles,** which may require hormonal or surgical treatment. Some boys born prematurely may have testicles that remain in the abdomen. These may descend on their own. A doctor should check any male with undescended testicles. The testes are of equal size, although, as we said above, one typically hangs lower than the other. The testes are sensitive to touch and pressure; they swell with blood during sexual arousal. Some men enjoy light caresses to the scrotum during sex, but others find them irritating. All males dread the pain of a blow to the testes. The euphemism for that blow, "a hit below the belt," has come to mean any sort of wounding, unfair attack.

The testes are the male **gonads,** or reproductive glands, and produce both hormones and sperm. The testes produce the male sex hormone, **testosterone** (one form of a class of the hormones called *androgens*), from **Leydig's cells.** These

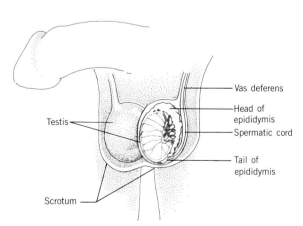

FIGURE 6.6

Internal structures of scrotum and testes.

FIGURE 6.7

Muscles of the male's pelvic floor.

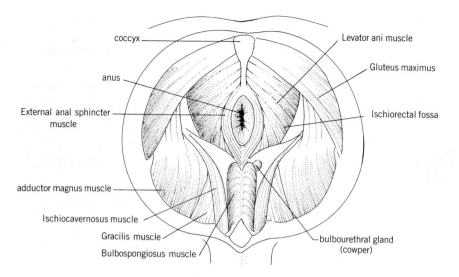

cells are close to blood vessels, through which the testosterone enters the blood-stream. Testosterone is one of the hormones that governs male sexual development, both before and after birth. (Chapter 3 sets forth the workings of testicular androgen in prenatal sexual differentiation.)

SPERM   **Sperm,** the male's sex cells, are manufactured and stored for a while in the **seminiferous tubules,** tiny ducts that are coiled tightly inside the testes. Once a male reaches puberty, he constantly produces new sperm, although the rate of production is likely to fall as he ages. In this way, males are different from females. A female's reproductive life (but not her sexual life) ends when she is middle-aged, and her menstrual periods stop. A male's reproductive life ends, theoretically at least, only with his death. (Old age may reduce sperm production in some men to the point of infertility.) Sperm carry 23 **chromosomes,** or half of the genetic instructions for making a baby. In a woman's body, a sperm will combine with an egg, which contains the other half of the genetic instructions. The sperm, however, always carries the single sex chromosome that determines the sex of the child.

Sperm production, or **spermatogenesis,** is a complex process of over 18 stages of development between the early, primitive form of the sperm and its maturity. The entire maturation process takes some 70 or more days at the end of which the sperm are microscopically tiny—only hundredths of an inch long—but fully formed. They are composed of a head, containing the genetic material and a chemical reservoir; a midpiece; and a tail, which extends from the midpiece and propels the sperm along after ejaculation. Sperm are not **motile,** that is, do not swim on their own, until ejaculation. Inside the male's body, they are thought to be moved along the production line either by hairlike cilia or by contractions of the various ducts where they are stored.

When a male ejaculates, up to 500 million sperm may be released, although 20 million per milliliter are considered the minimum necessary for fertility. Not all sperm are fully formed or motile. Deposited at the opening (cervix) of a

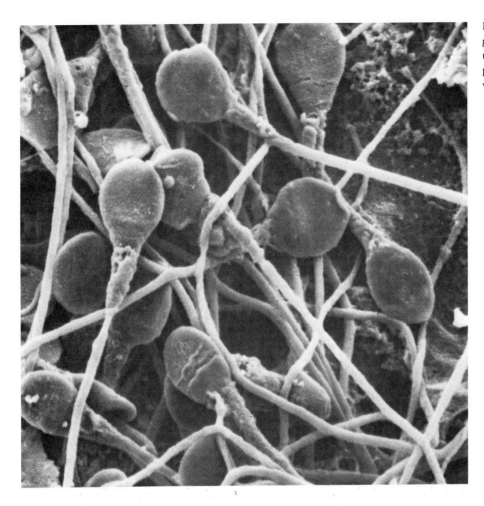

Human sperm. In this photograph of sperm, magnified 5000 times life size, the head, midpiece, and long tail are clearly visible.

woman's uterus, some of the sperm die immediately, some are malformed, some get lost, some swim too poorly to compete. But only one sperm has to swim to the egg for conception to occur. There is only one winner of the marathon race to an egg.

EPIDIDYMIS AND VAS DEFERENS   After the still immature sperm leave the seminiferous tubules, they go through small ducts to the **epididymis,** a tightly coiled tube that lies along the top and rear of each testis. Uncoiled, each epididymis would reach almost 20 feet. Sperm mature further in the epididymis, which incubates them for two to six weeks.

With sexual arousal, the now mature sperm are conducted out of the epididymis and bathed in secretions that ready them for their big journey. First they go into the **vas deferens,** one of the two tubes that ultimately will carry the ejaculate out of the body. Each vas (plural: vasa deferentia) loops upward out of the scrotum, over the pubic bone in the abdomen, along the bladder, and then downward along the **prostate gland.** There the sperm pass the **seminal vesicles,** lying behind the prostate, where they mix with secretions from both prostate and

THE PROSTATE PREVENTS URINATION AND EJACULATION FROM HAPPENING AT THE SAME TIME.

seminal vesicles that allow them to swim by themselves. The prostate has valves that function during urination and ejaculation (and prevents urination and ejaculation from happening at the same time).

Seminal Fluid

The seminal vesicles secrete **seminal fluid,** rich in sugars, proteins, and even an antibiotic substance. The sugars give energy to the sperm, needed for the long swim to the egg. Alkaline substances in the fluid from the prostate render the male's urethra and the female's vagina less acidic and therefore less hostile to sperm. The **prostaglandins** in the seminal fluid are hormones that make the uterus and fallopian tubes contract. Some women develop an allergic reaction to ingredients of their partner's seminal fluid, the symptom of which is an inability to conceive. Some men may also develop a kind of immune response to their own sperm in which their own system destroys or disables the sperm. Physicians who specialize in treating fertility problems can sometimes treat these conditions.

Seminal fluid also picks up secretions from the **Cowper's glands,** a pair of glands located just below the prostate. During sexual arousal, the Cowper's glands secrete a few drops of clear, alkaline fluid. This fluid may come out the tip of the penis before a man ejaculates, although some men never notice it. It may contain live sperm, and so a woman can get pregnant from this fluid even if the male does not ejaculate in her vagina. Once the vas deferens passes through the prostate, it becomes the **ejaculatory duct.** This duct opens into the urethra, the

FIGURE 6.8

Penis and scrotum self-examination. After a shower, which will relax the scrotum's muscles, sit or lie comfortably. Take your penis by the tip, and turn it with the other hand as you look for marks, swellings, or bumps. Look carefully and feel for any rashes or sores on the penis or testes. Hold your penis to one side as you feel the spermatic cord, which contains the vas deferens, on the upper part of each testicle. Press the testes gently against the scrotal sac to be sure there are no painful areas, bumps, or swellings. Squeeze the testes gently to see if they are unusually sensitive. Press gently on the area between your anus and scrotum to see if any spots are painful. If you feel anything unusual, tell your doctor right away. Your regular doctor may be able to treat you. If not, he or she can refer you to a urologist, a specialist in the male's urinary and genital tracts, or to another appropriate specialist.

A. TESTICULAR SELF EXAM

B. TESTES

Vas deferens

Spermatic cord

Head of epididymis

Testis

Seminiferous tubules

Scrotum

Tail of epididymis

passageway through the middle of the penis to the glans that delivers (separately) either seminal fluid or urine outside the body. Seminal fluid may be white, gray, or yellowish, and it is sticky. Immediately after ejaculation, it is viscous. It soon liquefies.

When a male ejaculates, roughly a teaspoon of seminal fluid squirts from the urethral opening of the penis, propelled in part by contractions of muscles surrounding the root of the penis. About a month after they have had their vasa deferentia cut in a simple operation called a **vasectomy,** men ejaculate only fluid and no sperm. Until that time, live sperm may still appear in their ejaculate.

Self-Examination

All males should examine their penis, scrotum, and testicles regularly (once a month is a good guideline) to identify any irregularities: lumps, sores, rashes, infections. Early treatment of infections and sexually transmitted diseases can mean the difference between effective control and possibly serious problems. Early treatment of tumors can mean the difference between life and death. Lumps in the testes can be malignant tumors. Although malignant tumors are not very common, late adolescence and early adulthood are the periods of highest risk for such tumors. Older men should see a physician for regular checks of their prostate gland.

SUMMARY

1 Male reproductive anatomy consists of penis, testes, scrotum, gonads, sperm-delivering and producing pathways, glands, and their surrounding structures.

2 The penis excretes urine, seminal fluid, and is sensitive to touch and pressure.

3 The tip of the penis has an opening called the *meatus*. The tip of the penis is the glans. The middle is the shaft, and the bottom is the root. The foreskin attaches around the sensitive ridge called the *corona*.

4 Internally, the penis consists of three parallel columns of spongy tissue that fill with blood and cause erections. These columns are called the *cavernous bodies,* of which there are two, and the *spongy body.* The urethra extends lengthwise through the penis and is the duct out of the body for urine and seminal fluid.

5 Male circumcision is the surgical removal of the foreskin of the penis. Some people advocate it for reasons of cleanliness and health. Others believe in it for religious or cultural reasons. Still others believe that routine circumcision is unnecessary and may impair sexual functioning. However, circumcision seems to affect neither health nor sexual functioning.

6 Many males feel anxious about the size and shape of their penis. But a big penis is not necessary for a woman's or a man's own sexual pleasure, and although unerect penises range in size from about 2½ to 4 inches long, most erect penises are about 6 inches long. Penis shape and coloring also vary

widely among individuals. It is normal for one testicle to hang lower than the other.

7 The scrotum is the loose pouch that hangs beneath the penis. Its smooth muscles contract on exposure to cold, during arousal and exercise. They relax on exposure to heat. These movements may protect the sperm inside the scrotum from extremes of temperature.

8 Inside the scrotum are the two sperm-producing and hormone-producing gonads of the male, the testes. They produce the hormone testosterone, which governs male sexual development before and after birth.

9 Sperm, the male's sexual cells, are manufactured and stored in tiny ducts within the testes. Sperm are produced constantly from puberty on. They contain half of the genetic instructions necessary for creating a human being, and the sperm always carries the instruction for which sex a baby will be.

10 Sperm production is a many-staged process that takes about 70 days from the primitive form to the fully developed, motile sperm. Sperm are visible under a microscope as having three parts: a head that contains genetic material, a midpiece, and a long tail for locomotion.

11 In the tube called the *epididymis,* the sperm mature for two to six weeks. Then they go into the vas deferens, which loops up and out of the scrotum, into the abdominal cavity, and toward the urethra.

12 Sperm can move under their own power only after they have been surrounded by seminal fluid. Secretions from the seminal vesicles, prostate gland, and the Cowper's glands contribute to seminal fluid. It is rich in sugars, amino acids, hormones, and even an antibiotic substance. Seminal fluid is alkaline, to reduce the acidity of the male's urethra and the female's vagina and make them more hospitable to sperm.

13 The ejaculatory duct is the narrow end of the vas deferens and opens into the urethra.

14 Males should examine their penis, testes, and scrotum each month to identify any unusual lumps, bumps, rashes, swellings, infections, sores, and the like.

KEY TERMS

genitals	undescended testicles
penis	gonads
urethral opening (meatus)	testosterone
glans	Leydig's cells
foreskin	sperm
corona	seminiferous tubules
frenum	chromosomes
shaft	spermatogenesis
root	motility
urethra	epididymis
corpus cavernosum	vas deferens
corpus spongiosum	prostate gland

circumcision
smegma
rite of passage
clitoris
congenital microphallus
scrotum
tunica dartos
testes

seminal vesicles
seminal fluid
prostaglandins
Cowper's glands
ejaculatory duct
vasectomy
spermatic cord
urologist

SUGGESTED READINGS

Jones, Richard E. *Human Reproduction and Sexual Behavior.* Englewood Cliffs, NJ: Prentice-Hall, 1984. Chapter 4 is an excellent explanation of male sexual anatomy and the hormonal controls over sexual development.

Julty, Sam. *Men's Bodies, Men's Selves.* New York: Dell (Delta Books), 1979. Inspired by the enormously popular *Our Bodies, Our Selves,* this book takes a close, engaging look at male sex and sexuality. It is especially sensitive to issues of heterosexual and homosexual identity, and its anatomy chapter is very helpful.

ROBERT DELAUNAY, "RHYTHM." COURTESY NATIONAL MUSEUM OF MODERN ART, PARIS.

Chapter 7

Stages of Arousal and Response

Sexual arousal is a series of physical changes, some of which we can feel and see directly and some of which we learn about indirectly, from laboratory observation. It is also a series of psychological changes in the form of sexual fantasies or feelings of pleasure. Sometimes sexual arousal lies dormant for weeks or months. Sometimes it is a mild yearning and sometimes an almost overwhelming urge. Sometimes it builds slowly; sometimes it pounces and takes us unaware.

> *I was walking down Fifth Avenue one afternoon a few years ago. The sidewalks were crowded. I spotted a guy who was perfect-looking, really sexy. He made me gasp. I still fantasize about him (22-year-old female college senior).*

We may be aroused by a friend or a stranger, by our self, a picture, or a thought. We may be aroused asleep or awake, in public or in private, to our embarrassment or great pleasure. Sexual arousal can absorb body and mind.

> *I get so horny at times that I can't think about anything else. Every girl turns me on. I can't concentrate in class. The feeling's so strong that I get to dislike it (21-year-old male college junior).*

But no matter the circumstances of the arousal, it is always both a psychological and a biological process.

PLEASURES OF MIND AND BODY

People may take sexual pleasure from caresses to any part of the body. Although people often focus on stimulating their sexual organs during sexual acts, skin elsewhere on the body can be stimulated pleasurably. Masters and Johnson (1979) found that many gay women know this and caress a sexual partner's skin unhurriedly during lovemaking. Some men and women are expert at masturbating and can bring themselves to a climax in a matter of minutes. But few people who masturbate caress their skin all over, rub themselves with lotion, or experiment with light, sensuous touches. Many heterosexual males ignore their breasts when they masturbate. In contrast, many homosexual men stimulate each other's breasts, knowing that they are erogenous. Homosexual men also know about the erogenous possibilities of the anus. Young children of both sexes often experiment with putting fingers or other things into their anus and thereby learn that it is a sensitive place. But when people later make the connection of anus with feces and, by extension, with dirtiness, they may shy away from considering the anus as sexual. The important thing, though, is that nature has programmed men's and women's bodies to respond pleasurably to light caresses virtually anywhere.

> *Sex with my girlfriend is sometimes slow and sweet. She'll run the tips of her fingers down my chest and stomach or kiss me lightly everywhere from my waist to the bottom of my feet. I get really turned on having the inside of my thighs touched (21-year-old male college junior).*

Few people of either sex make full use of the erogenous possibilities of their bodies.

Despite the temptation to think of special parts of the body as *the* sexual triggers, that honor belongs to the human brain. For regardless of touch, stroke, brush, lick, and push, the brain is the major on-off switch of all sexual behavior. One part of the brain controls the reflexes of sexual behavior; another part controls the thoughts that can enhance or inhibit those reflexes. In fact, the brain is probably the sexiest organ any human being possesses. The human brain allows us to think about, to relive, to imagine, and to invent highly arousing images. We can attach sexual meaning to many things and fantasize richly. When men masturbate, they may incorporate a wide range of objects and events into their fantasies. So powerfully sexual is the brain that some women can reach a sexual

The human brain is the most powerful sexual organ, for it allows us to think about, imagine, anticipate, relive, and invent highly arousing images.

climax by fantasizing alone. Usually, though, people combine their sexual fantasies with other, external means of arousal. The brain is not merely powerful in sexual matters; it is essential.

The brain also signals the rest of the body when it is time for the sexual developments of puberty to begin, when it is time for intense, frequent genital arousal. The brain's signal turns on the hormonal bath of puberty, when the light touch of a lover may feel like a bolt of sexual lightning. The brain colors our sexuality in another important way: through our subjective sense of our sexual self. How well people think they measure up can certainly affect how sexual they feel. When people think that something about their body is unattractive, not normal, or performs below par, the wound to their pride can inhibit their sexual performance. In short, the brain sends its sexual signals along many different routes. Some of these routes enhance sexual gratification, and some inhibit it.

DURING SEXUAL CLIMAX, TIME AND SPACE SEEM WIPED OUT.

STUDYING SEXUAL RESPONSE

Psychologists have wanted to investigate how the body changes during sexual arousal for a long time, but for years they were hindered by the social disapproval of watching human sexual acts. In 1855 Felix Roubaud published observations on human sexual intercourse; they were as good as most scientific observations of the period. Over the next hundred years, many others published small studies. Alfred Kinsey and his colleagues at Indiana University also directly observed some sexual acts, but they did not publish their findings out of fear of public opinion. But in 1954, Dr. William H. Masters of Washington University Medical School in St. Louis, Missouri, began the first large-scale, broadly based studies of human sexual response. His work would later be known as the Sex Research Project. In 1966, Masters and his colleague, Virginia E. Johnson, published *Human Sexual Response,* the first large-scale analysis of sexual arousal from start to finish.

Masters and Johnson chose volunteers who were reliably orgasmic, a mix of medical students, people from the scientific community, and prostitutes. Masters studied the sexual responses of 382 women between 18 and 78 years old and 312 men from 21 to 89 years old. The subjects included 276 married couples. Although the number of subjects was larger than that in earlier observational studies, it was not a **representative** or a **random sample** in that the subjects were volunteers (who often bias research findings), overwhelmingly white, relatively affluent, and highly selected.

Because Masters and Johnson published only a rough breakdown of subject participation, we do not know if all subjects participated equally or if a few supplied most of the data. Masters and Johnson's findings have become widely known by scientists and citizens alike and have profoundly affected modern ideas about human sexuality. They are assumed to describe the physiological sequence and some of the subjective events in sexual arousal. Readers should remember, however, that they will be reading about *average* and not individual responses.

Personal experience is rarely identical with the averaged results of many laboratory trials. Just as everyone's fingerprints are unique, so is everyone's sexual responsiveness.

Masters and Johnson studied how people responded to three major techniques for producing sexual arousal: heterosexual intercourse, solitary masturbation, and mutual masturbation (the last took place in twosomes with two different partners). These three techniques account for most (although not all) sexual acts in our society (Kinsey et al., 1948, 1953). In the first 12 years of their research, Masters and Johnson observed over 10,000 orgasms, mostly in women. They photographed their subjects with movie cameras and monitored them with instruments that recorded heart and breathing rate and muscle contraction. They studied the internal genitals of women with a clear-plastic penis substitute that could stimulate and photograph the vagina.

STAGES OF SEXUAL RESPONSE

Havelock Ellis: Natural Energy

The stages of sexual response have been characterized differently by various clinicians. One of the earliest models was offered by Havelock Ellis (1906), who spoke of sexual responses as the movement of energy within the body. Like other writers of his day, Ellis used imagery from the natural sciences to characterize human physiology. Thus he described sexual responses in terms of the natural energy in fuel and fire. He called the first stage of response **tumescence,** when blood flows to pelvis and genitals and when the bodily fuels are stoked. Ellis called the second stage **detumescence,** when sexual climax douses the fires of sexual energy and the "devouring flame" dies down.

Masters and Johnson

For purposes of analysis, Masters and Johnson divide the **sexual response cycle** into four stages and describe how the female and male bodies react during each stage. What we informally call "turning on" or "getting hot," Masters and Johnson called the first stage of the cycle. They found that some physical changes last for several stages and that others last for only one stage. (Figure 7.1 shows a summary view of the cycle in males and females.) We will first describe the

FIGURE 7.1

Male and female sexual response cycles. Three of many possible patterns of female responses are labeled *A, B,* and *C* (From Masters and Johnson, 1966).

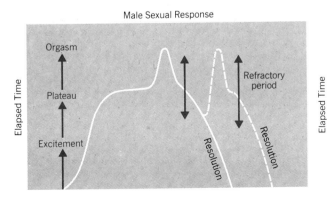

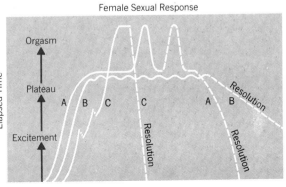

sequence of phases, and then we will describe the specifics of each phase in women and men.

Excitement is the first stage of the Masters and Johnson sexual response cycle. People may grow excited by physical stimuli—a warm caress, a kiss—or by psychological stimuli—an erotic picture or an imagined scene. During the excitement phase, the body begins to change in ways that allow for penis and vagina to unite in intercourse. (Intercourse is not *necessary* for any of the four stages.) The penis grows erect; the vagina gets wet and lengthens. In short, the primary signs of excitement are erection (in males) and lubrication (in females).

When my boyfriend and I start making love, I can always tell when I start getting turned on. All the tenseness leaves my mind, and my body starts to feel nice and warm (19-year-old female freshman).

Half the time, I see my erection first, and then I know that I'm turned on (18-year-old male freshman).

Plateau is the second stage of the sexual response cycle, when many of the changes that started during excitement continue. Other changes will follow. Some people think of plateau as the highest stage of arousal, a preparation for sexual

People may grow excited by a warm caress, a kiss, an erotic picture, an imagined scene.

climax, although climax follows only if stimulation continues. Some males do not perceive a definable plateau stage (Robinson, 1976).

Orgasm, or sexual climax, is the third stage of the sexual response cycle. Masters and Johnson define orgasm in both sexes as a distinct set of contractions of the genitals and a psychological change that is harder to define. For men, orgasm is usually a single ejaculation, quickly followed by the next stage, resolution. **Resolution** is the fourth stage of the sexual response cycle. It is when the events of the first three stages are reversed.

> *You know what I hate? A weak orgasm. It's worse than no orgasm at all (22-year-old female college senior).*

Speaking generally, the two sexes differ more in their responses during the orgasm phase than others. For women, continued arousal may lead to one of several different outcomes. Women may have several orgasms followed quickly by resolution. They may have no orgasm, but a long plateau followed by a slow resolution. They may have an orgasm quickly following plateau and quickly followed by resolution, a pattern most like a man's (these three possibilities, labeled A, B, and C, respectively, in Figure 7.1, are not the only possibilities for a woman). Adult men usually do not have more than one orgasm. But men in their teens or twenties may go through only 10 to 30 minutes of a **refractory period,** when ejaculation is not possible, no matter how strong the stimulation may be. Women do not necessarily have a refractory period between one orgasm and another. Similarly, some prepubescent males can have multiple orgasms (Kinsey et al., 1948), and some postpubescent males can keep from ejaculating by cutting the stimulation if they sense that they are about to ejaculate. They experience some of the involuntary contractions of orgasm, but no ejaculation. They can continue to have several (from 3 to 10) of these sets of contractions if they do not ejaculate.

> *When I'm really turned on, my penis gives this tiny little jerk. If I rest, I can keep going for a while. But if I keep on, I have to come (19-year-old male college sophomore).*

In contrast, when a male ejaculates and has an orgasm together, the orgasm feels intense, and a refractory period always follows (Robbins and Jensen, 1977).

DESIRE AND SATISFACTION

Masters and Johnson's four-stage model of arousal, plateau, orgasm, and resolution does not account for how some people say that they *feel*. Sex therapists have found that two more stages must be added to the sexual response cycle—desire and satisfaction. To be aroused sexually, a person must *want* to be aroused. Some patients show a pervasive loss of interest in sex. These are not people who have always had small sexual appetites; they are people who have instead lost their sexual appetites. These people could not care less about having sex, even though once upon a time they did care. **Hypoactive sexual desire** was first named by a psychiatrist at Cornell Medical School, Helen Singer Kaplan (1978). Most clinicians now include **desire** as a required first step toward arousal.

Out of the same interest in understanding the subjective elements of sexuality, two West Coast clinicians, Bernie Zilbergeld and Carol Rinkleib Ellison (1980),

FIGURE 7.2

Stages of sexual arousal. By combining the stages of sexual response suggested by Masters and Johnson, Kaplan, and Zilbergeld and Ellison, we see arousal building from the earliest, subjective state of desire; to excitement and, in some cases, a plateau of greater excitement; then orgasm; followed by a resolution period when physical responses reverse. A feeling of satisfaction then emerges; and a resting, refractory period sets in for several moments.

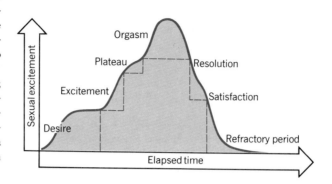

added a **satisfaction** phase. Zilbergeld and Ellison were seeing men who reach orgasm but found no pleasure in it. They also were seeing women who experienced great pleasure, but no orgasm. The functional part of sexual response may work as Masters and Johnson described, but the pleasurable feelings associated with those steps cannot simply be assumed. Clinics around the world are seeing some people with a satisfaction disorder: "Sure, I ejaculate, but what's so great about that?" they may say, or "Yes, I had an orgasm, but it gave me no pleasure." The new clinical model thus contains Masters and Johnson's four stages sandwiched between desire, the appetizer to start the sexual process, and satisfaction, the dessert after a sexual act (see Figure 7.2). (More people have trouble with desire than with satisfaction. We will discuss this topic more fully in Chapter 16, "Sexual Problems, Therapy, and Communication.")

Many new clinical findings have led physiologists to question the relationship between subjective sexual experience and physiology. Saying, "It's all in the brain" only intensifies the question of what *"it"* is.

HOW THE BODY CHANGES

Sexual arousal affects the whole body. Its whole tempo shifts as it moves from resting, vegetative functions such as digesting a meal or doing tomorrow's homework and into activity in many different areas. Masters and Johnson (1966) have divided the body's sexual responses into two broad categories: the **genital responses,** or all the responses of the reproductive organs to arousal, and the **extragenital responses,** or all the responses of the rest of the body. We might add a third category, *psychological responses,* which depend on and somewhat determine the other responses. The power of psychological responses is great—as anyone can attest whose phone has rung just as an orgasm was about to start.

People's muscles and blood vessels react to sexual stimulation. Muscle tension, or **myotonia,** increases throughout the body. The smooth, involuntary muscles are responsible for most of the movement and contractions of the genitals; the striated, voluntary muscles are responsible for large body movements. Involuntary muscles control the contractions one feels during orgasm, and voluntary muscles control the position one stands, sits, or lies in. The second major kind of response is the accumulation of blood in parts of the body. Blood congestion accounts for the swelling and erection of the clitoris and penis as well as any changes in color of the body during arousal. Blood congestion and myotonia of the involuntary muscles are controlled by the **autonomic nervous system.** The autonomic nervous system also contributes to control of the heart and other internal organs and the endocrine glands.

THE WOMAN'S RESPONSES

Both sexes experience muscle tension and blood congestion. Other aspects of their sexual response cycles are different. We will first describe how a woman's body changes when she is aroused.

Extragenital Responses

GENERAL BODY SYSTEMS   Sexual arousal increases the rate at which a woman breathes; in the late plateau stage, she may be taking 40 breaths a minute (instead of the normal, unaroused 12). Her heart beats more quickly, too, and by late plateau may be going 100 to 180 beats a minute (the normal, unaroused heart beats 60 to 80 times a minute). Blood pressure rises with sexual arousal and peaks late in the plateau phase. One convention of Oriental art was to depict people who were sexually aroused with toes tightly curled. Psychologists call this involuntary contraction of the hands and feet **carpopedal spasm.** Some women (and men also) get these spasms late in the plateau phase or during orgasm, because involuntary muscles tend to contract in spasms.

BREASTS AND NIPPLES   A woman's breasts and nipples change in size and color when she is sexually aroused (see Figure 7.3). During the excitement phase, the nipples grow erect; they increase in length and diameter at the base. Blood flow to the breasts makes the veins under the skin more visible and also increases the size of the breasts.

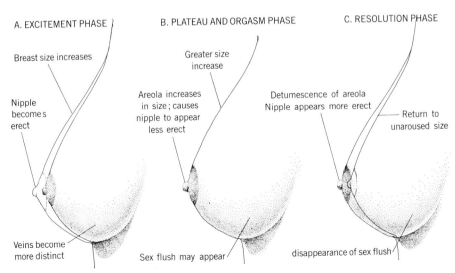

A. EXCITEMENT PHASE

Breast size increases

Nipple becomes erect

Veins become more distinct

B. PLATEAU AND ORGASM PHASE

Greater size increase

Areola increases in size; causes nipple to appear less erect

Sex flush may appear

C. RESOLUTION PHASE

Detumescence of areola
Nipple appears more erect

Return to unaroused size

disappearance of sex flush

FIGURE 7.3

Breasts and nipples change in response to sexual arousal.

During the plateau phase, blood congestion of the nipples and breasts continues. The breasts may be 20 to 25 percent larger during sexual arousal. The dark area around the nipple, the **areola,** fills with blood and swells so that the nipple seems to shrink.

During orgasm, breasts and nipples remain enlarged. During resolution, the areolae may shrink so rapidly that they make the still enlarged nipples look erect. This response follows orgasm. A woman's breasts remain enlarged for five or ten minutes, and the vein patterns may remain longer.

Some women's breasts and nipples are very sensitive to erotic stimulation. A few women reach orgasm from stimulation of their breasts alone. Other women's breasts are not sensitive, although they experience the usual physical changes of arousal. Part of the difference in sensitivity among women is probably the result of cultural learning—breasts are eroticized in our culture and in some others—and part is probably the result of biological factors.

Body Surface In three-fourths of Masters and Johnson's female objects, a **sex flush,** or a measle-like rash, spreads over the skin during sexual arousal. The flush, technically called a **macropapular flush,** results from increased blood flow to the skin. During the excitement phase, the flush colors the upper abdomen and may spread over the breasts. During plateau, the color extends over much of the body, including the face, thighs, buttocks, and the back. It remains stable during orgasm and fades rapidly, in reverse order of its appearance, during resolution.

Genital Responses

Many men and some women wonder whether a woman's genitals show that they are turned on, as a man's do so obviously with an erect penis. A number of changes do take place in a woman's genitals when she is aroused, but some of them are rather difficult to see with the naked eye.

Vagina and Labia During the excitement phase, the labia majora, which usually meet at the midline, flatten and rise slightly away from the opening of the vagina. During excitement or plateau, the labia minora may grow to two or three times their usual size and protrude through the labia majora, effectively adding an extra centimeter to the length of the vagina. The vagina also lengthens at its upper end during the excitement phase, as the uterus rises. The inner two-thirds of the vagina also expand in diameter, partly as a result of the uterus rising (see Figure 7.4).

Within 10 to 30 seconds after a woman begins to feel aroused, her vaginal walls begin to lubricate. They change from the purplish-red that is common in young women to a deeper purple (because blood supply increases). During the plateau phase, the labia majora do not change much, but the increased blood supply may turn the labia minora bright red. This dramatic color change precedes orgasm. During plateau, the outer vagina is so richly supplied with blood that its diameter shrinks by about one-third. The increased blood flow to the vagina and the labia minora mark the **orgasmic platform,** from which a woman may move into orgasm.[1]

[1] The term *orgasmic platform* is misleading. It is actually an expansion of the outer vaginal walls as they fill with blood. It is felt not as a platform, but as a reduction in vaginal diameter.

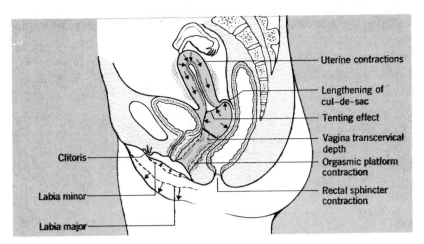

FIGURE 7.4

Female genitals during orgasm. During orgasm, the outer part of the vagina tightens, and the inner part expands.

Labels on figure:
- Uterine contractions
- Lengthening of cul-de-sac
- Tenting effect
- Vagina transcervical depth
- Orgasmic platform contraction
- Rectal sphincter contraction
- Clitoris
- Labia minor
- Labia major

An orgasm is an explosive peak and release of sexual tension. An orgasm consists of several parts. The vagina contracts rhythmically, beginning at about 0.8-second intervals, and continuing for 3 to 15 contractions. The number of contractions depends on and also affects the intensity of the woman's experience of orgasm. After the first three to six contractions, the intensity diminishes progressively. The events of orgasm may repeat two, three, four, or more times without loss of the orgasmic platform. Some women occasionally have a very intense orgasm, or **status orgasmus,** that lasts from 20 to more than 60 seconds.

During the resolution stage, first the outer third of the vagina loses the orgasmic platform and increases in diameter. The reversal of the expansion of the inner two-thirds of the vagina is slower to happen. The top wall of the vagina descends first, bringing the cervix close to the vaginal floor.

CLITORIS   The clitoris, which is the only organ in either sex that functions solely to afford sexual pleasure, is very sensitive to stimulation. Sexual fantasies and stimulation of other parts of her body will cause a woman's clitoris to show the changes characteristic of arousal. These changes may happen more quickly if the clitoris or the mons is stimulated directly (stimulation of the mons indirectly stimulates the clitoris). Because some women find direct stimulation of the clitoris painful, they grow aroused more easily if it is indirectly stimulated.

If anyone touches my clitoris when we are making love, it really hurts me. I move away, but it's hard for me to explain the problem in words (18-year-old female college freshman).

During sexual arousal, first the glans of the clitoris swells slightly. The shaft increases in diameter, and in some women doubles, and may lengthen in response to increased blood supply. Both of these responses are slower than the rapid erection of the penis early in the excitement stage. During the plateau stage, the clitoris disappears from view as it recedes under the protective clitoral hood. No specific changes in the clitoris have been found during orgasm. (See Figure 7.5 for illustrations of changes in the clitoris during arousal.) During the resolution stage and within 5 to 10 seconds after vaginal contractions end, the clitoris returns

FIGURE 7.5

The clitoris changes in response to sexual arousal.

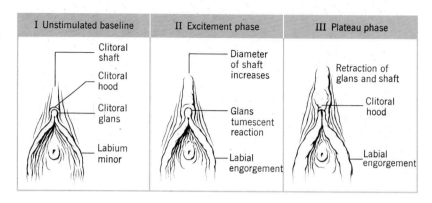

I Unstimulated baseline	II Excitement phase	III Plateau phase
Clitoral shaft Clitoral hood Clitoral glans Labium minor	Diameter of shaft increases Glans tumescent reaction Labial engorgement	Retraction of glans and shaft Clitoral hood Labial engorgement

to its exposed condition. The blood congestion usually takes 5 to 10 minutes to recede. Yet if a woman reaches plateau without orgasm, the blood congestion may take some uncomfortable hours to recede.

UTERUS   Although the uterus receives little direct stimulation during sex, it goes through a number of distinct changes when a woman is aroused. The three major changes are: the uterus increases in size; it becomes elevated from its resting position; and it contracts rhythmically at orgasm. Some women are intensely aware of uterine contractions during orgasm; others are not. Recently, some researchers have grown interested in local vaginal arousal (at a point in the vagina popularly called "the G-spot") as a source of uterine contractions. Later in this chapter, we will return to the G-spot and its hypothesized relation to uterine contractions.

Pregnancy and Sexual Response: General Findings

When a woman is pregnant, her uterus increases enormously in size, and blood congestion in the pelvic region increases as the pregnancy proceeds. Thus late in pregnancy, a woman's genitals may look as if arousal has already begun: vagina and labia may look constantly flushed and engorged with blood; vaginal secretions are the norm; breasts and nipples enlarge, their veining growing more prominent. Arousal may further intensify these changes. For some women, the pelvic blood engorgement during pregnancy increases their sexual arousal.

> *I was horny from the time I conceived until I went into labor. It didn't matter if I had a splitting headache. I wanted to make love. It didn't even matter if I was feeling sick. I still had to make love. My husband called me "Hotpants" (38-year-old pediatrician).*

For others, studies show that during the first trimester of pregnancy, sexual interest may drop, especially if a woman is feeling morning sickness, and in the last trimester of pregnancy, many couples find that their sexual activity diminishes (Calhoun, Selby, and King, 1981).

Women whose breasts were not particularly sensitive before may find that pregnancy makes them much more sensitive. Although a woman's bulk late in pregnancy may make it awkward, sexual activity until late in pregnancy still has

Couples may find that expecting a baby alters their sexual lives, making intercourse more or less frequent, pleasurable, and comfortable at different stages of a pregnancy.

medical approval. A couple may want to experiment with positions different from the usual ones. Side-by-side or rear-entry positions may still be comfortable late in pregnancy; or couples may choose mutual masturbation or oral sex. The contractions of uterus and vagina during orgasm may be especially intense during pregnancy, probably because the genitals are so enlarged and engorged. Some women who never had orgasms during intercourse find that they can do so after a pregnancy. Masters and Johnson believe that the reason is that the pelvis can fill more quickly and fully with blood after childbirth. Their belief remains a guess, but it is no guess that pregnancy permanently enhances some women's sexual responsiveness.[2]

What Does a Woman's Orgasm Feel Like?

Although it may be hard to say what an orgasm feels like, few people would try to describe it by saying, "Well, the vagina contracts at intervals of 0.8 seconds. . . ." A common (and not helpful) response to someone who asks what an orgasm feels like is, "Oh, you'll know when you have one." In fact, that is not always true. Some college women do not know whether they have ever had an orgasm (Clifford, 1978). They describe what probably is an orgasm: relief from tension and some contractions or flutters. Once they learn it is an orgasm, perhaps closer attention can help create a more obvious, more subjectively intense orgasm.

Masters and Johnson interviewed 487 women, some immediately after they had had an orgasm, and compiled this description of how a woman's orgasm feels:

Orgasm has its onset with a sensation of suspension or stoppage. Lasting only an instant, the sensation is accompanied or followed immediately by an isolated thrust of intense sensual awareness, clitorally oriented,

[2]More about sexual activity during pregnancy appears in Chapter 9, "Menstruation, Pregnancy, and Childbirth."

but radiating upward into the pelvis. Intensity ranging in degree from mild to shock level has been reported by many women within the context of their personal experience. A simultaneous loss of overall sensory acuity has been described as paralleling in degree the intensity and duration of the particular orgasmic episode (1966).

Women have described orgasm as a "suffusion of warmth" that starts in the pelvis and washes over the whole body. After that come "pelvic throbbing" and involuntary contractions in the vagina or lower part of the pelvis. Orgasm feels like it begins in the clitoris and then quickly spreads throughout the pelvis and the whole body. Masters and Johnson found that women could report an orgasm two to four seconds before instruments could measure any biological changes. Women reported feeling contractions even after instruments could no longer measure any. Usually, when women reported an intense orgasm, their pelvic contractions had been numerous and strong. But women also reported intense orgasms without intense contractions, and vice versa. Recent work on female orgasm finds no correlation between the number of contractions and the intensity of sexual pleasure a woman feels (Bohlen et al., 1982). Thus the relationship is quite loose between a woman's subjective feeling about orgasm and her biological response to arousal. Women generally reported that their orgasms were most intense when they masturbated, followed in intensity by those from mutual masturbation and then by intercourse.

The War of the Orgasms: Clitoral versus Vaginal

Sigmund Freud proposed that clitoral orgasms differed significantly from vaginal orgasms and that a woman's dependence on clitoral orgasms showed her failure to develop *mature* sexuality. Freud's enduring but incorrect idea has caused more than enough mischief. It is probably impossible to distinguish "clitoral" from "vaginal" orgasms with instruments. When women have (a "vaginal") orgasm in intercourse, they may well have arranged themselves so that their clitoris is stimulated, not so much from thrusts of a penis as from pressure on their pubic and clitoral areas. Many "vaginal" orgasms therefore probably involve indirect but effective clitoral stimulation. Said one college senior:

I can climax if I rub my pubic area against my boyfriend while his penis is inside me.

Although the inner two-thirds of the vagina has relatively few nerve endings and is therefore rather insensitive, a sizable minority of women do prefer vaginal to direct clitoral stimulation, and most women probably can distinguish the differences in feelings from these two kinds of stimulation. Women's descriptions of the two kinds of stimulation overlap, but clitoral stimulation is more often described as "sharp" or "hot" and vaginal stimulation as "deep," "soothing," or "uterine" (Fisher, 1973; Hite, 1976; Perry and Whipple, 1982). If all orgasms are essentially the same physiologically, as Masters and Johnson believe, and if the vagina has few touch receptors as compared to the clitoris, why can women ascribe different qualities to clitoral versus vaginal stimulation? We do not know the answer. Researchers like Julian Davidson at Stanford University are interested in the relationship between objective, physiological events and a woman's subjective experience. Davidson finds gaps in knowledge on both sides, but especially wide ones on the subjective, felt side (Bohlen et al., 1982; Davidson, 1981; see Graber, 1982, for recent work and speculation). Given our current state of knowledge, we do not know how women's varied descriptions correlate with the pattern of genital stimulation. So far, simple explanations—press here and it's felt there but not over there—have not panned out. Most of Hite's (1976) subjects reported that clitoral stimulation felt more intense, yet most preferred orgasm during intercourse to orgasm from manipulation of their clitoris alone. Most women (many of them feminists) seemed quite willing to sacrifice some sensual intensity for the sharing and intimacy of intercourse and intimacy that laboratory measurements of physiological responses cannot capture.

The G-Spot

The **G-spot** is named after Ernst Grafenberg, the physician who in 1950 found a spot on the vaginal wall that enlarged during sexual arousal. The G-spot is reputed to lie on the anterior (or front) wall of the vagina, with its long axis running along the path of the urethra (see Figure 7.6). When the G-spot is stimulated as a woman lies on her back—by hand, dildo, or by penile thrusting—it is said to increase to the size of a dime or larger (or up to 50 percent enlarged) and to make a woman feel the need first to urinate and then, with continued stimulation, to feel deep sexual pleasure. In 1981, the G-spot was rediscovered (Addiego et al., 1981) in a patient whose orgasm produced large quantities of a clear, transparent liquid—dubbed "ejaculation." (Later, the ejaculate was described as looking more like skim milk.) Most earlier investigators had assumed that fluid in such cases was urine and that the condition was "urinary stress incontinence," a tendency to pass some urine under certain conditions of excitement. Then a comparison of 24 women "ejaculators" and 23 nonejaculators was published (Perry and Whipple, 1981). The two groups were said to differ in their pelvic musculature. By 1982, *The G-Spot* was on the best-seller list (Ladas, Whipple, and Perry, 1982), challenging Masters and Johnson's view that all orgasms

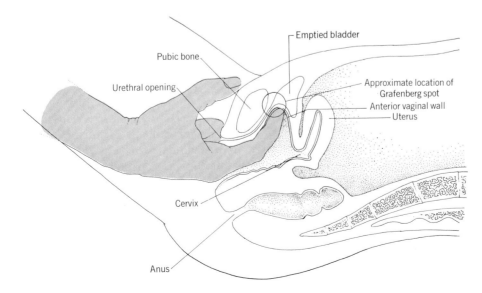

FIGURE 7.6

Finding the G-spot. The dime-sized G-spot lies on the front (anterior) wall of the vagina.

are physiologically alike. A new version of the vaginal orgasm had moved into public view.

John Perry, a clinical psychologist, and Beverly Whipple, a registered nurse, roposed two controversial "findings." First, they proposed that an estimated 10 percent of women, whom they call "ejaculators," have established a special kind of orgasm, based on stronger pubococcygeus (the muscles in the pelvic floor) and uterine muscles than nonejaculators have (see Figures 5.3 and 5.4). (This orgasm, Perry and Whipple [1982, p. 109] believe, involves the pelvic nerve rather than the pudendal nerve. Most other orgasms involve both nerves.) They believe that strengthening these muscles leads to uterine contractions, and biofeedback with an instrument to record vaginal muscle tone can teach orgasm. Whether this proposal is true for preorgasmic women has not yet been established. For 101 university women and for 92 women at routine gynecological checkups, respectively, no relationship was found between their measured muscular strength and the likelihood or intensity of orgasm (Chambless et al., 1982; Freese and Levitt, 1984). (The women's muscular strength was measured by a perinometer, the apparatus Perry has approved for clinical use.)

Perry and Whipple's second controversial finding is about "ejaculation." The volume of some reported and filmed ejaculations is well beyond the most semen ever recovered from *male* ejaculators. The composition of one such ejaculate was first reported to resemble the secretion from the male's prostate gland, and so a new structural-functional relation in females was inferred. The structure consists of glands from the **distal urethra,** said to be homologous to the prostate in males. The presumed function is ejaculation. In that no one actually knows what triggers female orgasm—or orgasm generally—scientific interest is lively.

The controversy over vaginal-versus-clitoral orgasm, which was thought to have been settled by Masters and Johnson, has been renewed as investigators hunt for new varieties of orgasm in the G-spot and vaginal musculature. Thus the first controversial hypotheses were that stimulation of the G-spot produced a deep, perhaps uterine, orgasm and ejaculation from an organ homologous to the prostate. But it has turned out that "ejaculate" by women resembles urine rather than prostate secretion (Alzate, 1985; Goldberg et al., 1983), and not all orgasms that proceed from stimulating the G-spot produce ejaculation. One investigator also has found arousable spots on *both* the anterior and posterior walls of the vagina (Alzate, 1985). When stimulated by hand, both spots can cause orgasm. The question of what triggers female orgasm is still not clear. New theories are appearing about the possible existence of spinal reflexes for arousal in women (already known for men) and the role of vaginal muscles in triggering the orgasmic reflex (Graber, 1982; Mould, 1982), but these too remain at the level of speculation.

The effect of the G-spot sensation has been to focus people's attention on the need for work on the underlying nerves and muscles of the female orgasm. Work on either sex is likely to improve our understanding of reflexes in the other, especially because so many of the sexual structures *are* homologous, because the timing of orgasmic contractions is alike in the two sexes, and because the two sexes also describe the experience of orgasm similarly (Vance and Wagner, 1976).

THE MAN'S RESPONSES

Because men and women have many organ systems in common, their responses to sexual excitement are usually similar, differing only in timing and degree. It is easy to think of the sexual responses of male and female as far less similar than they really are, but the many homologous sexual organs—clitoris and glans of the penis, inner labia and penile shaft, outer labia and scrotum—make clear how structurally similar the two sexes really are.

Extragenital Responses

The nongenital responses of men are much like those of women. Men experience muscular tension (myotonia) during late excitement or plateau phases. Spastic contractions of hands and feet indicate high levels of arousal and are more frequent during masturbation than intercourse. Men also develop a sex flush, and their breathing and heart rates increase.

Men's nipples may change in response to arousal and become sensitive to erotic stimulation. Nipples grow erect in the late excitement phase and stay erect for many minutes after orgasm. Few women directly stimulate men's breasts or nipples. More men do so in homosexual encounters, as we have said—a difference in sexual habits that again shows how strongly learning colors people's sexual perceptions and desires.

Genital Responses

Several changes in a man's genitals in response to sexual arousal are readily apparent, as many a teenager embarrassed by an unwanted erection can attest.

Penis   Erection of the penis is the first observable event in a male's sexual arousal. Newborn boys have erections, and Masters and Johnson observed an 89-year-old man whose penis became fully erect. The penis grows erect when its internal structures fill with blood. Controlled by the autonomic nervous system, **arterioles** (parts of blood vessels that can tighten or relax) in arteries leading to the penis open and allow blood to fill the spongy tissue. Erection disappears when the arterioles tighten, signaled by nerve impulses that pass from the brain or the genitals to integrating centers in the spinal cord. Thus a male may have an erection spontaneously and reflexively—as baby boys do when they are crying very hard, for instance, or as older males do when they dream even unerotic dreams—as well as in response to psychological stimulation. Thus erection is not always a sign of *sexual* arousal. It may also signal the arousal of fear or anxiety.

During the plateau phase, a male's erection may be completed with increased swelling of the corona or rim of the glans. Sometimes in late plateau stage the skin of the penis changes color, to a deep red or purple, a result of vasocongestion. During plateau, a few drops of fluid—from Cowper's gland—may seep from the tip of the penis. This fluid may contain sperm and is likeliest to appear if arousal at the plateau level continues for some time.

Men feel orgasm starting even before any contractions occur. One researcher has reported awareness beginning a full second before any contractions can be recorded (Bohlen et al., 1980). In the early stage of orgasm, the prostate gland, seminal vesicles, and vasa deferentia begin to contract rhythmically and involuntarily. The urethra then contracts from the prostate through the penis and expels seminal fluid. The first contractions happen at 0.8-second intervals; later contractions are separated by several seconds. Once the prostate and other organs have begun contracting, the orgasm almost always continues immediately to completion. Even the ringing phone won't interrupt the process. The volume and

FIGURE 7.7

Male anatomy during the stages of sexual response. (a) The male genitals in transition from unaroused to aroused. (b) The male genitals in an aroused state. (c) and (d) Emission and expulsion phases of orgasm. (e) The physical changes of arousal reverse during the resolution phase.

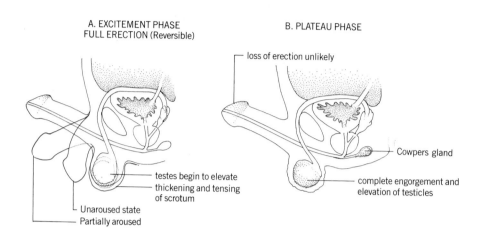

A. EXCITEMENT PHASE
FULL ERECTION (Reversible)

testes begin to elevate
thickening and tensing of scrotum
Unaroused state
Partially aroused

B. PLATEAU PHASE

loss of erection unlikely

Cowpers gland

complete engorgement and elevation of testicles

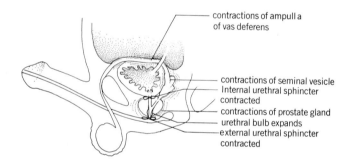

C. EMISSION PHASE OF ORGASM

contractions of ampull a of vas deferens

contractions of seminal vesicle
Internal urethral sphincter contracted
contractions of prostate gland
urethral bulb expands
external urethral sphincter contracted

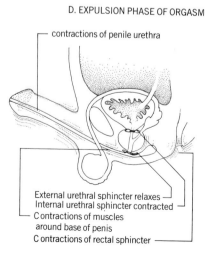

D. EXPULSION PHASE OF ORGASM

contractions of penile urethra

External urethral sphincter relaxes
Internal urethral sphincter contracted
Contractions of muscles around base of penis
Contractions of rectal sphincter

E. RESOLUTION PHASE

testes descend
scrotum thins and resumes wrinkled appearance
testicles return to unstimulated size
unstimulated state (second stage detumescence complete)
first stage of erection loss completed

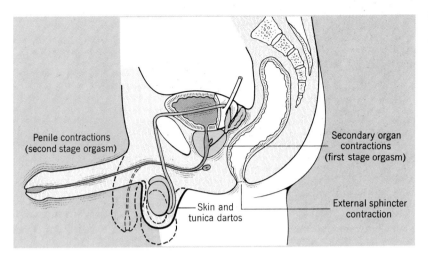

FIGURE 7.8

Male genitals during orgasm.

force of the ejaculation of sperm depend on how long it has been since a man previously ejaculated. The longer it has been, the greater the volume and force.

Right after they ejaculate, men enter the resolution phase. The first part of this phase is a refractory period when sexual motivation and arousal wane. The length of the refractory period depends on a man's age—the younger he is, the shorter the refractory period—and on whether he is still being stimulated. If he is, he may retain a partial erection. Men vary greatly in how quickly they lose their erection during the resolution phase, although if he exercises, urinates, or is distracted, a man will quickly lose his erection.

TESTES AND SCROTUM   When a man is aroused, the testes change in two ways. They increase in size and turn toward the body. The scrotum increases in thickness and contracts.

During the excitement phase, the testes elevate and partly rotate. To support the testes and in response to blood congestion, the scrotum decreases in internal diameter and thickness. During the plateau phase, the testes stay elevated and rotated. Just before ejaculation, the testes come closer to the body. When the testes are fully elevated, orgasm follows. During the plateau phase, blood congestion increases the size of the testes by 50 to 100 percent. The longer plateau lasts, the greater the increase in size. If plateau lasts for a long time and ejaculation does not follow, the testes may stay congested with blood for a while, a harmless but uncomfortable condition.

WHAT DOES A MAN'S ORGASM FEEL LIKE?

A man focuses erotically more on his genitals during arousal and orgasm than a woman does. Masters and Johnson (1966) drew a profile of "the psychology of male orgasm" after interviewing over 400 men. The consensus among men was that orgasm feels like a two-stage process. The first stage feels as if orgasm is impending and inevitable. It is probably stimulated by semen collecting in the prostate. In the second stage, semen goes from the prostate, into the penis, and is ejaculated from the body. Some men can have several spaced episodes of urethral contractions before they ejaculate (Robbins and Jensen, 1977). The first two or three strong contractions of the penis are very pleasurable. The later, milder contractions are felt to be weaker, less pleasurable, and may even go unnoticed. When men have several orgasms during one encounter, some report less intense pleasure with each ejaculation. Others like the prolonging of intercourse.

MEN'S AND WOMEN'S RESPONSES COMPARED

Men and women have many similar sexual responses. Both feel aroused throughout their bodies. In both, blood congests and muscles tense. Their genital responses are much alike, because many of the sexual organs grew from the same embryonic tissue. The timing of contractions during orgasm is the same in men and women. After orgasm, however, the male nervous system produces a refractory period that is longer than the female's. Men quickly lose their erections after orgasm and require some minutes to grow aroused again. The responses of both sexes slow—but do not stop—with age.

Psychological Responses

The physical signs of arousal, which are so much alike for males and females, are only half of the story. People's subjective, psychological responses to sexual arousal are, in part, learned. Stereotypes may suggest that women respond differently from men, but in truth, there are probably as many subjective sexual responses as there are individuals. For both men and women, sex is an interaction of mind and body. Arousal may grow from direct physical stimulation as well as from fantasies, memories, and dreams. Women and men may have orgasms in their sleep. Men and women report similar subjective experiences of orgasm: they identify orgasm anywhere from one to four seconds before rhythmic contractions of the genitals begin. The differences in how the sexes locate and appreciate orgasm may not be so great as Masters and Johnson (1966, pp. 177, 186) have suggested. In one study, judges read descriptions of orgasm written by male and female students. All words that might betray the students' sex were changed. The judges were professionals in fields related to sexuality, but they could not state certainly the sex of the authors of the descriptions (Vance and Wagner, 1976).

Yet men and women differ in their experience of orgasm in that women's orgasms are more vulnerable to interruption if stimulation ends, and many women require more stimulation than men to reach orgasm, at least during intercourse (Hite, 1976; Kinsey et al., 1953). Another difference is that men usually report their first (if they have more than one) orgasm is the most pleasurable; women sometimes report later orgasms as more pleasurable. Masters and Johnson also have reported (1975) another interesting difference. When women fall asleep after orgasm, many try to stay in close contact with their partner. But men do not.

Physiological Responses

Generally, when women and men share a physical system that responds to arousal, their responses tend to be similar in form, but not necessarily in duration. You can see how closely the responses compare in Figure 7.9.

FIGURE 7.9

A comparison of men's and women's sexual responses. In reality, the length of each stage varies greatly. Shown here, for the woman, are the changes for a single orgasm or several quick orgasms in a row. Men have either a quick or slow resolution of testicular changes (after Masters and Johnson, 1966).

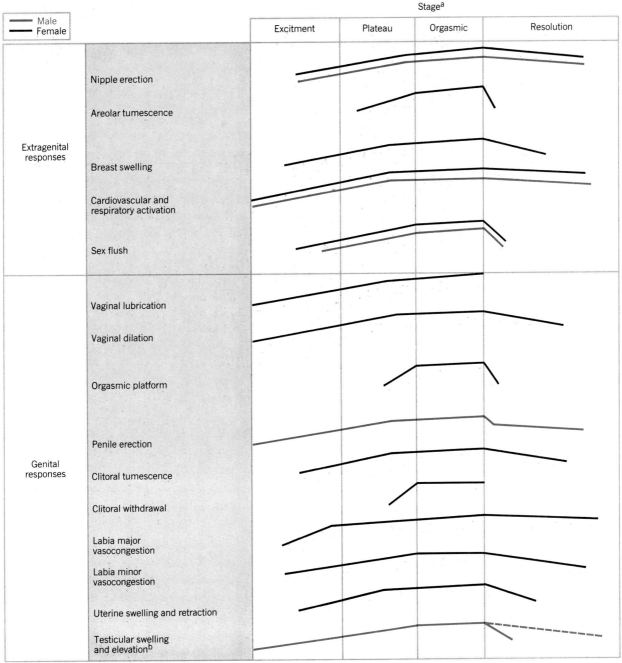

[a]The duration of each stage is highly variable; stages have been arbitrarily equated in length. For the female, changes for a single orgasm or a short series of rapidly occurring orgasms are depicted.

[b]Each man has either a characteristic fast or slow resolution of testicular changes.

Although in intercourse men can usually reach orgasm sooner than women, stimulation of the clitoris may erase this difference in timing of sexual responses. Many women reach orgasm as quickly as men during masturbation (Hite, 1976; Kinsey et al., 1953). Both sexes experience orgasm as a relief from the increased blood supply of the plateau phase, although the male's orgasm seems to reduce pelvic blood congestion more than the female's does. The female's capacity to become aroused again by stimulation after orgasm is in part due to remaining vasocongestion. It takes less additional stimulation to reach plateau and orgasm *after* the first orgasm. Once males ejaculate, no amount of added stimulation will arouse, for the brain is programmed for a resting period, the refractory phase.

During orgasm, both sexes experience rhythmic contractions in the genitals and secondary sex organs, and the initial interval between the contractions is the

SEXUALITY IN RESEARCH:
MULTIPLE ORGASMS: A CASE HISTORY

A 36-year-old woman who had no previous experience with orgasms offered researchers at the University of Minnesota Medical School (Bohlen et al., 1982) the chance to measure the objective and subjective development of her sexual responses. Raised in a strict Catholic home, the woman had had no overt sexual experiences until six months before she entered the research program. She had never masturbated and had only talked about sex with her younger sister. For six months, however, she had begun having intercourse once or twice a month and experimenting daily with self-stimulation. She volunteered for the program because she wanted to learn more about her body. She described the development of her sexual responses, including a pulsing orgasm, with a vibrator:

All I can say is that at first I felt good, and then I felt very, very good.

My response with digital self-stimulation of the clitoris, both before and after discovering the pulse, was quite different. In a typical session (including my first session in the physiology lab), a tingling sensation was there, but it was more generalized and varied in intensity. I was aware of muscle tension in the pelvic area and thighs, tension that became stronger and stronger. I continued stimulating the clitoris with my right middle finger until my whole body suddenly went rigid. I held my breath for what seemed to be 20 seconds or longer before my body would let go. This "letting go" was followed by feelings of relaxation and warmth. I felt very good all over.

In the first two sessions, the woman had a single orgasm. From the third session on, she had more than one orgasm. She reported tnat the first orgasm was same. But the female orgasm lasts longer and may entail more genital contractions. A group of physiologists at the University of Minnesota Medical School have used a computer to study orgasms in the laboratory (Bohlen, Held, and Sanderson, 1980; Bohlen et al., 1982). Eleven men and 11 women each masturbated three times to orgasm. Each wore an anal probe, and the women wore a vaginal probe as well. Pressure on the probes produced electrical signals that a computer turned into readable graphs.

The researchers found that each person's pattern of orgasmic contractions was very similar from one session to another but that each person's pattern varied significantly from that of the others. Women signaled that an orgasm was beginning anywhere from 4 to 1.5 seconds before regular contractions began. Some men also signaled that an orgasm was beginning before regular contractions began;

slightly more intense than later ones. The most orgasms she had in a single session was seven, in an interval spanning nearly 16 minutes. College women who can experience multiple orgasms through masturbating do so in only about one in ten sexual opportunities (Clifford, 1978a). The subject's later orgasms were not accompanied by a series of regular contractions as early ones were; later orgasms were accompanied instead by few and irregular contractions or even none at all. In each case, however, there was a pressure change at the start of each reported orgasm. The subject reported a feeling of "suspension" during these pressure changes. At the end of each orgasm, there was no distinct pressure change, and the subject herself had trouble saying exactly when an orgasm had ended. Her pleasure varied from one orgasm to another in no discernible pattern.

When the researchers later tried to correlate the subject's reports of the intensity of pleasure to other measures, they found that intensity of pleasure correlated highly with the number of orgasms she had and with the length of the span of multiple orgasms. But intensity of pleasure did not correlate with other of the subject's perceptions such as how long she felt the orgasms had lasted, how pleased she felt afterward, or how satisfying she had felt the orgasms to be. Among women who experience single orgasms in the laboratory, the researchers found no significant correlations between length of orgasm and its intensity, perceived duration, sexual pleasure after orgasm, or overall satisfaction.

Based on Bohlen, J. G., Held, J. P., Sanderson, M. O., and Boyer, C. M., "Development of a Woman's Multiple Orgasm Pattern: A Research Case Report," *Journal of Sex Research* (1982), 18, pp. 130–145.

others signaled only after the contractions had begun. The women showed three patterns of orgasm: a series of regular contractions; a series of regular contractions followed by a series of irregular contractions; and a series of irregular contractions. Most of the men showed a series of short, regular contractions. Others showed a series of regular contractions followed by irregular contractions; these men perceived their orgasms as lasting longer than the first group perceived theirs to last. One man showed an intermediate type: preliminary contractions followed by regular contractions that began in midorgasm.

BRAIN AND NERVOUS SYSTEM

To look at the physiology of arousal and orgasm, we must look to the nervous system as well as to the genitals. Erection and myotonia, in the male, and blood congestion and myotonia, in the female, follow from the vasocongestion **reflex**. Orgasm in the female and ejaculation in the male follow from the second reflex.

Erection Reflex

Males normally experience erection of the penis when two events take place. First, touching the penis or genital area sends a message to the **sacral** region of the spinal cord. Second, that region communicates through the parasympathetic di-

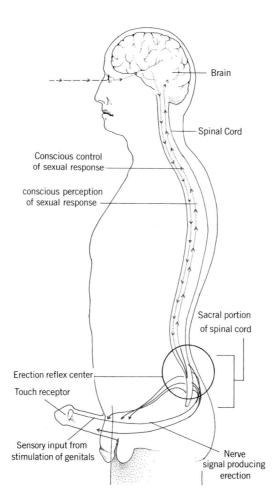

FIGURE 7.10

Nervous system control of erection.

vision of the nervous system to the muscles surrounding the blood vessels of the penis. That message creates the conditions for the arteries to expand and for the amount of blood to the penis to increase. In order to maintain an erection, the parasympathetic nervous system's message compresses certain veins and shuts certain valves so that blood does not leave the engorged penis (see Figure 7.10).

Erections occur under conditions besides the stimulation of touch. Irritation of the part of the nervous system that governs erection can lead to a chronic erection, a condition called **priapism.** (Priapism is named for Priapus, the Greek god of masculine fertility. He was traditionally represented as a grotesque little figure with a huge erect penis.) During the phase of sleep characterized by rapid eye movements (REM sleep), males routinely have erections. They also have erections with sexual fantasies. During these two "no hands" situations, somehow the erection center in the spinal cord receives a message from that master sex organ, the brain. (Females show nocturnal vaginal lubrication during REM sleep [Abel et al., 1979; Fisher et al., 1983].)

Ejaculation Reflex

Above the low, sacral section of the spinal cord with its special center for control of erection is the **lumbar** region of the cord. The lumbar region controls ejacu-

A. Emission stage

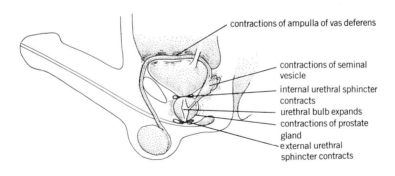

- contractions of ampulla of vas deferens
- contractions of seminal vesicle
- internal urethral sphincter contracts
- urethral bulb expands
- contractions of prostate gland
- external urethral sphincter contracts

B. Expulsion stage

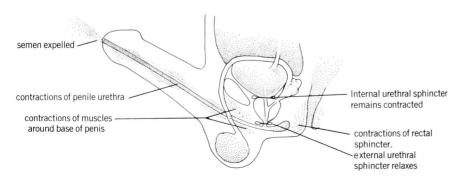

- semen expelled
- contractions of penile urethra
- contractions of muscles around base of penis
- Internal urethral sphincter remains contracted
- contractions of rectal sphincter.
- external urethral sphincter relaxes

FIGURE 7.11

Two stages of ejaculation.

lation. The sympathetic division of the nervous system transmits the message from the spinal cord to the muscles that contract during orgasm and ejaculation.

Spinal Cord Injuries

Spinal injuries more often occur among men in their twenties and thirties than among women. Car and motorcycle accidents, military battles, industrial accidents, and sports are leading causes of spinal injuries in men. Women most often suffer spinal injuries from car accidents, and as they participate increasingly in sports, their rates of spinal injury will in all probability also increase.

People do not lose their sexual feelings or sexual interest with a spinal injury. Yet over one-third of people with spinal injuries give up sexual activity. There are ways around such psychological barriers, and spinal injuries need not mean the end of a person's sexual life. The degree of sexual functioning that remains after a spinal injury depends on the severity of the injury. Thus men with upper motor neuron injuries may have reflex erections, but few ejaculate. Fewer men with lower injuries have erections, although one in seven or eight can ejaculate and experience orgasm. Some men (those with incomplete spinal lesions) can erect, ejaculate, and reach orgasm. Women with upper lesions retain the reflex for vaginal lubrication. Most spine-injured women enjoyed sexual activity before, and continue to enjoy it after, their injury. They remain fertile.

Men and women with spinal injuries must learn to deal with how the apparatus for handling bladder and bowel functions affects their sexual encounters. The first such encounter may be awkward, but couples who communicate well usually grow more comfortable with time. Counseling with the spinally injured typically includes workshops during which explicit sexual materials are used to diminish anxiety and to teach couples a wide range of techniques for sexual interaction. Like other couples, the spinally injured and their partners evolve their own forms of sexual arousal.

FIGURE 7.12

Sexual intercourse for people with spine injuries.

To be alive is to be sexual. It does not matter that a person cannot walk or hear properly, that his speech is slurred, or that her limbs contract involuntarily. People who have disabilities are entitled to sex and the practical information they need to act sexually with or without a partner. The problems the disabled face in leading a sexual life are many. Some are psychological. A person who is disabled from childhood may never have been expected to act sexually and may never have learned how to form the social relationships that turn into sexual relationships. Many people find once they are adults, with normal sexual desire, that they lack the social-sexual skills most people learn during adolescence. Parents of disabled children may feel so overwhelmed with other problems related to their care that they neglect to provide education about sex. They may think of their disabled child as a child forever and in this way avoid the uncomfortable prospects of sexual behavior and social rejection. Parents of disabled children may be much like other parents, too—embarrassed to discuss the mechanics of sex with their own children.

A disability undermines a person's self-confidence. Many are convinced that no one could find them sexually attractive, or that they are boring, or that the very mechanics of sex would turn off any potential partner. People whose disability strikes when they are adults may have had more social-sexual experience, but they, too, may not know how to act on their sexual wishes. The most common assumptions people make about disabled men's sexuality is that they cannot make love normally.

Even many health care professionals have had little or no training in the special sexual problems disabled people face, for the idea that everyone is entitled to a sexual life has been extended to the disabled population only in the last few years. Many professionals believe that the disabled need concrete, specific information about sexual responses. Even if they cannot engage in intercourse, they may be very responsive in other ways with their bodies. They recommend that intercourse not be considered *the* sexual goal. Many sexual pleasures take place outside of actual coitus. When people learn what feels good and how to communicate that, they have learned something extremely important about sexuality. Indeed, some disabled people are happy lovers, because they have been forced by circumstances to experiment and explore.

For Information on Sexuality and Disability

American Association of Sex
Educators, Counselors and Therapists
(AASECT)
5010 Wisconsin Ave., NW,
Suite 304
Washington, D.C. 20016

Sex Information and Education
Council of the United States (SIECUS)
1855 Broadway
New York, NY 10018

Spinal injuries or other disabilities need not prevent sexual thoughts, feelings, and expression.

The spinal-injured young man who is paraplegic may well feel acutely sexual, but the spinal break cuts off the sexual messages between his brain and his genitals. The spinal response to genital touching is erection in men and lubrication in women. In the intact nervous system, this is a two-way communication between brain and genitals. Arousal of the genitals is processed centrally. A sexual fantasy, thought, or image—brain events—usually make one feel genitally aroused. Spinal injuries interrupt this two-way communication between brain and genitals. But the sexual thoughts and fantasies remain intact after a spinal injury and direct what can still be a profound sexuality.

RESPONSES IN REAL LIFE

Real-life sexual encounters may be ecstatic, orgasmic, and romantic, or they may be somewhat less than perfect. Phones do ring, people do feel frightened, and they may fumble awkwardly. Only in movies do technicolor stars sink into perfectly coordinated embraces as violins play and fireworks light up the sky; only in novels does the earth move. Real people must contend with guilt, shame, years of sexual misinformation, inexperience, and discomfort.

The actor Jack Lemmon described his first experience with intercourse in terms unlikely to appear in any marriage manual:

> *The first time I had an affair I was in a parked car in a parking lot in Harvard Square. . . . We're in the seat and I can't get over this shift and I'm trapped and I'm going fucking crazy and I'm sweating and it's just the most uncomfortable goddamned thing you can imagine. Finally, I'm upside-down and my feet go through a rip that's in the goddamned canvas and one of them gets caught. . . . I'm saying, "My foot's caught,"*

and she's saying, "Wow, Oh, Ah" because I'm moving around to try to get my foot out. She thinks I'm terrific, right? I'm just trying to get my stupid foot out. And all of a sudden, a voice and a flashlight in front of us . . . I said to her, "Someone's coming." And she said, "Not yet" . . . and the guy came and shined the light at us and, oh, Christ, it's a wonder I ever did it again (Fleming and Fleming, 1975, p. 138).

Men and women are not born with the knowledge of how to give their partners sexual pleasure or of how to be "good in bed." Sex manuals that describe elaborate props or intricate positions are probably less good at teaching what is really necessary for sexual pleasure than one's own experience and receptiveness are. It takes time and experience to learn how your own body responds, what feels good or not good, what you like and don't like. It takes the same kind of time to learn about someone else's body, and it takes time to learn to trust someone in a situation of naked intimacy. In the matter of sexual response, mind and body act in unison; the psychological house sits squarely on the biological foundation.

SUMMARY

1 Sexual response consists of a series of biological and psychological changes. There are wide individual variations in sexual response according to age, experience, health, learning, mood, and other factors.

2 Masters and Johnson divided the sexual response cycle into four stages. During the excitement stage, the body begins to change in ways that allow for penis and vagina to unite in intercourse. The penis erects, and the vagina lubricates. During the plateau stage, the changes begun during excitement continue. Orgasm may follow the plateau stage if stimulation continues. Orgasm is a set of contractions of the inner and outer genitals plus a psychological change. During the resolution stage, the events of the previous stages are reversed.

3 The refractory period is the time following ejaculation when a male cannot ejaculate again. Women do not have refractory periods. To better understand the subjective elements of sexual arousal, clinicians have defined a desire phase—the earliest stage of sexual arousal, during which a person wants to be aroused—and a satisfaction phase—when positive feelings are associated with the changes characterizing sexual arousal. An absence of desire or satisfaction may be a sign of sexual difficulty.

4 Sexual stimulation increases muscle tension throughout the body and blood congestion in the genital region.

5 In women, sexual stimulation increases respiration, heart rate, and blood pressure. The breasts and nipples congest with blood, a sex flush may spread across the skin, and the external genitals also congest with blood. The vagina lubricates, lengthens, and expands in diameter. The clitoral glans swells, and the shaft increases in diameter. During plateau, the clitoris disappears under the clitoral hood. The increased blood flow to the vagina and labia minora signal the orgasmic platform, from which a woman may move into

orgasm. The uterus increases in size, elevates, and contracts rhythmically during orgasm.

6 An orgasm is an intense release of sexual tension consisting of rhythmic vaginal and uterine contractions. Although it is presently impossible to distinguish "clitoral" from "vaginal" orgasms with instruments, some women can distinguish differences in feelings from stimulation to the two areas. Masters and Johnson believe that all orgasms are essentially the same in physiological terms.

7 The G-spot is reputed to lie on the anterior wall of the vagina and to swell during sexual arousal. It has been proposed that about 10 percent of women are "ejaculators" who experience a special, deep kind of orgasm, involving their especially strong pelvic and uterine muscles, and who ejaculate a large volume of liquid. This view is still controversial.

8 In men, sexual stimulation increases muscle tension, heart and breathing rates, and a sex flush may spread across the skin. The erection of a male's penis is the first observable event in his sexual arousal. Erection is caused when the expandable bodies within the penis fill with blood. Men's nipples erect late in the excitement phase, and the testes elevate and partly rotate. Orgasm consists of regular contractions of the prostate gland, seminal vesicles, vasa deferentia, and urethra.

9 Men's orgasms depend on reflexes for erection and ejaculation. These reflexes in turn depend on communication between parts of the spinal cord, the genitals, and the brain. Less is known about females' orgasms, although they may not be structurally homologous to males' orgasms.

10 The location of a spinal injury will determine whether a man can still erect or ejaculate or whether a woman lubricates. Although many people with spinal injuries give up their sexual life, the loss of sexual desire and function is neither necessary nor inevitable.

11 Generally, when men and women share a physical system that responds to sexual arousal, their responses tend to be similar in form, although not necessarily in duration. Men and women report similar subjective responses to orgasms. After orgasm, however, women are likelier than men to seek close contact with their partner.

KEY TERMS

random (representative) sample
tumescence (detumescence)
sexual response cycle
excitement phase
plateau phase
orgasm
resolution phase
refractory period
attribution
hypoactive sexual desire

autonomic nervous system
carpopedal spasm
areola
sex (macropapular) flush
orgasmic platform
status orgasmus
G-spot
distal urethra
corpus spongiosum
arteriole

desire phase
satisfaction phase
genital responses
extragenital responses
myotonia

reflex
sacral region
priapism
lumbar region

SUGGESTED READINGS

Brecher, R. and Brecher, E. *An Analysis of Human Sexual Response.* New York: New American Library, 1966. A solid presentation of the 1966 Masters and Johnson book for a lay audience.

Graber, B. *Circumvaginal Musculature and Sexual Function.* New York: S. Karger, 1982. For the student with some biological background, this book presents new speculations on musculature, arousal, and orgasm.

AN INTERVIEW WITH SEX RESEARCHER JULIAN DAVIDSON*

Dr. Julian Davidson, a physiological psychologist, is an expert on the relations between hormones and behavior, and the behavior Davidson understood best from his laboratory work was rats' sexual behavior. More recently, Dr. Davidson has worked with humans, too, in an attempt to understand how hormones relate to people's sexual motivation. He has posed tough questions about how hormones affect human consciousness and sexuality. Although some scientists worry that the study of internal experience is problematical, Dr. Davidson believes that such study raises new and interesting questions about behavior.

QUESTION   Can you tell me, Julian, what you're trying to do, in general, in your laboratory?

DAVIDSON   We have programs in animal and human sexual behavior, and one goal is to see how data from the two compare. There is much about biological factors in sexuality that we can learn from rats and it's often well nigh impossible to find out the answers to those questions by experimentation in humans. Can you go from the rat to the human? My conviction that this is so comes from such simple but exciting facts as this: Vastly different species—probably including all the mammals—use testosterone to control the male's copulation. Ultimately, we'd like to understand the neural and hormonal regulation of sexual behavior.

QUESTION   Could you tell me something more specific about what is going on in your laboratory right now?

*Julian Davidson is Professor of Physiology at Stanford University.

DAVIDSON Well, in the rat laboratory we're trying to identify the particular neurotransmitters involved in different components of the male rat's sex behavior. Later we will go on to work on the female. That covers a lot of ground, and various labs have and are contributing in this area. At present we are on the track of picking out two components of behavior in the male rat which seem to be connected respectively to two different receptors in the central nervous system. But it's too early to make definitive statements about which individual behaviors depend on which individual neurotransmitters.

QUESTION How does this relate to humans?

DAVIDSON With animals you can "dissect" both the behavior and the brain to see *what* the effects are and *where* they are processed in the central nervous system. The work depends on the use of drugs that we suspect of having sexual effects. When these effects are identified, we can see if people with sexual dysfunctions are helped by these drugs in any way. It is ethically appropriate to do the early experiments only on animals; and it is clinically appropriate since the animal experiments give us clues about the effects we might expect in humans.

QUESTION What are you studying now on humans?

DAVIDSON In the human lab we have, for instance, a project on hormone replacement therapy in women past menopause. We're trying to find out whether female gonadal hormones or testosterone will correct the changes in female sexuality which many women experience at menopause, and we're trying out a couple of different combinations of these hormones. We're also following the relationship between testosterone and male sexual behavior. Here we continue to look for the behavioral "mechanisms of action" essential to the effects of testosterone on male sexuality. We are looking at previously not well studied, physiologically measurable processes, like the skin's sensory function and the conduction of neural impulses from genitals to the brain of humans.

QUESTION You have had some practical effects, have you not, from your work on hypogonadal males?

DAVIDSON Well, I hope so. I think it might be helpful if medical and psychological people, especially but not only those who specialize in sexual problems, understand that testosterone affects libido and not primarily potency. We know that castrated or testosterone deficient males might have full capacity for erections but view themselves as virtually asexual, because of their lack of drive and interest in sex.

QUESTION How do you relate your interest in conscious experience to your lab research?

DAVIDSON   As a physiologist by training, my goal would be to use physiological assessments and then try to connect them with self report ("subjective") measures. I'm interested in what the body is doing when people feel sexual. From the practical point of view, it helps to gain validation in the biomedical world to have data not just from self report but from numbers that machines can generate. The biomedical community has had a bad history with respect to interest in sexual problems, and such an approach is more likely to get its attention.

QUESTION   Could you tell me something about the things you wish you could tackle in the psychobiology of sexual experience, and whether you're ready to tackle them right now or later?

DAVIDSON   It's extremely hard scientifically to justify statements about body–mind relationships. My original concept was that, instead of looking at links between *behavior* and physiology, we would get people to try hard to describe accurately their *experience* in different conscious states, and we could put that together with the physiology. It seemed to me that could teach us a lot. It is very hard to get scientists (including myself) who work in labs and think reductionistically to deal with conscious experience *as data* without making them feel they're reneging on their basic philosophy as scientists. (Of course, I'm speaking of more than simple perceptions.)

   I think there's a lot to learn from simple physiology–experience correlations. When a person feels X, a set of neurons identified as Y lights up. That doesn't mean that the neurons are causing the feelings. In a sense, it could be the other way around.

QUESTION   Your chapter (in Davidson and Davidson, *The Psychobiology of Consciousness,* 1980) made me think that what you were trying to do was a Huebel and Wiesel on sexual behavior. Just as Huebel and Weisel studied how visual stimulation was reflected in particular brain responses in the cat, you'd like to do that with aspects of sexual behavior.

DAVIDSON   Yes, they were dealing with simple perceptions. Sex is an order of magnitude more complex. We're talking about what goes on inside when a sexual explosion appears outside. It is quite possible, of course, that when we know that, we still won't know much more about the interaction between the physical and the psychological. But intellectually, it is a fascinating task to correlate the different states of consciousness with physiological changes.

QUESTION   How would you get at this?

DAVIDSON   I don't even know the right strategy. The simplest tactic would be when we study sexuality, to collect more detailed information on what people *feel*. We should get them to describe their states of consciousness. Maybe only unusual people can do that. When I talk with people about their sex lives I'm surprised by how hard it is for them to do this. The dysfunctional people can't even compare adequately how they felt before and after their dysfunctions developed.

QUESTION   You surely mean more than just the kinds of descriptions in the Hite reports.

DAVIDSON   Well, the Hite reports say a little of it. A problem is that we can't get people to talk to us during the altered states of consciousness that sexuality represents. Perhaps we're dealing with something like state-dependent learning. [State-dependent learning describes the phenomenon by which something learned in *one* state—for example, one emotional state—can be more readily remembered within that state and may be completely unavailable to memory in another emotional state.] Perhaps, as in state-dependent learning, because you've changed the state you can't describe the feelings. But while having an orgasm, for example, you're not capable of communicating without changing the state. If the right hemisphere is working too hard on the orgasm, communication is impaired. So it's like a double bind.

QUESTION   Well, then, how could you get people to describe it?

DAVIDSON   Well, poets might be able to.

QUESTION   You surely mean more than that. Are there any approaches to the measurement of the subjective correlated with the physiological that you might feel comfortable with?

DAVIDSON   You could start with less intense sexual feelings and move the experiment out of the unnatural laboratory conditions. I'd like to see reporting throughout the day of feelings associated with the spontaneous erections which are fairly frequent, especially in younger people. We have a solid-state ambulatory monitor which could track those physiological events. If at each small erection an audible beep were triggered, the subject could write down immediately what he was thinking and feeling. One could look at mood states and see how they related to spontaneous sexual imagery under conditions of spontaneous physiologic arousal. This would be just a beginning, of course. It won't solve the mind-body problem, but it would be an interesting start.

QUESTION   Is there any work going on right now that looks like a positive approach to you?

DAVIDSON   Martha McClintock's lab is doing a beeper study related to mood in women throughout the menstrual cycle. On a very different tack, Benjamin Libet at the University of California at San Francisco has been working on how long it takes for neural processing of a stimulus to reach conscious perception. But he's dealing only with a flash of light or a sound. You see again that the perceptual things are doable, but this is an early essential part of a future physiology of consciousness. You don't have a problem of language there such as you would have in sex research, and you are dealing with very short times—milliseconds—but it is an important beginning.

QUESTION   Do you see some important things that are going to be found out about neurotransmitters in sex?

DAVIDSON   I think we will soon see specifically the different neurotransmitters involved in sexual function and the specific areas of the nervous system involved. Ultimately, that should lead to a new way of treating sexual dysfunction, what I like to call "neurotransmitter replacement therapy." If so, I hope neurotransmitters will never be used without simultaneous, adequate counseling. Drugs alone should not be used for sexual therapy.

QUESTION   Could you tell me a little bit about your life and how you came to this field of study?

DAVIDSON   I was born in Dublin, Ireland, but moved to Scotland when I was three and grew up in Glasgow. I got out of high school early and became an agricultural worker in England and in Israel on a kibbutz. Subsequently I studied agriculture at Hebrew University. After only a short bout of graduate work at the University of California, I found that my real interest was in physiology. Only later in life did I rediscover that it was in psychology. I've always been a psychologist, in the closet however, and I never took a psychology course for credit, but I'm not proud of that. My doctoral research and first postdoctoral (with C. H. Sawyer at UCLA) were on neuroendocrine physiology, but after another back and forth to Israel, I went to work with Frank Beach to see where testosterone acted on the brain to stimulate sex "drive." There I learned how to measure and evaluate rat sexual behavior; I've been doing it ever since. That was my way into psychology, by way of neuroendocrine training. I've changed the orientation of my career each decade since I began in the late 1940's, and the latest got me into working seriously with human subjects. I've been exhausted ever since trying to cope with the unending problems of assembling usable data from the world's worst experimental animals, but it's been fascinating all the time.

Chapter 8

Sexual Motives and Sexual Acts

SEXUAL MOTIVES

A few years ago, a 9-year-old boy and his 18-year-old sister were talking with an older friend. The 18-year-old was a college freshman home on a visit. She reminisced with amusement about the sex education films she'd seen in fifth grade. "Oh," she said, "It was all about menstruation and sanitary napkins and reproduction. But the juiciest part for us was when they told us how sex begins when a boy puts his tongue in your mouth."

"Yuk," said the 9-year-old. "That's disgusting. Why would anyone want to do that?" We all laughed. But he had asked a truly important question: why *do* we want to do sexual things? When psychologists ask college students that question, they find that people give varied answers and that men and women do not choose the same reasons in the same proportions. Women are more likely to choose love and attraction as their reasons, while men are more likely to want to experience what other men have experienced. Yet those answers are very different

Why *do* we want to do sexual things?

from the informal ones people give: "I'm so horny," or "When I haven't had sex for a long time, I just need it," or "I'm an English major and can't read a novel without getting turned on." (And these reasons are not exactly like those that researchers on love and attraction ferret out; see Chapter 13.) In this chapter, we will describe sexual motivation—drives and incentives—and the sexual behavior that we are motivated to learn and perform. For human beings to survive as a species, many of us must somehow be brought to the act of sexual intercourse. How do internal drives move the individual toward sexual behavior? How does the solitary, naive sexuality of childhood turn into the sophisticated, social sexuality of adulthood?

Biological Mechanisms

What happens when someone is aroused but performs no sexual act? What happens when someone is deprived of sex for a long time? What happens when a movie or novel turns on its audience but in the absence of any explicitly sexual events? In all of these cases, the people hanker, but they do not die. Other physiological drives are less benign. If we are kept hungry, in time we die. If we are kept thirsty or deprived of sleep for long enough, we die. But no one dies for lack of sex. Priests, nuns, followers of Gandhi, ascetics, and modern-day celibates often choose to redirect the energy that others put into sexual behavior. If there is a sexual drive, it is not altogether like other physiological drives.

Physiological psychologists tell us that our nervous systems, our hormones, and our genitals interact to keep us sexually motivated and active. When humans are **sexually motivated**, it means that they *will arrange their environments so that they can approach erotic stimuli or create them in fantasy.* We infer the motivation from what people do and say. An animal "tells" us how sexually motivated it is by how much effort it will expend or how many barriers it will cross to approach a sexually receptive animal of the other sex. Because ethics limit the experiments on human sexual motivation, we often turn to animals to study the physiology of sexual motivation. Of course, rats, guinea pigs, and monkeys perform sexual acts, but they cannot tell us how they feel. Thus information from experiments on animals suggests possibilities for mechanisms in human sexual motivation and behavior. Because no two species are completely biologically alike, and because consciousness plays a large part in human sexual behavior, psychologists expect similarities *and* differences in comparisons between humans and animals. The similarities tell us about our heritage as mammals; the differences tell us about our heritage as humans.

How Hormones Activate Sexual Behavior   Sexual motivation in humans is a product of both biological and psychological factors. One class of chemicals, the hormones, seems very influential in tuning the speed and degree of biological responses to erotic stimuli. A hormone, you will recall, is a chemical produced by the endocrine system and released directly into the bloodstream. It is tempting to think that sexual arousal resides in the genitals, but hormones have very powerful effects on the sex-related systems of the brain. Hormones not only organize biological events like the differentiation of the sexes before birth, but they also activate and maintain adult sexual function.

Only some parts of the endocrine system are thought to be relevant to sexual motives and acts (see Figure 8.1). The brain controls the entire endocrine system

FIGURE 8.1

Endocrine system. Shown here is a composite of the endocrine glands of both males and females.

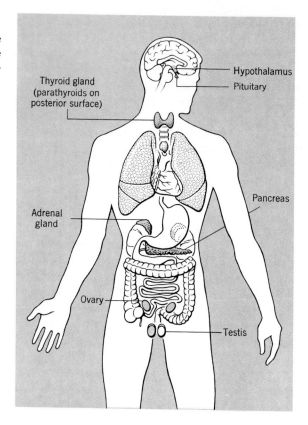

through the hypothalamus. The hypothalamus produces special neurohormones, called **releasing hormones,** which are directed to the pituitary gland. This organ, suspended from the hypothalamus, produces a set of hormones known as **gonadotropins.** As the name implies, these hormones stimulate the gonads (testes or ovaries) to produce and secrete their own hormones—called **gonadal hormones**—as well as to produce or to ready the sex cells. It may be that all of these classes of hormones play direct roles in sexual motivation, but most work has concentrated on the role of the gonadal hormones.

The gonadal hormones are **steroid hormones,** relatively small molecules with similar structures. (You may have heard of steroids in another context: some athletes take steroids for muscle-building.) Steroids are secreted by the testes (male) and ovaries (female) and also by the adrenal glands (both sexes). The steroids that influence sexual behavior are the androgens, estrogens, and progesterone. The most powerful androgen is **testosterone,** the most powerful estrogen **estradiol.** Both sexes have androgens and estrogens, but the ratio of androgens to other hormones is higher in males than females and the ratio of estrogens to other hormones higher in females than males. The roles of testosterone and estrogen are probably more complex than investigators once believed. You may have heard that androgen (or testosterone) is the "male hormone" and estrogen is the "female hormone," but this distinction is not valid. Testosterone is changed into other steroids in many places in the body. Two of these hormones, dihydrotestosterone (an androgen) and estradiol (a powerful estrogen), may act in combination to stimulate sexual behavior. Thus testosterone may have to be broken down into other compounds to produce its effects, just as table sugar (sucrose) must be broken down into simpler sugars (glucose and fructose) before the body can use it. Estrogen, likewise, is now thought to be the hormone created from testosterone in the brain of the male fetus. It programs his body *not* to cycle at puberty. (For more on this organizing role of hormones before birth, refer to Chapter 3.)

Research shows that some steroid hormones can alter humans' sensory thresholds. A **sensory threshold** is the lowest level of physical stimulus to which an individual responds. Many women's scent thresholds are lower during midmenstrual cycle, for example, when they may respond to smaller amounts of scents than at other times during the menstrual cycle (Parlee, 1983). When estrogen is at its height during the menstrual cycle, a woman may be sensitive to touch over a wider area of her genitals and thighs than at other times. Research shows, too, that androgens probably increase genital sensitivity. Thus hormones may contribute to human sexual interest either in the readier perception of erotic stimuli or in the increased probability of physical responses to them (Diamond et al., 1972; Levine, 1971; Money, 1961).

Scientists know more about what activates a rat's sexual behavior than a human being's. Rats are easier to experiment on, and no one requires a rat's approval for tinkering with its blood chemistry. Experiments show that androgens stimulate sexual behavior in male rats; estrogens and progesterone in females. For example, female rats not only passively attract and receive their male suitors, but they also actively solicit them. Female rats hop, dart, and wiggle their ears. They give off odorous chemicals (reflecting their hormonal state) that attract males. These chemicals, or **pheromones,** are olfactory stimuli that convey specific messages between animals of the same species. (See "Sexuality in Research: Pheromones.") To court actively, females apparently require a certain level of the hormone progesterone in their bloodstream (Tennent, Smith, and Davidson, 1980). If one removes the testes of mature males or the ovaries of mature female rats, their sexual behavior declines and eventually stops. The females stop cycling in and out of estrus; they

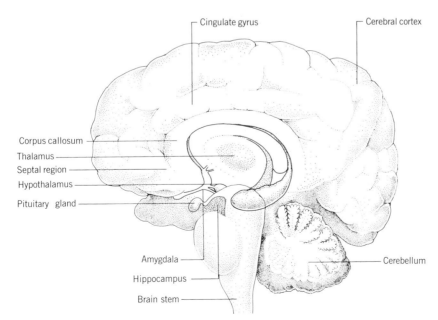

FIGURE 8.2

Limbic system of human brain.

stop attracting or accepting males; and males show no sexual interest even in receptive females. Injection of the proper hormones restores their sexual behavior by acting on the brain. Scientists also can increase aspects of sexual behavior in rats by creating lesions in certain areas of the brain. A lesion to the male's midbrain shortens the refractory period after ejaculation. A lesion to the female's septum, an area of the forebrain, makes her more than usually receptive to males. Males with such lesions mate better than others (Nance, Shryne, and Gorski, 1974). Electrical stimulation to one human male's septum and to limbic areas in one human female produced tumescence of the penis and clitoris, respectively, in two clinical cases (Heath, 1972).

SEXUALITY IN RESEARCH: PHEROMONES

It has been suggested that pheromones, the olfactory stimuli that carry specific messages between members of a species, are another kind of primary erotic stimulus. Some pheromones advertise a female's state of fertility, and some species, like the mouse and hamster, apparently cannot breed without these signals. Rhesus monkeys may have a sexual pheromone system. Vaginal secretions during the fertile period of the rhesus female contain odorous chemicals that direct the sexual activities of males (Michael and Keverne, 1968). Do human females produce pheromones? They do have some of the same chemicals in their vaginal secretions that are pheromones for rhesus monkeys, but there is currently no evidence that these chemicals actually affect human sexual behavior. Some theorists have proposed that humans do have sexual pheromones and that hair under the arms and pubic hair radiate them (Doty et al., 1975; Michael et al., 1974; Sokolov et al., 1976). We know that vaginally secreted substances that function as pheromones in rhesus monkeys are also secreted cyclically by women. Men's ratings of the pleasantness and intensity of vaginal secretions seem to correlate with the volatile fatty acid secretions in women, but that information does not establish that these secretions are human pheromones. There is no evidence that they act as sexual signals. Possibly, the chemicals in vaginal secretions are pheromones that affect sexual motivation indirectly. It has been found, for example, that the menstrual cycles of women living together in college dormitories tend to synchronize, perhaps by odor cues (McClintock, 1971).

We do know, however, that in human beings, hair in the armpits and genitals effectively traps the odorous solids produced by nearby sweat glands. Even though we Americans (to the amusement of people from some other cultures) wash, perfume, and deodorize our bodies, we still produce odorous sexual signals. The aftershave lotions, colognes, and fragrant soaps that we use are themselves sensual communicators. Although the question of whether humans produce pheromones remains unanswered, we know that as a species we respond sexually to other kinds of olfactory stimuli.

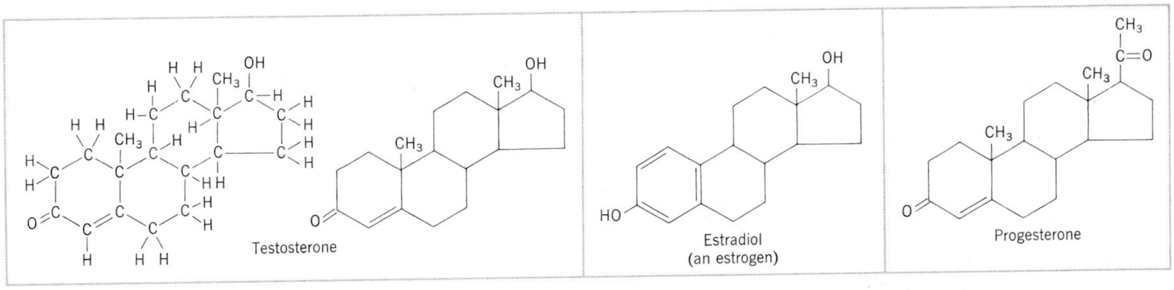

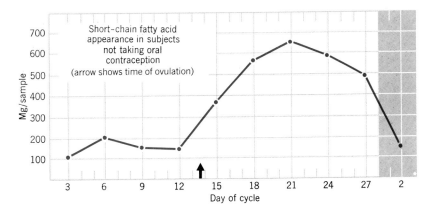

CH₃ structures — Testosterone, Estradiol (an estrogen), Progesterone

FIGURE 8.3

Structures of steroid hormones. Here *C* shows a carbon atom, *O* oxygen, and *H* hydrogen. (Most of the hydrogen atoms are omitted from all but the left-hand drawing as are the carbon atoms at the intersections of the bond lines.) These structurally similar hormones often turn into other steroid forms in the body. Progesterone becomes testosterone; testosterone becomes estrogen.

FIGURE 8.4

Pheromones and the human menstrual cycle. Top graph shows subjects' ratings of intensity and pleasantness of the odor of vaginal secretions from menstruation (phase 1), to ovulation (phase 3), to end of cycle (phase 5). Secretions were least intense and most pleasant around ovulation (from Doty et al., 1975). Bottom graph shows amounts of fatty acids in vaginal secretions across menstrual cycle (arrow = ovulation) (from Sokolov et al., 1976). Fatty acids act as pheromones in some primates.

Animals can also be turned off sexually by brain manipulation. By administering a lesion to a part of the hypothalamus called the medial preoptic area (MPO), scientists can prevent cats, rats, dogs, and rhesus macaques from copulating (Slimp, Hart, and Goy, 1978). Males with such lesions can get reflex erections and even masturbate, but they cannot carry out social sex. Females with lesions in the anterior hypothalamic-ventromedial region (AHVM) show no sexual behavior at all (Singer, 1968). In general, brain and hormone systems are closely interrelated (Naftalin and Butz, 1981).

HUMAN MALES   What about humans? The story of the human male's hormones is easier to tell than the story of the human female. Men need a blood level of testosterone within a certain range to maintain sexual interest and the ability to erect. (Men with 2 nanograms per milliliter or less of plasma testosterone show virtually no sexual interest.) But once above that range, there is no evidence that more testosterone produces greater sexual interest or activity (Brown, Monti, and Corriveau, 1978; Kraemer et al., 1976; Pirke, 1982; Pirke et al., 1974; Salminies et al., 1982). Below that range, men profit from exogenous (from an external source) testosterone. Men with underdeveloped (or "hypogonadal") testes rarely have spontaneous erections during sleep, masturbation, or coitus. But if they receive testosterone, their sexual interest and erections increase (Davidson, Camargo, and Smith, 1979; see also Figure 8.5). Older men whose free testosterone levels decrease (along with other hormones) show decreased erections during sleep and decreased sexual activity, but they still have an interest in and think about sex with pleasure (Davidson et al., in press). These changes in aging men are not the products of disease. Testosterone is clearly important to men's sexual arousal. Knowing this, endocrinologists look at a man's levels of blood testosterone and hormones that interact with testosterone when arousal or erections are impaired. Sexually experienced men who have been castrated to control cancer may function sexually for more than a year after their testes are removed. Sexually inexperienced

FIGURE 8.5

Androgen and sexual behavior in hypogonadal men. This graph shows how testosterone affected the frequencies of erections, attempts at coitus (successful and unsuccessful), masturbation, and orgasms in a group of hypogonadal males (Davidson, Camargo, and Smith, 1979).

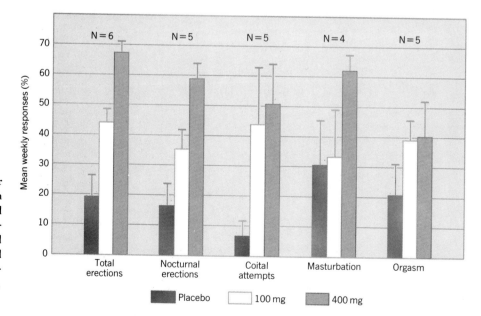

men, however, do not function sexually after their testes are removed. Similar results are found in many animals. When they are castrated, they lose their sexual function over varying periods of time, depending on the species (Hart, 1974). When they are given androgens, their sexual function returns. Thus testosterone is important in determining sexual behavior, but so is experience.

Men's testosterone levels seem to cycle rhythmically every 24 hours or so, with the highest levels early in the morning and the lowest at night. Do men's levels of sexual interest follow the same pattern? Not necessarily. Although men frequently have erections in the morning, sexual activity in the United States is highest at night (Kinsey et al., 1948). In short, sexual motivation in men may sometimes follow the daily testosterone peak, but it can easily be overcome by cultural and social factors.

The curve depicting testosterone levels over the life cycle seems to have many correlates in sexual behavior and feelings. Figure 8.6 shows the ascending side of this curve for boys at puberty. The flood of sexual feelings in boys between the ages of 12 and 16 is accompanied by—and probably in part caused by—more than a fivefold increase in testosterone levels. But sexual behavior and fantasies vary widely. Testosterone may fire up the sexual machinery, but experience and perhaps other biological factors determine its expression.

Individual men's testosterone levels vary from day to day. But men are not more likely to have sex on days when their androgen levels are high. Helena Kraemer (1976) and her colleagues at Stanford University Medical School found no significant difference in testosterone levels in the 24 hours preceding orgasm than in those that did not precede orgasm. Furthermore, testosterone levels went up *after* orgasm. Another study answers whether the drops in androgen levels, which are produced by psychological or physical stress, diminish sexual interest. Testosterone levels from male soldiers in officer training school were taken. The first weeks of the training were stressful, and testosterone levels were low. The later weeks were more rewarding, and androgen levels rose. The men's sexual interest and activity followed a similar pattern: low at the beginning of training and high at the end (Kreus, Rose, and Jennings, 1972). We do not know, however, whether the change in sexual interest relates directly to the testosterone levels or to the degree of stress.

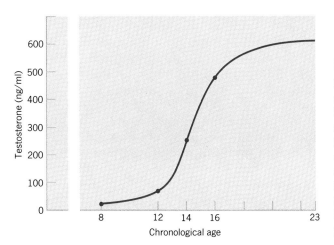

FIGURE 8.6

Fantasy and erection. The amount of testosterone in males' bloodstreams begins to increase at puberty. Puberty increases the incidence of nocturnal emissions, masturbation, and sexual fantasies (from F. W. Beach, in *Reproductive Behavior,* ed. W. Montagna and W. A. Sadler, New York: Plenum, 1974, p. 339).

HUMAN FEMALES   What about women's sexual arousal and excitement? The story is far from clear. Unlike the receptive female rat who is receptive only during the period of estrus, human females are receptive throughout their menstrual cycles. During the monthly cycle, levels of estrogen and progesterone vary considerably, but levels of androgen vary little and peak at about midcycle. It was once thought that women's sexual motivation increased during the first part of the cycle, peaked at midcycle and **ovulation,** and then fell during the latter part of the cycle (the **luteal phase**), and rose again at the end of the cycle (Udry and Morris, 1968). But by analyzing the same data with less questionable averaging techniques, one scientist concluded that most of the fluctuations in intercourse rates over the cycle could be explained in terms of abstinence around the menstrual period (James, 1971). Part of the difficulty in characterizing when females seek intercourse is that the human menstrual cycle is not very regular. Although conventionally the cycle is described as a regular 28 days long, only half of all women at the most are that regular (Kolodny and Bauman, 1979; Udry and Morris, 1977).

The search for the hormones associated with female arousal and pleasure continues. One research group has data suggesting that plasma androgen level (actually three different forms of androgen) is related to women's ability to feel sexual pleasure (Persky et al., 1979). Women who have lost their ovaries to surgery may contribute some answers. Sexual desire does *not* decline in women whose ovaries (and thereby, most of their estrogen, progesterone, and a small amount of their androgen) have been removed. When women's adrenal glands (which produce most of a woman's androgen) are surgically removed, however, sexual motivation typically plummets. But such surgery is usually a desperate attempt to stop a spreading cancer, and the depression women feel under those circumstances does not bode well for sexual motivation or its measurement. The perfect study of hormones and women's sexual motivation will take actual readings of hormone levels (multiple androgens as well as estrogen) and not estimates and will note whether women or men initiated coitus.

When nonhuman primate females are studied, other answers to questions about primate sexual motivation arise. Scientists find that removing the ovaries and adrenals of stumptail macaques does *not* curtail their active or receptive sexual behavior (Baum et al., 1978). But removing the ovaries and adrenals of another species, rhesus macaques, *does* curtail their sexual behavior. These studies tell us that at least one primate species exists in which female sexual behavior does not require the hormones that female rats require and that androgen is probably not the hormone for arousal in that primate species. But that is not true for all macaques. Only further studies will tell whether the female stumptail macaque's sexual behavior and motivation have more in common with the biological mechanisms in human females' motivation than that of the rhesus macaque. No data on hormones or behavior of our closer cousins, the female apes, exist to help us decide what to look for in the human female. Perhaps the human female's sexuality is less tied to hormones than the human male's and is more readily affected by learning and by aspects of the situation. But we do not know for sure yet: the mystery of how hormones affect the human female's behavior is yet to be solved.

NEUROTRANSMITTERS: THE NEXT SEXUAL FRONTIER?   The hormones, whose pervasive role in sexual function and behavior we have just described, are not the only messengers among cells of the body. Within the nervous system, chemicals called **neurotransmitters** carry signals between neurons and modulate the intensity of responses to such signals. Little is known yet about the specific roles of neurotransmitters such as dopamine, serotonin, or norepinephrine in human sexual response and behavior. Neurophysiologists surmise that such roles must exist, but the details remain to be clarified (Floyd Bloom, personal communication). Animal work has already begun.

A peculiar group of neurotransmitters, most likely to turn out to be involved in sexual behavior, is the "pleasure substances." This group includes endorphins and enkephalins, substances produced within the body. When minute amounts are injected into a rat or other mammal, they seem to cause acute pleasure and insensitivity to pain. Because pleasure and its anticipation are inseparable components of sexual experience, especially in humans, it would be surprising if the pleasure substances were not significantly involved in sexual activity. Many researchers are studying how this system might work.

EROTIC STIMULI   People learn about sexual motivation as they learn which stimuli arouse them. One person sees that stroking his penis makes it erect; one person sees that rubbing her vulva makes her nipples erect; another person feels distinctly aroused by pictures of nudes, or by women's shoes, or by thoughts of lovemaking. The number of erotic stimuli among adults is enormous, but all of them probably derive from a few basic erotic stimuli.

Lovely legs and behinds, faces and chests are all secondary erotic stimuli, the major determinants of adults' sexual motivation.

All humans have wired into them at birth pleasurable responses to gentle stroking of the genitals. No learning is needed for that. (In some repressive cultures, people learn *not* to notice such arousal or to label it as not sexual.) Thus the sensuality of human infants tells us that some stimuli may lead to sexual arousal without any prior experience or learning. We call these **primary erotic stimuli.** Light touch on any body surface (except those that are specially protected, like the corneas of the eyes), and particularly on the genitals, seems to be a primary erotic stimulus. In adolescence, people grow more sensitive to primary erotic stimuli. For example, in girls the increase in estrogen extends the receptive field of the nerve or nerves serving her genitals and thighs. This increases the range of her possible response.

In adults, a primary erotic stimulus—a light touch to the genitals, say—may lead to arousal, but it may also lead to revulsion, anxiety, or fear. The response depends on what the person being touched has learned about the source of the stimulation or the surrounding conditions. An American man probably does not respond sexually to a light touch from a female who also happens to be his mother. He has probably learned that feeling sexual arousal from this source of stimulation is not proper, and the bodily changes of arousal (and, therefore, sexual motivation) are inhibited by his brain. Learning, in short, can restrict erotic stimuli.

Secondary erotic stimuli are learned or conditioned, and they are the major determinants of sexual motivation in human adults. Primary erotic stimuli no longer are the sole influences on sexual motivation in adults; the light touch is transformed into more complex, secondary stimuli. It becomes the touch of a lover, of a parent, of a child, of an animal. The conditioning process by which things or events become secondary erotic stimuli can either *constrict* or *expand* erotic stimuli. The man who does not find his mother's touch sexually arousing has constricted the primary stimulus; the person who is sexually aroused by physical pain has expanded the primary stimulus. Secondary erotic stimuli largely determine adults' choices of sexual partners or objects. When we explore whether we are sexually compatible with someone or when we decide that a sexual partner cannot share our fantasies, we are actually assessing the fit between our own and our partner's responses to secondary erotic stimuli.

Humans have a striking capacity to choose and create the stimuli that are erotic, although each person develops a relatively restricted set. Our brains are our organs of fantasy, capable of introducing variety when it is needed for arousal or for dampening arousal when we might otherwise feel overwhelmed. The human ability to represent secondary erotic stimuli in fantasy has an enormous influence on the nature of human sexual motivation. Fantasy allows humans to manufacture at will the erotic stimuli that may in reality appear rarely or not at all. The human ability to fantasize may even contribute to a feature of sexual behavior that is uniquely human: the potential for sexual motivation in both sexes at any time in the female's cycle of fertility. The fruitful human imagination can conjure up exciting, erotic images. We go to great lengths to find commercial forms of sexual fantasy. Alone or in company, humans can imagine their way to intense sexual excitement.

Fantasy helps people of both sexes to play their sexuality to themselves in free, interesting, internal "home movies." Some of Woody Allen's movies (*Everything You Always Wanted to Know about Sex* and *Love and Death,* for example) are composites of such fantasies and inventions. In one such sequence, the great lover is Woody, and he explains to an aristocratic woman who praises his sexual technique,

TABLE 8.1
Common Sexual Fantasies

Listed in Order of Decreasing Frequency:

Heterosexual Men:

1. Replacement of established partner
2. Forced sex with a woman
3. Watching sexual activity
4. Sexual encounters with men
5. Group sex

Heterosexual Women

1. Replacement of established partner
2. Forced sex with a man
3. Observing sexual activity
4. Idyllic encounters with unknown men
5. Sexual encounters with women

Homosexual Men

1. Images of male anatomy
2. Forced sex with men
3. Sexual encounters with women
4. Idyllic encounters with unknown men
5. Group sex

Homosexual Women

1. Forced sexual encounters with women
2. Idyllic encounters with established partner
3. Sexual encounters with men
4. Memories of past sexual experiences
5. Sadistic imagery

Source: Coleman, D. Sexual fantasies: what are their hidden meanings? *New York Times,* Feb. 28, 1984, pp. C1 ff. (Based on Schwartz and Masters, 1984).

A study of 120 men and women, half calling themselves heterosexual and half homosexual, shows that fantasies are not necessarily congruent with actual sexual behavior or orientation.

"I practice a lot when I'm alone." So do people in other cultures, and so do members of other species (Ford and Beach, 1951). When David Barlow (Goleman, 1984) asked adults to monitor their sexual fantasies every day for several weeks, he found that the frequency ranged from 0 to over 40 fantasies a day, with most people having 7 or 8 a day. Most heterosexuals, he found, fantasize about "normal" sexual acts, and about one-quarter fantasize about variations such as homosexuality, group sex, sadomasochism, and the like. The survey of 120 men and women, half homosexual and half heterosexual, showed a similar variety in people's fantasies (Schwartz and Masters, 1984).

Humans find a large variety of apparently nonsexual stimuli erotic. It is easy to understand how the sight of genitals could evolve by natural selection to be erotic. But when a high-heeled shoe or a softly whispered word or a bar of music become erotic stimuli, it is likely that learning has taken place. The human capacity to learn, to symbolize, and to fantasize is itself a product of natural selection, and it takes humans far from the few biologically driven stimuli. But we should not entirely disregard biological contributions to human sexual motivation. Some writers have assumed that since sex has transcended purely reproductive purposes for the human, then human sexuality has transcended the biological foundations that are apparent in lower animals. Although many sexual encounters clearly are urged by nonsexual feelings, we must conclude that our biological programming for sexual behavior is still operating. Sexual behaviors are pleasurable and necessary for the survival of our species. Our genetic programming has ensured survival by making sexual behavior pleasurable. All other functions of human sexual behavior derive from that basic reproductive function and the biological mechanisms that have secured it. (These biological mechanisms include turning on as well as turning off. Reducing sexual motivation is important for survival, because a copulating animal is vulnerable. It cannot defend itself, find food, water, or shelter.)

SEXUALITY IN PERSPECTIVE:
SEXUAL FANTASY

Sexual fantasy is not reality. Indeed, many people would not want their sexual fantasies to come true. But their fantasies are nonetheless arousing. Although there are themes common to certain fantasies—being forced to have sex, quick and anonymous sex with a stranger, sex in exotic and alluring settings, and others—each of us embroiders our sexual fantasies to suit our own private erotic tastes. Below are a few sexual fantasies reported by college students.

Heterosexual male:

Lisa is gorgeous and really well built. One day at work, I am downstairs in the basement putting something away in the dressing room, when Lisa comes in. She has to change into her uniform before she goes to work. I start to leave, but she tells me to stay. She closes the door and slips off her dress. She comes over to me. By now I'm pretty nervous, but I turn to face her, and she puts her arms around me and kisses me. The next thing I know, she is taking my shirt off and working her way to my pants. Meanwhile I have taken off her bra and I'm just about to take off her panties. Her breasts are soft and sensual, and I start to caress them and suck on them. Now we are both naked, and she pushes me to the floor. She sits on my stomach and strokes my chest. Her breasts hang over my face. I fondle her breasts and buttocks. She slides down on me and begins to stroke my penis. Then she sucks on it and kisses me. She straddles me and guides my penis inside of her. She rocks back and forth, and I stroke and caress her stomach and breasts. All of a sudden, we start to rock and sway in unison. She gasps and moans and then stiffens slightly, and as she reaches orgasm, I come inside of her.

Homosexual male:

I sit on a ledge, looking out over the city. It's a sunny day, and the sunlight warms my body. A friend of mine appears in the picture. He is fair, not particularly athletic, just a bit on the frail side. I know him, and he knows me. One might ask whether one would die for the other, so close is our friendship. But he does not know about my . . . preference. I have decided to tell him this day, and I do, although such a fear (of rejection? loss?) runs through me that I actually begin to tremble. Will I lose him?

No. He accepts—and returns my feeling. I collapse against the wall, not knowing what to say, what to do. He moves closer, and I can feel his warmth through our clothes. My erection begins, and now we are touching. I can feel his erection. I place my arms awkwardly around his neck; he places his around my waist, and we kiss. It is strange at first. I fall back on the bed (out of nowhere, it seems), pulling him down over me. We kiss and neck. Shyly, we undress each other, smiling through the tension, absorbed in what we are doing. Now we are totally naked and quietly (only the sound of our breathing and moaning) go under the blankets. I masturbate him, and he returns the favor. Then he penetrates me, and at the same time, he masturbates me again, this time to orgasm, and he comes also.

We fall asleep. I'm cradling and being cradled by him in the bed as we watch the sunlight.

Heterosexual female:

My sexual fantasy is always, well usually, a very romantic one where the lights are very low, there is soft music being played, and the lovemaking takes a very long time: slowly undressing each other and then a lot of caressing, and kissing, and face-touching. Often a fire is burning in the fireplace. It is always a warm, wonderful experience.

Bisexual female:

Me and another woman—after eating sauteed shrimp and lobster in butter sauce with lots of wine to drink and music on the tape player. Both of us relax on a down comforter that has a satin cover. Each of us is in a silk camisole and loose panties. Giving each other massages, caressing, and kissing her neck ever so slowly, not missing a single spot. She gently bites my nipples as her hand finds its way to my vagina and starts to rub my clitoris. It seems to go on forever and starts to drive me crazy. I can't control myself any longer. Pushing her away, I start to lick her pussy, tasting her sweet juices. She comes in a fit of passion.

Sexual fantasies, whether privately imagined or shared with a lover, help to move us towards sexual arousal—and satisfaction.

Source: courtesy of Valerie Pinhas.

Sexual Motivation: An Incentive Theory

Sexual motivation is a drive, but it is a different sort of drive from hunger. In the case of hunger, the body continually burns up the food we eat to provide us with the fuel for life. Therefore we have ever-operating internal mechanisms to guide our behavior and to motivate us to eat. Monkeys and apes in the wild spend nearly all of their time searching for food. But sexual motivation seems provoked by an external stimulus, given an ability to respond to the stimulus. When motivation is inspired by an external stimulus rather than by internal states of need, it is known as **incentive motivation.** Sexual motivation largely fits that definition. (Hunger fits that definition, too, for those of us who cannot resist lovely looking food with its enticing odors, even if we've just eaten.)

In sexual motivation, certain external stimuli, as we have seen, have the power to arouse us, to guide our behavior, to produce sexual responses. Sexual responses can be both the results of contact with erotic stimuli and erotic stimuli themselves. For example, a woman who is sexually aroused will find her vagina getting wet, and in the Pacific Mangaian culture, the wet noises her body makes during sexual intercourse are considered especially arousing. They arouse the woman and her partner still further. One erotic stimulus, wetness, is enhanced by another, "wet" noises, in an escalation of arousal called a **positive feedback system.**

Positive feedback keeps people ever more motivated through the successive stages of arousal. But if arousal continued to build, people would be overwhelmed. The system needs brakes, a stopping point, and it has this in orgasm. With orgasm, the brain reverses arousal: blood vessels and muscles and internal organs revert to their unaroused state. Orgasm tends to return males to their unaroused state more forcefully than it does females, who often remain aroused (and vasocongested) after orgasm. With orgasm(s), the brain's electrical activity changes, further sexual stimulation is no longer pleasurable, and sexual motivation is low. What happens if no orgasm brakes the arousal? If there is no further stimulation, arousal will diminish, especially if fatigue or discomfort intervene. Really disruptive external stimuli—like the proverbial cold shower—as well as unpleasant feelings—like anger or anxiety—also reverse vasocongestion. Said one woman who had failed to climax, "I feel extremely frustrated. I'm almost doubled over in pain and I'm furious and would like to kill my partner" (Hite, 1976).

SEXUAL AROUSAL, ANGER, AND fear can do similar things to the human body.

Interpreting Body States

Suppose that a sophomore described how he felt: "My heart was pounding like a hammer, my cheeks felt hot, and my palms were soaked. As I stared at her, I felt a tightening in my gut." Does that sound like a young man with a crush? Certainly. But it also sounds like a furious young man, an anxious young man, or a frightened young man. Sexual arousal, anger, and fear can do similar things to the human body. As we saw in the previous chapter, social psychologists tell us that how people interpret these body changes can determine their motivation and feelings (Jones et al., 1975; Schachter and Singer, 1962). Because many of the body changes that occur during sexual arousal can be produced by nonerotic stimuli, people can be fooled into interpreting their responses as sexual arousal. This phenomenon is called **misattribution** or **mislabeling.**

Mislabeling can help to explain some puzzling questions about human sexual motivation. Why do some people find physical pain sexually arousing? Why do some men need a jolt of fear to perform sexually? Why is sex after an argument so satisfying? The answer to these questions may be that sexual motivation is heightened when the bodily arousal produced by nonsexual stimuli is (mis)labeled sexual arousal. Mislabeling may also explain chronically high and low levels of sexual motivation. People with very strong sexual motivation may mislabel internal and external events as sexual, and people with low sexual motivation may ignore their cues of arousal. In fact, the first stage in treating many sexual problems is to teach people to recognize their sexual arousal.

Mislabeling also may help to explain why some people find sex with a familiar partner less exciting than sex with a new partner. Meeting someone new tends to increase the level of physical arousal, especially among males. Women in our culture seem less susceptible to this kind of arousal (Kinsey et al., 1953), but this sex difference may be learned. Even male rats have shorter refractory periods following orgasm when new females are introduced into the mating arena, a phenomenon called the **Coolidge effect** (Bermant and Davidson, 1974).[1] New work by David Barlow (1984) and his colleagues at the State University of New York at Albany suggests that some kinds of anxiety heighten arousal. Similarly, Frank Beach discovered that when male rats were unresponsive to receptive females, shaking their cages aroused them just enough to move them toward the females (Julian Davidson, personal communication, 1984).

Learning to Be Sexual: A Socially Determined Developmental Sequence

The nine-year-old boy who responds to a description of French kissing with a heartfelt "Yuk," like most boys his age, has not learned how to respond erotically to kissing. A kiss does not shape his behavior toward a sexual act. Quite the opposite, in fact, for a kiss from a girl is likely to send him scurrying. How do people come to respond erotically to external sexual stimuli? When does this learning take place, and what do the "lessons" consist of? We will answer these questions in detail. In the meantime, the short answers are: people learn as adolescents how and in what order to undertake sexual acts and how to respond sexually. Masturbation, information from friends of one's own sex, and sexual exploration with a partner teach adolescents how to be sexual. Here is an explicit sexual lesson for adolescent males that catches the quality of such advice. The quotation is from a South African novel, but similar messages can be heard almost anywhere in the United States:

---

[1]The Coolidge effect takes its name from a joke about President and Mrs. Coolidge's separate tours around a model chicken farm. Mrs. Coolidge noticed the large number of chickens and remarked, "That rooster must be very busy." She tells the guide, "Show *that* to my husband." The guide recounts to Coolidge his wife's comments about the busy rooster. He asks, "Always with the same female?" "Oh, no, sir," the guide answers. "Well, tell *that* to my wife," says the President.

Now when you get this Trudy, only thirteen remember . . . You grab her, right? And then you don't French kiss her. That's nothing. No! Get hold of her neck and kiss around there for a while. Work your way up.

Get to an ear . . . OK? You listening, Harry? Right, do the lobe first, a few nibbles on the lobe, gently, take your time and THEN—zip! You push your tongue deep down into her ear. This is the bit you got to watch out for. She'll . . . go . . . CRAZY! Have you on the floor before you know it, panties around her knees, absolutely BEGGING for it. . . . (Hope, 1980, p. 37).

Many of us have partly funny, partly embarrassing memories of our first attempts to act like sexual adults. Even though we are capable of responding sexually all of our lives—infants are known to have erections, vaginal lubrication, and orgasm—most of us date ourselves as sexual beings from adolescence. We also tend to remember our early sexual experiences as confusing, as both exciting and disappointing, and as very important. Even if we fumble and bumble, learning to be sexual is *not* boring. It is more likely to feel like dangerous exploration through terrain our parents surely never traveled. And despite all the fumbling, a remarkably orderly process of sexual learning emerges. We learn that our bodies grow aroused, learn just what our bodies do when they are aroused, and we become increasingly proficient at getting to that state of arousal.

SOCIAL SEX: LEARNING THE STEPS   In the first Monty Python film released in the United States, *And Now for Something Completely Different,* an Eastern European tourist is shown entering a London shop to buy an English phrasebook. As he innocently practices his English, he is confused by people's peculiar reactions to his simple requests. It turns out that the phrasebook is a fraud, and he is not asking, "Where is the museum?" but "May I fondle your buttocks?" What makes the skit funny, of course, is that we know that one does not approach strangers on the street and ask to fondle their buttocks. Every culture teaches its members which actions are appropriate, and under which circumstances. We learn that only people on intimate terms may fondle one another's buttocks: sexual partners or parents to babies, for example. The degree of variation among cultures is wide in the matter of teaching people the rules for social sex. In our culture, we learn to approach sexual intercourse through a progression of what we consider increasingly intimate acts: kissing before French kissing, breast fondling before genital fondling. Yet the Mangaians move swiftly toward intercourse and do not consider our subroutines as separate behaviors, separate peaks to be scaled. Our learning of the sexual steps tends to be quite orderly, and social scientists have found that almost everyone follows a given sequence. Social scientists call this widely shared sequence **scaled behavior** (see Tables 8.2 and 8.3).

My memories of teenage sex are mostly of resting my hand on a girl's shoulder until I could slip it down to her breasts—over her blouse, of course—while we were kissing. Sometimes, she'd push my hand away. If she didn't, I'd wait a little while and then move my hand under her blouse. You had to wait at every move to see how far she'd let you go. Heaven forbid you should skip a step! She'd be indignant, and that would be the end of the whole game (22-year-old senior).

TABLE 8.2

Scaled Behavior of College Women, 1951–1978

| | Year | | |
Behavior	1951–1952	1973	1978
Deep kissing with a male	81%	90%	94%
Manual stimulation of breasts by a male	78	76	90
Oral stimulation of breasts by a male	11	57	82
Manual stimulation of genitals by a male	33	53	83
Manual stimulation of a male's genitals	33	48	75
Oral stimulation of genitals by a male	4	34	64
Oral stimulation of a male's genitals	(no data)	25	64

Source: 1951–1952 from Reevy, W. R. *Marriage and Family Living,* 1959, 21, 349–355; 1973 from Curran, J. Neff, S., and Lippold, S. *Journal of Sex Research,* 1973, 9, 124–131; 1978 from Mahoney, E. R. Unpublished paper, 1979. Cited in E. R. Mahoney, *Human Sexuality.* New York: McGraw-Hill, 1983.

One night my girlfriend and I decided to go parking, just for old time's sake. We drove to the country road where we used to make out as teenagers, turned on the radio, and lay down on the seat. It was awful. We were too used to going all the way on our comfortable bed. The charge was gone (21-year-old male junior).

SCALED BEHAVIOR: INTIMATE INCREMENTS   Learning the sexual steps in the order that our culture considers appropriate and deciding the circumstances under which our personal values allow us to act them out are very important tasks for adolescents. Sex with a partner usually begins with kissing. Young adolescents explore lips and the inside of a partner's mouth, which is rich in nerves and therefore responsive to sensation. They learn how to give erotic kisses, which are very different from the chaste kisses exchanged by parents and children, and to feel that the mouth is a place for sexual bonding.

When I was a teenager, I started thinking about growing up as a series of different kinds of kisses. When you're little you kiss your parents on the lips. When you're older, you kiss them on the cheek. Then you start kissing boys on the lips. Then you French kiss. Then you kiss your baby on the lips, and the cycle starts all over again (19-year-old female sophomore).

After kissing, adolescent couples explore a girl's breasts, clothed and naked. Biologists say that human breasts are, compared to other mammals' breasts, proportionately larger. These noticeable human breasts provide a focus for the visual and sensual exploration of the skin. Adolescents learn about the importance of touching not just the breasts but the skin generally: neck and back are rubbed and tickled; his chest is stroked. Real excitement often comes from having a "stranger" touch a girl's breasts—a violation of the privacy rule. Few people engaged in sexual acts analyze whether their excitement comes from the touching or the meaning of that touching. Excitement probably comes from both, especially in early sexual encounters.

TABLE 8.3

Scaled Sexual Acts

Females' Heterosexual Behavior Hierarchy		Males' Heterosexual Behavior Hierarchy	
Item No.	Behavior	Item No.	Behavior
1[a]	One minute continuous lip kissing	1[a]	One minute continuous lip kissing
2	Manual manipulation of female breasts, over clothes, by male	2	Manual manipulation of female breasts, over clothes
3[a]	Manual manipulation of female breasts, under clothes, by male	3[a]	Manual manipulation of female breasts, under clothes
4	Manual manipulation of female genitals, over clothes, by male	4	Manual manipulation of female genitals, over clothes
5[a]	Kissing nipples of female breasts, by male	5[a]	Kissing nipples of female breasts
6	Manual manipulation of female genitals, under clothes, by male	6	Manual manipulation of female genitals, under clothes
7	Manual manipulation of male genitals, over clothes	7	Manual manipulation of male genitals, over clothes, by female
8[a]	Mutual manual manipulation of genitals	8[a]	Mutual manual manipulation of genitals
9[a]	Manual manipulation of male genitals, under clothes	9[a]	Manual manipulation of male genitals, under clothes, by female
10	Manual manipulation of female genitals to massive secretions, by male	10	Manual manipulation of female genitals to massive secretions
11	Manual manipulation of male genitals to ejaculation	11[a]	Sexual intercourse, ventral-ventral
12	Oral contact with female genitals, by male	12	Manual manipulation of male genitals to ejaculation, by female
13	Oral contact with male genitals	13	Oral contact with female genitals
14[a]	Sexual intercourse, ventral-ventral	14	Oral contact with male genitals, by female
15	Oral manipulation of female genitals, by male	15	Mutual manual manipulation of genitals to mutual orgasm
16[a]	Oral manipulation of male genitals	16[a]	Oral manipulation of male genitals, by female
17[a]	Mutual oral-genital manipulation	17	Oral manipulation of female genitals
18	Mutual manual manipulation of genitals to mutual orgasm	18[a]	Mutual oral-genital manipulation
19[a]	Sexual intercourse, ventral-dorsal	19[a]	Sexual intercourse, ventral-dorsal
20	Oral manipulation of male genitals to ejaculation	20	Oral manipulation of male genitals to ejaculation, by female
21[a]	Mutual oral manipulation of genitals to mutual orgasm	21[a]	Mutual oral manipulation of genitals to mutual orgasm

A survey of college women and men, some married, between the ages of 17 and 29 showed this hierarchy of sexual acts. The frequencies of certain acts—numbers 13 and 14, for example, are very close. Note that for both women and men, several acts occur after sexual intercourse, many of them oral-genital in nature. The hierarchy for individuals with a homosexual orientation would be different from those depicted here. Recent findings in North Carolina put ranks 20 and 21 *before* 19. (Newcomer and Udri, 1985).

Source: Bentler, P. M. *Behavior Research and Therapy,* 1968, 6, 21–25, 27–30.

[a] = short scale .98.

Lord, the hours that my best friend and I spent discussing our sexual experiences with our boyfriends. If I had liked it, I called my boyfriend "sensitive." If I hadn't, he was "too gross" (23-year-old female senior).

Social sexual acts proceed from the least to the most private body parts (Curran et al., 1973; Mahoney, 1979; Reevy, 1959). Intercourse usually follows necking and petting. We have many informal ways of talking about this sequence: what we call "foreplay" comes before "the main event"; "getting to first (second, or third) base" comes before "scoring" or "going all the way." Petting under clothes—touching thighs, buttocks, and genitals—violates not only the privacy rule but the rule about staying clothed. Boys tend to move more quickly through the sexual steps than girls do, because boys usually have had more practice and peer support in viewing their bodies and their genitals as instrumental and frankly sexual. In the scaled sexual behavior of females in Table 8.3, touching a boy's

Social sex proceeds from the least to the most private parts of the body.

FIGURE 8.7

Relation of first intercourse to previous sexual experience. How quickly college students who are dating proceed to sexual intercourse depends on each partner's previous sexual experience (Peplau et al., 1977).

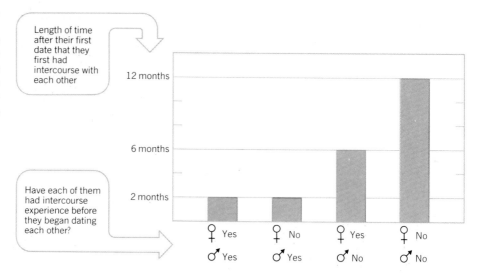

naked penis happens only five steps before sexual intercourse. Until girls touch the naked penis, the sexual exploration tends to have a provisional, potentially reversible quality to it. As one college junior said about her high-school experience,

> *When he took my bra off, I thought, "Well, that feels okay." But when he put my hand on his penis, I didn't like it. Not one bit. I was afraid even to look. So I started stammering, and he figured he'd gone too far. He apologized, and we went back to kissing and breast nuzzling. A month later I let him move my hand onto his penis. It felt less strange then.*

The last (and now sometimes the next-to-last) step before sexual intercourse, touching the girl's genitals, provides her with evidence of her own arousal. Vaginal lubrication wets the female genitals and readies them for comfortable intercourse. The partners have stimulated and aroused each other, although not necessarily to orgasm. No matter how sexually experienced people are, it is to their peril that they forget the lessons of these steps leading to intercourse. Sex therapy for people with sexual problems is based on rediscovering the skin as a sexual landscape, the mouth as a deep place of bonding, and the genitals, not as a stage for sexual performance, but places of delight and excitement.

SEXUAL ACTS

Male Masturbation: Fantasy, Fiction, and Friends

It may be the understatement of the century to say that adolescent boys are highly arousable, but they certainly are that. They experience erections to almost anything exciting, even being called on to recite in class or to join in a spitball fight. By age 16, most boys have explored their newly expanded sexuality by masturbating. What people learn about themselves from this "hands on" experience often forms an important part of what they will share with a sexual partner.

FIGURE 8.8

A man masturbating.

Most males masturbate simply and directly, and many boys learn a few simple techniques from their friends. Groups of friends provide explicit instructions or opportunities for imitation, as in "circle jerks," where boys masturbate together to see who ejaculates first or farthest. Adolescent boys learn that hand around the shaft of the penis and a rhythmic, up-down stroke put pressure on the shaft and a gentler, tugging pressure on the glans. Some males use oil, K-Y jelly, or soap and water to reduce friction, allow gentle glans stimulation, and vary the pressure.

As their arousal mounts, the rate of massaging increases, and orgasm usually follows within a few minutes of arousal. Orgasm and ejaculation usually end the reflexive thrusting. Most adolescent boys have practiced and learned about this sequence of reflexes—erection, pelvic thrusts, and ejaculation—before they have sex with a partner.

SEXUALITY IN PERSPECTIVE: MALE MASTURBATION FANTASIES

Masturbation is enormously gratifying, and to most boys, it is an exciting, risky violation of the rules. Many fantasize about the forbidden: sex with a stranger, with two women at once, with women who are forbidden, or with another male. The first and third of the following three fantasies are from heterosexual men; the second is from a homosexual man.

> *When I was a teenager, I liked to see if I could find pictures of naked men in the magazines that were always around the house.* National Geographic *sometimes showed tribesmen with their penises wrapped in long sheaths. I found those pictures very arousing, and I used them when I masturbated (19-year-old college sophomore).*

> *When I masturbate, I like to imagine being nibbled and sucked by a nameless, faceless stranger in a plush bed in a fine hotel (20-year-old male college junior).*

Aggressive fantasies, which are frequent, may make a boy feel guilty, but guilt may itself feed arousal.

> *I think about tying up the hands and feet of some attractive woman—either someone I've actually had sex with or someone I've just seen in passing or in class. I fantasize slapping her face with my erect penis and making her beg me to penetrate her (21-year-old college senior).*

Adolescent boys also share fantasy materials; they avidly pass around *Playboy* and *Hustler* magazines, and many a *Playboy* centerfold lives on in men's fantasies. By sharing fantasies and fantasy material with friends, groups of adolescent males come to share sexual imagery. This imagery changes with the generations: to the boys of the generation who idolized Joe DiMaggio, Marilyn Monroe was the woman of fantasy; today's fantasy woman may be leggy Darryl Hannah or Brooke Shields.

Female Masturbation: Fantasy and Friction

Adolescent girls learn to masturbate in a very different context from adolescent boys. For adolescent girls, masturbation is likely to be completely solitary and private. Boys are more likely than girls to masturbate socially at some time. Unlike males, adolescent girls do not usually teach each other about masturbating. Some women learn about vibrators from their mothers or friends, and feminist self-help groups may work to get women familiar with their genitals. But most young women discover masturbation on their own or learn it after sexual encounters with males. Today's West German women are masturbating earlier and more than they did 10 or 20 years ago (Clement et al., 1984). In Kinsey's day, more American women reported masturbating after sexual contact with males than before. Although fewer women than men masturbate, more and more women are learning to masturbate. Today's more numerous and explicit sources of sexual information probably influence the variety of methods women use to masturbate. German researchers conjecture that women have more varied outlets for emotional conflict than men do. They reason that men may masturbate as a way of dealing with many sorts of conflict and, therefore, they masturbate more than women do (Clement et al., 1984).

The many methods women use to masturbate are an ode to human invention. Some women use fantasy alone and can think their way to orgasm. Others tighten their buttocks or cross their thighs; others thrust; others stimulate their breasts and skin. Some use a running shower hose on the clitoris or a powerful vibrator. Almost all women masturbate by stimulating the clitoris and inner labia. Circular or up-and-down stroking at the side or shaft of the clitoris allow women to stimulate the clitoral glans indirectly. Some women begin at the glans and move away as it retracts, and some women stimulate the entrance to the vagina with their fingers. When the Kinsey report on women appeared in 1953, the world got its first large-scale evidence on how women masturbated. Despite common

FIGURE 8.9

A woman masturbating.

male fantasies of deep vaginal penetration with large penile objects, women typically did not use penis substitutes (dildoes). Kinsey found that many women who did use penis substitutes had begun doing so on the recommendation of a male psychiatrist so that the women might achieve the presumed "mature" vaginal orgasm. (For more on the controversy about vaginal versus clitoral orgasms, see Chapter 7.) Although some women do use dildoes in solo masturbation or in sexual encounters with other women, much of women's presumed interest in dildoes is a figment of men's fantasies.

Almost all women masturbate by stimulating the clitoris and inner labia.

The early European psychoanalysts were long concerned about the meaning of masturbation. One of their major concerns was a possible fixation on masturbation, which was considered less "mature" than heterosexual, genital sex. But people seem to prefer to combine social sex with solitary sex in their lives. Many married people do this. Some psychoanalysts suggested that masturbatory fantasies were pathological and avoided real life. But studies have shown that women who fantasize are sexually active, creative, and stable emotionally (Hariton, 1973). Considering certain fantasies pathological or criminal is to make the mistake of equating fantasy and action. They are not the same, and so long as people think about, rather than act out, taboo ideas, they do no harm.

Shared Touching

Touching—softly or roughly, as one's partner requires—is the ultimate turn-on, whether intercourse follows or not. A lover's sensitivity to a partner's changing needs shows most in touches. It is no accident that we say that we are "touched" when we are deeply moved. As children, we learn about our own and others' bodies by touching them. We grow attuned to our sensual preferences, and when we begin lovemaking, we communicate these preferences to a partner. Shared touching can be a powerful form of communication without words, for in the tension of muscles, the pressure of hands, the temperature of skin, our bodies reveal when we are content, relaxed, or aroused.

> *Touch is an end in itself. It is a primary form of communication, a silent voice that avoids the pitfalls of words while expressing the feelings of the moment. It bridges the physical separateness from which no human being is spared, literally establishing a sense of solidarity between two individuals. Touching is sensual pleasure, exploring the textures of skin, the suppleness of muscle, the contours of the body, with no further goal than enjoyment of tactile perceptions (Masters and Johnson, 1976, p. 253).*

Couples who do not want coitus may find sexual satisfaction and emotional closeness in stroking each other's bodies. Some stimulate each other to orgasm by the stroking of genitals. Others enjoy lying awash in sensual pleasure without the focus of orgasm.

FIGURE 8.10
Masturbating before a partner.

I love to be rubbed all over by my boyfriend. I just lie there passively, purring like a contented cat. He likes it when I rub my cheek and my hair all over him (18-year-old female freshman).

As their pleasure and arousal mount, a couple may move to stroking the places known to be sexually arousable, and orgasm may follow manual or oral caressing of the woman's labia and clitoris and the man's penis and testes. Couples sometimes enjoy masturbating together, sometimes masturbating in turn. The beauty of shared touching is that it imposes no rules of sequence or timing. It can free people to take time, to be sensual, and to listen to their bodies.

Gender Differences in Attitudes Toward Stimulation

Many men and women differ in their attitudes toward the pacing and sources of pleasure. In their study of homosexual and heterosexual couples, Masters and Johnson (1979) found that heterosexual pairs more often hurry toward intercourse and orgasm than homosexual pairs. Such rushing sometimes reflects the view that all touching and tenderness are preparation for the "real" action, the orgasm. Gay couples, whose physiology is similar, are likely to be more tuned into what gives pleasure to others like themselves. They may be less focused on the orgasm than on pleasuring. In sex therapy, women often report that their partners move to penetration and intercourse too quickly. These women find that their enjoyment rests on a slower pace, a good deal of touching and kissing, and a slower sexual "courtship." Although most experienced couples at some time have genitally focused "quickies," women—and especially young women—are more likely to dislike fast intercourse than are men. Young women especially value foreplay, sometimes more than intercourse itself (Denny et al., 1984; Pietropinto and Simenauer, 1977).

When discrepancies arise, many women find it difficult or impossible to tell their partners what stimulation they want (Hite, 1976), and so do some men. Not all sexual communication need be verbal, of course. A hand put over a partner's hand can indicate a preferred pressure or place of stimulation. The sounds of pleasure tell a partner what is arousing. Touch, murmur, and smile are all communications. So are simple words—"yes," "no," "harder," "softer," "ouch," and "more," "stop" and "don't stop."

Oral-Genital Stimulation

For most people surveyed in earlier studies, the sequence of sexual acts went from vaginal intercourse to oral-genital sex. This was the sequence that Kinsey found at a time when fewer than 10 percent of adolescents engaged in oral sex. By 1982, however, high school men and women were somewhat more likely to have engaged in oral sex before vaginal intercourse (Newcomer and Udry, 1985).

Some people find oral-genital stimulation so intimate that they engage in it only after they have had vaginal intercourse. (For people who wish to avoid intercourse, oral-genital sex can be another form of petting. Kinsey viewed it that way, as "the last of the petting techniques to be accepted." So did the Southern California and Southern high school students studied by Hass [1979] and by Newcomer and Udry, [1985].) It violates the rules about physical privacy in many ways, for during oral-genital sex, the genitals are flagrantly exposed to eye, mouth, and nose. Part of its very arousal value, of course, lies in the flagrant violation of rules about keeping one's genitals covered, clean, and untouched. Even genital union sexual intercourse takes place out of direct vision. Not so oral sex.

The first time my boyfriend went down on me I gasped, I was so shocked. I worried that I might smell bad, and generally I felt uncomfortable. But after a while, I got into it (21-year-old female sophomore).

For me, oral sex is the next best thing to intercourse. The pleasure is even more intense. I love to turn on my girlfriend that way, and I love to have her do it to me (22-year-old male senior).

How to handle ejaculation is a problem for some couples. Its importance psychologically is far greater than the matter of disposal of a spoonful of semen. Given the discomfort that many women experience about their partner's ejaculation during oral sex, the woman's decision is likely to carry the most weight.

When the mouth caresses a man's genitals, the act is called **fellatio.** When the mouth caresses a woman's genitals, the act is called **cunnilingus.** When two partners engage in oral sex at the same time, they are colloquially said to engage in "69," because of the configuration of their heads and bodies. Oral sex is stimulating for several different reasons. It provides visual stimulation. Physically, it is powerfully arousing, and it requires little previous arousal. The mouth lubricates the genitals. Oral sex lets partners take turns and adjust the pacing to their own wishes and needs. It is also popular because it does not cause pregnancy or require contraception.

Many, but not all, sexually experienced pairs engage in oral sex. In the 1940s and 1950s—Kinsey's day—oral-genital sex was more common among people with

FIGURE 8.11

Fellatio (oral caressing of man's genitals).

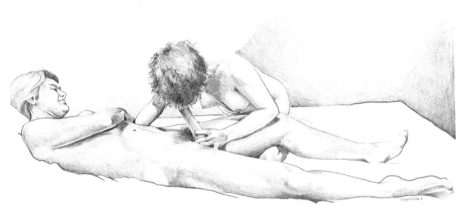

college degrees than among those with less education. Among those with less education, oral-genital sex was less likely to take place between husband and wife than between a man and a prostitute. College-educated men were likelier to engage in oral-genital sex with their wives. The less educated men in Kinsey's (1948) sample generally devalued both masturbation and oral-genital sex. Today, most of these class differences have disappeared or diminished (Hunt, 1974).

From their own experience with masturbation, women and men bring to oral-genital sex certain expectations about their partners' preferences. Some of these expectations may prove unfounded. Men may assume that women want firm pressure during cunnilingus, because firm pressure on the shaft of the penis feels best to most men during masturbation or fellatio. A woman may want, on one occasion, slow and light pressure to her genitals and, on another occasion, firmer and faster pressure. Women may assume that men prefer the same light pressure during fellatio. Guidance from their partners is helpful, in that the glans of the penis usually needs less stimulation than the shaft. Some men do like light nuzzling of the scrotum, perineum, and anus. Some women like light touching

FIGURE 8.12

Cunnilingus (oral caressing of woman's genitals).

FIGURE 8.13

"69"—mutual oral-genital caressing.

of the perineum, thighs, and anus. Whatever a person's preferences and whatever the expectations of one's partner, the most pleasurable sex happens when partners can signal to each other, by touch or word, what feels best to them.

The "How" of Sexual Intercourse

Human anatomy allows for a finite number of positions for sexual intercourse. Human cultural rules further limit the positions, frequency, duration, and acceptable partners for intercourse.

> ### Every culture favors one or two positions for intercourse.

Front-to-Front Positions (Ventral-Ventral)   Every culture favors one or two positions for intercourse. In the United States, the favored positions are front-to-front (ventral-ventral). These positions have the advantages of letting partners see, talk to, and kiss each other's faces and mouths. They therefore feel more intimate than in positions in which the male enters the female from behind. Most nonhuman mammals, in fact, use ventral-dorsal positions. Some copulate front-to-front in captivity, but rarely do so in the wild. Human females are built in such a way that ventral-ventral intercourse is easier for them than it is for, say, chimpanzee females. Human females have enlarged breasts and a vagina that is more ventral than other animals'. Jacob Bronowski, a scientist who turned to the study of language near the end of his life, believed that the evolutionary shift of the human female's vagina to a more ventral position and the development of language together permitted the close bonding of human sexual pairs. This evolutionary strategy loads the ventral surface with visual attractions, facial individuality, and personal and sexual intimacy.

MISSIONARY POSITION   The front-to-front position in which the male is above, also called the **missionary position** after the missionaries who endorsed it to the "heathens," is the most common position in most Western societies. The missionary position is very stimulating for the male and allows him to thrust deeply. For men who climax more quickly than they wish, the missionary position may be *too* stimulating. Some women like this position because of its intimacy, because of the genital stimulation it affords them, because it allows their partner to control the pace of thrusting, or because they like the symbolism of man on top and woman beneath. But for women who cannot position themselves to get enough genital (especially clitoral) stimulation, the missionary position may not work well. Thus for some couples, this position may make it difficult for one or both partners to achieve pleasure. For others, it is physically and emotionally satisfying.

> *I know some women who cannot climax unless they are on top of the man. I'm just the opposite. I can't climax unless I'm underneath. People really must be built differently. Or do they just get used to different patterns? (21-year-old female senior)*

WOMAN PRONE, MAN LYING ON HIS BACK   Some couples like to have intercourse with the woman atop the man. They prefer the woman to control the pace of thrusting and to position herself so that the man's body, and especially his pubic bone, provides clitoral stimulation as they thrust. This position may be less intensely arousing to the male than the missionary position, because his thrusting alone does not pace the intercourse and because his thrusting is shallower. Some men like the woman on top because they can fantasize with great pleasure that the woman is "taking" them. Some women like this position because intercourse seems expanded and extended when they can control the pacing. They may also like their greater freedom of movement and not bearing their partner's weight.

> *It took us 15 years to try out having sex with me on top. I had thought all along that I could only reach orgasm when I masturbated. But I came*

FIGURE 8.15

Sexual intercourse (ventral-ventral) with woman lying atop man.

the first time we tried. For some reason I told my mother this nice news, even though I'd never told her about the problem. She told me she'd figured it out three weeks into her marriage. Imagine what she could've spared me (51-year-old woman).

After nine years of using the missionary position, my wife and I finally decided to try making love with her on top. It was extremely pleasurable for both of us. But it tired my wife more than the missionary position did. Afterwards, she half gasped, "I think I took the advanced trail" (37-year-old man).

Being on top taught me how to come. Now it doesn't matter what position we take (26-year-old female graduate student).

FIGURE 8.16

Sexual intercourse (ventral-dorsal) with partners lying on their sides is especially good for those who are obese, pregnant, or who need to avoid causing pain to the chest or abdomen.

FIGURE 8.17

Sexual intercourse (ventral-ventral) with woman astride man.

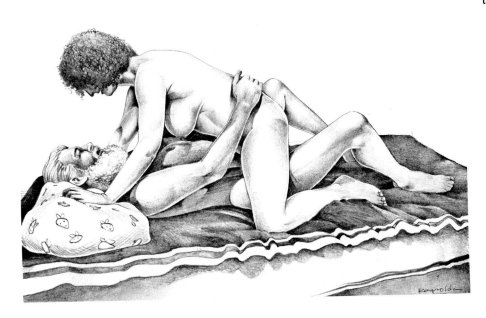

OTHER FRONT-TO-FRONT POSITIONS   People in other cultures use front-to-front positions that are less common in the United States. These positions include: female lying flat (supine) and male squatting above and drawing her close; partners side by side, especially good for partners with health or weight problems, during pregnancy, and after surgery that leaves the front of the body tender (for instance, after the removal of a breast, when it is important to a couple to find a position that gives pleasure but no pain). Side-by-side positions are excellent in all of these special circumstances, although they need not be used only then.

> *When I'm on my side, it's easier for me to play with my clitoris. That way, if my husband sounds like he's ready to come, I can come with him (31-year-old female graduate student).*

REAR-ENTRY POSITIONS (VENTRAL-DORSAL)   Rear-entry positions, with the man above the woman, have become marks of innovation, according to a 1983 Playboy survey of "avant-garde" sexuality. In the scale of sexual acts (see Table 8.3), note that rear-entry intercourse is several steps beyond ventral-ventral intercourse. Some women find vaginal stimulation increases when the man enters them from behind, and others like the sense of playfulness it gives them.

> *It makes me laugh every time my husband says, "Me Tarzan. You Jane," because I know he means for me to crouch. It's not my favorite position, but I find it fun because he's having so much fun (26-year-old woman).*

Hand stimulation of the clitoris is convenient in this position. Sex therapists who are persuaded of the importance of vaginal sensitivity (and areas like the G-spot) often recommend rear-entry positions.

FIGURE 8.18

Sexual intercourse (ventral-dorsal) with man entering woman.

Human inventiveness is such that within such neutrally labeled categories as we have just described, a whole range of imaginative behaviors may occur. People are known to have intercourse under water and on dining room tables, romantically in front of a blazing fire, or standing up and entwined like pretzels. Books and movies describe the pleasures of intercourse in the tiny bathrooms of airplanes and behind department-store model furniture. Now that both men and women travel in space, we expect soon to be treated to descriptions of intercourse without gravity.

Anal Intercourse

She returns and anoints him thoroughly [with Vaseline], with an icy expert touch. Harry shudders. Thelma lies down beside him with her back turned, curls forward as if to be shot from a cannon, and reaches behind to guide him. "Gently."

It seems it won't go, but suddenly it does. The medicinal odor of displaced Vaseline reaches his nostrils. The grip is tight at the base but beyond, where a cunt is all velvety suction and caress, there is no sensation: a void, a pure black box, a casket of perfect nothingness. He is in that void, past her tight ring of muscle (Updike, 1981, p. 417).

Some couples, both heterosexual and homosexual, enjoy anal intercourse, whether in addition to or instead of vaginal intercourse. Anal intercourse has been tried once or twice by many (25 to 45 percent, depending on the sample) heterosexual couples. About 2 percent of these couples engage in anal intercourse often (Hunt, 1974; Tavris and Sadd, 1975). Some people incorporate light stroking or finger penetration of the anus into their solitary or mutual masturbation. Anal sex involves stimulation of the buttocks and perineum, both sensitive areas of the body. The anus has many nerve endings that are sensitive to pressure and to touch. Unlike the vagina, however, the anus does not lubricate itself during sexual arousal. Thus, for ease of penetration as well as to protect delicate tissue, a sterile lubricant such as K-Y Jelly should be used. Mouth-to-anus stimulation, called **anilingus,** can be very arousing. But because the anus is also liberally supplied with organisms that should not enter the mouth or vagina, careful washing of body parts that have come in contact with the anus is in order. Men may want to use a condom during anal intercourse and remove (or change) it for vaginal intercourse. Although considerations of hygiene may cut into some people's full sexual enjoyment, they should understand the real possibility of disease that unprotected anal sex carries. Physicians have warned gay men of the diseases transmitted by unprotected anal intercourse.

Aphrodisiacs and Anaphrodisiacs

At least since the civilization of the ancient Egyptians, humans have sought substances to improve their sexual performance. Called **aphrodisiacs** (Aphrodite was the mythical Greek goddess of love), these substances have been sought for three different reasons: to enhance sexual motivation; to increase sexual performance; and to increase sexual sensation. People since time immemorial have believed in the sympathetic magic of animal testes or substances that looked like testes to enhance sex. In his *Ars Amatoria,* Ovid suggested that the goddess of love could be made to perform if a person ate white onions, eggs, or the nuts of a sharp-leaved pine tree. Similarly, raw oysters, thought to resemble testes, and the testes of the bull and buffalo have been consumed by those wishing to improve their sexual performance. Pliny described as aphrodisiacs: the dried and pulverized testes of a horse; the right testicle of an ass drunk in wine, worn as a bracelet, or dunked seven times in boiling oil and rubbed on a man's genitals. Although the hormones in testes are not chemically available to the person who eats them, sometimes the trick actually did work. Because of the **placebo effect,** when people believe that a substance is effective, they may feel the very effects they believe in.

In low doses, alcohol can enhance sexual arousal, especially because it overcomes feelings of inhibition. In higher doses, alcohol acts as a depressant and interferes with sexual performance.

Spanish fly, another aphrodisiac, is the pulverized exoskeleton of blister beetles. It irritates the ducts of the urogenital system and stimulates the genitals. It can lead to the irreversible and unerotic condition of perpetual erection known as **priapism.** Spanish fly may be assumed to be an aphrodisiac because it produces erection, even though the erections may feel uncomfortable. The discomfort can be treated, but the treatment prevents further erections. In high enough doses,

Spanish fly can cause diarrhea and changes in the cardiovascular system.

Many drugs have been believed to confer aphrodisiac powers. L-dopa, a drug used to treat Parkinson's disease, a neurological disorder that interferes with coordination, was thought to have a temporary aphrodisiac effect on about 20 percent of patients (in fact, it probably doesn't). In low doses, alcohol can enhance sexual arousal, especially because it overcomes feelings of inhibition. In higher doses, alcohol acts as a depressant and interferes with sexual performance. Even though a person may feel very sexy after a few drinks, alcohol interferes with spinal cord mechanisms for erection in males and arousal in females. Other depressants ("downs") like Quaaludes reduce sexual responsiveness. Stimulants ("ups") like cocaine and amphetamines in low doses seem to increase sexual motivation in laboratory animals, but in high doses they interfere with performance. Humans report that cocaine may produce a colder, more detached sexual experience.

Many "recreational" drugs (as opposed to prescription drugs) grow popular in part because people believe that they have aphrodisiac powers or because they hope that the drugs will enhance the sexual experience. A number of drugs combined with LSD affect sexual response. As with PCP ("angel dust") and mescaline, people's reactions vary widely. Some marijuana users say marijuana alters the sensations of sex. Some find their sexual pleasure changed for the better; others find it changed for the worse.

Sometimes sex when I'm high on grass is just wonderful—more intense and concentrated. But sometimes grass makes me really anxious. The only problem is that I can never tell in advance (18-year-old male freshman).

When I first told my parents that sometimes I got high on marijuana, my father was worried because he'd heard that it was an aphrodisiac. As usual, he was worried about his little girl's "reputation" (20-year-old female junior).

Heavy marijuana use (more than 10 joints a week) lowers androgen levels and occasionally produces breast enlargement in males. (Men with fertility problems therefore probably should avoid smoking marijuana). The active ingredient in marijuana, THC (tetrahydrocannabinol), has a weak estrogenic effect. The body eliminates it slowly, especially from fat. In response, the brain decreases reproductive organ hormones, and androgen levels drop (Kolodny et al., 1974). Marijuana is not dependable as an aphrodisiac.

Neuroscientists may soon know enough about the brain mechanisms controlling sexual activities to identify substances that are true aphrodisiacs. One laboratory recently analyzed **yohimbine,** a substance found in the bark of some plants. Yohimbine seems to be an aphrodisiac for male rats. New tests will show whether it works with people as well as rats, and whether it may prove helpful in treating people with low sexual interest (Clark, Smith, and Davidson, 1984).

Among gay males, amyl nitrate and other nitrates, called *poppers,* are popular for sniffing during sex. They increase heart rate and blood pressure and dilate blood vessels. Poppers give a rush that enhances the sensations of orgasms. But amyl nitrate can, because of its effects on blood vessels, cause headaches and other problems. Unfortunately, no drugs are known that selectively, dependably, and benignly alter or enhance the sexual experience for everyone.

On the street, MDA, a long-lasting hallucinogen related to both amphetamine and mescaline, has a reputation for being a "tactile" aphrodisiac. It supposedly enhances erotic response to touch. It is largely unexplored by mainstream investigators.

Other tranquilizers—Valium, Librium, and others—often can improve sexual performance by eliminating anxiety. Anxiety interferes with sexual responsiveness when it makes a person watchful and tense. However, the major tranquilizers disrupt sexual response. Some prescription drugs do interfere with sexual response, and people for whom such drugs are prescribed should experiment (with their doctor's help) to find a drug that does not interfere with their sexual performance. For people who need drugs to control medical problems, there are many drugs that do not cause erection or other arousal problems, and sexual dysfunction need not be the inevitable price of medical treatment.

In contrast, people on heroin or morphine are not much interested in sex, and these substances can be called **anaphrodisiacs.** In boarding schools, summer camps, and other places where males and females are expected to be chaste, rumor has it that saltpeter is added to their food to diminish lust. It isn't, and it doesn't. Centuries ago, Pliny noted that a liniment of mouse dung acted as an anaphrodisiac. He was probably right.

SUMMARY

1 When people are said to be sexually motivated, they will arrange their environments so that they can approach erotic stimuli or create them in fantasy.

2 Sexual motivation is a product of both biological and psychological factors. Chemical hormones produced by the endocrine system influence the speed and degree of biological responses to erotic stimuli. Steroid hormones—androgens, estrogens, and progesterone—are basic to sexual motivation.

3 Pheromones are odorous chemicals that transmit specific messages between members of a species. Pheromones reflect an individual's hormonal state. To date, there is no evidence that humans respond to pheromones.

4 Males' hormone levels cycle rhythmically over a 24-hour period and increase between birth and sexual maturity. Their levels of sexual interest do not necessarily follow the same patterns, however.

5 The relation between human females' hormone levels and sexual arousal and pleasure is the subject of several on-going investigations. Women whose ovaries have been removed surgically continue to experience sexual interest, but most women whose adrenal glands have been removed lose sexual interest.

6 Humans are the only animals we can be sure experience mental sexual events such as fantasies, special thoughts, or altered consciousness during orgasm.

7 Neurotransmitters are chemicals that act within the nervous system. Their role in sexual response has yet to be clarified.

8 Adults respond to many different erotic stimuli. Primary erotic stimuli—such as light stroking of the genitals—produce sexual arousal without any

prior experience or learning. Secondary erotic stimuli—the face of a lover— are learned or conditioned. The conditioning process by which stimuli become secondarily erotic can both constrict and expand the nature of erotic stimuli. The human ability to fantasize about secondary erotic stimuli powerfully influences sexual motivation. Sexual fantasies are common in heterosexual and homosexual males and females, during and apart from overt sexual activity.

9 Sexual motivation can be seen as incentive motivation, because it is powerfully inspired by external stimuli.

10 Because sexual arousal, anger, and fear all do similar things to the human body, social psychologists suggest that how people interpret these bodily sensations can determine their motivations and feelings. When people misinterpret nonsexual sensations as erotic or sexual arousal as unerotic, they are said to have mislabeled their arousal.

11 It is during adolescence that people usually learn how and when to respond erotically to external sexual stimuli. During masturbation, in information from friends of their own sex, and sexual exploration with a partner, adolescents learn how to respond to sexual stimuli.

12 Adolescent boys typically masturbate and learn about the sequence of reflexes—erection, pelvic thrusting, and ejaculation—before they have any form of sex with a partner. Adolescent girls are more likely to have social sexual contact before they learn to masturbate.

13 Many adolescents in this country typically proceed through a sequence of increasingly intimate sexual acts. These acts incrementally violate the privacy rules learned during childhood. Oral-genital sex once followed vaginal intercourse. Recent surveys of high-school students show oral-genital sex to occur before intercourse.

14 Humans may have sexual intercourse when they are front to front (ventral-ventral) or front to rear (ventral-dorsal). Individual inventiveness and cultural rules tend to influence the positions for intercourse that people assume.

15 Substances that enhance sexual performance are called aphrodisiacs; substances that impair it are called anaphrodisiacs. Superstitions and untested beliefs about these substances have existed for centuries.

KEY TERMS

sexual motivation	misattribution (mislabeling)
releasing hormone	Coolidge effect
gonadotropins	scaled behavior
gonadal hormones	fellatio
steroid hormones	cunnilingus
testosterone	69
estradiol	missionary position
sensory threshold	anilingus
pheromones	aphrodisiac
ovulation	placebo effect

luteal phase
neurotransmitters
primary erotic stimuli
secondary erotic stimuli
incentive motivation
positive feedback system

Spanish fly
priapism
yohimbine
anaphrodisiac

SUGGESTED READINGS

Bermant, G., and Davidson, J. M. *Biological Bases of Sexual Behavior*. New York: Harper & Row, 1974. Still the best single source on hormonal controls on sexual motivation in mammals. It is written clearly for those with some background in biology.

Boston Women's Health Collective. *The New Our Bodies, Ourselves*. New York: Simon & Schuster, 1984. In this updated version of the now classic resource book, the chapters on physiology and relationships are readable and helpful.

Davidson, J. M. "The Psychology of Sexual Experience," in J. M. Davidson and R. J. Davidson (Eds.), *The Psychology of Consciousness*. New York: Plenum, 1980. This provocative chapter first presents animal and human evidence on how biology controls sexual behavior and then poses questions such as how conscious processes like fantasy might influence sexual experience.

Hass, A. *Teenage Sexuality*. New York: Macmillan, 1979. This survey of adolescents in southern California and elsewhere is interesting for its comments on teenagers and their sexual experiences.

Hunt, M. *Sexual Behavior in the 1970s*. Chicago: Playboy Press, 1974. This flawed sample "replicates" the Kinsey Report and is saved by the master hand of a wise writer-researcher. It makes interesting reading, with numbers and case material on current sexual behavior.

Chapter 9

Life Begins: Menstruation, Pregnancy, and Birth

Why have we gathered menstruation, pregnancy, and birth into one chapter? One reason is to show the menstrual cycle as the preparation for new life. That leads to our second reason. If menstrual cycling is treated as a potential beginning of life, pregnancy and birth follow naturally. This chapter may seem to be about women and their reproductive biology, but pregnancy and birth concern couples, and reproducing couples include men. For many women the topics of pregnancy and birth may be frightening and loaded with misconceptions. Part of our aim in writing this chapter is to expose the misconceptions we learned as children along with the "facts of life."

MENSTRUATION: THE CULTURAL CONTEXT

When I was a young girl, I read in my mother's magazines about mysterious things called "sanitary napkins." I decided that they were for women who kept very clean houses (22-year-old female college senior).

In truth, menstrual flow is quite clean and smells only if it has been exposed to the air for some time. Yet many people, of both sexes, consider menstruating women somehow contaminated or dangerous. Many people avoid sexual intercourse during a woman's period.

The menstrual cycle conventionally is described as lasting 28 days, even though most women's cycles are shorter or longer and may vary from month to month. The word **menstruation** itself derives from the Greek word for month, and one informal term for menstruation is "the monthlies." The connection between menstruation and the calendar reveals an ancient idea about femininity. Twenty-eight days make a lunar month, and women's bodies and psyches were thought to respond to the phases of the moon. The menstrual cycle was believed to induce lunacy in women.

In our culture, the slang terms for menstruation are mostly derogatory: "the curse," "being on the rag," or "falling off the roof." Because in this and other cultures, menstruation is devalued, a woman may have mixed feelings about her periods. Her first menstrual flow may frighten as well as thrill her, embarrass as well as reassure. Very few women will forget how they felt when they first found that rusty red stain in their clothing. In her novel, *The Bluest Eye* (1970), Toni Morrison captures the moment when Pecola, a girl who is staying with two young sisters, Frieda and Claudia, first gets her period.

Suddenly Pecola bolted straight up, her eyes wide with terror. A whinnying sound came from her mouth.

"What's the matter with you?" Frieda stood up too.

Then we both looked where Pecola was staring. Blood was running down her legs. Some drops were on the steps. I leaped up. "Hey. You cut yourself? Look. It's all over your dress."

A brownish-red stain discolored the back of her dress. She kept whinnying, standing with her legs far apart.

Frieda said, "Oh Lordy! I know what that is!"

"What?" Pecola's fingers went to her mouth.

"That's ministratin'."
"What's that?"
"You know."
"Am I going to die?" she asked.
"Noooo. You won't die. It just means you can have a baby!". . .
Frieda was on her knees; a white rectangle of cotton was near her on the ground. She was pulling Pecola's pants off. "Come on. Step out of them." She managed to get the soiled pants down and flung them at me. "Here."
"What am I supposed to do with these?"
"Bury them, moron."
Frieda told Pecola to hold the cotton thing between her legs.
"How she gonna walk like that?" I asked.
Frieda didn't answer. Instead she took two safety pins from the hem of her skirt and began to pin the ends of the napkin to Pecola's dress (pp. 25, 27).

When a young neighbor spots the three girls, she yells to their mother, "They're playin' nasty." Thus Morrison shows the transformation of a child's discovery of a normal biological event into sexual anxiety over "playin' nasty."

THE MENSTRUAL CYCLE

The phases of the menstrual cycle prepare a female's body to conceive a child and maintain a pregnancy. Menstruation itself is the shedding of material that the body no longer needs because a pregnancy has not occurred. Immediately after

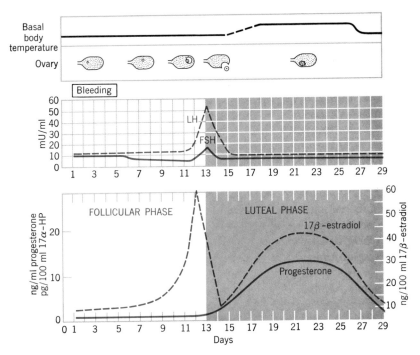

FIGURE 9.1

Human menstrual cycle. (Top) The pattern of temperature change across the menstrual cycle and the stage of development of the "egg of the month" in its follicle. (Middle and Bottom) The output of hormones (after Ganong, 1971 and G. W. Harris and F. Naftaolin, *British Medical Bulletin*, 1970, 26, 3–9).

the menstrual flow stops, the body begins to prepare again for a possible pregnancy. This cycling will continue for some three or four decades. Before birth, part of the female's brain, the hypothalamus, was programmed (by specific sex hormones, described in Chapter 3) to cycle in this way once a young woman reaches puberty. Therefore at some point typically between her eleventh and fifteenth birthdays, a young woman's first menstrual period, called the **menarche,** begins. Menarche is itself a response to hormones that flow in the bloodstream between the brain and the ovaries, a female's egg-bearing internal reproductive organs, and between the ovaries and her other reproductive organs. Several decades later, menstrual cycling will slowly diminish as hormone levels fall. Because the hormones that govern this cycling flow through the bloodstream, their effects are

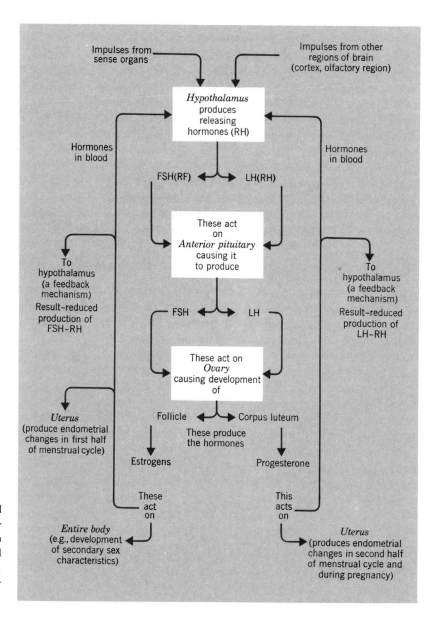

FIGURE 9.2

Hormones during the menstrual cycle. This chart shows the interactions of hormones and brain during a woman's menstrual cycle (from E.B. Steen and J.H. Price, *Human Sex and Sexuality,* New York: Wiley, 1977).

not restricted to the reproductive system. Hormones can influence, among other things, mood and sexual interest, appetite, and body temperature.

We turn now to the specific changes of each phase of the menstrual cycle.

Follicular Phase

The first day of the menstrual flow conventionally is called day 1 of the cycle. Then the **follicular** or **proliferative phase** of the cycle extends from about day 1 to day 12 or 14 (there is wide variation on the duration of this phase). During this phase, hormonal signals prepare an egg, or ovum, to ripen and the uterus to receive it.

At the beginning of the follicular phase, the pituitary gland, in the brain, secretes **follicle-stimulating hormone, or FSH.** This hormone stimulates the ovaries and their surrounding tissue, called **follicles.** Several ovarian follicles ripen each month, but only the dominant follicle will ovulate and be released. Each ovary produces the egg every other cycle. Each ovary contains thousands of un-ripened eggs that developed before birth, only a few of which will ever ripen in a women's lifetime, and of which even fewer are likely to be fertilized. Unlike males, who manufacture sperm continually after they reach puberty, females are born with all of the eggs they will ever have. During the follicular phase, the ovaries begin to increase their production of the hormone estrogen, and the es-trogen stimulates the cells of the uterine lining to proliferate (that is, to multiply).

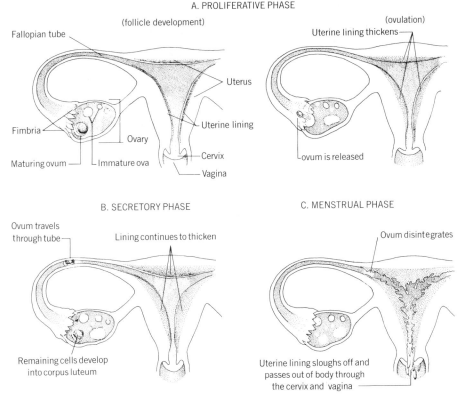

A. PROLIFERATIVE PHASE

(follicle development)

(ovulation)

Fallopian tube

Uterine lining thickens

Uterus

Uterine lining

Fimbria

Ovary

Maturing ovum — Immature ova

Cervix

Vagina

ovum is released

B. SECRETORY PHASE

C. MENSTRUAL PHASE

Ovum travels through tube

Lining continues to thicken

Ovum disintegrates

Remaining cells develop into corpus luteum

Uterine lining sloughs off and passes out of body through the cervix and vagina

FIGURE 9.3

Changes during the menstrual cycle.

This proliferation of the uterine lining, also called the **endometrium,** gives the name—**proliferative**—to the phase of the cycle that lasts from day 5 to 14.

Under the influence of the estrogen, the secretion of which peaks at about midcycle, the ripening egg and follicle move toward the surface of the ovary. Other changes occur at the same time to assure the egg a chance to be fertilized and survive. These changes are important to the reproductive success of the human species.

Ovulation

As the egg is released from the follicle in the ovary, a process called **ovulation** occurs. At this time, a woman's cervix secretes a slippery, clear mucus. Some women can tell that they are at or near ovulation because they see this wet discharge. This mucus makes the vagina less acidic and therefore less dangerous to sperm. A few days after ovulation, the cervical mucus thickens again and is much more difficult for the sperm to move through. Some women know that they are ovulating because they feel a twinge at one side of their abdomen. Called *Mittelschmerz,* German for "middle pain," it signals that the egg and follicle have burst from the ovary on that side. The ovaries alternate in providing the egg-of-the-month, and women with *Mittelschmerz* can tell which ovary has made the contribution. Not all women have *Mittelschmerz.* At ovulation, a woman's body temperature also rises by up to a full degree Fahrenheit. (For how to chart this temperature rise, see the section, "The Infertile Couple.")

The ovary releases egg and follicle in response to a burst of **luteinizing hormone, or LH,** from the pituitary. Ovulation usually takes place 14 days before the onset of menstruation. This 14-day interval is far less liable to variation than is the length of the follicular phase. The mature egg is gently waved into a fallopian tube by the fringed ends of the tube.

Not every woman ovulates during every cycle. It is normal for one or two cycles a year to be **anovulatory** in mature women. It is also normal for young women who are just beginning to menstruate not to ovulate for the first six

FIGURE 9.4

Development of ovarian follicle. Usually, one follicle matures during each menstrual cycle. When it ruptures, an ovum is released—the point in a woman's menstrual cycle, called *ovulation,* when she is likely to be most fertile.

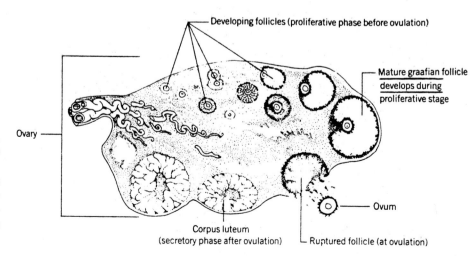

Developing follicles (proliferative phase before ovulation)

Mature graafian follicle develops during proliferative stage

Ovary

Ovum

Corpus luteum (secretory phase after ovulation)

Ruptured follicle (at ovulation)

months to a year and then, over the course of the next year or so, to begin to ovulate regularly (Gantt and McDonough, 1981). Once menstruation is established, well nourished young women have fewer anovulatory cycles than poorly nourished ones. During breastfeeding is another time in a woman's life when anovulatory cycles are normal. One caution: teenagers and nursing mothers may very well ovulate without knowing it—until, that is, they find themselves pregnant. Such women need birth control if they are sexually active and do not wish to conceive, even if they have not had a menstrual period.

Luteal Phase

The ripened egg, having been released into the fallopian tube, is now floating slowly toward the uterus. If sperm are present, they will ordinarily meet the egg in the outer third of the tube. One will join with the egg to fertilize it, and the resulting **zygote** will develop as it journeys through the tube and settles somewhere in the lining of the uterus. Once the fertilized egg has implanted in the endometrium, conception is completed.

After its five-day journey through the fallopian tube, the fertilized egg implants in the endometrium. To prepare for the implantation, the body has been sending hormonal signals. The ruptured ovarian follicle, having discharged its egg, has developed into a completely new organ, the **corpus luteum,** which is Latin for "yellow body." The corpus luteum secretes the hormone progesterone which, along with estrogen, stimulate the tissue, blood vessels, and glands of the endometrium to develop rapidly into a rich environment for the fertilized egg to implant itself in. If the endometrium cannot nourish the egg, the pregnancy will end—even before a woman suspects that she had conceived. If a pregnancy has begun, the corpus luteum grows and secretes both estrogen and progesterone throughout the pregnancy. These hormone levels will increase throughout pregnancy, dropping only just before birth. If a pregnancy does not begin, the egg leaves the woman's body with her menstrual flow, and the corpus luteum regresses. Progesterone levels drop.

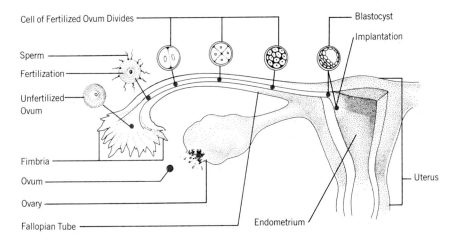

FIGURE 9.5

Egg from ovulation to implantation.

Menstrual Phase

As the hormone levels drop, the lining of the uterus is shed during the **menstrual phase** of the cycle. The body no longer needs this tissue, blood, and fluid. They leave through the vagina. Also in response to the lower levels of hormones, the body releases FSH and begins to prepare once again for ripening and releasing an egg. Menstrual flow usually amounts to no more than a few tablespoons of fluid, somewhat more in women who have an intrauterine contraceptive device, somewhat less in women who take oral contraceptives.

Premenstrual Syndrome

The levels of estrogen and progesterone in a woman's bloodstream are high at ovulation and the early luteal phase and then drop sharply just before menstruation begins. Some women report that for some or all of that time they feel headaches, abdominal bloating, painful breasts or joints, constipation, acne, sinusitis, asthma, cravings for sweets, salt, or alcohol. Psychological symptoms include fatigue, irritability, anxiety, lethargy, tension, depression, or violent outbursts. Quite a catalog. But how much of what has come to be called the **premenstrual syndrome,** or **PMS**—this mixture of various symptoms just before menstruation—is the result of negative cultural attitudes toward menstruation and female sexuality in general, and how much is unvarnished physiology?

To complicate matters, the whole problem has become heavily politicized. Some women used to argue that there is no physiological basis for premenstrual syndrome, that it is a convenient fabrication for keeping women down, another argument for not taking women's views seriously. At the other extreme are women who have used the premenstrual syndrome as a legal defense, arguing that it can so incapacitate a woman that she cannot be held responsible for her actions. But where does the truth lie?

In the medical community, one view of premenstrual syndrome is that "there is no formal proof that the syndrome exists, nor any real physiological basis to explain its symptoms" (*Research in Reproduction,* 1982, p. 1). This view rests on the fact that since the premenstrual syndrome was first described in the early 1930s, no one has collected solid data on the hormone levels of women who suffer from PMS and compared them with the hormone levels of a control group.

One London physician, Katharina Dalton, runs a clinic for women who suffer from PMS, and she is revered by many for taking the problem seriously. (Clinics also have begun opening in this country.) Dalton reports that symptoms can be relieved if women take natural progesterone four days before the symptoms usually start. The progesterone suppositories can be messy, however, and many women dislike the idea of taking hormones every month. For these reasons, some women prefer to treat PMS by a combination of diet—low salt and sugar, among other things—and exercise. On one side of the PMS debate are the medical skeptics. On the other are the women whose experience tells them that PMS is a fact.

Until we know what PMS actually is, we will not know how many women suffer from it nor how long it actually lasts. Many women report uncomfortable physical and psychological symptoms before and into the first 12 to 48 hours of their periods. Estimates range from 20 to 95 percent of women in their reproductive years, with only 5 percent suffering PMS symptoms severe enough to make them curtail their activities. But the estimated range probably is so large because PMS is still imprecisely defined. A tiny minority of women is described as reacting violently or in some other extreme way to PMS, and these are the exceptional, sensational cases that make the newspapers or that turn up in court. In these cases, a woman with PMS has acted more extremely, but not completely discontinuously, with her everyday behavior.

Given the confusion and the disagreements about PMS, what is one to conclude? Some women are very concerned that doctors' rejection of the existence of PMS is more of the same antifeminist attitude that held cramps to be a woman's rejection of her femininity. It is likely that within the very broad list of symptoms and their duration lurks a narrower clinical entity. PMS may even turn out to be more than one disorder. It is certainly possible for the hormone fluctuations of the menstrual cycle to alter women's behavior, and physicians have had success in treating them. But until behavioral data attest to its existence, the jury on PMS, officially at least, is still out. It is also true that many people—including doctors—are taking menstrual pain seriously when once they did not. Fewer women today are being told that their cramps are "all in their head."

Mood and the Menstrual Cycle

Closely related to the issue of the premenstrual syndrome is whether and how women's moods vary during their menstrual cycles. Our culture has deeply rooted beliefs about how menstruation makes women "moody." The late Senator Hubert Humphrey's physician, Dr. Edgar Berman, was widely quoted after he said that women were unfit to hold high government office because they were subject to "raging hormonal influences." In the ensuing conflict between Berman and some feminist critics, much heat but little light was generated.

It seems like a simple enough question to ask: do women's moods vary with the menstrual cycle? But simple it is not. To answer it, we would need to characterize one or more women's moods every single day. We could not just rely on women's reports of their own moods, because studies have found that women who *believe* that their periods are near, when they are not, report more fluid retention, pain, and changes in eating patterns than other women do (Ruble, 1977). These women, of course, are products of the same culture that believes in those "raging hormonal influences."

Most studies of women's moods during the menstrual cycle have in fact used women's own reports or projective measures like fantasies, stories, and reactions to pictures. Gloomy stories are interpreted to reflect gloomy moods, cheerful stories to reflect cheerful moods. The inference is that the cheerful (gloomy) stories come from women who also act cheerfully (gloomily) at work that day, at home, at play, and so forth. The issue badly needs clarification by behavioral measures as well as self-reports. Self-reports are valuable, for no one knows her moods better than a woman herself, but they do not tell the whole story.

To answer the "simple" question, we also need measurements of a woman's daily hormone levels. (Much of the current literature on the subject relies on women's memory of when their last menstrual period began, a badly flawed point of departure.) When reliable hormone measurements are in hand, and when reliable measurements of behavior are also in hand, then researchers can decipher *whether* and how the two may be connected.

Women do suffer from distress that may well be hormonally based: premenstrually, after childbirth, and as their menstrual cycling ultimately declines with age. In all of these instances, estrogen and progesterone decline markedly. We know that hormones affect how the nervous system functions, but we are only at the beginning of understanding how hormones and **neurotransmitters,** the chemicals that travel between nerve cells, affect each other. Ultimately, we will probably learn that people inherit different sensitivities to neurotransmitters, hormones, and their fluctuations. No one denies that some women experience unpleasant changes of mood over the menstrual cycle. No one denies that some women experience changes in sensory thresholds over the menstrual cycle (Parlee, 1983) as well. But we do not yet know enough about the relationship of moods and hormones in either sex to understand how the menstrual cycle affects women.

MENSTRUAL DIFFICULTIES

Menstruation is a normal response in a healthy body, and most women go through their years of menstrual cycling without any problems. But when menstrual problems do crop up, they tend to be problems of irregular, absent, or painful periods. Each has a different cause and cure. Most minor menstrual difficulties require little or no treatment and little or no adjustment of daily routine. Some women who have minor cramping or fluid retention find it helpful to cut salt from their food for several days before they expect to menstruate. Others swear by regular, moderate exercise; still others tout the curative powers of an orgasm. It probably does no real good (but no real harm either) to take special vitamins or to avoid hot baths and heavy exercise, as some people advocate. For any serious discomfort, a woman should see a doctor. Painful menstruation is treatable.

One serious problem associated with menstruation is toxic shock syndrome, a systemic infection that menstruating women (as well as children of both sexes, men, and nonmenstruating women) may develop. For a description of its probable cause and how best to avoid it, see "Sexuality in Perspective: Toxic Shock Syndrome."

Painful Menstruation

Painful menstruation, or **dysmenorrhea,** means sharp and quite uncomfortable pain in the abdomen and sometimes in the lower back and thighs or intermittent cramping. It is more than the mild cramping that a cup of tea and a catnap will cure. Some painful menstruation is a response to hormones secreted at ovulation, and some is a response to pelvic pathology.

Primary Dysmenorrhea   Cold comfort that it may be, **primary dysmenorrhea** is a sure sign that a woman has ovulated. It is also rare among women who have been pregnant. When a young woman begins to menstruate, her periods probably will be painless for the first year or so, before she has begun to ovulate regularly. But once she is ovulating regularly, she may begin to feel mild or severe pain just as her menstrual flow begins and into the next day or two. She may also feel heaviness in her abdomen (from vasocongestion), diarrhea, nausea, tender breasts, and perhaps psychological symptoms like anxiety or depression. Dysmenorrhea is not psychological in origin. It sometimes runs in families (Gantt and McDonough, 1981). A woman should see her doctor to rule out the presence of any other

**SEXUALITY IN PERSPECTIVE:
TOXIC SHOCK SYNDROME**

Several years ago, the makers of Rely tampons took them off the market after a blast of publicity implicated these and other "superabsorbent" tampons in a sometimes lethal illness called **toxic shock syndrome (TSS)**. At the time, no one really knew what caused toxic shock; all they knew was that several menstruating women who had used superabsorbent tampons had been hospitalized with very serious illnesses. Now it is known that two fibers contained in some tampons—polyester foam and polyacrylate rayon—can bind magnesium. When magnesium is present in the vagina, it creates an environment in which the TSS bacterium can multiply rapidly (Altman, 1985). The women had developed a sudden and high fever, headache, sore throat, vomiting, and diarrhea. They soon went into shock. Their hearts beat irregularly. Their kidneys stopped working. A reddish rash later developed over their whole body, even the palms of their hands and the soles of their feet. Then their skin peeled. Cultures showed a massive infection by a common bacterium, *Staphylococcus aureus*. Staph proliferates in many places: in household garbage, in nicked fingers, and in the warm, moist, magnesium-binding tampons that can be left in the vagina for many hours because they are extra-absorbent. The staph organism breeds and multiplies, and when it enters the bloodstream it releases a toxin, or poison, that causes a person to get sick—very sick.

Toxic shock syndrome is not confined to women who use tampons. Children come down with it, and so do adult men and nonmenstruating women. A postmenopausal *New York Times* reporter who contracted TSS nearly died. The tips of her fingers had to be amputated, and although she returned to work after some months, she is permanently disabled. Doctors treat TSS with antibiotics and fluid replacement. But because the toxic shock bacterium is known to grow in tampons, particularly superabsorbent ones, doctors recommend that menstruating women take a few precautions to lessen their chances of getting this rare but serious disease.

1 Wear sanitary napkins during sleep.

2 During the day, alternate tampons and sanitary napkins.

3 Change tampons at least every six hours.

4 Do not use superabsorbent tampons containing polyester foam or polyacrylate rayon.

5 For those who have had TSS, avoid tampons entirely for two menstrual cycles and until cultures for staph are negative.

Based on Gysler, M. "Toxic Shock Syndrome—a Synopsis," and Gantt, P. and McDonough, P. "Adolescent Dysmenorrhea." In Carol A. Cowell, M.D. (Ed.), *The Pediatric Clinics of North America* (May 1981) Vol. 28, No. 2; Philadelphia: Saunders, 1981.

contributing cause, but primary dysmenorrhea itself is the result of a uterus that is contracting painfully in response to hormones called **prostaglandins.** The prostaglandins make nerves in the uterus and surrounding tissue especially sensitive to pain.

For mild primary dysmenorrhea, doctors often prescribe nonaddictive painkillers. Aspirin is actually quite effective in some cases (it inhibits prostaglandins). For more serious pain, they prescribe medication that blocks the formation of prostaglandins. Known by the names Motrin, Indocin, Ponstel, and Anaprox, these prostaglandin inhibitors are taken for the first day or two of a menstrual period and for some women effectively combat the pain (Gantt and McDonough, 1981).

SECONDARY DYSMENORRHEA   Painful menstruation that is caused by some pelvic pathology is called **secondary dysmenorrhea.** In younger women, secondary dysmenorrhea usually results either from infection or from a condition called **endometriosis,** in which tissue from the uterine lining grows elsewhere in the pelvis, sometimes on an ovary or fallopian tube, on the exterior of the uterus, intestines, or bladder. Endometriosis may be congenital or the result of surgery or pelvic infection. It deserves medical attention because, like **pelvic inflammatory disease,** or **PID,** it can cause infertility. Some women with endometriosis also find sexual intercourse painful.

PID may cause not only painful menstruation but also general tenderness of the abdomen, fever, and painful intercourse. If it scars the internal reproductive organs, particularly the extremely narrow fallopian tubes, it can prevent a woman from ever getting pregnant. Painful menstruation can also be caused by intrauterine devices, obstruction or malformation of the genitals, endometrial polyps, cysts or tumors (Gantt and McDonough, 1981).

ABSENT MENSTRUATION

When a young woman has not menstruated by the time she is in her late teens, she has **amenorrhea,** or absent menstruation. This term, like dysmenorrhea, covers a variety of problems. Menstruation may be absent because a woman's hymen, the membrane that covers the vaginal opening, is impassable; it may be absent because of hormonal irregularities; it may be absent because of genital blockages or malformation; it may be absent because a woman is malnourished, fatigued, under emotional or physical stress or because she is pregnant or breast feeding. **Primary amenorrhea** describes the failure to begin menstruating, from whatever cause, and **secondary amenorrhea** describes the disappearance of menstruation once a woman has already had one or more menstrual periods.

MENOPAUSE

After 30 or 40 years, or 480 menstrual periods after menarche, a woman's menstrual cycles begin to taper off. Some time in her forties or early fifties, a woman begins producing fewer sex hormones, her menstrual periods grow shorter, irregular, and eventually cease, and she may feel certain transitory discomforts from the falling hormone levels. The end of menstruation is called **menopause.** It need not mean that she is sexually inactive, however. Many women actually feel relieved of the burden of worrying about contraception or pregnancy and continue to enjoy sexual relations well into old age. The diminished estrogen levels can produce certain minor problems, however. The vagina may lubricate less effectively during sexual arousal (and so may need local estrogen cream or K-Y sterile jelly for more comfortable sexual activity) and may be more prone to infection than before menopause. More serious problems believed to stem from the lower hormone levels include higher incidence of heart disease (approaching those of men, who have never had estrogen's presumed protection), cancer of the reproductive organs, and brittle bones. Some physicians believe in prescribing pills to replace the lost estrogen.

Estrogen Replacement and Osteoporosis

After menopause, all women show a substantial loss of estrogen. For a minority of women, this loss is associated with recurrent, uncomfortable hot flashes. Some women feel so overheated that they claim they could solve the world energy crisis. Others think the worst problem comes from mates who fail to appreciate cold nights without blankets. Most women have some hot flashes and consider them a minor annoyance.

Doctors first used estrogen replacement therapy on a large scale to treat bothersome hot flashes. Estrogen also had been used (without solid evidence) to treat skin wrinkling and depression. Estrogen goes to any organs that have estrogen receptors, and these include the lining of the uterus and the breasts. Estrogen can make cells multiply, and that is the source of its therapeutic value as well as its potential for causing cancer. (Estrogen should not be used in women who have or have had estrogen-sensitive cancers.) Women on long-term estrogen therapy have an increased risk of uterine cancer and must be checked every six months by their doctor. In contrast, current data show that estrogen does not increase the risk of breast cancer (for women who have never had breast cancer). Estrogen does help treat vaginal symptoms and hot flashes, but it does not keep skin from wrinkling.

One serious effect of menopause is **osteoporosis,** the loss of calcium from the bones. Osteoporosis is associated with aging in both sexes, but it is accelerated by menopause. Osteoporosis afflicts about one postmenopausal woman in four. It can produce the characteristic "dowager's hump," easily fractured bones, pain, and restricted activity. The catch-22 is that restricted activity accelerates the calcium loss. The current treatment for osteoporosis is low doses of estrogen, combined with increased calcium, increased fluid intake (for better absorption of the calcium) and some kind of weight-bearing exercise like walking, jogging, or dancing (Whedon, 1981). Women who must choose between the cancer-causing possibility of estrogen and the disability of osteoporosis face a dilemma. They must weigh the opposing risks and benefits. Women who fear the intake of any hormone will choose increased exercise plus calcium. Women who have had hysterectomies—surgical removal of the uterus, sometimes with removal of the ovaries (parahysterectomy)—will probably choose estrogen, calcium, and exercise.

Psychological Effects of Menopause

For a long time, psychiatrists viewed the menopausal woman in terms of what she had lost: reproductive ability, youth, and dependent children. She was considered at risk for "involutional" depression ("involutional" describing those disorders in which old people turn inward). But research on menopausal women paints a different picture.

True, few women welcome the physical changes of menopause—changes in hair, skin, waistline, bones, and vagina—but most women welcome the time given to them and their own needs once reproduction and child care have passed. Out of the empty nest emerge women who look for jobs or other activities that interest them, not depressed mother hens (Baruch et al., 1981). Studies show no increase in depression among women after menopause compared to women before menopause. In fact, the women at highest risk for depression are mothers at home with two or more preschoolers and husbands with whom they cannot communicate (Brown et al., 1975). One study of Manhattan households (Srole and Fischer, 1980) found that even when compared to young women, middle-aged women showed remarkable mental health. The investigators attributed that health to the fact that the recent changes in women's place in the working world hit middle-aged women after they had made decisions about marriage and family, and so they could add plans for working to their more traditional plans. Getting older meant moving into new and interesting areas.

Another study has shown that women between 43 and 53, the years of menopause, think that sex is as good or better than it was earlier in their lives. Only one woman in six felt that sex was less important after menopause than before. Menopausal women worry not about losing their own reproductive ability but about cancer and their husbands' health (Neugarten, 1963). Those are realistic concerns: by age 65, half of married women have been widowed. Older women are interested in sex, but the supply of sexual partners is limited, as are the socially acceptable ways for women to seek men.

Menopausal women cannot fairly be viewed in terms of losses, because they are not mourning the passing of menstruation, childbirth, or child rearing. That does not mean that they do not love their families, partners, children, or friends. They remain sexual beings, usually experienced sexual beings. Some are single, some married, some divorced, some cohabiting, some lesbian. Menopause is the loss of reproductive ability, but most women certainly do not consider it pure loss (Luria and Meade, 1984).

PREGNANCY: THE DEVELOPMENT OF NEW LIFE

When sperm and egg unite, and when the fertilized egg implants itself in the lining of the uterus, conception is complete, and a pregnancy has begun. A woman may first suspect that she is pregnant when her menstrual period does not arrive, or she may suspect it if her breasts grow tender, or if she has to urinate frequently, or if she feels tired. If she has been taking her resting temperature every morning to pinpoint her ovulation, she will notice that it has remained high. Some doctors suggest that a woman presume that she is pregnant if her basal temperature stays over 98 degrees Fahrenheit for 18 days or more. Acting on these **presumptive signs** of pregnancy, she is likely to have a pregnancy test.

From her urine or blood, the test will detect the presence of **human chorionic gonadotropin**, or **HCG**, a hormone secreted by the cells of the developing embryo, as the human infant is called for the first third of the pregnancy. (Some women buy home pregnancy test kits to test the urine excreted first thing in the morning. These tests work only when at least nine days have passed since a missed menstrual period and have a fairly high incidence of false results. A second test may therefore be in order. Home tests are appealing because they can be used in privacy. In contrast, blood tests performed by a laboratory can detect pregnancy much earlier, only a few days after conception.) By four weeks after conception (two weeks after a missed period should have started), an internal gynecological exam will show the characteristic changes of early pregnancy—a softening of the uterus and a bluish coloring of the cervix. These physical signs, plus a positive pregnancy test, are **probable signs** of pregnancy.

When she suspects or learns that she is pregnant, a woman should consult a doctor or midwife to learn how to keep herself and her embryo healthy. She may have to decide whether to continue or to end the pregnancy. (For more on abortion, see Chapter 10.) To the woman whose pregnancy continues to term, a baby will be born approximately 280 days after the first day of her last menstrual period.

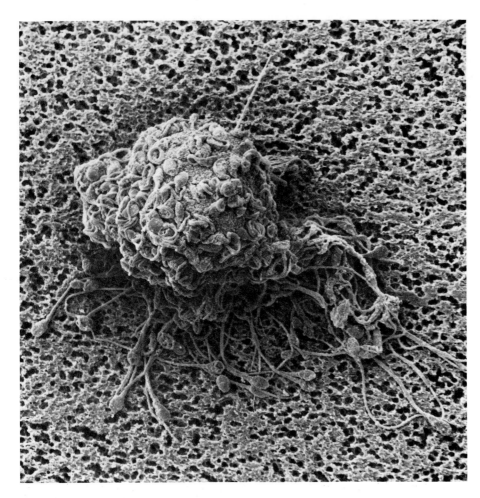

Human sperm cluster around an ovum (magnified 1650 times).

Human egg about to be fertilized (magnified 1000 times). Only one sperm swims through the zona pellucida (wavy band) and merges with the ovum itself. The ovum's covering appears as the white band.

Psychological and Social Aspects of Pregnancy

Pregnancy ushers in a series of changes and adjustments for the pregnant woman and for her partner. Pregnancy changes a woman's relationships to herself, her fetus, her partner, and others, as surely as it changes her body. From the moment she learns that she is pregnant, a woman may begin to behave on behalf of her fetus. She is no longer independent in quite the same way as she was before: she is already a mother, even though she will not feel the fetus for weeks or see it for months to come. She may begin to judge every morsel that she eats, every brisk walk, every catnap, for its effects on the pregnancy. Pregnancy imposes responsibilities for the fetus's well-being that the mother cannot escape (although she can ignore them), and these thousand daily reminders reinforce her in her new role.

Even if she rebels against the restrictions that pregnancy imposes, and even if she keeps up her familiar daily routine, she is irrevocably a mother-to-be now. Many pregnant women feel a mixture of positive feelings like pride, excitement, pleasure, and eager anticipation and negative feelings like anxiety, fear, restlessness, and frustration. Some women welcome their pregnancy, and others regret it, but few women escape the ambivalent feelings that accompany so profound a change in their lives.

I was proud of myself for getting pregnant. It meant I was a real woman and my husband was a real man (22-year-old mother).

I didn't want the baby. It was the wrong moment in our relationship. It took me weeks to decide for an abortion (24-year-old female graduate student).

By the eighth month of pregnancy, the *anticipation and preparation phase* begins. A woman may feel weighted down and bulky. Her thoughts move ahead to the delivery and the child she soon will meet. She will soon leave her job and increase her medical visits. With childbirth, one developmental stage ends and another, parenthood, begins.

The Expectant Father

What about the pregnant woman's partner? He (or she, in the case of homosexual pairs) also faces a series of adjustments to pregnancy and parenthood. He, too, faces adjustments that are psychological, social, and, yes, even physical. He feels changes in his relationship with both the pregnant woman and with the developing fetus. It may take an expectant father some time to feel that the pregnancy will result in a real child. He may feel jealous of the intimate relationship between his partner and the fetus within her. He may feel temporarily left out, shunted aside, and neglected.

As a pregnant woman's appetite for food and sex change, her partner may have to accommodate these not altogether pleasant changes in her. He may worry that the fetus will be born abnormal or malformed. It is not unusual for expectant fathers to experience some of the same physical discomforts that pregnant women feel. Many an expectant father feels nausea, tiredness, and mood swings—psychological reactions to the stresses of pregnancy and impending parenthood. Many men also feel deep pleasure, pride, and tenderness about the pregnancy from the start.

> *When we got the news that my wife had conceived, the world seemed to fall into place. I had been slightly troubled all during my twenties. But now I felt* right. *That feeling has never gone away (35-year-old college professor).*

People of either sex may wonder how they will do as parents when they still feel like children themselves.

Thus pregnancy confers on parents-to-be a number of psychological and social issues for resolution. They must adjust to their new roles and to changes in their own relationship. Finally, they must adjust to the inner, psychological demands of parenthood.

> *When I was pregnant, I used to think: "This all feels so complicated. I'm glad that the physical development is automatic" (25-year-old mother).*

The couples who adjust best to the dislocations of pregnancy—the perhaps infrequent sexual intercourse, the physical and psychological stresses—are those who are affectionate and cooperative. Strong and intimate bonds can help parents, expectant or actual, both to cope with the difficulties and to exult in the pleasures of parenthood.

First Trimester

A full pregnancy lasts 40 weeks. For purposes of discussion, it is divided into three trimesters.

The human egg ordinarily is fertilized in the outer third of one fallopian tube, the part nearest the ovary. As the fertilized egg moves slowly through the tube and toward the uterus, it divides repeatedly. The **blastocyst,** as the group of dividing cells is now called, implants in the uterine lining. Those that do not implant will flow out of the body during the next menstrual period. Some implant but soon detach, perhaps because the endometrium is insufficiently nourishing.

Such missed pregnancies happen so early that a woman has not had time to suspect that she was pregnant. Once the blastocyst attaches securely to the uterine wall, its cells continue to divide rapidly and soon begin to specialize. A **placenta** evolves out of some of the cells. This remarkable organ connects mother and fetus through their circulatory systems. Their bloodstreams do not actually mix. Instead, they circulate independently on separate sides of a barrier membrane in the placenta, exchanging oxygen, nutrients, and waste products from the developing embryo. The embryo is attached to the placenta by its umbilical cord, a translucent rope of tissue. (When the umbilical cord is cut at birth, its stump heals to form the **navel,** or bellybutton.) Blood vessels in the umbilical cord are connected to the embryo's circulatory system. The placenta produces increasingly large amounts of the hormones estrogen, progesterone, and HCG as the pregnancy continues. These hormones account for many of the physical changes a pregnant woman feels (among them, enlarged breasts and uterus, constipation, sleepiness, and so forth).

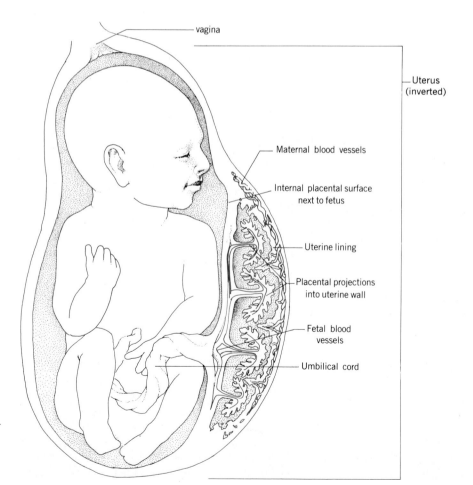

FIGURE 9.6

Fetus, placenta, and uterus. The fetus is attached to the nutrient-rich lining of the uterus via its placenta and umbilical cord. Although the bloodstream of mother and fetus do not mix, they exchange materials through thin cell walls.

A RELATIVELY NEW TEST, CALLED CHORIONIC VILLUS SAMPLING, CAN DETECT GENETIC DEFECTS IN THE FETUS AS EARLY AS THE EIGHTH WEEK OF PREGNANCY.

A relatively new test, called **chorionic villus sampling,** can detect genetic defects in the fetus as early as the eighth week of pregnancy. This sample consists of a villus: a tiny bump on one of the membranes (the chorionic membrane) that surrounds the fetus and forms part of the placenta. First, a thin needle is inserted into a pregnant woman's vagina and cervix. While a detailed ultrasound picture of her uterus and the fetus appear on a screen, a doctor guides the hollow needle toward a chorionic villus and snips it or suctions it off. Chorionic villus sampling may prove preferable to other diagnostic procedures (especially **amniocentesis**) for several reasons. Unlike amniocentesis, it can be performed in the first trimester. If genetic defects show up, it is still early enough in pregnancy for a woman to choose a relatively uncomplicated and safe abortion procedure. The biopsy can be performed early enough in pregnancy that the mother will not have felt the fetus's movements. The biopsy also offers more fetal tissue and faster results than amniocentesis (Schmeck, 1983).

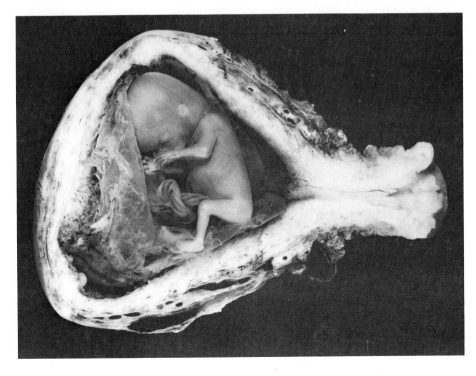

Human embryo in the first trimester of pregnancy, with placenta and surrounding membranes.

During the first 12 weeks of development, the **embryonic period,** the embryo develops three different layers of cells, ectoderm, endoderm, and, later, mesoderm. From the ectoderm will develop the nervous system, skin, and sensory organs. From the endoderm will develop the respiratory and digestive systems. From the mesoderm will develop muscles, skeleton, circulatory system, and reproductive organs. (For a full discussion of the development of reproductive organs, see Chapter 3.) By the end of the first trimester, the fetus's organ systems and major structural features have formed. It looks like a tiny human, with a large head, arms and hands, legs and feet, and a functioning placenta. (Earlier it looked like a tiny amphibian, with a tail, large head, and no neck.) The fetus swims in a warm, cushioning liquid, called **amniotic fluid,** contained within two membranes. The amniotic fluid buffers the fetus from extremes of noise and temperature and from hard shocks. A securely lodged fetus is nearly impossible for a woman to displace solely by falling or getting bumped. Protected by warm fluid, attached by a lifeline, the fetus hears the rush of blood through its mother's heart, the sounds of her digestion, her voice, as all of its needs are automatically met. Toward the end of the first trimester, the fetus's heartbeat—fast and high-pitched, sounding more like a bird's than a human's—can be detected. To hear their child's heartbeat can deeply move a mother and father.

Second Trimester

During the second and third trimesters, the embryo is called a **fetus.** The structures that developed during the first trimester now enlarge and specialize further. For instance, the fetus's face grows more human-looking, its genitals become clearly male or female, its hair and eyebrows fill in. The fetus goes through periods of rest and activity, darting and rolling through the amniotic fluid. By the sixteenth week, a woman may feel the faint tapping of the fetus's movements, a development called **quickening.**

The second trimester is not only when the heartbeat can be heard and movement felt (by those who feel her uterus as well as by the mother), but also when tests to determine the size, health, and position of the fetus(es) may be performed. (Heartbeat, movement, and sonograms of the fetal skeleton are all **positive signs** of pregnancy.) **Sonograms** are procedures in which sonar waves are bounced off the fetus. The sonogram shows how big the fetus is (sometimes helpful for confirming how far advanced the pregnancy is), its position in the uterus, how many fetuses there are, and may reveal certain abnormalities in development. Amniocentesis is another procedure, in which a sample of amniotic fluid is taken through a hollow needle inserted into the abdomen and amniotic sac and then examined. Because the fluid contains cells from the fetus, the chromosomes can be examined for abnormalities. Amniocentesis is ordinarily conducted between the sixteenth and twentieth weeks of pregnancy, a time when there is enough fluid to sample and also a time when abortion is still legally available, should parents decide to end the pregnancy of a deformed fetus. (Results from amniocentesis take about four weeks.) Amniocentesis poses small but real risks to the fetus: the needle may puncture a vital organ, or a mother may spontaneously abort. Usually, therefore, it is performed only on women over 35 or others whose fetuses are at risk for chromosomal disorders (such as Down's syndrome or gene mutations such as sickle-cell anemia, or hemophilia).

SEXUALITY IN PERSPECTIVE: SEX DURING PREGNANCY

Pregnancy is a normal and healthy state, having sex is a normal and healthy activity, and so the two may be quite compatible. But in actual practice, for many couples pregnancy means less frequent sexual intercourse and orgasm (White and Reamy, 1982). During the third trimester especially, sexual interest and activity decline (Calhoun, Selby, and King, 1981). But this decline is not universal. For many expectant couples, sex is welcome. Women should ask their doctor's advice about sexual activity during pregnancy. Most physicians will recommend that in an uncomplicated pregnancy, so long as a woman is sexually interested, she can masturbate or have sexual relations with a partner.

For those times during a pregnancy when intercourse is uncomfortable or inadvisable for medical reasons, couples may want to use techniques of mutual masturbation or oral-genital sex. The male-above position is likely to be uncomfortable as the pregnancy progresses, and couples may therefore want to experiment with side-to-side, rear-entry, or woman-above positions.

Many couples enjoy lovemaking during pregnancy for its very newness and for its freedom from worries about birth control. Others are made uncomfortable, especially in late pregnancy, by the presence of the fetus. As one prospective father said:

> *When we made love in the eighth month or so, I could feel the baby's head with my penis. It made me feel inhibited, even though I knew I was being silly. So we decided for oral sex, taking turns. We got very inventive (33-year-old male chemist).*

After the child is born, most physicians advise that a woman wait three to six weeks to resume intercourse. By that time, a woman's body ordinarily has recovered enough from childbirth to have passed the danger of infection, and episiotomies probably have healed. Women who are breast-feeding may find that their breasts now respond differently to stimulation and are either more or less sensitive. A sexual partner may find their milk-filled breasts very erotic—or quite the opposite. Rather to some people's surprise, the breasts may leak milk in response to sexual arousal and fairly spurt milk during orgasm.

Some women find that they can have orgasms for the first time after childbirth, probably because the increased capacity for vasocongestion remains after pregnancy ends. Other women find that they have to tone up their vaginal and perineal muscles in order to feel a satisfying orgasm. The specific exercise for toning these muscles—and it may enhance sexual pleasure for all women—is called a **Kegel** (rhymes with "bagel"), after the doctor who popularized it. To Kegel, a woman tightens the muscles that stop the flow of urine and then releases them. She should repeat this procedure a couple of dozen times a day over a period of weeks.

FIGURE 9.7

Mutual masturbation during pregnancy. Some couples find sexual satisfaction during pregnancy from mutual masturbation.

Third Trimester

The last third of the pregnancy is when the fetus develops all of the finishing touches that will help it to survive in the world. Under its translucent skin, insulating pads of fat are deposited; its lungs develop so it will be able to breathe after birth; it rapidly gains weight and length. The fetus who is born early in the third trimester has a better than even chance of surviving, given sophisticated medical care. Every day closer to term improves its chances of survival. Thus the seven-month fetus who weighs only 2 pounds has less chance of surviving than

FIGURE 9.8

Sexual intercourse during pregnancy. A pregnant woman with a bulging abdomen may find it helps to sit astride her partner during intercourse. Partners lying side by side (shown in Figure 8.16) is another possibility during pregnancy.

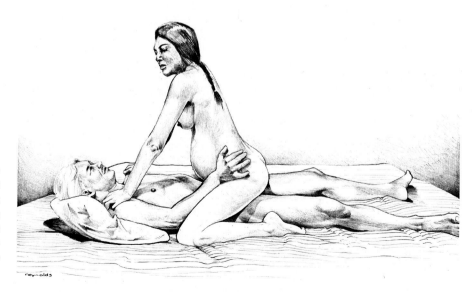

the eight-month, 5 pounder or the nine-month, 7 or 8 pounder. At some medical centers, doctors can save most of the "thousand grammers," the tiny premature infants who weigh only about 2 pounds. When infants weigh less than that at birth, their chances for survival are poor. During the last trimester, the fetus has grown large enough so that the uterus is a tight fit. Now, instead of swimming freely, most fetuses settle head down in the uterus. Their mothers now feel the pokes from feet and hands and the bumping of a head on their pelvic floor. Late in pregnancy, it is quite common for parents even to notice the fetus hiccoughing!

By the last months of pregnancy, the mother's hormone levels are very high, she has gained 20 or 30 pounds or more, and she may feel huge and ungainly. The uterus is so large that it presses against her lungs, stomach, bladder, and intestines, causing shortness of breath, indigestion, frequent urination, and constipation. Her heart has enlarged to handle the increased volume of blood pumping through her system. She may be retaining fluid and feeling puffy.

I continued jogging until 10 days before delivery. Towards the end, I felt as if I were drowning in fluid as I breathed. Finally, I just couldn't heave my bulk around any more, so I rested, feeling like a beached whale, until the baby arrived.

Her uterus contracts painlessly and irregularly in rehearsal, **Braxton-Hicks contractions** that firm the uterus up for the work of delivery. Her breasts are large and may secrete a clear fluid called **colostrum,** a precursor to breast milk that will nourish the newborn baby for its first day or two and provide it with immunity to disease. A few weeks before delivery, the fetus's head is likely to drop down into the pelvis. Sometimes called "lightening," this movement takes pressure off the woman's lungs and upper body. It will soon be time to deliver.

Problem Pregnancies

Some pregnancies are plagued with problems. Early in a pregnancy a woman may **miscarry,** that is, spontaneously abort the fetus. The reason for miscarriage is not always clear. Sometimes an egg or sperm is abnormal. Sometimes the fetus is abnormal, and miscarriage is nature's way of aborting a deformed being. In other cases, miscarriage results from problems with the mother's hormones or physiology: for example, the cervix may open too early in pregnancy and allow the premature infant to be born. Many women have a single miscarriage and no other problem pregnancies at all, but a few women repeatedly miscarry, and they require special medical treatment. The more miscarriages she has had, the greater a woman's chances of miscarrying again.

Miscarriages can happen at any time during a pregnancy; if they occur during the final trimester, they are usually termed "stillbirths." Signs of a miscarriage include abdominal cramping, pain, and bleeding. If a pregnant woman notices any of these symptoms, she should call her doctor right away. Some miscarriages can be averted. Some are inevitable. Many a miscarriage is emotionally painful, and many parents need to complete a mourning process for their lost child.

I had accidentally gotten pregnant when our son was just a few months old. Early in my second month, I caught a virus. I had a high fever, and a few days later I had a heavy period. Another pregnancy test confirmed that I had miscarried. I was surprised that we were so sad about it (27-year-old mother).

ECTOPIC PREGNANCY   An **ectopic pregnancy** is a pregnancy in which the embryo implants somewhere besides the uterine lining. Usually ectopic pregnancies take place in one of the fallopian tubes—a tubal pregnancy. More rarely, they take place in the cervix, ovary, or abdominal cavity. Ectopic pregnancies may progress without symptoms for some weeks, supported by the normal hormones of pregnancy that circulate in the mother's bloodstream. However, when the fetus grows too large for the fallopian tube or other organ to accommodate it, the pregnancy comes to an end. (There are a few documented cases of abdominal pregnancies that proceed to term and that produce normal, healthy infants. Rare as these cases are, they demonstrate that hormones essential to pregnancy will flow wherever the mother's blood flows.) With a tubal pregnancy, a woman feels sharp abdominal pain as the tube bursts. Bleeding then follows, and the fetus is miscarried. In most cases, the fallopian tube (or ovary, in ovarian pregnancies) must be surgically removed.

THE RH FACTOR   The **Rh factor** is a substance found in human (and *Rh*esus monkeys, hence the name) blood cells. Most people (86 percent) have this substance, and they are termed "Rh positive." Some people don't have it, and they are termed "Rh negative." An Rh-negative mother can pose problems for her child *if* the father of the child is Rh positive. If both parents are Rh negative, the child will be Rh negative also, and the problems of incompatibility will not crop up. Problems occur during the birth of a child with Rh-positive blood, when a small amount of blood from the baby leaks into the Rh-negative mother's bloodstream (as the placenta separates from the uterus, for example, or at other points during delivery). Her Rh-negative blood will treat the baby's Rh-positive blood like a foreign substance and will build antibodies against it. This first baby suffers no damage, but any subsequent babies meet the antibodies in the mother's bloodstream.

Early in pregnancy, a blood test will confirm the parents' Rh status. If the mother proves Rh negative and the child Rh positive, she will be given an injection immediately after delivery to prevent her blood from producing antibodies (and will be injected also after all future deliveries, abortions, or miscarriages). If she has already produced antibodies, her baby may receive a complete transfusion of blood immediately after birth. This is a dangerous procedure for the newborn, and not all survive it. The best treatment for Rh-negative mothers is early detection, with a simple blood test, and early treatment.

INFERTILITY AND STERILITY

Some people choose not to have children, out of commitment to religious, professional, or other values that are incompatible with parenthood. But other people, who want to have children, have to contend with the problems of infertility or sterility. One in seven couples is **infertile** and cannot maintain a pregnancy to term or conceive a child after having intercourse for a year without birth control. In slightly over half the cases, the problem resides with the female, and in slightly fewer than half, with the male. In many couples with a fertility problem, it turns out that both partners are marginally fertile, and the combination of their problems eventually brings them to fertility specialists. Infertility differs from sterility in that **sterility** is an absolute condition, the absence of the ability to reproduce. Thus a male who has no testes or the female who has no uterus is sterile. Their choices for having children are necessarily limited to adoption, to artificial insemination of the female by a donor (AID) in cases of male sterility, or a pregnancy by a surrogate mother in cases of female sterility. The latter remains a controversial and relatively uncommon procedure. Two limiting factors are that not many women want to act as surrogates, and the legal consequences of the procedure remain largely untested. AID is a more common procedure, used in cases of male sterility and infertility. Sperm banks will even mail frozen donor sperm to physicians, who insert it into a woman's vagina in a simple, painless procedure.

THE APPARENT INCIDENCE OF INFERTILITY HAS BEEN INCREASING.

Many cases of infertility can be treated successfully. In the last few decades, the apparent incidence of infertility has been increasing, a trend ascribed to several possible sources.

1 A high incidence of pelvic inflammatory disease (PID)—especially **chlamydia** and **gonorrhea**—and other sexually transmitted diseases, which can scar delicate reproductive organs. (See Chapter 17.)

2 An increase in numbers of people who are postponing parenthood until their 30s, an age when women take significantly longer to conceive than they might have in their 20s.

3 An increase in infertile couples who seek medical help for infertility because better diagnoses and treatment are available today.

Infertility in Males

In males, sperm must develop fully (through 18 steps of development) and swim strongly, must travel through all the necessary internal pathways and into a partner's vagina, and must be delivered in sufficient numbers for a pregnancy to result. Men may be infertile if too many of their sperm are malformed—some may have two tails or broken tails, for instance, or even two heads—or if the sperm swim poorly (called poor **motility**) or if there are too few sperm in the ejaculate. Men average about 100 million sperm per milliliter of ejaculate. Pregnancies are extremely unlikely if there are fewer than 20 million sperm per milliliter of ejaculate; and half of the men with sperm counts between 20 and 40 million per milliliter are infertile. A common cause of infertility in males is a faulty valve in the spermatic vein. Called a **varicocele,** and more often found in the left than the right spermatic vein, the vein allows blood to circulate around the internal sperm-producing pathways rather than conducting it away and toward the heart. Whether because this blood is too warm or because it is toxic to developing sperm, doctors do not know, but the blood effectively irritates the sperm and causes them to be ejaculated before they are fully mature and therefore before they can swim strongly enough to reach the woman's egg. Most varicoceles can be surgically corrected relatively simply.

Other men may be infertile because their body mistakenly targets their sperm as foreign bodies and attacks them, much as it would attack an invading disease-bearing organism. This kind of reaction can sometimes be treated successfully with medications that suppress the body's immune response to the sperm. Some men have low sperm counts because their scrotum gets too warm—sperm thrive only when the scrotum is slightly lower than body temperature—whether from hot baths, tight clothing, fever, or another cause. Sperm count, motility, and shape can also be adversely affected by long-term marijuana use, poor general health, and other usually reversible causes.

> *When we found out that it was me who was causing our infertility, I may not have shown it as much as my wife, but it certainly hurt. After a while, I had to go through something much like a mourning process, to let go of the idea that I would ever be a father, before I could begin to heal (36-year-old professor).*

Infertility in Females

In females, the causes of infertility may be located in nearly any part of the reproductive organs. For a female to be fertile, she must ovulate, the egg must merge with a sperm cell and travel into her fallopian tube, the tube must be open and able to conduct the egg toward the uterus, the egg must implant in the uterine lining, the lining must be able to support the embryo, the vagina and cervix must admit sperm, the cervical mucus must allow sperm to pass, hormones must be released at the right times and in the right amounts throughout the menstrual cycle and pregnancy, and the uterus must be able to support a growing fetus.

Some women have an allergic-like reaction to their partner's sperm that interferes with conception. Condoms sometimes succeed in correcting this problem because they prevent semen from coming in contact with a woman's body and therefore may allow it time to desensitize to the sperm. Common causes of infertility in females include: endometriosis; pelvic inflammatory disease, which scars and closes the fallopian tubes; failure to ovulate, usually because of hormonal problems; and failure to maintain a pregnancy to term.

Endometriosis is sometimes (inaccurately) called "the career woman's disease," because it tends to increase in severity with the number of menstrual cycles a woman has. It is believed that endometriosis is congenital. Probably when the chemical instructions go out for building the upper reproductive tract in the fetus, part of the program is faulty and causes endometrial tissue to form elsewhere besides the endometrium. When a woman reaches menstrual age, the hormones that cycle in her body and cause the endometrium to build up each month also congest the "misplaced" endometrial tissue. But the body has no way to shed the misplaced tissue, as it does with the endometrium during the menstrual flow, and so the endometriosis grows progressively worse with each cycle, until it may scar or cause pelvic organs to adhere to each other. It may, for example, cause the fallopian tubes to adhere to part of the uterus or intestines so that eggs cannot enter to be fertilized, or it may scar and close the tubes themselves. Therefore, women who (try to) get pregnant relatively late in their reproductive life are at greater risk for having problems with endometriosis than are younger women. (The progressive nature of endometriosis is one reason why its other symptoms—painful menstruation, premenstrual discomfort, or painful intercourse—may worsen over time as well.) One treatment for endometriosis is hormone therapy that prevents menstrual cycling and the building of any endometrial tissue. Another treatment is oral contraceptive pills that disrupt the menstrual cycle and prevent endometrial build´up. But this treatment is not used for women who want to get pregnant, and the side effect require monitoring. Yet another treatment is surgery to break adhesions and remove excess tissue. Pregnancy is nature's own remedy: it prevents menstrual cycling for months. In human history, when women were pregnant or nursing for much of their reproductive lives, endometriosis had little chance to cause them problems.

The treatment fits the problem, but not all forms of infertility are yet curable. Some, but not all, blocked fallopian tubes can be surgically repaired. In an increasing number of cases where the tubes are absent or not functional, treatment may consist of removing a woman's egg, fertilizing it in a laboratory, and implanting it in her uterus. (Known as **in vitro fertilization,** literally "in glass" fertilization after the glass laboratory dish in which ova are fertilized, this procedure is gradually becoming more widely available in the United States. Some in vitro fertilizations and artificial inseminations involve surrogate mothers.) Failure to ovulate can sometimes be treated with a "fertility drug" such as Clomid that induces eggs to ripen. Sometimes these drugs cause several eggs to ripen, and newspapers show pictures of the overwhelmed parents with their five or six tiny blessed events. In in vitro procedures, doctors may extract several ripened eggs from a prospective mother, to increase the chances of success. Multiple births are therefore relatively common among the ranks of these infertile couples as well. To date only a minority of couples have succeeded in producing a child with in vitro procedures.

Much of the frustration of infertility, however, lies in how slowly the problem is unraveled. Diagnosis, not to mention cure, may take years or may never come. A doctor who says, "I'm sorry, but there is nothing more we can do," or "We just don't know what the problem is in this case" can bring a couple to despair. Fertility specialists, like all conscientious doctors, proceed from the least invasive to the most invasive diagnostic procedures and treatments. Thus they will insist on charting a woman's temperature to see that she ovulates before they will perform exploratory surgery, and they often insist on a few months' wait between each different procedure to give a couple time to get pregnant after each. Diagnostic procedures themselves often cure the problem: for example, flushing the fallopian tubes with an opaque solution for X ray can sometimes open them. Fertility specialists are working to cure the problems that still elude them. Among other questions, they are trying to answer: what role the coating of the ovum (the **zona pellucida**) may play in conception; under what circumstances (such as advanced age) men or women contribute genetically faulty germ cells; how to help certain men to produce motile sperm; and how to increase the success rate of in vitro fertilizations.

The Infertile Couple

The waiting and the menstrual period that each month announces "no pregnancy" can be emotionally devastating. More than one marriage has faltered on a partner's failure to produce children. More than one fully grown man or woman has felt helpless, incompetent, or worthless because of an infertility problem.

The worst thing was not knowing why I couldn't conceive. Every test on both of us checked out. The doctors said that sometimes they just can't find the cause. "There's so much we still don't know," they would say (34-year-old male lawyer).

After four years of failing to get pregnant, the seventh doctor we saw diagnosed endometriosis and said it could be treated. When I didn't menstruate, because I was pregnant, I was so happy that time stood still. I will never forget those hours. I felt like I had rejoined the living (37-year-old female professor).

At a time in their lives when young adults deeply wish to build a family, to extend themselves and their relationship in the generativity of parenthood, infertility may be anguishing. Infertility often feels like a death does and evokes from people many of the same feelings—denial, rage, depression, and perhaps a final acceptance—as more conventional mourning. At any point in their medical quest for a child, a couple may decide to abandon the struggle. Some opt for childlessness and the very real pleasures of an adult life. Some develop a close relationship with a niece or nephew or another child. Some plod through the thicket of more tests and procedures. Some adopt a child.

A couple can take some steps to improve their chances of conceiving even before they consult a physician. (An internist, general practitioner, or gynecologist can refer people to specialists in fertility problems.) They should make sure that they are having intercourse around the time when the woman ovulates, for she is most fertile at that time. If she does ovulate, it will be about 14 days before the onset of her menstrual period. If her cycles are regular, counting the days may work. For some women, a more accurate method of pinpointing ovulation is to chart their body temperature. A woman does this by keeping a thermometer and graph paper by her bed. First thing every morning, before she leaves bed or ingests anything, she takes her temperature orally and records it, to the tenth of a degree, on the chart labeled along the vertical axis for temperature readings between 97 and 99 degrees. Along the horizontal axis, the date is charted, day by day. Ovulation will show up as a slight dip in temperature, followed within 24 hours by a rise of up to one degree. After ovulation, the temperature will stay at 98 or higher until just before menstruation. (This method may not work well for women whose temperatures do not show the telltale drop and rise.) A couple should time their intercourse for once in about 48 hours (giving the sperm time to replenish themselves; more frequent intercourse tends to produce diminishing returns) and should alternate so that one month they have intercourse on even-numbered days and the next month on odd-numbered days. (Here is another instance in which sex can become homework rather than pleasure.) It goes without saying that they should not use birth control. Women who have been taking oral contraceptive pills may need an extra six to eight weeks for their menstrual cycles to become ovulatory again. Most couples succeed in conceiving within a year. For those who cannot and for those who conceive but miscarry, the road ahead may be rocky going. Just as childbearing forces adults to make a host of psychological adjustments, failure to bear children can bring on its own psychological adjustments. Many couples ultimately decide that the freedom of life without children has rewards. Infertile couples are not miserable all their lives.

How long labor lasts varies from woman to woman and from pregnancy to pregnancy.

BIRTH

During the suspended animation of late pregnancy, a woman is focused on giving birth, and the couple is focused on meeting this intimate stranger. Finally, labor begins. In some women, labor starts slowly, the contractions of the uterus that have been happening for weeks now gradually building in intensity. In others, labor starts suddenly, with the rupture of membranes and a rush of warm amniotic fluid from the vagina. Still other women discover the mucous plug that has sealed the cervix, the so-called "bloody show" that signals labor is beginning. How long labor lasts varies from woman to woman and from pregnancy to pregnancy. First labors tend to be longer than subsequent labors, but some first labors themselves last only two or three hours. Others, slower to build, take nearly a full 24 hours. No one knows exactly what triggers labor, although there is speculation that a hormonal signal from the fetus is the trigger. Hormonal signals in the mother begin contractions of the uterus. These contractions gradually open her cervix and press the baby downward through the birth canal.

First Stage of Labor

Labor has begun when the uterus is contracting regularly and effectively. The cervix thins out and opens to permit the eventual passage of the baby into the vagina. Contractions may begin at 10- or 15-minute intervals and increase to 5- or 7-minute intervals, although the timing of contractions and the duration of early first-stage labor vary enormously among individual women and according to the position of the baby in the uterus. By the time the baby is ready to emerge, contractions will come only a minute apart. Many women prefer to stand or walk around during the first stage of labor, and many are advised to stay at home (if they are not having a home delivery), in familiar surroundings, until they are uncomfortable enough to need medical care.

First-stage labor is defined by the cervix thinning out and dilating from closed to about seven centimeters open. At some point during the first stage, women who have learned techniques of relaxation and breathing will begin to apply what they have learned in order to cope with the increasingly intense contractions. Many men, now actively involved in coaching their partner through these breathing and relaxation exercises, participate in and contribute to their child's birth rather than staying passively and anxiously in some waiting room. Not all males and not all hospitals encourage these "labor coaches" in the labor or delivery rooms, but recent years have seen increased participation by fathers in the birth of their children.

The first stage of labor.

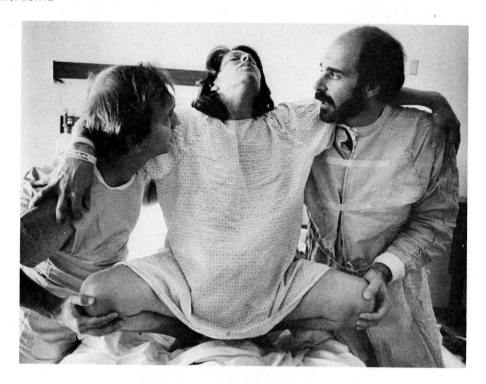

When I found out my wife was pregnant and expected me to stay with her during the delivery, I thought, "No way." I didn't want to watch a gory spectacle. But there is nothing gory about birth, and if I hadn't been there I would have missed the most moving experience of my life (27-year-old father).

TRANSITION   Defined as the period when the cervix opens from 7 or 8 to 10 centimeters, at which point it is considered fully dilated, transition usually is the most difficult part of a woman's labor. Contractions are intense and follow closely on one another. A woman may feel hot and cold, exhausted, irritable, nauseated, even fearful, and transition is when she may need the most encouragement and support from others. Transition is shorter than earlier first-stage labor, lasting from only a few contractions to an hour, and it ends when the presenting part (usually the head) of the baby can begin to ease out of the uterus and into the vagina.

SECOND STAGE OF LABOR

As the baby's head presses through the fully dilated cervix, the second stage of labor has begun. After transition, which may have been very difficult, this part of labor comes as a relief to many women. The second stage is shorter than the first stage, and most women now feel a deep and powerful urge to push the baby out along with their contractions. For many women, being able to push relieves much of the earlier pain of labor. As they bear down, the baby moves along the vagina, its head gradually becoming visible. When the widest part of the baby's head is visible and does not recede with each successive contraction, a point called

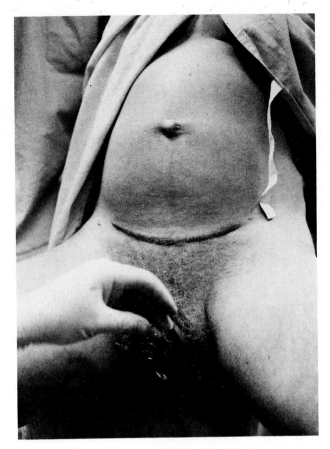

The second stage of labor. The baby's head is crowning. Notice the Caesarean scar from an earlier delivery. Today some women who have had Caesarean deliveries can later deliver vaginally.

crowning, the birth attendant may ask the mother to stop pushing for a moment. (The vast majority, about 98 percent, of babies are born head first. The others are born bottom first, in the **breech position**, or with some other body part—shoulder or leg, for example—presenting itself first. Some of these babies can be turned so that they are born head first. Because births of babies in unusual positions are much more likely to run into complications, many are now delivered by **Caesarean section**, a surgical procedure in which the baby is removed from the uterus through an incision in the mother's abdomen.)

My wife had a Caesarean, but I was allowed into the operating room with her. When our daughter was born, they handed her to me. She was awesome. I just held her and looked and looked at her and cried from joy (24-year-old law student).

The increase in the number of Caesarean births over the past several decades has caused controversy. Obstetricians argue that Caesareans reduce the incidence of birth-related injuries to infants and save lives of infants and mothers. Opponents argue that too many Caesareans are done arbitrarily—for the convenience of medical staff or for fear of malpractice charges—rather than for legitimate reasons.

In vaginal deliveries, some attendants make an incision from the vagina and along the perineum (the area between the vagina and rectum), called an **episi-**

The baby's head is born first. Its body slides out after another uterine contraction or two.

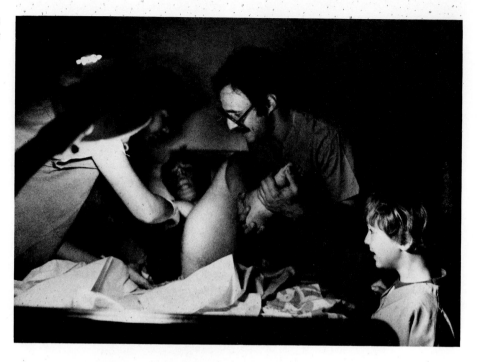

otomy, to allow the baby to be born without tearing the mother's tissues. Others do not perform an episiotomy. All attendants support and guide the baby out of the vagina: head first, then shoulders, trunk, legs, feet, and umbilical cord. Some women have questioned the need for routine episiotomies, claiming that they are not always necessary and that recovering from an episiotomy is often more difficult than recovering from childbirth itself. Those who favor episiotomy say that it prevents a woman's vagina from tearing and that the neat incision is easier to repair than a ragged tear would be.

The newborn is likely to be covered in a whitish, creamy substance called **vernix** that insulates its skin. Vernix is made up of shed fetal skin cells. The attendants may wipe the baby off and suction mucus from its nose and throat. Once it starts breathing, its coloring is no longer bluish. The attendants quickly assess the baby's condition for five obvious signs—heart rate, respiration, color, muscle tone, and responsiveness—immediately after birth and five minutes later. This assessment is called the baby's **Apgar score** (named after Virginia Apgar, the pediatrician who devised it). The Apgar test gives a good, quick reading of the newborn's condition.

When the umbilical cord, which has tied baby to placenta, stops pulsing, it is clamped and cut. In a few weeks, the remaining umbilical stump will heal into the baby's navel.

Third Stage of Labor

The last stage of labor consists of a few contractions that expel the placenta from the uterus. Many women do not feel these contractions, especially in the excitement of greeting their child. The attendant examines the placenta to make sure that all of it has detached from the uterus. Remaining parts might create infection or bleeding. At this stage, too, the attendant will stitch up the episiotomy, if one has been performed. For the next several weeks, the new mother will have a discharge of **lochia,** much like a long menstrual period, as her uterus sheds it thick lining and returns to its prepregnant state.

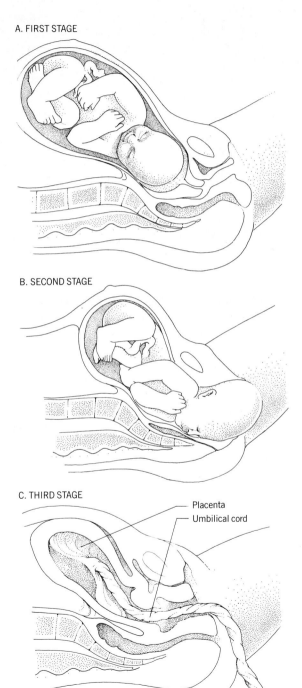

A. FIRST STAGE

B. SECOND STAGE

C. THIRD STAGE

Placenta
Umbilical cord

FIGURE 9.9

The three stages of childbirth. In the first stage, the cervix thins and opens to permit passage of the infant. In the second stage, the infant passes through the vagina and is born. In the third stage, the placenta and fetal membranes are expelled.

NEW ATTITUDES TOWARD CHILDBIRTH

Until early in this century, many infants were born at home. Then custom shifted, and the scene of childbirth moved from the bedroom to the hospital delivery room. The hospital setting offered obstetricians sanitary surroundings and greater control over the course of labor, especially in case of emergency. Husbands were relegated to a waiting room, and women often labored alone. Many laboring women received enough pain medication to render them groggy or even unconscious. Thus in many instances, neither parent was alert nor present to greet the birth of their child. Yet in terms of declining mortality rates for infants and mothers, the advantages of hospital births were real enough.

Home Birth

Today many people want to return childbirth to the family, be that in the family home or a home-like birth center. In the past 10 to 20 years, many prospective parents and many medical professionals alike have acted to undo the perceived drawbacks of hospital births. Their objections have tended to center on the clinical atmosphere of the hospital; the isolation of the laboring woman; the widespread use of medication with its possibly adverse effects on laboring women and their infants; and the frequency of medical interventions in the natural and healthy process of birth. Home births are less expensive than hospital or clinic births, and birth centers too are usually less expensive than hospitals. Costs are lower because many women go home from a birth center or hospital birthing room sooner than they would after a traditional or more complicated delivery.

After screening out those pregnant women whose deliveries might present complications, some trained midwives and obstetricians willingly attend births in family homes or birth centers. There, a woman is in familiar surroundings.

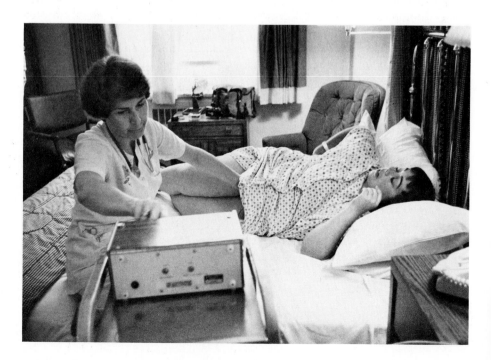

A birthing center.

Instead of a cold and clinical setting filled with unfamiliar equipment, the room is homey and inviting. Many hospitals and birth centers now offer birthing rooms complete with television set, a shower, couch and end tables, wallpaper on the walls, and a small refrigerator.

Emergency equipment is out of sight (but nearby just in case). Reputable professionals make sure that they have ready access to emergency equipment should the labor turn difficult. Father, midwife, obstetrician, and other helpers—even brothers and sisters—attend and support the woman. The use of medication is minimal, for the emphasis is on birth as a natural and healthy course of events. When no medication has been used, infants often emerge alert and curious. For some time after birth, their eyes remain open. They may nurse at their mother's breasts and curl their hands around a proffered finger.

Several other recent developments have made many hospital deliveries less impersonal.

As one childbirth educator remarked, "Is there any such thing as *unnatural* childbirth?"

Natural Childbirth

When people talk about **natural childbirth,** they usually have in mind several different things: an unmedicated delivery, a mother and labor coach who have learned techniques for coping with pain, and perhaps a delivery somewhere besides a hospital delivery room. As one childbirth educator remarked, "Is there any such thing as *unnatural* childbirth?" Natural, or prepared, childbirth proceeds from these assumptions: a woman who is psychologically prepared for birth can cooperate in delivering her child and can deal more effectively than an unprepared woman can with the discomfort of labor; the perception of pain is heightened by tension and fear and diminished by calm and comprehension. Thus many pregnant women and their labor coach (usually a husband or friend) attend classes or learn from cassettes or books how to relax between contractions, how to breathe through contractions, how to push the baby out, and generally what to expect during the course of labor and delivery. By rehearsing several possible situations—an arduous labor, an emergency Caesarean, a medicated delivery, etc.—people can reduce their fear and their experience of pain and can greatly enhance their enjoyment of this natural biological event.

Some advocates of natural childbirth object to the use of drugs during labor, arguing that they are often unnecessarily administered to the mother, dimming her perception and her ability to cooperate in the delivery as well as posing a possible danger to the fetus, who is still attached to its mother and susceptible to whatever enters her bloodstream. Others object to the **lithotomy position** commonly used for delivery, in which a woman lies on her back, legs up, and feet in metal stirrups. Some women are more comfortable and can work with rather than against gravity if they labor in other positions: squatting, sitting up, kneeling, crouching on all fours. Some advocates of natural childbirth prefer the comfort of home or home-like surroundings to the cold, clinical hospital. They ask that monitors, probes, vaginal examinations, drugs, episiotomies, and the like not be administered routinely, that the birth proceed with as little "unnatural" interference as is consistent with the health and safety of mother and child. After the child is born, many mothers like to be awake, to hold and nurse their baby right away. Immediately after birth, when the baby is alert and curious, can be a time when parents and child begin to form the intense attachments that will later cement their relationship.

In uncomplicated, straightforward deliveries, many of these conditions can be met. A woman should certainly feel free to shop early in her pregnancy for a birth attendant whose philosophy of childbirth is compatible with her own. Likewise, knowing how to relax and to breathe through contractions can be genuinely helpful during labor, and many women have avoided medication or anesthesia because they could cooperate rather than fight their contractions. But rigid adherence to ideals of natural birth is probably as ill advised as rigid adherence to most philosophies, because it leaves no room for maneuvering in case of complications. The health of mother or child may be risked inadvertently in an attempt to avoid clinical techniques. Women need psychological room to maneuver, too. It is sad when a woman whose labor is different from what she expected, as many labors are, does not feel she can accept medication when, in fact, a respite from pain might offer her a respite from exhaustion, a chance to regroup her energy before she begins to push the baby out. Some women feel that they have failed shamefully if they accept pain relief, medication to speed a slow labor, or a Caesarean. The wisest course is probably for a woman to learn the techniques of prepared childbirth as well as the possible forms of medical intervention so that she can make intelligent, informed choices during the course of her labor and delivery.

Fathers and mothers usually feel strongly attached to their babies, and babies may grow emotionally attached to both parents.

GENTLE BIRTH

A French obstetrician, Frederick Leboyer (1975), has advocated an approach to childbirth "without violence." In many routine hospital deliveries, the newborn is greeted by harsh lights, the clanging of metal instruments, and brisk handling. Leboyer believes that this radical departure from the warm, dark, muffled uterus must terrify the newborn. Surely, he suggests, an easier transition would benefit infant and parents. In the **gentle birth** advocated by Leboyer, the lights of the delivery room are dimmed and noises hushed as the infant emerges. The infant is placed on its mother's soft abdomen, as the pulsations of the umbilical cord cease. Immediately after birth, most babies are alert and curious. They look around, grasp a parent's finger, suckle at the breast. Only later will they fall into a deep sleep.

When the cord is cut, the baby is gently lowered into a warm-water bath reminiscent of the warm fluid of the womb. Treated in this gentle fashion, Leboyer believed, infants seemed peaceful and content. Although long-term differences between infants subjected to gentle as opposed to traditional birth methods are unlikely (Sorrells-Jones, 1983), many parents enjoy gentle birth.

POSTPARTUM PERIOD

Labor and delivery usher in deep and rapid changes in a woman's body and mind. These continue during the period following birth, the **postpartum period**. Labor is so strenuous that some women have said that running a marathon is less taxing. Because her body has to recover from the birth, a woman is likely to ache for several weeks. She may have a painful episiotomy to contend with and, especially in second and subsequent births, sharp contractions of a uterus gradually returning to its prepregnant state. Her breasts swell as they prepare to produce milk. On the second or third day after delivery, milk comes in.

On the third day after birth, many women "return to earth," that is, get over the floating elation many experience right after delivery. Many women's emotions then are very changeable and intense; they find it easy to cry and to laugh. Several days after delivery, many women feel a transient depression, probably because of the rapid drop in hormones. The "progesterone bath" of pregnancy has in a matter of hours run dry. The hormonal shift from pregnancy to birth may be the sharpest in a woman's life (short of surgery to remove ovaries). If the depression lasts for more than a few days, and if it becomes a mood of bleakness and despair, a woman should seek professional help. Some postpartum depressions do not develop until weeks or months after childbirth. Some researchers think of this period as a kind of natural developmental crisis, a period of intense, sudden, physical and psychological adjustment. For women unhappy about their pregnancy in the first place, the postpartum period can be especially difficult, a time to worry about how to support this new and demanding person, a time to face the realities of caring for a baby, perhaps a time to relinquish the baby to an adoptive family. None of these is an easy option. For many parents, of course, the postpartum period is a thrilling time when they get to know their child.

BREAST FEEDING

About the only thing that a father cannot do for his child that a mother can do is to breast-feed it. As her labor progresses, the pituitary gland secretes hormones, **prolactin** and **oxytocin,** that cause a woman's breasts to make and release milk. When the baby is put to the breast, it instinctively begins to suck (very small or premature babies may have poor sucking reflexes and may need to be coaxed to nurse well). This sucking on the nipple stimulates the breast, via the pituitary, to release its collected milk. As the milk begins to flow, most women feel a "let-down response" (so called because the milk is let down from the milk-producing ducts to the nipple). Often the mere hunger cries of an infant cause a nursing mother's breasts to leak milk. The baby's suckling also causes the uterus to contract to its former state.

Breast milk has the advantages of being sterile, portable, convenient, always at the right temperature, and formulated perfectly for human infants. Breast-fed babies usually have fewer stomach upsets or allergic reactions than bottle-fed babies, and pediatricians now recommend that women breast-feed if they possibly can. Breast milk also gives the baby immunity to many illnesses (because the

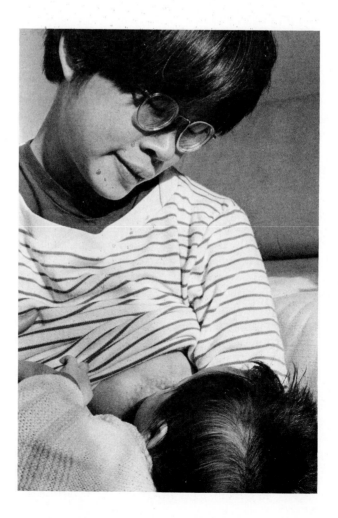

Breast feeding.

mother has developed immunity, which she passes on to the baby in her milk) at a vulnerable time. One drawback to nursing is that whatever the mother ingests may enter her milk, and so she must continue to avoid many drugs and even certain strong-tasting foods, such as garlic, fish, onions, and the like, that might give her milk an off taste. Many women find nursing physically pleasurable (some even find it sexually arousing) and a time of special closeness with their child. Mothers who do not breast-feed can, of course, hold and cuddle their infants just as lovingly. Formulas that replace mother's milk provide adequate nutrition for most babies, although sometimes parents have to experiment to match formula with child. Even mothers who do not nurse can often let the newborn suckle their colostrum.

Some mothers do not want to nurse. Some find that for no apparent reason they run out of milk after a few weeks. No woman should be made to feel inadequate for choosing how she wishes to nourish her child. Whether and how long a mother nurses is a personal decision. But she will need instruction and support at the beginning. A woman who nurses her child for the first two or three months of its life has protected it well from illness. That many women continue to nurse for many months afterward attests to its pleasure and convenience. But all parents may use feeding times as oases in their busy schedules for enjoying feeling close, and loving their infant.

SUMMARY

1. The menstrual cycle, a normal biological process, prepares the female body for conception and pregnancy. During the follicular phase, hormones prepare an ovum for ripening and release in the ovary. The uterine lining also proliferates during this phase. The ovum is released from the ovary at ovulation, a point 14 days before the start of menstruation.

2. The ripened ovum floats from the ovary, into the fallopian tube, and then into the uterus. If it joins with a sperm, the fertilized ovum becomes a zygote. The ruptured ovarian follicle, the corpus luteum, secretes hormones that help to prepare a rich endometrial environment for the zygote. If a pregnancy occurs, hormone levels keep rising. If no pregnancy occurs, hormone levels drop, and the ovum leaves the woman's body with her menstrual flow.

3. During the menstrual phase, the endometrium is shed through the vagina. In response to lower ovarian hormone levels, the body releases follicle-stimulating hormone, and the menstrual cycle begins anew.

4. Premenstrual syndrome is a mixture of various unpleasant symptoms preceding menstruation. Many reasons have been offered to explain its occurrence, but no behavioral data have yet shown exactly what this entity is. Many doctors nevertheless undertake to treat PMS in women who complain of it. Some women also suffer mood changes during the menstrual cycle, although the precise relationship of mood and hormones has not been charted yet.

5. Dysmenorrhea is painful menstruation. Primary dysmenorrhea is painful uterine contractions in response to prostaglandins. Secondary dysmenorrhea is caused

by some pelvic pathology such as endometriosis or pelvic inflammatory disease. Absent menstruation, diagnosed when a woman has not menstruated by her late teens, may have many different causes.

6 As hormone levels fall, menstrual periods eventually taper off when a woman is in her forties or early fifties. The end of menstrual cycling is called menopause. Side effects of the lowered estrogen levels may include minor annoyances like skin wrinkling or dry vagina and more serious problems like osteoporosis. Psychologically, women usually do not experience menopause purely as loss.

7 Pregnancy is signaled by the absence of menstruation or other presumptive signs. A pregnancy test can detect human chorionic gonadotropin, a hormone secreted by the embryonic membrane. Pregnancy changes a woman psychologically and socially as well as physically.

8 During the first trimester of pregnancy, the embryo's cells are dividing and specializing, and its major organ systems and structural features are developing. Teratogens are substances that can cause malformations of the embryo. Tests such as amniocentesis and chorionic villus sampling can determine whether the embryo has certain genetic defects. During the second trimester of pregnancy, the structures that developed during the embryonic period develop further and enlarge. The fetus's movements can be felt by the mother-to-be. Growth and development continue during the third trimester of pregnancy.

9 Because the bloodstream of mother and child communicate during pregnancy through the placenta, the mother should avoid ingesting any substances that might harm the fetus's development. She also needs to eat a high-protein, balanced diet to assure the fetus of adequate nutrients for growth and development.

10 Birth takes place in several stages. Strong uterine contractions thin and dilate the cervix so that the baby's head and body can pass through the vagina. After the baby is born, the placenta is delivered. Hormonal changes in the mother's body induce lactation and the return of the uterus to its unpregnant size.

KEY TERMS

menstruation
menarche
follicular (proliferative) phase
follicle-stimulating hormone (FSH)
follicle
endometrium
ovulation
Mittelschmerz
luteinizing hormone (LH)
anovulatory cycle
zygote

embryonic period
amniotic fluid
fetus
quickening
positive signs (of pregnancy)
sonogram
vasocongestion
Kegel
Braxton-Hicks contractions
colostrum
teratogen

corpus luteum
menstrual phase
premenstrual syndrome (PMS)
endorphins
neurotransmitters
toxic shock syndrome (TSS)
dysmenorrhea (primary and
    secondary)
endometriosis
prostaglandins
pelvic inflammatory disease (PID)
amenorrhea (primary and
    secondary)
menopause
osteoporosis
presumptive signs
human chorionic gonadotropin
    (HCG)
embryo
probable signs
blastocyst
placenta
navel
chorionic villus sampling
amniocentesis

fetal alcohol syndrome
miscarriage
ectopic pregnancy
Rh factor
infertility
sterility
chlamydia
gonorrhea
motility
varicocele
in vitro fertilization
zona pellucida
crowning
breech position
Caesarean section
episiotomy
vernix
Apgar score
lochia
natural childbirth
lithotomy position
gentle birth
postpartum period
prolactin
oxytocin

SUGGESTED READINGS

Ingelman-Sundberg, Axel; Wirsen, Claes; and Nilsson, Lennart. *A Child Is Born: The Drama of Life before Birth in Unprecedented Photographs.* New York: Delta/ Seymour Lawrence Book, 1980. A small gem of a book with uniquely beautiful photographs of fetuses inside the uterus at various stages of development.

Kitzinger, Sheila. *The Complete Book of Pregnancy and Childbirth.* New York: Knopf, 1980. Very well illustrated and written in an accessible style, this book describes pregnancy in detail. Among the information it presents are week-by-week development of the fetus, diet and exercise for the mother, relaxation and breathing techniques for mother and labor coach, what to look for in an obstetrician, and many other helpful topics.

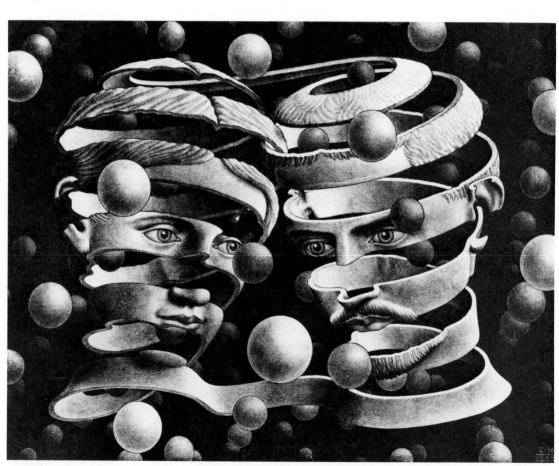

Chapter 10

Contraception and Abortion: a Shared Responsibility

HISTORY AND BACKGROUND

Deep in a cave in Combarelles, France, thousands of years ago, an early human painted along the cave walls scenes of daily life. Among the pictures of domestic routine, a couple embraces intimately. Over the man's penis is a covering: contraceptive protection against a cave-baby (Finch and Green, 1963). For thousands of years, people have fashioned condoms to cover the penis and prevent conception, fashioned them out of animal gut and cloth, leather, horn, tortoise shell, the pods of seeds, and, in recent history, out of rubber and plastic. People have blocked conception in other ways, too. An ancient Egyptian papyrus (the *Petri* or *Kahun Papyrus,* dated about 1850 B.C.) recommended blocking the cervix, which is the entrance to the uterus, with honey, gum, or crocodile dung. Three centuries later, the *Ebers Papyrus* would recommend inserting into the vagina a tampon made of linen shreds and containing tips of branches from the acacia shrub. (The acacia contains gum arabic, which turns into lactic acid in the vagina—exactly the sperm-killing substance that would be rediscovered early in the 1900s, or roughly 34 centuries later.)

Today, if you walk into a drugstore anywhere in the United States, you will probably find an open display of condoms, contraceptive creams and foams and sponges, all slickly packaged to lure buyers. An entire display may offer condoms. The choices are bewildering: what *is* the difference between "ultra-thin" and "thin but safe"? Madison Avenue has shaped the contraceptive market just as it has shaped the market for detergents.

But contraceptive merchandising has been legal in this country for only a short time. The last state law against distribution of contraceptives was struck down by the Supreme Court as a violation of privacy only in 1965 in *Griswold* v. *Connecticut.* The educated rich who had traveled to Europe in the first few decades of this century could bring back early barrier contraceptives like condoms and diaphragms. A few American shopkeepers also kept a small stock, well hidden from view, but contraceptives never reached the poor. (See "Sexuality in Perspective: the Diaphragm on the Frontier.") In her autobiography, writer Kate Simon (1982) describes some of the birth control methods used in the 1920s. She reports that her mother had 13 abortions, all illegal, all administered in the family apartment in the Bronx. Her mother actually was lucky: she lived. Her abortionist was a well-trained, licensed, upper-class Boston doctor for whom each abortion was an act of civil disobedience. Many poor women paid dearly for dangerous, often botched, illegal abortions. Many died.

People the world over, people since earliest historical time, have sought to foil nature's troublesome way of following sexual intercourse with pregnancy. With typical human inventiveness in their many different methods, they have sought to separate the cause from the effect. People have not always known, however, that semen and conception are connected. In some cultures, people have not believed that man plays any role in conception; others have believed that his semen nourished the already growing fetus. **Contraception** describes any method of preventing pregnancy, ranging from mechanical or chemical blocking of the union of sperm and egg, to preventing the production of sex cells (sperm or ovum), or preventing people from having intercourse in the first place. Just as human societies contracept, nature does too.

In every society ever studied, births have been regulated in some fashion. Among the Dani of New Guinea, low sexual interest limits births. In contrast,

SEXUALITY IN PERSPECTIVE:
THE DIAPHRAGM ON THE FRONTIER

Historians who study the development of America have charted fascinating changes in family size between one era and another. Historically family size has varied with the rates of infant and childhood mortality. Although various forms of birth control have been available since the beginning of recorded history, it is only in the last century that reliable, safe, and inexpensive contraceptives have been available to large numbers of people. Condoms and diaphragms in their modern form have been available only since the advent of rubber and, more recently, plastics and the technologies for working with them.

Lillian Schlissel, an American historian who has studied the families who crossed the country in wagon trains to the West, has found that birth rates began falling toward the second half of the 1800s both in the cities and on the frontier. (It was also happening in England at the same time [Degler, 1980].) By studying the letters and diaries of frontier women, Schlissel has found that they shared information about birth control. A letter written in 1885 from Rose Williams in Ohio to Lettie Mosher in North Dakota imparted important news:

> *You want to know of a sure preventative [to pregnancy]. Well plague take it. The best way is for you to sleep in one bed and your Man in another . . .*

> *Well now [there is] the thing. . . . I do not know whether you can get them out there. They are called Pessairre or female preventive if you don't want to ask for a 'pisser' just ask for a female preventive. They cost one dollar when Sis got hers it was before any of us went to Dak[ota] The directions are with it.*

Pessaries are any kind of vaginal suppository, and the letter makes clear that vaginal diaphragms were available to rural women. Women farther west probably had to wait for some time after 1885 to find diaphragms in the local store, and they are likely to have relied on abstinence (especially during the actual journey west, when privacy was minimal) or withdrawal, common methods of limiting birth in the absence of more sophisticated, and more costly, methods. At the very same time, the illiterate immigrant women of New York who asked their physicians how to prevent further pregnancies were being told to have their husbands "sleep on the roof" (Sanger, 1938).

Based on Lillian Schlissel, *Women's Diaries of the Westward Journey,* New York: Schocken Books, 1982, pp. 109–110.

FIGURE 10.1

Spontaneous abortions. Nature herself limits births. By the seventh month of pregnancy, 95 percent of all chromosomally defective fetuses have been spontaneously aborted. The frequency of chromosome abnormalities spontaneously aborted decreases from 60 percent in the second to third months to 7 percent at the end of the sixth month of pregnancy. (From J.G. Lauritsen, "The Cytogenetics of Spontaneous Abortion," *Research in Reproduction,* vol. 14, no. 3, July 1982, p. 3.)

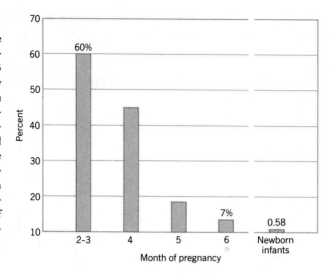

the Chinese use strong social pressures to limit births: pressures against premarital sex and in favor of small families. Nature has her own effective ways of contracepting. Poor nutrition and hunger, for example, limit population in several ways. They delay **menarche** among women; they increase susceptibility to disease, so fewer fetuses and newborns survive. Long nursing of infants, a custom in many societies, in the aggregate reduces fertility. Age also reduces fertility in the aggregate: lower rates of sexual intercourse, hormonal changes, and infections following childbirth or abortions render older women less fertile than younger women. The rough figure is that for every month of increasing maternal age, it takes .07 percent longer to conceive (Potts, in Austin and Short, 1972). That is not a staggering amount, but it will be felt across large groups of people. It means that the sexually active woman of 30 who uses no contraception is about 10 percent less likely to conceive than the 18-year-old woman.

Nature reduces fertility in other ways, too. In the United States and Britain, 7 to 10 percent of couples are known to be infertile. Ten to fifteen percent of sperm are abnormal. Half of all fertilized eggs fail to implant properly in the uterus, and of those that implant, one-fifth spontaneously abort (Potts, in Austin and Short, 1972). Although exact figures for all spontaneous abortions remain unknown, we do know that 15 percent of all recognized pregnancies end in spontaneous abortion. Many of the spontaneously aborted fetuses are chromosomally abnormal, and nature eliminates over 90 percent of these by the last trimester of pregnancy (Lauritsen, 1982; see Figure 10.1).

People's reasons for using contraception or abortion tend to center either on the family or on society at large. Family-centered reasons include: the wish to space children, to have no more children, to avoid health problems in a susceptible woman from pregnancy or birth, and to avoid health problems in an infant (such as Down's syndrome or other congenital problems). Some people contracept to limit the strain that childcare exerts on parents' time and resources. It has been found, for example, that the younger a woman is when her first child is born, the likelier her first marriage is to dissolve; if she is under 20, she is more likely than an older first-time mother to see her second marriage dissolve as well (McCarthy and Menken, 1979). Society-centered reasons include the wishes to limit population or to avoid famine. Although people use contraception to prevent (or to delay) pregnancy, the particular method they choose is likely to depend on how old they are, how much money they have, whether they are married or not, how often they have intercourse, which methods they can actually get, and other such individual factors. For example, teenagers who have intercourse in a car and must keep it secret from their parents are likely to use very different (or no) contraception from the 30-year-old married couple who has intercourse regularly and privately at home. The very psychology of contraception differs enormously for two such couples. Motivation is a critical factor when people choose whether or which type of contraception to use. For couples who do not want a pregnancy, contraception is a shared responsibility.

> BECAUSE HUMAN LIFE IS PRECIOUS, PEOPLE INEVITABLY DEVELOP STRONG FEELINGS ABOUT WHETHER IT IS MORAL OR JUSTIFIABLE TO PREVENT OR TO END PREGNANCY.

THE POLITICS OF CONTRACEPTION

Like the psychology of contraception, the politics of contraception are important determinants of who does or does not use which methods of birth control. (See Figure 10.2) Because human life is precious, people inevitably develop strong feelings about whether it is moral or justifiable to prevent or to end (as in the case of abortion) pregnancy. This passionate debate is particularly trenchant for poor, overpopulated countries. Pakistan and India, for example, are countries without enough resources to handle their populations. There and in other countries where population outruns resources, governments have begun family planning programs: propaganda and education, mass sterilization, free contraceptives, free abortion, and similar attempts to limit pregnancies. Where governments know that to feed their people they must control population, as in China, that control can be grim and invasive. Neighbors and coworkers become agents who enforce national policy. Whereas in the developed world, abortion is considered a private decision, in China it is considered a civic duty subject to public pressure (Butterfield, 1982). The problems that face family planners are deeply rooted, here in custom, here in religion, here in ignorance. A farmer and his wife who want sons to till the soil, provide for them in their old age, and carry on the family name are unlikely to limit their family to one or two, especially if the first children are females. Rather, they will reach for "an heir and a spare," a strategy that leads to an average family size of four. A peasant who cannot count or read is a poor candidate for the surest form of contraception, birth control pills, which require counting the days of the menstrual cycle. A confirmed Roman Catholic, fundamentalist Protestant, or Orthodox Jew is not likely to use birth control, even to prevent a seventh or eighth child. In short, the stakes are always high in the psychology and politics of contraception (Djerassi, 1979).

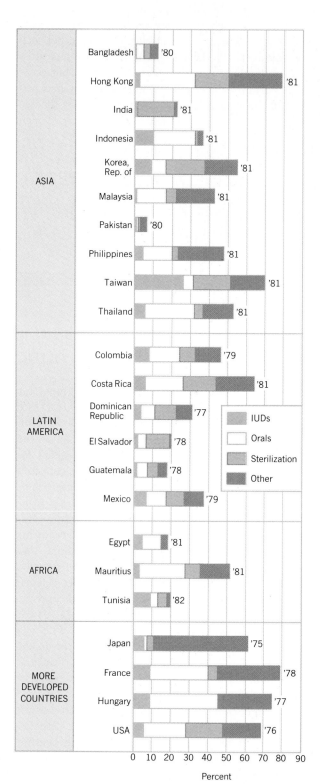

FIGURE 10.2

Contraceptive methods by married women, ages 15-44.

Family planning in India.

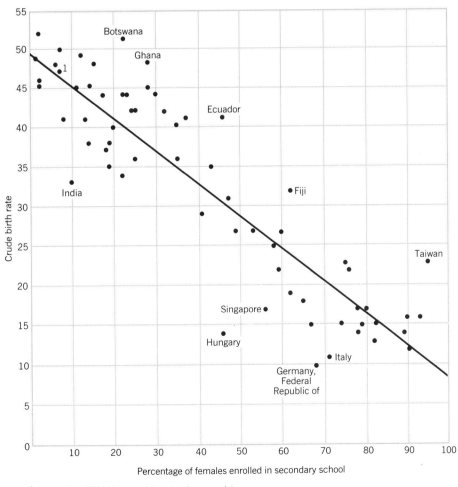

FIGURE 10.3

Birth rate and education. The birth rate in various countries is shown as a function of the percentage of women enrolled in secondary school.

FIGURE 10.4

How effective is each contraceptive method? The failure rate shows how many women out of 100 "typical users" will be pregnant at the end of one year. For corresponding lowest rates, see Table 10.1. (Sources: Hatcher et al., 1982, p. 5; Norplant, *Family Planning Perspectives,* 1984, p. 48.)

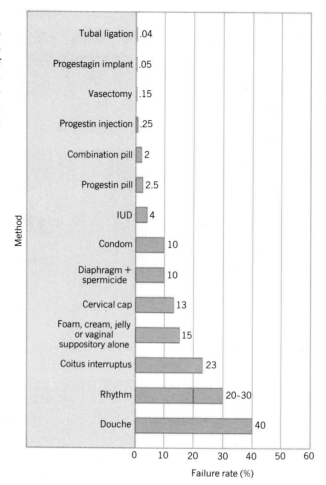

THEORETICAL VERSUS ACTUAL FAILURE RATES

In the best of all possible worlds, the ideal contraceptive would work despite the human tendencies to forget, to take chances, to miscalculate, or to indulge in wishful thinking. The effectiveness of many contraceptives depends on users' motivation: the woman must remember to take her birth-control pills, to put in her diaphragm and spermicide, just as the man must remember to put on his condom and to remove it with care soon after he ejaculates. People must understand under which conditions intercourse can cause pregnancy. Some people believe, for example, that they have intercourse too infrequently, or that they are too young, or that the woman must have an orgasm to get pregnant. The ideal contraceptive, which does not yet exist, would be cheap, simple to use, independent of the act of intercourse, utterly effective, and without side effects. The ideal contraceptive would also somehow bypass human frailty.

When population researchers talk about contraception, they distinguish between a particular method's **theoretical failure rate** and its **actual failure rate.** For example, the theoretical failure rate for birth-control pills is less than one

TABLE 10.1
Failure Rates of Contraceptives

Method	Lowest Observed Rate (%)	Typical Failure Rate
Tubal ligation	.04	.04
Combination pill	.05	2
Progestin implant	.05	.05
Vasectomy	.15	.15
Progestin injection	.25	1.25
Progestin pill	1	2.5
IUD	1.5	4
Condom	2	10
Diaphragm and spermicide	2	10
Cervical cap	2	13
Foam, cream, jelly, or vaginal suppository alone	3–5	15
Coitus interruptus (withdrawal)	16	23
Rhythm and related methods	2–20	23–30
Douche	—	40
No method (chance)	90	90

Source: Hatcher et al., 1982, p. 5; Norplant, *Family Planning Perspectives,* 1984, p. 48.

percent. In other words, fewer than one woman in one hundred, all of whom take the pill exactly as prescribed, will get pregnant in a given year on oral contraceptives. But the actual failure rate is higher, about 4 percent. Real women (as opposed to ideal women) forget to take their pills sometimes, or they find themselves unexpectedly away from home when they need to take their pills, or they vomit from the flu and lose a pill without realizing it, and so on. Besides inadvertent errors are the contraceptive failures that come when people take chances. It's the rare human being who does not, in the heat of passion, say, or in the heady afterglow of alcohol or high spirits, decide, "Forget the diaphragm (condom, foam, etc.). I want you *now*," or "Don't put that on. I like you bareskinned," or "It's already day 23 of my cycle; I'm not fertile."

For those who do not want to conceive, contraceptives must be used for *every* act of intercourse. Women cannot assume that they are not fertile, even if they are menstruating. Stranger things have happened than an egg being released from the ovaries when no one would have expected it. Contraception dropped "just this once" because people are tired, or have run out of foam, or they're at her place but the condoms are at his place all invite pregnancies. "Just this once" feelings are understandable and eminently human; they are also feelings acted upon by many women later interviewed at abortion clinics (Luker, 1977).

NONREPRODUCTIVE FORMS OF SEX

One possibility (that is not technically contraception) for couples who want to avoid conceiving a child is to engage in nonreproductive forms of sex. Sweden,

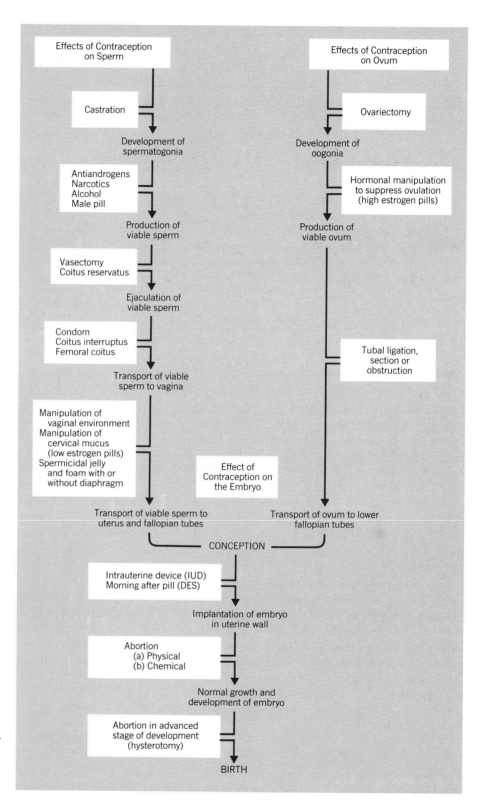

FIGURE 10.5

Points of contraception. The steps in the development of sperm, ova, and an embryo, with points shown at which contraception may be used effectively.

for example, a country of permissive sexual values, officially encourages teenagers and older couples as well to engage in nonreproductive forms of sex both to experience intimacy and to avoid pregnancy. There are other gratifying forms of sexual activity besides intercourse, and they can be a good solution for people who cannot or will not use other forms of birth control. Even for people who do use contraception, touching and stroking, without pressure for sexual performance, can be intensely intimate and sexual. (See Chapter 16 for a description of sensate focus, which is precisely this kind of unpressured and pleasurable caressing.) Oral-genital sex and mutual masturbation are just two sexual possibilities that allow couples to stimulate each other to orgasm, if they wish.

ABSTINENCE

For some people, abstaining from sex is a feasible way to prevent unwanted pregnancies. Both inside and outside of marriage, people may find that periods of abstinence meet important needs. Abstinence gives people breathing space, time out from the demands of intimate relationships. It requires neither expense nor special equipment. For many people, abstinence solves the problem of lives temporarily overcrowded by the demands of jobs, family, and interests elsewhere. Historians reveal that during the eighteenth and nineteenth centuries, when no methods of contraception were widely available, abstinence was the method of birth control among "respectable," middle-class married couples in the United States and Europe (Gay, 1984; Schlissel, 1982). Many couples who consider themselves happily married abstain from sex for considerable periods of time, time they devote to children or other shared or solitary pursuits. When the pursuit of a lifelong ambition—to get a degree or to do one's "personal best"—requires all of one's efforts, abstinence from sex can seem sensible to someone who views a sexual relationship as temporarily too costly in time and energy. Although it is not dependable as a social policy for population control, because not everyone can or will abstain from sex, abstinence can be satisfactory birth control for many.

CONTRACEPTIVES MALES USE

For a couple to conceive a child, a sperm cell from the male must join with an egg cell from the female. At any point in their journey toward each other, a contraceptive may prevent conception. (See Figure 10.5 for an illustration of this principle.) Logically, therefore, preventing a male from producing any live sperm at all would seem to be very effective as contraception. One way to prevent sperm production is to remove a male's **testes,** or sperm-producing organs, in short, to castrate him. Such a radical step is seldom used for contraception. Testes produce hormones necessary to maintain secondary sex characteristics and sexual appetite.

Blocking Sperm Production

An acceptable contraceptive would prevent a male from producing viable sperm but would allow his testes to continue producing the sex hormones that affect his secondary sexual characteristics and sexual arousability. It's a logically appealing approach, but not a feasible one. No safe method presently exists to make all men's sperm reversibly infertile without interfering with sexual interest and functioning (Schearer, 1978; Schearer et al., 1978). Heating the testes kills sperm, but in some men the effects seem irreversible. At high, chronic doses, drugs like alcohol and morphine derivatives can limit sperm production. They do so by interfering with hormones that influence sexual arousal. Researchers in the United States and other countries are looking for a male contraceptive that would contain the right hormone(s) to stop sperm production reliably without causing many men unacceptable side effects such as loss of sexual appetite (libido), nausea, and breast enlargement.

Thus when it comes to contraception that works by preventing the testes from producing living sperm, no acceptable method yet exists. What about blocking conception a bit farther down the production line: by preventing a male from ejaculating live sperm?

Blocking Ejaculation of Sperm

Conception can occur only if a male ejaculates live sperm. One possible contraceptive procedure is to prevent ejaculation of sperm.

Vasectomy   There is one simple, effective, relatively inexpensive, and widely available means of removing sperm from the ejaculate: **vasectomy.** In this uncomplicated surgical procedure, often performed right in a doctor's office, the vasa deferentia, the two ducts that carry sperm, are severed in the scrotum. It is so simple a procedure that many men schedule a vasectomy for a Friday and return to work on Monday morning. The doctor injects a local anesthetic into the skin of the scrotum, makes an incision through which each vas is elevated and severed, takes a few stitches to close the incision, and repeats the process on the other testicle. A man may want to apply ice packs to control swelling, but the discomfort is not severe, and complications are infrequent. Vasectomy takes about a half-hour, is the most common surgical procedure performed on men, and is quite inexpensive compared to other contraceptives. Vasectomy does not interfere with sexual pleasure or intercourse. In a large, 1982 survey of American women's contraceptive habits, 15 percent, or some 4.9 million women between 15 and 45, reported relying on a partner's vasectomy. Although vasectomy was not popular among men under 24, it accounted for 17 percent of contraception among 25- to 29-year olds, 25 percent among 30- to 34-year olds, fully 31 percent of 35- to 39-year olds, and 23 percent of 40- to 44-year olds. Vasectomies were also reported more popular among white than black men (Forrest and Henshaw, 1983).

Vasectomy is extremely effective in preventing pregnancy if a man takes a few simple precautions right after the procedure is done. Right after the vasectomy, some live sperm remain in the upper part of the vasa deferentia; if they are ejaculated, they can cause pregnancy. To prevent pregnancy, men are advised to use other methods of birth control for the 15 successive ejaculations after the vasectomy. When two semen samples, taken a month apart, prove free of sperm, a man can dispense with supplementary forms of birth control.

Vasectomy is permanent. It is a form of sterilization that a man should undertake only when he is certain that he does not and will not in the future want children. Thus vasectomy is rarely performed on college students or young adults.

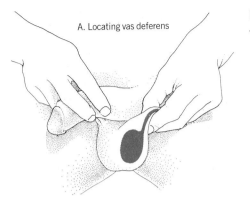

A. Locating vas deferens

FIGURE 10.6

Vasectomy.

B. Vas deferens exposed

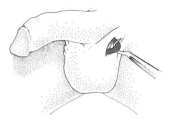

C. Vas deferens cut and or cauterized

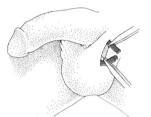

D. Incision closed and procedure
repeated on other side.

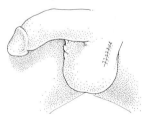

In up to 50 percent of cases, it is true, surgeons have been able to rejoin the severed ends of the vasa deferentia. But it is not yet known whether full-term pregnancies will routinely result from these reversals (Harvard Medical School Health Letter, 1977). They require tricky, delicate, expensive microsurgical procedures. Even if the vasa are restored—and surgeons continue to experiment with procedures for making vasectomy reversible, including clips, valves, and Teflon-covered magnets that can be moved to open or close passages—a man's fertility may not return. Some men apparently produce antibodies to their own sperm following vasectomy, and the overall fertility rate of men who have had vasectomies reversed is only 25 percent. The major drawback to vasectomy, then, is that it must be considered permanent.

The long-range safety of vasectomy is an open question. Researchers have monitored its long-range effects on large mammals, and early evidence suggested that many vasectomized animals develop antibodies to their own sperm. So do many human males who have vasectomies. But when work with monkeys showed that vasectomized males had a slightly higher risk than others of developing atherosclerosis, or hardening of the arteries, a serious health issue was raised (Clarkson and Alexander, 1980). To date, none of the health problems found in animals has turned up in humans, despite many years of vigilance (Walker et al., 1981). A larger study, conducted in the United States among nearly 1600 men vasectomized for 10 or more years, showed no more atherosclerosis among this group than among men with intact vasa (*Family Planning Perspectives,* January/February, 1983, pp. 30–31). Although the antibody question about humans is not answered fully for periods beyond ten years, many medical people are betting that humans and animals are sufficiently different that vasectomy is acceptably safe.

Psychological Effects of Vasectomy   Vasectomy produces no obvious physical changes in humans: a man still feels sexually aroused, still ejaculates, still has intercourse as he is accustomed to doing. His hormones and nervous system function as before. But vasectomy may produce psychological changes, both positive and negative, subtle and gross.

First the good news. Thousands of vasectomized men have been interviewed at various times after their operations, and 90 to 100 percent from each study are pleased with vasectomy and would do it all over again. Some men even become evangelical about vasectomy, and high proportions of men in certain work and social groups choose vasectomies. Few want the procedure reversed; few report changes in their feelings, health, or personal habits (Ferber et al., 1967). Many wives of vasectomized men report that *they* feel better, probably a result of not having to worry about pregnancy. Couples often report that they feel freer about their sexual behavior after a vasectomy, that their sexual desire, pleasure, and frequency of intercourse all increase. Very few couples report a decrease in sexual enthusiasm. The overwhelming majority report either no change or very positive changes after a vasectomy.

The bad news is that vasectomy can cause some few men subtle psychological problems. These stem from the close association some men make between fertility and virility, that is, between being able to impregnate a woman and being manly. One study of 48 couples with vasectomized husbands and 48 husbands with wives on birth-control pills found that over a four-year period, the vasectomized group reported more assertiveness in the husbands and more submissiveness in the wives than among the pill group. Why? Although the vasectomized husbands said that they were happy with their choice, they may have been subtly worried about their virility and, in consequence, acted more assertive—a trait that in our culture is part of the stereotype of the masculine role. The vasectomized group also had intercourse more often than the pill group, perhaps to assuage the husbands' worries about their masculinity. Perhaps, of course, they felt sexually freer. By the end of the four-year study period, most of the differences between the groups had disappeared (Ziegler et al., 1966; Ziegler et al., 1969). So the bad news turned out to be not so bad.

In short, the good news is that vasectomy is simple, effective, and, as far as we can tell, safe. The not so good news is that it must be considered a permanent form of sterilization. Vasectomy can temporarily undermine an occasional man's sense of his virility, and no one yet knows how to be sure who that occasional man is.[1]

Blocking Sperm from Entering the Vagina

Two quite different forms of contraception operate—one well and one badly—to prevent ejaculated sperm from entering the vagina.

Withdrawal   Withdrawal, also called **coitus interruptus,** is the contraceptive practice by which the male withdraws his penis from his partner's vagina before he ejaculates. Withdrawal is simple, reversible, widely available, practiced all over the world, free, and without harmful side effects. Unfortunately, it is a poor way to prevent conception. First, as we have mentioned already, fluid filled with live sperm seeps from the tip of the penis even before ejaculation. Second, withdrawal requires careful timing, frustrates both partners' enjoyment, and is especially difficult for males who ejaculate quickly once they enter the vagina. Only using no contraception at all has a higher pregnancy rate than withdrawal.

Withdrawal is appealing because it is simple and available. To teenagers who are embarrassed about buying contraceptives because they might thereby seem too sexually available; to people who are naive about the effectiveness of withdrawal; and to millions of people too poor to buy contraceptives or without any available source of contraceptives, withdrawal is very appealing. It has been practiced in ancient Greece, Islamic nations, and in medieval Europe (Himes, 1936). The Bible describes it as the sin of Onan, who spilled his seed on the ground, an act "evil in the sight of the Lord." A recent survey shows that in the United States about 3 percent, or about 900,000, sexually active women of childbearing age (that is, 15 to 44 years old) rely on withdrawal to prevent pregnancy. More women—5 percent—who rely on withdrawal are between 15 and 19 years old than any other age (Forrest and Henshaw, 1983).

Condoms   Far more effective than withdrawal and similar to it in preventing ejaculated sperm from entering the vagina, is the condom. Condoms are sheaths that cover the penis and collect sperm. Today they are made in a number of styles and materials: "rubbers" (latex), "skins" (animal gut), smooth, textured, with and without reservoir tips. Some couples complain that condoms decrease sensation during intercourse, although "skins" are reputedly better than "rubbers" in this respect. Textured condoms, such as those covered with tiny protuberances, are said to provide extra stimulation (to the female).

Condoms are safe, without side effects (an allergic reaction can usually be countered by changing brands), reversible, highly effective if used properly, and may offer protection against many sexually transmitted diseases. They are relatively popular among American couples who use contraception: 4.5 million women, or about 8 percent, rely on condoms. Condoms are popular among teenagers (21

[1]The Association for Voluntary Sterilization, 708 Third Avenue, New York, N.Y. 10017, provides information about vasectomy and other sterilization procedures and keeps a national roster of qualified physicians.

FIGURE 10.7

Condom. To use a condom correctly, it must be unrolled completely, slipped onto the erect penis before any drops of fluid seep from the penis, and held at the base as the male withdraws so that it doesn't slip off.

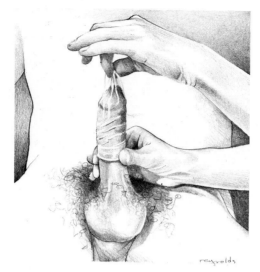

percent of those who are sexually active use them), people in their early twenties (13 percent), late twenties (12 percent), and their early thirties (12 percent) (Forrest and Henshaw, 1983). A condom's effectiveness depends on two different factors, both within the user's control. The first is motivation: condoms don't work if they aren't put on, a fact that may be obvious in the coolness of reading this textbook but that may grow less compelling in a passionate moment. The second factor is proper use: a condom has to go on before a male is fully aroused to catch the early drops of fluid from the penis and later should be held at the base as the male withdraws from the vagina so that the condom does not slip off the now flaccid penis. Some people find that this kind of maneuvering interferes with their sexual pleasure, some dislike the reduced sensation condoms offer, and some find them expensive in the long run. Others incorporate the donning of the condom right into their lovemaking. More than three-quarters of married women in Japan choose condoms for contraception. Their condoms are half as thick as the American types (*Consumer Reports,* 1979; Haberman, 1986).

Aside from certain experimental forms of contraception, these few methods—vasectomy, withdrawal, and condoms—are available to males. Why so few? Because no safe block for the continual production of sperm yet exists. For example, one promising gonadotropin (synthetic LHRH) blocked sperm production very well, but it produced erectile dysfunction and hot flashes in half or more of the men who received it (Linde et al., 1981). The paucity of choices may also grow out of the widespread belief in this and other cultures that pregnancy and its prevention are feminine concerns.

CONTRACEPTIVES FEMALES USE

Just as contraceptives can, in principle, act anywhere along the male's sperm-manufacturing and delivering "production line," they can also act anywhere along the female's egg-manufacturing and delivering "production line." One advantage of contraception for females rather than males is that only one egg need be dealt with rather than millions of continuously produced sperm. Furthermore, females

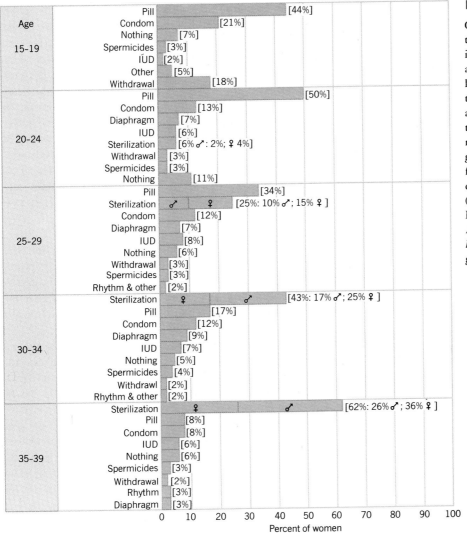

FIGURE 10.8

Contraception among women in the United States, ages 15–39, in 1982. The pill is most popular among women under 30. Sterilization accounts for nearly two thirds of the contraception among those over 35. Unprotected intercourse is most common among young women. In general, Americans are well informed and sophisticated in their choices of contraceptives. (Source: J.D. Forrest and S. K. Henshaw, "Contraception in America," *Family Planning Perspectives,* vol. 15, July/August 1983, Table 5, p. 163.)

can choose contraceptives that act on sperm deposited in the female reproductive tract during intercourse or contraceptives that act on the fertilized or unfertilized egg.

Keeping Sperm from the Uterus

Once sperm have been ejaculated in a female's vagina, several forms of contraception can prevent them from reaching an egg.

Spermicides **Spermicides** are substances that kill sperm. Although many different substances kill sperm, acceptable spermicides must be easy to apply, quick to act, must spread easily throughout the vagina, must not be irritating or harsh, and must not have offensive odors or tastes. Many modern, chemical spermicides meet these criteria. They work by altering the acidity of the vagina so that it is inhospitable to sperm. If one brand of spermicide proves irritating to either partner, another brand can be substituted. Homemade spermicides like vinegar or salt should not be used, because they can injure the lining of the vagina.

Commercial spermicides are available in several different forms: cream, jelly, aerosol foam, and vaginal inserts. Foam is the most effective for contraception, followed by jellies and creams.

Vaginal inserts are the least effective form of spermicides. Spermicides are far less effective when they are used alone than when they are combined with diaphragms, rubber barriers that cover the cervix. Spermicidal foams are 60 to 80 percent effective (Ryder, 1973), when used by couples wanting to delay or to prevent pregnancy, respectively. Four percent of the sexually active women in the United States between 15 and 44 rely on spermicides. Among them are many more—7 percent—15 to 19-year-olds than older women (Forrest and Henshaw, 1983).

The advantages of spermicides are their ease of application, their reversibility, safety, and their availability without prescription. The disadvantages are their only moderate effectiveness and the need to apply extra spermicide for repeated intercourse. That can be messy, and stopping to insert the spermicide can interfere with a couple's pleasure. As with so many other kinds of contraceptives, the nuisance value of the spermicide means that it is less likely to be used during lovemaking.

In 1983, the Food and Drug Administration (FDA) approved the general sale of **contraceptive sponges.** These soft, disposable plastic sponges are inserted in the vagina. They work in several ways at once: the chemical they contain inactivates sperm; they block the entrance to the uterus; and they trap and absorb sperm. In clinical trials, the sponge was about 85 percent effective in preventing pregnancy. Sold over the counter under the brand name "Today" in a package that gives instructions for use, the contraceptive sponges do not require a doctor's prescription. The advantages of the sponge are that it is not messy, it is cheap, and it is effective for 24 hours after insertion. The disadvantages are that it must be inserted correctly and left in place long enough after coitus for the spermicide to affect all the sperm in the vagina; it requires continual, if small, expense; and it relies on the motivation of the user. It may be displaced by vaginal contractions during orgasm, and some women find the sponge irritates them. Currently, the Food and Drug Administration reports one case of toxic-shock syndrome for every two million sponges, when used properly. The Centers for Disease Control reported this risk to be "far lower than the risk of dying from birth-related causes alone," particularly among 15- to 19-year-olds ("Health Official," 1/10/86).

Douching One of the older forms of contraception is **douching,** flooding the vagina with water or other solution *after* ejaculation. Douching, which is reversible, convenient, inexpensive, and many other good things, is an abysmal contraceptive. Its failure rate is so high that roughly half of the couples who use it exclusively will conceive within a year (Ryder, 1973). Fewer women report relying on douches to prevent pregnancy than other methods of contraception: only 150,000 women, or fewer than 1 percent, in a 1982 national survey (Forrest and Henshaw, 1983). Douching is ineffective because the sperm move so quickly into the uterus after ejaculation. If a woman could douche within seconds of her partner's ejaculation, a gymnastic feat worthy of the Olympics, she might prevent a pregnancy. In an emergency a better try is a quick application of spermicide.

CERVICAL CONTRACEPTIVES   Barriers that cover a woman's cervix only or the cervix and surrounding area are especially effective contraceptives if they are combined with a spermicide.

DIAPHRAGMS   A **diaphragm** is a thin, flexible circle of rubber with a bendable, springy rim. Diaphragms were one of the earliest reliable forms of contraception available to women and have been relatively popular for most of this century. By pinching together the sides of the rim, a woman can insert the diaphragm at the top of her vagina. There it opens out and mechanically seals the entrance to the uterus. The rim of a diaphragm should be coated with a spermicide, and a dab of spermicide also should be placed in the concave center of the diaphragm to kill any sperm that might cross the barrier. Spermicide and diaphragm should be inserted before intercourse and left in place for 6 to 8 hours following intercourse. For subsequent acts of intercourse while the diaphragm is in place, more spermicide should be applied, but the diaphragm should not be removed. A properly fitted diaphragm should not cause a woman or her partner discomfort. Like virtually every form of contraception, diaphragms appeal to some people but not to others. Researchers have found, for example, that as family income climbs, so does the percentage of women who rely on the diaphragm. Among all sexually active women of childbearing age in the United States, 5 percent rely on a diaphragm. Very few teenagers (1 percent) use diaphragms; they are more popular among women between 20 and 34 (7 percent use them) (Forrest and Henshaw, 1983). One couple in their thirties felt differently about the wife's move from the pill to the diaphragm.

I hate my wife's diaphragm. I feel like I'm making love to a plastic bag.

I feel safe with my diaphragm. If I had stayed on the pill at my age, I'd be worried.

Diaphragms are fitted by a doctor or other medical professional according to the size of a woman's upper vagina. Diaphragms range in size from 45 to 100

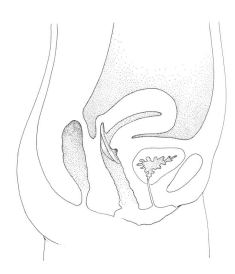

FIGURE 10.9

Diaphragm. Combined with spermicide, the diaphragm is a highly effective contraceptive.

millimeters (about 2 to 4 inches across). A woman's size may change after child-birth, breast feeding, gynecological surgery, or weight change of more than 10 pounds, and so at these times she should go for another fitting. Some diaphragms are made with rims that bend at only two points, rather than all around, and may be recommended to women after childbirth to lessen the chance that the diaphragm will slip during intercourse (the postpartum vagina may have less muscle tone than the "prepartum" vagina).

Diaphragms combined with spermicide are very effective contraceptives. But they require proper insertion, and if they are inserted incorrectly or not inserted at all, pregnancy can result. Some women find the fitting process a small nuisance. Diaphragms are not expensive, and properly cared for, one should last several years. (After use, they should be washed with soap and water, rinsed, and left to air dry. Then they are stored in their plastic container. Some women dust them with cornstarch to keep the rubber supple. Any tiny holes that develop can be detected by filling the diaphragm with water or by holding it up to a light and gently stretching it. Pinprick-size holes may result from the rubber drying out, from a fingernail scratch, or from rough handling. A diaphragm with holes is useless.) The great advantages of diaphragms are that they are without side effects, reversible, and quite reliable when used conscientiously with spermicide.

Cervical Caps   A cervical cap is a variation on the barrier method of covering the entrance to the uterus. The cervical cap is fitted by a medical professional and just covers the cervix itself. Popular in Europe, but not yet approved by the United States FDA, cervical caps are nevertheless available from some doctors. They have advantages over diaphragms that make them quite attractive to some women. Like diaphragms, they are reversible and without side effects, but unlike diaphragms, cervical caps can be inserted and then left in place for several days at least (a feature that worries some gynecologists, given that anything that remains for long in the vagina may put a woman at risk for toxic shock syndrome), do not need any attention during subsequent acts of intercourse, and are less likely to be felt by either partner. In recent FDA tests, however, cervical caps have had a high rate of failure. Of 87 women followed for six months, seven had become pregnant, and 39 percent had stopped using the method. Approval for widespread use is therefore unlikely, although the FDA will approve some research (*Family Planning Perspectives*, 1981, p. 48).

The diaphragm, cervical cap, and spermicides are methods available to women by which sperm can be kept from the egg. Of all of them, only the diaphragm plus spermicide has a dependably low failure rate, although the sponge may eventually prove equally effective. In theory at least, it would seem easier to detour a single egg (or, more rarely, more than one egg) from its rendezvous with one sperm than to detour the millions of sperm. But it is still a complex task to interfere with the egg. Now we will describe the contraceptive methods that interfere with the egg's development, release, travel, or implantation.

Blocking Development of Eggs

Women are born with all of the eggs, or ova, they will ever have already in place in their two ovaries. But each egg has to go through a process of development before it matures, leaves the ovary, and travels into the fallopian tube possibly to be fertilized. True, removing the ovaries surgically would be an effective kind of contraception. But, like castration, it is far too radical a procedure to be used for that purpose. Surgical removal of the ovaries (called ovariectomy or oophorectomy) removes their hormone-producing capabilities as well as their eggs, and secondary sexual characteristics are adversely affected. Like the male who unhappily loses his testes to surgery (for cancer, for example), the young woman who loses her ovaries often finds her resulting sterility a deep psychological wound. (Loss of one ovary or testis does not produce sterility.)

PREVENTING OVULATION   Several contraceptive methods rely on preventing the ovaries from releasing an egg. They interfere with the hormonal mechanisms that control **ovulation.**

LACTATIONAL AMENORRHEA: BREAST-FEEDING AS BIRTH CONTROL   A woman who is breast-feeding a child is likely not to have menstrual periods or to ovulate, and this **lactational amenorrhea** is sometimes used, especially in underdeveloped or developing nations, as an aggregate form of birth control. Breast-feeding interferes with the hormonal cycling necessary for ovulation, but it does so unreliably for any particular woman. A woman may ovulate and conceive before she has had a menstrual period following childbirth, and so this kind of contraception is very unreliable. Nursing mothers or their partners are strongly advised to use another form of contraception, usually a barrier method.

BIRTH-CONTROL PILLS   Scientists have long known that if a woman ingests large enough doses of the hormone estrogen, she will not ovulate. Over 146 plants have been identified that affect estrogen. Sheep and birds that eat these plants show lowered fertility. In the folk medicine of the Navajo Indians, a plant called "stoneweed" (*Lithospermum ruderale*) is used for contraception. Laboratory tests on animals have confirmed its efficacy (see Farnsworth et al., 1975a; 1975b; Finch and Green, 1963.) Progesterone, produced by the ovaries (like estrogen), and testosterone, produced by the adrenal glands of both sexes, are other hormones that affect fertility. Once scientists had identified these hormones and their structure, they began a 40-year search for a safe, effective, inexpensive oral contraceptive.

The birth-control pill has come to be emblematic of the modern age. It is *the* most effective (reversible) contraceptive known. Today's young users cannot recall a world without dependable contraception: it was the pill that ushered in this age of high expectations. From the expectations of perfect contraception, rage grows when it proves imperfect. Inevitably, the pill, like all the other reasonably effective contraceptives, poses hard choices to possible users. It requires intelligent consumer decisions about acceptable risks. The risks of the pill must be compared with the risk of unprotected intercourse. Deaths in pregnancy to unprotected women far outstrip deaths from any contraceptive, including the pill, until women reach the age of 39. (See Figure 10.10 for data on estimated mortality among women users and nonusers of contraception.) A 1982 survey showed that the pill was the most popular method of contraception after sterilization: among sexually active women 15 to 44, 27 percent used the pill. Most of these women were under 35, with the highest rate (50 percent) among 20- to 24-year olds. One and one-half million teenagers—44 percent of those sexually active—also use the pill (Forrest and Henshaw, 1983).

FIGURE 10.10

Deaths among protected and unprotected women. The death rates per year for every 100,000 fertile women between the ages of 15 and 44, according to type contraceptive used or not used. (Data from Alan Guttmacher Institute, 1981.)

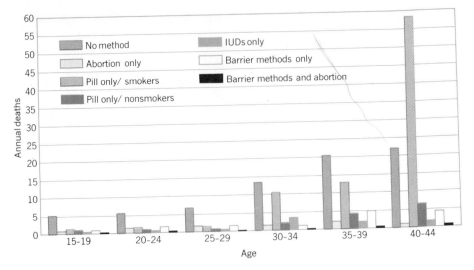

The first contraceptive pill, which combined estrogen and a synthetic form of progesterone (called "progestin"), was mass tested in 1956 and worked better than any other reversible contraceptive. This pill was a **combination pill,** in which the synthetic progesterone prevented ovulation and the addition of estrogen prevented irregular bleeding (caused by progesterone). Women took the pills from the fifth day after their menstrual period began until the twenty-fourth day. Menstrual bleeding began three or four days later. Although dosage levels have decreased significantly, the basic design of today's pill is like that of the first model.

Dosage and formula determine the contraceptive action of the pills. High doses of progesterones and estrogens inhibit ovulation. Pills with the high doses, once the norm, today are rare. Alternatively, pills with lower doses and with fewer side effects can keep the cervical mucus at the time of ovulation too thick for sperm to penetrate. Finally, combination and **mini-pills** (the latter made of progestin alone) may prevent a fertilized egg from implanting in the lining of the uterus—strictly speaking, not a contraceptive effect, and therefore a method some women wish to avoid.

Oral contraceptives taken properly and consistently are over 99 percent effective as contraception, and they are convenient. (The theoretical failure rate is 1 percent, but the actual failure rate is 4 percent. In real life, women forget to take pills.) But pills require continuing medical supervision of possible side effects or complications, and they are a small, continuous expense. The pills must be taken every day. Contraceptive protection with the pill begins from the first cycle, if the pill is started on the fifth day. However, doctors usually recommend a supplementary means of contraception for the first cycle, especially for women with short cycles. A woman should take a pill every day at about the same time. If she misses one pill, she should make it up as soon as possible or take two as her next dose. If she misses two or more pills, she should continue to take them but should use another method of contraception for that cycle.

WOMEN WHO dEfiNiTEly should *NOT* TAKE THE pill ARE THOSE WITH HiGH blood pRESSURE, diAbETES OR A RISK Of dEVElopiNG iT, ANd SMOKERS (ESpEciAlly OVER 30).

Side Effects of Birth-Control Pills   For some women, birth-control pills are worrisome. They fear altering their own hormonal cycling. Others fear the possible side effects of the pill. Women who definitely should *not* take the pill are those with high blood pressure, diabetes or a high risk of developing it, smokers (especially over 30), or women with past or present cancer of any estrogen-sensitive tissue such as breast or endometrium. Others who should not take the pill are women with histories of blood clots, migraine, liver disease, undiagnosed vaginal bleeding, angina pectoris (severe chest pain, associated with cardiovascular disease) or stroke. Very young women should avoid the pill also, because estrogen taken early can stunt growth.

The uncomfortable but not especially serious side effects of birth-control pills can often be treated simply by a change in brands. Estrogen can produce the following side effects: nausea, bloating, weight gain, breast tenderness, broken capillaries, excessive menstrual flow, headache, and other problems. A synthetic progesterone (progestogen or progestin) can produce: sparse or infrequent menstruation, acne, hairiness, weight gain, increased appetite, fatigue, depression, reduced sexual interest, hair loss, and vaginal infections (Kreutner, 1981b). Some of these side effects are like those pregnant women experience; in that the hormone levels of birth-control pills create a kind of mock pregnancy, it is not surprising that the side effects would be similar.

New forms of contraceptives may ultimately solve some of the pill's inherent problems. A long-acting implant may replace the daily pill and give more continuous, lower hormone dosages. In 1983, the Finns began using an implant of progestin, with the tradename "Norplant." This formula is not yet licensed in the United States. A study commission ruled against the implant (called Depo-Provera in this country) because of uncertainties about the risk of cancer. Six small rubber containers are implanted in a fan shape under the skin of the forearm. The implant's great advantage is its extended protection against pregnancy. It is easily inserted and removed through a small incision made by a medical professional; it is reversible; it is not dependent on the act of intercourse; and it avoids estrogen's side effects. Its side effects may include reduced menstrual bleeding and reduced sexual desire. Based on five years of test placement, pregnancy rate with Norplant was 0.5 per 100 years of use, the same as the pill's theoretical failure rate (*Studies in Family Planning,* 1983, 1984; Sivin et al., 1982). Because user error is unlikely with the implant, theoretical and actual failure rates should be nearly identical.

Because side effects depend on dosages, low hormone dosages are desirable. In fact, today's pill has significantly lower hormone dosages than the early combination pills had. Hormones deposited right at the cervix, as with the experimental vaginal ring, or in the uterus or bloodstream rather than swallowed could avert many problems by lowering dosages and delivering the hormones right to their intended site. A mini-pill of progestin alone, which is already available, can help women who must avoid estrogen, although it is less effective than either the combination pill or the intrauterine device (IUD). Finally, "morning after" pills can prevent pregnancy if they are taken for five days after unprotected intercourse. The form of estrogen in these pills, however, is **DES (diethylstilbestrol),** which has been implicated in cancer of children born to mothers who took it over time to maintain a pregnancy. (In fact, we now know that DES does not help to maintain pregnancy.) Many women experience severe nausea from its high estrogen level.

CLOTS, CANCER, HEART ATTACKS, AND THE PILL   The pill has been in use long enough to permit long-range studies of its effects on women's health. Most of its side effects, serious and otherwise, derive from its estrogen content. The best studies have been on the risk of blood clots, and the best technique has been to compare large numbers of women who never have used the pill with those who have. The comparison group provides a base rate of the incidence of blood clots. Estrogen increases blood clotting. Named for where they strike, blood clots cause: phlebitis in leg veins, with the possibility of ensuing pain and impaired circulation, and pose graver dangers if they travel to lung or brain; pulmonary embolism in the lungs; and stroke in a brain artery, with ensuing brain damage, paralysis, cognitive loss, and even death, all of these depending on the location and severity of the clot. The risk of death from blood clots, including stroke, is four to ten times greater in pill users than nonusers. The risk of stroke is seven to nine times greater for pill users, but the risk of stroke in absolute terms is low. Four times as many women die of stroke during delivery as die from pill use (Collaborative Group for the Study of Stroke in Young Women, 1973, 1975; Vessey, 1974).

As women taking the pill get older, their risk of heart attack increases, although recent research indicates that almost all the increased risk of heart attack occurs among pill users who smoke. British studies found a fivefold risk of heart attack for women over 40 on the pill compared to those not on the pill (see Figure 10.11). As a result, the U.S. FDA has recommended that women over 40 use another form of contraception. High blood pressure and obesity add to the pill's risks. If one adds these risk factors to the medical contraindications to the pill, a substantial number of women—especially those over 35—will be advised to seek alternative forms of contraception.

Some women worry about the increased risk of cancer from the pill. In Chapter 9, we discussed how estrogen stimulates cell growth in certain sites, especially the breasts and endometrium. High levels of estrogen increase the risk of cancer in parts of the body with estrogen receptors. But today's pill has quite low dosages of estrogen. The news about the pill and cancer is much better than people once thought. Evidence consistently shows that women on the pill actually cut their risk of ovarian or uterine cancer in half. They also reduce their risk of breast cancer and probably their risk of benign (noncancerous) breast tumors as well. A series of recent studies have found no evidence of greater risk of breast cancer among pill users. The pill also seems to reduce the incidence of pelvic inflammatory disease and rheumatoid arthritis (*Harvard Medical School Health Letter,* November 1982; Lincoln, 1984).

How is a young woman without any condition that contraindicates taking the pill to assess its risks to her? First, she can assess the risk of death. It is in the range of 0.3 to 3 per 100,000 users. Then she can compare that risk with that from other contraceptives. Only the IUD among reversible contraceptives approaches the pill in effectiveness. The risk of death from the IUD is 1.5 per

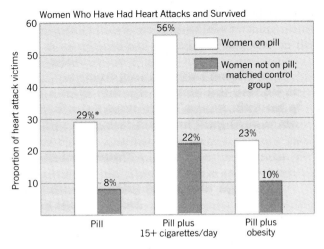

Women Who Have Had Heart Attacks and Survived

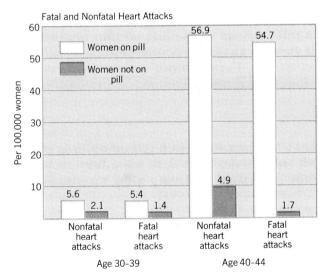

Fatal and Nonfatal Heart Attacks

FIGURE 10.11

(Top) Women who have had heart attacks and survived. (Bottom) Fatal and nonfatal heart attacks per 100,000 women. In British studies, birth control pills increased the risk of heart attack. Cigarette smoking was a strong risk factor, obesity somewhat less of a risk factor. The risk of heart attack to women over 40 was so great that the United States FDA has advised them to use other forms of contraception (Mann et al., 1975; Mann and Inman, 1975.)

100,000 users (Hatcher et al., 1978). What about contraceptives that are less effective than the pill or IUD? Here she must include the risks from abortion and pregnancy, the alternatives if a contraceptive fails. The risk of death from legal abortion is 0.4 in 100,000 abortions if it is performed in the first eight weeks of pregnancy, 16 per 100,000 if it is performed at 21 weeks or later in pregnancy. Bearing a live baby kills about 8 women per 100,000 live births (Tietze, 1981). Choosing contraceptives can sometimes feel like walking through a mine field. Given the mortality figures above, only late abortion equals or surpasses the risk of death from childbirth. Thus, when these risks are taken into account, many young, healthy women choose to take the pill at least during those years when they most want to minimize their chances of getting pregnant (Ford, 1980; Zelnik and Kantner, 1980).

Oral contraceptives remain the most effective of the temporary, reversible methods. Even so, they are not right for many women: those with medical conditions that make taking oral contraceptives too risky, those whose personal values militate against birth control, those whose sexual encounters are infrequent enough to make daily hormone doses problematic. But all women who use contraceptives face the dilemma that forms of contraception besides the pill and IUD pose greater risks of pregnancy (and its serious attendant risks). Even with the best of contraceptives, women face the possible need for a back-up abortion if their contraception fails. Risk may not seem high, but some failures are inevitable.

> *I got married when I was 27 and had been on the pill for six years. I also smoked cigarettes. My gynecologist had wanted me off the pill, but I insisted on waiting until I was married. She reassured me that a properly fitted and inserted diaphragm had a very low failure rate, but I didn't want to take any chance of conceiving before I got married because I simply could not have gone through with an abortion. I figured if I were married and accidentally got pregnant, I would have the baby, and it would have a family to be born into. Before that, any risk of pregnancy had been too high.*

Blocking the Fallopian Tubes

If the two fallopian tubes, each of which leads from an ovary to the uterus, are not open, eggs cannot pass through them to be fertilized. Blocked tubes, a fairly common form of infertility, may result from congenital malformation, endometrial tissue that grows in the tubes rather than the uterus, or scarring from pelvic infection or sexually transmitted disease. But some women whose fallopian tubes are open elect to have them closed as a form of birth control. The procedure must be considered permanent, a form of sterilization, although it can sometimes be reversed surgically. (Doctors are working on tiny valves or chemically inert implants that can be reliably reversed.) This kind of sterilization has no serious side effects and is very attractive to women who have completed their families. They are freed from years of inconvenience with other contraceptives and from worries about pregnancy. About 19 percent of sexually active American women under age 45 and 26 percent of married women had been sterilized for contraceptive purposes as of 1982 (Forrest and Henshaw, 1983; Shipp, 1985).

FEMALE STERILIZATION   As we have already said, removing a woman's uterus or ovaries is too radical a procedure to be done for purposes of contraception. But ligating (tying off) the fallopian tubes, an operation called **tubal ligation,** is a fairly simple and effective means of sterilization that does not interfere with normal menstrual cycling, hormones, or sexual interest. The surgical procedure itself is classified by where the incision is made.

Laparotomy, a major operation in which an incision is made through the abdomen, until the late 1960s was the way that surgeons performed tubal ligations. Because it was a major operation, with risks and great stress to the patient, it was usually performed when a woman was already hospitalized and when her motivation for birth control was high: after an abortion or childbirth. Other surgeons entered the pelvis through an incision in the upper vagina, a procedure called a **culdoscopy.**

Recently developed simpler procedures for tubal ligation have made it far more popular, far less stressful, and far less risky. One such procedure is the **laparoscopy,** sometimes called "the bandaid operation" because the incision is small enough to be covered by a bandaid (see Figure 10.12). Some laparoscopies are

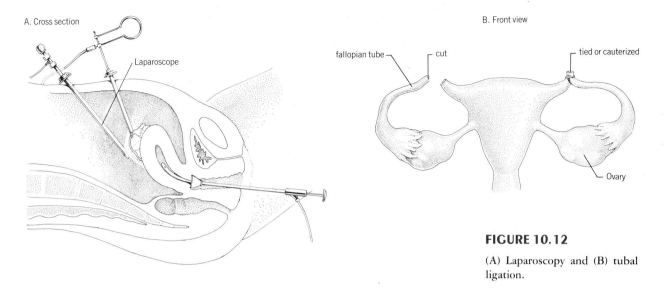

A. Cross section

Laparoscope

B. Front view

fallopian tube — ⌐ cut

tied or cauterized

Ovary

FIGURE 10.12

(A) Laparoscopy and (B) tubal ligation.

performed with local anesthesia, some are performed with general anesthesia, and many are performed without the woman even having to stay overnight in the hospital or clinic. Laparoscopy is still more complex and expensive than vasectomy, but it is just as effective and quick. First a woman is given a tranquilizer and temporary narcotic to relax her and deaden pain. Local anesthetics are injected around the navel and cervix. Alternatively, a relatively short-lived general anesthetic is administered. The surgeon makes a small incision just below the navel, introduces carbon dioxide into the abdominal cavity to separate the abdominal wall from the organs for a better view, and then inserts a laparoscope through which to see the internal organs. Sometimes through a second incision, usually just above the pubic hair, and sometimes through the first incision, the surgeon ties off the ends of one tube and then another. The surgeon may also cauterize (heat seal) the ends, use clamps, or implant one of the newer valves or silicon plugs. Then the carbon dioxide is released, the incision(s) stitched and covered with bandaids. The whole operation takes about half an hour. It is immediately effective. The woman rests for a few hours in bed at the clinic or hospital and then goes home, where she should rest for another few days. Intercourse can be resumed in a week. Another such procedure is the **mini-laparotomy,** which is also growing popular. In these, the incision is made above the line of the pubic hair and is much larger than that in the bandaid operation. This incision allows for the insertion of the laparoscope and surgical instruments. But no carbon dioxide is used.

Side effects with laparoscopy are infrequent but include burns or perforation of internal organs (from poor surgical technique), internal bleeding, or gas pains from residual carbon dioxide. Any surgery is stressful to the body, and some women, especially if they have had general anesthesia, feel tired for several weeks after the procedure. The mini-laparotomy has many fewer side effects and risks and is likely to displace all other sterilization operations, especially where medical attention is in short supply (McCann and Cole, 1980).

BECAUSE STERILIZATION STILL MUST BE CONSIDERED PERMANENT, WOMEN SHOULD CAREFULLY CONSIDER ITS POSSIBLE PSYCHOLOGICAL EFFECTS.

Psychological Effects of Sterilization   Because sterilization still must be considered permanent, women should carefully consider its possible psychological effects. Is sterilization going to make them feel freed from worry, or are they going to mourn their fertility? Is it going to seem a blessed relief or a loss of essential womanhood? Although in the United States, female sterilization is more popular than male sterilization (and especially among blacks) (Forrest and Henshaw, 1983), the question of psychological problems in women has received less attention than it has in men. One study done at the Centers for Disease Control (Grubb, 1983, in Forrest and Henshaw, 1983) found that about 2 percent, or some 14,000 women, regretted their sterilization within a year. Other studies are under way. Some sterilization procedures are undertaken for unhappy reasons: when another pregnancy would be dangerous, when cancer of the uterus or cervix has been found. But most women who have been sterilized for contraception report great satisfaction with the procedure. (Slightly fewer of such women than vasectomized men say that they are happy with sterilization.) Some women report greater frequency and enjoyment of sex.

A review of 20 years of studies in 12 countries revealed that women with fewer than four children were more likely to regret sterilization than women with four or more children (Schwyhardt and Kutner, 1973). In a world where four children is considered a *large* family, these results would likely change. Other firm conclusions are hard to come by. When possible, decisions about abortion and sterilization should be independent. A decade ago, more white males than females were sterilized, but as the laparoscopy has been perfected, increasing numbers of women have chosen sterilization. In the United States today, more than four couples in ten contain a partner who is sterilized (Shipp, 1985). The majority of couples married 15 years or longer and still practicing birth control have chosen sterilization (Westoff and Jones, 1977a).

Sterilization and the Retarded   Sterilization may be performed on women deemed retarded or incompetent by civil authorities. One of the effects of "mainstreaming" the retarded, that is, moving as many as possible out of institutions and into the community, has been to increase sexual problems in this population: unwanted pregnancies, sexually transmitted diseases, and sexual exploitation. Whereas the institutionalized "mentally incompetent" might once routinely have been sterilized, public opinion now opposes this course. The involuntary sterilization of two Alabama sisters on welfare, one of whom was mentally retarded, created a furor and led the federal government in 1973 to prohibit the use of federal funds for sterilizing the mentally retarded. This ban has been interpreted broadly, and the number of sterilizations has been cut (penalizing some poor families who might have legitimate claims to sterilizing a mentally retarded individual who cannot understand enough to protect herself)—although no clear guidelines for sterilization have emerged.

What should those guidelines be? Few people would disagree that a severely handicapped person should not have children if that person will require custodial care all her (or his) life and has no possibility of nurturing a child within a family or other social network or of taking responsibility for that child. But sterilization is a radical choice to visit on someone who cannot take part in the decision. Under what conditions is sterilization warranted, and for what reasons? Is it ever justifiable solely for the convenience of the custodian? How is a physician to obtain the necessary informed consent from the patient? At what point should a person be judged fit to indulge in social sexual behavior? Is that point to be measured in IQ points? Many moderately and even severely retarded people are capable of giving and receiving love, enjoying sex, reproducing—and in some cases reproducing their mental handicaps. For them, what is the right choice—contraception or no? abortion? sterilization?—and who is to make that choice? By what enlightened set of guidelines is society to proceed? One physician (Kreutner, 1981a) has proposed that retarded people of reproductive age be sterilized if: they feel that they should not have children; they cannot take care of themselves even minimally (for example, a woman who cannot manage to change sanitary napkins or bathe during her period). Some physicians believe that a person whose IQ is over 70 can give informed consent to sterilization and that it is medically advisable to sterilize people with IQs under 50 or those with severe emotional or physical handicaps in addition to retardation, although laws prevent it. Sterilization, because it is permanent and prevents reproduction, raises questions about the sexuality of retarded people in an essentially compelling way.

Preventing the Embryo from Implanting

Some birth-control methods work not by preventing conception but by preventing the fertilized egg from implanting or from developing in its earliest stages. Thus these methods are not, strictly speaking, contraception. To some people, these methods of birth control are akin to early abortion and are therefore unacceptable. Neither the morning-after pill, by which high doses of DES halt pregnancy, nor abortion is recommended as a continuous form of birth control. But the **intrauterine device,** or **IUD,** can be an effective means of birth control for some women. Six percent, or 2.3 million, of sexually active women of childbearing age, rely on IUDs. They are most popular among women between the ages of 20 and 34 (Forrest and Henshaw, 1983).

The IUD (Intrauterine Device) The principle on which the IUD works is simple. The IUD prevents the embryo from implanting in the lining of the uterus, although the exact mechanism is not understood. Probably any sizable solid object in the uterus can prevent pregnancy. Ancient Arab tribes were said to place stones in the uteruses of camels to prevent their pregnancy during a long journey. The IUD is reversible, inexpensive, and some are nearly as effective as the pill. Apparently, the greater the surface area of the IUD, the greater its effectiveness. Only 1 to 3 percent of users become pregnant with the IUD in place. The IUD has the advantages of needing very little attention and of depending not at all on motivation after it is inserted. It does not interrupt the act of making love.

Most IUDs today are plastic, some with copper wrapping. Some release synthetic progesterone to increase their effectiveness. They come in various shapes, loops and coils, and have string-like tails that project into the vagina to let a woman make sure her IUD has not slipped out. A medical professional has to insert the IUD, usually during menstruation, when the opening to the uterus is most dilated. Insertion is quick, although many women find that it is painful. IUDs also cause bleeding. An IUD is checked about six weeks after insertion. Removal is just a reversal of the insertion procedure.

The side effects and possible risks of the IUD can be extremely serious. Expulsion rates range from 5 to 35 percent, depending on the type of IUD, and pregnancies are frequent after unnoticed expulsions of the IUD. Expulsions are more common in women who are young or who have had no children than in other women. An improperly inserted IUD may perforate the uterus and enter the intestines or abdominal cavity. Perforations can cause serious infections and interfere with future pregnancies. One kind of IUD, the old Dalkon Shield, is riskier to women who get pregnant with the IUD in place than other types marketed in the United States. Spontaneous abortion usually happens in such cases, but if it does not, the old Dalkon Shield poses a greater risk of possibly fatal uterine infection to the mother than other IUDs. The old Dalkon Shield was withdrawn from the U.S. market in 1974, but many women still had it in place after that. It also has remained available in other countries.

Two recent studies (Cramer et al., 1985; Daling et al., 1985) on IUDs and infertility sound an alarm. About 20 percent of the cases of infertility among 550,000 couples in the United States may be due to tubal problems in the women. Of these, 16 percent (or about 88,000) probably were caused by IUDs. Most women on IUDs do not suffer these effects. But for the unlucky woman who does, the route seems to be as follows: IUDs heighten the risk of pelvic inflammatory disease. Infection in the fallopian tubes narrows and finally closes the tubes, blocking sperm and egg, and causing infertility. One of the two studies, based in Boston (Cramer et al., 1985), has shown that the rate for the risk of infertility mounts in the first few months on the IUD and then diminishes. The number of a woman's sexual partners also alters the risk. Regardless of their type of contraception, women with one sexual partner have fewer tubal infections than women with more partners. The second study, based in Seattle (Daling et al., 1985), has shown a similarly increased risk of tubal infertility among women who use IUDs. (See Table 10.2.) For these and other reasons, women have taken IUD producers to court. As a result, in 1986 the major producers of IUDs announced that they would no longer produce for the U.S.

Occasional side effects of the IUD include painful menstrual cramps, pelvic

TABLE 10.2
IUDs and Infertility

Total Infertile Women		Women with Tubal Infertility	
		Percentage on IUD	Percentage Not on IUD
Boston	283	31.4	16.7
Seattle	159	35.2	13.8

Source: Cramer, D. W., et al., *New England Journal of Medicine,* 1985, *312,* 941–947; Daling, J. R., et al., *New England Journal of Medicine,* 1985, *312,* 937–941.

discomfort, and increased menstrual flow. The newer, smaller, copper-clad IUDs produce a smaller increase in menstrual flow. Cramps usually subside after some weeks, but a number of women ask for their IUD to be removed because of the pain or bleeding. Now that IUDs are less widely available, women must turn to other methods, some with higher failure rates.

CONTRACEPTION BY THE RHYTHM METHOD

The **rhythm method** of contraception relies on a couple to abstain from sexual intercourse during the part of the menstrual cycle when a woman is most likely to be fertile (see Figure 10.13). Conventional wisdom holds that the life of each egg is 24 hours and the life of sperm in the upper reproductive tract is 48 hours. Thus, in theory, if a woman with a regular cycle avoids intercourse for 72 hours before the time of ovulation and for 48 hours after ovulation, she will not conceive. To allow for error in ascertaining the day of ovulation, an extra day of abstinence is added before and after the presumed time of ovulation, for a total of eight days. Women with irregular cycles abstain longer. In practice, unfortunately, this safe, natural, cost-free, reversible method of preventing conception has a high rate of failure. No one has ever taught an ovary to honor a calendar, and most women ovulate too irregularly, especially in their earliest and latest menstrual years, to make the rhythm method very effective. The assumptions about the length of time egg and sperm survive are also questionable. The rhythm method, also called "periodic abstinence," is the only form of birth control approved by the Roman Catholic Church. Catholic couples are more likely than couples of other religions to rely on the rhythm method, but only a tiny minority of American Catholic women—1 percent, or 500,000 women in a large national survey—reported using the rhythm method. Two percent of sexually active women between 15 and 44 rely on rhythm, and most rhythm-method users are over 35 (Forrest and Henshaw, 1983).

Shortest cycle (days)	Day fertile period begins	Longest cycle (days)	Day fertile period ends
22	4	23	12
23	5	24	13
24	6	25	14
25	7	26	15
26	8	27	16
27	9	28	17
28	10	29	18
29	11	30	19
30	12	31	20
31	13	32	21
32	14	33	22
		34	23
		35	24

Source: After E. Havemann. *Birth Control.* New York: Time-Life, 1967, p. 23.

FIGURE 10.13

Calendar rhythm method of birth control. This method shows women when during their menstrual cycles they must abstain from sexual intercourse. If a woman's cycles vary from, say, 27 days to 32 days, she may be fertile between days 9 and 21. She therefore must abstain from sexual intercourse between days 9 and 21.

COUPLES MUST BE HIGHLY MOTIVATED FOR THE RHYTHM METHOD TO WORK.

Couples must be highly motivated for the rhythm method to work. They must abstain from intercourse when it is not safe—a period of many days in the cycle of some women—and they must carefully chart ovulation. A woman can do this by taking her resting temperature every morning before she arises and noting the increase of about 1 degree Fahrenheit that follows within 24 hours of ovulation. (At this point, she has *already* been fertile for one day, and sometimes two.) She can also watch for telltale changes in cervical mucus: it is clear, thin, and stringy at ovulation. A couple abstains from intercourse from the time when cervical mucus turns white and cloudy, through the few days of clear, stringy mucus that signals ovulation, and resumes intercourse when the mucus is again white and cloudy. The point of all of these exercises—charting temperatures, checking cervical mucus, and the like—is to localize ovulation.

NEW TRENDS IN CONTRACEPTION

New contraceptives in various stages of readiness for market abound. A few will be available soon; the problems with some of the others may never be overcome. For instance, one intriguing contraceptive that is still years away is a nasal spray containing hormones that depress sperm production in males and ovulation in females. Researchers are also investigating the possibility of vaccinating women against getting pregnant by inducing them to form antibodies to the **zona pellucida,** the covering of the ovum which sperm must penetrate. The vaccine would work by preventing the sperm from penetrating the zona pellucida. It has been found that some women whose infertility cannot otherwise be explained have high levels of antibodies to zona pellucida while few or none occur in fertile women or men (Marx, 1978). Such a vaccine, which may teach doctors more about treating infertility as well as about contraception is, however, some years away. The same is true for a vaccine to raise antibodies against human chorionic gonadotropin, without which pregnancy cannot continue.

For women, the **disposable diaphragm** may turn out to be popular and effective. Available already in some parts of the country, the disposable diaphragm comes with a premeasured amount of spermicide and is used like its nondisposable cousin, the traditional diaphragm. But once used, it is discarded. It does not need to be cleaned, dried, or stored. Estimates are that the theoretical failure rate of the disposable diaphragm plus spermicide is only 2 percent and the actual failure rate, 20 percent. Inserted and worn correctly, it can be an effective and convenient form of contraception. One drawback, however, may be its cost. At about $2 each, the disposable diaphragm may be an expensive proposition for some sexually active women. But it may solve the dilemma of women new to contraception—a group that historically has had high rates of unintended pregnancies.

By the late 1980s, a new kind of oral contraceptive may be available to women that works very differently from the present combination pill. French and American researchers are testing pills that women would need to take only just before their menstrual cycle or if they find that they have missed their period. They would therefore be exposed to much lower total doses of hormones than with present contraceptive pills. The pill would not prevent ovulation, as combination pills do, but would either occupy the body's progesterone receptors or would interfere with the body's progesterone production. Either pill is said to cause expulsion from the uterus of any egg that might have been fertilized. This form of birth control would be convenient, practical, safe, and extremely effective, if it works as promised. As of 1985, clinical tests on the antiprogesterone agent X showed almost 90 percent of women successfully ended pregnancies. Dosage problems are said to be the cause of the 10 percent failure rate. The drug is called Epostane. The French drug, RU 486, works by occupying progesterone receptors (*Business Week,* April 1, 1985).

A **vaginal ring** worn at the cervix and containing progestin and natural estrogen will avoid the side effects of oral doses of hormones and still, it is hoped, protect women from pregnancy. The doughnut-shaped ring will be worn for three weeks and then removed for one week, to allow menstrual bleeding. Each ring will last for six months. The natural estrogen, which cannot be taken by mouth, is thought to be safer than the synthetic estrogen in contraceptive pills. The ring, which has been tested internationally, is about as effective as low-dose birth-control pills and is likely to be available in the United States within a few years.

Reliably reversible sterilization procedures are likely to help many women in the very near future. One interesting device being tested on a limited number of humans is the **fimbrial hood.** It fits over the fimbriae, the fan-shaped projections at the end of each fallopian tube that pick up the egg as it leaves the ovary. Tests on animals show that the hoods can be removed without damaging the fallopian tubes, an important consideration for women who want eventually to conceive. Silicone plugs that fill the fallopian tubes and that can later be removed are another contraceptive possibility that may be available to women in the near future.

A discovery made by chance in China holds promise for eventually providing a contraceptive for males that depresses their production of live sperm. The substance that researchers are working with is called **gossypol,** a derivative of cottonseed oil. Gossypol lowers sperm production enough to limit fertility, although it has not yet been made to do so reliably. Gossypol also has problematic side effects, including nausea, loss of libido, and some cases in which sperm production has been irreversibly affected (Lobl et al., 1980). Even so, gossypol is being tried in a variety of forms. It is intriguing because it halts sperm production in 99 percent of men.

ABORTION

Abortion is standard procedure in many countries, and two-thirds of the world's people live where abortion is legal (*Family Planning Perspectives,* 1979). In the United States, abortion has been legal since a Supreme Court decision in 1973 held that states could not rule against abortion in the first 13 weeks of pregnancy, could rule on abortion in the second 13 weeks in ways consistent with maternal health, but could rule against abortion after 24 to 28 weeks of pregnancy. The ruling, which national polls show is widely supported, transferred the decision about abortion to doctor and patient.

IN THE politics of ABORTION, POWER, MONEY, AND passion ARE THE WEAPONS of All PARTIES.

The Politics of Abortion

In the politics of abortion, power, money, and passion are the weapons of all parties. Members of groups that call themselves advocates of "the right to life" argue that abortion is murder and a sin and should be banned. Some, but not all, would allow abortion in cases of incest or rape. The Roman Catholic Church opposes abortion on moral and religious grounds, claiming that the embryo is a living human being with a soul from the moment of conception. Some other religious groups view abortion as a violation of the moral absolute that all human life is sacred. They argue that life is given by God and must be taken only by Him.

Proponents of legal abortion call themselves "pro-choice." They make very different arguments from those of right-to-life advocates. They are moral relativists who hold that a woman, and not the state, has the right to decide whether and when she will bear a child. It is she whose body goes through pregnancy, and it is she who must raise the child. For the state to interfere is tyranny. Those in favor of choice argue also that the rights of the mother outweigh the rights of

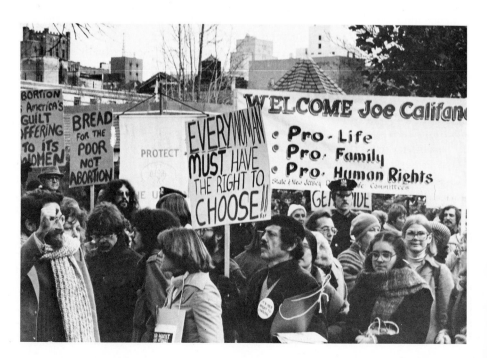

The politics of abortion.

a potential human being, and they do not agree that the embryo is a complete human being at conception.

The point at which the fetus has been defined as human has shifted historically. Once it was believed by the Church that the fetus took on a soul at about the middle of pregnancy, when the mother felt the "quickening," the fetus's first noticeable movements (Mohr, 1978). Current Catholic views on first-trimester abortions are only about a century old. Yet designating when human life begins is a question of values rather than science.

Proponents of choice also claim that women will have abortions whether they are legal or not. Illegal abortions are performed under poor medical conditions, often bringing hemorrhage and infection, sometimes bringing sterility or death. Finally, they argue that the quality of life of unwanted children and their families is diminished and that the burden of a law against abortion falls most heavily on the poor. Wealthier women have always been able to finance safer illegal abortions, whether in this country or abroad. In 1977, the Supreme Court ruled that states need not pay for "nontherapeutic" abortions, and Congress soon thereafter limited public financing of abortion. In 1977, one-quarter of all legal abortions were paid for by Medicaid, but after the court ruling, the number of Medicaid-supported abortions plummeted by 98 percent. Although the political maneuvering in the wake of these decisions continues, the effect is to limit the availability of abortion to poor women and to send them to illegal abortionists or to strapped private charities.

Even before abortion was legal, it was frequent. Figures from the Institute of Sex Research in 1958 showed that from one-fifth to one-fourth of pregnancies of white women had been aborted. Among widowed, separated, or divorced women of all ages, three out of four pregnancies had been aborted (Gebhard et al., 1958).

The problem with abortion is that the issue pulls so many people in several directions at once. Some people feel truly unconflicted on the abortion issue, but

Garry Trudeau's modern couple is not happy about their limited choices.

DOONESBURY   by Garry Trudeau

some can believe the justifications of *both* sides. Some people believe that abortion should be available, but they would have a hard time themselves going through the procedure. It is not a simple question; there are no easy answers. Our personal values influence how we feel about contraception, abortion, and the nature of human life. In specific, personal situations, some people may feel truly free from doubt or pain on the issue: they are *for* or *against* their own abortion. The issue of abortion, moral and practical, is worth thought, for it will not go away. It is an integral part of the dilemma our sexual and reproductive knowledge confers upon us.

Prevalence of Abortion

In 1969, there were an estimated 22,000 legal abortions in the United States. In 1980, there were 1.5 million (Cates, 1982). This increase in legal abortions has had important effects on public health: deaths and surgical complications among women of childbearing age have decreased; safe procedures for ending pregnancies have burgeoned; and low-cost, outpatient gynecological services have also increased (Cates, 1982). A large questionnaire survey of married and unmarried women between the ages of 15 and 44 in the United States posed questions about abortion (Forrest and Henshaw, 1983). The answers reflect opinions and attitudes toward contraception and abortion as of Spring, 1982. When women were asked whether they would *consider* having an abortion if they accidentally got pregnant, about 50 percent of unmarried women and about 33 percent of married women said that they would consider abortion. Among unmarried women between 18 and 30, 49 percent say that they would have an abortion. Among women between 30 and 44, 56 percent of the unmarried and 37 percent of the married women would consider having an abortion. Not surprisingly, women seem to base their decisions about abortion both on how a child would affect their lives and on their own basic attitude toward abortion. Women of all income levels answered similarly. But religious differences were significant: 33 percent of Roman Catholics, 42 percent of Protestants, 64 percent of Jews, and 66 percent of those without a religious affiliation said that they would consider having an abortion. Forty-eight percent of black women and 40 percent of white women would consider abortion. Ambivalence about abortion seems to have declined significantly, with about half of those who were once (in 1973) ambivalent favoring and about half opposing abortion. Overall, 40 percent of adult women of reproductive age will have had abortions by the time they are 45, if current rates of abortion continue.

In the first five years after abortion was legalized in New York (the state legalized it in 1970, three years before the Supreme Court ruling of 1973), nearly one in five New York City women of reproductive age had had at least one legal abortion (Parker et al., 1975). Nationally, as legal abortions increased, illegal abortions decreased, although, only when we know how many *illegal* abortions had been performed can we compare the difference. One estimate is that about 70 percent of legal abortions in New York City between 1970 and 1972 replaced illegal abortions, the other 30 percent replacing unintended births (Tietze, 1973).

Since legalization, New York City's fertility rate, especially among blacks, has declined rapidly. The size of the black family has been larger than black women have sought; there has been a gap between intention and experience. One researcher has concluded:

By enabling blacks to avert what must have been a substantial number of unwanted births, and thereby to reproduce at a rate more compatible with the well-being of the family, abortion legalization may rank as one of the great social equalizers of our time (Kramer, 1975).

Some people worry that women come to depend on abortion as their primary means of birth control. In fact, evidence suggests that women use contraceptives more effectively after an abortion because they have been given advice about contraception at abortion clinics. Women who have more than one abortion are not necessarily lax about contraception. A woman having a repeat abortion generally is using better contraception than she did in the first instance, yet she may be using a form of birth control with a substantial failure rate (Berger et al., 1984; Tietze and Bongaarts, 1982). Studies show that the proportion of American women using birth control has risen and risen faster since abortion was legalized than before and that more couples are using the most effective forms of birth control—the pill, sterilization, and the IUD (Westoff and Jones, 1977). One demographer has calculated that even on the pill, which is over 99 percent effective, a woman has a 20 to 50 percent chance of needing two abortions, 10 years apart, in her 30-year reproductive life (Tietze, 1974). Contraceptive methods with higher failure rates than the pill's will produce even higher rates of back-up abortions. In short, abortion does not necessarily imply that a couple has not been using contraception.

Following an abortion, women are more likely to use contraception. Many women who have abortions are inexperienced with contraception, and studies show that they are considerably more careful to use contraception after their abortion. Thus the evidence indicates that legal abortion does not make women lazy about contraception, indeed, that legal abortion improves the rates of contraception of those who have had abortions (Stubblefield et al., 1984). Even the most careful people may sometimes need an abortion to back up a contraceptive method that has failed. No contraceptive, save sterilization, approaches perfection.

Hazards of Abortion

The physical hazards of illegal abortion are grave—sterility, infection, and death—but the hazards of legal abortion are usually less serious. Some short-term side effects such as pain, fever, and bleeding are fairly common after abortions. Because abortion is a surgical procedure and grows more complicated as a pregnancy advances, the earlier in pregnancy an abortion occurs, the safer it is and, in general, the less physically stressful. Legal abortion in the first third of pregnancy is very safe. Legal abortion in the second trimester grows seven times riskier. (See Figure 10.14 for a comparison of the risks for abortion and various contraceptive methods.) But the risks of abortion should be considered in context: how do they compare with the alternative, the risks of pregnancy? Childbirth is eight times riskier to a woman's life than first-trimester abortion is. Childbirth is even more risky in the second trimester than abortion is. For young women, childbirth is riskier than it is for older women, and so for young women, abortion is safer. Although abortions in the second trimester account for only a small proportion of all abortions, older women and blacks are at higher risk for second trimester abortions. (Part of the reason is that women at the beginning and end of their menstrual histories may not know when they became pregnant, because irregular periods are common at both times.)

FIGURE 10.14

Deaths from legal abortions and childbirth, 1970–1978. Figure shows deaths per 100,000 legal abortions and per 100,000 live births. Childbearing posed a greater risk to women's health than abortion did. In 1978, there were 0.5 deaths per 100,000 abortions but 8 deaths from childbearing. (Source: C. Tietze, *Induced Abortion: a World View, 1981* 4th ed., New York: Population Council, 1981.)

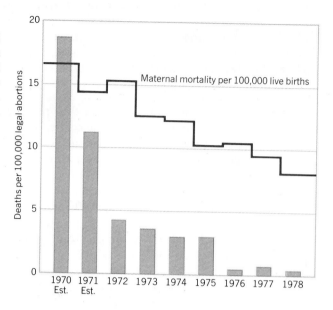

Some people have been concerned about the effects of abortion, and especially repeated abortions, on women's health. They have worried about the effects on later pregnancies or about the relationship between abortion and breast cancer. Whether abortion will cause later miscarriages depends in part on the method of abortion. The World Health Organization suggests that sharp curettage and wide dilation of the cervix, not the suction method used in the United States, may have long-range fertility effects. Of eight studies assessing risk of harm to future childbearing, six found no long-term effects from abortion (cited in Cates, 1982). Similarly, a recent study of Boston-area women shows that abortion does not cause sterility (Stubblefield et al., 1984). In this study, the rates of pregnancy and contraceptive use were compared in three groups of women: (1) those who had had first- and second-trimester abortions; (2) those who had recently given birth; and (3) those who had visited clinics for contraceptives. The investigators found that abortion did not cause sterility. The major difference between the postabortion group and the other women was that the postabortion group later had fewer pregnancies, because more of them were using contraception.

Abortion can pose women and their partners with hard choices, but it rarely threatens mental health. Early abortion in particular rarely causes psychological disturbances. Few women experience either guilt or regret in the wake of abortion (Osofsky and Osofsky, 1975). But they may experience conflict in deciding to undergo abortion (Gilligan, 1982). When her partner supports the decision to abort, a woman finds the experience easier than when he does not (Freeman, 1978). Childbirth poses a greater psychological risk: serious depression after abortion is one-fifth as common as it is after delivery. The Joint Program for the Study of Abortion, surveying 73,000 legal abortions in 1970 to 1971, concluded that although "abortion may elicit feelings of guilt, regret, or loss in some women, these reactions tend to be temporary and appear to be outweighed by positive life changes and feelings of relief" (quoted in Lincoln, 1975).

Placing unwanted babies for adoption once was widespread. As late as 1969, 80 percent of babies born out of wedlock were placed for adoption (U.S. Senate

Report, November 4, 1975). In 1983, only 4 percent of such babies were placed for adoption (Alan Guttmacher Institute, 1981). Follow-up studies of parents who surrender their babies show that they feel emotional burdens from the adoption. Many feel depressed. A significantly higher incidence of secondary infertility (infertility that follows a previous pregnancy) appears among such parents than in the population as a whole (Deykin et al., 1984; Rynearson, 1982). Placing a baby for adoption is not a guilt-free, problem-free solution to unwanted pregnancy.

Techniques of Abortion

Legal abortions are performed in one of several different ways. The procedure generally depends on how far advanced the pregnancy is. If they possibly can, women who seek abortion should do so during the first trimester of pregnancy, because abortion then is easiest, cheapest, and safest. Most women suspect that they are pregnant very early in pregnancy, and pregnancy can always be determined in the first trimester by laboratory test. Women whose fear makes them prolong the agony of not knowing make it harder on themselves if they finally decide they do want an abortion. Of course, some women must wait to decide if they wish to abort. Only during the second trimester are results of **amniocentesis** available, a test by which fetal cells shed into the amniotic fluid are examined in order to find chromosomal and other birth defects. Amniocentesis is performed between the sixteenth and twentieth week of pregnancy, when enough fluid is available, and results take several weeks. If the fetus is known to be abnormal, some women elect to have a fairly late but still legal abortion. Women who are at risk because they have had earlier defective offspring or women who are over 35 and therefore at risk for producing Down's syndrome babies are candidates for amniocentesis. Many such women who are found to be carrying defective fetuses choose to abort and try again for a normal child.

How Far Has the Pregnancy Advanced? (and What *Is* an Abortion?)   During the first trimester of pregnancy, abortion can be performed in a brief and benign procedure called **vacuum aspiration** or **suction curettage.** This method accounts for 96 percent of all curettages performed in the United States (*Abortion Surveillance,* 1978). It can usually be performed in a doctor's office or clinic and does not require general anesthesia. Aspiration is the most common and the safest kind of abortion. First a physician may locally anesthetize the cervix, then insert a tube into the uterus that is attached to a vacuum pump, and remove embryo and placenta. The procedure takes about two minutes, blood loss is minimal, and complications (temporary drop in blood pressure, pain, or fever) are uncommon. A woman then rests for a few minutes and is free to resume her normal activities. Aspiration costs from $80 to $150.

Late Abortion   After the first trimester of pregnancy, abortion can become a more complicated procedure. Recently, research has shown that aspiration can be used safely through the twentieth week of pregnancy. Based on a review of 10 years' experience with legal abortion, actual obstetric practice will probably be to use aspiration at least until the sixteenth week of pregnancy (Grimes et al., 1977; Grimes and Cates, 1981). From then through the twenty-eighth week of pregnancy, the recommended procedure has been **saline infusion.** In this procedure,

FIGURE 10.15

Pregnancy and abortion time-tables. Types of abortion and the period during pregnancy when they are generally performed are shown. Abortions are legal until 24 weeks gestation, but in rare instances, fetuses born at 23 weeks survive. As the limits between fetal viability and abortion blur, physicians and patients face troubling dilemmas. (Source: D. Kleiman, "When abortion becomes birth," New York *Times,* February 15, 1984, pp. B1, B4.)

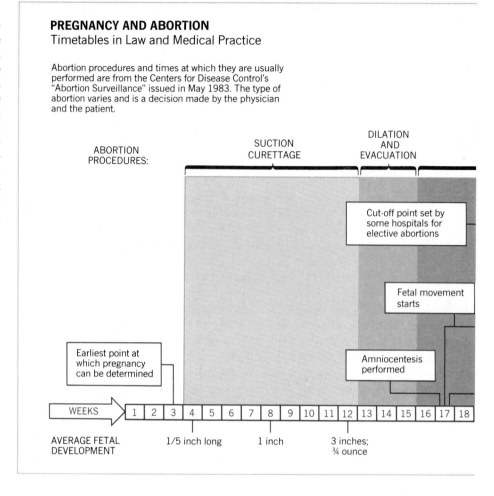

PREGNANCY AND ABORTION
Timetables in Law and Medical Practice

Abortion procedures and times at which they are usually performed are from the Centers for Disease Control's "Abortion Surveillance" issued in May 1983. The type of abortion varies and is a decision made by the physician and the patient.

which is the most common for late abortions, a strong salt solution is injected into the amniotic fluid surrounding the fetus. In most cases the fetus dies, and through mechanisms not fully understood, the salt solution causes the uterus to contract and deliver the fetus. The process takes 24 to 35 hours, and so a woman must be hospitalized for at least a day. Complications of saline abortion include fever, infection, or hemorrhage. It is riskier than aspiration during the first 20 weeks of pregnancy. Some doctors therefore prefer to use **prostaglandins,** hormone substances that also cause premature labor and expulsion of the fetus. The drawback to late prostaglandin abortions is that the fetus, in very rare instances, may survive. In the most controversial procedure, **dilation and evacuation or D and E,** the fetus is dismembered in the uterus. The advantages of this method are its low rate of side effects to the mother and the certainty that the fetus will not survive. Its disadvantages are that D and E can be psychologically painful to the medical staff (Kleiman, 1984). As specialists in newborn care have improved the survival chances of fetuses as young as 25 weeks gestation, the possibility of a fetus surviving a late abortion raises serious ethical questions for doctors and patients alike (see Figure 10.15).

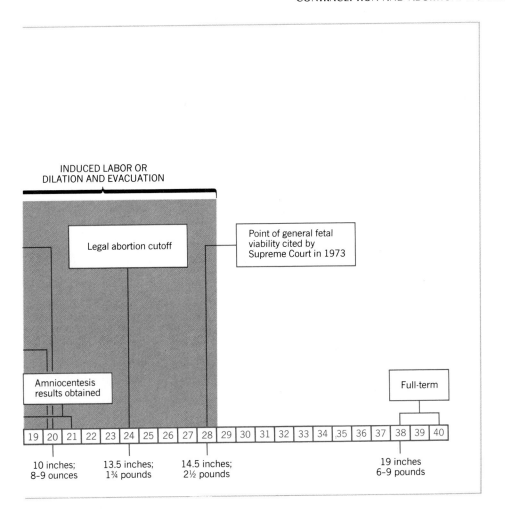

INDUCED LABOR OR
DILATION AND EVACUATION

Legal abortion cutoff

Point of general fetal
viability cited by
Supreme Court in 1973

Amniocentesis
results obtained

Full-term

| 19 | 20 | 21 | 22 | 23 | 24 | 25 | 26 | 27 | 28 | 29 | 30 | 31 | 32 | 33 | 34 | 35 | 36 | 37 | 38 | 39 | 40 |

10 inches;
8-9 ounces

13.5 inches;
1¾ pounds

14.5 inches;
2½ pounds

19 inches
6-9 pounds

After 28 weeks, a fetus must be removed by a surgical procedure called **hys-terotomy.** Hysterotomy is like a Caesarean section, in which a woman is given a general anesthetic and the fetus is removed directly from the uterus. Of all the forms of abortion, the risks are highest with hysterotomy, for it is surgery, and it requires a general anesthetic, which itself carries risks.

MENSTRUAL REGULATION   **Menstrual regulation** or **menstrual extraction** is per-formed when menstruation does not begin 14 days after it is expected or up to 42 days since the beginning of the last menstrual period. It is a simple, out-patient procedure that is like vacuum aspiration. It takes just a few minutes to perform, half an hour to recover from, usually requires no anesthesia, and poses less risk even than the very safe vacuum aspiration. Many menstrual regulations are performed *without* a pregnancy having been confirmed, to avoid placing doctor or patient in the ethical dilemma of knowingly performing an abortion. (In other words, menstrual regulation is not necessarily a form of abortion.) In fact, for this reason, the procedure is legal in some countries that ban abortion. Because menstrual regulation can pose a small risk to a woman, it is preferable for medical

FIGURE 10.16

Contraception by sexually active Americans, 1982. Ninety-two percent of sexually active Americans use some form of contraception, and 65 percent use the most effective methods: sterilization, pills, or IUDs. Sterilization is the most popular choice; pills are popular for women under 30. Condoms are the third most popular choice, especially among teenaged couples. (Source: J.D. Forrest and S. K. Henshaw, "Contraception in America," *Family Planning Perspectives*, vol. 15, July/August 1983. Effectiveness figures from A. L. Schirm et al., "Contraceptive failure in the U.S.," *Family Planning Perspectives*, vol. 15, 1982, pp. 68–75.)

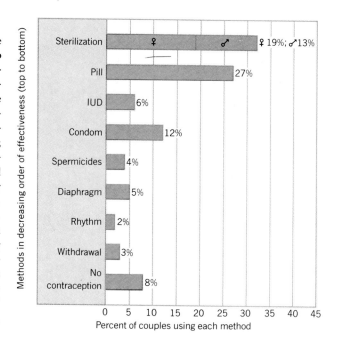

reasons if a pregnancy test is performed beforehand. Of course, women who do not want to know whether the menstrual regulation has aborted an embryo may want to avoid a pregnancy test.

Abortion-Inducing Substances

An **abortifacient** is a substance that causes abortion when introduced into the body. Abortifacients abound in folk medicine and among illegal abortionists. Some of them are harmless; others kill. But some abortifacients are used legally by physicians when aspiration and saline methods are otherwise inappropriate. The most common abortifacient is made of prostaglandins, hormones that may play a part in natural delivery. Abortion by prostaglandin requires a hospital stay. Although the death rate for prostaglandin abortion is lower than for saline abortion, the risk of side effects—diarrhea, vomiting, and fever—is higher. Researchers are working to refine the technique and reduce these side effects.

BIRTH CONTROL PRACTICES IN THE UNITED STATES

The United States is composed of groups that differ vastly in social values and behavior. From surveys of Americans that inquire into their use of birth control, we can make certain generalizations about large groups in the population. For one example, in the United States Roman Catholics whose church condemns abortion and all forms of contraception except the rhythm method, are just as successful as non-Catholics in preventing pregnancy. (They are less successful than non-Catholics in *delaying* pregnancy. Statistics show that virtually all groups intending to delay pregnancy are less successful than groups intending to prevent it.) Catholics in the oldest age groups intending to prevent conception are among the most successful of all Americans (Ryder, 1973). For women under 45 who believe in using contraception, religious beliefs do not seem to influence significantly the contraceptive methods that they choose. Small differences do exist: Jewish women are the most likely to use the pill, Protestants to be sterilized, and Catholics to use the rhythm method (Forrest and Henshaw, 1983).

Not all women of childbearing age use contraception, however. About 8 percent, or 3 million, women of childbearing age who are exposed to the risk of pregnancy, do not contracept. Many of them are teenagers (about 18 percent) and women in their early twenties (11 percent). Their reasons for not using protection vary. Some (especially younger women) fear side effects, and some do not believe in birth control. Hardly any (0.4 percent) say that they rely on back-up abortions. Some women simply are not at risk for pregnancy: a full one-third of the 55 million women in the United States between 15 and 44. About two-thirds of teenagers, for instance, are not sexually active. One-fifth (19 percent) of the women between 15 and 44 are not sexually active (among these are 7.9 million women who have never had intercourse), 8 percent are pregnant or trying to be, and 7 percent are sterile or past menopause. Black and white, Protestant and Catholic women are equally represented in the groups of women not at risk for pregnancy. Still, most women of fertile ages are sexually active. Survey figures show that the numbers of women who are at risk for pregnancy increase by age groups. Among 15- to 19-year-olds, 37 percent are sexually active; among 20- to 24-year-olds, 73 percent; among 30- to 34-year-olds, 76 percent. Of women past 40, 67 percent are sexually active (Forrest and Henshaw, 1983). What are these sexually active women doing about contraception?

In the United States, the most popular method of contraception is sterilization. One in three couples (32 percent) uses this method. Nineteen percent of sexually active women under 45 have had a tubal ligation, and 13 percent of the men have had a vasectomy. Sterilization is the most common method of preventing pregnancy among married women over 30, regardless of the number of children they have. But for women under 30, sterilization is most popular only for those with two children or more already. Twenty-seven percent of the sexually active women surveyed used birth-control pills. Condoms were the third most popular method (12 percent), followed by IUDs (6 percent), and diaphragms (5 percent). Rhythm, withdrawal, and douching come next in popularity (9 percent). (See Figure 10.17.) In 1982, fully 92 percent of all potentially fertile couples in the United States who were not pregnant and wanted to avoid getting pregnant were using contraception or had been sterilized (Forrest and Henshaw, 1983). The old gaps between rich and poor and between Catholics and non-Catholics are closing (*Family Planning Perspectives*, January 2, 1979). That is a real revolution.

Better-educated Americans want and produce fewer children than less-educated Americans. The 1970 National Fertility Study showed that between 1966 and 1970, fully 44 percent of births for married women under 45 were unplanned and 15 percent unwanted. Although the least educated women want only slightly more children than the most educated, they actually bear twice as many as the most educated women do. About 27 percent of the women who are at risk for pregnancy but use no contraception are 24 or younger. The women between 15 and 44 who are at risk but do not contracept get 27 percent of the abortions performed every year in the United States (Forrest and Henshaw, 1983).

FIGURE 10.17

Contraceptive Factsheet

	Pill	IUD	Diaphragm with Spermicide	Disposable Diaphragm (with Spermicide)	Condom	Spermicide	Rhythm
What is it?	Oral contraceptives that suppress ovulation or prevent implantation of fertilized ovum	Plastic device with string-like "tail," inserted by doctor into uterus	Flexible rubber cup with bendable rim; spermicide applied to rim and inside center before intercourse	Like traditional diaphragm; spermicide included	Flexible, thin covering for penis, made of rubber or animal membrane	Chemical cream, foam, jelly, or insert that kills sperm in vagina	Abstinence from coitus during woman's fertile period
Prescription needed?	yes	yes	yes	no	no	no	no
How does it work?	Combination pill (estrogen plus progestin) taken 21 days a month; mini-pill (progestin only) taken daily	Prevents ovum from implanting in uterus	Creates barrier at cervix that sperm cannot cross; spermicide kills any sperm that do cross barrier	Like traditional diaphragm	Reservoir tip collects semen; must be carefully removed so semen does not enter vagina	Immobilizes and blocks sperm from entering uterus	Charting body temperature shifts and changes in cervical mucus helps predict ovulation; coitus avoided for some days thereafter
Failure rate[a]	Combination pill: 2 women/year; progestin pill: 2–3 women/year	4 women/year will get pregnant	Inserted correctly: 2–4 women/year; inserted incorrectly, 10–20 women/year	—	10 women/year	15 women/year	20–30 women/year

Advantages	Independent of coitus; may protect against PID, acne, benign breast disease, and ovarian cysts	Independent of coitus	Poses no health risks; very effective when used properly and with spermicide	Like traditional diaphragm but disposed of after use	Protects against STDs; widely available	Some protection against STDs; widely available; easy to use	Sanctioned by Roman Catholic Church
Disadvantages	Daily pill; some health risks, especially to smokers and women over 35	Painful insertion; can increase menstrual flow and cramps	Dependent on coitus; new spermicide needed for each act of coitus	Expense	Interrupts lovemaking; must be carefully removed	Interrupts lovemaking	Requires regular periods of abstinence by both partners; ineffective
Side effects and risks	Possible nausea, weight gain, bloating; possible heart attack in smokers and women over 40	Heavy menstruation; risk of PID	Allergy to rubber or spermicide can often be cured by switching brands	Same as traditional diaphragm	Same as traditional diaphragm	Local irritation *may* be associated with higher incidence of birth defects	None; abstinence may strain a relationship
Who should or should not use it?	Excellent for women under 30 with no risk factors (see text for risk factors)	Excellent for women who have completed their families; not for women with heavy periods, multiple partners, or who have not completed their families	Unsuited for women with loose vaginal muscle tone or those inhibited about touching their genitals	Same as traditional diaphragm	Suitable for all men, except those allergic to rubber	Good for women who have sex occasionally	Unsuitable for women with irregular menstrual cycles

[a]Failure rates based on number of women per 100 using method per year who become pregnant using the method. Of 100 women using no contraception, up to 90 would be pregnant within a year. Effectiveness increases when methods are combined——condom plus spermicidal foam, for example.

Birth Control and Race

The National Fertility Study of 1970 showed that black women on the average want only slightly more children than white women do but bear considerably more. Why? The answer is confounded by racial differences in education and socioeconomic status. In fact, highly educated black women actually want and bear fewer children than comparably educated white middle-class women.

Some of the difference in the size of black and white families may reflect choice rather than failed contraceptives. On sterilization, for example, interesting differences show up in the numbers of black men versus black women and blacks versus whites who have been sterilized for contraceptive purposes (some 9 percent of all surgical sterilizations are carried out for reasons other than contraception) (Ford, 1978). Between 1973 and 1976, among men and women 35 to 44 years old, 13 percent of women and 16 percent of men had been sterilized. But when those figures are broken down by race, we see that more whites (20.1 percent) than blacks (12.9 percent) had been sterilized and, furthermore, that far more black women (11.0 percent) than men (1.9 percent) had been sterilized. For whites, men had only a slightly higher rate than women (10.5 percent versus 9.6 percent, respectively). In the years 1973 to 1976, when many people were worried about the pill's side effects, the highest rates of sterilization occurred among high-income white couples. In the same period, one-third of black couples, regardless of income, shifted from birth-control pills and IUDs to "nonmedical" and less effective forms of contraception (Ford, 1978). More recent survey results bear out these differentials: more white women than black, of similar age and marital status, are sterilized, and fewer black males than white males are sterilized. More black women than white women use the pill.

Birth Control for Adolescents

Young men and women who are just beginning to be sexually active are, as a group, very lax about using contraception. A large study of sexually experienced American teenage girls between the ages of 15 and 19 showed that more teenage girls were using contraceptives in 1979 than in 1976, but more in 1979 were using the least effective methods—withdrawal and rhythm—and proportionately fewer were using the most effective methods—the pill and IUD (Kantner and Zelnik, 1980). Survey results from 1982 show that 18 percent of exposed 15- to 19-year-old women used no contraception. Forty-four percent used the pill, and 21 percent used condoms (Forrest and Henshaw, 1983).

Teenage pregnancy hits more than a million U.S. teenagers every year. In 1983 alone, unmarried women 15 to 19 years old bore 261,260 babies. Of those who marry *after* the pregnancy, 60 percent divorce within 3 years (Johnson, 1986). Most teenagers get pregnant within the first six months after they begin having intercourse. In 1979, 33 percent of sexually experienced girls between 15 and 19 had been pregnant (Kantner and Zelnik, 1980). One estimate, published by the Alan Guttmacher Institute (1981) of how many teenagers are sexually active is 12 million, or 80 percent of males and 70 percent of females by age 19. Most teenage girls wait until they have had intercourse for a while or until they have gotten pregnant to ask for contraception (Schlage et al., 1973, cited in Kreutner, 1981b).

Why do so many teenagers get pregnant? There are several reasons. Women between 15 and 24 worry about side effects (6 percent) or don't believe in birth control (2 percent). Almost none say that they rely on abortions or can't afford contraception (Forrest and Henshaw, 1983). Ignorance is another reason.

Seven out of 10 women in one Kantner and Zelnik (1973) survey did not believe that they could get pregnant (Shah et al., 1975). Some teenagers (half in the Zelnik and Kantner survey of 1977) simply do not know when their fertile periods occur. Some think that they are sterile (Luker, 1977). Some think that they are too young or that it takes many sexual encounters to get pregnant. Sexual guilt interferes as well. Some feel so much sexual guilt that they do not learn well about contraception (Schwartz, 1973) or do not even want to think about it (Allgeier, Przybyla, and Thompson, 1978). Sexual guilt makes buying contraceptives especially embarrassing (Fisher, Fisher, and Byrne, 1977). Sexual guilt also makes people shy away from contraceptives that require touching the genitals—spermicides, diaphragms, condoms, IUD strings (Byrne, 1977). Over 30 percent of sexually active teenagers can't find contraception (Shah et al., 1975). Some have sexual encounters too rarely or unexpectedly to plan for contraception. Some disapprove of contraception or believe that it interferes with spontaneous sexual pleasure (Kreutner, 1981b). Some use contraceptives ineffectively: the same condom more than once, long after its expiration date, only partly unrolled, inside out (Pinhas, personal communication, 1985). Only a few teenagers want to be parents yet they are more fertile in their teens than they may be in their thirties.

In Baltimore, where state statistics show that teenage mothers account for 25 percent of all the city's births, workers from Johns Hopkins University Hospital are distributing free contraceptives to students in sex education programs at local junior and senior high schools. The aim is to curb pregnancies (*New York Times,* September 27, 1983).

The Guttmacher Institute estimates (1981) that contraceptives have prevented 680,000 teenage pregnancies every year since 1976. Although more teenagers are using contraception, many use less effective forms of contraception. The number of teenage pregnancies, numbers of abortions among teenagers, and the numbers of teenagers keeping their babies all have risen over the last 10 years. The prospects for a lasting marriage begun during adolescence are very poor. The positive side of the story is that teenagers use more reliable forms of contraception once they

The rate of pregnancies among unmarried teenagers in America is higher than in any other industrialized nation, even though few teenagers want to be parents.

SEXUALITY IN PERSPECTIVE:
BUILDING A FAMILY—UNPLANNED EVENTS

This chapter reveals a host of facts and figures about contraception and family planning. Although these facts may seem complex, people's real lives are even more complex and filled with many unknowns. In reality, when people plan for their future, they sometimes do well to let the past serve as a guide. Here is how one investigator (Bongaarts, 1984) envisions the dream of building a family. Imagine, if you will, a fairly conventional scenario. A couple marries. The wife is 25 years old. They plan to have two children, spaced three years apart, and they hope for a boy and a girl. Like any parents, they want their children to be healthy. How likely is this series of events, should the couple stay married for 20 years? That was the question posed by John Bongaarts. The answers appear in Table 10.3. There is only a 6 percent chance that the couple will avoid all unplanned events—all infertility, miscarriage, babies born sick, or born later than wanted, or babies born who were not wanted at all. Divorce and death take their own tolls of this all-American dream.

TABLE 10.3

Unplanned Events

Events	Probability of Experiencing Events (%)	Probability of Avoiding Events (%)
Contraceptive failure before		
First birth	13	87
Second birth	13	87
Involuntary childlessness		
Primary	6	94
Secondary	2	98
Conception delay longer than one year before		
First conception	9	91
Second conception	9	91
Intrauterine death after		
First conception	20	80
Second conception	20	80
Congenital malformation		
First birth	2	98
Second birth	2	98
Undesired sex combination		
(2 boys or 2 girls)	50	50
Unwanted birth	30	70
Divorce	43	57
Death of parent	9	91
Death of child	4	96
Probability of avoiding all unplanned events	—	6

Source: Bongaarts, J. "Building a Family: Unplanned Events," *Studies in Family Planning,* January/February, 1984, Table 1, p. 18.

enter stable relationships. Sex education may be especially useful in decreasing sexual guilt, opening minds to contraceptive knowledge, and—if the information is mastered—in increasing contraceptive use. Sex education carries no risk, for it does not alter whether teenagers have sex or not. Sex education about contraception increases the likelihood that teenagers will use contraception, even when they first have intercourse, and it decreases the likelihood of pregnancies among sexually active teenagers (Zelnik and Kim, 1982).

SUMMARY

1 Contraception is any method of preventing pregnancy, from the mechanical or chemical blocking of the union of sperm and egg, to preventing the production of sperm and egg, to preventing sexual intercourse. Nature and human beings both contracept.

2 Nonreproductive forms of sex and abstinence from sex are both forms of birth control. They have the advantage of being freely available, simple, and effective. They also accord with the values and needs of many people, in many walks of life.

3 Contraceptives have both theoretical and actual failure rates. The ideal contraceptive, which does not yet exist, would never fail, and it would be cheap, simple to use, independent of the act of intercourse, and without side effects.

4 Contraceptives used by males include those that block sperm production or ejaculation. Vasectomy, or the severing of the sperm-carrying ducts in the testes, is a popular, effective, and widely available means of removing sperm from the ejaculate. Other ways of preventing sperm from entering a partner's vagina include withdrawal, which has a very high failure rate, and condoms, which are safe and effective.

5 Contraceptives used by females include spermicides and douching, to prevent sperm from entering the uterus, as well as the safe, effective diaphragm and cervical cap. Blocking the development of eggs and preventing ovulation are two other contraceptive principles. Birth-control pills prevent ovulation; they are highly effective and, for many women, an excellent form of birth control. Some women have their fallopian tubes surgically closed, a permanent and effective form of sterilization. The intrauterine device prevents a conceptus from implanting in the uterus.

6 New trends in contraceptives include nasal hormone sprays, vaccinations against sperm penetrating ova, oral contraceptives that need be taken only a few times during a given menstrual cycle, the fimbrial hood, a vaginal ring that contains progestin and estrogen, and gossypol, a cottonseed derivative that lowers sperm production.

7 Abortion is both a health issue and a political issue. As legal abortions have become more prevalent, deaths and surgical complications among women of

childbearing age have decreased, and safe procedures for ending pregnancies have increased.

8 Abortion's side effects usually depend on how late in pregnancy it is performed. The earlier in pregnancy the abortion is performed, the safer it is and, in general, the less physically stressful. Abortion in the first trimester of pregnancy is very safe. Most early abortions are conducted through vacuum aspiration or suction currettage. Abortion in the second trimester is riskier. Later abortions are conducted through aspiration, saline infusion, dilation and evacuation, or hysterotomy. Some women who miss a menstrual period and fear pregnancy undergo menstrual extraction. The alternative, childbirth, poses greater physical and psychological risks to women.

9 In the United States, sterilization is the most popular form of contraception. Next in popularity are birth-control pills, condoms, IUDs, diaphragms, rhythm, withdrawal, and douching. Sterilization is more popular among whites than blacks. Birth-control pills are more popular among black women than white. But black women who want to prevent pregnancy are less likely than white women to use contraception.

10 Teenagers who are just beginning to be sexually active are generally lax about birth control, as the high pregnancy rates among teenagers attest. Many teenagers use no contraception or use some of the least effective methods. Many wait until they have had intercourse for a while, until they have gotten pregnant, or until they have entered a stable relationship to ask for contraception.

KEY TERMS

contraception
menarche
theoretical failure rate
actual failure rate
testes
vasectomy
coitus interruptus
spermicides
contraceptive sponge
toxic shock syndrome
douching
diaphragm
ovulation
lactational amenorrhea
combination pill
mini-pill
diethylstilbestrol (DES)
tubal ligation
laparotomy

culdoscopy
laparoscopy
mini-laparotomy
intrauterine device (IUD)
rhythm method
zona pellucida
disposable diaphragm
vaginal ring
fimbrial hood
gossypol
amniocentesis
vacuum aspiration
suction curettage
saline infusion
dilation and evacuation (D and E)
hysterotomy
menstrual regulation (extraction)
abortifacient
prostaglandins

SUGGESTED READINGS

Djerassi, C. *The Politics of Contraception.* New York: Norton, 1978. A chemist who helped develop the pill looks at the contraceptive scene with a critical eye on the gap between the technological, ethical, and political aspects of contraception.

Hatcher, R.A., et al. *Contraceptive Technology, 1980–1981.* New York: Irvington, 1982. A thorough coverage of contraception today.

Mohr, J.C. *Abortion in America: The Origins and Evolution of National Policy 1800–1900.* New York: Oxford University Press, 1978. This is the fascinating story of how abortion policy was turned around.

PART IV

SEXUAL DEVELOPMENT
AND ORIENTATION

Pablo Picasso, "First Steps." Yale University Art Gallery.

Chapter 11

Sexuality Through the Life Cycle: Childhood

When people think about "sexual experience" in the abstract, they are very likely to think of two adults, probably male and female, engaging in foreplay and sexual intercourse. But in reality, human sexual practices are varied. Not only do the sexual acts themselves vary, but they vary over the course of human life.

NATURE AND CULTURE INTERACTING

The story of human sexual development is the story of nature and culture interacting. Part of human sexual development is biological, of course. Biological development is influenced heavily by genetic and hormonal controls on the fertilized egg, fetus, child, and adult. But sexual development also depends on the interplay between organic or hormonal controls and external, socially determined mechanisms. For example, it depends on relationships with family members and peers, on religious traditions and taboos. Sexual development also depends on interaction with others, in fantasy or in reality, and in this way it is unlike purely biological development.

THEORIES OF SEXUAL DEVELOPMENT

When does human sexuality begin, and how does it *develop* over the course of a person's lifetime? Is it an unbroken and continuous stream, or does it progress in fits and starts? Does sexuality develop in stages or not, and are the stages invariably ordered? Can a person "go back" and make up for lost development? In this chapter, we will examine these questions. We should recall our definition of sexuality: *it is sexual behavior plus all of the human feelings, attitudes, and actions generated by one's understanding of one's own and of others' sex.*

Some theories of human sexual development depict sexuality as a process continuous from infancy to old age. Others hold that culture creates important discontinuities. Sociologists John Gagnon and William Simon offer a "discontinuity" theory: they suggest that the contexts for childhood and later sexuality are quite distinct (as we will detail). The influential psychoanalytic theory of Sigmund Freud is an example of a "continuity" theory: it posits strong continuity between the experiences of early childhood and the sexual experiences of later life. Most psychologists remain unconvinced that the evidence proves Freud's development theory, but Freud's enormous influence on western views of sexuality makes his theory important. Freud's theory is perhaps best characterized as an intuitive, literary one. Some parts of the theory cannot be fully evaluated by truly scientific criteria. There have been many disconfirmations of the developmental theory. Yet even beyond his theory, Freud has provided metaphors that western societies use to describe sexuality and that shape social visions of sexuality.

Freud's Theory of Sexual Development

Sigmund Freud's theory of human behavior assumes that children's first five years form the basis for later relationships, including sexual ones. Freud shaped our culture's thinking about sexual experience and childhood, for he was the first to assert that sexuality—which he defined as a striving for bodily pleasure that is localized in special body zones—is, from earliest infancy onward, a lifelong and deep source of motivation. Freud believed that the sources of bodily pleasures were, first, the mouth; then the anus and urethra; then, for boys, the penis and, for girls, the clitoris and vagina. How children experienced and mastered these zones of bodily pleasure constituted the sexual experiences of infancy and early childhood. Freud considered these childhood experiences the precursors and subtle sculptors of sexual feelings, responses, and relations during puberty and adulthood.

The central idea in Freudian theory shocked the post-Victorian world: *all* human behavior, sexual and nonsexual, derives from an initial, built-in, instinctive striving for sensual pleasure. Freud believed that basic human behavior is driven by a self-centered **pleasure principle:** maximize sensual pleasure and minimize pain. This selfish striving is at odds with the requirement of cooperation that makes human society possible. Therefore, society must teach the child to inhibit sensuous selfishness as well as other forms of selfishness.

Freud postulated that the distinction between male and female psychosexual development begins during the phallic stage. He viewed childhood anatomical differences between the sexes as creating inevitably different psychological experiences for boys and girls. Freud's view is captured in his aphorism, "Anatomy is destiny."

Adult, **genital sexuality** comes with the hormonal changes of puberty. If all the pregenital periods have gone well, the adult integrates oral, anal, and phallic elements into foreplay. But "normal" genital pleasure is derived—for Freud— primarily from heterosexual intercourse. If the child does not move smoothly through the stages, one of two conditions will appear in adulthood. If an exclusive oral or anal sexuality remains the adult's central source of pleasure, Freud diagnosed "perversion." Neurosis is the second possible condition. Neurosis is more complex than perversion. It is a symbolic, unconscious transformation of oral, anal, and phallic conflicts, not yet worked through in the course of development. Thus from the centrality of the sexual motive, Freud developed concepts of normality and neurosis.

Not all followers of Freud believe the orthodox theory that we have cited. But to all Freudians, early relations between mothers and children are the underpinnings of later relationships, sexual relationships among them. If that early relationship goes awry, later stages will be unstably grounded. Let us turn to actual sexual behavior and to studies of children and their mothers.

Sigmund Freud

SEXUALITY IN RESEARCH: CRITICAL PERIOD, SENSITIVE PERIOD

Parent and infant gaze into each other's eyes, luxuriate in warm embraces, nuzzle and kiss, bill and coo. It is no wonder that Plato, Freud, and many others (Bowlby, 1951; Fraiberg, 1977; Klaus and Kennell, 1976) believed that the first relationship between infant and parent permanently shapes all others. This belief rests on the assumption that infants go through **critical periods** of development. Critical periods, as biologists originally defined them, are points during prenatal development when some event *must* occur or development is forever after altered. Does the attachment of infants and caretakers rely on a critical period? Research says no. Nature gives children more than a single chance (Clarke and Clarke, 1977).

The critical period hypothesis of attachment has been replaced by a weaker, less deterministic formulation, that of the **sensitive period.** Whereas the critical period is a matter of now or never, the sensitive period hypothesis is that some development occurs *most readily* during certain periods but can also occur, if less readily and perhaps less well, at other times. Thus if a baby does not attach during infancy, the sensitive period hypothesis predicts that it will have a smaller (but real) chance of attaching later. Such a hypothesis is harder to test than the critical period hypothesis.

A sensitive period hypothesis would predict that more adults who had had secure attachments would have solid sexual relationships than would those adults with poor early attachments. It would also predict that those who were securely attached would have better sexual relationships than those who were less securely attached. Ethics prevent anyone from experimentally introducing attachments at six-month intervals to previously unattached children for the purpose of learning how long a child is "sensitive" to learning relationships. Within ethical bounds, recent work has tracked infants as they enter preschool. Psychologists at the University of Minnesota compared infants with differing types of attachment to their mothers as they entered preschool (Waters, Wippman, and Sroufe, 1979). Securely attached infants later made friends more easily with their peers than did less securely attached infants. Over a period of three years, these patterns remained stable. (Children's temperaments, which are also stable over time, and continuity in parent–child interaction may of course contribute to the observed results [Waters, 1978].)

Only one study, and a provisional one at that, tests the proposition that early relations between infant and caretaker predict intimate relations between adults. Arlene Skolnick, a psychologist at the University of California at Berkeley, asked an ambitious question: are children who have had good relationships as infants likely to have good relations with their peers and good marriages, too? She found fewer than 100 cases (in the longitudinal Berkeley Guidance Study) with all of the necessary data (that is, data on four relationships: child with mother, with childhood peer, with spouse, with adolescent peer, and with spouse). Some lucky people had four good relationships. Some few poor souls had only bad relationships. But—and here's the rub!—most fell in between. Some people started well, then zigzagged from doing well to doing poorly. Others started badly and improved; others started well and zigzagged through the other three relationships. The first relationship—mother to child—was not a good predictor of later relationships (Arlene Skolnick, 1986). Luckily, the die is not cast with one's first relationship in life.

What is the connection—if any—between a solid sexual relationship in adulthood and a secure early attachment to a loving parent?

SEXUAL BEHAVIOR IN THE FIRST FIVE YEARS: EVIDENCE

At birth, the human infant seems to "know" only one area of its body. It knows its mouth, lips, and cheeks. Touch the newborn there, and its mouth turns toward your finger. The newborn's reflexes orient it to nursing. After a baby nurses, sucks, and feels full, it usually relaxes its body, and blissfully nods off to sleep—an attitude that most parents read as genuine pleasure.

> *No one who has seen a baby sinking back satisfied from the breast and falling asleep with flushed cheeks and a blissful smile can escape the reflection that this picture persists as a prototype of the expression of sexual satisfaction in later life (Freud, 1905, p. 182).*

As real as these oral pleasures are, only confirmed Freudians feel free to call them sexual, because the Freudian definition of sexual encompasses any sensual pleasure.

Do babies have *any* responses that everyone can agree are sexual? Yes, they do. Babies already have bits of the reflexive sexual responses that will last through adult life. Baby boys are born with the spinal reflexes for erections (Halverson, 1940), and presumably baby girls are born with the reflexes for vasocongestion and vaginal lubrication. (Because boys' erections are more obvious to caretakers and require no measuring instruments to be put inside their bodies, these responses are better documented.) These early erections seem to be associated with sensations from a full bladder or bowels, sensations that many babies seem to find unpleasant—or so their wailing would imply. The erections—and usually the wailing, too—go away when the bladder or bowel is emptied. As the nervous system develops during the early months, babies begin to explore by touch and sight the accessible parts of their bodies. Toe-nibbling, finger-watching, and ear-pulling are all signs of the infant's explorations of itself. Some baby boys find their penis during their explorations, and they are likely to give it an experimental tug or two. A girl's clitoris is not so easy to find, but some baby girls do find and play with their genitals in the first year. This exploration is a normal part of development.

In time, babies learn that touching or rubbing their genitals feels pleasant. They have become sexual people—very young and not terribly well coordinated—but sexual for all that. In some cultures, mothers routinely touch or mouth a baby's genitals in order to quiet or distract it. From all accounts, and psychologists must rely on parents' accounts of infant sexuality, many babies masturbate from a very early age. In one study, 36 percent of one-year-olds were reported by their mothers to play with their genitals; the incidence was higher among the boys than the girls (Newson and Newson, 1963).

> *By the time she was a year old, my daughter could get blissful all on her own. She'd clamp her thighs together rhythmically while sucking hard on a nipple (mother of a 3-year-old).*

> *When I change my son's diaper or put him in his bath, he sometimes likes to play with his penis. It used to be a more hit-or-miss affair. Now he gets an erection 5 seconds after he finds his penis. And he's much better at finding it now (mother of a 2-year-old).*

Few babies engage in fully developed, rhythmic masturbation. Usually their activity is less elaborate and more diffuse. Boys may tug at their penis; girls may finger their vulva or rub their thighs together. Mothers have reported what looked like orgasm in male and female babies as young as 5 months old, although in most children, orgasm appeared later (Kinsey et al., 1948, 1953). Alfred Kinsey, who observed a sample of boys from infancy until late childhood, believed that their sexual reactions as infants resembled those they would show in childhood. Boys' orgasms, unlike those after puberty, produced no ejaculate and required no resting, **refractory period** between orgasms. Some young boys reportedly had several orgasms in a row (without ejaculating, of course) (Kinsey et al., 1948).

Between the ages of two and five, children become increasingly interested in their genitals. One interview study of the mothers of middle-class, New England preschoolers found that half of the mothers had noticed their children playing with their genitals or playing sexual games (Sears, Maccoby, and Levin, 1957). The incidence of genital play is probably higher than one-half, some mothers noticing, others probably suppressing what they notice. An older study, among younger children, found that 55 percent of boys and 16 percent of girls masturbated (Levy, 1928). By the time children are four or so, many like to play sexual games like "Doctor" or "Mother and Father."

A friend's 4-year-old daughter often grabbed her teddy bear, plunked herself in a corner of the couch, and started rubbing her vulva. She'd get a glassy look and embarrass her poor mother. But when her mother tried

to make a deal with her: "Niki, if you stop doing that, you can have the great big teddy you want so much," Niki thought for a minute and replied, "No, I like this better."

Preschoolers want to know what their bodies are like and what other children and adults look like. They like to show off and to look. They may masturbate, or they may try to fondle their mother's breasts. At five or six, children may associate urination with sexual activities (a reasonable idea, because the places for urinating and sexual feeling are so close together).

Given the chance, children in all societies examine one another's bodies, whether within their family or with friends. In sexually permissive cultures, sexual games and love-making are common at ages five or six (Malinowski, 1929; Ford and Beach, 1951). In our society, too, many children learn to masturbate and even to mimic intercourse. Even where sexual exploration is forbidden and carefully watched, children may still explore—but with added anxiety and excitement. The Kinsey group interviewed 432 children between the ages of 4 and 14 and found that 56 percent of the boys and 30 percent of the girls had already masturbated (Elias and Gebhard, 1969; figures from the Kinsey group date from the 1930s and 1940s but were published in the 1960s). An earlier published survey of 13-year-old boys (Ramsey, 1943) found that at age 5, fewer than 5 percent of boys had played sexually with a girl; at age 8, one-third had done so. By the age of 13, more than 80 percent of boys had masturbated, and 66 percent had engaged in sex play with girls. The findings are similar for girls, although the rates are lower than for boys.

Childhood sexuality is strongly exploratory in nature, and much of this exploration is playful. Play, after all, is children's work, and their sexual explorations are embedded in their play. Although some of this play may *look* sexually advanced—two 6-year-olds kissing and rubbing genitals in imitation of intercourse can look quite realistic—children have only limited understanding of the context of sexual behavior. Just as children's cognitive understanding of physical reality is limited, their understanding of sexuality is limited as well. Young children often understand only parts of the story of sexual behavior. They misunderstand or fail even to imagine other parts of the story. Young children, for example, define a boy or a girl by hair length, clothes, and body build. Only at about age seven do they begin to show that they understand that genitals alone tell a person's sex (Thompson and Bentler, 1971). Thus genitals are not always *primarily* sexual to young children, and sex differences are not as clearly understood as adults (including Freud) may believe.

Mislabeling Children's Sexual Acts

In their study of preschoolers mentioned above, Robert Sears, Eleanor Maccoby, and Harry Levin found that mothers reported that half of the children had engaged in sexual play. They also found that many of the mothers showed some anxiety over the children's sexual behavior. For example, to prevent sexual exploration, many mothers forbade their children to use the bathroom with a friend. Many mothers viewed their children's sexual exploration as dangerous behavior. Mothers often distract children or relabel their children's activities in order to change unwanted behavior. Relabeling also reclassifies the behavior out of the sexual domain and into familiar territory, where the child's behavior already has been legitimately subject to adult controls.

Parents who see children touching their genitals may mislabel it as, "Oh, your pants must be too tight. Let's change them," or, "Do you need to go to the bathroom?" Parents may also say, "You'll get all dirty and smelly with your fingers there," or "Is something itchy in your panties?" Because children do not yet have acceptable language for their masturbatory activities, they may adopt the adults' mislabelings instead. When parents mislabel, they usually are not being consciously devious. They are often acting out of their own sexual anxieties, and they are teaching their children what they hope is self-control, modesty, and postponement of sexuality. Many parents believe that "next year" or at some other time in the future, their child will be "old enough" or will be "ready" to hear about sex. Parental mislabeling of children's sexual exploration makes parents underestimate its incidence and frequency.

Adults similarly underestimate when they try to remember their own childhood sexual play. Many adults forget that they masturbated as children. The Kinsey group found that when they asked *adults* whether they had masturbated before they were 12 years old, only 12 percent of the women and 21 percent of the men remembered having done so. When the Kinsey group asked *children* (by using different words in their questions), 56 percent of boys and 30 percent of girls said that they had masturbated.

Children's Same-Sex Play

One-third of girls and one-half of boys among the 432 children Kinsey interviewed remembered some form of sexual play with children of their own sex (Elias and

Lots of childhood sexuality is exploration.

Gebhard, 1969). Most of the children looked at and touched the genitals of children of their own sex. Only a few engaged in mouth-genital play or some form of penetration. Yet this early and transient same-sex activity often had little effect on adult sexual identity (West, 1968). Why? To answer that, consider for a moment the lowly laboratory rat.

Before they reach sexual maturity, rats practice almost all parts of what will later be the full adult sexual response. Usually, sexually mature rats stop practicing the sexual behavior of the other sex. But young rats can mimic the sexual acts of the other sex, and a young, "sexy" rat, one who shows lots of sexual behavior, may well show lots of both sexes' behaviors. When a partner of the other sex is available, all adult rats prefer that partner to one of their own sex. Human children seem to learn sexual behavior in pieces, just as rats do. Pieces of their learning may consist of homosexual *acts*, but most children go on to develop heterosexual and not homosexual *identities*. Because children have not yet solidified their sexual identities and will not do so until after puberty, many of the sexual acts of childhood do not mean what the same acts would mean in adulthood.

During the grade-school years, parents usually relax their watch over their children. Children are allowed to play by themselves and to make certain of their own decisions. Children do not stop their sexual explorations at this stage. Indeed, they tend to carry them into any groups they participate in: school, neighborhood, family, or other common groups. Once past nursery school, children tend to play in single-sex groups, and so their sex play tends to be with children of their own sex and age.

EVALUATING THE EVIDENCE

What can we safely conclude about childhood masturbation and sex play? The evidence suggests that many infants and children masturbate. Surveys among children plus reports from parents indicate that more than half of boys and slightly fewer girls masturbate and play sexually during middle and late childhood.

Learning the precise incidence of sexual activity among children is difficult, for interviewing young children on sexual topics is often tabooed, the techniques are not well defined, and many adults have safely forgotten their childhood sexual experiences. Psychologists also must be cautious in observing children's sexual behavior. Children have rights to privacy. Thus much of the information about childhood sexuality must come indirectly, through parents. Kinsey was invited by some mothers to observe their infants at home, and from these observations he drew data on infant sexuality to bear out his interview data (Kinsey et al., 1948; 1953). Given the importance of his findings on infants, one wishes that other investigators had replicated Kinsey's findings.

Although Freud's theory of childhood sexuality is important, the actual evidence for it is unfortunately skimpy. Yes, children do act interested in their own and other people's bodies. Yes, they can take pleasure from their own bodies, and they can be curious about the bodies of their friends. Certainly they are motivated by their curiosity and their wish to explore. But Freud meant more than that when he said that children are sexual. He meant that there were three definable foci of sexual interest built on oral, anal, and masturbatory pleasure. What little data we have suggest that genitally focused masturbation starts as early as motor coordination allows and continues throughout childhood. It is not renounced in late childhood during the stage Freud called **latency.** Genitally oriented masturbation cannot be localized in the phallic period alone. Data on oral and anal pleasure-seeking are rare outside of clinical histories. Oral reflexes are ubiquitous in the first months of life. Lack of oral pleasure has not been associated with failure to grow and develop (Sears and Wise, 1950). In summary, we are left believing that Freud correctly stated how strong a child's search for sensual pleasure is, but that the orderly progression from oral to phallic pleasure seeking is unproved.

Beside the sexual development theory, Freud postulated a complex relationship between childhood and later experiences. Freud predicted that there is an important *continuity* between life's first relationship—baby and mother—and all later relationships, even the sexual relationship of lovers. That prediction is even more complex than the assertion that children are sexually driven. To investigate Freud's prediction, we first have to detour to explain the process of attachment.

Psychologists say that an infant has "attached securely" when, in the second half of its first year: the infant shows mild distress when its mother leaves; approaches her when she returns; and is quickly soothed by her (Ainsworth et al., 1978). Babies attach to fathers or other primary caretakers as well, and they can attach to more than one person. How does secure attachment develop? What happens if it does not develop?

Body contact is warm. It is soft, for flesh is soft, and it is comforting. The physical warmth of a mother's breast or a father's arms provide their baby with essential contact comfort.

EARLY ATTACHMENT AND ADULT LOVE

Observation of human babies tells us that from the moment of birth, they have definite social and biological needs. All babies need to be fed, kept warm and safe from harm. Unless these biological needs are met, no baby can survive. But babies have other needs, too: to be held, to feel the physical warmth and closeness of another body. Body contact is warm. It is soft, for flesh is soft, and it is comforting. The physical warmth of a mother's breast or a father's arms provide their baby with essential **contact comfort.** Humans are programmed to find bodily contact pleasurable and soothing from the very moment of birth. Most primate babies in nature—whether monkey, ape, or human—would die without contact with another's body. From birth, the human baby's eyes can focus on the face of the person who holds and feeds it. In the laboratory, isolated primates are known to create their own sensory inputs: to rock back and forth, to play with their bodies, and so forth. By programming babies to be attracted to the eyes and face of their caretakers—because of their movement and contrast—nature also increases the odds of gratifying, mutual admiration sessions.

Such exchanges are important if parents and children are to form bonds of attachment. In meeting their baby's needs, caring parents handle and relate and grow attached to it. Mothers and babies play at this reciprocal gazing. To mothers, the baby's gaze and smile make their baby seem a real person who knows them (Robson, 1967). Babies and (usually) mothers enjoy listening to each other's sounds and making faces. Babies and parents have a rhythm to their play. One research psychiatrist at Cornell Medical School, Daniel Stern (1977), calls this relationship a "dance." In their dance, the parent and child learn about timing and what to expect of the other.

A baby's attachment to its first caretaker in many ways resembles the loving sexual relationship. The mutual gazing and smiling of infancy are present between lovers, who gaze more at each other than at acquaintances (Rubin, 1973). Lovers comfort and please each other through bodily contact, as babies and caretakers do. In both sorts of relationships, contact comfort and a loved one's presence are reassuring. As mothers do to their babies, lovers give each other special and often nonsensical or baby-like names. Those who watch the dance of mother and infant say that it looks like a love affair. It does.

> *Love of a partner and sensual pleasure experienced with that partner begin in infancy and progress to a culminating experience, "falling in love," the finding of a permanent partner, the achievement of sexual fulfillment.* **In every act of love in mature life, there is a prologue which originated in the first year of life** (*Fraiberg, 1977, pp. 31–32; our emphasis*).

But many features of the two relationships differ significantly. In both age and maturity, lovers are far more equal than infant and caretaker are. Compared to the baby, both lovers enter a relationship with a far better developed capacity to relate to others, and they can each invent new ways of interacting within their relationship. Babies are limited in the ways they have of stopping or shifting the nature of interactions. Mothers carry more of the burden of keeping the dance alive.

SEXUALITY IN RESEARCH: MONKEY LOVE

In laboratory experiments with rhesus monkeys that are now considered classics of their kind, University of Wisconsin psychologist Harry Harlow and his associates asked how love, attachment, and sexual activity develop. Most primates are very sociable. They need others in order to survive, to learn essential forms of behavior, and, of course, to reproduce. Ordinarily, the mother cares for her young within the social group of her species. To learn how to find food, how to copulate, how to carry young, or other necessary skills, the youngsters watch, play, and experiment. They have many and repeated chances to learn; no skill is won or lost at a single stroke.

Given the great importance of social interaction to normal development among primates, Harlow devised a series of experiments to tease out just what that social interaction teaches monkeys. To do so, he isolated monkeys from their mothers and studied the effects of the isolation. After separation from their mothers, both monkey infant and mother showed signs of stress and disruption. The babies adapted by rocking, huddling, and stimulating themselves to make up for lost sensory input. If the separation went on for a long time, the babies later grew alienated and withdrawn from other animals, including their mothers (see Cairns, 1979).

Harlow later offered the babies mother-substitutes. One substitute was made of wire and gave milk through a nipple. The other substitute was made of terrycloth and gave the baby a soft place to cling to but no milk. History was made when the babies spent far more time with the soft mother-substitute than the fast-food mother. Harlow had demonstrated that monkeys are born with a need for cuddling and closeness.

Harlow's work also says something about the development of adult sexual relationships in primates. Harlow concluded that adult heterosexual love is the fourth in a series of steps. The first step in this series is the mother's love for her infant. She shows her love by cuddling, grooming, gazing, and providing her infant with safety. The second step is the infant's love for its mother. The third step is love between peers or agemates. The fourth step is heterosexual love. Each step requires reciprocal responses: the infant must cling to its mother if she is to support it; peers must interact to be friends or playmates; sexual partners must invite and receive each other to carry through an act of copulation.

Harlow found that infant monkeys who had been deprived of the first two steps, mother love and infant love, had real trouble achieving heterosexual love. These early forms of love provide practice in giving and getting as well as contact comfort. Deprived of this comfort, monkeys later feared close contact with others.

That fear made interaction with peers of the other sex very difficult for the deprived monkeys. The basic security—the knowledge and lack of fear—afforded by the interaction of mother and infant are normally the social antecedents for the easy development of peer love. Female monkeys deprived of *both* mothers and peers tend to become poor mothers, at least to begin with. Males have trouble being good copulators. Motherless mothers are very hard on their first babies, who do well even to survive. But with subsequent babies, they come to resemble other, normal mothers (Seay et al., 1964). Their later competence is not the result of their greater age or even of motherhood itself. It is a result of the youngster's teaching the mother to interact: the baby resocializes its mother.

An infant monkey hugs a soft, terrycloth "mother."

Harlow's work suggests that monkeys can more easily climb the ladder to heterosexual love if they get boosted to the rung for peer love. Peers can give security, too. Play with peers involves body contact, exploration, fun, sham aggression (in roughhousing), and social control of aggression. Body contact and control of aggression are needed during sexual contact. Play also involves practicing pieces of the behavior that later will become the sequences of copulation. An infant deprived of maternal love can learn from close contact with its peers which touching feels good, which hurts, and how much is enough. Perhaps all of these attributes help an individual to come closer to another and to expose vulnerable body parts in sexual acts.

In natural surroundings, primate mothers (here, a gorilla) show their infants love by cuddling, grooming, gazing, and keeping them safe.

If the human primate is like the rhesus macaque, then we can draw several conclusions: interaction between mother and child normally teaches the young how to interact without hurting or being hurt, and it teaches the young how to jostle painlessly in play. The young then transfer these abilities to their play with peers, sexual interaction, reproduction, and, later, care of their own young. When interaction between mother and child is lacking, interaction with peers can supply the necessary learning. Individual primates who lack interaction with both mother and peers face problems reproducing and rearing young, but as adults they can *still* learn, from their own young, how to interact.

GAGNON AND SIMON: CHILDHOOD'S SCRIPTS

Freud's is not the only influential theory of sexual development. From the field of sociology has come another, counterbalancing theory, which emphasizes the *dis*continuity between childhood and adult sexuality. Perhaps children learn aspects of sexuality that are not *directly* sexual. Perhaps they learn some nonsexual framework that later supports the sexual structure. So say two sociologists (mentioned in Chapter 4), John Gagnon of the State University of New York at Stony Brook and William Simon of the University of Houston.

Gagnon and Simon have proposed that sexual development follows **sexual scripts,** one for females and one for males. Like scripts in a play, sexual scripts tell what is to happen: who the potential partners are, when one may interact with them, and how to interact. Lines may be scripted, too: from a female's, "I'd love to go to the football game," to a male's, "You would if you loved me." Over time, scripts change along with the larger society. Today, a female may do some of the inviting to a football game or the sexual wooing.

Sociologists focus on people as members of groups, and they look for uniformities in groups. Children can be treated sociologically, as a group. One can ask what this group learns that they later incorporate into their sexual lives. First, children learn their **gender identity** (in a process described in Chapter 3). By the age of two, they are learning which parts of their body to keep covered. By the time they are five, it is relatively rare for children in this society (who are not raised in nudist families, of course) to wander about naked, even on beaches. Preschool girls with skimpy bikinis are not only rehearsing the modesty of adolescence, but also come to feel that their chests have special meaning. Learning to be modest means in part learning to feel ashamed of showing one's body, for moral values are usually attached to modesty training: "Only naughty children take off their clothes, Jennifer." "Don't be a nasty boy, Justin. Cover yourself up."

Children's knowledge of sexual words or acts is often vague and imprecise. They may know sexual words like "fuck" and "fag," may even use them as insults, but they may not know what they mean. When researchers pressed a 10-year-old boy to define "fag" and "queer," he said, "Oh, you know, boys who don't play ball" (Luria and Herzog, 1983). "Fuck," one boy declared, means "damn."

Gagnon and Simon (1970) consider childhood sexuality to be significantly different from adolescent and adult sexuality. Children who masturbate or have orgasms do not understand these experiences in the same way as they will after adolescence. Although the biology of children's masturbation is like that of adolescents', the symbolic meaning of the sexual experience is different.

When my son was 3, he called masturbating "tickling." I don't think he thought of them as two separate categories of activity (25-year-old male graduate student).

Children may know vaguely that a word or deed is "bad" or exciting because of the way that others react, but their own understanding of sexuality is quite limited (see Table 11.1).

Gagnon and Simon believe that the story of sexuality is not primarily biological but is instead mainly the story of rich cultural and social meanings. Those meanings change as people move from childhood to adolescence. Children learn from their family and friends how boys and girls are supposed to act. They learn about **gender roles** in their society (a process described in Chapter 4). In grade school, children are aware of older brothers and sisters and of (those sophisticated) junior high-schoolers. In their sexually segregated peer groups, fifth-grade girls are clearly

Children learn the modesty rules of their culture. In our culture, it is unusual to see children much over 5—those here are 4 and 6 years old—wandering around naked.

Children learn first which sex they are. Then, between ages 3 and 11, they learn other aspects of gender identity. Children learn sexual words but not their meanings, sexual acts but not their names. They play sexual games without sexual motives. (For later steps in a sexual career, see Table 12.1.).

TABLE 11.1

Outline of a Sexual Career, Part I

Stages & Ages	Agents	Assemblies
1. Infancy: ages 0–3	Mother to family	Formation of base for conventional gender identity.
2. Childhood: ages 3–11	Family to peers, media	Conventional gender identity consolidates; learning about modesty and shame; learning of general moral categories; nonsexually motivated sex play; learning about sexual acts without naming; mass media reinforce conventional gender, sex, and family roles and prepare for participation in youth culture

Gender Identity (arrow spanning stages 1 and 2)

Source: Gagnon and Simon, 1973.

concerned with how they look. They also can manage interpersonal problems in the classroom with great tact (Thorne and Luria, 1986). Interest in appearance and close attention to interpersonal cues are two important parts of the sexual script for females in this society, and they use them for both friendly and hostile interactions. Although romances are known among fourth-graders, the "lovers" typically are eager to disown their feelings. Barrie Thorne, a sociologist at Michigan State University, heard a girl respond to teasing that she "liked" a certain boy by saying, "I don't like him. I hate him. I like him for a friend" (Thorne and Luria, 1986). Children from blue-collar families have romances earlier on average than children from white-collar families, just as later, after puberty, they will have their first intercourse and marry earlier (Vener and Stewart, 1974). Thus in some schools, children begin to rehearse adolescent sexual behavior in fourth or fifth grade. Others wait until the end of sixth grade or later. Boys' groups experiment with pornography and, in the process, teach boys not only the acceptable cues for what is sexual but also the acceptable ways of acting sexual. Girls' groups prepare girls for the sexual experiences they will meet as adolescents. In their groups, boys and girls learn which sexual acts will be forbidden and which allowed. Peer scripts rarely agree totally with parents' scripts on permissible rates for climbing the sexual ladder. The heady sexual excitement of adolescence will define a new set of sexual and gender relations.

Most of Gagnon and Simon's theory of sexual development applies to later stages, when adolescence begins. Gagnon and Simon try to account for why males and females take different paths and why they assign different meanings to sexual acts. As sexual scripts change, some norms remain stable, and others change. Gagnon and Simon's theory also proposes that the overtly sexual may hide nonsexual motives. (For Freudians, the reverse is true: the nonsexual hides the sexual.) In the next chapter, we will return to Gagnon and Simon's conception of sexual scripts and how they interact with gender roles.

Earlier we reviewed children's sexual behaviors. Now we are ready to ask what they *know* about sex.

CHILDREN'S IDEAS ABOUT SEX

Psychologists use two different terms for what children know: **competence** describes all of a child's knowledge; **performance** describes that part of a child's knowledge shown in response to a direct question. Performance typically is an imperfect and diminished measure of competence. Intellectual and motivational factors both contribute to the gap between competence and performance. Thus an interviewer may learn some of what a child knows, but the interviewer can never be sure of what the child does *not* know, even when the child says blankly, "I don't know" (Gelman and Gallistel, 1978).

Children's Ideas about Sex Differences

Two Australian social scientists, Ronald and Juliette Goldman (1982), have tackled these problems in interviewing children from Australia, England, North America (a mixed sample from the United States and Canada), and Sweden. They wanted to know what grade-school children know about the differences between the sexes, how babies are made, about sexual intercourse, and about birth control. The Goldmans interviewed 20 boys and 20 girls, all in public schools, all with two married parents and a sibling, at each of the ages, 7, 9, 11, 13, and 15. In all but the North American sample, they had 40 children at each age level. They had fewer North American children. The total number of children answering any given question was about 800. The Goldmans found, not surprisingly, that children's information about sex improves as the children get older.

If it's got a penis . . . it's a boy. Girls have a virginia."

The Goldmans' interviews revealed that it takes children many years to sort out the differences between males and females. Young children say things like, "Girls are soft, and boys hit." More of the teenaged English-speaking children in the sample could cite the differences between boy and girl babies than younger children could. One-third of the children sampled were 9 years old before they could explain the physical differences between the sexes. By age 11, another one-third could explain the differences. Among 11-year-olds, however, about one-third lacked the vocabulary to describe the differences. Others could describe the differences in idiosyncratic words. Said one 11-year-old English boy, "If it's got a penis . . . it's a boy. Girls have a virginia" (p. 196). Swedish children, who have sex education from preschool on, were more likely than the English-speaking children to have the necessary vocabulary. Children who had siblings of the other sex identified sex differences more accurately than children with siblings of the same sex.

Some children answered the Goldmans' questions creatively, even when they did not know the proper words. Boys, said a 7-year-old Australian, have "something sticking out like a hose." As one 13-year-old North American boy put it, boys have "a round tube." Girls have "chest things," said an Australian boy of 9. Many children, and girls especially, did not know the meaning of "uterus" and "puberty." Fewer than 60 percent of English-speaking 15-year-olds claim to understand that puberty means changes in sexual characteristics and the advent of fertility. But as noted above, we must draw such conclusions cautiously, for it is possible that children cannot or will not express what they do know—out of embarrassment, lack of vocabulary, or other performance factors. To avoid embarrassment and problems related to children's ignorance of terms, interviewers asked questions in the children's own words. One such interviewer asked, "Apart from wanting a baby, why is it *a mum and a dad* will have a *you-know-what together in bed?*" (the boy's own words are in italics; Goldman and Goldman, 1982, p. 260).

Children's Ideas of How Babies Are Made

Children may learn about the differences between the sexes by observing the bodies of males and females at home or among friends. But they cannot directly observe how babies are made. To understand that process, children must have both specific information ("Sperm from the father joins with egg from the mother. Only one sperm . . . ") and the cognitive abilities to understand a long chain of causes and effects. Understandably, it takes most children years to learn the complicated—and hidden—story of fertilization, pregnancy, and birth. The pieces fall into place but slowly—and charmingly.

When our son was 4, my wife and I thought it was time to start teaching him where babies come from. In a quiet moment, I ever so carefully explained that babies grow inside a mother's uterus, which is a special place inside of her. Only ladies have uteruses, I explained, and uteruses are not the same as tummies. The next morning he explained to his mother that when he was a baby, he had lived in Mommy's tummy, in Daddy's tummy, and in Mr. Rogers's tummy. So much for my careful teaching! (33-year-old male high school teacher).

In the developing world, children who sleep in the same room as their parents are very likely to learn the mechanics of how babies are made, with or without the information about genetics. There are many such children. In the United States, children from different social classes tend to have different levels of sexual knowledge. Two investigators from the Kinsey group, James Elias and Paul Gebhard (1969), found that grade-schoolers from blue-collar families were likely to understand the mechanics of sexual intercourse but not fertilization. In contrast, grade-schoolers from white-collar families were likely to understand fertilization but not intercourse. When two investigators (Bernstein and Cowan, 1975) more recently asked 11- and 12-year-old, middle-class, California Bay Area children, "How does the baby happen to be inside the mother's body?" fewer than half could tell the whole story.

When such children are asked how babies are made, most understand that sexual intercourse is the answer. But they tend to fill in some of the blanks quite creatively. Instead of saying that they don't know part of the story about fertilization, many children jump to faulty conclusions. Thus children hear about

Mommy's eggs and conclude that they are like hens' eggs: brittle and fragile. They hear about Daddy's seed and conclude that, like grass seed, it needs water to sprout, and they think of semen as this water. One Australian boy of 7 explained that fathers buy seed at seed shops and put it into mothers. An 11-year-old North American boy said that the father's warmth in bed makes the baby grow. Of course, given the way many children are taught about reproduction, their mistaken impressions are no surprise. Many children never receive any formal sex education at all. Family members may be too shy or feel inadequate to the task; peers may be full of misinformation themselves; teachers may not have the legal authority or even the desire to teach about sex. Said one university professor,

Given all the mystifying tales kids hear about where babies come from, it's a wonder they ever get it straight. This culture is full of tales about "the birds and the bees," about storks, about babies being found under cabbage leaves in the garden.

Most of the Swedish children interviewed knew by age 9 that people find intercourse pleasurable. (Some 7-year-olds even thought so.) The Swedish program of sex education includes this information, and the fact that the children learn it without obvious distortion demonstrates that, in a nonjudgmental environment, even 7-year-olds can master this kind of sexual information. (After all, children can become experts on fantasy lands, dinosaurs, and other creatures totally outside the realm of their actual experience.) Outside of Sweden, only 1 in 5 children thought that there were nonreproductive reasons for intercourse. Only at age 13 did many of the English-speaking children say that intercourse is pleasurable. Most children, showed gender differences in explaining why people have intercourse for reasons beyond reproduction. Girls said that the reason is love; boys said the reason is pleasure.

The Goldmans also asked children about birth control. They asked "what people do if they don't want to have [or to start] a baby." When children are younger than 11, about one-fourth (and especially boys) say that nothing can be done to prevent a baby. Children older than 11 answer otherwise. Few Swedish children, only those 5 to 7, think that having babies in inevitable. Swedish 9- and 11-year-olds know about the contraceptive devices males and females can use. English-speaking children know about contraception by age 13 to 15. By that age, many English-speaking girls know about birth control pills. At age 11, most children know something about abortion. By age 15, all the children interviewed knew about it. Thirteen- and 15-year-old girls tend to describe abortion more vaguely than boys their age. Why? The Goldmans suggest that the girls are more aware of cultural disapproval of abortion.

In sum, children slowly master the complicated story of sexual reproduction. Where sex education is thorough and age-graded (as in Sweden), even young children can understand some facts as well as subtleties of sexual behavior. Where they have to string the facts together on their own, children make mistakes, create erroneous (if sometimes inventive) explanations, and generally muddle through until they understand something about the biology of sex differences and reproduction.

SEXUALITY IN PERSPECTIVE: SEX EDUCATION

In an ideal world, parents would talk comfortably with their children about all aspects of human sexuality. They would openly answer questions; they would easily communicate facts and values; and they would readily and realistically discuss the details of sexual choices. But in this less than ideal world, children learn not to ask embarrassing questions of their parents. Many parents feel uncomfortable using the language of eroticism with their children, and it may be hard for them to accept their children as sexual people. Long interviews with 1400 parents in Cleveland, Ohio—a city with many Roman Catholics and relatively few divorces—showed that 85 to 95 percent of the parents had never mentioned any aspect of erotic behavior to their children (Roberts, Kline, and Gagnon, 1978). Most parents who *had* managed to talk about sex did so only once.

Even though parents have a hard time teaching their children about sex, they want them to know about it. For example, a Gallup Poll taken in 1977 showed that 70 percent of adults wanted contraception taught in the schools (twice the number who wanted it in 1970). Similarly, a National Opinion Research Council survey in 1974 found that 78 percent of adults wanted sex education and birth control available to teenagers who asked for them. School superintendents reported that few parents opposed sex education; fewer than 5 percent removed their children from such programs (Kirby et al., 1979).

When sex is taught in schools, the goals of the program may be broad or narrow. Thus in Sweden, children begin in nursery school to learn about sexuality and family, the first small steps toward the knowledge necessary for making responsible sexual decisions and for forming intimate and family relationships. Swedish children continue to learn about sexuality as they go through school. In the United States, many schools teach about sexually transmitted diseases (STDs), contraception, menstruation, and teenage pregnancy. New York City public schools now teach prekindergartners to second-graders about how "animals and humans need families." Third- and fourth-graders learn how "in order for family life to continue, living things must mate and reproduce." Fifth- and sixth-graders learn about puberty and conception. Junior-high students learn about adolescence, "a time of rapidly changing needs," and about sexual abuse. High-schoolers learn about genetic and sexually transmitted diseases, about starting and maintaining a family, single parents, and teenage pregnancies (Purnick, 1983). Generally, the most common form of sex education in the United States is a high-school course that lasts a week or two and covers only a few topics (Kirby et al., 1979). In a 1979 survey, half of the unmarried 15- to 19-year-olds had been taught about contraception, 60 percent about STDs, and 70 percent about menstruation (Zelnik and Kantner, 1981). (That 70 percent figure is the highest ever found in the United States.)

Sex education can be very effective outside of school. For example, The British Broadcasting Corporation ran an excellent education film for 8- to 12-year-olds. It showed a live birth and named the genitals fully. A follow-up inquiry showed that after the film, children knew more about sex than they had earlier and their attitudes toward nudity and childbirth had changed (Himmelweit and Bell, 1980). Another sex education program, this one for junior-high students, is presented in churches by the Unitarian Universalist Alliance. Real people have been recorded as they talk out their positive and negative feelings about sexuality. The recordings are so realistic and compelling that parents (who go through the program before their children do) are helped to talk about sexual issues that they otherwise never would have mentioned to their children (such as homosexuality or pornography).

When the results of all the studies and inquiries are tallied, how effective is sex education? First, students who have had sex education know somewhat more than they knew before their sex education courses and somewhat more than students who haven't taken such courses. Second, although sexual values do not seem to change as a result of sex education, there is some evidence that sex education improves tolerance for other people's sexual values (Kirby et al., 1979). Third, thorough coverage of contraception improves use of contraception, and pregnancy rates are likeliest to drop when sex education is taught in schools tied to clinics that dispense contraception. Fourth, teenagers who have taken sex education courses are no likelier to have had sexual intercourse than teenagers who haven't taken courses (Zelnik and Kim, 1982). Finally, as you may have suspected after hearing those wild and crazy tales in the school cafeteria, friends are the poorest—if common—source of good information about sex (*Family Planning Perspectives*, 1981).

SUMMARY

1 Human sexuality is a product of both biological development and social learning. People learn from others—especially their parents and peers—how to act sexual.

2 Some theories of sexual development consider it to be continuous from infancy to old age. Freud's theory of psychosexual development, for example, posits that childhood sexual experiences shape those of adolescence and adulthood. In contrast, the theory of sociologists John Gagnon and William Simon posits a significant discontinuity between childhood and adult sexual learning. Gagnon and Simon stress the social aspects of sexual learning; Freud stresses the biological aspects.

3 Infants and young children show many exploratory sexual behaviors. They masturbate and play sexually with others of their own and the other sex. But many adults mislabel, ignore, underestimate, or simply forget the sexuality of childhood.

4 Human and other primate infants enjoy contact comfort from their care-taker—usually, but not necessarily, their mother. Some psychologists predict that infants must attach securely to their caretaker in order to avoid problems in their adult sexual relationships. Research implies that nature gives the young many chances to learn the forms of behavior—sexual and otherwise—necessary for intimate relations later in life.

5 For many reasons, adults have trouble learning just what children do and do not know about sex. Children seem to learn the complicated stories of sex differences and reproduction slowly and with increasing accuracy as they grow older. Sex education can help even young children understand some of the facts and subtleties of sexual reproduction.

KEY TERMS

pleasure principle
Oedipus complex
genital sexuality
critical period
sensitive period
refractory period
latency

contact comfort
sexual scripts
gender identity
gender roles
competence
performance

SUGGESTED READINGS

Goldman, R., and Goldman, J. *Children's Sexual Thinking: a Comparative Study of Children Aged 5 to 15 Years in Australia, North America, Britain, and Sweden.* London: Routledge & Kegan Paul, 1982. National differences and individual differences in what children know about reproduction and sexual behavior are clearly, often amusingly, presented.

Rutter, M. *Maternal Deprivation Reassessed.* 2nd edition. Middlesex, England: Penguin, 1981. A British psychiatrist presents the evidence on children deprived of mothering. Michael Rutter defends the position that it is never too late to intervene on behalf of children once deprived.

Stern, D. *The First Relationship: Infant and Mother.* Cambridge, MA: Harvard University Press, 1977. A lovely book about interaction between mothers and infants, written with the clarity of a fine researcher.

Chapter 12

Sexuality through the Life Cycle:
Adolescence and Adulthood

In general, although adult sexuality does develop from the behavior and values forged during adolescence, most adults add few sexual behaviors to their repertories. Instead, adulthood is a time when people tend to consolidate their sexual patterns and to learn through experience their sexual values and choices. For many people, the sexual choices, attitudes, and frequencies of particular sexual acts during young adulthood strongly color the sexuality of middle and old age.

ADULT SEXUAL IDENTITY

Adolescence is a time when people learn new sexual acts (such as petting and sexual intercourse), acts that carry special, socially prescribed meanings. Adolescence is also a time when people complete the work, which they began as children, on their **gender identity** (their private sense of femaleness or maleness). As adolescents, they fantasize about and decide whether (in reality) they prefer sexual partners of their own or the other sex. In sum, **adolescence**—a period broadly defined as ranging from puberty to the early twenties—is a time of new sexual acts, new sexual fantasies, and a new context within which these are interpreted.

The physical changes that turn girls into fertile young women and boys into fertile young men are called, collectively, **puberty**. During puberty, the differentiation of the two sexes is completed. Partly in response to these biological developments, and partly in response to psychological, cognitive developments, adolescents begin to identify themselves as sexually adult women or men.

In our dreams, daydreams, and romantic or erotic reveries, we meet people we desire sexually.

Forming a full adult gender identity, Money and Ehrhardt (1972) believe, includes choosing the sex of one's sexual partners, a choice that clinicians believe most people make first at the level of fantasy. In our dreams, daydreams, and romantic or erotic reveries, we meet the people we desire sexually. Most people are not aware of having chosen the sex of their desired partners, because the "choice" feels so automatic and natural. Yet for some adolescents, 5 to 10 percent, this choice feels difficult, because their imagined sex partner is of their own sex. Many of these adolescents feel painfully conflicted over the sex of the partners who appear in their sexual fantasies. Even so, the imagined partner seems to such adolescents as automatic and natural as the opposite-sex images are to other adolescents. Although many aspects of adolescent sexuality can be hard to handle, some people find that defining their sexual orientation—heterosexual or homosexual—is especially difficult.

The sexuality of adolescence, therefore, is not just a product of biological urges. It proceeds from several necessary components: actual physical maturation; social interaction; and psychological pressures. In response to all of these, adolescents actively *construct* the kind of sexual people they will become. This construction is not necessarily conscious or studied. Rather, adolescents build their sexuality on society's **gender-role** definitions and on the norms that prevail in their peer groups. They build in response to social pressures and the sexual imagery available from books, movies, friends, and other *social* sources. Important pieces of this construction come also from the adolescent's sexual opportunities and from something we might call "sexual interest." In short, adolescents shape their sexual selves by watching others in their groups, by heeding and incorporating spoken and unspoken codes of behavior for each gender, and by expressing (or denying) felt psychological needs.

STORM AND STRESS?

Many clinicians and writers in the popular press customarily have described adolescence as a period of great sexual, emotional, and even religious turmoil. But is this description of adolescence as a time of *Sturm und Drang*—storm and stress—an accurate one? When psychoanalytically oriented researchers study adolescents today, they find instead remarkable stability and continuity of personality throughout adolescence. They find few storms and relatively short-lived stress. For example, only a small minority of adolescent boys in a privileged midwestern sample was found to fit a stormy, or "tumultuous," pattern of development. These boys tended to come from less favored family backgrounds than most of the other boys in their class. Thus opportunities that other boys took for granted were closed to them (Offer and Offer, 1975). An earlier study of high-school students of both sexes came to remarkably similar conclusions (Douvan and Adelson, 1966).

SOCIAL AND MORAL AGENDA

Sociologists Patricia Miller and William Simon (1981) argue persuasively that to understand adolescent sexual behavior, one must understand the meanings attached to it, both by adolescents themselves and by others. Sexuality does not develop in a fixed sequence the way that baby teeth give way to a fixed order of second teeth. No, they suggest, adolescent sexual behavior and commitment reflect ideas about sex that are shared, social constructs. Many of these ideas bear on gender roles. For instance, young women bring to sexuality concerns about love and relationships; young men may devalue emotional commitment but have explicit sexual goals, at least to begin with.

Immediately sexual acts end up serving social and psychological ends. Petting, Miller and Simon point out, certifies a pair as adequately feminine and masculine. The emblems of going steady—a boy's ring on a girl's finger, a girl's picture in a boy's wallet—serve similar social and psychological ends. The meanings attached to sex can be as important as any sexual act itself. Just being seen with a date implies sexual competence.

In our high school, you were cool if you showed up at a certain diner late on a weekend night with your date. The usual procedure was to go somewhere early in the evening, maybe a movie, or to someone's house, or just cruise around in a car. Then to the diner. Then parking (21-year-old male college junior).

In some adolescent groups, intercourse or heavy petting signify love and commitment, but in other groups, they signify pleasure. In every group, adolescents keenly feel the weight of social expectations on their sexual lives, expectations from peers, parents, and themselves.

In adolescence, more than any other period of life, managing one's sexual behavior takes on a moral cast.

Moral judgments tend to add significance to sexual activity. The sexual encounter during adolescence (or its anticipation) provides one of the few instances where ordinary people doing relatively ordinary things experience themselves as extraordinary actors in the moral universe (Miller and Simon, 1981, p. 392).

Society broadcasts another mixed message to adolescents. They learn to fear sexual inexperience *and* sexual experience (Miller and Simon, 1981).

If I went out twice or three times a week with my boyfriend, my parents warned me to "slow down." If I stayed home, they asked where all the boys were. My best friend never dated until college, and her parents were frantic. They were too embarrassed to ask directly, but you could tell they were worried she was a lesbian. Every once in a while, they asked her if she needed to see a shrink (22-year-old college senior).

WHEN ANd WHETHER TO HAVE INTERCOURSE, ESpECIALLY fiRST INTERCOURSE, OCCUPiES A CENTRAL PLACE IN THE AdOLESCENT'S MORAL UNIVERSE.

When and whether to have intercourse, especially first intercourse, occupies a central place in the adolescent's moral universe. Several studies (Cairns, 1973; Jessor and Jessor, 1975; Chilman, 1983; Hass, 1979) support the contention that although more adolescents than ever before have had sexual intercourse, they continue to attach traditional moral values to it. There are strong correlations between very early sexual intercourse and other forms of behavior considered deviant, such as delinquency or taking drugs. There are also strong correlations between very early intercourse and alienation from family, church, and school (Schofield, 1965). Not only does very early intercourse tend to be considered deviant, but casual sex—maximizing the number of partners—tends to remain largely the province of a minority of males (Sorenson, 1973; Vener and Stewart, 1974).

Society has put adolescents in a bind. They are supposed to commit themselves to a heterosexual identity and to emerge from adolescence with the social and psychological skills necessary for marriage and parenthood. But, to some degree, they are not supposed to *act* sexual, especially if they are female. For example, "good girls" traditionally have been allowed lots of romance but no heavy sex. Only "bad girls" were said to have sexual intercourse before they married (or at least engaged to be married). Today, traditional good girl–bad girl conventions seem more widespread among younger adolescents—13- to 15-year-olds—than among older adolescents. When they occur among older groups, we know that we are in a setting of strict (usually religious) values. In the updated version of these conventions, today's "bad girl" has had intercourse with "too many" men. Today's "good girl" has had intercourse with "a reasonable number" of men. Exactly how many are "too many" and "a reasonable number"? No one can say exactly. Such numbers are the product of social conventions; they are cultural and moral measurements, not measurements of physical or biological properties.

Sexual intercourse hangs over adolescence like forbidden fruit. Overvalued because it is forbidden, intercourse attracts swarms of psychological and social meanings. Decisions about intercourse render it not merely a physical act, not merely a biological appetite, but a ritual surrounded by symbolism and mystique. Adolescents who have had intercourse may assume special status and prestige.

GENDER SCRIPT FOR ADOLESCENCE

As people emerge into adolescence, they bring with them their personal styles, developed in childhood, of coping with and meeting the world. They enlist these personal styles of adaptation in their sexual and social behavior. To most adolescents, sexuality now *feels* sharply different from that of childhood. For many boys, for example, the boosted testosterone of puberty prompts more frequent erections. To paraphrase comedian Richard Pryor,

> *First thing in the morning, my erect penis banged on my chest so I'd take it to the bathroom. It got hard all the time,* hard as diamonds! *I could come—boom, baroom, baroooom—twenty times a day.*

For many girls, sexual fantasies run through their imaginations like serial dramas. The words and images of desire drown out lecturing teachers and parents.

> *Somehow the teachers always knew when you fell into a daydream. Then they'd call on you, and you'd have to say, "I'm sorry. I wasn't paying attention." The whole class would snicker (18-year-old female college freshman).*

Today's Gender Script

Gender scripts are not static any more than teenagers' topics of conversation are static. As gender roles within the larger society change, so may adolescent gender scripts. Compared to the scripts of the 1940s and 1950s (Kinsey's day), the scripts for adolescents today are heavy with changes. One such change is that the distinctions are blurring between what is acceptable or possible for the two genders (Miller and Simon, 1972). For example, many adolescent women want careers, traditionally part of the masculine script. As adults, these women will therefore marry later than the women of their mothers' generation. They are less likely to follow the old feminine script, in which women wanted a promise of marriage in return for sex. An emotional commitment traditionally has made sex more acceptable to unmarried women. At the same time, men who want such women as sexual partners must focus less on scoring and more on the social skills necessary for attracting and holding a partner. For both sexes, living together and late marriage are common alternatives to the older norm, early marriage.

TABLE 12.1
Outline of a Sexual Career, Part II

Stages & Ages	Agents	Assemblies
Gender Identity → 3. Early Adolescence: ages 11–15	Family, same-sex peers, media	First social identification as conventional sexual performer; first overt sexual activity with self and others; development of fantasies; beginnings of male-female differences in sexual behavior; application of gender package and moral values to sexual acts; sexual acts become private; same-sex peers reinforce homosocial values; family begins to lose moral control; media reinforce conventional adult gender roles; attachment to youth culture forms.
Sexual Identity → 4. Later Adolescence: ages 15–18	Same-sex peers; increasing cross-sex peers; media decreasing family	Increasing integration of sexual acts with nonsexual social relations; heterosocial relations; media reinforce sexual and gender roles; sexual activity increasingly frequent; family control declining.
5. Early Adulthood: ages 18–23	Same- and cross-sex peers; media; minimal family of origin	Mate selection; increased sexual practice; males commit to love and females to sex; insulation from family and peers' judgments; pressure to marry; relief from competition with same-sex peers as cross-sex ties stabilize; peers and romantic code legitimize sexual activity; media reinforce youth culture values of romance and virtues of marriage; falling in and out of love; end of protected student status.

← Family Formation →		
6. Final mate selection—early marriage, ages 20–27	Fiancé(e); spouse; same-sex peers; family of origin increases	Sexual activity regularizes and rates stabilize; variation in kinds of sexual activity; children born; increasing sexual anxiety about children; family values reinforced by children and family of origin; eroticism declines and maternal feelings increase; sexual behavior becomes routine; decreased contact with unmarried cross-sex peers; interaction in groups of couples; pregnancy, children, and work restrict sexual activity.
← Reproduction →		
7. Middle marriage; ages 28–45	Spouse; same-sex peers; family of origin; married peers	Marital sex declines; some extramarital experimenting; children mature; conflict of erotic and parental; sexual dissatisfactions emerge; physical energy and beauty decline; job commitment increases; marriage moves to nonsexual basis.
8. Post-young children; ages 45 +	Spouse; same-sex peers; married peers	Sexual activity declines further; some extramarital sex; substitution of nonsexual commitments other than children as basis of marriage; physical strength and beauty decline further; further desexualization of gender identity; exit from public sexual arena.

During adolescence, a sexual identity and overt sexual activity continue to develop. Adolescents adopt sexual values and become actively sexual. Adulthood's scripts call for forming families and bearing children.

Source: Gagnon and Simon, 1973.

DOONESBURY
by Garry Trudeau

A Cross-Cultural Perspective   Until recently, we had no western samples in which females—like males—reaching puberty, became sexually active. Today, we do. In Upsaala, Sweden, girls at puberty are sexually active and have *more* sexual partners than boys their age do. The girls are younger when they first have sexual intercourse than boys are (Lewin, 1982). Similarly, in a sample of West German students (Clement, Schmidt, and Kruse, 1984), the young women have sexual intercourse more often than the young men and, outside of long-term relationships, as often as young men. Although neither the Swedish nor the West German study is nationally representative, both are harbingers of change in sexual scripts. In both studies, the traditional gender differences in masturbation persist. But the meaning of the sexual acts still differs for males and females. The German researchers suggest an extension of the sexual scripts: young men use their sexual experiences to confirm their masculinity and identity as males, and they use masturbation also as a context within which to express their nonsexual emotions. Young women, given their script, use their sexual experiences to confirm their femininity and identity as females, but they rely less exclusively on masturbation to release tension or to express emotion.

Another change in the sexual script for adolescents stems from the suffusion of *adult* social life with sexual elements (Miller and Simon, 1981). Today adolescents see adults—their ultimate models—as sexually active and sexually interested. Adolescents mix with adults who are slim, trim, and bedecked in designer jeans, who meet at bars, who dance seductively, and who go on dates. Often, adults seeking to marry or remarry play the same kinds of courtship games as adolescents do—but with even more explicit sexual overtones. The 50-year-old man on a Cape Cod beach, wooing a 19-year-old woman, uses a sophisticated psychological ploy, easier for him than for a 19-year-old man:

> *You are very beautiful. A real woman. You have such a strong self. That really turns me on. (He strokes her hands, arms, and face.) You know yourself. That's beautiful.*

Many adults have shed the tentativeness and coyness toward sexual invitations that are common among adolescents. These adult models imply that in the new and improved script, sex can take center stage. Said a college sophomore about his divorced father's dating,

I'm not sure if I like my dad's dating or not. Sometimes I think he tries to act too young, like when he borrows my clothes or my records. Sometimes he is totally out of it, like when he wears stiff new jeans or buttons his shirts all the way up. If he brings a date home, I'm supposed to act like everything's just ordinary. But it's embarrassing to eat breakfast with some strange lady you know spent the night in your house.

ADOLESCENTS' SEXUAL BEHAVIOR

Compared to adolescents of earlier generations, adolescents today are more likely to think they should be interested in sex, to have sex earlier, and to be sexually competent once they have experience. Adolescents from all social classes have all forms of social sex earlier today than adolescents did in the 1940s and 1950s. They proceed through the steps—kissing, light petting, heavy petting—to intercourse more quickly as well. In Kinsey's day, young women who married did so within a year or two of their first experience with intercourse. Today, young women have intercourse when they are younger and marry when they are older. They have intercourse outside of marriage for a longer period, on average, than women used to do. Moreover, more young women today have intercourse with more than a single partner. These women are not likely to have many sexual partners at the same time. They are likely to have a series of loving, monogamous relationships (Hunt, 1974; Sarrel and Sarrel, 1979; Sorenson, 1973).

My parents simply cannot understand that I have slept with half a dozen guys since freshman year in college. Being in love six times in twelve years isn't outrageous. But my poor mother worries that I'm promiscuous and "ruined for marriage" (30-year-old lawyer).

WHEN SEX IS A BURDEN

Human beings do not glide along in mindless conformity. Many adolescents enjoy sex physically, socially, and emotionally, but not all do. Sex may intrude in some lives like an unwelcome, demanding guest. Many high-school boys are far more interested in cars, or computers, or basketball than in girls (Offer and Offer, 1975). Sports long have offered boys a way to prove their masculinity to their male peers without having to demonstrate sexual prowess. Most teenage boys have masturbated extensively, yet some are not ready to make the social advances toward girls that the adolescent male's script calls for. Similarly, not all adolescent girls feel ready for the demands of teenage sexual interaction. Some girls can take refuge in schoolwork or in the role of confidante.

I always avoided the make-out parties in high school. They seemed gross. But when I hit college, I couldn't seem to find a place for myself. I found a quiet guy who was a virgin like me, and we decided to hell with it, we'd kill two birds with one stone. It was awful. We ended up comforting one another, but we both felt terrible, mortified, ashamed. I thought, if this is sex, you can have it. It was two years before I wanted to try again (college senior describing events at age 19).

In high school, I felt fat and ugly, so I acted like everybody's "just a friend." That worked for a while. I felt protected from having to act sexy or make the decisions about whether to do this or that with boys. But I was glad to get to college and drop that neutral pose. I guess I finally just got old enough to handle sex (20-year-old college sophomore {female}).

It is not surprising to learn that the higher the social class of adolescents, the more acceptable they find delaying sexual experience or postponing some of the later steps, like sexual intercourse. Making a serious investment in school work is more acceptable to adolescents in a college-oriented, middle-class community than in poorer communities (Chilman, 1983).

THE SEXUAL FANTASIES OF ADOLESCENCE MAY BRING SPECIAL AGONIES. IF THEY DEPICT SCENES OF RAPE, OR VIOLENCE, OR BONDAGE, ADOLESCENTS MAY FEAR THAT THEIR SEXUAL DESIRES ARE "PERVERTED" AND UNNATURAL.

The sexual fantasies of adolescence may bring special agonies. If they depict scenes of rape, or violence, or bondage, adolescents may fear that their sexual impulses are "perverted" and unnatural. They are surprised to be told how common such fantasies are. (Adult rapists report far more sadistically violent and more

The sexuality of adolescence *feels* sharply different from the sexuality of childhood.

obsessive rape fantasies than adolescents of either sex.) If their fantasies depict scenes of homosexual acts, adolescents may conclude that they are "queer." As one 19-year-old said,

> *My sexual fantasies are vivid but confusing. Sometimes I'm making out with a man, sometimes a woman. Meanwhile, I've been seeing a lot of one guy I like a lot. When I told him about these dreams, he thought I was being funny. But I'm still worried that maybe I'm a lesbian.*

Of course, fantasies do not dictate actions. As we have seen, fantasies of same-sex partners are common—among the top five—in a sample of heterosexual adults, just as fantasies of other-sex partners are common among a sample of homosexual adults (Schwartz and Masters, 1984).

The adolescent sexual scene is not easy for all adolescents. Some interviews with girls who mature and date early show that they are unhappy with their inability to handle the social and sexual pressure that somewhat older boyfriends exert. Said one junior high school girl, "I don't really like to be kissed, you know." Said another, "I don't like a guy trying to touch me, and that's what they tried to do" (Simmons et al., 1979, p. 964). On average, girls manage the transition to adult sexuality with self-concept and self-esteem intact. To the girl who *wishes* that she could get into the world of dating and sex, such statements may sound incredible. But the modesty training of childhood cannot be turned off like a light switch; girls *and* boys must learn a new framework within which to interpret their bodies in social interaction.

Masturbation

The fantasies that develop while an adolescent masturbates may last a lifetime. For boys, this may mean that an internal symbolic system for sex is worked out while their social experiences are primarily with other boys (that is, during the period when boys masturbate actively before they have any form of social sex). Common sexual fantasies among males in the early 1970s pictured intercourse with a stranger, or forcing a woman to have sex, or having sex with two or more partners. Two themes run through such fantasies: first, male sexual power (in overcoming women) and women's belief in that power; second, women's lack of sexual assertiveness. By the 1980s, differences between men and women in their fantasies appear to have diminished, at least in one smaller-scale comparison by gender and sexual orientation (Schwartz and Masters, 1984).

Masturbation is probably the most guilt-inducing, hidden, and denied sexual act in most people's lives. The guilt reflects our culture's ambivalence toward sex for pleasure as opposed to sex for procreation. Young adolescent boys today who are already sexually experienced often report little or no masturbation in their histories. Given the rates of intercouse, it is highly unlikely that they masturbated so little in their early teens. Yet teenage boys often are embarrassed to report their experience with masturbation, although they freely admit their sexual ex-

FIGURE 12.1

Masturbation. The greatest increase in masturbation was reported by white females, especially young adolescents. Kinsey interviewed 5300 males and 5940 females between 1938 and 1949. Hunt, trying to replicate the Kinsey studies, questioned 982 males and 1044 females (Hunt, 1974; Kinsey et al., 1953).

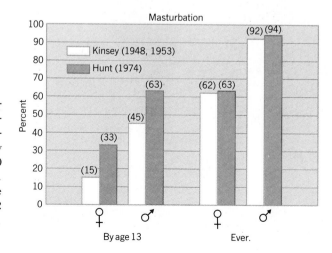

periences with women (Sorenson, 1973). Respondents to a survey in France often returned their questionnaires without answering the questions on masturbation but answered the questions on oral sex (Gondonneau et al., 1972). Not only do adolescent boys try to hide their solitary pleasures, but adult men regularly answer survey questions or clinical interviews on how often they masturbate by saying something like, "X times a week—but not often enough to hurt myself." Because there is no evidence that masturbation hurts anyone, these qualified answers suggest that old, guilt-laden attitudes towards masturbation are intact, perhaps only cosmetically altered since the nineteenth century.

HETEROSEXUAL ACTS AND IDENTITY

At some time between the ages of 14 and 16, most high-school students have moved in their social-sexual lives to petting below the waist. They have arrived there by scaling the sexual steps already discussed. Figure 12.2 shows the per-

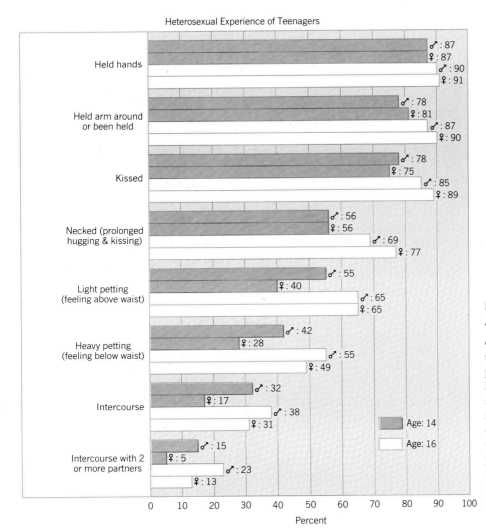

FIGURE 12.2

Teenagers' heterosexual experience. When teenagers were asked to report their heterosexual experiences as of 1973, both sexes had proceeded from least to most intimate sexual acts. By age 16, more males than females had engaged in heavy petting and intercourse. This figure shows the percentage increases between ages 14 and 16 for both sexes as well as the differences between the sexes (Vener and Stewart, 1974).

centages of students in 1973 in a lower-middle-class midwestern high school who had already performed each act between the ages of 14 and 16 (Vener and Stewart, 1974).

Today's figures would be somewhat higher given the decline in age at first intercourse found by Zelnik and Kantner between the early and late 1970s. Among women under 25, however, the incidence of petting changed significantly between the 1940s and 1972—from about 50 percent to a rate right up there with men.

The movement through the sequence of steps is not preordained by biology, and not every adolescent breezes through it. Many young women feel conflict at every point of decision. They choose how to proceed on the bases of sexual curiosity, their view of their relationship, the status and age of their partner, and their ideas about the sexual activity among peers. Many adolescent girls use an interesting language about sex. It implies that they do *not* choose. "He swept me off my feet," or "I was overcome," they may say, implying that sex is completely spontaneous, unplanned, a matter of romance and passion rather than cold-blooded, premeditated decisions. Even so, many young women report greater ease with petting than with intercourse, reaching orgasm most reliably under the conditions that pose no risk of pregnancy (Chilman, 1983).

SEXUAL INTERCOURSE   No area of sexuality has been more thoroughly researched than the first act of sexual intercourse by women. Today, many agents of society—parents, legislators, educators, clergy, and the like—state that they want to control adolescent intercourse in order to avoid large numbers of pregnancies outside of marriage. Therefore, the U.S. government and private foundations have supported a good deal of research into adolescent intercourse and pregnancy, contraception, abortion, and sex education.

What does all this research say? Are the experiences of today's adolescents uniquely different from the experiences of their parents and grandparents? No, they are not. It is true that more unmarried adolescents today have had intercourse, but a significant number of parents and grandparents themselves had intercourse outside of marriage. In Kinsey's day, by age 25, 71 percent of single men and 33 percent of single women had had intercourse. As of 1972, by age 25, 97 percent of all single men and 67 percent of single women have had

FIGURE 12.3

Sexual intercourse by unmarried college students. Between the 1940s and the 1970s, the incidence of sexual intercourse increased steadily among college men and women. (Some two dozen studies have been compiled to produce these figures. They have been included regardless of sample adequacy, representativeness, or age range.) (Based on Table 5.5 in Chilman, 1983, "College-Level Females and Males Reporting Nonmarital Intercourse," pp. 81–85.)

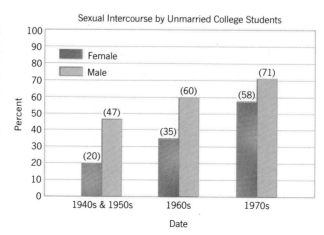

intercourse. Those increases translate into about one-third more single men and twice as many single women having intercourse today. Kinsey found that about half of all married women had had intercourse before marriage. In short, the *rates* of increase (versus the absolute figures of incidence) have been steeper among women—in part because rates among women had more room to climb (Hunt, 1974).

The research attention directed at the age when young women have their first sexual intercourse has revealed several trends. In 1979, a national **probability sample** of 15- to 19-year-old women in metropolitan areas was surveyed. (Recall that a probability sample matches the distribution of *all* women 15 to 19 with respect to that population's demographic characteristics.) The average age for the first intercourse of these women was a bit over 16. Young black women tended to start intercourse earlier than young white women. Most women—both those never married and those married—have had intercourse while single. Table 12.2 shows a steady rise, from 30 percent to 50 percent, in the numbers of sexually active unmarried teenaged women between 1971 and 1979. The term "sexually

TABLE 12.2
Sexual Behavior Among College Students

Have you ever engaged in the following behavior with a member of the opposite sex?	Percentage of males saying yes	Percentage of females saying yes
1. One minute of continuous kissing on the lips?	86.4	89.2
2. Manual manipulation of clothed female breasts?	82.7	71.1
3. Manual manipulation of bare female breasts?	75.5	66.3
4. Manual manipulation of clothed female genitals?	76.4	67.5
5. Kissing nipples of female breast?	65.5	59.0
6. Manual manipulation of bare female genitals?	64.4	60.2
7. Manual manipulation of clothed male genitals?	57.3	51.8
8. Mutual manipulation of genitals?	55.5	50.6
9. Manual manipulation of bare male genitals?	50.0	51.8
10. Manual manipulation of female genitals until there were massive secretions?	49.1	50.6
11. Sexual intercourse, face to face?	43.6	37.3
12. Manual manipulation of male genitals to ejaculation?	37.3	41.0
13. Oral contact with female genitals?	31.8	42.2
14. Oral contact with male genitals?	30.9	42.2
15. Mutual manual manipulation of genitals to mutual orgasm?	30.9	26.5
16. Oral manipulation of male genitals?	30.0	38.6
17. Oral manipulation of female genitals?	30.0	41.0
18. Mutual oral-genital manipulation?	20.9	28.9
19. Sexual intercourse, entry from the rear?	14.5	22.9
20. Oral manipulation of male genitals to ejaculation?	22.7	26.5
21. Mutual oral manipulation of genitals to mutual orgasm?	13.6	12.0

Source: From Curran, "The Social Psychology of Sexual Behavior," Table 7.1, in Deaux and Wrightsman, 1984.

When male and female college students were asked about the kinds of personal relationships within which they would approve of sexual intercourse, they most favored *sexual* intimacy in relationships of greatest *personal* intimacy. In each case, males' attitudes were more liberal than females'.

FIGURE 12.4

Intercourse among adolescents, aged 13–19. Surveys in the 1970s among metropolitan-area femaled, ages 15 to 19, and males, ages 17 to 21, show that the incidence of intercourse increased over time among females who had been married, were married when sampled, and who never had been married. The age of females' first intercourse dropped slightly, from age 16.4 in 1971 to 16.2 in 1979. Males sampled in 1979 had a higher incidence of intercourse than females. (M. Zelnik and J.F. Kantner, "Sexual Activity, Contraceptive Use, and Pregnancy among Metropolitan-Area Teenagers: 1971–1979," *Family Planning Perspectives*, 1980, *12*, 230–237.) A study of 1641 conservative midwestern university students showed that some young women had oral sex before intercourse. Overall, frequencies of sexual behavior were similar for men and women.

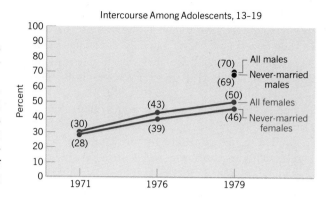

active" defines incidence ("Have you ever . . . ?") of sexual intercourse. In 1979, 50 percent of 15- to 19-year-old women had had intercourse. They are all reported as sexually active. In truth, one in eight of these women had had intercourse only once (Zelnik and Kantner, 1980). If "sexually active" meant having intercourse twice or more, the incidence would be 44 percent.

One psychologist called a 50 percent incidence of any behavior a "tipping point." Once more than half of any group did something, Ruth Hartley declared, it became expected, even coercive to those who might wish to act otherwise. Like wearing designer jeans or staying up late, sexual intercourse, too, can tip into the realm of the obligatory for many adolescents. Table 12.2 shows the results of a recent survey on a variety of sexual acts by college students. Rates for the two sexes are fairly similar.

For a long time, adolescent men have been pressured by their peers to have intercourse. The same researchers who studied the 15- to 19-year-old women studied a sample of 17- to 21-year-old men (a two-year age difference between the sexes that is typical of teenage pairs). Well over half of these men—70 percent—had had intercourse before marriage. The percentages among black men were higher at all ages than among white men (Zelnik and Kantner, 1980).

Do the numbers on sexual experience reflect great promiscuity among adolescents? Not at all. All surveys of adolescents (as well as adults) show that they value fidelity (Hass, 1979; Hunt, 1974; Pietropinto and Simenauer, 1977). But fidelity does not mean one partner forever. It means one partner at a time, a pattern of serial monogamy that contrasts with the promiscuity of "sexual adventurers." These adventurers—few, but not rare—are most often men who play the field widely, trying to have as many sexual partners as they can (Hass, 1979; Sorenson, 1973). More than half of the sexually experienced teenagers in Sorenson's early-1970s sample believed that sex without love was immoral. About 40 percent were in monogamous relationships at the time of the study. Given the unusually large numbers of teenagers who reported having sex to Sorenson, the most reasonable conclusion is that teenagers expect—realistically—to love many people before they marry. Promiscuity does not have wide approval, even among college students (see Table 12.3).

ORAL-GENITAL ACTS   Oral sex to orgasm traditionally had been seen as more intimate than intercourse between men and women. As the age at first intercourse has decreased, so, apparently, has the age at which people engage in oral sex.

TABLE 12.3

Attitudes of College Students Towards Sexual Intercourse

Relationship	Men approve	Women approve
Partners are married	100%	99%
Partners are engaged	90	83
Partners are in love	85	74
Partners really like each other	67	42
Partners are friends	42	13
Partners are casual acquaintances	34	9
Partners are unacquainted	37	7

Source: Adapted from Mahoney, 1979.

Among high-school students in tenth, eleventh, and twelfth grades in a southern city (Newcomer and Udry, 1985), and among a sample of teenagers—90 percent from southern California (Hass, 1979)—more report engaging in oral sex than in intercourse. This pattern is more likely among girls, for oral sex requires no contraception and invokes no fear of pregnancy. Among adolescents, fellatio appears somewhat later than cunnilingus. Among boys, there is no analog for the technical virginity sought by girls. In Kinsey's day, as we have seen, oral sex was for "bad" women among the less educated, and for wives among the better educated. Today, oral sex is more widely practiced, regardless of education—among whites, that is. Oral sex still has a bad name among many blacks (Hunt, 1974). One study from the 1970s, of conservative, midwestern universities presaged today's findings on high-school students, for a few college women had oral sex before intercourse (Curran, 1975). But most men and women in this earlier college sample had not yet experienced mutual oral sex to orgasm. That may have been a postgraduate experience.

PREGNANCY OUTSIDE OF MARRIAGE   The sheer numbers of unmarried teenagers having intercourse today reflect changes in the sexual environment: greater social acceptance today of sex outside of marriage, the earlier ages at which people begin to have sex, and the shorter time it now takes adolescent couples to move from

A 19-year-old unmarried father and his newborn son.

FIGURE 12.5

Unmarried mothers, ages 15 to 19. Pregnancies among unmarried metropolitan-area teenagers increased from 1971 to 1979. Many pregnant teenagers gave birth to live babies, although white women chose abortion more often than black women (45 versus 20%, respectively), and slightly more white than black women had miscarriages or stillbirths (16 versus 9%, respectively). (M. Zelnik and J.F. Kantner, "Sexual Activity, Contraceptive Use, and Pregnancy among Metropolitan-Area Teenagers: 1971–1979," *Family Planning Perspectives*, 1980, *12*, 233, 234.)

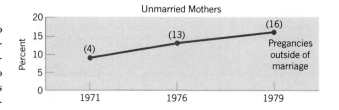

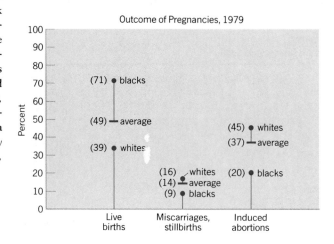

petting to intercourse. Not only has the incidence of nonmarital intercourse gone up, but the absolute numbers of teenagers have gone up as well since the "baby boom" generation hit adolescence in the late 1960s and early 1970s. Thus more unmarried adolescents are having intercourse, and they are having it earlier. They are also, in the aggregate, more fertile than adults and, once regularly sexually active, many are more active than adults are. Finally, it takes many young couples some time to learn how to use contraceptives reliably. The sporadic nature of some adolescent sexual relationships interferes with steady contraception. The result: pregnancies (see Figure 12.5).

Although the number of adolescents who get pregnant and bear a child seems high, the *proportion* gives a somewht different impression. In 1979, 16 percent of all 15- to 19-year-old women had become pregnant. Of these, half bore a child—8 percent of the age group. (Even 8 percent is too high, of course, when such a pregnancy is unwanted or forecloses a couple's or a woman's opportunities in later life.) Among teenage girls who had *ever* had sexual experience outside of marriage, 33 percent had at some time gotten pregnant. That figure breaks down into a 29 percent incidence for whites and 45 percent for blacks (Zelnik and Kantner, 1980). These figures should be interpreted in the context of associated factors. We have mentioned the relatively great fertility of teenagers and their rates of sexual activity once they are in stable relationships. Other factors that affect teenage pregnancies include: the low likelihood that they will be legitimized by marriage; and the increasing availability of legal abortions, which has lowered the percentages of live births among teenagers. Any discussion of teenage pregnancies must also take into account contraception and abortion in teenage culture.

Contraception and Abortion

Most teenage girls—82 percent—say that they do not want to get pregnant. In 1971 and 1976, about one in four did want to get pregnant. By 1979, the proportion had decreased to 18 percent, fewer than one in five. Between 1971 and 1976, more teenagers began using contraception, a good sign that they did not want to get pregnant. Of those who did get pregnant, half never used any contraception, and 14 percent always used it, another 36 percent had used contraception, but only some of the time (Zelnik and Kantner, 1980). A more recent survey has shown that 18 percent of sexually active 15- to 19-year-old women currently use no contraception at all. Of those who currently do use contraception, 44 percent use the pill, and 21 percent use condoms (Forrest and Henshaw, 1983).

Concern today for teenage mothers and their children is warranted. Raising a baby is an exceptionally demanding task, but it is particularly so in a society that offers teenagers precious few material resources. Babies can be hard on young marriages. Regardless of the circumstances of the birth, children born to teenagers are at risk of: spending part of their childhood in single-parent households (which are common after parents of any age divorce, of course); and of being teenage parents themselves when they grow up. The combination of young mother, disrupted education, poor job prospects, and the cost of the child to the mother's economic prospects are all associated with intellectual deficits in children of teenagers. Researchers once thought that the intellectual deficit might be biological in origin, that teenage mothers were biologically unready to reproduce. But research today suggests that the deficit is of social and economic origin. Many teenage mothers, dragged down by their babies, do not finish high school and do not keep pace with their contemporaries in either schooling or jobs (Baldwin and Cain, 1980; McCarthy and Radish, 1982; Mott and Marsiglio, 1985). The cost to their children is intellectual development that falls below that of other children their age.

Legal abortions are not rare among adolescents. Of every 100 teenage pregnancies outside of marriage, 37 end in legal abortion. Modern abortion facilities are available almost universally in large cities, and counselors at these facilities advise women about contraception. Statisticians have calculated that abortions could be reduced by 75 to 83 percent if all women used the medically reliable contraceptives that some women learn about after they have had an abortion. (But even if every woman were on the pill or IUD—which would be unsound medically—there would still be about 450,000 unintended pregnancies a year, simply because sexual acts occur in very large numbers and because no contraceptive method or user is perfect.) Unfortunately, an abortion clinic may be the first place an adolescent gets any reliable sex education. Young women who seek abortions are typically an economic and religious cross-section of their communities. Studies have found virtually no negative long-term effects from abortion. (No work of any substance has been done on how abortion affects their sexual partners.) Although women's contraception improves markedly after abortion, some women do have repeat abortions. The mathematical models for repeat abortions suggest that they follow contraceptive failure at about the rate expected for the method used, not that young women consider abortion trivial, to be risked carelessly. Only sterilization is 100 percent effective, and no responsible person would advise adolescents to be sterilized.

Homosexual Acts and Identity

At some time during childhood or adolescence, people who will adopt a homosexual identity decide that they are alienated from some part of the accepted gender roles for their biological sex. Although such alienation is common among adolescents, people who will later decide that they are homosexual report having felt strongly, significantly different from others of their sex (Bell, Weinberg, and Hammersmith, 1981). The early genital focus of males means that many young men act on their crushes and move toward a homosexual identity. Some men decide that they are homosexual without having had *any* sexual experience, except fantasized male lovers. Some of these men marry and father children while maintaining a homosexual identity. Others may marry and only later assume a homosexual identity. Some men try marriage as an escape from their homosexual feeling, hoping that a heterosexual life will alter a homosexual identity. Many homosexual men also have had heterosexual experience.

The later genital focus of the feminine sexual script spells a different development toward lesbianism. A minority of women adopt a lesbian identity during adolescence, most of these *after* having had heterosexual intercourse. Many later-to-be-gay women marry, bear children, and adopt a lesbian identity only afterward. Some of these women aver that they have been lesbian for some time; others feel that they go through a change in sexual identity.

HOMOSEXUAL ADOLESCENTS HAVE MUCH THE SAME TERRAIN TO COVER AS HETEROSEXUAL ADOLESCENTS DO: HOW TO DEAL WITH SEXUAL INTIMACY, HOW TO BE SEXUAL WHILE LIVING WITH PARENTS, HOW TO KEEP FRIENDSHIPS WITH PEOPLE OF BOTH SEXES.

Homosexual adolescents have much the same terrain to cover as heterosexual adolescents do: how to deal with sexual intimacy, how to be sexual while living with parents, how to keep friendships with people of both sexes. To all of these problems for the homosexual adolescent are added the huge problem of living with a socially devalued identity. Today, many adolescents find support in the organized gay community. In the past, most tried to shake off their homosexual fantasies and experiences. They struggled with psychotherapy, hypnosis, celibacy, penance, and confession. Adolescence may be for some a rocky road to a homosexual identity. Some young people spend years uncertain of their sexual orientation. A subset of young people—probably fewer than identify with the gay community—become bisexual, or *equally committed* to male and female partners. No one has carefully studied the development of such a truly shared commitment.

When does adolescence end and adulthood begin? Does adulthood begin on a certain birthday, or at college graduation, or when a person takes a job, or marries, or has a child? For many, the transition is long and slow, seen clearly only in hindsight. The work of adolescence gradually gives way to the work of adulthood, but there are no simple markers to this passage. Some traditional markers, especially for women, have changed. Some women now consolidate their careers and reach their thirties before they settle into marriage or parenthood, a path traditionally followed by men only.

> *I used to think that on my 21st birthday, I would suddenly be an adult. I would all of a sudden know who I was and what I wanted in life. It hasn't happened yet, and I'm 25! (female graduate student)*

Adulthood has been said to begin when a person has settled into an occupation (Erikson, 1980). For those who go straight from high school to a job, adulthood effectively arrives earlier than for college students. Given graduate and professional training, the long moratorium from paid work can extend into the late thirties.

Changing Sexual Standards for Adults

Adults are creatures of their time, and their sexual behavior is shaped by prevailing social norms. Thus we find important differences between the sexual experiences of the generation born before 1900, as reported by Kinsey and his colleagues, and the present generation of adults. The oldest people in Kinsey's sample, who would now be in their 80s or older, lived in a world of sexual values that included: a strong double standard, a strong tie between heterosexual intercourse and reproduction, and strong distinctions between sexual behavior before and after marriage. Informally, about half of all couples in the total Kinsey sample who planned to marry exercised their sexual rights before the marriage ceremony. If a man broke off the relationship after having had intercourse with his fiancée, he was

For Better or For Worse   by Lynn Johnston

considered an immoral cad. He had "taken advantage" and "broken his promise."

Among our grandparents' or great-grandparents' generation, only the exceptional woman lived with a man who was not her legal husband. Homosexual love was barely acknowledged: some called it "the love that has no name." Unmarried pregnant women were hidden during their pregnancies, and their babies were taken to be placed in suitable families. The formal standard was that all sexual behavior took place in marriage; it was to be heterosexual, reproductive, monogamous, and forever. Homosexuals, divorcées, and birth-control advocates existed, but they had to struggle to find others like them.

Cohabitation

Today's adult sexuality looks quite different from that of our grandparents. The sharp division between unmarried and married life has blurred, most men *and* women arrive at marriage with sexual experience, including coitus, and the old gap between male and female sexual experience has narrowed. Many young adults furnish their own apartments, live with a lover, and post two names on the mailbox. This sexual freedom is less widely accepted among older than younger adults, but the trend among young adults is quite real (Wilson, 1975).

> *My wife and I lived together for four years before we got married. We were both in our twenties, working hard, and not ready to commit ourselves to marriage. What changed? Age, I guess. It felt like time to make it legal and to stop swimming against the stream. We were both 30, and it was time to stop being adolescents (36-year-old sales executive)*

> *My husband and I lived together for several months before we got married. I cared about what our children would think, but not all that much. We had earned our independence (67-year-old remarried woman)*

The U.S. Bureau of the Census defines **cohabitation** as *an unmarried man and woman sharing their living quarters.*[1]

Between 1970 and 1980, the number of cohabiting couples tripled, to 1.6 million. This enormous change can be traced to at least three social phenomena. First, people are marrying later, and the pool of young unmarrieds has increased. Second, the high divorce rate produces another large pool of people who are accustomed to regular sex. Cohabitation answers their needs for sex and companionship as well as reassurance about their desirability. Third, the Social Security set uses cohabitation as a test and a short-term replacement for marriage. Cohabiting couples of all ages typically are monogamously committed to each other, although not all plan marriage. Researchers tell us that cohabitation is no guarantee of a happy later marriage. Cohabitors are as likely to divorce (Newcomb and Bentler, 1980) and to be as satisfied with their marriages as noncohabitors.

---

[1]The Census Bureau calls cohabitors *POSSLQs: Persons of Opposite Sex Sharing Living Quarters.* Oddly enough, that unsexy phrase is the only official one we have. Everyone seems to have trouble with the terminology for live-in lovers. "Girlfriend" and "boyfriend" seem too pale; "lover" seems too torrid; "roommate" seems evasive. "Partner" sounds like a business arrangement.

Sex in Marriage[2]

The United States has become a marrying nation. By 1978, the Census Bureau reported that 95 percent of us marry at some point in our lives. Given the already diversified sexual lives of unmarried young adults, why do they bother to marry? Recent surveys find that people do not think marriage *defines* people, especially women, as they once did. But people do think that their major life satisfactions come from family life (Veroff and Feld, 1970; Veroff, Douvan, and Kulka, 1981). For many, marriage as a commitment probably looms larger than marriage as a sexual playground. One scholar of love through the ages has seen marriage as a pledge to give one's time to another in the hope of warding off loneliness (De Rougemont, 1940). Interviews with a variety of American couples support this view. Married couples (including stable gay couples) who commit time to one another report greater satisfaction and more stability than other married (and stable gay) couples (Blumstein and Schwartz, 1983). Sexual interaction is certainly one way that people ward off loneliness.

Only when couples live together (in marriage or otherwise) are their sexual partners so conveniently available for sex. No one needs telephone, negotiate an evening out, or fumble through cat-and-mouse games. The average couple's first year of marriage, in fact, has the highest rates of intercourse of any period in marriage. Today's married couples also probably have intercourse more frequently than their parents' generation did.

But with age, the rate of intercourse declines today, as it did a generation or two ago (Kinsey et al., 1948; 1953). After the first four years of marriage, the rate of intercourse drops—even among young couples, where wives are under 30 (Udry, 1980). Both husbands and wives contribute to the decline, as competing activities—career demands, hobbies, extramarital sex—the arrival of children, and lack of sexual variety take their toll.

Once we had a child, sex became just another chore around the house. Friends say that it will get better, but I worry. The romance is D-E-A-D. We talk only about the baby (33-year-old mother, married five years).

Sex is more comfortable and familiar now than it was when we first married. Then it was overwhelming passion. I remember how my heart would pound when she walked into the room. Now it's more reassuring, more tender somehow. It's different but still good (29-year-old husband, married seven years).

But do long-married people enjoy intercourse? Many say yes. In the 1950s, 70 percent of the long-married husbands and 57 percent of the wives said that sex brought them "great enjoyment." A further 25 percent of the husbands and 33 percent of the wives said that sex gave them "mild pleasure" (Ard, 1977). It might seem reasonable to report, on the basis of surveys of magazine readers (like those of *Redbook* [Tavris and Sadd, 1975]) or of other nonrepresentative samples (like Morton Hunt's [1974] survey) that people in happy marriages say that sex

[2]For survey material on sex in marriage, see Chapter 2.

The arrival of children, the demands of careers, and the long familiarity of a sexual partner all can make intercourse less frequent among long married couples.

is satisfying and people in unhappy marriages say the opposite. But that is not always so. (See "Sexuality in Perspective: Sexual Problems in 'Normal' Couples," in Chapter 16.) Somehow people come either to value other aspects of married life over sex or to change their expectations of sex. Many men and women agree, for example, that love is more important than sex. But married men, in fact, report the highest levels of sexual satisfaction, when compared with single, divorced, and separated men (Miller and Simon, *Playboy* Study, 1978). A *Psychology Today* survey (July 1983) showed that 29 percent of men and 44 percent of women (both married and unmarried) considered sex without love unappealing (Rubinstein, 1983).

One of the best predictors of whether someone, especially a man, will be sexually active in later adulthood is the amount of that person's sexual activity—solitary and social—in adolescence and early adulthood. Early sexual experiences seem to represent a temperamental level of activity for a person; the early experiences probably also frame our attitudes toward sexual enjoyment and shape our expectations about sexual activity. Thus men who enjoyed making love as adolescents or young adults are likely to seek out and to enjoy sex in middle and old age. Young men who seek lots of sexual expression—from masturbation to sex with partners—are more likely to seek sexual expression when they are older and married than those who were less sexually active as adolescents. For today's middle-aged and older women, the pattern is somewhat different. We will delay describing that pattern until later, in "Part Biology, Part Sociology," because today's older women may not be so reliable predictors for today's younger women as tomorrow's older women (Luria and Meade, 1984).

SEXUALITY IN PERSPECTIVE:
SEX AND THE WORKING-CLASS MARRIAGE

In a popular book called *Worlds of Pain,* clinician Lillian Rubin has captured the feelings of 50 working-class couples about their sex lives. Two worlds emerge in these interviews, one of husbands and one of wives. The husbands were raised to seek and feel entitled to sexual variety and satisfaction. The wives were raised to seek expressions of intimacy and feel entitled to expressions of feelings.

Few working-class wives said they enjoyed oral sex without reservations or guilt. Said one wife:

> *I sure wish I could make him stop pushing me into that (ugh, I even hate to talk about it), into that oral stuff. I let him do it, but I hate it. He says I'm old-fashioned about sex and maybe I am. But I was brought up that there's just one way you're supposed to do it. I still believe that way, even though he keeps trying to convince me of his way. How can I change when I wasn't brought up that way? [With a pained sigh.] I wish I could make him understand (p. 138).*

Husbands and wives wish for understanding, but their very different socialization into sex makes understanding elusive.

> *Either I'm forcing my way on her or she's forcing her way on me. Either way, you can't win. If she gives in, it isn't because she's enjoying it, but because I pushed her. I suppose you could say I get what I want, but it doesn't feel that way (p. 139).*

> *I don't like to think he might think I was being aggressive, so I don't usually make any suggestions. Most of the time it's okay because he can usually tell when I'm in the mood. But if he can't, I just wait (p. 143).*

One couple struggles with the problem of orgasms: as the wife has an orgasm for the first time, her husband suddenly loses all interest in sex. For another couple, the woman's lack of orgasm frightens them. She worries that he'll find a woman who has orgasms—even multiple orgasms—regularly. Rubin's couples know that the world today is more accepting of sexual variety. But they are troubled about how and whether to change the old sexual scripts of how men and women are supposed to act in bed.

Based on Lillian Rubin, *Worlds of Pain,* "The Marriage Bed," New York: Basic Books, 1976, pp. 134–154.

Divorce: Single Again

If Americans are a marrying nation, they are also a divorcing nation. At today's rates, the lifetime risk of divorce (conservatively measured) is close to 40 percent. (See Figure 12.6) Although that numbers means that there are three stably married couples for every two divorced couples, a 3:2 ratio is cold comfort to people raised on fairy tales that end, "and they lived happily ever after." For many couples, today's stories end, "and they had 5 or 10 or 20 good years together."

The personal consequences of divorce are great; it breaks the most intimate of ties. Sexual intimacy and the sense of personal worth attached to such intimacy begin to dissolve even before the divorce. When a couple is dissatisfied with their marriage, they have intercourse less often. As intercourse diminishes, they begin to seek sex outside of marriage (Edwards and Booth, 1976). Extramarital sex probably serves to bolster wounded egos at least as much as it answers directly sexual needs. Although some couples divorce after one spouse has found another sexual partner, many more find themselves shopping for new sexual—and marital—partners only after divorce. (See "Sexuality in Perspective: Extramarital Sex.")

SEXUALITY IN PERSPECTIVE: EXTRAMARITAL SEX

It is entirely possible that the history of extramarital sex extends as far back as that of marital sex. From ancient laws and codes of ethics that have survived, we know that extramarital sex was forbidden to ancient Inca, Maya, Egyptian, Hebrew, and Christian wives but not their husbands. By the time that Europeans began to colonize the United States, laws against adultery applied to husbands as well as to wives. To the Puritans, death was the fit punishment for adulterers, although such executions were uncommon and eventually disappeared altogether. Today, people in most western societies accept sexual fidelity as a formal standard for married people (Hunt, 1974). In a survey (Broude and Green, 1976) of 116 contemporary cultures, the double standard prevailed in a majority. Extramarital sex is considered permissible for husbands but not for wives in 43 percent of the cultures, and in another 22 percent, extramarital sex is punished more harshly for wives than for husbands. Only in 11 percent is extramarital sex considered permissible for both sexes, and only in 23 percent is it considered equally wrong and punished equally severely in both sexes. When people age 18 and over from the United States were sampled in 1973, 1974, 1977, and again in 1980 on their "opinion about a married person having sexual relations with someone other than the marriage partner," 70 to 74 percent thought that it is always wrong, and between 12 (in 1974) and 16 percent (in 1980) thought that it is almost always wrong. Only 3 to 4 percent thought that it is never wrong. Attitudes toward extramarital sex thus were quite stable over time. As we saw earlier, attitudes toward extramarital sex vary according to factors of age and religion. People with strong religious values are more likely to condemn and avoid extramarital sex

Divorced people are different from others who are single. They may be less coy (but more apprehensive) than high-school or college students in looking for social sex. Divorced people have more sexual experience than young people entering their first marriages. They may have complex lives: children, job, an apartment or house, sole responsibilities that used to be shared. There are no virgins in this group, and their presence in the singles world makes it more frankly sexual. Many divorced people have suffered blows to their self esteem as well as to their romantic and sexual illusions. A successful reentry into sexual life can soften those blows. In the absence of good, longitudinal, **ethnographic studies** of the singles world, journalists and research firms have tried to fill the vacuum. (A journalist pair, Bernice and Morton Hunt [1977], observed and described "the world of the formerly married." A research firm interviewed some respondents who had answered questionnaires and summarized its findings in *Singles: the New Americans* [Simenauer and Carroll, 1982]. Some of their results appear here.)

Divorced men and women who begin to socialize must learn a new sexual script, a script that is more difficult for some than for others. For the formerly

than are others (Kinsey, 1953; Tavris and Sadd, 1975), and young people, especially young men, are more likely to engage in extramarital sex than older people (Edwards and Booth, 1976; Glass and Wright, 1977). Happily married people engage in extramarital sex, as well as unhappily married ones. People with liberal attitudes toward sex may engage in extramarital sex that is intensely meaningful to them. Kinsey found that 10 percent of his female respondents, and Tavris and Sadd found that 6 percent were reportedly happily married and intensely committed to an extramarital affair at the same time.

Extramarital sex may consist of simple flirting, teasing, or fantasizing, without overt sexual acts. It may consist of petting but not sexual intercourse, as was the case among 9 percent of Kinsey's sample of white, college-educated males and white, college-educated females (Gebhard and Johnson, 1979). Extramarital sex may consist of a brief interlude—a business convention, a vacation, or another such "open space" in a married person's routine—of casual sex. Exciting and novel as this brief interlude may be, it rarely evokes an emotional commitment from the participants. The extramarital affairs that entail secrecy and risk are those in which the participants invest emotion, time, and energy. As time passes and emotional commitments deepen, casual extramarital affairs may grow intense and serious, and they may threaten the marriages of either or both partners. Many fewer men told Kinsey (1948; 1953) that their own adultery had affected their marriages than answered that their *spouse's* had seriously affected their marriages. In cases where a spouse is ill, absent, or otherwise unavailable, a long-lasting, stable extramarital affair may turn into a way of life (Brecher, 1984).

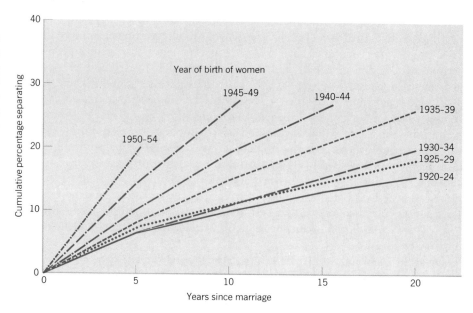

FIGURE 12.6

Probabilities of divorce. This figure shows the cumulative probability of separating after a first marriage, by years since marriage and years of birth for whites living in the United States (from Bongaarts, 1984, Figure 5, p. 17).

married, dating moves to sexual relations much faster than it does for the never married. Remnants of grief over their divorce holds some people back. Some divorced, middle-aged women choose to leave the sexual scene (Lowenstein et al., 1982) and stay celibate. The pressure for sex often comes from men: the longer a divorced man stays single, the more likely he is to expect a date, even a first date, to include intercourse. The same holds true for twice-divorced women. One sex therapist has described the pressure that some divorced women feel:

> *They are driven to [having sex early on] by the myth that if you don't have sex by the third date, you will lose the man. Many single women are just coming out of marriages and are terrified by what they view as a kind of sexual "pressure cooker." They feel pushed and even compelled to perform sexually (Dr. Richard Samuels, cited in Simenauer and Carroll, 1982, p. 134).*

Another woman had sex on her first date after a divorce and then, impelled by the rules and values of her premarital days, scrubbed her whole body with scouring powder (Mavis Hetherington, personal communication). Men are not immune from such feelings of disgust in situations they never expected to face.

Not all women or men abhor casual sex. About one-third of the single women in the Simenauer and Carroll (1982) sample found that liking a man was enough of a reason to have intercourse with him on a first date. On average, however, single women are more conservative than men. They are less willing to try out new sexual acts and less often enjoy sex without love than do men. But many men and women agree that casual sex and maintaining many sexual partners at one time are not rewarding. Men and women, it seems, still operate with different sexual scripts. Thus few women over 45 reported ever making direct sexual invitations, yet most of the men reported that they approved of such invitations. As among adolescents, serial monogamy seems to be more highly valued (Simenauer and Carroll, 1982).

After the divorce, I felt too timid for bars and too lonely to sit at home. At the local art museum, at my synagogue, and in locally sponsored cooking classes and Caribbean cruises, I found a lot of people in the same boat I was in (39-year-old divorced woman).

Even before I was divorced, I knew that I wanted to move to California and enjoy myself. That's just what I did. Now I play tennis every day, go out most nights, and generally do all the things I could never do when I was a husband and father of growing children (44-year-old divorced man).

The formerly married are not a uniform group, and their adaptation to the sexual world after divorce depends on many factors.

Celibacy

People choose to abstain from sex for many different reasons. Some divorced people, as we saw above, recoil from the pressures toward sex in the singles world. Others are too tired or too devoted to their work to care much for social sex. The medical student who opts out of the social sexual scene will reenter that scene when work demands decrease. Still others choose celibacy for religious or ethical reasons. The followers of Gandhi, Roman Catholic clergy, and the Shakers are examples of those, some of them sexually experienced, who choose celibacy.

People sometimes worry that celibacy is harmful. It isn't.

People sometimes worry that celibacy is harmful. It isn't. If people tie their self-esteem to social sex, then celibacy will pain them. Human sexuality, after all, is not like hunger or thirst, drives that must be satisfied in order for life to continue. Some people choose to put their energies elsewhere. Sex need not be now, or always, or ever.

SEX IN MIDDLE AGE

The story of sex during middle age is an interesting one, but it is also a story likely to change significantly. Today's younger women, for example, are marrying and having (fewer) children later than their mothers and grandmothers did. More of them have orgasms than the older generations did. Both men and women value physical fitness more, and medicine itself is learning to control conditions like diabetes and high blood pressure that can interfere with sexual functioning in middle age. Will we be a nation of sexually active, physically fit 80-year-olds—with bad knees?

Female Sexual Response

At some point between the time that they are about 45 and 55 years old, women experience important changes in their reproductive and hormonal systems collectively known as **menopause.** (Usage of the terms "menopause" or "climacteric" varies. Technically, a woman is menopausal when she has not menstruated for a year.) But many women's menstrual periods stop and start rather than stopping abruptly. After menopause, the ovaries produce lower levels of hormones, menstruation stops, and women can no longer get pregnant. More than a few people believe that a woman's sex life or interest in sex ends with menopause. A California sample of women nearing menopause not only had irregular menstrual periods but also hot flashes and lower estradiol (an estrogen) levels than women with regular periods. The former group also had less frequent sexual intercourse. But the observed effects are correlations; they do not explain how the hormone levels relate to sexual behavior (McCoy et al, 1985). Some aging women can and do have fully satisfying sexual lives. William Masters and Virginia Johnson (1966) have studied eight women over 60 and three women over 70 (of whom the oldest was 78) and found them all to be sexually responsive. Surveys of retired people indicate that the availability of a partner and good health are related to today's older woman's continued sexual activity. Among women over 50 in one educated sample, sexual interest remains high (Brecher, 1984).

As the body ages, most physiological events get slower and weaker. Sexual response proves no exception. Thus although the older woman shows most of the same responses to sexual arousal as the young woman, many happen more slowly (for example, vaginal lubrication), more weakly (orgasmic contractions), and reverse more slowly (nipple erection). Older women can accommodate these physical changes. They can, for example, lengthen the period of foreplay until they are fully aroused (a technique that helps the slower, aging male as well). Some women may need to use topical estrogen cream to moisten a dry vagina. (But with increasing numbers of aging women taking oral estrogen, thought to prevent **osteoporosis,** or thinning of the bones, fewer will experience such vaginal problems.)

Masters and Johnson (1966) found that a group of women past menopause responded sexually in ways that were more typical of younger women. In general, these older women had had active sex lives throughout adulthood. Although it is impossible in these cases to tell cause from effect, experiments with animals suggest that sexual exercise keeps the sexual responses fit. As with any form of exercise, the principle seems to be, "Use it or lose it."

Male Sexual Response

Like women's, men's sexual responses may slow and decrease some with age. Arousal takes longer, erection is slower and weaker, orgasm and ejaculation feel less intense. The normal changes of aging can frighten some men into swearing off sex altogether—but unnecessarily. Duke University researchers found that when middle-aged couples stopped having intercourse, typically the reason was the husband. Men who feel unhealthy are likely to show lower levels of sexual enjoyment and interest than healthy men. In general, a man's physical functioning tends to relate significantly to his level of sexual interest and enjoyment (Pfeiffer and Davis, 1972). Erections symbolize masculinity to many men: to them, a weak erection means a weak man. Older men who understand how sexual responsiveness changes with age can judge their bodies accurately; they can avoid falling into the trap of thinking that their sexual function has failed when it has not.

Middle-aged men do not typically go through a marked shift in hormone and reproductive status, as women do. But they do show a hormonal decrease; free testosterone goes down with age (Davidson, 1983). (Free, or unbound, testosterone is distinguished from bound testosterone.) Some men have erection difficulties that stem from vascular problems: blood apparently flows into the penis but flows out of it—for reasons unknown—too soon (Karacan et al., 1983). In the popular press, a change of life or **climacteric** has been proposed to exist for males in their forties or fifties to account for some men's pronounced, sudden shifts in attitude and feelings. But if this climacteric exists, it is less grounded in physiological changes than is the female climacteric (menopause), in that men rarely experience the same rapid hormonal declines that women do. It is more likely that the popular diagnosis of male climacteric reflects men's fears about the passing of opportunities at work, in the bedroom, and in the family, opportunities seen as available only to the powerful, successful young man.

Part Biology, Part Sociology

Between the ages of 40 and 60, men and women feel many of the small signs of aging. Bad backs and arthritis do their share of reducing the frequency of intercourse. Joints and vertebrae that once worked effortlessly can make even favored coital positions a trial when people hit their sixties and seventies. Even so, most postmenopausal women remain interested in sex. In one study of 100 women between the ages of 43 and 53, all at varying points in the stages of menopause, two-thirds of the women thought that menopause had no effect on sexuality. The other one-third was split: half thought that sexual relations grew less important, and the other half thought that sex improved as fears of pregnancy ended (Neugarten, 1963). Similar results came from a catch-as-catch-can volunteer sample of 484 women of all ages found by the Boston Women's Health Collective (*Our Bodies, Our Selves,* 1984).

Menopause is, of course, a set of changes in hormones. A Swedish study compared premenopausal women (mostly around age 46) and postmenopausal women (mostly around age 54, all having had a year without menstrual periods). Interviews with 800 women, all of whom were living with a partner, revealed that age alone did *not* account for patterns of changes in sexual interest or behavior. Rather, menopausal status accounted for the sexual decline. But before the researchers concluded that hormones were determining the whole sexual decline, they tested the women's levels of the hormone estrogen. They found that estrogen output was unrelated to sexual interest. Women of higher social class showed much less decline in sexual interest than women of lower social class. Sexual decline was most common among women who got little emotional support from their husbands; whose relations with their husbands were poor; whose husbands were in poor physical health; and who had suffered many stressful events within the previous year. This sounds like a recipe for producing a depressed woman. In contrast, women whom personality tests showed to be outgoing and "rationally dominant" tended to remain sexually interested. Thus we see a picture emerge of the woman who loses sexual interest after menopause. She is married to a man of lower social class; she has little emotional support from and poor relations with him. He has been sick recently, and the family has been unusually stressed within the last year. She is introverted, unaggressive, and unlikely to put herself forward.

In short, hormones make a difference, but social factors make an important difference as well (Hallstrom, 1979). It is important to remember that today's older women have been shaped by the double standard of their youth.

What *is* a woman's experience of sex in middle age? Much of that experience depends on her earlier sexual history, which in turn depends on what she and her peers were doing sexually when they were all younger. Earlier sexual experiences shape a woman's expectations, of course. All of these factors make for wide variation in sexual attitudes and experiences. But above all, a woman's sexuality in middle age depends on the availability of a stable sexual partner. Thus married women have intercourse more often than their unmarried counterparts. (Kinsey-vintage data on middle-aged women who never married are sketchy. Questionnaires on sexuality tend to produce many unanswered questions from such a group.) When a middle-aged woman's marriage ends, whether in divorce or death, it profoundly affects her sex life. Even in Kinsey's time, the postmarital sex lives of middle-aged divorced and widowed women under 50 (and matched for age) showed some interesting differences. More divorced women than widows had intercourse after their marriages had ended. Fewer widows remarried. When either type of woman entered the social sexual world, she typically had more than one partner. But after 50, the differences between the groups diminished, and age took over as the central factor in sexual behavior (Gebhard, 1971). That apparent age effect may reflect the sexual marketplace, of course. Perhaps the market responds to age, rather than age determining the changed behavior. If so, the expectations that women and men remain sexual all their lives may change the sexual marketplace and change sexual behavior among middle-aged women.

When Sex Declines

Older men can learn to work with rather than against their slowed responsiveness. Longer, more intense stimulation can help arousal. Sex with a familiar partner may have grown stale and not arousing enough for both men and women. Older men sometimes turn to a new partner. The excitement and anxiety of a new liaison dramatically increase the level of arousal. (In fact, older people with heart disease are sometimes advised by their physicians to avoid sex with new partners, for it may prove *too* stimulating to their cardiovascular systems.) Sometimes shifting to new techniques (turn-taking, mutual masturbation, oral-genital sex, or to a new use of erotic materials that spur fantasy) can provide the necessary spur to arousal. Older couples vary tremendously in their sexual responsiveness. Physical and mental health, willingness to experiment, interest in sexual relationships, attitude toward work, and the frequency of sexual activity as young people all affect aging people's sexual responsiveness.

By the age of 65, half of all married women are widowed, given today's Census data. One might expect masturbation to increase among this group. Many older women continue to masturbate (Brecher, 1984). But although formerly married women do masturbate more than married women of their age, they do not masturbate as often as their married sisters have intercourse. Kinsey attributed this discrepancy to the domination of the husband in determining sexual frequency. Remove the male from the pair, and sexual frequency drops, Kinsey would say. Will today's young women, with their greater feelings of entitlement to genital sexuality, masturbate more later in their lives than today's middle-aged women have done? For at least one sample in the Northeast, about 1 in 4 men *and* women of 60–85 were, in fact, still masturbating (Adams and Turner, 1985).

The Baby Boom Comes to Middle Age: A Lifespan Perspective

The members of the baby-boom generation are about to become the 40-year-olds of the 1990s. Their sexual histories are markedly different from the middle-aged people studied by Kinsey's group or by the Duke University researchers. The baby-boomers have more liberal sexual views and more extensive sexual practice and are more likely to have dual-job or dual-career marriages and families with few children. These factors can pull their sex lives in either of two ways: toward more and longer-lasting sex or toward less sex, because of the drain of work and other commitments. Clearly, the experience of middle age can vary from one generation to another.

Few people doubt that the middle-aged will be considered sexual beings longer into their lives than once was the case. Women gain especially on this score, for men traditionally have been considered sexual longer than women. Given the declining ratio of men to women as age mounts, the sexual middle-aged woman may find few marriageable sexual partners. A pattern of more short-lived sexual liaisons may soon become more common for such sexually active women. Current evidence suggests that older women (sampled through their 80s) remain interested in sex, at least so they report on some survey questionnaires (Brecher, 1984).

SEX AFTER 80

More of us are living well into old age today, and many of us would like to know what sex is like at 70, or 80, or even 100. The sex lives of healthy old people between the ages of 80 and 100 had never been studied before two intrepid physiological psychologists began their investigation (Bretschneider and McCoy, 1983). They found and gained the cooperation of 102 white women and 100 white men ranging in age from 80 to 102 (average age, 89) who lived in 10 retirement facilities in northern California. The participants were in good physical and mental health and were taking no medications known to affect sexual interest or functioning. They were middle- or upper-class, 99 percent of whom had graduated from college (and obviously not a random sample). Before retiring, 30 percent had been professionals or semiprofessionals. Two-thirds of them had been married; they'd had an average of three children. More men than women were still married at the time of the study. More women than men had never been married or had been divorced. All participants answered a questionnaire that was part demographic, part sexual.

What were the findings? More men than women still masturbated, and more men than women who masturbated found it enjoyable. Many more women (70 percent) than men (38 percent) did not have intercourse. Of course, many more women (75 percent) than men (47 percent) had no regular sexual partner. About twice as many men (76 percent) as women (39 percent) who had intercourse enjoyed it. There was no difference between men and women on frequency or enjoyment of intercourse when they were young.

Men more than women liked touching and daydreaming and thought sex was important. But both sexes reported that sex was less important than it once had been. Even from their 80s to their 90s, some people reported that they less often enjoyed touching and caressing without intercourse. For men and women, the importance of sex in youth and old age correlated highly, a confirmation of the generalization that frequent, enjoyable sex early in life goes along with frequent, enjoyable sex late in life. Both this study and the Duke University research show distinctly different patterns for men and women. At every age, women express less interest in sex than men. Whether this difference will reappear in the next generations of older people, no one can yet say. Is the double standard with which

FIGURE 12.7

Many older men and women consider sex important and fulfilling.

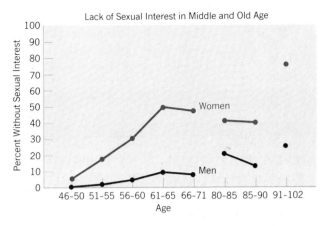

Lack of Sexual Interest in Middle and Old Age

FIGURE 12.8

Lack of sexual interest in middle and old age. At every age from 46 to 102, women reported less sexual interest than men. The pattern of decline continued over time, although not for every age group. Respondents over 80 were asked whether sex was or was not important to them (Bretschneider and McCoy, 1983). Respondents under 72 were asked whether they had sexual interest (Pfeiffer, Verwoerdt, and Davis, 1972). (Sample size for oldest group—shown as dots—was only 9 women, 15 men.)

today's women and men over 60 grew up enough to explain this difference between the sexes? If so, later generations who grow up with a weakened or moribund double standard should show a different pattern in older age. (See Figure 12.8.)

In sum, the evidence on sex and aging supports several important points about human sexuality. First, sexuality can continue throughout life, even though sexual response slows with age. Second, human sexual behavior is largely independent of reproduction. Third, substantial declines in sex hormones are associated with declines in sexual interest and activity. But not all loss of sexual interest and erection is determined by hormones alone. In women, social factors like social class, attitudes, and a sharing sexual partner probably avert or mask such declines.

Fourth, and most important, at all ages and in both sexes, sexual interest has a wide range. At all ages, some adults are sexually active and interested. Health, the availability of a partner, and genetic and temperamental factors all play a role in the maintenance of sexual interest and activity.

SUMMARY

1 Adolescents complete their fully adult gender identity, first in fantasy and then in reality, a process that includes choosing the sex of their sexual partners and reinterpreting the exploratory sexual acts of childhood in a context more like that of adults. Adolescent sexual behavior and commitment reflect socially shared ideas, many of which bear on gender roles.

2 The sexual scripts for the two sexes indicate how adolescents are supposed to behave sexually. Today's scripts for both sexes are more similar than in the 1940s and 1950s. Many women no longer wait for marriage to begin having sexual intercourse, although most females still begin to masturbate later in life and do so less often than males. Today, adolescents from all social classes are more likely than adolescents of previous generations to think they should be interested in sex, have sex earlier, and be sexually competent once they have experience.

3 Adolescents may feel conflict as they decide whether to engage in increasingly intimate sexual acts. By early adulthood, nearly all males and females have petted. By age 25, 97 percent of single men and two out of three single women have had sexual intercourse. Since Kinsey's day, the rates of increase in sexual intercourse among single women have been steep, and the average age of first intercourse has been declining. These numbers do not reflect promiscuity; instead, they reflect a pattern of loving several people monogamously and serially before marriage.

4 As more unmarried adolescents have intercourse and have it earlier, the numbers—though not the proportions—of pregnancies have increased. Adolescent couples may not wish to or know how to use reliable contraception.

5 Some adolescents adopt a homosexual identity. They feel alienated from parts of the accepted gender roles for their sex and strongly different from others of their sex. Like adolescents who adopt a heterosexual identity, homosexual adolescents must learn how to deal with sexual intimacy, how to be sexual while living with their parents, and how to keep friendships with people of both sexes.

6 Today, no sexual acts are exclusively new to adults. Like everyone else, adults' sexual behavior is shaped by prevailing social norms. The double standard has been strongest in the lives of people who today are in middle and old age. Today, more liberal sexual values, cohabitation, and the glorification of the youth culture all have blurred the once-sharp distinction between married and single life.

7 In marriage, a sexual partner is conveniently available. In the first year of marriage, the average couple has the highest rates of intercourse of any time

in marriage. After the first four years of marriage, frequency of intercourse declines.

8 When a marriage ends, as about 40 percent do, sexual intimacy has dissolved, and the newly single, sexually experienced partners must learn new sexual scripts.

9 Some adults choose celibacy, whether after a divorce or for religious, ethical, or career reasons.

10 The story of sex in middle age is likely to change significantly as today's young people grow older. With age, physiological sexual responses slow, but sexual interest need not disappear. A man's or a woman's earlier sexual history—especially frequency and enjoyment of sex—is often a good predictor of sexual interest and practice in middle and old age. As young people age, attitudes are likely to change: people (especially women) are likely to be considered sexual beings for longer into their lives.

KEY TERMS

gender identity
adolescence
puberty
primary sexual characteristics
sex hormones
core gender identity
adult gender identity
secondary sex characteristics

gender role
Sturm und Drang
sexual scripts
probability sample
cohabitation
ethnographic studies
menopause
climacteric

SUGGESTED READINGS

Brecher, E.M. *Love, Sex, and Aging.* Boston: Little, Brown, 1984. An interesting and upbeat book, full of quotations from respondents to a Consumers Union survey of sex among older men and women.

Hunt, M. *Sexual Behavior in the 1970s.* Chicago: Playboy Press, 1974. Still the best overall popular update of the Kinsey Reports. Respondents over age 18 tell about adult sexuality.

Miller, P. Y. and Simon, W. "The Development of Sexuality in Adolescence." In J. Adelson (Ed.), *Handbook of Adolescent Psychology.* New York: Wiley 1980. A thoughtful, provocative review that traces from preadolescence to adolescence the concerns of young people meeting social sexuality.

Simenauer, J., and Carroll, D. *Singles: the New Americans.* New York: Simon & Schuster, 1982. A wide-ranging survey of 3000 people in 275 metropolitan areas that covers the social and sexual experiences of singles of all ages.

Chapter 13

Love and Attraction

Love is the deep and precious bond between parent and child, between lovers, between dear friends, between husband and wife. Some feel love as passion, some as tenderness, some as poignance, some as comfort; some feel no love at all. Although people feel love so variously, most would agree that love draws people together: to love someone means wanting to be near, to touch, to gaze on. We all recognize at a glance the outward signs of love: the young couple walking with arms entwined, the child nestled in a parent's lap, the sweet stolen kiss of two 70-year-olds. We all recognize, too, the signs of dislike: the studious avoidance, the cold warring, or the cool disdain. Love draws people together, just as dislike divides them. Psychologists call the way we evaluate others positively or negatively, **attraction,** and through some ingenious experiments, social psychologists have measured attraction and have begun to understand the features that attract one person to another. Love is a strong, positive form of attraction. It is harder to isolate than attraction for purposes of study, but psychologists have made some interesting inroads in understanding loving and liking as kinds of attraction.

One of the psychologist's first tasks has been to define and distinguish among several closely related behaviors: loving, liking, and attraction. Many people have felt all of these but have trouble specifying where one feeling leaves off and another begins.

LIKING OR LOVING?

During the presidential races of 1952 and 1956, Dwight Eisenhower's campaign slogan was, "I Like Ike." It seemed that the voting public did indeed like Ike, for twice he won the presidency. What made Ike so likable? He had a famous winsome smile, he had been a victorious general in Europe during World War

Love is a strong, positive form of attraction.

II, his past was clear of scandal, and his politics seemed conservative and safe. Ike was perceived as intelligent, respectable, responsible, and admirable, the very qualities that people associate with *liking* (Rubin, 1970). As social psychologist Zick Rubin found, the traits of people one likes are different from the traits of people one loves.

Rubin's work at the University of Michigan led him to devise a 13-item Love Scale and a 13-item Liking Scale. Responses could vary across nine degrees of agreement or disagreement. Rubin set out with the idea that liking and loving were interrelated but that each also had unique aspects. Rubin checked the validity of his scales by asking 158 dating couples (University of Michigan undergraduates) to complete the questions. He asked members of couples not to sit next to each other while they were answering the questions; each filled out the questionnaire about his or her dating partner and again about a close friend of the same sex. Rubin's findings are intriguing. First, he found that people liked their dating partner and their friend about the same amount but loved their dating partner significantly more than their friend. Second, he found that women loved their friends more than men did. As they are growing up, girls interact in pairs more than boys do. Friends in pairs are more likely to share secrets and more personal information than friends in larger groups (Taylor, 1979; Taylor et al., 1981).

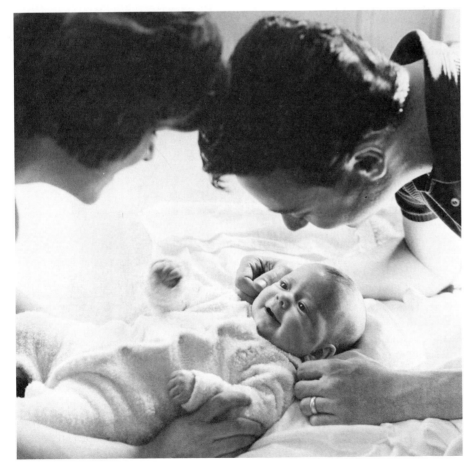

Storgé—the love between parents and children.

Rubin found that men rated liking and loving their girlfriends more alike than women did for their boyfriends. Why? Rubin speculated (1973) that because interpersonal feelings are more important to women throughout life than to men, women may make finer distinctions between liking and loving than men do.

In the retest of the dating couples six months later, Rubin found from interviews that the more intensely in love the couple had been, according to the Love Scale, the more likely they were still to be dating, and the more likely they were to describe their love as equally or more intense than it had been six months before. Rubin also predicted that the more intense the love between a couple, the more gazing into each other's eyes they would do. Observation in the laboratory bore out his prediction.

LOVING

All of us intuitively understand the difference between the love we feel for a new baby, a grandparent, an old friend, or a mate. We all understand, too, the difference between the love we feel for the people in our lives and the love we feel for abstractions like country or God. The English language actually has several different nouns for these different kinds of love—affection, lust, passion, fondness, infatuation, rapture, adoration—and modifiers as well—mother love, brotherly love, platonic love, and Christian love. The Greek language distinguishes among four different kinds of love: **eros** is passionate love and is related to the English words "erotic" and "erogenous"; **agape** is the selfless, charitable love personified in Jesus, Mahatma Gandhi, and in the everyday kindnesses of everyday people; **philia** (related to the stem in words like "Franco*phile*" and "*phil*anthropy" and "*phil*anderer") is the love between good friends; and **storgé** (*stor-gay*) is the love between parents or grandparents and children. To say "I love you" can have many different meanings, depending on to whom, when, where, and why we say it.

Passionate or Companionate Love?

Many people would agree that the early love between a couple is, in most instances, qualitatively different from the love they share when their relationship is older and settled. In a culture like ours, where romantic love is considered by many people a desirable beginning for an enduring relationship like marriage or cohabitation, couples usually must navigate an important transition at some point, if their relationship is to survive. They must move from the early, strong physical attraction and all-consuming desire to possess their beloved that social psychologists have called, logically enough, **passionate love** to the later, cooler **companionate love**. Companionate love is the friendship, caring, and deep attachment of established couples (Walster et al., 1978).

Passionate love is the heart-pounding, tight-embracing, mooning, lusting stuff of poetry and romance. Companionate love, by contrast, is sober, gentler, longer-lived. For the thousands of years of human history when marriage was largely a formal, economic arrangement for the disposition of property and production of heirs, passionate love was neither assumed nor expected to exist between husband and wife. If, out of a marriage contracted by their families, they forged companionate love, they were lucky. Thus the Greek or Roman husband looked outside marriage, to a mistress or a young boy, for passion. The medieval woman looked to a lover, not her husband, for passion. (Romance, furthermore, as idealized by medieval poets and singers of courtly love, was chaste and not typically the stuff of physical passion.) To centuries of married pairs, our current notion that love, especially passionate love, belongs within marriage would have sounded absurd and astonishing. Some historians locate the wide acceptance of the idea of romantic love to the end of the seventeenth century. Love is no less an historical and cultural variable than standards of attractiveness, or marriage customs, or gender roles. Modern views of love and, especially, falling in love, marrying, and parents accepting the power of love as a basis for marriage are products of the flowering of the Industrial Revolution (Reiss, 1967). (For a discussion of the rules for choosing a spouse, see Sexuality in Perspective: "Marriage: the Market Rules.")

Companionate love.

SEXUALITY IN PERSPECTIVE:
MARRIAGE: THE MARKET RULES

Bridal veils and organ music cannot mask the fact that in our society, like all others, people choose a marriage partner of the correct class and caste. Those who violate this implicit but powerful rule do so at their peril. In storybooks, Cinderella may nab the prince, and the farmer's son may win the princess, but in real life, people tend to marry within their own social class. Beauty and charm, it is true, give women good bargaining position for marrying upward. Some women with beauty and charm are also likely to be more mobile in their work than their less favored sisters. Handsome, charming heterosexual men have less mobility in the marriage market; rules in homosexual markets are somewhat different.

The courtship and marriage market is not a free market. Sociologists describe it as actually comprised of many small markets—ethnic, religious, and economic—that are carefully monitored by elders within families. The pool from which we choose our partners is restricted in part so that families can control property arrangements. After all, marriages are certainly economic relationships; each partner brings assets to the marriage and will contribute goods and services, real and potential, throughout his or her lifetime. Each partner also may stand to inherit property from his or her family of origin. Indeed, much wrangling in a failed marriage is over money: alimony, child support, the disposition of the house and furnishings. In an age where 30 to 40 percent of marriages end in divorce, women with jobs effectively carry a form of unemployment insurance.

Sociologists also tell us that women marry for the first time on an average two years younger than men do. When both husband and wife come from relatively traditional backgrounds, they are more likely to say that they are contented in marriage than couples without such traditional backgrounds. Table 13.1 shows some of the background patterns associated with long-lived marriages.

What does the table tell young, educated, nontraditional couples? Waiting until your twenties to marry, knowing your partner for two years or so before marrying, planning an engagement of six months, choosing a partner from a similar background—of whom your family and friends are likely to approve— and working out with your partner your various obligations within marriage are all within the power of nearly any couple to achieve. As for having happily married parents, that is beyond a young couple's control.

TABLE 13.1
Background Factors and Divorce

Greater Likelihood of Divorce	Less Likelihood of Divorce
Urban background	Rural background
Marriage at young age (15–19 years)	Marriage at older ages (males—23; females—22; or older)
Brief acquaintance before marriage	Acquaintance of 2 or more years before marriage
Short engagement or none	Engagement of 6 months or more
Unhappily married parents	Happily married parents
Couples who do not attend church or who come from different faiths[a]	Couples who attend church regularly, are Catholic, or come from the same faith
Low social rank	High social rank
Kin and friends disapprove of marriage[a]	Kin and friends approve of marriage
General dissimilarity in backgrounds[a]	General similarity in backgrounds
Disagreement about role obligations	Agreement about role obligations

Source: Adapted from W.J. Goode, *The Family*, Englewood Cliffs, N.J.: Prentice-Hall, 1982, p. 161.
[a]Indicates a violation of the rule that spouses should have similar backgrounds.

Certain social factors in people's lives are associated later on with higher or lower probabilities of divorce.

Love as Culturally Determined

Just how does romantic love work? Two social psychologists, Elaine Walster and Ellen Berscheid (Berscheid and Walster, 1974), have studied the conditions in our society under which passionate love grows. They found that three conditions are necessary, the first of which is that a person live in a culture that believes in passionate love. People who do not believe in love will neither expect to nor fall in love. The second condition is that an appropriate person be available to love. This person must be physically appealing as well as available. People tend to love those who are available to them but keep themselves from others (Walster et al., 1973). The third condition is that people must feel something that they label "love," whether those feelings result from a loved one's sexual attractiveness or from qualities only indirectly associated with a loved one. To fall in love passionately, then, we must live in a culture that leads us to believe in love's existence, we must find someone who is an appropriate object of our feelings, and we must label those feelings "love."

Sexual Love

In our culture, people who are passionately in love are very likely to have strong sexual feelings about their beloved. Part of the desire to merge with the beloved is sexual. Through deep kissing, intimate caress, and sexual intercourse, bodies merge and boundaries between them blur. Whether people gratify their wish for physical union, that is, whether they act out their love sexually, depends on their sexual values, their gender, and, of course, the nature of their relationship. All of these, in turn, depend on the particular place and time in history in which people live. Unrequited love and love from afar are not likely to lead to sexual consummation. Likewise, those who are not married but believe that intercourse belongs within marriage are likely to express their love in other ways.

Of course, not every sexual relationship is loving. Some people guiltlessly separate sex and love; others find loveless sexual encounters physically pleasing but emotionally lacking. In our culture, people of both sexes prefer sex and love together, but women are more likely than men to require that sex be accompanied by love. Because the female **gender role** focuses on the interpersonal—how to be intimate, how to relate, how to love—skills women share with men in intimate relationships, women are especially likely to consider the connection between sex and love essential.

Self-Disclosure

Whether people want love to accompany sex probably relates to their view of intimacy and self-disclosure. **Self-disclosure** is the revelation of oneself to another, and many women require it in an intimate relationship. Self-disclosure can mean making oneself vulnerable, exposing oneself to another, or sharing valuable information about oneself. It tends to draw people together, to enhance intimacy, and it therefore requires trust. Just as the gender script for females teaches them to value mutual self-disclosure, so adolescent sexual interaction permits females to teach males how to disclose themselves in relationships. Girls learn this art early and practice it with their girlfriends. They learn how to integrate it within intimate relationships. Grade-school boys have significantly less experience disclosing themselves to their male friends.

On our third or fourth date, my boyfriend told me about his father's suicide. I knew then he loved me, because he could tell me something so personal. Up until then he talked about school or basketball. That was when I knew I meant something special to him (20-year-old female college sophomore).

What information gets disclosed has a bearing on attractiveness. Men who disclose to others—male or female—about family secrets or personal competitiveness are not always viewed by others as attractive. In contrast, women who disclose family secrets, but not competitiveness, enhance their attractiveness (Derlega and Chaiken, 1976). Once relationships are underway, however, college men disclose to their female partners and not to their male friends. Their disclosures are a measure of their comfort with the loving relationship (Komarovsky, 1976).

MEN find self-disclosure more difficult than women do in our society.

Social psychologists have noted that men find self-disclosure more difficult than women do in our society (Cozby, 1972). Gender stereotypy tends to pressure males to present themselves as competent, never self-doubting people. In stereotype, self-disclosure is weak, at best a distraction from the tasks at hand. Luckily, most men are not Clint Eastwood types and achieve some flexibility in their personal relationships, enough to permit the reward of intimacy. Part of that reward is the freedom to disclose themselves more fully to a lover.

People in a relationship tend to disclose information about themselves mutually and to about equal degrees (Davis, 1976), because self-disclosure generates trust and boosts self-esteem, and these in turn create an atmosphere conducive to further self-disclosure (Taylor, Gould, and Brounstein, 1981). In one interesting experiment, Zick Rubin (1975) showed how people reciprocate self-disclosures. He sent student interviewers to a lounge at Logan Airport in Boston where people were waiting for flights to depart. Each student approached a lone passenger and asked for help in a study purportedly about handwriting. For passengers who agreed, students then jotted a few sentences about themselves on paper and asked the passenger to reciprocate by writing something down. Half of the passengers were led to believe that the students were copying the sentences they wrote and half that the sentences were generated spontaneously by the student. In fact, the degree of self-disclosure of the sentences was manipulated by the interviewers. Some wrote highly intimate sentences: "I think that I'm pretty well adjusted, but I occasionally have some questions about my sexual adequacy." Some wrote nonintimate sentences: "I'm in the process of collecting handwriting samples." For the most part, passengers tended to reply in kind, either with highly intimate sentences—"I've just been attending . . . my fortieth [college] reunion. I still feel sexually adequate—never felt otherwise."—or with nonintimate sentences. However, passengers reciprocated the most intimate statements *only* when the interviewers seemed to be copying sentences someone else had written, not when the sentences were "spontaneous." In personal relationships, disclosure usually is geared to the level of intimacy a pair has reached together. "Copying" sentences made the intimate statements less intimate. In everyday life, the implicit reciprocal norm is violated when one person discloses and the other does not, and disclosure can be seen as a bid for disclosure from another person. Such violations of the norm probably help people to learn which settings and which relationships invite self-disclosure and which do not. A relationship with a lover invites self-disclosure; that with a friend may invite it; that with a boss rarely does.

Liking and Arousal

Various experiments have demonstrated that how we feel physically—good or bad, mildly or intensely aroused, and so forth—strongly influences how we feel about the people around us at the time. It may be a bit unsettling to learn that we tend to like people or find them more attractive if we are in a comfortable rather than an overheated room (Griffitt, 1970); the funnier the slapstick comedy we have just seen (Gouaux, 1971); the more we like the music we have just heard (May and Hamilton, 1977); or even the better the news of the day (Gouaux, 1971; Veitch and Griffitt, 1976). For those of us who like to think that we are good judges of people, that we choose our dear ones wisely, it can be disconcerting to learn that thoroughly extraneous factors so readily influence our feelings. But it does make sense that if we are feeling good, for whatever reason, we will find the people we're with more likable than if we are feeling bad. In fact, that tendency is what we act on when we ask someone to dinner. There we arrange a pleasant setting, a good meal, and a compatible group of people. Some religious cults, for example, eager to be found likable, place great emphasis on meals and mealtime talk with potential recruits. Hosts and guests, by this reasoning, should like each other more for having broken bread together than people who have only conversed in an office hallway or in a cafeteria line.

The Label "Love"

One theory of human emotion holds that first a person feels physiologically aroused and then looks to the situation for a label for that arousal; it may be labeled "love," "anger," "fear," or the like. This theory dates back to the nineteenth century and psychologist William James. How people label the diffuse sensations they feel was the subject of a famous laboratory investigation conducted by Stanley Schachter and Jerome Singer (Schachter, 1964; Schachter and Singer, 1962). They found that when people felt their faces flush, their palms sweat, and their hearts pound, not only did those people believe that they were excited, but they also labeled that excitation according to their interpretation of their situation.

For their investigation, Schachter and Singer injected male college students with epinephrine, a drug that increases arousal by acting on the nervous system to produce the sweating, flushed face, and heart pounding. They told some subjects to expect the drug's effects; they told others nothing about expected effects. Another group was told to expect the wrong effects (itching and numbness), and a final (control) group received neither injection nor any information about effects. A confederate of the experimenters then manipulated the various groups of subjects in different ways. Half were made angry, and half were made very happy. Schachter and Singer found that subjects who had been told what to expect from the injection could label their arousal and did *not* follow the confederate's lead. The same was true of subjects who had received neither injection nor information. Subjects who had not been told what to expect from the injection, in contrast, found themselves aroused but with no ready explanation for their arousal. They were therefore susceptible to the confederate's emotional suggestions. The conclusions the investigators drew were that emotions start as states of general arousal and then are labeled according to the information available or from situational cues. (This experiment was done before the days of strict rules about using drugs and minimizing deception with human subjects. Today, investigators might not get committee approval for such an experiment.)

If Schachter and Singer were right, then if you find your heart leaping, your breathing fast, and your palms sweaty, you may call your arousal "love" if your girl- or boyfriend has just appeared; you may call it "rage" if you have just hung up on an obscene phone call; you may call it "fear" if you have just been awakened by a loud crash. Such labels seem altogether reasonable, given the situation. Schachter and Singer's findings about attributions of emotion following epinephrine arousal may or may not reflect how people label emotions in real life. (Other theorists hold that emotions precede the physical feeling [for example, Izard, 1977].) But their model is nonetheless interesting. Let us turn now to the work of Berscheid and Walster, which uses the Schachter and Singer model of arousal to explain love. Ellen Berscheid and Elaine Walster (1974) extended the Schachter and Singer model to love and sexual feeling. Sexual arousal is certainly a form of physiological arousal. Berscheid and Walster theorized that this physiological arousal in the right setting might be labeled "love." Is arousal in any sexy situation likely to be labeled love or attraction? Perhaps. But a more powerful demonstration of the attribution theory would be to create arousal under conditions highly *un*likely to be considered sexy, but in the presence of mild sexual cues to which the arousal might be attributed. If such arousal then can be attributed to love or to sexual wishes, with minimal sexual provocation, then we may conclude that the model is reasonable.

Such a study gave some support to the model. Men tested on a high, frightening suspension bridge produced more sexual imagery to a projective test than did men tested over a stable, low bridge. The tester, an attractive woman, also was contacted after the experiment by more of the men in the frightening than the safe condition (Dutton and Aron, 1974). Concluding that social psychologists can get *anyone* to make *any* attribution about arousal—including sexual attributions—would be wrong. Instead, people seek reasons for any arousal they feel. What they can't explain is felt to be negative. When people are unaroused or have ready explanations for their arousal, they feel neutral or a bit positive. What people *do*, however, is cued by the behavior or mood of others around at the time of test. For behavior in a situation, people seek cues for how to behave in their situations. Psychologists set up behavioral cues via confederates. But in arousal-attributions made by subjects, confederates determine far less how subjects think about their situations (Marshall, 1976; Maslach, 1977).

A form of behavior found among male primates and humans shows just how closely related sexual arousal and aggression can be. In fact, sexual arousal and aggression stem from excitation of neighboring parts of the brain. The display of an erect penis can mean, according to the context in which it is presented, sexual invitation or threat, appeasement or greeting. The male squirrel monkey (*Saimiri sciureus*) responds to other monkeys with vocalizations, spread thighs, erect penis, scratching, and urinating in certain situations that evoke strong feelings. It also responds in this fashion when it sees its own image in a mirror. What the gestures mean depend on their context. Thus when the male monkey stands in a group of other males, his penile display toward a female is a kind of courting that

FIGURE 13.1

Penis sheaths turn penile display into everyday dress among Papuan men.

precedes his attempts to mate with her. But when the male displays to another, nearby male, it is an act of aggression and dominance. If the other does not respond submissively, he may be attacked. When two males are at some distance from each other, the display can be a greeting, or it can be a sign of appeasement, made by a dominant male to calm an agitated other. Certain New Guinea tribesmen use similar signals to express agitation, aggression, dominance, appeasement or greeting, and erotic feeling. When boys or men of the Asmat or Auyu tribes are frightened, joyous, surprised—in other words, thrown into a state of general arousal—they may spontaneously break into a dance of penile display: vocalizing, spreading their thighs, grasping and rubbing their genitals, erecting, and thrusting their pelvises. The same gestures are ritualized in erotic night dances. The males may present this display when strangers arrive or depart or in response to an exciting, agitating, or frightening event such as a house burning down, a violent thunderstorm, or victory in battle. Among other New Guinea tribes, the boys and men have incorporated a form of penile display into their everyday dress. The men wear sheaths over their penises that are made of nuts, shells, braided fibers, or gourds. Some of the gourds are extremely elongated or huge spheres. For certain ceremonial occasions, the penis covering is so extreme that it interferes with the wearer's vision (see Figure 13.1). For us, the irony of this exaggerated genital display is that the tribesmen claim to wear the coverings out of modesty, even sexual prudery.

PHYSICAL ATTRACTIVENESS

Cultures vary dramatically on what they hold to be physically attractive in men and women. In the United States, women's breasts and buttocks are considered attractive. The modern young American male may lift weights to develop muscles, and he and the modern American female jog or diet to idealized thinness. Among some Polynesian and Hawaiian peoples, extremely obese women have been con-

TABLE 13.2

The Erotic Code of Feminine Attractiveness

Culture	Sexual attractions
Truk, Micronesia, Caroline Islands	Affection-pain
Tahiti, Polynesia, Windward Islands	Erotic dancing
Old Hawaiian aristocrats	Extreme obesity
East Bay (Pseudonym), Melanesia	Thigh tattoos
Mangaia, Polynesia, Cook Islands	Flower fragrances
Australian Aborigines	Sight of female genitals
United States	Breasts, buttocks

Source: Davenport, 1977.

Standards of attractiveness vary from culture to culture.

sidered attractive (see Table 13.2). Members of one New Guinea tribe bind infants' skulls so that the forehead slopes sharply backward, which to them is attractive (see Figure 13.2).

The means are many, but the end is always the same: to influence how others feel about us with our physical appearance. They see more good in us if we are attractive and more negatives if we are not (Solomon and Saxe, 1977). Studies show that physically attractive people are more persuasive than people who are less attractive (Chaiken, 1970). For better or worse, how we look strongly influences how we fare: "beautiful is good," or so it is because many of us believe it to be so.

FIGURE 13.2

In each culture people are trained to see beauty differently. In this New Guinea tribe, infants' skulls are bound so that their foreheads will slope backwards.

In our culture, young men and women jog and diet to an idealized fitness and slenderness.

Male and female college students rate attractive people as more socially desirable, happier socially and professionally, and more marriageable than less attractive people (Dion, Berscheid, and Walster, 1972). Physically attractive people are more successful in everyday social interactions than less attractive people are. Attractiveness also is the key factor in how people rate their dates after the first date (Walster et al., 1965) as well as the fifth (Mathes, 1975). Attractive men interact more with women and are more satisfied with the quality of those interactions (Reis et al., 1980).

Attraction and Proximity

It is a truism that we must know someone before we can feel attracted to him or her. The people we get to know, of course, are those whom we see. Living near someone makes acquaintance more probable, for the nearer we live to someone, the likelier that we will see that person repeatedly. Many years ago, a sociologist (Bossard, 1932) studied 5000 marriage licenses issued in Philadelphia. He plotted the addresses of the newlyweds and found that about one-third of the couples had lived within five city blocks of one another. About one-fourth had lived within two city blocks. The same tendency holds true for college students who live near each other (Festinger et al., 1950). Students on the same floor or in the same dormitory rate one another as more attractive than those who live farther away (Evans and Wilson, 1976; Nahemov and Lawton, 1975). The power of proximity to induce and augment attraction extends to adults in apartment complexes and to elderly people in urban housing projects. Social psychologists believe that proximity increases attraction because of repeated exposure. Not "absence," but "nearness makes the heart grow fonder." People grow increasingly positive toward another person the more they see that person, at least if they started out feeling positive. Even if they viewed another person somewhat negatively from the start, repeated exposure only creates more positive feelings.

But people do not find dates or partners at random, whether in their neighborhood, college dorm, or housing project. What directs such choices?

Attraction and Similarity

We all know of dramatic cases in which opposites attract: the 15-year-old who falls in love with the 22-year-old "older man"; the dark-haired Italian teenager who swoons over the blond, Swedish visiting student; the white graduate student who marries her black professor. But these are relatively infrequent occurrences. The frequent occurrences, so the Census tells us, are that like marries like: whites marry whites, and blacks marry blacks. People marry within their religious groups. Sociologists have many explanations for why people are attracted to and marry others like themselves. We tend to live near people like ourselves, to be exposed to them, and to find them attractive. Families usually support such choices, too.

The extent to which similarity attracts extends across interests, values, and behavior. College students form friendships with those in their dorms who are majoring in subjects like their own, with liberal arts and engineering majors forming different social groups (Newcomb, 1961). People also are attracted to those who behave as they do, social psychologists have found. Accordingly, non-smokers prefer to be with other nonsmokers, smokers to be with smokers (Polivy

Similarity attracts.

et al., 1979). Another study has shown that best friends in high school are usually in the same grade, of the same race and sex, feel similarly toward school and their teachers, parents, and even their future plans. But above all, best friends do things similarly; if one smokes, the other does, too; if one takes illegal drugs, the other does, too. This pattern of similarity holds for drinking, cutting classes, time spent on homework, going to church, reading, watching television, listening to music, and other activities (Kandel, 1978). Even when experimental subjects have only to judge whether they would like someone whose views on a subject they know only from a questionnaire reference, they like the hypothetical other more when the answers to the questionnaires agree more with their views (Byrne, 1971).

Similarity holds couples together, too. In one study of 22 married couples (Murstein and Christy, 1976), the physical attractiveness of the pair, whether rated by the pair members themselves or by independent judges, matched very closely. Other studies have shown that the similarity between members of a couple correlates with the degree of satisfaction they feel about their marriage (Hendrick, 1971; Meyer and Pepper, 1977). Gregory White (1980) sought couples of varying degrees of commitment and correlated each pair's attractiveness. The highest correlations occurred among seriously committed couples and those who were engaged or married. Casual dates showed the least similarity.

The findings from one study of dating couples illustrate several points about attraction and the conditions under which it flourishes (Hill, Rubin, and Peplau, 1976). Among an original sample of 231 dating couples, 103 eventually broke up. From the answers to questionnaires, the researchers concluded that dissimilarities of age, educational goals, intelligence, or physical attractiveness occurred most often among couples who eventually broke up. In contrast, dissimilarities of religion, attitudes toward gender roles, and preferred family size did not correlate with breaking up. Few couples agreed about breaking up. Slightly more women than men perceived problems in the relationship and wanted to end it. By analyzing the data from these same couples, Abigail Stewart and Zick Rubin (1976) found that men who scored high on a need for power were more likely to be in relationships that broke up—and to have predicted the break up—than men who scored lower on a need for power. Women's need for power did not correlate with the survival of their relationship, another demonstration that gender may influence the stability of relationships differentially. Men and women do not fulfill *all* their needs in relationships with members of the other sex. Perhaps the need for power is expressed in different settings for men and for women. In any case, some similarities matter far more than others in the maintenance over time of dating relationships.

In our relationships, we constantly give up a little here to get a little there.

Loss and Gain

In our relationships, we constantly give up a little here to get a little there. We make endless mental calculations and adjustments, giving here, pulling back there, to keep our relationships in accord with our sense of their proper balance. For example, if people think that they are far more invested in a relationship than their dating partner is, they are quite likely to break off that relationship (Hill, Rubin, and Peplau, 1976). Equal investments tend to hold people together most strongly. When people directly benefit from a relationship, they are more attracted to another than when they do not benefit (Clark and Mills, 1979). Although it may sound terribly calculating to say that people like others better when they think they can get some advantage from an association with them, one theory holds that it is nonetheless true.

EXCHANGE THEORY   A California sociologist, Glen Elder (1969), published a study on marriage mobility. He had followed a group of high-school women years after graduation. In high school, the women's physical attractiveness had been rated. Elder was interested in the economic and social status of the men they later married. He found that the more physically attractive women had married men of higher status than the less attractive women.

Elder's study embodies the principle of **exchange theory**. This theory holds that marriage (or a serious romantic relationship) is an exchange of resources, a kind of trade. A woman's resource is her appearance, a man's his success or potential success. The theory does not require that people consciously or callously calculate the value of the exchange. All that is needed is for men to feel good when they date the most attractive woman they can and for women to find striving, successful men more attractive than others. For exchange theorists, the nature of the couple is critical, and the process by which the coupling is produced is less critical. Lonelyheart advertisements show that people are aware of market factors: females describe their youth and physical attributes; males describe their education and credentials. Exchange theory has been supported by a good deal of psychological and sociological research since Elder's study, although occasional studies and some recent theoretical work challenge the theory (see Taylor and Glenn, 1976; Walster, Walster, and Berscheid, 1978).

But market factors certainly can influence dating. When one set of researchers (Coombs and Kenkel, 1966) set up computer dates for a dance and then checked both before and after the date for the desired characteristics in a date and degree of satisfaction, respectively, they found that people liked their dates more when they were more attractive. But when people were asked to choose a date whom they would have to invite, they tended to choose someone about as attractive as they were. The latter situation entails a risk of being turned down, given the dating marketplace; the computer date entailed no such risk. Thus similarity as a factor in choosing a partner may be partly determined by market factors.

Although exchange theory seems plausible, it also sounds a bit cold-blooded. Few of us perceive our relations with others as driven completely by market considerations. It seems likely that long-term, committed relationships can tolerate periods of emotional imbalance better than short-term dating relationships can. People do sacrifice for a loved one. Staying in a relationship because it has lasted a very long time may be viewed as entrapment by some exchange theorists, but it rarely can be explained in exchange terms alone. To deal with such objections, equity theory has been proposed.

EQUITY THEORY   Exchange theory is more adequate as an explanation of casual relationships. **Equity theory** is more adequate to explain intimate, long-term relationships in which people behave altruistically. Parents care for babies, mates care for each other during illness, religious people devote their lives to God. Equity theory is an attempt to explain relations when the exchange is not equal, but equitable (or fair, in other words).

People in intimate relationships disclose things about themselves and engage in exchanges for long periods. The inequities in these relationships, equity theorists suggest, are temporary, for people tend to balance their accounts. Like exchange theorists, they note that factors of time and the different notions that males and females hold about reward and punishment create different tallies between intimates from those maintained in casual relationships. For many situations, exchange and equity theories would lead to identical predictions. Married couples, for example, engage in many equal and equitable exchanges. If you pick up the laundry, they say, I'll pick up the pizza. If you pick up the babysitter, I'll do the dishes.

When people compared themselves and their partners on current income, love, and willingness to sacrifice for the other, researchers (Berscheid, Walster, and Bohrnstedt, 1973) found that many trade-offs appeared. One partner's greater attractiveness may be balanced by the other's higher income or more loving nature. When inequity occurs in one area, equity requires greater contributions in another area such as self-sacrifice, lovingness, or the like. Because exchange theory could predict this pattern as well, equity theorists turned to couples at the University of Wisconsin to test their theory. They asked the couples to rate the equity of their relationships and then how they felt about their relationships. The couples rated their contentment, happiness, anger, and guilt within the relationship. Those who reported their relationship as more equitable also rated themselves as happier and more content than did those in less equitable relationships. But— and exchange theory would not predict this—when subjects felt that they were getting far more out of a relationship than their partners, they were less content, less happy, and much more guilty than the more equitably situated. In essence, people who are "overbenefited" are less comfortable than those in more equitable relationships.

Equity theory is young enough so that its challenge to exchange theory has not been tested fully yet. It is unlikely that dating and marriage relationships work according to the same rules of equity. But equity theory has the advantage

TABLE 13.3

How Important Are Love and Sex to Adult Men?

	Single	Married	Divorced
Love is more important than sex for a happy, satisfied life.	45%	50%	57%
My current life is satisfying.	33%	66%	42%

When men were polled for a Playboy survey on their attitudes towards love, family life, and sex, the results showed that a full 85 percent of all men considered love *very* important to a happy, satisfied life. Married men were most satisfied with their lives and were twice as likely as single or divorced men to say that they were *very* satisfied with their lives.

Source: Simon, *Harris Poll: The Playboy Report on American Men,* 1979.

over exchange theory of bearing out intuitions that the rules we use to measure loving relationships are more elastic than those we use on casual relationships.

Gender Differences in Romantic Strategies

According to their responses to psychologists, men want in women something very different from what women want in men. Some sociologists like to characterize male and female differences in relationships by the difference in reproductive investment of the sexes. The male contributes a spoonful of semen, and the female contributes a nine-month, temperature-controlled home for the young, followed by months to years of nursing. The long pregnancy and nursing, by this reasoning, limit the female's ability to leave as many copies of *her* genes as the male, given his copious supply of semen (Trivers, 1972). Her investment is in high quality but relatively few births. Few modern men are motivated by the wish or need to leave the most copies of their genes; modern western values reinforce the motivations underlying large investments of time, energy, and resources in small numbers of offspring. But sociobiologists respond by arguing that remnants of the early strategy influence the sexes in their differential strategies today in relationships. Of course, many factors combine to lead to sex differences in romantic strategies.

OVER AND OVER AGAIN, THE SAME RESULTS APPEAR: feelings of strong attraction are likely to strike males earlier in relationships than females.

Over and over again, the same results appear: feelings of strong attraction are likely to strike males earlier in relationships than females. Almost twice as many college men as women report being "very easily attracted" to people of the other sex (Kephart, 1967). Many more men than women are satisfied by their computer-chosen partners at a dance; and more of the women than men in the same computer dance had higher demands of their dates. Why? Men, it seems, are more romantic than women are. They fall in love more easily than women. Although men have higher demands for attractiveness in a partner than women (Coombs and Kenkel, 1966), they are more likely than women to remain satisfied with an ongoing relationship. Women size up and seek more attributes than men, and they break off relationships more readily than men do. Zick Rubin (1973) found that college men in relationships endorsed more romantic statements than their female partners did.

Males and females get jealous about different matters in relationships, too. Men get jealous about their partners' sexual activity, women about intimacy and their partner's psychological ties to another (White, 1981).

Two or three years into our relationship, my girlfriend admitted that recently she had slept with a classmate of hers. I knew the guy vaguely. When she told me, I felt like she had punched me. I wanted to kill him, but I wanted to punish her even worse. We broke up not too long after that. That was betrayal (21-year-old male junior).

Jeff and I decided that we would have an open relationship. I slept with another guy and told Jeff about it. He hasn't slept with anyone else yet. But he goes out nearly every night with some political group full of politico-females who hang all over him and talk Spanish. Jeff says that they're "just friends," but I doubt it (19-year-old female freshman).

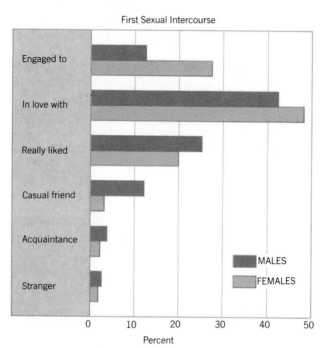

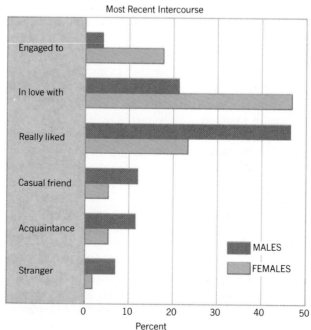

FIGURE 13.3

Here we see the percentages of college students of either sex who were engaged in more or less intimate relationships when they first and most recently had intercourse.

TABLE 13.4

What the Two Sexes Look for in a Partner

What males want in females	What females want in males
1. Physical attractiveness	1. Achievement
2. Erotic ability	2. Leadership
3. Affectional ability	3. Occupational ability
4. Social ability	4. Economic ability
5. Domestic ability	5. Entertaining ability
6. Ability to dress well	6. Intellectual ability
7. Interpersonal understanding	7. Observational ability
8. Art appreciation	8. Common sense
9. Moral-spiritual understanding	9. Athletic ability
10. Art, creative ability	10. Theoretical ability

Source: Centers, 1972.

Men consider a woman's physical attractiveness her most important ideal quality. Women consider a man's achievement and leadership his most important ideal qualities.

Women's serious relationships are conditioned by how women evaluate long-term partners: love and marriage must be measured not only by sexual and personal compatibility but other criteria as well. Sociologists have long known that women marry more than a man; they marry a standard of living for themselves and their children-to-be (Waller, 1937).

When men and women are asked to rate in order of importance the ideal qualities of a long-term partner of the opposite sex, men consider physical attractiveness first and foremost. For women, physical attractiveness does not even make it into the top ten. As Table 13.4 shows, the ideal female is physically stimulating, supportive, and nurturant. The ideal male is economically and socially successful (Centers, 1972). It seems that the stereotyped gender roles that people fill in our culture are very powerful: men are seen as dominant breadwinners, women as their physical and spiritual supporters. It is probably too early to expect that attitudes among young people today have changed since the 1970s to reflect changing gender expectations. The best evidence about how men choose

FIGURE 13.4

Some primate females have mock genital displays on their chests that may serve as releasers of sexual behaviors for males who approach from the front. (Left) Gelada baboons. The female (center) and the male have mock genital displays on their chests. The male's display may appease other, aggressive males (from Wilson and Nias, 1976). (Right) It has been proposed that women's breasts act as sexual releasers for men by mimicking buttocks.

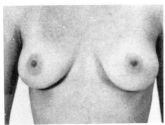
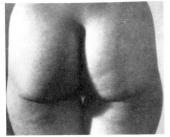

partners is still that they choose on the basis of attractiveness. The best evidence about how women choose partners is that they choose on the basis of future promise.

Biological Basis of Attractive Features

Because we discuss at length the physiology of the sexual drive in Chapter 8, here we will only mention the interesting ideas of those students of human and animal behavior who believe that humans are born with the tendency to find sexually attractive certain physical characteristics of the opposite sex.

Desmond Morris, a popular writer and ethologist, has proposed that the swollen buttocks of female primates act as inborn releasers of sexual behavior for males of their species. Morris has also proposed (1967) that the human female's prominent breasts—buttock displays "relocated," so to speak—release males' sexual energy and that evolution has favored prominent breasts because humans sexually invite and generally copulate face to face. Morris's idea remains untested, if intriguing. Not all human societies, after all, attach erotic significance to the female breast (for example, Mangaia does not). Even if Morris were right about the female breast as a universally erotic signal, the inventive forebrain of humans assures that somewhere in the world, some culture will divest it of appeal and turn to some other sexual signal. Mangaians have no shortage of erotica, even if some people find it mysterious that breasts are not erotic to them.

PEOPLE ARE woefully iNACCURATE wHEN it COMES TO gUESSiNG wHAT tHE OTHER SEX likes.

In a survey of readers of the New York newspaper, the *Village Voice,* (see Gagnon, 1977), men and women stated both what they sought in a heterosexual partner and what they believed people of the other sex sought in a partner. The results showed that people are woefully inaccurate when it comes to guessing what the other sex likes. First of all, men *thought* that their most sexually attractive attributes, in descending order of importance, were: muscular shoulders and chest, muscular arms, large penis, and tallness. But women thought men's most attractive features were, again in descending order of importance: small and sexy buttocks, slimness, flat stomach, and expressive eyes (see Figure 13.5).

In a classroom survey at Tufts University, students of sexuality showed the same discrepancy between what they wanted in the physical characteristics of a partner and what the other-sex partner thought was wanted. Men were most interested in buttocks and faces. Women assumed, however, that they were most interested in breasts. Men underestimated women's interest in their eyes, shoulders, and chests and overestimated their interest in their face (Luria and Rose, 1978). (See Table 13.5.)

It is interesting to note that a survey among homosexual men (Bell, 1974) found them in agreement with women on many of the physical attributes they find attractive in their male partners, such as buttocks and eyes. But like heterosexual men, homosexual men believe that women are attracted by an athletic build, tallness, and a large penis. (See Figure 13.6.)

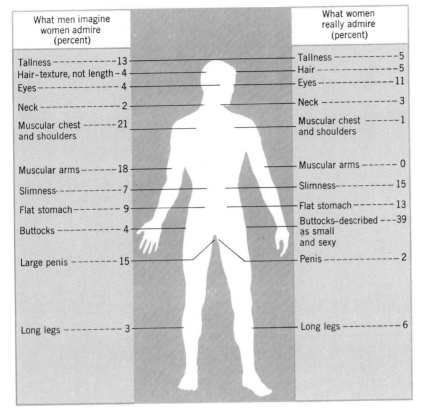

What men imagine women admire (percent)	What women really admire (percent)
Tallness ———— 13	Tallness ———— 5
Hair-texture, not length – 4	Hair ———— 5
Eyes ———— 4	Eyes ———— 11
Neck ———— 2	Neck ———— 3
Muscular chest and shoulders ——— 21	Muscular chest and shoulders ——— 1
Muscular arms ——— 18	Muscular arms ——— 0
Slimness ———— 7	Slimness ———— 15
Flat stomach ——— 9	Flat stomach ——— 13
Buttocks ———— 4	Buttocks-described ——— 39 as small and sexy
Large penis ——— 15	Penis ———— 2
Long legs ———— 3	Long legs ———— 6

FIGURE 13.5

What men think women find attractive in men. Data are from a small and informal *Village Voice* survey. Such exaggerated misunderstandings probably develop in same-sex peer groups before and during adolescence (after Wilson and Nias, 1976).

TABLE 13.5

What College Students Look for in a Sexual Partner

	Males want in female (actual)	Females think males want	Females want in males (actual)	Males think females want
1. General looks	7%	1%	3%	11%
2. Overall body	15	17	20	27
3. Torso	—	—	7	9
4. Face	20	4	7	14
5. Hair	5	—	7	—
6. Mouth	—	1	3	3
7. Eyes	3	1	13	7
8. Breasts	17	49	—	—
9. Buttocks	25	17	6	5
10. Legs	3	5	5	4
11. Thighs	3	—	2	1
12. Waist	1	2	—	—
13. Hips	1	2	2	—
14. Stomach	—	1	—	—
15. Shoulders	—	—	17	7
16. Chest	—	—	14	4
17. Arms	—	—	—	1
18. Beard	—	—	—	1
19. Hands	—	—	—	1
20. Genitals	—	—	—	4

When Tufts University students in a human sexuality course were asked, "What is *the* characteristic you look for in a potential sexual partner?" they replied as this table shows.

FIGURE 13.6

Erotic features desired in a part-ner. This profile, as listed by 575 white, male, homosexual men, seems to combine the features of what heterosexual men and women find erotic about men (from Bell, 1974; after Wilson and Nias, 1976).

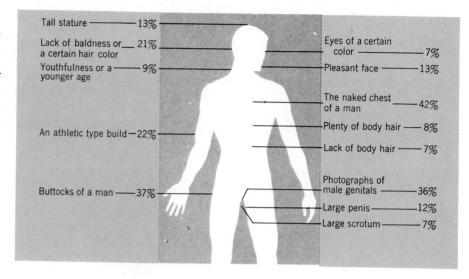

Tall stature — 13%	Eyes of a certain color — 7%
Lack of baldness or a certain hair color — 21%	Pleasant face — 13%
Youthfulness or a younger age — 9%	
	The naked chest of a man — 42%
	Plenty of body hair — 8%
An athletic type build — 22%	Lack of body hair — 7%
	Photographs of male genitals — 36%
Buttocks of a man — 37%	Large penis — 12%
	Large scrotum — 7%

TABLE 13.6

Factors Sought by Heterosexual Partners

Men (%) believed that women looked for:

23 Arousal to multiple orgasm
15 Delays his orgasm
12 Man domineering
9 Arousal to orgasm
0 Man gives good oral sex
0 Man matches woman's rhythm

Women (%) believed that men looked for:

14 Good use of vaginal muscles
13 Woman slavishly submissive
9 Woman performs advanced techniques of fellatio
7 Woman horny and aggressive
1 Woman has orgasm
1 Woman has broad range of sexual techniques

Women (%) believed that women looked for:

13 Delays his orgasm
11 Man gives good oral sex
11 Man matches woman's rhythm
6 Man takes forceful control
3 Arousal to orgasm
0 Arousal to multiple orgasm

Men (%) believed that men looked for:

15 Woman performs advanced techniques of fellatio
8 Woman very submissive
8 Woman adventurous, kinky, ready for anything
2 Woman energetic but not aggressive
2 Both have orgasm
1 Tight vagina

Source: Reported in J. H. Gagnon (Ed.). *Human Sexuality in Today's World.* Boston: Little, Brown and Company, 1977.

Are women attracted to a large penis? Many men apparently believe—mistakenly—that women consider the size of a man's penis important to his attractiveness. This belief may tell us more about men's feelings than women's. Bernie Zilbergeld, a Berkeley, California, clinical psychologist who has written extensively about male sexuality, has said that men are haunted by the fantasy that their penises should be "two feet long, hard as steel and can go all night" (in Herman, 1982, p.191). He believes that the following passage, from Harold Robbins's *The Betsy,* captures some of the impossible expectations men have of themselves:

> *Gently her fingers opened his union suit and he sprang out at her like an angry lion from its cage. Carefully she peeled back his foreskin, exposing his angry red glans, and took him in both hands, one behind the other as if she were grasping a baseball bat. She stared at it in wonder, "C'est formidable. Un vrai canon. . . ."*
>
> *Naked, he looked even more an animal than before. Shoulders, chest, and belly covered with hair out of which sprang the massive erection. . . .*
>
> *She almost fainted looking down at him. Slowly he began to lower her on him. Her legs came up . . . as he began to enter her. . . . It was as if a giant of white-hot steel were penetrating her vitals. . . . She began to climax almost before he was fully inside her. Then she couldn't stop them, one coming rapidly after the other as he slammed into her with the force of the giant body press she had seen working in his factory. . . . the man and the machine, they were one and the same (quoted in Herman, 1982, p.191).*

The male fantasy worships the fierce penis—the "angry lion"—and it worships the huge penis—the "cannon," the "giant of white-hot steel," "the giant body press," "the machine"—that penetrates the woman and causes her (rather improbably) wave upon wave of orgasms. Here is no negotiation of tentative partners, no progression from less to more intimate sexual acts. Reality hides under the bed.

In this culture, many men believe that a sexual partner wants a man with a large penis and that a large penis is especially satisfying during intercourse. (See "Sexuality in Perspective: 'A Giant of White-Hot Steel.' ")

WHAT IS ATTRACTIVE IN BED? In a survey related to the one described above, the *Village Voice* asked 100 "friends and acquaintances" of the journalist (in other words, this was more of a happenstance sample than a representative sample) what they sought from a heterosexual partner in bed and what they believed people of the other sex sought in bed. Again, the misapprehensions were enormous (see Table 13.6). In this sample, men, for instance, vastly overestimated the importance to women of multiple orgasms and underestimated the importance of fore-play. In turn, women overestimated the importance to men of vaginal muscle control and underestimated the importance to men of sexual assertiveness and oral sex. The survey's results may not be representative, but they imply that sexual communication between the sexes is fairly distorted, even in this happenstance sample.

The popular magazines' material on gender differences in what attracts and arouses often reads as if it were engraved in biological stone. Students of human sexuality know enough history and anthropology to understand that tastes change over time and that time is often measured in small chunks of only a few years' duration (Brownmiller, 1984). In the last 30 years, men's hairstyles, for example, have shifted from crewcuts to long hair and back to short hair. Idealized breast styles have shifted from large, pushed up, and tightly controlled to small, min-imized, and bralessly "natural." Definitions of what is attractive may be short-lived, but no culture lacks a concept of attractiveness. Once that concept and a standard of attractiveness exist, people are motivated to approximate the standard as closely as they can.

SUMMARY

1. Attraction is the way we evaluate others negatively or positively. Love is a strong, positive form of attraction.

2. The qualities people associate with liking include intelligence, respectability, responsibility, and admirableness. People tend to like others who seem to have good judgment, to be well adjusted, and whom they think others would evaluate favorably. They associate loving with intimacy, caring, and attach-ment. Females tend to love their friends more than males do, perhaps because many female friends interact in pairs, an arrangement that favors intimacy.

3. Psychologists once believed that mothers and children learned by association with breast feeding how to cuddle and seek closeness to each other, but more recent work suggests that human and other animal infants are genet-ically programmed to find interaction with their soft, warm caretakers to be attractive and comforting.

4. Feelings of love are subject to cultural norms and expectations. Passionate love, for example, grows in cultures where people believe in its existence. It also requires the availability of an attractive person as its object and the labeling as "love" of the feelings toward that person.

5. In our culture, sexual feelings often accompany the feelings labeled as love. Self-disclosure, the revelation of oneself to another, may accompany intimate relationships.

6. One theory of human emotion holds that people first feel physiological arousal and then look to their situation for a label for that arousal. Higher physical arousal may lead to more sexual labeling.

7. Cultures vary (and cultural fashions themselves change) in what is considered attractive in males and females. But the goal is invariably to influence through physical appearance how others feel about oneself. People see more good in those who are attractive and more negatives in those who are not attractive.

8. Attractive people are considered by others to be more socially desirable, happier, and more marriageable than less attractive people. Attractive people

are also more successful in everyday social interactions and, often, more satisfied with the quality of those interactions than less attractive people are.

9 People tend to feel attraction for those they know and see repeatedly, so long as their first feelings tended in a positive direction. Proximity can induce and enhance attraction.

10 Although opposites attract in the minority of instances, it is far more common for people to feel attracted to those who are like them. For the most part, people marry within their racial and religious groups.

11 People are likelier to feel attracted to those from whom they may derive some benefit, and equal investments in a relationship tend to hold people together most firmly. Exchange theory holds that marriage or other serious romantic relationships are exchanges of resources. Traditionally, those resources have been women's looks and men's success.

12 Men and women often say that they want different things from their relationships. Some sociobiologists classify this difference according to the different reproductive investments of the sexes. Men tend to be more romantic than women; more of them report being easily attracted to women and feeling satisfied with their partners than women do.

13 In choosing partners, men rely heavily on physical attractiveness; women rely on future promise. Men and women perceive inaccurately what people of the other sex find attractive.

KEY TERMS

attraction
eros
agape
philia
storge
passionate love

companionate love
gender script
self-disclosure
exchange theory
equity theory

SUGGESTED READINGS

Berscheid, E. and Walster, E. *Interpersonal Attraction* (2nd ed.). Reading, MA: Addison-Wesley, 1978. These two authors make this an authoritative source on people's attraction to each other.

Brownmiller, S. *Femininity*. New York: Simon and Schuster (Linden Press) 1984. The changing view of what is considered feminine in bodies, movement, hair, clothes, voice, skin, emotion, and ambition. Brownmiller asks whether this ever-changing roster makes women feel inadequate.

Singer, L. *Stages: the Crises that Shape Your Marriage*. New York: Grosset & Dunlap, 1980. What happens when a marriage hits a crisis? Patterns of crises and responses are presented in this book.

Tennov, D. *Love and Limerence: the Experience of Being in Love*. Briarcliff Manor, NY: Stein and Day, 1979. This book compares intimacy of people in love and not in love to highlight what a special cultural invention love actually is.

Walster, E.. and Walster, G. W. *A New Look at Love*. Reading, MA: Addison-Wesley, 1978. Two experts tell a coherent story, with good case histories, of the social psychological findings on love and attraction and what they mean in everyday interactions.

FERNAND LÉGER, "TWO MEN." HIRSHHORN MUSEUM AND SCULPTURE GARDEN.

Chapter 14

Homosexuality

In cultures the world over, some men and women choose members of their own sex as sexual partners. In our own society, homosexuals are found in every social class and occupation. Kinsey and his associates estimated that 4 percent of males and 2 to 3 percent of females were exclusively homosexual as adults (1948, 1953). If these percentages hold today, then about 5 million Americans above the age of puberty have chosen sexual partners exclusively of their own sex. This number is equal to or greater than the total population of the United States at the time of the American Revolution.

HOMOSEXUAL ACTS AND HOMOSEXUAL IDENTITY

Whom should we consider a homosexual? In this book, we have used the terms **homosexual** or **gay** to mean either a man or a woman who voluntarily has sex with members of his or her own sex. Other writers use the term "homosexual" to refer only to gay males and the term **lesbian** to refer to gay females. ("Lesbian" derives from the name of the Greek island, Lesbos, an important cultural center in the sixth and seventh centuries B.C. and home of the lyricist, Sappho, whose poetry celebrated love among women.) Should a definition of homosexuality include people who have sex *occasionally, mainly,* or *exclusively* with people of their sex? No matter which standard we choose, we arbitrarily separate people into two groups: homosexual and heterosexual. We ignore degrees of commitment to partners of a given sex and, especially important, how people think of themselves.

Kinsey and his colleagues realized the faults in sorting everyone into two categories of identities, and they proposed that *acts* and *stimuli,* not people, be characterized as heterosexual or homosexual (1948). They drew up a seven-item scale that could locate the proportion of homosexual to heterosexual acts in each person's experience. The scale extends from 0, exclusive heterosexuality, to 6, exclusive homosexuality (see Table 14.1).

But Kinsey's approach ignores how people define themselves. Some people define themselves as homosexual, perhaps proudly and perhaps guiltily, but never with indifference. Some people are labeled by society as homosexual and accorded particular treatment. For these people, the homosexual acts that they perform

TABLE 14.1

Kinsey's Continuum of Sexual Orientation

Scale Point	Description	Males (%)	Females (%)
0	Exclusively heterosexual behavior	52–92	61–90
1	Incidental homosexual behavior	18–42	11–20
2	More than incidental homosexual behavior	13–38	6–14
3	Equal amount of homosexual and heterosexual behavior	9–32	4–11
4	More than incidental heterosexual behavior	7–26	3–8
5	Incidental heterosexual behavior	5–22	2–6
6	Exclusively homosexual behavior	3–16	1–3

may have little direct effect on their lives, but the negative labels they or society bestow may have enormous influence on how they feel about themselves and even on how they behave. When we come to defining our terms, then, we think it is important to distinguish between behavior and identity:

A **homosexual act** is an erotic practice or feeling directed toward a member of the same sex; homosexual acts are common throughout most human culture.

A **homosexual identity** incorporates into one's self-definition the acceptance of an erotic or romantic attraction to a person of one's sex.

One applies the homosexual label to oneself if one has a gay identity; it can not be given directly by society, although society may influence one's adoption of the label.

A homosexual identity is not the absence of a heterosexual identity; it is an active choice.

Homosexual identities are less common than homosexual acts or heterosexual identities.

In this chapter, we will use the label "homosexual" or "gay" for someone who has formed a homosexual identity and the label "heterosexual" for someone who has formed a heterosexual identity.

Under certain circumstances, people may consider homosexual acts to be independent of homosexual identity. For example, in the New Guinea culture of East Bay (see Chapter 1), every young male is expected to have extensive homosexual experience with an older male before he eventually marries a woman. Among adults, heterosexual marriage is considered superior to homosexual pairings, and these do not occur among adult males in their prime. It seems that homosexual identities are never formed in the East Bay cultures. (In contrast, some women in our own western culture are known to define themselves as homosexual, because they are emotionally attached to women, before they have engaged in homosexual acts [Schafer, 1976].) One young historian has offered another example, this one from western culture, of the distinction between homosexual acts and homosexual identity. He has argued that in the permissive atmosphere of Europe before 1100 A.D., homosexual behavior flourished, yet people who were sexually involved with those of their own (as well as the other) sex apparently did not assume homosexual identities (Boswell, 1980).

People usually do not define their identity from a single experience. No one is forever after fated to be homosexual or heterosexual after a particular sexual act. By taking a two-part definition, we can understand the sexual histories of many people who, for example, turn to homosexual acts when they are in sexually segregated situations like military service, sheep or cattle-tending, children's play groups, boarding schools, prison, or at sea. When the sexual segregation ends, most people choose partners of the opposite sex. Few have formed homosexual identities, although they have performed homosexual acts. Homosexual activity that is the product of segregated situations is called **situational homosexuality.**

In humans we may account for some homosexual behavior, but not identities, by our species' mammalian heritage. Higher mammals often require practice before they can copulate successfully. Many young mammals practice with other

SEXUALITY IN PERSPECTIVE: GAY IDENTITY

The poet Adrienne Rich has remarked that the person who names an experience decides how people will see that experience. Nowhere is this more apparent than in the study of homosexuality. Over time, the views of physicians, psychologists, and sexologists change, and we are given new names and new perceptions of sexual behavior and experiences (Foucault, 1980). Some people talk about homosexuality in numbers (as Kinsey did); some talk about it as an orientation; some as a preference. Some (like us) talk about it as an identity.

This chapter explains the real discrepancy between homosexual identity and acts with a homosexual partner. That people's labels for themselves are powerful is attested to by those who identify themselves as gay without having performed a single sexual act with a partner of their own sex. Gay people who marry, have children, and maintain a gay identity produce another kind of discrepancy between act and identity. So do the bisexual women who shift identities, depending on their primary relationship (Blumstein and Schwartz, 1976). Many homosexuals speak of a commitment toward people of their own sex that they do not feel in heterosexual acts (which most gays have experienced).

All of these explanations lead us to choose the term "homosexual identity." We apologize for any confusion of this term with "gender identity." They are different phenomena indeed. *Identity* is a strong word. It's needed for double duty. People feel their core gender identity strongly, and they feel their sexual identity strongly, too.

young mammals of either sex. Among mature animals, homosexual acts can be induced by separating them from the other sex. It is likely that humans share the basic mammalian tendency for widely directed sexual play before puberty.

BISEXUAL ACTS AND IDENTITY

Some people define themselves as **bisexual.** In other words, they are romantically and sexually attracted and committed to members of both sexes. Their sexual fantasies contain images of partners of both sexes (Storms, 1980). As with homosexuality, to understand the distinctly human form of bisexuality, one needs a two-part concept that takes into account the difference between acts and identity. Many people in our society have had bisexual *experience.* The Kinsey group, in studying males, found (1948) that 50 percent of adult males had exclusively heterosexual histories and 4 percent exclusively homosexual histories, leaving 46 percent in the bisexually experienced category. Among single women, 17 percent had bisexual histories (Kinsey et al., 1953). But bisexuality is also a self-selected identity and label, just as homosexuality or heterosexuality are. People may feel that they are bisexual, even though they have had sexual relations with partners of only one sex. Other people, with significant amounts of sexual activity with both sexes, may label themselves either heterosexual or homosexual (Blumstein and Schwartz, 1976). People make active choices when they label their own sexual orientation.

As an interesting complement to Kinsey's one-dimensional scale for categorizing sexual behavior, social psychologist Michael Storms (1980) proposes a two-dimensional scale for sexual desire. The advantage of Storms's model is that it can account more fully for bisexuality. The two-dimensional model proceeds from the premise, borne out by research, that many people have *both* some homosexual desire and some heterosexual desire. Storms categorizes a person's homosexual desire as somewhere between none and high; he does likewise for a person's heterosexual desire. As the matrix in Table 14.2 shows, someone with low homosexual and heterosexual desire is *asexual.* Someone with low heterosexual desire and high homosexual desire is *homosexual.* The reverse pattern characterizes a *heterosexual.* Finally, a person with high heterosexual and homosexual desire is **bisexual.**

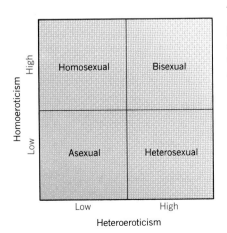

TABLE 14.2

Sexual orientation matrix. When sexual orientation is considered two-dimensional, *bisexuality* describes people with high homosexual and heterosexual interest. *Heterosexuality* describes those with high heterosexual but low homosexual interest. *Homosexuality* describes high homosexual but low heterosexual interest. *Asexuality* describes low sexual interest in general (Storms, 1980, in Mahoney, 1979, p. 314).

Deviance Theory

To understand the transition among humans from homosexual behavior to homosexual identity, we turn to a perspective developed by sociologists that explains how people who deviate from the norms of a society handle their difference. Heterosexuality is still the norm in every human society, despite widespread homosexual activity. Therefore, homosexual activity is **deviant** (from a statistical norm) according to this sociological perspective. Homosexual *behavior* is an example of what sociologists would call **primary deviance.** Primary deviance can occur in many settings and in very incidental fashion, as when teenage boys compete in a "circle jerk" to see who ejaculates first or farthest. If the deviant behavior is considered unimportant, it is likely to pass without consequence to the identity of the person who has engaged in it. But when the person labels the behavior as deviant and comes to consider it as a basis for self-definition, the behavior has become **secondary deviance.** An act has then been elaborated into an identity. In other words, the difference between primary and secondary deviance is the presence or absence of the self-definition of deviance. Secondary deviance can have enormous consequences, because deviants are stigmatized.

Once deviants label themselves, they try to find new norms to deal with the social stigma. They may search for a community that offers these new norms. Among organized homosexuals of both sexes, one of the ways the stigma is fought is by a relabeling of common terms. "Homosexual" or other, insulting terms become "gay" or, less often, "homophile"; "heterosexual" becomes "straight." The gay community also establishes new norms to replace the stigmatizing norms of the straight world. "Gay is good" serves the same purpose for homosexuals that "black is beautiful" serves for blacks: it restores self-worth to people stigmatized by definitions made by the majority. With the support of new norms, a person may firmly establish a valued homosexual identity.

A brief, important digression before we continue. Social scientists have offered various theories—deviance theory, biological and environmental theories (discussed in the "Development of Homosexuality" section of this chapter)—to account for the nature of homosexuality. But some members of the gay community fear that "purely" sociological theories, such as labeling or deviance theories, put gays at a disadvantage in court cases against them. They fear that courts will judge gays as having "chosen" to be homosexual, when gays feel that no such conscious choice has been made. (Gay males and females differ to some extent on this issue of choice.) Some researchers (Whitam, 1981) believe that a biological theory will help courts to be fairer to gays and will help them avoid court judgments that depict gays as failing to "shape up" and become heterosexual. Regardless of the theory that finally best fits the data—the usual basis on which informed people say that they choose among competing theories—social scientists must guard against unwittingly feeding phobias about homosexuality. Modern social scientists so far have not done so for the most part, but the possibility remains open and therefore to be guarded against.

HOMOSEXUALITY AND CULTURAL VALUES

Historically, most cultures have approved of homosexuality, if in a limited way (Ford and Beach, 1951). Even the Judaic tradition, which later established strong antihomosexual moral and legal codes that still exist in the Western world, once encouraged homosexuality. The ancient Hebrews were expected to form religious homosexual liaisons with priests in the era before the Babylonian Exile. The later Jewish tradition, out of which Christianity was born, became more ascetic and restricted sexual behaviors of all types, including homosexual ones.

In ancient Greek civilization, homosexuality was an accepted and desired part of life for men. A close relationship between a man and a boy, perhaps including physical love, was considered an ideal educational experience. Sappho, whom we have mentioned above, was the Greek poet who established a colony of women on the island of Lesbos. Although we do not know whether they practiced homosexuality, we do know that they established a strong sense of sensual feminine identity. **Sapphic love,** the physical or sensual love between women, is named after Sappho. Past and present, we find that most of the world's civilizations have tolerated homosexual relations, at least for part of their population, for part of their lives. No civilization has ever advocated homosexuality as an exclusive substitute for heterosexuality; that civilization would soon die out.

About two-thirds of twentieth-century societies seem tacitly or explicitly to approve of some homosexuality (Ford and Beach, 1951). Homosexuality exists in the great majority of the world's civilizations. It is, in fact, likely that researchers could not find a society in which homosexuality is completely absent, but in societies where it is strongly condemned, the behavior is kept well hidden (Davenport, 1965; Marshall, 1971).

The range of social values concerning homosexuality is very wide. At one pole are peoples like the Siwan of northern Africa, whose males universally engage in homosexuality:

Strong relationships between men were important in ancient Greek society. Some of these relationships were sexual. This scene is from a Greek vase of the fifth century B.C.

This table shows the attitudes of a national sample of Americans towards homosexuality. The sample covers the years 1973 to 1980. The general trend, over time, was towards greater acceptance.

TABLE 14.3

How Americans Feel about Homosexuality, 1973–1980

Attitude	Percentage of National Sample		
	1973	1977	1980
Are sexual relations between two adults of the same sex			
Always wrong	74	72	73
Almost always wrong	9	6	6
Wrong only sometimes	10	8	6
Not wrong at all	15	15	15
Should an admitted homosexual male be allowed to make a speech in your community?			
Yes	63	64	68
No	37	36	32
Should an admitted homosexual man be allowed to teach in a college or university?			
Yes	49	51	59
No	51	49	41

Source: Davis (1980).

Prominent Siwan men lend their sons to each other, and they talk about their masculine love affairs as openly as they discuss their love of women. Both married and unmarried males are expected to have both homosexual and heterosexual affairs (Ford and Beach, 1951).

A Siwan man is regarded as "queer" if he does not have sex with other men. Although homosexuality for women is almost certainly less common around the world, in some societies, such as the Australian Aranda, it is widely distributed.

At the other pole are societies that disapprove of homosexuality and use punishments that range from the rejection of homosexual behavior to the threat of death. Ridicule seems the most common form of negative reaction to homosexuality throughout the world. Ostracism, harassment, and social and economic embarrassment also threaten homosexuals in Western society. **Homophobia** describes an intense dislike of homosexual people and practices, typically in the absence of much information or contact with homosexuals. In our society, people with strict, even rigid, notions about how males and females ought to act are more likely than people with more relaxed actions to be homophobic.

Most Americans dislike or disapprove of homosexuality, attitudes that often go along with little or no contact with people who are gay. Whenever people hold an extremely negative opinion about those they know little of or not at all, some clinical psychologists dub their irrational, uncontrollable fears *phobias*. Irrational fears, unresponsive to accurate information about homosexuality, are dubbed *homophobia*.

Researchers who have compared people with strongly intolerant views of homosexuality to those with tolerant views have found interesting differences between the groups (Larsen, Reed, and Hoffman, 1980; McDonald and Games, 1974). Those in the intolerant group are more likely to view the purpose of sex as procreation, to be active in fundamentalist churches, to live in rural areas, and to view homosexuality as a threat to the family. Members of this group are also likely to have rigid views about what males and females ought to do. In contrast, those in the tolerant group are more likely to be urban, young, educated, to view sex as recreational, and to be less active churchgoers (and not to go to fundamentalist churches if they do go to church). Members of this group are also more likely to have flexible ideas about gender roles.

But to cast one group as the villains in black hats and the other as heroes in white hats is to miss the different world views of the two groups. Those who are for and against legal abortion divide along many of the same issues as those who are tolerant and intolerant of homosexuality (Luker, 1984). The social problem is how to get members of the two groups to hear and talk with each other. Taunts, derision, and violence do *no one* good.

GAY MEN: SEXUAL
AND SOCIAL BEHAVIOR

Our society is rife with stereotypes and misinformation about the sexual and social behavior of homosexual men. As for sexual behavior, most of the body's erotic zones are common to both sexes, and so it is not surprising that many forms of sexual behavior are common to both heterosexual and homosexual acts. Many homosexual encounters among men do not involve penetration with the penis but rely upon fondling, mutual masturbation, femoral coitus (penis between partner's thighs), or genital friction. Oral stimulation of the penis, mutual oral-genital stimulation (colloquially called "69" for the positions of the partners), and anal intercourse do involve penetration by the penis. None of these forms of behavior is foreign to heterosexual encounters (Kinsey et al., 1948). One form of sexual behavior practiced (apparently exclusively) in the world of gay males is **fisting**. Once anal reflexes to penetration are stilled, larger and larger objects can penetrate. Fisting is penetration of the anus with hand or fist, and it is a sexual behavior that invites the testing of limits. Anal fissures and large tears accompany fisting, and these may allow infection to enter the bloodstream. Health leaders in gay male communities have urged men to pay attention to these risks. (AIDS is discussed fully in Chapter 17.) One of the few sexual techniques used far more by male homosexuals than heterosexuals is stimulation of the nipples (Masters and Johnson, 1966).

FIGURE 14.1

The heterosexual stereotypes of the "active" or giving male and the "passive" or receptive female have been so widespread that early investigators of male homosexuality felt obliged to designate one member of a homosexual partnership as the active role player and the other as the passive role player. It was assumed that each gay man preferred one role or the other. The active, giving man was seen as more masculine, and the passive male was seen as less masculine. But most gay men do not fit the stereotypes (Hooker, 1965; McWhirter and Mattison, 1981). Their preferences (like those of heterosexuals) change with different partners and over time. The stereotypes of active and passive only cloud the study of homosexuality.

Another stereotype of homosexual men is that they are extremely promiscuous, that they have sex with many partners to whom they have no deep commitment. Although many homosexual men have many different partners, and although very casual sex appeals to many of them, many other homosexual men are interested in longer lasting and more committed relationships with their sexual partners. They form stable, enduring, monogamous pairs. Yet in studies where the researcher has tried to gather as representative a sample as possible from the gay community (Bell and Weinberg, 1978), it has been found that some, but not all, gay men do have trouble sustaining long-term relationships. Why? First of all, our society firmly opposes the public display of male couples. Except in certain cities with large homosexual populations—San Francisco is the most notable— gay couples are constrained from expressing their attachment in public.

Privileges that members of heterosexual couples take for granted—holding hands publicly, sleeping together when visiting parents, and even such trivialities as family-plan discounts for airline or sports tickets—often are not afforded to homosexual couples. Such pressures undoubtedly jeopardize many relationships. Socializing with colleagues is often a regular part of a job or career, but it is a part often denied to homosexual couples. Many such couples must hide their homosexuality. One prominent New York physician with a long-standing relationship saw it fracture under the weight of the socializing that was required in his job as a public health official but that excluded his male lover (Brown, 1976).

Another reason such relationships founder is because the financial, legal, and childrearing responsibilities that preserve many struggling or otherwise lifeless heterosexual relationships do not operate within gay relationships.

SEXUALITY IN PERSPECTIVE: GAY MALE COUPLES

Many preconceived notions that straight people hold about gay male couples are inaccurate. So say David McWhirter and Andrew Mattison (1984), in their book *The Male Couple: How Relationships Develop*. Among the myths to be exploded, McWhirter and Mattison include the one that says: in a long-term gay male couple, one man assumes the social, sexual, and emotional role of "wife" and the other assumes the role of "husband." From their interviews with more than 150 gay male couples, the authors learned that they assume equal, interchangeable roles. One partner may prefer housework and the other may prefer cooking, and so they divide tasks according to personal preference rather than some nonexistent sexual division of roles.

McWhirter and Mattison have found that gay couples break up sooner than many straight couples. After a year or so, passion may cool. "Gay men lose their passion, infatuation, and romance within one year in many cases." Why? The authors can only speculate. Perhaps it is because there are not any children to keep the partners together. Perhaps it is a matter of self-fulfilling prophecy: the partners never expected their relationship to last. Which gay couples stay together longest? In general, when one partner is at least five years older than the other, the couple is likeliest to stay together. (In the wake of AIDS, many gay couples are likelier to be monogamous than before this scourge visited the gay community. At least so say McWhirter and Mattison on the basis of their sample of 150 gay male couples.)

Like all people in intimate relationships, gay men turn to their partners for emotional sustenance. The sharing and closeness of the gay couple, like those of the straight couple, sustain each partner and strengthen their bonds. Says McWhirter, "What counts most in any relationship, homo- or heterosexual, are the building blocks of shared experiences which lead to trust and tolerance and love."

Based on D. McWhirter and A. Mattison, *The Male Couple: How Relationships Develop*, Englewood-Cliffs, NJ: Prentice-Hall, 1984.

Male couples may separate because women tend to provide most of the bonding power in a relationship. Women, heterosexual or homosexual, may be more likely to preserve a long relationship than men and to preserve it despite sexual or other sorts of difficulties. Women are trained in our culture to view their major occupation as marriage; men are trained to earn a living. Therefore, a homosexual relationship of two men may be inherently less stable than a relationship of two women or of a man and a woman.

A recent development that may have the effect of diminishing promiscuity and reinforcing longer-lasting sexual relationships is **Acquired Immune Deficiency Syndrome (AIDS)**. In San Francisco, with its exceptionally concentrated and politically powerful gay community, warnings about AIDS have cut down on the anonymous, promiscuous sex that used to thrive in public bathhouses, restrooms, and other such popular spots. Although many men have been concerned that the dire warnings about the link between AIDS and gay contacts were promulgated by "sexual fascists" or homophobes, others believe that the changes in behavior forced by fear of AIDS actually will enhance gay men's relationships. Only time will tell. Almost all research on gay men is pre-AIDS.

Meeting Partners

Homosexual men may find partners in many of the ways that heterosexual men conventionally do: through business and professional contacts, through athletics, through mutual friends, through organizations and clubs. But the gay community also has certain specialized institutions that help men meet. Silent, impersonal sexual encounters between men in public places like highway truck stops, restrooms (or "tearooms," described below), or parks typically have a different flavor from private sexual encounters.

The Gay Bar   Any moderately large city is likely to have one or more bars that are focal points for the gay male community. Some gay bars are neighborhood bars where friends can socialize and relax. Other bars cater to a more specialized clientele such as **drones,** slang for gay men who dress in leather and other very masculine fashions, or advocates of **sadomasochism,** or other subgroups in the gay community. Singles bars for heterosexuals bring people together much as gay bars do. Gay bars offer immediately available sex without commitment, but some enduring relationships start in bars as well. Men may initiate contacts through smiles, stares, or drinks. (The gay community has a fairly high incidence of alcoholism, in part a result of so much social life taking place in bars, and counseling is offered to gay alcoholics by some gay community groups.) The interchange may result in sex at either partner's home or in a secluded public place. The partners may spend the night together or separate after sex, perhaps to return to the bars.

The Baths   Steam baths that cater to homosexuals provide quick and anonymous sex. Each bath has a large "general activities" room where men make themselves available for various sexual acts. Small, individual rooms afford more privacy. Men may be considerably less discriminating about their choice of partners in the baths than in the bars, and they may have sex with a number of partners during the course of an evening. The baths also may provide a place for entertainment,

"Cruising" in New York's Greenwich Village.

and some celebrities of the straight world got their start entertaining in the gay baths. A few clubs for heterosexuals are beginning to approximate the range of sexual activities available in the steam baths.

TEAROOMS   Public toilets provide the least complicated and most direct route to impersonal sex for men. Toilets known to the homosexual community as centers of homosexual activity are called **"tearooms."** There are no heterosexual equivalents to tearooms.

Laud Humphries studied (1970) the patrons of a park restroom that was a popular tearoom (as we described in Chapter 2, "Sexuality in Perspective: Observing the Tearoom Trade"). Elaborate rules of decorum hold sway in the tearoom. Men are almost never approached, unless they make their sexual intentions clear. Juveniles are rigorously excluded from the practices. Words are rare; the tearoom trade runs smoothly on gestures and unspoken understandings. It is completely anonymous, and the dominant activity is fellatio. Humphries once witnessed 20 acts of fellatio in one hour in a single restroom. Another researcher interviewed a man who had fellated 17 men consecutively and remembered none of them (Delph, 1978).

Who is in the tearoom trade? Humphries directly interviewed the men in their homes a year after he had observed them. Fifty-four percent of the men were married and living with their wives and children. One regular at the tearoom, a physician in his late fifties, visited the tearoom punctually every day (except for Wednesdays) for fellatio. The tearoom routine was segregated from the rest of his heterosexual life, which consisted of a long, stable marriage and grown children, but it was still a regular feature of his existence. Another heterosexually (self-) labeled man used the tearoom as an outlet for sexual frustrations caused by the periodic abstentions required by the method of birth control he and his wife used. The man considered visiting the tearoom an acceptable alternative to "cheating" on his wife with other women.

OTHER PUBLIC PLACES   Most large cities have particular areas, such as parts of parks, where gay men congregate in search of sex. Some beaches have gay areas, and some vacation spots are gay in season and straight out of season. Cruising (searching for a partner) in public areas may be similar to the meetings in gay bars, or the partners may have sex in a public spot. Anonymous partners can be dangerous; gay men are beaten and robbed more often than they report to police. The gay community tries to function as a network for maintaining safety and warning gays of such dangers. Sex in public places is a violation of the law that says sexual acts should be private. The public act therefore may increase risks—and arousal—just as sex with a stranger may do.

HUSTLERS   Not all gay men can find partners when they want to. The premium on youth in the gay community can mean that some homosexual men have trouble attracting the young men they desire. They may therefore resort to exchanging money for sex. Young male **hustlers** (male prostitutes), who are called "trade," flourish in the gay community and may operate in bars, baths, or public places. They usually assume the receiving role in fellatio and evince no pleasure or affection in their business relations. Many hustlers do not think of themselves as homosexual and maintain that they have homosexual relations only for the money. Among gay men, however, the contrary view is sometimes expressed: "Today's trade is tomorrow's competition." (John Rechy's haunting novel, *City of Night,* [1963] is an excellent fictional portrayal of a male hustler's life.)

GENDER ROLE IN MALE HOMOSEXUALS

Most men with homosexual identities have firm gender identities as males. They do not wish to be females, and they do not look like females. Contrary to stereotype, not all male homosexuals are feminine (and not all feminine men are homosexual). Gay men generally find masculinity attractive and femininity less attractive in their partners. Obviously or exaggeratedly masculine characteristics like broad shoulders and narrow hips or a large penis are valued in most of the gay world (Rechy, 1963; Tripp, 1975).

A man in drag.

SEXUALITY IN CONTROVERSY:
LESBIAN MOTHERS AND CHILDREN'S GENDER IDENTITY

Many lesbians have children. Because the problem of whether lesbians are "fit" mothers has been brought into so many courtrooms, it would be especially helpful if data were available to answer the question. When the decision has not evolved out of an automatic assumption that lesbian mothers are automatically unworthy of keeping their children, the court has asked whether lesbians can rear children to be heterosexual. Although everyone knows that most homosexuals, male and female, came from heterosexual parents, the reverse is indeed a different question.

Three studies, all well designed, two done in the San Francisco area, can now give us at least a provisional answer about the school-aged children of lesbian mothers. (Older children can be questioned directly on gender issues by the court. No data on adolescent children raised by gay parents are available.) The studies tell us that for children between 5 and 12, gender identity is like that of most other children their age. Matched groups of children of lesbian mothers and children of single heterosexual mothers (the mothers themselves matched for age and education) prefer similar toys. There are no differences in gender identities between the two groups of children; boys in both groups prefer "boy things" and girls, "girl things" (Hoeffer, 1981). When the evaluation techniques are even more sophisticated (intelligence and inkblot tests; human figure drawings; and psychiatric interview, conducted in a playroom, about childhood memories, plans for the future, and gender-related interests), and when the study is *double blind*— neither interviewers nor scorers of data know the mothers' sexual orientation— then no significant differences in gender identity turn up between children of lesbians and children of heterosexual mothers (Kirkpatrick, Smith, and Roy, 1981).

These studies may make a difference. Courts have awarded lesbian mothers custody of younger children, typically in cases where fathers do not contest custody. Where there is a contest, lesbian mothers do not have an easy time.

Based on Hoeffer, B. "Children's Acquisition of Sex-Role Behavior in Lesbian-Mother Families," *American Journal of Orthopsychiatry,* 1981, 51, pp. 536–544; Hotvedt, M., Green, R., and Mandel, J. "The Lesbian Parent: Comparison of Heterosexual and Homosexual Mothers and Children," *Archives of Sexual Behavior,* 1986, in press; Kirkpatrick, M., Smith, C., and Roy, R. "Lesbian Mothers and Their Children: A Comparative Survey, *American Journal of Orthopsychiatry,* 1981, 51, pp. 545–551.

Only within a few gay subcultures—some in Latin America—is femininity considered erotic. In the United States, men are most likely to affect feminine behavior (if ever they do) right after they have **come out,** that is, have accepted a homosexual identity. However, the feminine behavior often subsides as the gay identity solidifies (Gagnon and Simon, 1973). Some gay men use feminine pronouns or names to refer to peers or outsiders ("she," "Mary"), often humorously, sometimes cruelly. Gender stereotyping is the subject of dirty jokes, artful digs, and faithful mimicry among gay entertainers.

A minority of gay men are **transvestites,** that is, take sexual pleasure from dressing in women's clothing. (Most transvestites are not homosexual. For more on transvestism, see Chapter 15.) Homosexual men who habitually dress as women are known as **drag queens.** They may pass as stylish, attractive women or parody the role with great humor. The movie and play, *La Cage Aux Folles,* capture that parody well in sympathetically presenting the dilemma of an aging drag queen. The dilemma is funny to gays, not only because of the gender incongruity, but because in truth it is a dilemma common among older heterosexual women who want to stay young and attractive.

GAY WOMEN: SEXUAL AND SOCIAL BEHAVIOR

Although lesbianism is more widely accepted around the world than male homosexuality (Ford and Beach, 1951), the lesbian must nonetheless defy social norms. Her place in the world may be just as shaky as the male homosexual's. She may be excluded from employment by the same rules and social pressures that limit the male homosexual's opportunities. Many lesbians have children from previous marriages. Although there are no laws that explicitly say that lesbians may not have custody of their children, lesbians may be legally declared "unfit mothers" and lose their children for no reason other than their sexual orientation. (See "Sexuality in Controversy: Lesbian Mothers and Children's Gender Identity" for more on this issue.)

Some people believe—wrongly—that lesbian relationships are somehow asexual because no penile penetration is involved.

Some people believe—wrongly—that lesbian relationships are somehow asexual because no penile penetration is involved. Kinsey and his colleagues (1953) found that lesbians actually had a higher rate of orgasm during each sexual contact than did a comparable sample of married women. People can better arouse a partner when they know what pleases that partner, and it may be easier to know what a partner of one's own sex will find arousing. Lesbians have developed sexual acts that others might call "foreplay" to a height unknown to most heterosexuals. The preferred pace of sexual stimulation for women is generally more steady and leisurely than that of men. (Masters and Johnson have found [1979] that homosexual pairs of both sexes rush less to climax than do heterosexual pairs.) Lesbian

FIGURE 14.2

relationships typically involve considerable body contact, caressing, and kissing. These techniques may complete the sexual repertoire of some lesbian pairs for a considerable time, perhaps years (Kinsey et al., 1953; Saghir and Robins, 1973). Most of the lesbian techniques resemble **sensate focus** and "pleasuring," the foundations of modern sex therapies.

Most lesbians do ultimately move on to breast and genital stimulation in their lovemaking (Kinsey et al., 1953; Saghir and Robins, 1973). Both manual and oral stimulation may be used as they are in heterosexual foreplay. Most genital manipulation is confined to the clitoris, labia minora, and the entrance of the vagina. Penetration of the vagina or anus does not seem to be centrally important in fact or fantasy for lesbian pairs, although penetration with **dildoes,** or penis substitutes, may be important to some pairs. Lesbians do not share the strong genital focus of male homosexuals or heterosexuals. Actually, lesbian sexual practices do not seem especially different from what heterosexual women find most pleasing in their sexual relationships.

Early reports on lesbian pairs divided the women into two types: the male-role player, or the "butch," and the female-role player, or the "femme." Butches were to wear masculine clothing, act in masculine fashion, and make the sexual advances. Femmes were to wear feminine clothing, act in feminine fashion, and be sexually passive. Indeed, some lesbians adopted such stereotyped exaggerations of the heterosexual pattern. Stereotyped choices are often made in response to social expectation rather than to personal choice. One lesbian told interviewers about her initial search for a role as a lesbian:

> *I would ask people, "What do you think? Am I butch or am I femme?" Some would say I looked femme and acted butch; others would say I looked butch and acted femme. Because I couldn't be typed, I was always looked on with suspicion and sometimes believed to be a policeman (Abbot and Love, 1972).*

Although some lesbians have adopted some male mannerisms, lesbians generally have feminine gender identities. Many of the younger lesbians in the United States are trying to break out of butch-femme role stereotypes in their relationships. The desire to release sexual and romantic partners from the arbitrary, restrictive patterns that have evolved in our culture is not limited to homosexuals but seems to be a new general trend in our society, sparked in part by the women's movement.

It could be argued that the masculine behaviors of some lesbians are traces of their probable histories as tomboys. In other words, most lesbians (two out of three) report having been tomboys as children, but so have many heterosexual women (one out of six) (Saghir and Robins, 1973). Many more tomboys become heterosexual than homosexual. Most lesbians, whether they have been tomboys or not, experience the heterosexual patterns of dating and sexual relations. A great many have children. Thus most lesbians have shared with heterosexual women the typical social-sexual history of females in our society. It is therefore difficult to maintain that lesbianism arises from a simple confusion of gender identity or gender role (Blumstein and Schwartz, 1976; Saghir and Robins, 1973; Schafer, 1976).

As we noted above, relationships between homosexual women last longer, in general, than those between homosexual men. In a large San Francisco study conducted in 1970, the dominant living arrangement of gay women was described as **close coupled**, or stable, monogamous pairs (Bell and Weinberg, 1979). Such

Like other women, lesbians invest their relationships with affection.

relationships may last because of women's greater bonding abilities (whether these abilities are biologically or socially based) or because social interference in relationships between two women is less pronounced than it is for two men. Probably as a result of this difference, lesbians have fewer sexual partners than male homosexuals. Their social networks do not converge on gay bars as much as male homosexuals' social networks do, although there are lesbian bars. The general unpopularity of quick, anonymous sex among lesbians—as among other women, too—has prevented the development of baths or tearooms in the lesbian community. (Some baths do have "women's nights.") The social science literature suggests that lesbian women are more like all other women than they are like any group of men, homosexual or heterosexual. Lesbians are like other women in the affection they invest in relationships, the duration of these relationships, and in their attitudes toward sexual fidelity. If women in general change their views, lesbians are likely to do so (Peplau et al., 1978). Like gay women, gay men in closed, exclusive pairs differ from those in open pairs. Gay men in closed pairs have more concern than those in open pairs about issues of jealousy. Open couples are more concerned about variety. Most open and closed pairs have relationships on the side, though the number is smaller among closed couples. Such pre-AIDS findings reflect the presence of similarities and differences among gay men (Blasband and Peplau, 1985).

BISEXUALITY

Because we have no studies on the incidence of bisexual identification, we can only speculate on trends in bisexual identification and behavior. One sex researcher, Wardell Pomeroy, has estimated the number of people interested in the active bisexual life at about 5 percent of the population. But this number probably waxes and wanes with certain social trends. For instance, as the stigma of homosexuality diminishes, more people might translate their feelings for friends of their own sex into active sexual relationships. The effect of this trend would be to increase the incidence of bisexual behavior without necessarily increasing the incidence of bisexual identification. In addition, as stigmatization diminishes, and homosexuals move from exclusively homosexual social circles, the incidence of bisexual experience may increase (Gould, 1974). Some homosexuals may choose to relabel themselves bisexual after heterosexual contact. In contrast, one trend that could decrease the number of people who consider themselves bisexual is pressure from gay movement counselors to have bisexuals redefine themselves as homosexuals. In short, as social attitudes toward homosexuality change, bisexuality will also be affected. The effects are more likely to show up on behavior than on identity. If bisexuality means an equal commitment to men and women, then the number of bisexuals is unlikely to increase very fast. But labeling oneself as bisexual is not just a matter of having both male and female sexual partners. Women with these sexual experiences sometimes label themselves by which sex partner they are currently seeing. One woman considered herself not bisexual, just not discriminatory! (Blumstein and Schwartz, 1976; Coleman, 1985; Dixon, 1985.) Recent work on married, bisexual men suggests that where major problems arise they concern the issue of the open marriage and the issue of the husband's sexual identity (Brownfain, 1985; Coleman, 1985; Gochros, 1985; Matteson, 1985; Wolf, 1985).

THE GAY MOVEMENT

Minorities that are socially ostracized and deprived of legal rights may ultimately organize to advance their cause, to right wrongs, and to socialize openly. Gay men and women are no exception. Although the cause of homosexual rights has a long history, the movement began to show its effectiveness in the 1950s. The gay rights groups provide many services, including legal advice, consciousness raising, and psychological counseling. Many groups sponsor publications, provide meeting places, and promote public marches.

Gay organizations have remained largely segregated by sex. The largest gay male organization in the United States is the Society for Individual Rights (S.I.R.), which is based in San Francisco. The Mattachine Society, another large gay male organization, modeled itself on civil rights groups. In 1969 the more militant Gay Liberation Front was organized in response to a brutal, "routine" police raid on a New York Greenwich Village gay bar, the Stonewall Inn. Gay liberation groups have also appeared on college campuses. The largest lesbian organization is the Daughters of Bilitis, which was founded in San Francisco in the 1950s as a social club. The group has since become concerned with providing legal and social support. Lesbian groups tend to be active in the women's movement.

Catholic gay men and women demonstrate for acceptance of homosexuality within their religion. Protestant and Jewish gays also have demonstrated.

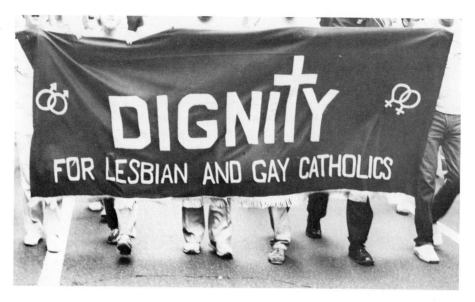

The range of political and religious opinions among homosexuals probably mirrors that of the heterosexual world. Nevertheless, gay groups in large cities like San Francisco or Boston control enough votes that local candidates seek their endorsement. Dianne Feinstein was elected mayor of San Francisco in part because of her willingness to deal with gay politicians and their supporters. San Francisco is unusual in the large size and strong organization of its gay community. Many religious homosexuals have been reluctant to abandon the religions that often have rejected them. Some religious homosexuals have pushed for acceptance of homosexuality in their own religions. One such group among Catholics is "Dignity." Some homosexuals remain within their religion but seek segregated, homosexual congregations. Some Jewish organizations and Protestant denominations have accepted such congregations, but highly centralized church authorities in the Presbyterian and Episcopalian churches have not. Gay couples have tried to get their relationships legitimized as marriage. A pair of Minnesota men went to court to achieve that end, but they lost. Such couples have legitimate fears about their unrecognized status costing them inheritances, houses, and other possessions willed to them by a homosexual partner. The legal solution to this dilemma is a well-drawn legal contract, with two lawyers, one for each party to the agreement (Weitzman, 1981).

THE DEVELOPMENT OF HOMOSEXUALITY

How do people come to think of themselves as homosexual (or heterosexual, for that matter)? Are we born predisposed by our genes to one sexual orientation or another, or do we learn to love our own sex in the social situations that envelop us when we are young? Which factors, if any, appear in the early lives of homosexuals and bear on the creation of a homosexual identity? Most researchers have looked for the answers to questions about the origins of homosexuality in the environment rather than in biology. We will look at both sets of theories.

Environmental Theories

One place to look for the beginnings of homosexuality is in a child's early sexual experiences, for what one learns early in life often has lasting effects. We acquire our tastes for certain food and music, for example, early in life. One tenet of developmental psychology is that early learning can be very powerful. It seems only common-sensical that the powerful rewards of sex with someone—whether of the same sex or not—might lead a person to choose later sexual partners of the early partner's sex. But sexual orientation cannot be simply ascribed to early sexual contacts. For example, in the East Bay cultures of New Guinea, young boys are initiated into sex by men but ultimately form heterosexual marriages. In our own culture, 60 percent of prepubescent boys and 33 percent of prepubescent girls have participated in some form of same-sex play (Elias and Gebhard, 1969), yet very few of them identify themselves as homosexual when they are adults. Much of that activity is exploratory, "horsing around," or social comparison.

Another possibility is that unpleasant sexual experiences in childhood or adolescence act as powerful deterrents (Feldman and MacCollough, 1971). Not only homosexuals but heterosexuals, too, often report terrible early sexual experiences. Thus although many people have unpleasant sexual experiences, many try again repeatedly. The histories of homosexuals and heterosexuals do not differ significantly in this way (Bell, Weinberg, and Hammersmith, 1979).

The history of many homosexual women affirms the lack of connection between early sexual experience and adult sexual orientation. Many women adopt bisexual or homosexual identities only after years of exclusive heterosexuality and, often, unhappy marriages (Bell, Weinberg, and Hammersmith, 1979; Saghir and Robins, 1973; Schafer, 1976). In many cases then, early homosexual play is neither necessary nor sufficient to determine adult homosexual identity. But a retrospective study of 2835 male students in Germany (Giese and Schmidt, cited in Schmidt, 1978) leads to a different conclusion—at least for that segment of the sample that had had extensive homosexual experience as boys. About 10 times as many of these students had homosexual contacts as adults as did students who reported no homosexual contacts in boyhood. No one can determine whether their extensive early homosexual experience was satisfying to those students and therefore led them to continue it past puberty or whether some kind of homosexual orientation was manifesting itself early in life. No one can rule out that gay men *recalled* their homosexual experiences better than other men did, because they felt less pressured to repress their childhood memories, or that they restructured their memories to fit better with their present lives. But regardless of the interpretation, the German study is a warning against the automatic application of conclusions drawn from the experience of one sex to the other. It is also a warning against equating children's exploratory, not necessarily extensive, same-sex play with same-sex play that is extensive. The German study provides more questions than answers.

Clinicians have used the sex of the partners fantasized about in adolescence and adulthood as the best clue to a person's sexual orientation. But recent data (Schwartz and Masters, 1984) suggest that the issue is not so clear-cut. Although gay men and women fantasize more about people of their own sex, they also fantasize about people of the other sex. Heterosexual men and women report just the opposite: most have fantasies about the other sex but some about their own sex. But no one yet knows the origins of these sexual fantasies. Some clinicians believe that homosexual identities may be fostered by childhood experiences other than exploratory sex play. Most environmental theories of homosexuality have looked to the relationship of parents and child (rather than the relationship of child and peers). The most influential of these theories derives from psychoanalysis.

PSYCHOANALYTIC VIEWS Sigmund Freud's clinical observations of homosexual patients led him to believe that homosexuality originated in a complex relationship between the biological processes of development and the experiences of life. His theory was essentially as follows: Newborns have a bisexual nature and respond with full pleasure to any erotic stimulation, regardless of the sex of the person stimulating them. Psychosexual development restricts the stimulators and forms of stimulation to a socially acceptable few. Shaping is accomplished by loosely programmed biological events that can be reinforced—or opposed—by those who care for the child. Finally, the nature of the erotic object (male or female) remains a matter of choice. The needs served by a homosexual choice are not necessarily explicitly sexual.

How did Freud account for a homosexual's development? He believed that homosexuality is an arrest, or stoppage, at the stage before heterosexual development. What accounts for such an arrest? A dominant mother, Freud believed, who fosters an unusually strong bond with her son and at the same time rejects his father may influence her son's sexual relationships. A young boy must want and be able to be like and identify with his father, in order to move on to heterosexual relations. For this reason, too strong a struggle by a son against his father—who is perceived as the boy's rival for his beloved mother's love—can lead the son to reject the father's heterosexual role as a woman's lover. Freud studied the origins of female homosexuality less, a neglect that characterized the social science literature in general until recently. Freud loosely applied his theories, based on males, to females.

Freud saw many factors as influencing the homosexual choice, some biological. Contemporary psychoanalysts have focused on only one approach to homosexuality (see following section) and have ignored most of the others. Few social scientists today hold a narrow psychoanalytic view of homosexual development.

THE FAMILY PATTERN HYPOTHESIS There is no doubt that psychosexual development can be affected by a child's interactions with the world. Many important factors in the establishment of gender identity begin to exert their influence after birth. (See Chapter 3 for a full discussion of how gender identity develops.) Usually parents and peers show approval of behavior considered acceptable for a child's gender and disapproval for behavior considered unacceptable. But do some families "teach" homosexuality to children by relaxing the early training in gender roles?

The evidence for a particular family pattern being associated with homosexuality is found in a study performed by a group of psychoanalysts on their male patients (Bieber et al., 1962, 1976). The patients were divided into two groups. The H-group had a homosexual orientation; the comparison group, the C group, had a heterosexual orientation. The patients' therapists made the comparisons between the two groups and completed a 450-item questionnaire on the patients' past relationships to their parents and their current adaptations. From these answers, Bieber and his colleagues formed a profile of the family patterns among many homosexual patients:

The outstanding characteristics of these mothers was an extraordinary intimacy with their H-sons. Pathological sexual attitudes and behavior were frequently expressed, covertly or subtly, and constituted central aspects of the relationship. The CBI (close-binding-intimate) H-mother exerted a binding influence on her son through preferential treatment and seductiveness on the one hand, and inhibiting, overcontrolling attitudes on the other. In many instances, the son was the most significant individual in her life, and the husband was usually replaced by the son as her love object.

About 30 percent of the heterosexuals and 70 percent of the homosexuals had CBI mothers. Homosexual patients more frequently reported fathers who were hostile, detached, and rejecting than did heterosexual patients. However, not all homosexuals had both CBI mothers and hostile-detached fathers, or even one such parent. Some heterosexuals had one or both of these types of parents.

The Bieber study is marred by two significant flaws. First, the men were all analytic patients (including the control group). Thus they were not representative of either heterosexual or homosexual men. Second, the information on the childhood family patterns was reconstructed by therapists. Even if their reconstructions were accurate, an open question, their findings may apply only to men disturbed enough to seek psychoanalysis. When the Bieber study was redone with men sampled who were not in therapy and who themselves answered the questions, the results were similar to those from the Bieber study (Evans, 1969). It is possible, however, that these men were disturbed although not in therapy (Hooker, 1969). In the only study that actually excluded subjects who were overtly disturbed, homosexual men rated their parents as equivalent and rated them positively (Greenblatt, 1966). How the subjects were selected seems to have been a factor in determining the results.

An early history of disturbed relations with one's parents is probably not a sufficient explanation for homosexuality in men. Could early gender roles somehow be a better lead than the complex family dramas depicted by psychoanalysts? Although gender roles are shared ideas about how males and females "should" behave, not all men or women are alike. The reason that most people slip into gender roles so easily is that the latitude in fit is fairly—though not infinitely— wide. But for some people, that latitude is not enough. A six-year-old boy who wants to wear a wig to school or a six-year-old girl who cuts off all her hair to look like a boy is not likely to avoid notice by other children. The boy and the girl are making statements about their gender identities. Are they *automatically* to be considered prehomosexual? No.

GENDER ROLES   One variant on the learning hypothesis is that as boys, gay men found themselves on the fringes of peer groups (Tripp, 1975). Isolated from other boys, these prehomosexual boys eroticized their powerful, forbidden peers: the unknown and the desirable were transformed into the erotic. This hypothesis is provocative, for two out of three gay men report having been considered a "sissy" at some point. Yet the hypothesis does not seem to describe the origins of female homosexuality. Although two out of three gay women report having been tomboys, they were not shunned by other girls. Tripp, who suggested this learning hypothesis, does not believe that gay women are eroticized in the same way as gay men are. Thus he does not try to extend his hypothesis to the development of female homosexuality.

Few homosexuals have distorted core gender identities; as we have seen, most are well within the limits our society prescribes for gender roles. But some individuals may come to a homosexual identity through a particular set of early childhood experiences. Investigators have studied young boys who show traits that **transsexual** and some homosexual men have reported in their own childhoods. Often these boys say that they *are* or want to be girls. These feminine boys dress in women's clothing, most before the age of four. Feminine boys selected girls more often as early childhood playmates and were not accepted by other boys (Green, 1977). Boys who want to be girls usually become not transsexual, but homosexual in identity (Money and Russo, 1981). It should be noted that some studies of male homosexuals who did *not* display childhood or adult feminine behavior also found that they report poor early social interaction with other boys (Grellert, Newcomb, and Bentler, 1982; Saghir and Robins, 1973). In one study, boys who were gender-disturbed and dressed as girls avoided rough-and-tumble play and sports generally. The feminine boys preferred girls' toys to boys'. In fantasy play, they usually adopted the role of "mother" or other female roles that are studiously avoided by most boys in our culture. Finally, in psychological tests that tap gender roles, feminine boys' scores were remarkably similar to girls' scores.

We do not know exactly what leads feminine boys to begin acting feminine, although Richard Green did identify (1986) certain critical experiences that reinforced feminine behavior in some of his subjects once that behavior appeared. Some boys were not discouraged from practicing feminine behavior. In a few cases, a family member encouraged feminine behavior by photographing the boys in women's clothing, wigs, and makeup and mounting the photographs in the family album. Some (but not all) mothers also overprotected their sons and helped them to avoid rough play. In sum, adults may support cross-gender role and identity, but feminine boys may be particularly responsive to that support. Lots of families fight the cross-dressing, to no avail (Zuger, 1966). Parents of feminine boys report that their sons show unusual abilities in play-acting and role-taking, different reports indeed from those offered by parents of masculine boys.

Is there a link between acting highly feminine in boyhood and acting homosexual in adulthood? In three studies that followed a total of 27 feminine boys from childhood through adolescence or beyond, half emerged as homosexual, heterosexual transvestite, or transsexual adults (Lebovitz, 1972; Money and Green, reported in Green, 1974; Zuger, 1966). That is a substantially higher proportion than those three groups combined represent in the general population. A similar result has appeared in recent work by Richard Green (1986). Building on the three smaller studies of the 27 feminine boys, Green tracked a group of 55 boys with the same early feminine behavior as well as a comparison group of nonfeminine boys matched with the feminine boys on every possible demographic and family variable. The boys are now young men, and, based on the part of the group interviewed as adults, the feminine boys are about four times as likely to be gay or bisexual than to be heterosexual. All of the boys in the comparison group have become heterosexual. One feminine boy became transsexual. Despite the childhood cross-dressing, no boy became a transvestite.

Green has a powerful case for the conclusion that cross-dressing feminine boys are twice as likely to become homosexual, transvestite, or bisexual as heterosexual. The reverse conclusion—that homosexuals and bisexuals are, at childhood root, feminine—is far from warranted by the evidence. Underlining the possible complexity of the route from childhood to adult sexual orientation is Green's research group's finding (Williams, Green, and Goodman, 1985) that intensely *masculine* little girls are not distinguishable from their matched controls at puberty. Female sexual orientation takes longer to ascertain than male, however, and steps in reaching a homosexual identity are not the same for men and women (Shafer, 1978). But the major difference in life course for feminine males and super-tomboys is that the girls are not punished by other girls. Boys are. If feminine boys found a comfortable place in male peer groups, would they end up like the other boys in sexual orientation? No one knows, for boys typically isolate feminine boys.

Conflicts about gender *identity* are not reported by homosexuals as primary reasons for homosexuality. But conflict about gender *roles* is beginning to look central. When researchers at the Kinsey Institute tested out all hypotheses about the origins of homosexuality by comparing men's and women's responses to 200 questions on their sexual histories, both homosexual and heterosexual, the only significant difference between homosexuals and heterosexuals was that homosexuals described themselves as feeling or being nonconforming about gender, alienated from the gender roles they were supposed to play from childhood on (Bell, Weinberg, and Hammersmith, 1981). Gender nonconformity applies to feelings as well as behavior. It does not mean that all gay men avoided athletics as boys or that all gay women avoided playing with girls. But gays report that they *felt* different from others of their sex. Discomfort with aspects of gender role must be widely distributed among heterosexuals as well as gays. Perhaps gays remember those feelings better, given their sexual orientation as adults.

Despite any such feelings, there are probably many more masculine than feminine-looking homosexuals; many feminine-looking boys are heterosexual adults; and some feminine boys even become masculine homosexuals. The questions being asked are about the origins of homosexual identity; the questions of masculinity or femininity of demeanor need not have the same answers.

Biological Theories

Some early researchers proposed that homosexuality and transsexualism might be caused by a particular set of genes or abnormality of chromosomes. But there is no convincing evidence for this theory. Other researchers proposed that homosexual behavior might arise when levels of sex hormones are atypical in adulthood. Because male homosexuals were considered insufficiently masculine, the question was whether their levels of male hormones (androgens) were too low. Similarly, because female homosexuals were considered insufficiently feminine and overly masculine, the question was whether they had too little estrogen or too much androgen. Data on hormones do not support these theories. Such simplistic theories can no longer be defended. When male homosexuals are given supplements of male hormones, they not only do not become heterosexual, they may become more easily aroused by another male. The levels of male hormones in blood and urine do not differ in groups of male homosexuals and heterosexuals (see Meyer-Bahlburg, 1977, for an excellent review of this literature). Fewer studies have compared the androgen levels of female homosexuals and heterosexuals, but consistent hormonal differences of any sort have not turned up (Meyer-Bahlburg, 1978; 1984).

Despite the lack of a simple biological correlate to homosexuality, many investigators and many gays (especially men) believe in a biological model for the origins of homosexuality. One line of reasoning presented in a volume by a gay task force is: prenatal hormonal events indirectly program how individuals will respond to some events in childhood. Aspects of personality like activity level, energy expenditure, and fearfulness are probably hormonally influenced. These kinds of behavior may be important in gender role assumption. Failure to feel at ease in one's gender role and preference for cross-gender play go along with erotic attraction to people of one's own gender in childhood and before puberty (Paul et al., 1982; Whitam, 1977, 1981). The outcome of this path in adulthood is homosexual orientation.

Unfortunately, *direct* biological testing of this hypothesis on humans would be ethically impossible (see Sigusch et al., 1982). Work with animals, where male and female sexual *behavior* is clear and different, cannot provide an adequate model of homosexual *identity* (Beach, 1977). Some social scientists in the male gay community have informally endorsed a hormonal hypothesis (Paul et al., 1982), and gay men increasingly have accepted this hypothesis. Many gay women, however, see *their* sexual preference as a less biologically driven choice. Findings based on memories of childhood are not inevitably true reflections of childhood events. "Memories" are susceptible to later reconstruction, especially when people share a theory about childhood determinants of later sexuality. (This tendency occurs not just among gays, of course, but among virtually all people who try to recall how childhood events affected development. Life is less orderly than our theories would make it.) The hormonal theory may hold some truths, but inventive new ways of testing it will be needed. Green's large sample and longitudinal evidence from early boyhood to early adulthood are very powerful, for childhood events in his study are known to be true, but his sample of cross-dressers is not representative of all male homosexuals.

Follow-up studies of females exposed prenatally to male hormones and males prenatally exposed to female hormones test a biological hypothesis (see Chapter 3). Preliminary results have not supported any *simple* biological hypothesis for females (Money and Mathews, 1982). A small sample of prenatally androgenized females has recently turned up about 1 in 4 bisexual or gay by their mid 20s (Money and Schwartz, 1977; Money et al., 1984). Some of these girls have trouble navigating friendship and romance in early adolescence.

A more common test of prenatal hormonal error as a cause of homosexuality would be an investigation of brain differences between homosexuals and heterosexuals. We cannot directly observe prenatal sex hormones' effects on the human brain, but we can see residues of their earlier presence or absence in normal adult physiology. In the adult woman, during the early follicular phase of the menstrual cycle (see Chapter 9), rising levels of the hormone estrogen provoke a two-phase response in the secretion of the pituitary hormone **luteinizing hormone (LH)**. First LH decreases and then increases sharply. In virtually all men studied, only one phase in response to exogenous estrogen has been found—a brief decrease in LH. This phenomenon has been taken to mean that the male brain is not programmed prenatally for the second phase, the increase in LH necessary for menstrual cycling. Hormonal tests such as these are done by priming males with estrogen, to reproduce the mounting estrogen levels in females before the rise in LH.

Investigators (Gladue, Green, and Hellman, 1984) gave single injections of an estrogen to men and women and measured their LH secretions. Some of the men were exclusively heterosexual, and some were exclusively homosexual. All were healthy, drug free, and free of other factors known to affect normal hormone responses. The results were interesting (see Figure 14.3). The LH response of the homosexual men was intermediate between the heterosexual men's and women's, and it included the rise in LH. The investigators also looked at testosterone responses to the estrogen injections. The homosexual men's testosterone decrease from the estrogen injection lasted significantly longer than did the heterosexual men's, even though the initial testosterone levels were virtually identical. The work on the LH burst among homosexuals grew out of work on male animals given hormones at critical periods of development. German work comparing heterosexual, homosexual, and bisexual men seemed to support the animal work (Dorner et al., 1975).

Work on the LH response is an effort to trace adult homosexuality to prenatal organizing hormones acting on the brain. But behavioral endocrinologists find that LH response in non-human primates reflects adolescent and adult hormones, not prenatal hormones. Highly feminine androgen-insensitive XY females show LH suppression—just like the heterosexual males—after estrogen priming (see Meyer-Bahlburg, 1984). Researchers are likely to continue to search for biological causes of homosexuality in prenatal masculinization and defeminization.

Conflicting evidence comes from male-to-female transsexuals and from bisexuals. Endocrinologists at Tufts University tested a small sample of women interested in a sex change but not yet taking male hormones (a usual preliminary step to sex change surgery) (Seyler et al., 1978). One group of the women appeared to have a masculine-like LH burst, and another did not (Seymour Reichlin, personal communication). Bisexual men, whose hormone responses might be expected to be intermediate between homosexual and heterosexual men's responses, did have the same LH drop as heterosexual men but *less* of a rise (Dorner et al., 1975). The work on LH intrigues researchers of homosexuality. As for conclusions, past work on hormones and homosexuality cautions us to await replications of the studies.

FIGURE 14.3

Responses to hormone injections. This graph shows the luteinizing hormone (LH) responses to estrogen injections in three groups of subjects (12 female heterosexuals, 14 male homosexuals, and 17 male heterosexuals). The response of the male homosexuals were intermediate between those of female and male heterosexuals (Gladue, Green, and Hellman, 1984).

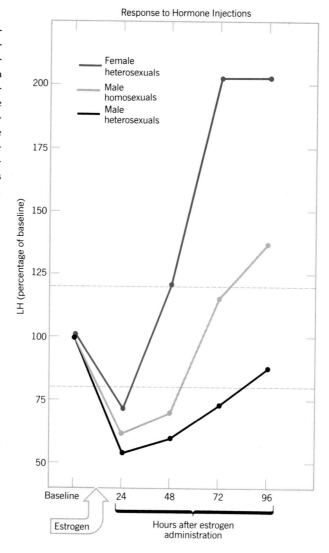

IT is possible THAT sEVERAL paTHways lEAd To HomosEXuAliTy. IT is also likEly THAT THE fAcTors THAT conTribuTE To HomosEXualiTy for MEN ANd womEN diffEr siGNifiCANTly.

How does one make sense out of the conflicting theories of the origin of homosexuality and out of the differences between homosexuality in the two sexes? It is possible that several pathways lead to homosexuality. It is also likely that the factors that contribute to homosexuality for men and women differ significantly. Biological factors, perhaps unusual levels of sex hormones, may turn out to play a role in homosexuality, but there is no solid, direct evidence for them right now. Social factors or a combination of social and biological factors are much more likely, we believe, to steer someone's sexual orientation in one direction or another.

Michael Storms: Timing of Sexual Development

Michael Storms (1981) suggests that one's erotic orientation develops from the interaction of sex drive and social development in early adolescence. Early adolescence is a period of strong erotic feelings and strong sexual fantasies. Storms believes that children who reach sexual maturity earlier than age 13 will be overrepresented among those who form homosexual attachments, because they are at an age when they probably have friends only of their own sex. (The Kinsey Reports noted that many gay adults had engaged in sexual activity, especially masturbation, at younger ages than many heterosexual adults.) Children who reach sexual maturity after 13 and after the sexes typically have begun mixing will tend to form heterosexual attachments. In both cases, early and later maturing, most children will become heterosexual. But of those who become homosexual, there will be larger proportions of early maturers with homosexual attachments. The famous personality theorist Harry Stack Sullivan proposed a theory of homosexual development that resembles Storms's. Sullivan believed that young adolescents must separate sexual desire from their close same-sex friendships if they are to develop a heterosexual orientation. When sexual desire and close friendship are joined early in development, a homosexual preference is likely to develop.

The hypothesis of Storms (and Sullivan) has the advantage of accounting for heterosexual as well as homosexual preference. It also has the advantages of positing the development of sexual preference just before or at sexual maturity, and it avoids positing a family pattern or dormant childhood determinant of later sexual preference. But as with the hormonal hypothesis, Storms's maturation theory fits better with data from males than females. Most girls are sexually mature by age 13. One would expect a higher incidence of lesbians, according to this reasoning, than of male homosexuals. But that is not found, and so Storms's theory is forced into postulating that biological dampers affect females' sexual drive. Storms's theory is eminently testable, and new work is likely to appear soon that tries to answer the question: how does homosexuality develop?

Bell, Weinberg, and Hammersmith: a Repudiation

Homosexuals, male and female, whose responses to 200 questions (Bell, Weinberg, and Hammersmith, 1981) about their lives are compared to those of heterosexuals provide repudiation of most clinical, psychological, and sociological theories about homosexuality: cold, detached fathers, close, binding, intimate mothers; choice of cross-sex parent as role model; poor relationships with peers; bad experiences with the other sex; seduction by an older child of their own sex; and so forth. Instead, studying the interrelated paths of the interview responses leads researchers who in 1970 conducted an excellent, large San Francisco sample of gay and straight men and women to find:

> By tracing the various causal chains . . . we can see that if a certain circumstance arises, it may predispose a subsequent one that in turn

might give rise to a third phenomenon and eventually lead toward the development of a homosexual preference. But at any point along the chain, the process can stop. For example, the path model for the males shows that if a boy identifies very little with his father, he is more likely to dislike traditional boys' activities, develop homosexual inclinations, and become a homosexual adult. But this outcome is not inevitable. A boy who, for whatever reason, did not identify very much with his father might well go on to enjoy boys' activities and accept himself as "properly" masculine anyway; in metaphorical terms, such a boy could get off the train at the station marked "Identification" and not continue his journey to "Homosexuality." Or another boy may engage in genital homosexual sex play during childhood, but then discontinue it by adolescence and go on to become a heterosexual adult. The fact that such interruptions can occur accounts in part for our inability to explain all the variance in sexual orientation. Another reason, of course, is that some people simply do not fit at all into the causal chain. . . .

No particular phenomenon of family life can be singled out, on the basis of our findings, as especially consequential for either homosexual or heterosexual development. You may supply your sons with footballs and your daughters with dolls, but no one can guarantee that they will enjoy them. What we seem to have identified—*given that our model applies only to [known] theories and does not create new ones*—is a pattern of feelings and reactions within the child that cannot be traced back to a single social or psychological root *(Bell, Weinberg, and Hammersmith, 1981, pp. 191–192).*

Only one predictor divided gays from straights: as children, male and female gays felt that they were not like others of their sex. Some aspects of gender identity or gender role felt untrue to their sense of self.

Significantly, this Kinsey Institute investigation shows that homosexual men who have been in therapy give data consistent with the viewpoint of their therapists. Female homosexuals who have been in therapy give more varied stories, just as one might expect, given that Freud left the route to female homosexuality less well defined than that to male homosexuality. It may also be that homosexuals in psychotherapy are a special population, whose lives tend to conform to the psychoanalytic hypothesis. It may be that psychotherapy patients' beliefs about themselves are conditioned by the therapies. In any case, these results alone should serve as warning: what people say of their lives must be listened to, but we must seek additional data for confirmation. Asking parents alone may not do: mothers tend to forget their children's early behavior, especially when that behavior violates gender norms (Radke-Yarrow et al., 1970). To the credit of recent researchers, samples of homosexuals have been large and broad enough to invite credibility. Some gay researchers *who know the gay world well* have themselves begun publishing work on homosexuality. Both changes bode well for future research, because they offer new sources of information.

MENTAL ILLNESS AND ADJUSTMENT

Are homosexuals mentally ill? Until 1973 they were considered ill by the American Psychiatric Association. In that year, homosexuality was removed from the

Surveys have shown that homosexual men are self-accepting. Some have less faith in others than heterosexual men, perhaps in reaction to those who might expose or harass them.

official list of mental illnesses after a vote by the APA members. This "science by election" shows how truth in human sexuality so heavily relies on which way the winds of opinion happen to be blowing. (For a fascinating history of the issues behind the changed viewpoint, see Bayer 1981.) Although Freud considered homosexuality less mature than heterosexuality, he did not think that it was either neurosis or psychosis (the two classical categories of mental illness). Other psychoanalysts have reached different conclusions, however.

To determine whether homosexuals as a group show more mental illness than heterosexuals, we would need certain information. We would need a sample representative of all homosexuals and of all heterosexuals (not just those in psychotherapy). We would need to screen these groups with an objective and reliable measure of pathology. This perfect study simply does not exist. In one of the better studies, groups of 30 male homosexuals and 30 male heterosexuals—none in psychotherapy—took a battery of standard psychological tests (Hooker, 1957, 1958). All subjects chosen seemed well adjusted and functioned well in society. If one assumes that pathology is common, then the sample is unrepresentative. If it is uncommon, then the sample is more acceptable, because the *extent* of pathology is what is being studied. Random or truly representative sampling should be required, but stigmatized groups do not readily yield up representative samples to researchers. As a compromise in Hooker's work, groups were matched for age, background, and intelligence. The test results were submitted to "blind" raters, who were not told of the subjects' sexual orientations. The raters could not distinguish between members of the two groups on the basis of their test scores. The ratings of adjustment were equivalent for the two groups. Hooker concluded (a generation ago) that male homosexuals may fall within the range of psychological normality.

A large-scale questionnaire survey of male homosexuals in three Western cultures, the United States, Holland, and Denmark, answers more questions about mental illness in homosexuals. Although the samples again were not representative of all homosexuals, they were large. We will report here only the responses for the U.S. sample, which comprised over 1000 men. (The answers of the European men were similar.) Most men were self-accepting, and most (85 percent) did not see themselves as failures. Yet psychological problems were common among them. One-fourth of the men considered themselves depressed and unhappy; 42 percent said that they had at some time felt on the verge of a nervous breakdown. Only 10 percent considered homosexuality an illness; 43 percent had consulted a psychiatrist, although only 8 percent were in therapy at the time of the study. Most men had minor psychosomatic complaints such as sleeplessness and anxiety (Weinberg and Williams, 1974).

How should we interpret these results? The authors of the study compared them to the results of another survey of the general male population in the United States (which, of course, would include a minority of homosexual and a majority of heterosexual men). The homosexual men report less happiness and faith in others than do the men in the general survey, but there is little difference in ratings of self-acceptance and psychosomatic symptoms. It is likely that the personal disappointments homosexuals suffer and the wariness they may adopt toward those who might expose or harass them can generate depression and lack of faith in others. Other studies have confirmed these general trends (for example, Sisson, 1975).

CHANGING HOMOSEXUALITY: THERAPY

Some homosexuals come to psychiatrists or psychologists wishing to change their sexual orientation. Although that wish might seem to present an appropriate task for therapy, it actually raises significant ethical questions. If a therapist treats someone for homosexuality, isn't the therapist implying that homosexuality is a mental illness or, at least, a maladjustment? Does the patient really want to change orientation, or is the patient really responding to prejudices against homosexuality (Davison, 1976)? Gay groups protest that society forces gays to see themselves as abnormal and hateful. The solution, they maintain, is not therapy but an organized, powerful gay community. For therapists, there is no easy way out of the ethical dilemma. Some therapists flatly refuse to undertake such conversion treatments. Others believe that gays who seek help either in changing their sexual orientation or in dealing with sexual dysfunction deserve that help. The observant and sympathetic therapist usually explores with the potential patient the whole range of options—including making a more satisfying adjustment to homosexuality—before beginning a course of therapy aimed at sexual reorientation.

The chances of successfully reorienting are not high. But the chances depend on many factors: the sincerity of the wish to change, the extent of homosexual and heterosexual experience, and sexual orientation in fantasy. The two critical

TABLE 14.4
Sexual Reorientation Therapy

	Number of cases	Immediate treatment failures	Follow-up treatment reversals	Assumed failure rate
Males				
Conversion[a]	9	2	1	33%
Reversion[b]	45	9	3	27
	54	11	4	28
Females				
Conversion	3	0	0	0%
Reversion	10	3	1	40
	13	3	1	31

Source: Masters and Johnson, 1979, Table 17.2.

[a]Conversion therapy concerned patients with exclusively homosexual histories.

[b]Reversion therapy dealt with restoring heterosexual functioning to those patients who did not have exclusively homosexual histories.

Therapy to restore heterosexual functioning—here labeled "reversion"—succeeded more often than therapy to convert homosexual to heterosexual functioning. The precise number of successes is difficult to state, because 16 males out of 43 successes and 3 females could not be found for later follow-ups. The "assumed" failure rate, which assumes no reversals among the missing clients, actually might be slightly (10%) low. (Source: Masters and Johnson, 1979, Table 17.2)

factors for success are the homosexual's own wish to change and a history that includes substantial heterosexual feelings. William Masters and Virginia Johnson (1979), for example, choose clients who are seriously motivated to change or who have a partner of the other sex to whom the client is committed. (Some married clients try to shake off a covert homosexual past.) Therapy is conducted by a male and a female. Masters and Johnson refer 20 to 23 percent of clients elsewhere, for not meeting their criteria for successful therapy. The process of reorientation itself has two goals: the weakening of homosexual identification *and* the strengthening of heterosexual identification. They are such difficult goals to achieve that a totally successful reorientation is very rare.

Therapists find it easier to help homosexuals move toward a greater proportion of heterosexual relations than toward exclusive heterosexuality. Kinsey knew that, and the same conclusion is evident in Masters and Johnson's work (1979). Success rates are higher for dysfunctional gays than for those seeking sexual reorientation. One study of psychoanalytically treated homosexual males reports a 27 percent shift to exclusive heterosexuality (Bieber et al., 1962). Half of the bisexual men shifted. No one since has duplicated these results or followed patients for a reasonably long period. Most sex researchers remain skeptical about reports of such success. One sex researcher, Wardell Pomeroy, has issued a public challenge: his money for any exclusive homosexual made exclusively heterosexual. He has not yet paid anything. Behavior modification therapy has also been used to change homosexual orientations. (The standard procedures of behavior modification are described in Chapter 15). When we compare the studies that followed patients for a reasonable period after their therapy ended, we find that about 40 percent of men shifted toward heterosexuality (although not necessarily toward heterosexuality exclusively) after behavior modification (Bancroft, 1974).

Researchers have not concentrated on studying change of sexual orientation among female homosexuals. Sometimes women go from years in an exclusively gay to years in an exclusively straight relationship (Blumstein and Schwartz,

1976). Master's and Johnson's success in reorienting three gay women (see Table 14.4) is only a bare beginning for understanding such a shift in sexual orientation.

SUMMARY

1 Homosexuals, or gays, are people who voluntarily have sex with members of their own sex. Some people use the term "homosexual" exclusively for males and the term "lesbian" for females.

2 Homosexual acts and homosexual identity are not the same things. In some cultures, they are considered quite independent of each other. Homosexual acts are erotic acts or feelings directed toward a person of one's own sex. Homosexual identity incorporates into one's self-definition the acceptance of sexual attraction to another person of one's own sex.

3 Homosexual acts that are the products of sexually segregated circumstances are called situational homosexuality.

4 People who define themselves as bisexual are romantically attracted and committed to members of both sexes. As with homosexuality, bisexual acts and bisexual identity are not the same things.

5 One sociological theory to account for the nature of homosexuality is deviance theory. It attempts to describe how people who deviate from social norms handle their difference. Homosexual behavior in the form of primary deviance—a person's first or earliest homosexual acts—may be incidental and not considered important. When people label their behavior as deviant and incorporate it into their self-definition, the behavior has become secondary deviance.

6 Most cultures historically have allowed for homosexuality. About two-thirds of modern-day cultures approve of homosexuality in some form. But the range of social values concerning homosexuality varies widely. In some cultures, homosexuality is nearly universal (among males) and quite conventionally accepted. In other cultures, homosexuality is stigmatized and punished.

7 Many homosexual encounters among men rely less on penetration with the penis than on fondling, mutual masturbation, femoral coitus, oral stimulation, and genital friction. Some gay males practice fisting—anal penetration with large objects—although the possibility of contracting infections through the resulting anal fissures has led many gays to avoid fisting.

8 One false stereotype of gay couples is that one partner acts feminine and passive while the other acts masculine and aggressive. Another false stereotype is that gay males are extremely promiscuous. Some gay males do not commit themselves to enduring relationships, it is true, but gay couples face social barriers that tend to undermine their relationships.

9 Homosexual men meet sexual partners in many of the same ways that heterosexual men do: through business and professional contacts, athletics, mu-

tual friends, organizations, and the like. Specific to the gay community, however, are gay bars, baths, tearooms, public areas where gays congregate, and gay hustlers.

10 Most men with homosexual identities have firm gender identities as males. Only within a few gay subcultures is effeminacy considered erotic. A small minority of gay men dress as women.

11 Lesbianism is more widely accepted around the world than male homosexuality, but lesbians still face social stigmatization in the United States and other cultures. Lesbian sexual encounters typically involve much body contact, caressing, and kissing and a steady, leisurely pace of stimulation. Vaginal or anal penetration does not seem centrally important for many lesbian couples.

12 Most lesbians have some heterosexual experience, in dating, marriage, and motherhood. Most lesbian relationships are more stable and enduring than those of gay males, and lesbians tend to have fewer sexual partners than gay males do.

13 Many different gay organizations exist to provide social, medical, legal, psychological, or other kinds of services to members of a community that have long suffered stigmatization and discrimination.

14 Various theories exist on the origins of homosexuality. Environmental theories typically explain the development of homosexuality in childhood sexual experiences. There is debate among social scientists about the importance of early, exploratory same-sex play to later sexual development. Psychoanalytic theory locates the origins of homosexual development in complex interactions between biological maturation and social relationships. Some social scientists believe that patterns of family interaction influence the development of homosexuality.

15 Some young boys who act feminine as children are more likely than other boys to emerge as homosexual, heterosexual transvestite, bisexual, or transsexual adults. But the reverse conclusion is not warranted: that homosexuals and bisexuals are fundamentally feminine.

16 There is no convincing evidence for the theory that particular genes or abnormality of chromosomes cause homosexuality or transsexualism. An explanation based on prenatal hormonal events has been accepted by some gays, although the evidence to support this theory is still tentative and controversial. In sum, it is likely that people reach homosexuality via several different paths and that the factors that contribute to homosexuality differ significantly for men and women.

17 Homosexuality once was classified as a mental illness by psychiatrists, but in 1973 it was removed from the list of mental illnesses by the American Psychiatric Association. The personal disappointments homosexuals suffer and their wariness toward those who might aggress against them can generate depression or pessimism, but the gay community in general is not characterized by higher than average rates of mental illness.

18 The question of whether therapists should help homosexuals reorient themselves sexually raises ethical questions. In practice, the chances of successful reorientations are low. Two factors critical to success seem to be extensive heterosexual feelings and a personal, voluntary wish to change.

KEY TERMS

homosexual
gay
lesbian
homosexual act
homosexual identity
situational homosexuality
bisexual
deviant
primary deviance
secondary deviance
Sapphic love
fisting
Acquired Immune Deficiency
  Syndrome (AIDS)

drones
sadomasochism
tearooms
come out
transvestite
drag queen
gay hustlers
sensate focus
dildo
close coupled
transsexual
luteinizing hormone (LH)

SUGGESTED READINGS

Boswell, J. *Christianity, Social Tolerance, and Homosexuality*. Chicago: University of Chicago Press, 1980. Boswell's book about early views of homosexuality and their sudden change is like a mystery story. Be prepared for an ambiguous ending.

Califia, P. *Sapphistry: the Book of Lesbian Sexuality*. Tallahassee, FL: Naiad Press, 1980. A lesbian feminist describes the many ways women relate sexually to one another.

Claiborne, C. *A Feast Made for Laughter: a Memoir with Recipes*. New York: Doubleday, 1981. A delicate boy tells his story. Well-born but poor, beloved and babied by all, the boy comes to share his father's bed. Discovering his father's autoeroticism leads him into erotic activity with his father. A book utterly without self-pity.

Sisley, E. L. and Harris, B. *The Joy of Lesbian Sex*. New York: Crown, 1977. The book's subtitle calls it "a tender and liberated guide to the pleasures and problems of a lesbian lifestyle." In format at least, the book is influenced by Comfort's *The Joy of Sex*.

White, E. *A Boy's Own Story*. New York: Dutton, 1982. This novel of a boy growing up in the 1950s catches the way sexual fantasy, romance, parents, conflicts, and a boy's own views of homosexuality lead him a very long way around to growing up gay.

PART V

SEXUAL PROBLEMS
AND SOLUTIONS

LYUBOV SERGEEVNA POPOVA, "ARCHITECTONIC PAINTING." Collection, THE MUSEUM OF MODERN ART, NEW YORK.

Chapter 15

Sexual Variations

Sexual "variations"? Variations on what? The kinds of sexual behavior that we will talk about in this chapter are variations on the "standard" form of sexual behavior around the world—heterosexual intercourse. A sexual variation is any sexual activity that a person prefers to or substitutes for heterosexual intercourse or a sexual activity that involves unusual methods of arousal. Thus exhibitionism ("indecent exposure") and voyeurism ("peeping") are forms of sexual variations. But nude sunbathing or watching a strip show are not, because these activities are not substitutes for intercourse and are not considered, in our culture today, to be unusual. Variations also have been called "deviations" and "perversions," terms that have come to imply moral judgment, and they have been called, more neutrally, "atypical behavior." The current, standard definition of which forms of sexual behavior are variant comes from the diagnostic bible of clinicians, the American Psychiatric Association's *Diagnostic and Statistical Manual of Mental Disorders, Third Edition* (1980), or *DSM III,* for short. This manual defines categories of psychosexual disorders, and under the heading, "paraphilias," it lists sexual variations. Interestingly, the definitions have changed over time (see Table 15.1). That these definitions are not fixed tells important truths about sexual variations: even the experts do not always understand them very well, and the sexual variations themselves are subject to cultural definition, like other sexual behaviors.

VARIATIONS IN DEGREE OR KIND?

Are sexual variations extremes of behavior that most of us understand, or are they qualitatively different from ordinary sexual behavior? When one reads the Amer-

TABLE 15.1

DSM 3 Categories of Psychosexual Disorders

Gender identity disorders
Transsexualism
Gender identity disorder of childhood
Atypical gender identity disorder
Paraphilias
Fetishism
Transvestism
Zoophilia [rare]
Pedophilia
Exhibitionism
Voyeurism
Sexual masochism
Sexual sadism
Atypical paraphilia
Psychosexual dysfunctions
Other psychosexual disorders
Ego-dystonic homosexuality
Psychological disorders not elsewhere classified

Source: *Diagnostic and Statistical Manual of Mental Disorders*, Third Edition (1980), American Psychiatric Association.

ican Psychiatric Association's list of paraphilias, or sexual variations, some do seem far from ordinary imagination. For instance, zoophilia (sex with animals) is relatively rare in our citified population. Yet other variations—fetishism, exhibitionism, and voyeurism come to mind—are extreme forms of what many of us do from time to time. Thus at one end of a continuum of the role of objects in sexual arousal is fetishism; at another end is the piece of clothing or jewelry we wear to look attractive, land a date, or just to feel lucky in love. At one end of another continuum, that of showing and looking in sexual arousal, is exhibitionism; at other points on that same continuum are the slow, erotic undressing of lovers or purposely skimpy shorts and tight jeans. Just as this sort of exhibitionism is socially acceptable, some forms of adult lust for children are similarly extolled. Vladimir Nabokov's *Lolita* is a famous example of the older man's infatuation with a young girl; Brooke Shields played a barely pubescent New Orleans prostitute whose virginity was very valuable to an older male customer in the movie *Pretty Baby*. Where does permissible sexuality end and pedophilia (sex with children below the legal age of consent) begin?

SEXUAL VARIATIONS diffER fROM TYPICAL SEX IN THEIR COMPULSIVE QUALITY.

Sexual variations differ from typical sex in their compulsive quality. Often, the script of the variation must be performed in a precise way, over and over again, with certain special sights or props under certain special conditions. Without the leather boots, or the sight of a woman through her window, or the protests of a "slave," there is no sexual excitement. Compulsion is not choice. The people who perform these acts often would prefer *not* to, for these acts may make them feel uncomfortable and—given the illegal nature of some sexual acts—disrupt their lives. But they may not be able to stop themselves.

VIOLATION OF SOCIAL RULES

Even when a sexual variation causes nobody any harm, a person who is known to practice atypical sexual behavior may meet with society's strongest rejections. The cruelest of names—"pervert," "queer," "sickie"—and the strongest of rejections are commonly hurled at people whose sexual behavior differs from the social norm. In some places, people who practice sexual variations have been considered mentally ill or morally degenerate.

Sexual variations tend to violate certain widely held sexual values. First, and foremost, laws insist that sex should be private, yet some variations violate rules of privacy. Exhibitionism, for example, forces the victim to look at a stranger's genitals, a part of the body our rules of privacy and modesty dictate remain covered except to one's intimates. Voyeurism violates the privacy of the person being watched. By invading their sexual privacy, these variations make many victims feel "violated"—even though there has been no physical contact at all.

In voyeurism, the eye has become symbolically transformed into an aggressive sexual instrument, and its victims react to it as such. Second, laws on sexual consent generally refer to hands-on sex, usually with penetration. The victims of voyeurs or exhibitionists have not consented, but they are not protected by laws on consent. Instead, the offender's *behavior* in and of itself is considered illegal.

Third, and closely related, is the rule that sex be between consenting *adults*. Sexual activity with children violates this rule. We acknowledge the power of sexual feelings by wanting to protect children from adult sexuality. It is in its laws that a society sets the outer limits for what defines privacy, proper modes of dress, consent, and the age of sexual partners. Society has an interest in regulating sexual behavior, even sexual behavior that ostensibly does no physical damage, for by punishing some, others are warned not to stray beyond the limits of the acceptable.

"Lewd and lascivious conduct" is the legal name for any sexual acts or solicitations that violate the rule that sexual behavior must be private. Couples kissing on the street, men ogling passing women, workmen whistling at teenage girls all are frankly sexual acts. The law does not consider these "lewd and lascivious." Why not? They all fall within heterosexual norms, and all the people remain fully clothed. No genitals show. If the kissing couple were two men, some state laws would label their behavior as public and sexual, hence lewd and lascivious. (Men picked up in Boston in separate, locked stalls in a library toilet, reputed to be a center for homosexual acts and pick-ups, have been charged with lewd and lascivious conduct [Katherine Triantifalou, Esq., personal communication, 1984]. The police try to control such spaces as resolutely public, despite the fact that a closed stall is hardly public.)

Societies may stigmatize variant sexual behavior on the grounds that for strictly biological reasons, sexual variations that do not culminate in reproduction of young are maladaptive. The claim may be that for a species to evolve and survive, it must reproduce. If people exclusively practiced a form of sexual behavior that led to masturbation, as many variations do, rather than to heterosexual intercourse, the human race would have run its course. But for psychological or social reasons, parenthood is certainly not a prerequisite to everyone's productiveness, success, or happiness. Some cultures attach no stigma to sexual variations: the transvestite in certain American Indian tribes was well accepted and sometimes revered, and among shepherds, for another example, intercourse with sheep is often understood as an outlet for sexual needs during long periods of isolation. Societies, not evolution, make judgments about morality and mental health, and what is considered variant in one society may be common, accepted, perhaps even mandatory or a ceremonial rite in another society.

Because ideas about what is normal and what is deviant vary so much from place to place, we will only discuss variations relatively common within our culture. We will discuss six common variations: fetishism, transvestism, exhibitionism, voyeurism, sadomasochism, and pedophilia.

THE NATURE OF SEXUAL VARIATIONS

Before children reach the age of sexual socialization, when their sexual behavior falls under social limitations, they derive erotic pleasure from a great variety of sources and acts. Sigmund Freud thought young children were "polymorphous perverse" (*poly* meaning many, *morphous* meaning form). In other words, Freud thought that childhood sexuality took many forms before it was ultimately chan-neled into heterosexual and genital activity. Freud believed that sexual variations in adulthood were childhood sexuality magnified and elaborated. Given the prim-itive state of our evidence on childhood sexuality, such a theory cannot be tested. Freud thought that the normal sequence of sexual development somehow had stopped early in those who practiced "perverse" sexual acts. In Freud's view then, variations were not so very distant from "normal" sexuality; they were, so to speak, younger, less adult in form.

Frank Beach (1977), the pioneer investigator of animals' sexual behavior, has looked at human sexual variations from the perspective of animal behavior. Beach's two-part classification is often used in the study of motivated animal behavior: first, **appetitive behavior,** which brings an animal closer to something that it needs or wants; second, **consummatory behavior,** which is fairly regularly per-formed and acts on the thing sought. For example, an animal searches for food—appetitive behavior—and then eats the food—consummatory behavior. Applied to variant sexual behavior, Beach see no difference in the consummatory behavior of more typical, nonvariant sexual acts and that of the variations: they culminate in orgasm, from masturbation or intercourse. But the appetitive behavior asso-ciated with sexual variations—what brings people closer—differs markedly from that associated with more typical sexual acts.

In typical sexual acts, Beach sees arousal growing out of consenting adults sharing their excitement. Such acts tend to mutually reinforce the pleasurable bonds of intimacy between sexual partners and to escalate the intensity of arousal. But in many variant sexual acts, arousal grows either in the absence of any partner or in blotting out much of the partner (as in transvestism or fetishism) or without a partner's consent (as in exhibitionism and voyeurism). These categories literally eliminate or "reduce" the partner. Some variations such as sadomasochism and pedophilia keep a partner but change the nature of the acts (and the fantasies of consent). Beach suggests that the avoidance of shared erotic feelings may char-acterize many variant sexual acts. Sharing may be too intense for people who practice some variations. This theory has not been widely tested. In the laboratory, exhibitionists are not aroused by films of the usual sorts of preparations for erotic contact while most nonexhibitionist men are aroused (Kolářský and Madlafousek, 1983). This finding might allow one to label voyeurism, exhibitionism, and obscene phone-calling, among others, as "courtship disorders" in which the men are not inclined to have intercourse. But researchers tested a group of 16 exhi-bitionists and 16 men as controls on their arousal to the four phases of typical sexual interaction: finding a suitable partner, erotic interaction before any touch-ing, touching without intercourse, and intercourse. A narrative described each phase. Both groups of men showed the same degree of arousal, and their arousal was highest during the description of intercourse (Freund et al., 1984). So much for an interesting hypothesis. Researchers are left describing variations as inade-quacies in sexual approach for reasons as yet unspecified. Before we continue with the research on sexual violations, we should say a word about the research pop-ulations.

Research Populations

Which people practice sexual variations? Psychologists really know very little about who, among the general population, makes up this group. Much infor-mation on sexual variations has come from men—more men practice variations than do women—who have been arrested and jailed. These men, who are convicted sex offenders, are unlikely to be representative of practitioners of sexual variations as a group. Many wealthier and influential offenders who run afoul of the law can afford the legal or psychological help that keeps them out of jail. Those who are jailed probably have the fewest resources. Many have a profound lack of social skills. They may be so isolated and socially inept that therapy may have to begin with teaching basic skills like how to make conversation or ask for a date. However disadvantaged this group is, it is the source of most of the available information. Because people who practice variations may feel sexual guilt and may also fear social and legal reprisals, they keep themselves well hidden from the inquiring eye of social scientists. Of all the research cited in this book, the work on sexual variations is the most likely to have been conducted on unrepresentative populations.

EXHIBITIONISM

My mother and I were riding the subway when all of a sudden she stood up, grabbed my arm, and marched me into the next car. When I asked her what was going on, she said, her lips pursed with anger, "That man was exposing his private parts." Our family always used affectionate Polish terms for genitals, and when I heard that "private parts," boy did I know it was bad. I never even saw the guy.

Exhibitionism is the act of exposing one's genitals to an unwilling audience for one's sexual pleasure. Often committed by males in front of female children or adults, the act of exposure often is accompanied by masturbation. To some men, their victims' shock is very exciting, and they incorporate images of their shocked expressions into their masturbatory fantasies. Not all exhibitionists do so, however (Kolářský and Madlafousek, 1983). Most people who engage in exhibitionism quickly leave the scene afterward, and so subway cars, public hallways, parks, or other spots with easy escape routes may appeal to them. But for other men, getting caught is privately gratifying. In fact, the Kinsey group found (1948) that the largest proportion of convicted sex offenders had been imprisoned for exposing themselves.

The act of exhibition is usually sexually arousing and rewarding in and of itself rather than a means toward further sexual activity. Many men who exhibit themselves are shy, retiring, and socially inept. They may be young and serious, with deep worries about their masculinity, men who want to regain their confidence about their sexual abilities in a way that feels unthreatening. Exposing oneself forcibly to strangers, as is usually the case, may feel less threatening than risking exposure before someone familiar. Running away afterward may feel less threatening than sticking around a scene fraught with sexual anxiety or failures: many such men have suffered repeated failure to get or maintain an erection (Gebhard et al., 1965). Sometimes men or women who are mentally ill or disoriented expose themselves. The following case history captures many of the typical elements of exhibitionism (after Stoller, 1977):

Mr. A., a married man, has had a history of unsatisfactory relationships with women, even with his wife. He is shy and passive around women and does not object to being dominated by his wife. Their sexual activity is infrequent and flawed by his inability to keep an erection. Mr. A. has been exhibiting his erect penis to females passing on the street for five years. He takes little care to protect himself from being caught: exposing himself in the daytime in his own neighborhood. These activities have led to arrest, imprisonment, and erosion of his professional and family life; yet he still feels the compulsion to expose himself again.

If his audience has not witnessed the act, Mr. A. will relocate to make sure that he is seen. He has not run when noticed, except on one occasion when two teenage girls actually approached; he then fled the scene.

Often called "indecent exposure," exhibitionism is the single most common sex offense in the United States, according to law enforcement records. It accounts for one-third of all sex violations. Exhibitionism may violate local mores and outrage society. A 44-year-old man who had been arrested in Oklahoma for exposing himself was sentenced by a jury to 99 years in prison—twice the sentence given to a murderer convicted in the same court (*New York Times*, March 11, 1982). Such a sentence is surely not a punishment that fits the crime, but it does reflect the disgust that people may feel at the violation of sexual norms.

In one study by psychologists at Indiana's Kinsey Institute (1965), it was found that men in prison for exhibitionism had a number of qualities that would tend to make heterosexual relationships difficult for them. Relatively few of these men marry, and even those who do rely heavily after marriage on prostitutes and on masturbation. Although the study found that most sex offenders have a low rate of repeat offenses, especially compared to those who commit nonsexual offenses, men who exhibit themselves tend to do so repeatedly. Many reported feeling compelled to expose themselves; that is, for them, exhibitionism had a compulsive quality. Although exhibitionism itself is usually harmless, leaving its victims shocked but not otherwise harmed, a small minority of men who exhibit themselves are also convicted of offenses involving force against a woman. Although most exhibitionism (80 percent) is not accompanied by acts of aggression, no one knows how to predict which men will on some occasion become aggressive (Gebhard et al., 1965; Rooth, 1973).

In a Toronto study of 138 men who exposed themselves, 381 men who showed other sexually anomalous behavior, and 75 male control subjects (Langevin et al., 1979), the investigators found that in the laboratory, men who exposed themselves were no more or less sexually arousable than other men. The subjects appeared on self-report tests as introverts but were not more likely than the controls to have been divorced or to have had marriage problems. Their exhibitionism was not associated with homosexuality, rape, or **frottage** (rubbing up against women for sexual pleasure). Langevin and his colleagues did find, however, that subjects who practiced sexual variations were more likely than the controls to report feelings of inferiority about their bodies. Men who practiced exhibitionism were more likely than men who practiced other variations to say that they wanted more athletic bodies and more likely than the controls to want larger penises and better looks.

VOYEURISM

Voyeurism is the act of watching people undressing or having sex without their permission or knowledge, for the purpose of sexual gratification. "Voyeurs," which in French means "ones who look," do not engage in the socially accepted kind of looking that people do at X-rated movies, and they do not have a typical curiosity about a sexual partner's body. People who engage in voyeurism in fact hardly respond to pornography or to the voluntary exhibition of bodies that goes on at nude beaches or strip shows. Unlike those who expose themselves publicly, those who watch others usually do not want to be discovered (Gebhard et al., 1965). Colloquially called "Peeping Toms," most are males who work alone, secretly, and who masturbate as they observe. Most are not interested in observing a woman whom they know, unless she has not given her permission, and they may scour whole neighborhoods for the sight of a woman undressing or, more rarely, engaged in sexual activity.

> *As a group, peepers are persevering optimists. In this way they remind one of ardent fishermen, undaunted by failure and always hoping that the next time their luck will be better. Just as the fishermen will wait patiently for hours, so will the peeper wait patiently for a female to finish some interminable minor chores before going to bed. . . . (Gebhard et al., 1965).*

The following profile of voyeurs has been found (Gebhard et al., 1965). In childhood, many voyeurs were poorly socialized with the opposite sex. However, most had about an average amount of preadolescent sex play with partners of both sexes. The voyeurs' masturbatory patterns are not unusual (except during peeping), but they have bizarre masturbatory fantasies and high masturbatory guilt. As in many other sex-offender groups, many voyeurs have had deficient heterosexual adjustment in adolescence and adulthood. Only a relatively small proportion of the men marry. As a group, the peepers have an unusually high incidence of homosexual behavior when compared to other sex offenders, although they report little excitement at observing men. Although they rate their response to pornography as low, voyeurs are unusually aroused by thinking about or observing women.

As juveniles, the voyeurs had very frequent encounters with the law, although a majority of their offenses had been for peeping. A small number of voyeurs had raped; the how and why of that transition from the less intrusive to the highly intrusive and violent sexual act we do not yet know.

FETISHISM

Fetishism describes a person's use of an object or body part for sexual arousal; often the object—a shoe, a piece of women's clothing, a furry object—is preferred for solitary sex rather than incorporated into social sex. Many people with fetishes thus lead sexual lives devoid of personal relationships. Even their fantasies tend to be solitary, centering around the objects they find sexually exciting rather than the people who might be related to these objects. Fetishes are of two types. **Partialism** describes a fetish for a particular part of the body, perhaps the foot.

Leather garments may be object fetishes. This woman's leather and whip imply that she is interested in sadism.

With partialism, the dividing line between "normal" and variant patterns of arousal is not always clear. Clinicians are likelier to label a sexual pattern fetishistic as the arousing body part gets farther away from breasts or genitals. Here is a description of a foot fetish (after Stoller, 1977):

> *Mr. B., a young single man, is sexually aroused only by viewing or fantasizing women's feet, naked or clad with shoes. He comes to orgasm if a woman steps on his penis or if he imagines this act in a masturbation fantasy.*

The second type of fetish is the **object fetish,** in which an inanimate object is sexually revered. The clinical literature reports a wide list of object fetishes— flowers, pillows, satin, sounds, smells, and so on—but the most common objects are women's clothing, especially underwear or footwear, furry objects, rubber and leather garments. People usually have a favorite object fetish, one that excites them sexually, and incorporate that object into masturbation or masturbate in its presence. Some people have large collections of fetishes or find several types of fetishes sexually exciting.

People who are sexually attached to fetishes show three striking characteristics, according to Gebhard and his colleagues (1965). First, the men's heterosexual lives are underdeveloped. As children, they had not played with girls and had been very attached to their mothers but weakly attached to their fathers. Second, their sexual activities, which are highly varied, seemed to substitute for heterosexual relationships. Third, their fetishes had taken on erotic meaning early in the men's sexual development, usually before puberty. Clinicians tend to view fetishists as immature, sexually fearful, and actively wary of heterosexual encounters.

TRANSVESTISM

From the Latin roots for "cross" and "dressing," **transvestism** describes the practice of dressing in the clothes of the other sex in order to achieve sexual pleasure. Transvestites often masturbate or engage in intercourse after dressing up. In contrast to **transsexuals,** people who feel that their core gender identity is at odds with their biological sex (discussed in Chapter 3), transvestites usually do not have a basic disturbance of gender identity. They are usually not homosexuals; most are heterosexuals whose sexual activities are more pleasurable when they are dressed in women's clothing (Kinsey et al., 1948). (See "Sexuality in Perspective: Cross-Dressing.") A few cases of women cross-dressing have been found in the psychological literature (Stoller, 1982). Although it is far more acceptable socially for women to dress in men's clothing than for men to dress in women's, there is a difference between most women, who wear mannish clothing for style, and female transvestites, who find sexual pleasure in their cross-dressing and who usually favor a particular man's suit or pair of slacks for arousal. Said one 34-year-old woman, "Simply putting on my suit can provoke an orgasm" (Stoller, 1982, p. 101).

In contrast, male homosexuals who dress as women, known as **drag queens,** are usually not sexually aroused by this dress and may appear in drag either to

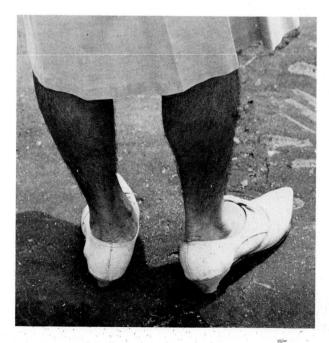

Men who dress in women's clothing for sexual pleasure are transvestites. Most are heterosexual and therefore quite different in orientation from the homosexual men—drag queens—who dress as women.

fulfill role expectations, to attract a male partner, or to spoof gender roles. The same pattern holds true for female homosexuals who dress as men. Neither group of homosexuals, according to our definition, is transvestite. Among one group of cross-dressing men who were in prison (and who therefore represent poorly all cross-dressing men), Gebhard and his colleagues found (1965) that most had come from broken homes and had been unhealthy as children. Like men with fetishes, the cross-dressing men in prison had had little luck with heterosexual relationships, few partners or encounters, and a high rate of failing with women.

SEXUALITY IN PERSPECTIVE: CROSS-DRESSING

People's tensions about aspects of their gender roles may take many different forms. One such form is cross-dressing, that is, dressing in the clothes of the other sex for sexual pleasure. Below is a letter from an Ann Landers column and her reply. It ran in the newspaper under the headline, "Father's Odd Dress."

Dear Ann Landers:

I am 6 feet, weigh 200 pounds and look like a football player. No one would ever suspect that I am a transvestite. I don't feel I am an "oddball." I accept this fact of my personality as an outlet for my tensions. Everybody needs some outlet, and cross-dressing happens to be mine.

My hang-up is limited mostly to wearing women's panties or panty-hose, which I do every day under my street clothes. If I am alone during the evening, I sometimes dress further.

I have been married for ten years, and although my wife is not particularly happy about my "outlet," she tolerates it well and never says anything.

The problem is this: we have a 4-year-old son and are expecting another child soon. How do we handle the situation so the children can come to accept my inclination to be "different" and not develop a neurosis or think Daddy is "strange"?

Since there are many others who would ask the question if they had the courage to do so, please answer in the paper for all of us.

Great in Numbers

Ann Landers answered:
I see no reason for the children to be told. It would only confuse them. This matter is strictly personal. It involves no one but you. Keep it to yourself.

From the Boston *Globe,* December 8, 1978.

Some people consider transvestism an extreme form of fetishism. Yet many transvestites report that their wish to cross-dress formed considerably before puberty and, therefore, earlier than other males report that their fetishes developed. In a study conducted at Washington University's Medical School, most men said that they had begun cross-dressing before they had turned 10 years old; others had begun by midadolescence. They continued to cross-dress continuously through adulthood and middle age, and the cross-dressing was almost invariably sexually arousing, leading to masturbation or intercourse. Only in late adulthood did the cross-dressing grow less sexually arousing (Croughan et al., 1981). Transvestites may begin to cross-dress when they first develop a strong erotic attraction to a particular piece of women's clothing. The 70 subjects in the Washington University study were members of cross-dressing clubs, in which men regularly meet to dress up and to give each other support and advice on dressing and making up. In a similar eastern group, the same early pattern was found. Many of the men were married and had children (Feinbloom, 1976).

The Washington University psychiatric team wanted to know what made transvestites seek psychological help. They found that the men who seek treatment are likelier than those who do not: to fantasize themselves as female during sexual intercourse; to have cross-dressed during intercourse; to prefer sexual activity, whether heterosexual or homosexual, while cross-dressed; and to have experienced more adverse consequences for cross-dressing. Those consequences probably motivated the men to seek help. Transvestites may lose wives who cannot accept the cross-dressing or fear that their children will find out about it (Croughan et al., 1981).

SADISM AND MASOCHISM

Most people find elements of **sadism,** the infliction of pain for sexual arousal, and **masochism,** the acceptance of physical or mental pain for sexual arousal, within their sexual behavior. In our culture and many others, pinching, scratching, and biting are common during sexual activity. Among higher animals in general, a bit of exaggerated stimulation during mating seems to be the rule rather than the exception (Ford and Beach, 1951). Only when physical aggression or submission in sexual activity is extreme and dominating do psychologists consider them to be variant.

Sadism may be actually or symbolically cruel. At one end of the spectrum are people who act out their violent sexual fantasies but only threaten harm. At the other end of the spectrum are people who are sexually excited by torturing people, sometimes even killing their victim. Some people believe that rape (discussed in Chapter 19) is a form of sadism. Sometimes these fantasies become truly destructive. Here is one extreme case history (after Stoller, 1977):

Mr. B., a young married man, had an increasing interest in binding and torturing women, beginning in adolescence. He introduced mild elements of these fantasies into sex play with his wife. The binding has become progressively less symbolic and more physical, twice resulting in unconsciousness for Mrs. B.

Mr. B. is a repairman and is greatly tempted to bind and torture women whom he meets at work. He is afraid he might have to kill the victim if he actually succumbs to his fantasy. So far, he has avoided involvement with these women by returning to his truck and masturbating while looking at pictures of bound and tortured women.

Masochists become sexually aroused from receiving painful stimulation or being threatened with it. Pain is usually introduced ritualistically: it must be applied in a form and place precisely specified by the person experiencing it. Some psychoanalytic theorists believe that women are more often masochistic than men (the only instance of sexual variation in which women supposedly outnumber men), but there is no solid evidence on this point. Most sadists engage in masochism, and most masochists engage in sadism. **Sadomasochism** (sometimes abbreviated as S/M) is the composite variation. Sadomasochism, in its enactment of elaborate fantasies, most often resembles a drama, complete with roles, props, sets, costumes, acting, and direction. The props, often of leather or rubber, may serve as fetish objects. A couple's sadomasochistic activities, whether heterosexual or homosexual, may begin with an agreement about roles. One person accepts the role of dominant master, and the other accepts the role of submissive slave. The slave may have to "earn" punishment for some concocted crime. Then the

This demonstrator at a San Francisco gay rights parade is rigged up in the paraphernalia of sadism.

punishment or threat of punishment begins, only to end in sexual pleasure. (For an interview with a professional master, see "Sexuality in Perspective: Dialogue with a Dominatrix.") Such rituals may be sexually stimulating enough for some people, although others require actual pain for their sexual satisfaction. When the participants consent to sadomasochistic sex, there may be no unwilling victims.

Sadomasochistic activities are usually social, but some people do practice what seems to be extreme cruelty when they are alone. One example is of eroticized bondage hangings, in which men arrange elaborate straps and slings to seek the thrill of orgasm in dangerous circumstances. These men tend to be seriously depressed, lonely, isolated, and fascinated with death. Many are homosexual, fetishistic, and unable to maintain any personal relationships, sexual or otherwise (Litman and Swearington, 1972). But some are only adolescents trying out a new masturbatory act (Burgess, 1982), and their deaths are shocking to their parents and friends.

SEXUALITY IN CONTROVERSY: DIALOGUE WITH A DOMINATRIX

New York's *Village Voice* in 1979 ran an interview with Toni Rose, a 19-year-old professional dominatrix, or master, in sadomasochistic sex. Trained by her mother, who was also a dominatrix, Toni Rose (T) was described in superlatives by her "victims" (and paying clients). Below are excerpts from the interview, which was conducted by Howard Smith (S).

S. What reasons do men give for seeing you?

T: A lot of the men who have sessions with me believe they should be disciplined for being chauvinistic. Since they've been sadistic toward women, they want a woman to be sadistic toward them. Some tell me they should be punished for no other reason than the fact that they were born; others say all men should be disciplined simply because women are superior. . . .

S: So then, is this just a job to you?

T: No, being a dominatrix isn't just *some* job. I am very into what I do. Instead of feeling men are inferior, I believe they deserve to be disciplined and dominated for being so rude in the past to women. On another level, I feel like I'm acting as a form of therapist. Men come to see me and I do what they want. Then, after the session, they smile and walk out, ready to conquer their world again. A lot of men who see me are important with heavy responsibilities for making a lot of difficult decisions. They come to me so that they can release some of the pressure and tension of having to be the one who's always in charge. With me, they can finally be submissive. They get off on having someone else finally telling them what to do—sort of a reverse in roles.

One study of 245 sadomasochistic West German men, who anonymously completed a questionnaire on their sexual behavior, revealed that 30 percent were heterosexual, 31 percent bisexual, and 38 percent homosexual (Spengler, 1977). The subjects had been found through ads they had placed for sexual partners or through sadomasochistic clubs. The heterosexual males had more difficulty finding opportunities to act out their sadomasochism than the males in the other groups. Opportunities to act out sadomasochism are more easily found in the community of gay than straight males. In fact, some heterosexual men frequent gay bars and choose partners whose clothing reveals their interest in sadomasochism. The choice of sexual *act* is strongly enough felt for these men to move across the line between hetero- and homosexuality. Clubs to serve people who practice sadomasochism tend to draw men predominantly. One club owner explained the absence of women from such clubs as a reflection of the ease with which men in this society will accept women who wish to be passive and masochistic. Men, he said, are not so lucky, and so they need clubs where they can buy the right to be passive, ma-

S: Do you ever have total novices call you?

T: Sure. Most of them, of course, are usually very shy. They'll call seven times or so to make an appointment before they ever show up. Their session is basically just worshiping my body, getting verbally abused, a slight spanking, or dressing up as a transvestite. I start them off very mildly.

S: Do they always move on to the harder stuff?

T: Oh, no. With a lot of them, the fantasy is just bondage, the act of getting tied up.

S: Do they tell you what they want in advance?

T: Right, and before the appointment we work out a rough script, and then at the session I add my own improvisations. . . .

S: Do you ever see women?

T: Yes, I currently have two female slaves.

S: Are there any differences between a male and a female slave?

T: With a female slave, it's just more erotic and sensual in nature. A male is more oriented toward punishment. . . .

Taken from Howard Smith and Cathy Cox, "Dialogue with a Dominatrix," *Village Voice,* January 29, 1979, p. 19.

sochistic, and dominated by women. One study of the S/M subculture in the United States turned up a ratio of 5 women to 13 men (Breslow, et al., 1985). Recently, some lesbian groups have been urging that feminist groups defend women's rights to explore their own sexuality, including sadomasochistic sexuality. Because some feminists consider sadomasochism by its very nature to be exploitative and sexist, this discussion has been a lively one. The following quotation is especially interesting because it is written by a woman who is a lesbian and a feminist:

> *Since there is so much confusion about what S/M is, I want to describe my own sexual specialties and the sadomasochistic subculture. I am basically a sadist. About 10 percent of the time, I take the other role (bottom, slave, masochist). This makes me atypical, since the majority of women and men involved in S/M prefer to play bottom. . . .*
>
> *Because sadomasochism is usually portrayed as a violent, dangerous activity, most people do not think there is a great deal of difference between a rapist and a bondage enthusiast. Sadomasochism is not a form of sexual assault. It is a consensual activity that involves polarized roles and intense sensations. An S/M scene is always preceded by a negotiation in which the top and bottom decide whether or not they will play, what activities are likely to occur, what activities will not occur, and about how long the scene will last. The bottom is usually given a "safe word" or "code action" she can use to stop the scene. This safe word allows the bottom to enjoy a fantasy that the scene is not consensual, and to protest verbally or resist physically without halting stimulation.*
>
> *The key word to understanding S/M is fantasy. The roles, dialogue, fetish costumes, and sexual activity are part of a drama or ritual. The participants are enhancing their sexual pleasure, not damaging or imprisoning one another. A sadomasochist is well aware that a role adopted during a scene is not appropriate during other interactions and that a fantasy role is not the sum total of her being (Califia, 1981, pp. 31–32).*

Califia is describing S/M as a community that is self-regulating and that warns newcomers about unsafe partners. Any S/M culture is likely to be varied. Clinicians see some cases in which serious injury and even death are the ends of acts that began as S/M fantasies. The arousal that accompanies the threat of a painful act pales for some, and arousal spills over to the threatened act itself. The movie *Midnight Cowboy* shows such a sequence, with a hustler throwing a masochist down a steep stairway, provoked by his insistence and followed by his orgasm.

PEDOPHILIA

Pedophilia is sexual attraction to children. Most people who take children as sexual partners (and are imprisoned for it) do not necessarily prefer them as sexual objects but find them less threatening and more readily available than adults (Gebhard et al., 1965). Men who have sex with children are not distinguishable from the rest of the population in looks or (other) actions. Some are otherwise respectable and accomplished citizens. The stereotype of the pedophile is the "dirty old man" who lurks about a playground for likely sexual targets among the children at play. But the stereotype is not especially accurate, for the target of pedophilia is rarely an absolute stranger, and a few may cooperate or invite the older man's attentions. Most sexual contacts with children are premeditated. In fact, in a follow-up study on males who as adolescents had had sex with older men, the older men had been acquaintances of the boys—a family friend, an employer, even a minister (Tindall, 1978).

Pedophilia may be homosexual or heterosexual, physically aggressive or not. Homosexual males who are attracted to young boys generally seek orgasm and accept boys of all ages. Although homosexual males make up 10 percent of the male population, they make up 20 percent of the population of child molesters. Unlike heterosexual males, who generally take children as sexual objects after failing with adult sexual partners, homosexual males are genuinely attracted to young boys. Some homosexual males who practice pedophilia are indiscriminate about the age and sex of their sexual objects (Gebhard et al., 1965). There is no evidence that adult oriented male homosexuals regress to take child victims (Groth and Burgess, 1978). Heterosexual males who practice pedophilia are more numerous than homosexual males, and they differ also in rarely seeking orgasm and in preferring younger partners. The heterosexual male's behavior actually resembles the immature sexual behavior of his young victims: he looks, touches, fondles, and shows his own genitals. He often masturbates afterward. But some men are brutal with and penetrate their victims.

Some men, both homosexual and heterosexual, are pedophiles—sexually attracted to young boys.

Studies show that heterosexual males who sexually victimize children tend to be impulsive and flighty. They marry rather impulsively and, therefore, rather often. As adults, they masturbate often and have long histories of sexual problems in their relationships (Gebhard et al., 1965). Here is a sad case history from the Gebhard et al. study:

The boy felt awkward and embarrassed with girls his own age, a typical early teenage situation, but unlike the typical teenager he responded by reverting to males of prepubertal age. This led to his first arrest, and when news of this spread through his high school his stunted heterosexual life with girls of his own years was blighted still more, which served to engender more pedophilic activity. His own pedophilic activity was confined to petting during which he did not ejaculate; instead, he would go home and masturbate. The petting was emotionally satisfying. As an adult on parole, he attempted to follow the prison psychologist's advice and establish a relationship with women. His first attempt was evidently so clumsy and uninspired that the woman refused a date saying, "I don't go out with queers." This had a crushing effect upon his morale and he turned again to children who were more likely to accept him.

The male who is aggressive toward his child victims seems to have a different history from the nonaggressive male. The aggressive male tends to be heterosexual and to have been poorly socialized. His views about sexuality tend to be conservative: he sees women as either very good and Madonna-like or as very bad and whorish. He makes liberal use of prostitutes and insists that his wife be a virgin. About 75 percent of the aggressive acts against children in the Gebhard et al. (1965) study had been committed by men while they were drunk. Many of these showed signs of psychological disturbances. Unlike unaggressive men who use children sexually, the aggressive men rarely knew their victims and more often sought intercourse with them. Below is a case history of aggressive pedophilia:

A 49-year-old Boston schoolbus driver was arrested in May 1977 for the rapes of a 12-year-old boy and a 13-year-old girl. The driver had lured the students to his home for the sexual activities. Both children were retarded. The driver had spent at least eleven of his last twenty-six years incarcerated in prison or treatment centers for offenses legally defined as sodomy, abuse of a female child, being a lewd person, open and gross lewdness, unnatural acts, assault and battery of a minor child, and contributing to the delinquency of a minor child. The bus company was unaware of the driver's history of repeated sex offenses because of a Massachusetts law that forbids law enforcement agencies from disseminating information about a person's criminal record. The driver was convicted of these and related crimes and sentenced to life imprisonment.

Investigation revealed that the driver was part of a group that used boys as homosexual prostitutes and models for pornographic films. Among the twenty-four men indicted in the group were a child psychiatrist and a psychologist.

THE ORIGINS OF SEXUAL VARIATIONS

Psychologists do not fully understand how sexual variations originate, but most agree on three points. First, sexual variations result from learning rather than from biological mishaps. No variation has ever been linked to a chromosome, gene, or hormone, although occasionally variant sexual behaviors emerge following brain damage. Second, sexual variations usually have roots in experiences before or during puberty, although psychologists disagree about the nature of those experiences. Third, the overwhelming majority of people who engage in sexual variations are men. In fact, the sex difference is probably the single most solid piece of evidence on variations. Given these three points, any theory that explains the origins of sexual variations must account for formative sexual experiences among boys.

Two influential theories of sexual variation include the psychoanalytic and conditioning theories. But we begin with an early, and now discredited, theory for historical interest.

Krafft-Ebing: Masturbation and Genes

Richard von Krafft-Ebing (1840–1902) was a German neurologist, psychiatrist, and author of a famous volume on sexual psychopathology called *Psychopathia Sexualis*. Krafft-Ebing, who presented the first detailed theory of sexual variations, believed that they had two sources. The first source was masturbation, in any form, including what he called "psychical onanism" and "nocturnal pollutions." (A modern conditioning theory, discussed later, also considers masturbation to play a critical role, although only the masturbation that accompanies variant fantasies.) The second source was genetic predisposition. Many of Krafft-Ebing's case histories begin by presenting "taints" in the subject's family. There is no evidence today for genetic predisposition toward any sexual variation. Although inaccurate in these ideas, Krafft-Ebing did introduce ideas about sexuality that have received support. Even so, he was a prime example of a Victorian sensibility, that could not view sexual behavior with detachment.

Freud: Arrested Development

A near contemporary of Krafft-Ebing (1856–1939) and, like him, a neurologist and psychiatrist, Sigmund Freud's attitudes toward sexual behavior were nevertheless quite different from Krafft-Ebing's. Freud believed that the roots of perversions, his name for variations, occurred in every childhood. He also believed that the prime motivation for everyone was sexual energy, or **libido,** and that biologically programmed events normally bring everyone through infantile, "perverse" sexuality into "normal," heterosexual, adult sexuality. Events that might disrupt this course of development might be, first, excessive gratification at one level of development that prevents progress to another level or, second, failure to resolve important conflicts, with the result a regression to early states of sensual gratification. The latter process Freud called "neurotic." A **neurosis** was created when a person failed to resolve a significant conflict and repressed from consciousness the conflict and the feelings attached to it.

Freud believed that perversions and neuroses were closely related. Because conflicts, which were at the root of neuroses, were inevitably sexual in nature, their repression meant the repression of sexual energy. Repressed sexual energy, Freud theorized, is expressed either as neurotic symptoms or as perversions. Most Freudian psychoanalysts believe that sexual variations are the consequences of unresolved **Oedipal conflicts,** in which the young child falls in love with and wants an exclusive relationship with his or her opposite-sex parent and fears punishment by the same-sex parent for this usurpation. In real-life variations, these translate into young boys fearing that their father will castrate them in punishment for the boys' desire for their mother and rivalry with their father. Thus psychoanalysts may interpret exhibitionism as a way for a man, unconsciously plagued with fears of punishment by his father, to reassure himself that his genitals are intact and potent. (Robert Stoller's theory of the origin of variations, described later in this chapter, is grounded in Freudian theory.)

Freud tried to explain why certain fetishes are very popular. He wrote that boys who fear castration wish to inspect their mothers' genitals to make sure that they are intact. When they discover that their worst fear seems to have come true, that some people lose their penises, they are severely distressed. The last object viewed before their horrible discovery becomes a symbol for the missing penis and is adopted as a fetish. Thus shoes, the foot, underwear, pubic hair and its look-alikes are all strong candidates for fetishes, and they are all in fact popular fetishes. This interesting theory does not account for the origins of fetishes that are unrelated to the lower half of a woman's body or the occasional fetishism among women. A conditioning theory can explain the same events more simply.

Psychoanalytic theory sees sexual and aggressive energy as closely linked, and in the adult sadomasochist, the normal balance between them has somehow grown distorted. Experimental evidence (see Chapter 13 on the labeling of arousal) does suggest that aggression can increase sexual arousal, and vice versa, but these relationships may be understood in terms of misinterpretations of physical arousal. Because all of the sexual variations are socially disapproved, acting them out might be expected to arouse people from fear, guilt, or anxiety, feelings that might be misinterpreted as sexual arousal. Thus we may be able to understand why sexual variations can increase sexual excitement for some without resorting to Freud's complex and unproven hypotheses. Finally, psychoanalytic theory does not easily account for the one solid finding on variations: the preponderance of males among those who engage in them.

Stoller: the Erotic Form of Hatred

Robert Stoller, a psychoanalyst at the University of California at Los Angeles, has offered the most recent psychoanalytic theory of the origins of sexual variations. He believes that the compulsive quality arises from a person's continual need to satisfy unconscious wishes and to repair childhood injuries to self-image and self-esteem (1975). Stoller believes that variant sexuality is "the erotic form of hatred," a sexual fantasy of revenge. In such sexual fantasies, a person imagines revenge on people to repair deeply felt, unconscious sexual injuries. Thus the boy who fears castration—a normal fear during all early male development, according to psychoanalysts—may as an adult compulsively exhibit his penis so that women will be shocked and thereby reassure him of his "manliness." The greatest excitement in the triumphant revenge comes from the variant act as risk-taking.

Because the sexual fantasy concerns rage and revenge, the sexual object is dehumanized and degraded. Thus, Stoller believes, variations are hostile at the core. In sadistic sex, the hostility is easy to see; in fetishism or **necrophilia** (sex with corpses), the dehumanization of the object is clear. Stoller believes that all sexual variations contain hostility, revenge, triumph, and a dehumanized object. The sexual behavior is pleasurable because it undoes trauma, guarantees a happy ending, and produces orgasm.

Conditioning Theories

Many clinicians have rejected the psychoanalytic explanations of variant sexual behaviors in favor of simple conditioning theories. Conditioning theorists explain the origin of sexual variations as the learning of unusual connections. (The notion that sexual variations are learned is not new. The originator of the first intelligence test, Alfred Binet, advanced such a theory early in this century.) Conditioning theory might explain the acquisition of a variation as follows. A boy comes into contact with a previously unerotic article just before he feels sexually aroused. The object then becomes arousing because of its chance pairing with the sexual arousal. Just as a bell can come to make a dog salivate in anticipation of food (by a process of pairing called "classical conditioning,") so an article of clothing can come to arouse a person sexually.

But this theory is too simple to relate the facts that we know about sexual variations to the dynamics of learning. Variations often seem to be powerfully ingrained in the sexual lives of their owners. They are very difficult to overcome: men may risk their reputations, jobs, and marriages to fulfill their variant sexual interests. How can so powerful a learned pattern of arousal grow out of an accidental, and probably rarely repeated, experience? Most powerful habits are gradually acquired and require considerable repetition.

A more complex theory of conditioning may help to explain sexual variations. According to this theory (McGuire, Carlisle, and Young, 1965), before any heterosexual play or intercourse, the young child comes into contact with a random stimulus or situation that is followed by the first significant sexual arousal. This single coincidence of arousal and stimulus is not enough to make the variant behavior permanent. The necessary learning takes place *after* the critical arousal, when the memory of the arousal is incorporated into a masturbation fantasy and locates the remembered stimulus right before orgasm. If the fantasy is repeatedly summoned during masturbation, the variant stimulus could eventually take on great erotic power. Other fantasies, such as those about intercourse, could eventually pale by comparison. Certain events might serve to reinforce the variant fantasy. Early failures at more typical sexual behavior, which are far from uncommon, might convince the person who enjoys a variant sexual fantasy that a typical sex life is neither possible nor even potentially rewarding.

A theory of variance that emphasizes masturbation fantasies may also be able to account for the reported differences between women and men. In all Western societies studied, women masturbate less than men, and they do so later in life, generally after they have had heterosexual experience (Kinsey et al., 1953). Therefore women are likely to develop predominantly heterosexual behavior and fantasies. Kinsey also reported that fewer (64 percent) females fantasize during masturbation than males (89 percent) do. The Hite Report (1976) found that some, but not all, women consider fantasy to be distracting from sexual arousal. For these reasons, women would be less likely than men to develop variant sexual behaviors. The problem with this theory of the source of variations is that it does not account for the low incidence of variations among the 64 percent of women who do fantasize during masturbation (Stoller, 1982). On the basis of McGuire and his colleagues' conditioning theory, we might predict that the few women who do practice variations will be found to resemble male practitioners in sexual development. Thus they should be found to share a background of early and continued masturbation, with variant fantasies, and an early sense of heterosexual relationships as unrewarding. Our prediction has not yet been tested for the simple reason that cases of females practicing variations are most unusual.

Conditioning theory needs more empirical support before it can be said to explain acceptably the origins of sexual variations. Masters and Johnson's early clinical reports (1970) suggested that early sexual practices might serve to imprint sexual dysfunction, and by inference, variations. The hypothesis has not been borne out by further clinical work, however. Many people overcome debilitating beginnings to their sexual lives. No one can yet account for why some such beginnings end happily and some dysfunctionally. An analog to a variation has been conditioned in the laboratory. A British researcher (Rachman, 1966) produced a boot fetish in three married psychologists. He did this by showing a slide of a pair of women's boots and then a slide of sexually arousing nude women. It took between 24 and 65 pairings for the three men to show erections to the boots alone on five successive trials. This classical (Pavlovian) conditioning model of variations seemed promising, but the effect has not been replicated, and it may have little to do with a real fetish or the ways real fetishes are created. Thus we are still left with little confirmation of the conditioning theory. Even so, it remains a popular view among behavioral researchers. The successes of clinical reconditioning strategies in sex therapy (see Chapter 16) no doubt keep hope of conditioning—and reconditioning—alive among researchers working in prisons with men whose variations have lost them their freedom.

THE SEXUAL VARIATION ITSELF MAY MAKE A PERSON ANXIOUS, GUILTY, OR EMBARRASSED.

TREATMENTS FOR SEXUAL VARIATIONS

Why do people who practice variations seek treatment? For some, with truly dangerous and publicly offensive sexual behavior, treatment is necessary for their own and for society's sake. For others, who voluntarily seek treatment, their sexual practices may not only risk legal reprisals but also personal disruption. A wife may, for example, tire of adapting to her husband's fetishistic practices and threaten to leave him. A man may fear disgrace if his behavior is made known to his children or employer. The sexual variation itself may make a person anxious, guilty, or embarrassed. Below we will describe the three major forms of treatment for sexual variations: psychoanalytic treatment, behavioral therapy, and biological therapy.

Psychoanalysis and Psychoanalytic Therapy

Psychoanalysis was once considered the classic treatment for sexual variations. A long, expensive, often traumatic course, psychoanalysis seeks to undo the repression that psychoanalysts believe causes sexual variations. The patient is led to recreate memories of the conflicts and situations that formed his sexual preferences (such as the sexual trauma, unconsciously retained, which Stoller believes to motivate the variant act). Once these repressed problems emerge, the patient can dissipate fears in other ways and begin maturing sexually (and to orthodox Freudians, heterosexuality is mature). Freudians are not sanguine about the use of psychoanalysis in patients who practice variations, because in psychoanalysis the defenses must be laid bare. Many people who practice variations lack the insight and kind of perseverance necessary for successful psychoanalytic treatment. Even the less involved therapies, which have evolved out of psychoanalysis, have not been very successful with the variations.

Behavior Therapy

Behavior therapists today are leading the attempt to devise new treatments for variant sexual behavior in willing patients. The therapists understand their interventions in terms of three major learning procedures.

Extinction Procedures   A therapist may arrange a procedure whereby the links between particular undesired behaviors and their rewarding consequences are weakened. Generally, when a behavior is not reinforced, it becomes less frequent and finally is extinguished. A therapist might, for example, note that a man who exhibits himself is reinforced by the reaction of his audience. Perhaps the women to whom he exposed himself ran away or screamed. The therapist might arrange for a long series of trials in which the man exposes himself to a nonreactive audience. This procedure might decouple the exhibitionism from its reinforcing consequences.

Punishment   Another approach to treating variant sexual behavior is punishment. Punishment can suppress the occurrence of undesired behaviors by linking a previously neutral or rewarding behavior with an aversive consequence. A man who cross-dresses might, for example, be punished by painful but harmless electric shocks after he has donned women's clothing. Because physical punishment by a therapist raises ethical concerns, behavior therapists currently use punishment imagery whenever possible rather than actual punishment. This kind of imagery procedure is known in general as a covert procedure. When a previously rewarding stimulus is linked with a fantasy of punishment—such as public humiliation— the procedure is called **covert sensitization**. Covert procedures can be very effective. (To feel the power of a covert stimulus, try the following: Settle yourself into a relaxing and comfortable position in a room with very little stimulation. Then imagine a lemon. Make the image very clear. Imagine cutting into the lemon. Then imagine biting into the juicy lemon. Now note what is happening in your mouth.)

Clearly, covert sensitization requires a patient's cooperation, for the patient must produce the fantasy. Although overt punishment is easier for a therapist to control and might seem more powerful than imagery, the effects of overt punishment often do not transfer beyond the punishment situation. Covert sensitization transfers more readily beyond the confines of the treatment room.

LEARNING AND REINFORCEMENT   As we have seen, many people whose typical sexual behavior is variant have been found to be deficient in the adult social skills that can lead to more typical sexual behavior. Educating them in these appropriate skills and reinforcing their exercise can be an important component of behavioral treatment. Merely extinguishing or suppressing variant sexual behavior never automatically leads to the acquisition of more appropriate sexual behavior.

CASE HISTORIES

Although some of the treatment approaches described seem cut and dried, actually they are not. They require lots of feedback about treatment progress and lots of inventiveness from the therapist. One can best get the flavor of behavior therapy for sexual variations by studying some case histories. We present two case histories, one successful and one unsuccessful.

> *Mr. C. was a 19-year-old, unemployed, ex-student who was referred to one of the authors by a state rehabilitation service for treatment of exhibitionism. Mr. C. had been picked up near his home several times by local police for exposing himself and masturbating in public. According to Mr. C., the police had threatened him with violence and arrest if they caught him again, yet he continued his exhibitionism. Mr. C. had been in special education classes and was mildly retarded, but he understood the consequences of his acts and feared his family's reaction if they found out about his behavior. He also feared the police.*
>
> *Mr. C. wanted a more typical sexual life but lacked any dating skills and many social skills. His sexual outlets, besides exhibitionism, were masturbating at home and occasional unsuccessful searches for prostitutes (one such search had led to his mugging in an alley). He had recently begun to fondle children in his neighborhood. Each of these behaviors seemed to be motivated not just by sexual needs but by the wish to overcome the humiliation he felt from being teased for his odd ways of interacting with his peers.*

The goals of the treatment for Mr. C.'s specific problems were to reduce the frequency of his exhibitionism and emerging pedophilia and to increase the frequency of appropriate sexual behaviors such as private masturbation, courting and dating behavior, and perhaps less risky searches for prostitutes. The therapist devised a broad treatment plan that addressed not only the sexual acts themselves but also the behavior that precipitated them. Included in the plan were:

1 Job skills—Mr. C.'s variant behavior seemed to stem in part from his boredom and shame at having no real work.
2 Social skills—if Mr. C.'s social awkwardness could be reduced, he would be teased less by others and would have a better chance of meeting and dating suitable partners.

3 Sex education—Mr. C. was ignorant of many facts about sexual functioning. In consequence, he was afraid of approaching adult partners.

4 Reduction of exhibitionism—Of the two variant behaviors, exhibitionism was the first addressed, because it was the most firmly established.

Covert sensitization was the treatment of choice. Because Mr. C. feared the police and his family's reaction, the therapist devised the following fantasy: Mr. C. is exposing himself to a group of girls at his customary location. The police approach from all sides, and they have barking, menacing dogs. The police and the dogs hold him at bay, and the police verbally abuse him. They fetch his family, who then taunt and humiliate him.

For this treatment plan to succeed, the procedures must be flexibly applied, and the treatment must last for a long enough time. Mr. C. did not report approaching any children during the time of treatment, and he made gains on most of the other goals of treatment. But he did not find a job. When Mr. C. reported new fantasies about exposing himself, the therapist shifted to a new covert fantasy: The police pick him up and report his arrest to his family. As Mr. C.'s behavior grew more acceptable to his peers, his variant fantasies diminished. It would be reasonable to expect Mr. C.'s progress to be stable. Mr. C. comes into therapy periodically for booster sessions. These sessions renew his contact with his therapist and reinforce the covert sensitization.

Not all cases are as successfully treated as Mr. C.'s. But his case demonstrates what clinicians commonly find: real people do not fit simple clinical labels. Mr. C. was an exhibitionist turning to pedophilia. In real life, many police cases referred for outpatient therapy are interrupted by courts or social workers before the therapy has had time to proceed very far, or by the client's lack of cooperation. Even if the treatment is mandated by a court, it is unlikely to be successful unless the client cooperates. The case history of Mr. D. is from Barlow and Wincze's (1980) description of a case that can be adapted to the general treatment of pedophilia. Pedophilia and incestuous pedophilia are not identical. But the therapists in this case, by making clear their treatment methods and goals, show how pedophilia also can be treated.

Mr. D. was a 52-year-old skilled workman who reported a 10-year history of sexual involvement with his daughter. She was 22 years old at the time treatment began. At the time that he became sexually involved with his then 12-year-old daughter, Mr. D.'s sexual adjustment with his wife was quite poor. The incestuous activities began with light kissing and fondling and proceeded to mutual masturbation. When the daughter was 16, her mother learned of the incestuous relationship and divorced Mr. D. The daughter lived with her mother, and Mr. D. remarried. His adjustment in the second marriage, sexual and otherwise, seemed good. After a 5-year separation from his daughter, Mr. D. visited her, and their sexual relationship resumed. Mr. D. grew depressed and confessed the relationship to his new wife. With her support, he entered behavioral treatment.

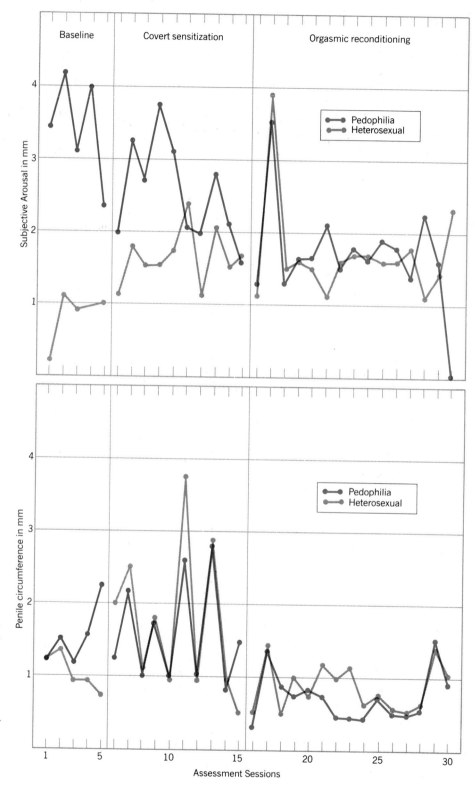

FIGURE 15.1

Behavioral treatment of sexual variations. Baseline refers to penile measurements before treatment. Covert sensitization shows penile measurements during imaging. Orgasmic reconditioning shows penile measurements during sessions of reconditioning to heterosexual stimuli. (Source: Barlow and Wincze, 1980)

The treatment's goal was to reduce Mr. D.'s incestuous fantasies but to preserve his capacity to relate appropriately to his daughter. (The daughter was also in therapy at the time.) The therapist assessed Mr. D.'s incestuous sexual arousal in two ways: one subjective and one physiological. For the first, the therapist devised several scenes of Mr. D. interacting sexually with his daughter and asked Mr. D. to rate his degree of arousal to each scene. To assess Mr. D.'s desire to interact appropriately with his daughter, the therapist devised several scenes for him to rate as well. For the physiological assessment, the therapist measured changes in Mr. D.'s penile circumference (easily done with a strain gauge around the penis, the gauge attached to a polygraph machine) as he looked at photographs of his daughter and heard descriptions of incestuous activities with her. These assessments were made often during the course of treatment and after it ended, to provide measures of Mr. D.'s progress.

The covert sensitization of Mr. D. centered on fantasies of his punishment upon being discovered by his second wife and the family priest in sexual relations with his daughter. The fantasies then depicted Mr. D. being rejected by these three people, who were important to him. Mr. D. was treated as an in-patient, and the therapist of Mr. D. created the punishing scenes five times a day for 15 days. After he was discharged, Mr. D. continued to present these scenes to himself.

The results appear in the two graphs of Figure 15.1. The graphs show Mr. D.'s changes in penile circumference (a measure of degree of erection) and his psychological arousal during the imaging before treatment—the baseline segment—during treatment—the covert sensitization segment—and after treatment. The reduction in variant arousal shows clearly.

Sexually atypical behavior may become a highly personalized expression of the self, hard to modify at will.

A CURRENT PERSPECTIVE

The state of the art in treating sexual variations can be represented by Barlow and Wincze's (1980) three-part model. These clinical researchers take a problem-oriented approach to treatment. They repeatedly measure progress before, during, and after treatment. The first part of their approach consists of assessing and reducing any problems of sexual arousal or behavior. They might, for example, intervene to strengthen adult, heterosexual arousal and to weaken pedophilic arousal. The second part aims at the social skills and emotions associated with their client's sexual functioning. (In Mr. C.'s treatment, this second part was prominent.) The third part of the treatment aims at deviations from accepted gender roles. Some clients with sexual variations are confused about aspects of gender roles. They may have rigid ideas about how to dress or act; they may not understand what others consider cross-gender ways of acting or speaking.

For treatment of sexual variations to succeed, the evidence suggests that flexible and individually tailored therapy is necessary. Partners and even children may need to be included in treatment, and a client's overall adaptation may need to be considered and modified. Therapy may have to eliminate or reduce typical triggers for variant sexual acts—fights between husband and wife, for example, or particularly wounding taunts. By taking a broad and problem-oriented approach, therapists may be able to help clients reduce or eliminate the most extreme and threatening sexual variations. Sometimes, artful and hand-tailored therapy can successfully treat forms of behavior that typically are very resistant to therapeutic modification. Incestuous behavior and rape fall into this category. (See Abel et al., 1978, for a description of treatment for rape.)

But it is good to keep in mind that despite real advances in treating sexual variations, the task is a formidable one. Sexual behavior has many underlying motives, some difficult to understand and not all related to what might be considered normal sexual motivation. Sexually atypical behavior may take on the qualities of a signature; it may become a stable and highly personalized expression of the self, hard to modify at will.

Biological Therapies

Attempts to deter atypical sexual behavior that rely on biological methods are socially and ethically questionable. They are also not always effective. Denmark, for example, treats sex offenders by castrating them. (Castration of violent, repetitive sex offenders was once fairly common in the United States and in England.) Although technically the offender is given the choice between long imprisonment and castration, the choice is probably not a live one for most men. A study of 900 Danish men who had been castrated over a 30-year period (with a median follow-up period of at least six years) showed that sexual arousability and erections declined over time in most of the men. After castration, further conviction rates dropped to around 1 percent (compared to 18 percent with uncastrated sex offenders) (Sturup, 1972). But in the short run, castration does not turn off sexual behavior. Some male animals and humans who are castrated can retain their sexual capacities for years (Bermant and Davidson, 1974; Hart, 1974). Castration may work in some cases to reduce socially offensive sexual behavior, but its human costs are high. A study of 39 sex offenders released from West German prisons showed that sexual thoughts, coitus, and masturbation all declined after castration, but not *soon* after. The study also noted that castration seemed to have a strong effect only if it had been performed on males between the ages of 46 and 59 (Heim and Hursch, 1979). In the United States, as recently as 1970, the attorney general of California ruled that it would be unethical for men to trade castration for parole or a lighter sentence.

BECAUSE lobotomies and castration are so questionable ethically, clinicians have looked to reversible drugs and hormones.

Lobotomy, a surgical procedure that cuts connections to the frontal lobe of the brain, was once performed on men who were considered sexually deviant. Like castration, psychosurgery is permanent. But psychosurgery alters more than sexual behavior; it affects the entire personality. Lobotomies are rarely prescribed today. Because lobotomies and castration are so questionable ethically, clinicians have looked to reversible drugs and hormones. Often, clinicians combine biological drug treatment with psychological treatment. At Baltimore's Johns Hopkins Hospital, for example, hormone injections (of medroxyprogesterone acetate—also called Depo-Provera—which alters the hormone ratios that presumably govern male sexual desire) plus counseling have reportedly helped some sex offenders to regulate their behavior. Said John Money, the medical psychologist who ran the program, the men get a vacation from the sex drive (Coakley, 1979, p.3A), with time out to learn how to manage their antisocial fantasies and acts. Relapse rates after one year are reported to be low (Berlin and Einecke, 1981). In Europe, an antiandrogen drug called *cyproterone acetate* has been used on sex offenders with presumably promising results. The drug, however, reduces sexual arousability as well as curbing antisocial sexual tendencies. Newer antiandrogens are being tested in the United States. Recent European reports of a new major tranquilizer, Benperidol, attest to its ability to reduce variant behavior *without* reducing arousability. But these reports should probably be met with skepticism until we have more evidence.

Evaluating Treatments

A recent summary to evaluate treatments for variations concluded that studies too often lacked control groups and relied too heavily on what the men reported rather than on a large number of independent measures. The good news lay in behavioral treatment tailored to individual clients' arousal patterns. Combining treatment to eliminate variant patterns with that to foster appropriate sexual behavior seems a promising approach. In men with long histories of variant behavior, booster treatment sessions seem necessary (Kilmann et al., 1982).

SUMMARY

1 Sexual variations are sexual activities that are preferred to or substituted for heterosexual intercourse or that involve unusual methods of arousal. Sexual variations tend to have a compulsive quality.

2 Most people who practice sexual variations do no harm to others or involve a willing partner. But some force their victims' participation, psychologically or physically harming them. More men than women practice sexual variations. Many of those apprehended by police have few social skills or other resources, but it is from this disadvantaged group that most information on sexual variations has been drawn.

3 Sexual variations violate widely shared values about sex—that it be private, for example, and confined to consenting adults. Ideas about what is normal and deviant vary from culture to culture.

4 One theory (Freud's) holds that sexual variations are childhood sexuality magnified and elaborated. Another (Beach's) holds that variations differ from typical acts in the appetitive behavior that brings people closer together. Yet another (Stoller's) sees variations as vengeful attempts at repairing old, unconsciously remembered traumas.

5 Exhibitionism is the act of exposing one's genitals to an unwilling audience for one's own sexual pleasure. It is the single most common sex offense in the United States.

6 Voyeurism is watching people undress or have sex without their permission or knowledge. Voyeurs do not want to be discovered. Most are males who operate alone, in secret, and who masturbate as they observe.

7 Fetishism is the use of an object (object fetishism) or body part (partialism) for sexual arousal, usually solitary arousal. Those who practice fetishism seem immature, fearful of sex, and wary of heterosexual encounters.

8 Transvestism is the practice of dressing in clothes of the other sex to achieve solitary or social sexual pleasure.

9 Sadism is the infliction of pain for sexual pleasure. Masochism is the acceptance of pain for sexual pleasure. The composite variation is called sadomasochism. The cruelty may be actual or symbolic; often it is ritualized and enacted in fantasy.

10 Pedophilia is sexual attraction to children. Children may appeal to some people as less sexually threatening and more readily available than adults. Pedophilia may be homosexual or heterosexual, physically aggressive or not.

11 The origins of sexual variations are not entirely clear to psychologists. But they know that variations result from learning rather than from biological mishaps, their roots go back to puberty or before, and many more men than women practice them. Both psychoanalytic and conditioning theories have been offered to explain the origins of sexual variations.

12 Psychoanalytic therapies are not very successful in treating sexual variations, perhaps because of limitations in those who practice variations, or perhaps because the variation is intensely rewarding.

13 Behavior therapy individually tailored to the needs of the client can in some cases reduce or eliminate the practice of variant sexual behavior and introduce more socially acceptable patterns of behavior.

14 Biological therapies for variations are controversial. Some are permanent (like castration) and of questionable value. Antiandrogen treatment may prove promising for some men.

KEY TERMS

sexual variation
appetitive behavior
consummatory behavior

drag queens
sadism
masochism

exhibitionism
frottage
voyeurism
fetishism
partialism
object fetish
transvestism (cross-dressing)
transsexual

sadomasochism
pedophilia
libido
neurosis
Oedipal conflicts
necrophilia
covert sensitization
lobotomy

SUGGESTED READINGS

Bancroft, J. *Deviant Sexual Behavior: Modifications and Assessment*. New York: Oxford University Press, 1974. An overview of attempts to modify and evaluate variations in sexual behavior.

Gebhard, P. H., Gagnon, J. H., Pomeroy, W. B., and Christenson, C. V. *Sex Offenders*. New York: Harper & Row, 1965 (New York: Bantam, 1967). A technical and comprehensive Kinsey-style investigation of convicted sex offenders. It is the largest study of its kind.

Lester, D. *Unusual Sexual Behaviors*. Springfield, IL: Thomas, 1975. A nontechnical review of forms and presumed causes of sexual variations.

Stoller, R. J. *Perversion: the Erotic Form of Hatred*. New York: Dell (Delta Books) 1975. A psychiatrist known for his command of research and clinical evidence provides his own psychoanalytic version of perversion. An interesting and controversial book.

VICTOR VASARELY, "GOTHA." COLLECTION, THE MUSEUM OF MODERN ART, NEW YORK.

Chapter 16

Sexual Problems, Communication, and Therapy

DEVELOPMENT OF SEXUAL PROBLEMS

Sometimes our sexual imaginings exceed our bodies' abilities to carry them out. Orgasms may come too soon or not at all; erections disappear when put to the test; vaginas clamp shut before penetration. Complete sexual enjoyment is never certain, even with a desirable and beloved partner. In real life, all sorts of problems may interfere with people's sexual fulfillment. If people feel, after extensive sexual experience, either that they repeatedly are failing to enjoy sex or to share enjoyment with a partner, **sexual dysfunction** may be the problem. Dysfunction does not happen only to "other people"; most people have temporary sexual problems at some time or other.

Mind and Body

Conventional wisdom would steer us to the genitals for the origins of sexual problems. After all, they're the parts not doing their job. But if we started with the genitals, often we'd be starting at the wrong end of the body. Many sexual problems are psychological in origin; some are physiological. Sometimes the distinction is blurred, because psychological events can modify physiological responses. It is important for a sex therapist to diagnose the cause of the patient's sexual symptoms.

Some sexual problems are not psychological in origin (although they may have strong psychological consequences). In fact, sex therapists have been modifying their estimates downward of the proportion of sexual dysfunctions that are psychologically caused. They once believed that the vast majority of cases of erectile dysfunction were psychological in origin. But today, evidence suggests many cases with clear physiological causes. Medication, hormonal, vascular, and neurological problems today are implicated frequently in cases of erectile dysfunction. The treatment for sexual dysfunctions of physiological origin is, of course, quite different from the treatment of sexual dysfunctions with a psychological origin. But in any case of sexual dysfunction, the whole person—mind *and* body—is affected. The feedback runs in both directions: just as mental events constantly modify the behavior of the organs, glands, and muscles, physiological events constantly affect sexual moods, attitudes, and motivation. Just as hormones affect behavior, behavior may affect hormones. Stressful events measurably modify hormone levels (Rose et al., 1972).

SEXUAL COMMUNICATION

Sexual interaction is not merely organs grinding. It is a complex mix of fantasy, friction, and communication. All of us have had years of getting to know our own bodies before we enter into mature sexual interaction. Each sexual episode of the present echoes past sensual and sexual experiences. To each sexual episode, we bring our personal histories, our attitudes and values, likes and dislikes, information and misinformation. Part of our sexual pleasure or displeasure will follow from how thoroughly we communicate our sexual needs and wishes.

The student who asked that question was sure that we had an all-purpose answer. We don't. But we can give some general advice.

Sex is usually best when people really trust and care about one another. Most of us go through life with a public self that seems far less sensitive than our private self. Society demands this facade, but it can cause trouble in bed. Many people feel that they should seem knowing when in fact they are uncertain. In a sexual relationship, we are naked and vulnerable, and when we feel this way, we tend to respond especially well to someone who is truly considerate and understanding. People get to be considerate and understanding by tuning in to how their partner is feeling. The intimacy between people who are honestly sharing their feelings is a fertile place for sexual desire to grow. So, to be good in bed, it's worth the effort to be honest and considerate with your partner.

If you know something about sexual responses, you know areas of particular sensitivity. Women should know that many men feel tired and want to disengage after orgasm. Men should know that stopping stimulation before or during a woman's orgasm can stop it dead in its tracks. Start-stop works better for men than for women; women may feel that it is inconsiderate. Many women need nongenital foreplay before they can enjoy genital stimulation. Men's fantasies about penetration usually translate into foreplay techniques that focus on the vagina. The entrance and outer parts of the vagina are more sensitive than the inner parts, but the clitoris is much more sensitive. Two out of three women need clitoral stimulation to reach a climax. But many women are shy about saying just what they like. Yet men say that they want to know what gives women pleasure and are surely happier when their partner responds more to sex (Fisher, 1973; Hite, 1976; Pietropinto and Simenauer, 1977).

Some women think it is unromantic and unspontaneous to discuss contraception. An abortion or an unwanted child is not romantic either. Some men— Norman Mailer talks about such fantasies in his *Prisoner of Sex*—think good sex is ejaculating into a ready space where an egg waits for their sperm. They should tell their partner in case she does not want to act out their fantasy. It's her decision, too, in that the "ready space" contains her egg, and it's her "space" that's filled when she becomes pregnant.

Good sex does not always require new variations or new positions, although most people do like some variety now and then. If life outside of bed is bewildering, the good old, same-as-always way in bed may feel just right. Good sex does not always mean intercourse. Sometimes just being close is best. Sometimes going back to sex play without intercourse is fun. At other times, a new position is attractive. Inventiveness may be fun, but to be really good in bed, a person needs to be open, honest, and considerate. That's harder than making love while standing on your head, but it's much more of a turn-on.

It is a tribute to humans that, despite temporary setbacks, most do enjoy sex. The mystery for psychologists is to understand which factors allow some people to communicate and work out their sexual worries and difficulties, despite unfavorable histories and despite cultural repression of sexuality, when other people, with similar backgrounds, cannot. Said one sex therapist, "I wish I could tell you that good sex always happens between two people when profound feeling exists, but it's not necessarily so" (Offit, in Gittelson, 1980, p.20). Even early experience, which intuition assures us might lead to later sexual dysfunction, may not be an accurate predictor.

COMMUNICATION ENRICHES AND ENHANCES SEXUAL INTERACTION.

FOUR CAUSES OF SEXUAL DYSFUNCTION

Partners who can continue to communicate with one another—by word or gesture, during or after, in bed or out—about what works for them and what does not are both likely to enjoy their sex and, eventually, to reach orgasm at the desired moments. Communication enriches and enhances sexual interaction. Women who trust their partner and feel genuinely loved and cared for are more likely than others to become orgasmic (Fisher, 1973). It may be reassuring to new couples who are working out their sexual experience to know that sexual therapists do not consider them to have sexual dysfunction, even if they have symptoms of what would be considered dysfunction in established couples. Therapists usually will treat couples only after their relationship is well established and they have had many occasions for intercourse and other forms of sexual interaction together.

Some people's lives contain more than their share of obstacles to sexual pleasure. An absence of communication about sexual and other issues is often one such obstacle. In the case history that follows, you will see other common obstacles to sexual pleasure.

Mr. and Mrs. A. were referred to Masters and Johnson for treatment. Mrs. A. had grown up in a very formal and controlled family. Privacy connected with dress and toilet was the rule without exception. The father censored any mention of sex in the reading material coming into the home. Mrs. A.'s mother was a dutiful housekeeper, mother, and servant to her husband. The family was a place where pleasure and talk about pleasure were absent.

Mrs. A. and her sister were both told by their mother after they started menstruation to expect "the curse" with bad pain every month. Both young girls confirmed their mother's expectations.

In her teens, Mrs. A. was allowed by her father to date in groups at school or church events where adult chaperoning was assured. The father selected a college for Mrs. A. where male and female undergraduates, when together, were required to keep a minimal 18 inches distance between them at all times. Mrs. A. met her husband while working as a secretary in a firm specializing in religious publications. Her only bodily contact with her future husband consisted of three kisses, the only kisses she had received from any man.

On Mrs. A.'s wedding day her mother told her that Mr. A. would soon have a husband's "privileges" and Mrs. A. would soon have a wife's "duty." According to the mother, Mrs. A. could expect to be hurt by her husband but "it" would get better over time. Mrs. A.'s reward for submitting to "it" would be children.

With this preparation for marriage, Mrs. A.'s first night with Mr. A. was a nightmare: he frantically searching for where to put his penis; she protecting her modesty with bedsheets and nightgown. Her pain whenever her husband attempted penetration finally led to his renunciation of trying. He finally resorted to masturbation, of which she was not aware. In the three years before they consulted Masters and Johnson, he made attempts at intercourse about once every three or four months, sometimes ejaculating while trying to penetrate. Mrs. A. assumed that this was satisfying for him.

Mrs. A., on examination in St. Louis nine years after marriage, was found to have an intact hymen and a severe case of vaginismus, a disorder in which an involuntary spasm of the vagina prevents penetration. Treatment of vaginismus starts with a demonstration to the husband of the totally involuntary nature of the spasm. This occurs dramatically when a vaginal examination is attempted by the doctor. During this examination, Mrs. A.'s husband—for the first time in his life—saw his wife without clothing (after Master and Johnson, 1970).

Four factors crop up frequently in the histories of people, like Mr. and Mrs. A., who consult sex therapists:

1 Ignorance about biological and sexual functioning.

2 Shame about sexual behavior.

3 Lack of communication about important, not necessarily sexual, issues.

4 Fear of failure in sexual encounters that leads to anxious watchfulness about performance.

Performance anxiety leads to a phenomenon called **spectatoring,** in which a person becomes a spectator at his or her own sexual events. Because people feel inhibited and respond poorly when they are watching their every move, spectatoring is incompatible with pleasure. Similarly, sexual ignorance in people with strict and judgmental backgrounds or in people who have been taught that sex is permissible only for procreation, may lead to sexual problems. Here is a case history of one such couple:

Both Mr. and Mrs. B. came from strict religious homes that provided no sexual education. At marriage, both were virgins. Mr. B. had tried twice to gain sexual experience with prostitutes. Both contacts ended disastrously. One prostitute humiliated Mr. B. by laughing at him for his lack of knowledge. The second coitus never occurred because Mr. B. ejaculated prematurely while trying to figure out how to use a condom. Mr. B.'s premarital sexual knowledge consisted of occasional masturbation during his teens and some peer-group instruction of a vague sort. He had never seen a woman—not even in a picture—fully undressed. Only after 9 months of marriage did Mr. and Mrs. B. manage to have intercourse. The sporadic coital episodes typically ended in premature ejaculation. This gave Mrs. B. no chance at sexual satisfaction. Mr. B. was mortified and watchful at each of the infrequent, widely spaced sexual encounters. Neither partner knew how to talk to the other about the situation. The virtual disappearance of intimacy and of sexual encounters led Mrs. B. to become a shrew within the family. Finally she turned to an extra-marital affair where she experienced some gratification. Mr. B. also turned to an extramarital affair, which did not work for him. After ten years of marriage, and after having three children, they sought the advice of their pastor. Unfortunately, he minimized the importance of the problem, leading Mr. B. to abandon the church. Later the couple consulted Masters and Johnson (after Masters and Johnson, 1970).

Working Harder

Many people react to sexual dysfunction by working harder. Although this can be an excellent solution for a weak tennis backhand, it is a poor solution for sexual dysfunction. Overconcern about sexual performance usually generates failure, and a vicious cycle begins. The paradox is that we must let go to perform. We must let the reflexes happen. Once we start actively willing them to happen, telling ourselves to feel excited, to become erect, or to lubricate, the more elusive the desired responses grow. Most sexual dysfunction comes from inhibition, from not letting the body express itself in sexual release. Like sleep, sexual reflexes visit a body that is comfortable and ready to allow those reflexes to evolve naturally.

Trying harder usually does *not* lead to sexual pleasure. People then have two choices. They can suffer in silence, or they can seek professional help. Many—perhaps most—people choose the first alternative, because seeking help is not easy. One's sexual behavior is private and fraught with emotion. It is hard for people to see their sex lives as impersonally as they see their difficulties with objects like cars, objects that they take to be repaired without judging themselves harshly. Most people view their sexual experiences as a special, unique, even if troublesome, part of themselves. People cannot rearrange their histories, but they can sometimes rearrange their futures. Many people decide that they want more from their sexual lives, or they want to regain what they have lost. Sexual therapy can provide real help.

SEXUAL DYSFUNCTION IN HOMOSEXUALS

Heterosexual men and women do not have an exclusive claim to sexual dysfunctions or their treatment. Homosexuals share most of the sexual problems of heterosexuals: problems of desire, arousal, and orgasm, problems of sexual shame, lack of knowledge, failure to communicate, and anxiety that leads to spectatoring. Many gay people suffer enormous guilt about their sexuality, and guilt and shame feed sexual problems. Gays are treated according to the same therapeutic principles as heterosexual couples. Sex therapy is available to gays in some clinics or private

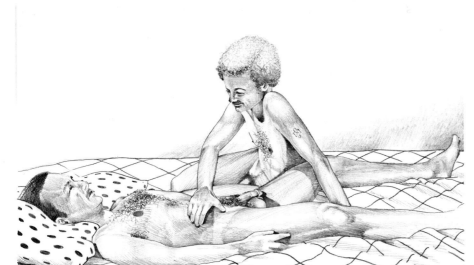

FIGURE 16.1

Therapy for gay couples.

practices that treat heterosexual couples as well as in clinics run by the gay community. Clinics set up by members of the gay rights movement to serve the special needs of gay men and women are becoming sources of new knowledge about homosexual functioning in and out of bed (Paul et al., 1982).

MALE DYSFUNCTION

The most common sexual problems for men are erectile dysfunction and premature ejaculation. Erectile problems once were called "impotence," a term that has been dropped because of its inaccurate connotation, as if a problem with erection meant the loss of all of a man's power.

Erection Problems

Erectile dysfunction describes a man's repeated inability to get or keep an erection of his penis. Erection problems are embarrassing; they wound a man's self-esteem. He may come to dread that his erection problems signal the end of his virility and youth. Irrational fears may abound. He may worry that his "excessive" masturbation has come back to haunt him, for example. Self-esteem can go the way of the erection. One man reports his pain at erectile loss in this way:

> Once I was having intercourse with a woman I loved and respected. She was about to orgasm. . . . I could feel my erection going soft. I got scared. I fell out of her vagina. . . . I felt subhuman, a total, miserable failure, the worst lover and person on earth (Hite, quoted in Herman, 1982, p.265).

Clinical psychologists recognize that catastrophic assaults on self-esteem, such as the one reported by this man, go hand in hand with depression. Indeed, a man worried about his erectile failures can become depressed, even if he has never been seriously depressed before. He usually is depressed most when he is with the very person he cares about, who knows most intimately about his problem—his partner. If the partner feels that she (or he, in homosexual couples) is the cause of the erection problem, she (or he) may feel threatened and contribute to the other's guilt and frustration. A vicious cycle has begun.

When a man has never been able to have an erection in vaginal or anal intercourse (in the latter case, regardless of his partner's sex), his dysfunction is called **primary erectile dysfunction.** Much more common is the form of erection problem, called **secondary erectile dysfunction,** in which a man has lost his ability to have erections. Masters and Johnson diagnose secondary erectile dysfunction when a man cannot erect on one-quarter or more of his sexual opportunities. Another kind of erection problem, **transient erectile dysfunction,** is temporary

SEXUALITY IN PERSPECTIVE: SEXUAL PROBLEMS IN "NORMAL" COUPLES

Psychologists know most about the sexual problems of people who present themselves for treatment, people who form the clinical population. But what about the sexual behavior of "normal" people, those who consider themselves happily married and sexually functional? Do they have sexual problems, and if so, of what type, how often, and with what effects on their personal relationships? Three psychologists from the University of Pittsburgh happened on some answers to these questions (Frank et al., 1978). The volunteers were predominantly white, middle class, Christian, and well educated. Of the 100 couples, 84 had children, 12 reported having had marriage counseling at some previous time, and their average age was the mid-30s.

When asked questions about how happily married they were, 83 percent of both husbands and wives rated themselves happily or very happily married; 88 percent of husbands and 89 percent of wives said that they would marry the same person again; and the majority considered their marriages better than other marriages.

But when they began answering questions about their sexual behavior, the couples showed a surprisingly high number of problems, surprising, that is, for people who considered themselves happily married. The investigators had divided sexual problems into two categories. "Dysfunctions" included problems with erection and ejaculation in husbands and problems of arousal and orgasm in wives; in other words, these were performance problems. "Difficulties" had more to do with the emotional tone of sexual relations and included "partner chooses inconvenient time," "inability to relax," "turned off," "too little foreplay before intercourse." Among wives, 48 percent reported difficulty getting excited, 46 per-in nature. It may be caused by too much alcohol, by distraction, or by fatigue. Unlike secondary erectile dysfunction, it passes when the fatigue, distraction, or alcohol does.

A survey in the mid-1950s uncovered that more than one-third of men married for a long time who enjoy sexual pleasure in their marriage report occasional erection problems (Ard, 1977). Even in a happily married, well educated sample of 100 couples, 16 percent of the husbands had problems getting or maintaining an erection (Frank et al., 1978). (See "Sexuality in Perspective: Sexual Problems in 'Normal' Couples.") Among the 7200 men who responded to Shere Hite's questionnaire for the *Hite Report* (1981), 39 percent reported rarely having erection problems; 17 percent reported sometimes having erection problems; and 13 percent reported frequently, regularly, or always having erection problems (Herman, 1982).

cent reported difficulty reaching orgasm, and 33 percent difficulty in maintaining excitement. Among husbands, 36 percent reported ejaculating too quickly, and 16 percent reported erectile problems.

Was there any relationship between sexual problems and the amount of satisfaction the couples reported: yes and no. The answer really depended on the nature of the problem. "Dysfunctions" seemed not to dampen satisfaction; these were products of inhibitions, ignorance, and physical problems and were tolerated well. But "difficulties," which reflected problems between the partners, did dampen satisfaction. The sexual problems that were least well tolerated were a wife's sexual "difficulties." In general, the wives' reports of sexual *difficulties* in themselves and their husbands were more strongly related to feelings of sexual dissatisfaction in both partners than were reports of sexual *dysfunctions*. Husbands tended to underestimate their wives' dysfunction, a finding that can be interpreted in two ways. First, husbands tend to assume that all is well so long as their wives neither complain nor refuse intercourse. Second, wives tend to want emotional sensitivity in sex more than their husbands do. Despite the incidence of sexual problems, 86 percent of the wives and 85 percent of the husbands considered their sexual relations moderately or very satisfying. That the couples felt happily married and sexually satisfied implies that this group, chosen for its normality, can tolerate a fairly large number of sexual problems. The conclusion: how a couple feels about the emotional tone of their marriage determines, far more than sexual virtuosity, how satisfied they are with their sexual relationship.

Based on E. Frank, C. Anderson, and D. Rubinstein. "Frequency of Sexual Dysfunction in 'Normal' Couples," *New England Journal of Medicine*, vol. 299 (July 20, 1978) pp.111–115.

ORGANIC CONTRIBUTIONS   Although many cases of erection problems are psychological in origin, reputable sex therapists first try to rule out any organic (biological) causes. If an organic cause turns up, it is addressed first. For example, early, undiagnosed diabetes can cause difficulty in erection, and insulin treatment can help restore lost function. Hormone disorders that lower androgen levels also

SEXUALITY IN PERSPECTIVE: CAUSES OF ERECTION PROBLEMS

One of the problems that has plagued researchers in sexual dysfunctions has been the elusiveness of the cause of erection problems in men. When researchers looked at studies from endocrinologists, they found that most cases of erectile dysfunction had endocrinological origins. When they looked at studies from neurologists, they found cases with neurological origins. The same thing happened with studies from urologists, psychiatrists, and so on. To eliminate this obvious selection bias, researchers from the Minneapolis Veterans Administration Medical Center questioned 1180 men at a general medical clinic. Of this group, 34 percent (401 men) answered that they were suffering from erection problems. Their average age was 59 years. Of these 401 men, 188 agreed to have the cause of their erection problem evaluated further. Physicians find it hard to convince men with erection problems to seek help. It is not easy for men to live with an erection problem, but it is not easy for them to ask for help with it either. Keep in mind that this sample had its own bias, in that the men were patients at a medical clinic. The results were as follows:

TABLE 16.1
Source of Erection Problems

Endocrine problems (diabetes, pituitary or thyroid disease, malfunctioning testes)	38%
Medication	25%
Psychological	14%
Neurological	7%
Urological	6%
Other/unknown	11%

The researchers concluded that when erection problems strike, doctors and laypeople alike should first consider whether the cause is a new drug. A check for diabetes and other hormonal disorders would come next. Perhaps the most interesting finding of this study was the relatively small proportion (14 percent) of cases attributed to psychological causes.

Based on Slag et al. "Impotence in medical clinic outpatients." *Journal of the American Medical Association,* 1983, 249, 1736–1740.

can cause erection problems, and so can certain disorders of the nervous system or blood vessels, certain surgical procedures, some medications, and narcotic or alcohol use (Kaplan, 1974, 1983; Masters and Johnson, 1970). In a very few cases, a tumor interferes with sexual interest and performance (Kaplan, 1984, personal communication).

Although transient erection problems are not themselves serious, they can trigger enough performance anxiety to make a man dread any sexual encounter. Fear and anxiety can turn transient problems into true secondary erectile dysfunction. About half of the men treated for secondary erectile dysfunction by Masters and Johnson developed the problem after a history of either premature ejaculation or fairly heavy drinking.

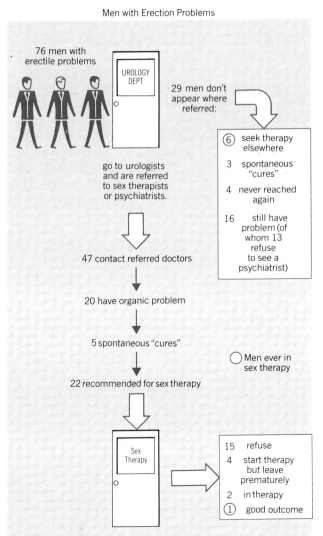

FIGURE 16.2

Men with erection problems. Urologists may see more men with erection problems than either sex therapists or psychiatrists see. Of 76 urological patients referred to a psychiatrist or sex therapist, only 13 (17%) entered sex therapy; 20 (26%) had an organic problem; 7 (9%) got better spontaneously; and 28 (36%) refused therapy although their problems remained (based on Seagraves et al., 1982).

FIGURE 16.3

Penile implants. An inflatable pump can be surgically implanted in certain men who suffer erection problems. The device consists of a reservoir (*A*), silicon tubes, a bulb attached to a pump, and (*B*) two silicon cylinders that can be pumped full of liquid from the reservoir.

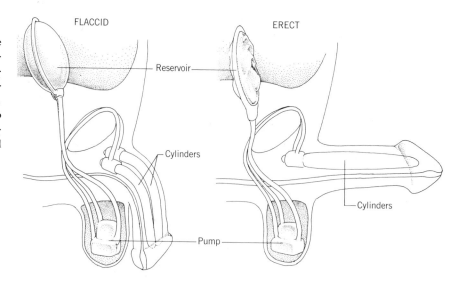

DIAGNOSING THE CAUSE OF ERECTION PROBLEMS   A differential diagnosis of erection problems establishes whether the cause is psychological or organic.[1] But for the clinician to reach the diagnosis is tricky and often uncertain. Although physicians already had studied the effects of the nervous system and blood vessels on erections by the turn of the century, that sort of work was eclipsed by Sigmund Freud's new psychoanalytic theory of sexual problems. More recently, successes in treating men with normal testosterone levels led Masters and Johnson to believe that virtually all erection problems were psychological in nature. But that belief has proved untrue. About 30 percent of erection problems have an organic cause (Schrome et al., 1979), a figure derived by measuring the reflexive erection of sleeping men. Most men know that they often wake up with an erection. When they are asleep, they have up to five periods of erection, called **nocturnal penile tumescence (NPT)**. These NPTs coincide with rapid eye movement sleep in men whose nervous system and blood vessels support reflex erections. Men who do not have erections during three nights of sleep in a laboratory, who do not have early morning erections, and who are having sexual problems are likely candidates for physiological explanations for their erection problems (Karacan, 1978). A simple home test has been suggested: if a man encircles his penis with a strip of stamps before he goes to sleep, any erection during the night will break the strip.

Laboratory studies have shown that in some men, blood flows normally into the penis but then drains out too quickly (Karacan et al., 1981; 1983). The effect of the vascular problem, of course, is an erection that is not firm enough to penetrate the vagina. New techniques for assessing blood vessel damage hold promise for treating erection problems that have an organic cause. Two of these procedures, called **infusion cavernosography** and the **Xenon-washout blood flow test**, consist of injecting the genitals with radioactive substances and monitoring the movement of the tagged radioactive substances. The course and rate

[1]Centers that investigate sleep disorders perform NPT evaluations. Addresses of such centers are available from the Association of Sleep Disorder Centers, TD-114, Stanford University School of Medicine, Stanford, CA 94305.

of flow of blood in the penis show up, and blood pressure and pulse within the penis can also be measured (Wagner and Green, 1983). By these methods, blood flow to the penis and firmness of erection can be monitored.

Some men with irreversible damage to blood vessels or nervous system choose a surgical implant that allows them to induce erections mechanically. Because erection and ejaculation are separate reflexes, some men have fathered children thanks to the implant. Current estimates are that between 6000 and 10,000 men have had the implant; much of the cost is covered by insurance policies (McLin, cited in Donovan, 1985). (See Figure 16.3.) When reproduction is not an issue, oral arousal of the penis is a satisfactory path both to sexual arousal and orgasm with ejaculation. (Erection is not the only route to arousal and ejaculation.) For some men with inadequate blood flow to the penis, an artery can be transplanted to restore function. Men with normal testosterone levels who have erection problems remain as interested in sex as they were before their problem developed.

Treatment of Erection Problems   The behavioral treatment of both primary and secondary erectile problems is designed to reduce a couple's anxiety about a particular sexual performance by *prohibiting* that performance as therapy begins. The quickest way to diminish anxiety about sex, paradoxically, is for a professional authority to forbid its performance. But today's therapists are not the first in medical history to prescribe abstinence for erection problems. Here is Sir John Hunter, a British physician of the late 1700s (cited in Zilbergeld and Evans, 1980, p. 29):

> *I told him that he was to go to bed with this woman but first promise himself that he would not have any connection with her for six nights, let his inclinations and powers be what they would: which he engaged to do. About a fortnight after, he told me that this resolution had produced such a total alteration in the state of his mind that the power soon took place, for instead of going to bed with fear of inability, he went with fears that he should be possessed with too much desire. And when he had once broken the spell, the mind and powers went on together.*

Sex therapists today reinvent this wisdom that the quickest way to diminish sexual anxiety is to forbid sexual performance. A couple in therapy is told that the erection reflex will occur when the man is aroused and responding to sexual stimuli. Their attention therefore is directed away from erection and towards what gives each partner pleasure. One major technique for teaching this is **sensate focus.** Figure 16.4 shows the positions for sensate focus. The partners are told to take turns helping one another experience pleasure, at first without touching the genitals or breasts. The goal is for them to discover the great pleasure that comes with touching and being touched. Each partner is allowed to be "selfish" in turn. Each partner guides the other's hand to show the best spots and best pressures for stimulation. In this fashion, each teaches the other what is sensually agreeable and disagreeable.

The sexual excitement generated by the sight and sound of a partner's pleasure is a further source of sexual excitement for both. The process turns the man's attention to his partner, away from his own performance, and allows his own excitement to build to erection. Because intercourse is forbidden, the overconcern

FIGURE 16.4

Sensate focus allows partners to discover the sensual pleasures of places other than the genitals.

about maintaining an erection is forgotten. After a few days of sensate focus, which is slowly extended to breasts and genitals, the man can get an erection without concentrating on it.

Following the sensate focus exercises, the woman uses the new knowledge of her partner to tease her partner's penis to a firm erection and then to stimulate him no more until the erection wanes. She repeats this process several times at each session. This method helps a man lose his fear of losing his erection. As in the sensate focus exercises, the emphasis is on closeness and sensual enjoyment, not performance. Once the couple feels comfortable with this procedure, the therapists direct the man to lie on his back. The woman then sits straddling his thighs, to stimulate him to full erection. She then directs his penis into her

TABLE 16.2
Improvement of Sexual Dysfunction in Therapy

	Masters and Johnson	German group
Female dysfunctions		
Orgasmic dysfunctions	81% (N = 342)	69% (N = 108)
Vaginismus	100% (N = 29)	78%[a] (N = 27)
Male dysfunctions		
Premature ejaculation	98% (N = 186)	84% (N = 31)
Erectile dysfunctions	72% (N = 245)	79% (N = 57)
Total successes	83% (N = 802)	75% (N = 223)

Source: Kolodny, 1981; Arentewicz and Schmidt, 1983.

[a]This figure includes both vaginismus and desire disorders.

vagina. All of these events are under the woman's control and therefore do not distract her excited, fully erect partner. She thrusts slowly. Then she is still and her partner thrusts slowly. If his erection wanes, they repeat the whole process. The focus remains total sexual pleasure, not performance. With psychological pressures towards erection gone, full intercourse usually follows without further therapy.

All of the exercises are performed by a couple in complete privacy. Therapists give instructions or descriptions only after the couple describe events to the therapists. During discussions, the therapists transmit a sexual value system: the right to pleasure is assumed, and the taboos against sexual pleasure are examined. The couple also communicates during discussions with the therapists and alone together. This treatment of erectile dysfunction has been better and faster than any other psychological methods used before. As Table 16.2 shows, about three-quarters of men respond well to this type of combined behavioral and psychological treatment.[2]

PREMATURE EJACULATION CAN ROB bOTH PARTNERS Of SEXUAL PLEASURE.

PREMATURE EJACULATION

Another common sexual problem for men is **premature ejaculation,** that is, ejaculation that occurs just after or even before a man's penis enters his partner's vagina. Premature ejaculation can rob both partners of sexual pleasure. The woman's loss may frustrate or anger her; it can even induce her sexual dysfunction. When women expect themselves to submit to sex because it is their husband's privilege, premature ejaculation may be a blessing to them. But when women want sexual pleasure of their own, premature ejaculation is no blessing at all. For

[2]A national self-help and referral network, with many local chapters, serves couples with erection problems. Impotents Anonymous can be reached at 5119 Bradley Blvd., Chevy Chase, MD 20815.

the man, premature ejaculation foils sexual pleasure and causes performance anxiety. Although some people think it is primarily a problem of the young and anxious man with a powerful sex drive, premature ejaculation discriminates against no group of men. It happens to older men and to men of all circumstances. Premature ejaculation does not have any known organic cause.

Some therapists diagnose premature ejaculation if a man climaxes before his partner more than half of the time they have intercourse. This definition assumes that his partner can reach orgasm in intercourse. It is both a useful and troublesome definition. It is useful because it focuses on the needs of the couple. It is troublesome because all women reach climax in their own fashion, and so a man who might be defined as a premature ejaculator with one woman might not be so defined with another woman, even if the time between erection and ejaculation were exactly the same. Helen Singer Kaplan, a physician who specializes in the diagnosis and treatment of sexual problems, offers a definition of premature ejaculation as a condition in which a man lacks voluntary control of ejaculation once he is highly aroused.

No one knows all the reasons for premature ejaculation. Masters and Johnson have speculated that for men who ejaculate prematurely, early sexual experiences may have been rushed: fumbling in the back seat of a car with a partner anxious to be finished; intercourse with a prostitute who praised him for climaxing quickly (to a prostitute, like anyone else at work, time is money). But these early, rushed sexual experiences are not sufficient explanation. Too many sexually functional people have had the same early experiences, and not all dysfunctional people have experienced the early rushing. But sex therapists have found that they need not thoroughly understand the cause to cure the problem.

TREATMENT OF PREMATURE EJACULATION   Common sense might dictate that the man who wants to avoid ejaculating prematurely should distract himself. If he doesn't want to climax, the logic goes, he should think about sports or multiplication tables or buying socks. Wrong. He should do just the opposite. In 1956, James Semans discovered that premature ejaculators need to focus on the sensations that occur just before ejaculation in order to gain voluntary control over it. Much as a child being toilet trained must learn how a full bladder feels, the man must pay *more* rather than less attention to how full arousal feels. Semans devised the **stop-start technique** for treating premature ejaculation. With it, a man's partner first brings him to a full erection. As he feels he's about to ejaculate, his partner stops stimulating him, and the erection is allowed to wane. The process is repeated several more times. Semans reported that the stop-start technique produced cures within a month. Masters and Johnson developed a variation of Semas's technique and called it the **squeeze technique.** The man lies on his back, and the woman sits facing him. His legs straddle hers. She stimulates him to full erection, and when he says that he is about to ejaculate, she stops the stimulation and firmly squeezes his penis just under the rim of the glans for three or four seconds. (See Figure 16.5.) The squeeze makes him lose part of his erection and relieves the urge to ejaculate. (It does not hurt.) The couple repeats this process several times before the man finally ejaculates, and the period before ejaculation (also called the **plateau phase** of arousal) gradually lengthens. A man may learn to tolerate 15 to 20 minutes of arousal at this level without ejaculating. That kind of control is enormously rewarding to a couple who may have long suffered silent shame, frustration, and helplessness.

FIGURE 16.5

Basilar squeeze technique.

The **basilar squeeze technique** may also be used by a man alone or with a partner. With this technique, the squeeze is applied to the base of the penis rather than at the ridge of the glans. When the couple moves on to intercourse, the position in which the woman sits or half-lies on top of the man is best. The missionary position, with the man lying atop the woman, is the worst for premature ejaculation, because it may be too intensely stimulating for the male. With the woman on top, she inserts his penis into her vagina, but she does not thrust. This quiet time lets the man experience vaginal containment without ejaculating. As he feels about to ejaculate, he withdraws his penis. His partner applies the squeeze technique and inserts his penis into her vagina again. With the basilar squeeze technique, complete withdrawal is unnecessary. When the man has succeeded at this exercise several times, he may begin to thrust slowly to maintain his erection. Many women have orgasms in intercourse themselves for the first time during this unhurried pleasuring. When the couple can tolerate containment and thrusting for some time, they are taught the side-by-side position for intercourse (each lying on a side, facing one another, legs entwined). The couple may choose to stay with the woman on top. The couple is told to continue using the squeeze technique from time to time after therapy.

The treatment of premature ejaculation has been very successful in many different settings. The original Masters and Johnson, St. Louis treatment with two therapists and a two-week, vacation-like concentrated treatment had a 98 percent improvement or success rate with a five-year follow-up. A German sex therapy group reports partial or full improvement in 84 percent of their male patients (Arentewicz and Schmidt, 1983). Similarly high rates of success have been achieved with group therapy at New York Hospital with as many as four married couples meeting in a group (Kaplan et al., 1974) for six weekly, 45-minute, outpatient sessions. (Each participant's history is taken individually before group treatment.) Couples usually required three or four practice sessions at home to control the problem. One man in the group had 10 years of psychoanalytic therapy aimed at solving his sexual problem, had achieved a good deal of insight into his problems, but only after four months of group treatment with a combination of psychotherapy and the Semans exercise did he overcome his premature ejaculation.

Retarded Ejaculation

Seemingly at the end of the spectrum from premature ejaculation is **retarded ejaculation,** a dysfunction once considered infrequent. It is characterized by fear of ejaculation *inside* the vagina. Clinicians have speculated that men who suffer retarded ejaculation may fear impregnating their partner, may have moral concerns about intercourse, or may fear sexual abandonment. Whatever the fuel for the dysfunction, sex therapists treat it with **systematic desensitization** to the anxiety-producing situation. It is treated as a **phobic** response, an irrational fear that the man cannot control by reason alone. Instead, therapy desensitizes the anxiety in small steps, with good rates of success.

FEMALE DYSFUNCTION

Women suffer from sexual problems of both psychological and physiological origin. Women get trapped in their anxieties over abandoning themselves to pleasure, over communicating what does and does not feel good to them, and over leaving an impression of lacking control. Women suffer particularly from the view that only "bad" women are sexual.

Orgasmic Dysfunction

The major sexual problem for women is not reaching orgasm. Some women have never had an orgasm; they are considered to have **primary orgasmic dysfunction.** Others have once been able to reach orgasm regularly but no longer can. They have **secondary orgasmic dysfunction.** Many women can reach orgasm in solitary or mutual masturbation, in situations other than intercourse. They have **coital anorgasmia.** Many women's sexual problems derive from our society's conflicting sexual values. If sex outside of marriage has always seemed the province of "easy," uncontrolled teenage girls, a woman (married or unmarried) may have enormous trouble retraining herself to let go, to give in to sexual abandonment.

No one can simply order a woman to abandon herself or relax. (That's as useful as telling someone who's worried, "Don't worry!") A woman needs to accept herself and her right to sexual pleasure, and her partner must also accept that right. When a woman does not accept her right to pleasure, she does not ask her partner for stimulation that gratifies her. Some women also think that they must pretend to have orgasms in order to hold onto a man. With that kind of miscommunication and dishonesty, those women cannot enjoy sex. Fears of rejection and of losing love in this age of widespread divorce lead many a dysfunctional wife to "do her duty" by faking pleasure during and after intercourse. For women to be truly orgasmic, the faking of pleasure must be replaced by honest communication.

Treatment for Orgasmic Dysfunction   Sex therapists can treat women whose problem is orgasmic dysfunction. The treatment proceeds in two steps. First, therapists try to help a woman to understand that she has the right to sexual pleasure and that her partner wants this for her as well. Second, the couple learns specifically what gives the woman sexual pleasure. Women who have never masturbated nor reached orgasm may not know what feels good. They and their partners must learn, often through sensate focus. At first, they avoid breast and genital contact. They add them after they have experienced the pleasures of sensate focus. They also communicate what they find arousing. These sensate focus sessions are important, for they create an atmosphere in which a woman can feel free to be sexual, and they free her from the pressure to reach orgasm. In fact, all attention is turned away from orgasm as a goal.

A woman's partner learns along with her what kind of stimulation—of the skin, mons, clitoris, or vagina—arouses her and causes lubrication. Clitoral stimulation is usually important for a woman's arousal. Even among women who reach orgasm regularly, two out of three want clitoral stimulation during foreplay, although they often find this difficult to tell their partners (Fisher, 1973; Hite, 1976). Yet most men want to know what their partners would like them to do (Pietropinto and Simenauer, 1977). Women usually find that stimulation of the clitoral shaft is more pleasurable than stimulation of the head, or glans, of the clitoris. During sensate focus, a woman communicates to her partner the right rhythm and pressure for touching to give her pleasure. Secretions from her vagina help to lubricate the clitoris; oral stimulation of the clitoris, if a woman wishes it, also lubricates the clitoris.

By the time that arousal from body and clitoral stimulation are well established, a couple is usually confident that their particular body and genital play works well for them. They are then instructed to continue this genital play; the woman inserts her partner's penis in her vagina as she sits or half-lies on top of him. This exercise, which precedes the active thrusting of intercourse, teaches the woman that the penis is hers to play with and directs her attention to the sensations from vaginal containment of the penis. After she has felt these sensations, she is instructed to try thrusting at her own pace. (During the course of the exercises, allowance is made for her partner's ejaculation. He would otherwise be under great strain.) The couple may go through teasing, mounting, and dismounting several times as the woman's sexual arousal builds.

Masters and Johnson report about an 80 percent improvement rate with this method for treating female orgasmic dysfunction. That is a high rate indeed. The Hamburg group reports comparable improvement, of 69 percent, for orgasmic dysfunction. The techniques that seem to work best with women suffering from secondary orgasmic dysfunction—who once had orgasms but no longer did—heighten their arousal before any coital activity. They can often reach orgasm if little stimulation is left to coitus itself. Some women also like to stop during coitus for clitoral stimulation or to continue clitoral stimulation during intercourse. Sex therapists do not consider women dysfunctional if intercourse without any clitoral stimulation does not lead to orgasm.

Special Methods for Treating Primary Orgasmic Dysfunction   The woman who has never had an orgasm is like the person who is trying to reach an object she has never seen. Before she is likely to have an orgasm, she must learn her own cues for getting aroused. Because masturbation teaches a woman the early signs of her arousal, she may need to learn this technique before moving on to her orgasms. (Nearly all men first learn the signs of arousal from masturbation. To them, the woman who does not know how to masturbate or climax seems strange.) The

FIGURE 16.6

Women who suffer from orgasmic dysfunction may learn about orgasms by masturbating with a vibrator.

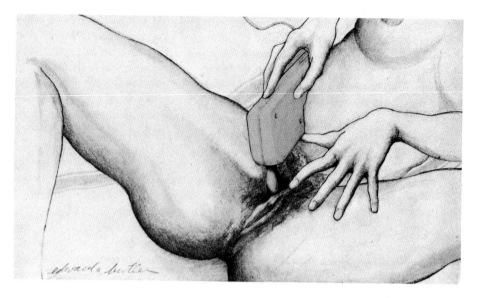

Kinsey Report (1953) and later studies have made clear that many women report not masturbating to orgasm before marriage. Sex therapy teaches a woman, either individually or in a group, how to masturbate (Barbach, 1975; Kohlenberg, 1974; LoPiccolo and Lobitz, 1972). The exercises are performed by a woman or couple privately, at home.

The therapy begins with lessons about genital anatomy. A woman is told to study her own naked body at home in a mirror; many have never looked at their genitals before. Therapy continues as the woman is told to find her sensitive areas and learns techniques of stimulating herself with her hand, lubricated with sterile jelly. For many women, these simple steps produce orgasm. When couples are treated, the woman teaches her partner what she has learned about herself, and the couple integrates this into their lovemaking. She may also be taught how to tighten the muscles around her vagina, an exercise that improves sexual pleasure during intercourse for some people.

If a woman still does not reach orgasm, she is taught how to increase both the intensity and duration of masturbation. Erotic materials help stimulate her fantasies. She may also be taught how to use a vibrator. One kind of vibrator straps onto the hand and makes the fingers vibrate; another kind directly vibrates the body. The woman uses whichever kind she prefers. Vibrators are less tiring than masturbating by hand, and therapists encourage a woman to stimulate herself for as long as she wishes. She is encouraged to be patient, to give herself pleasure, and not to worry about time limits. If orgasm is still inhibited, a therapist may discuss with a woman her fears about orgasm: private worries about looking undignified, ugly, or convulsive, even about involuntarily urinating or defecating. The therapist may help a woman to role play or privately act out having an orgasm. In treating orgasmic dysfunction, therapists build in several successive methods. For some women, orgasm first happens after a long period of continuous masturbation. With time and practice, it may happen more quickly. Orgasms during masturbation are usually followed in a matter of weeks by orgasms during intercourse. The success rates for treating orgasmic dysfunction with directed masturbation are as high as 80 to 100 percent. The usual treatment period is about two months or less (Barbach, 1975). About 5 to 10 percent of women feel sexual arousal but do not experience orgasm at any time—for no known psychological or physiological reason. Some sex therapists consider this group to be a normal variation.

Many women who have never had orgasms do read popular, self-help books (like Lonnie Barbach's *For Yourself* [1976] and Heiman, LoPiccolo, and LoPiccolo's *Becoming Orgasmic* [1976]). Since books and television programs on female orgasm have become common, fewer women go to clinics for treatment of primary orgasmic dysfunction. Instead, most clinics treat persons with secondary orgasmic problems or those who may have difficulty transferring their masturbatory discoveries to sex with a partner. Many therapists endorse sex education via the media, for it gives permission to be sexual as well as information that helps functioning.

Vaginismus

Women and men feel that the moment when the penis penetrates the vagina is important. Penetration may signal the end of virginity or fear of the unknown, and it may be accompanied by an anxious mixture of fear and arousal. When the penis penetrates an unlubricated vagina, a woman may feel pain. Some women fear pain from penetration even though they have never actually experienced any. Under both circumstances, women may experience a reflexive, conditioned clamping of their vaginal muscles in response to anticipated penetration. Called vaginismus, this reflex is her body's way of protecting a woman from pain and threat. Because a penis cannot penetrate a tightly shut vagina, some women with vaginismus may live for years in relations where intercourse is but rarely attempted. Some of these women are fully orgasmic during petting.

Treatment for Vaginismus   Vaginismus, a strongly fearful response, is a condition that responds well to behavioral therapy. A couple is shown and assured that the tight clamping of the vaginal muscles is reflexive in nature and that the woman cannot prevent it. Therapy follows the course of systematic desensitization (described in "Behavior Therapy"). Following masturbation or oral arousal, a couple is taught how to introduce a thin glass rod into the vagina. The principle behind the exercise is to give the woman a minimally anxiety-provoking object to insert in her vagina. After she has become reasonably comfortable with this form of penetration, she successively introduces slightly thicker rods. This process continues until she feels ready to introduce her partner's penis into her vagina. If she grows seriously anxious, she returns to penetration with the size of rod that she had already mastered. This form of treatment is remarkably successful. Among the women treated by Masters and Johnson for vaginismus, all learned to accept penile penetration. Among the women treated by a German group, 78 percent improved (Arentewicz and Schmidt, 1983).

SEXUAL DYSFUNCTION IN AGING PARTNERS

Masters and Johnson believe that middle-aged men and women stand to profit most from the recent advances in knowledge about sexual behavior and dysfunction. For people over 50, erection and lubrication are slower and require longer, more intense stimulation. Older men also need more stimulation to ejaculate than younger men, and women may need longer stimulation to feel adequately aroused. Older men are prime candidates for secondary erectile dysfunction (the type in which a man once could have but no longer gets or keeps his erection), for many face not only these changes in sexual functioning but also problematic changes at work and at home. If they feel depressed in spirit, if their self-esteem drops, if their sexual functioning grows increasingly less satisfying, they may be unhappy men indeed. If they do not understand the normal changes in physiology that age brings, men may stop having sex altogether. Lacking an explanation for a partner's loss of sexual interest, older women may assume that they have grown unattractive. Both older men and older women may need reassurance. People who know and deal with the aging of sexual responses can continue their sexual lives well into old age.

Healthy couples can have sex well into their 70s or beyond. Knowing the changes that age brings can help people of both sexes to gauge their own responses accurately. Intercourse can continue into old age, especially if the partners understand how to apply longer and more intense stimulation. Age brings orgasms that are less intense, with fewer contractions. But sexual desire need not wane. Partial erections and diminished lubrication do not mean that the pleasures of ejaculation or orgasm have vanished. Couples need not confine their physical pleasure to intercourse; stimulation of nongenital parts of the body, petting, and oral sex provide sensual pleasure as well. Like younger people, the older couple can feel free to try what they like without hurrying. Sensate focus, taking turns, and active participation by both partners all help to maintain an active sexuality and to minimize the effects of aging in males. Some people even increase their sexual activity after they turn 60 (Pfeiffer et al., 1969), and some women reach orgasm for the first time after menopause, when fears of pregnancy have vanished.

DISORDERS OF SATISFACTION AND DESIRE

During the 1970s, sex therapists were optimistic. The effect of Masters and Johnson's *Human Sexual Inadequacy* in 1970 on the treatment of sexual problems had been enormous. Psychotherapists were using all their clinical skill to find the least intervention necessary for the greatest improvement in sexual functioning. Behavior therapists developed displays, films, and original methods to provide patients with permission to be sexual, to impart information about sexuality, and to defuse anxiety. Systems therapists helped couples to see the payoffs to their relationship that were hidden in their sexual problems. They helped couples devise ways to cooperate and to avoid sexual dysfunction, and they were quite successful (showing success rates of from 40 to 60 percent with primary erectile dysfunction and 90 to 95 percent for vaginismus and premature ejaculation [LoPiccolo and Hogan, 1979]).

But in time, sex therapists began seeing new problems. For example, two California psychologists, Bernie Zilbergeld and Carol Rinkleib Ellison (1980) reported seeing sexual problems that were quite different from those that had been described by Masters and Johnson. In fact, the California patients would have been considered sexually *functional* in Masters and Johnson's terms: they could become aroused and reach orgasm. But most of them either were not interested in doing so or took no pleasure from it. Zilbergeld and Ellison challenged the Masters and Johnson model of sexual response. They said that it described only objective, physiological responses and failed to account for people's *feelings*. Zilbergeld and Ellison said that they were seeing patients who were suffering, in effect, from a *disorder of desire*. In other words, there was a discrepancy between their physiological responses, which seemed to be in working order, and their subjective feelings, which were not. Meanwhile, at New York Hospital in Manhattan, Helen Singer Kaplan was also seeing patients with this new type of sexual disorder. She called it **hypoactive (low) sexual desire** (Kaplan, 1978). In Masters and Johnson's model of sexual functioning, sexual desire was assumed always to precede sexual arousal—a logical enough description of events. But it simply did not describe what was happening to many people. These people turned off at the first hint of desire. Instead of following their fantasies or sexual wishes, they suppressed them, although they were quite unaware that they were doing this. Instead of focusing on a partner's attractive features or lovely voice, people with desire disorders might focus instead on the partner's flabby thighs or cigarette-smoke breath. A partner might turn into a block of ice or remember an appointment with the dentist when approached for sex. One woman wrote to a newspaper columnist that her husband's sexual advances made her think compulsively about gin rummy. Many came to sex therapists complaining that they "felt nothing" or that sex had become unbearably anxiety-provoking. Although they wanted to want sex, they could not, for they rarely wanted to make love. Many were brought to sex therapists by their dismayed partners. Furthermore, a few of Zilbergeld and Ellison's patients showed a disorder *after* orgasm, a **satisfaction disorder,** characterized by feelings of, "So I climaxed. So what?" Many more people with desire disorders came (or were brought) to clinics than people with satisfaction disorders.

Desire disorders may be more common than sex therapists once believed. One estimate of how widespread desire and satisfaction disorders are comes from Helen Singer Kaplan (personal communication, 1984). She estimates that at some point in their adult lives, about 50 percent of all Americans will suffer a sexual dysfunction. Of these, about 40 percent (or 20 percent of the total) will suffer low sexual desire. Those estimates add up to a population in the *tens of millions—* certainly no small matter. These problems appear in homosexual as well as heterosexual couples. Other investigators support the magnitude of Kaplan's estimate.

A Pittsburgh group studied 100 stable, happily married couples who were *not* candidates for any kind of therapy. They found that 35 percent of the wives and 16 percent of the husbands had little interest in sex and that 28 percent of the wives and 10 percent of the husbands got turned off easily (Frank et al., 1978; see "Sexuality in Perspective: Sexual Problems in 'Normal' Couples"). Another set of figures, these from the Sex Therapy Center at Stony Brook, New York, shows that among couples who came for therapy of any sort between 1974 and 1981, 38 percent of the husbands and 49 percent of the wives were diagnosed as having problems of low desire. Some 18 percent of the wives but no husbands were diagnosed as having an aversion to sex. It is interesting to note that the more recent clients were more likely to have desire disorders than the less recent clients (Schover and LoPiccolo, 1982). German sex therapists are finding that many women who seek treatment for anorgasmia require treatment for aversion toward sex (Arentewicz and Schmidt, 1983). Kaplan believes that because of more liberal public attitudes toward sex and because people are generally better informed about sexual functioning, the simple cases for therapists to treat—problems of performance anxiety that lead to premature ejaculation, for example—are far less frequent. They are being replaced by more patients who have more serious disorders (Kaplan, 1978).

Patients with desire disorders, therapists have found, get turned off easily.

Patients with desire disorders, therapists have found, get turned *off* easily. The wrong word from a partner, an odd odor in the bedroom, a distracting thought all are turnoffs. Sexual partners usually arrange their sexual encounters so that distractions are kept to a minimum. They unhook the phone, lock the door, make sure the children are asleep, and the like. Although it is not always possible to banish every distraction, and although everyone has intrusive thoughts from time to time, most people have ways of returning themselves to arousing, rather than unarousing, thoughts. But people with desire disorders *follow* their sexually negative, distracting thoughts. Those thoughts and fantasies can make a sexual encounter feel "not worth the effort" or, to others, even revolting.

People who feel revolted by sex suffer from a form of desire disorder called an **aversion disorder.** Therapists treat aversion disorders by exploring the current sources of the aversion at the same time that they strengthen a client's permission to be sexual. Many people with aversion disorders come from families that dealt with bodily pleasures sternly, judgmentally, and punitively. Treatment aims at increasing a client's *interest* in sex. German sex researchers report seeing more women than men who are averse to sex. In one instance, a German woman whose family had treated her as worthy only to scrub and serve developed an aversion disorder and felt revolted by her husband's sexual demands. Once therapists encouraged her to reclaim her life—by finding a paying job and beginning to pursue her own wishes—she could begin to pursue her own feelings of pleasure as well. In effect, her aversion had served a positive purpose; it held more promise for her later sexual pleasure than silent aversion would have done (Arentewicz and Schmidt, 1983).

Dr. Kaplan finds that many people with desire disorders come from "anti-pleasure" families and fear losing control (which their stern parents would not approve of) or feel anger in sexual situations. Some cases seem to be triggered by the birth of a child, others by the loss or change of a job, others by ovarian surgery. The event somehow has made sexual functioning a danger area.

Desire disorders do not respond so rapidly or successfully to sex therapy as sexual dysfunctions. Perhaps because desire disorders reflect deep angers and anxieties, therapists as yet seem to be less successful in treating them than they have been with disorders of the excitement or orgasmic phases of sexual response. Indeed, the closer are a problem's roots to sexual motivation, the more difficult it may be to treat. People with desire disorders are not simply people with small sexual appetites. Most of them once enjoyed sex but somehow lost interest. These are the people with **secondary desire disorder,** a typical example of which is the husband who desired intercourse with his wife twice a week for many years but who lately has desired intercourse once every two months, and then only so that his wife won't feel rejected. A typical case of **primary desire disorder** might be this: a male, 20 years old, has rarely been attracted to women, rarely has sexual thoughts or fantasies, and does not masturbate. If he forms a relationship, it is his partner who is likely to insist on sex therapy. Partners suffer not only the stress of diminished sexual expression, which can occur between any two partners of unequal sexual interest and for which sex therapists have good remedies, but also the stress of the unaccountable absence of sexual interest even when sexual interaction takes place. Understandably, partners feel that they have grown less attractive when intercourse takes place less and less frequently.

When sex is infrequent or absent from a relationship, it does *not* necessarily mean that the partners do not love one another or even that they feel the need for more sexual activity. Likewise, not all cases of low sexual desire have a psychological origin. Low desire can be the effect of purely physical causes like vascular problems, certain medicines, prolonged stress, or depression. In those cases of low sexual desire that do have a physiological cause, there is usually a component of anxiety or hostility. Many people with low sexual desire fear intimacy and may unconsciously use their negative feelings about sex to fend off an unwelcome partner. Just as it is quite common for people to turn off at the first stirring of desire because they are afraid to be intimate and therefore vulnerable to a partner, it is also common for people to turn off because they are afraid of losing control during sexual abandonment. The therapist must diagnose whether the case is one of low desire within an anxious but essentially sound and loving relationship or a case of withholding sex in a rejecting relationship. The forms of treatment and the prognosis for the two differ, of course.

How do therapists deal with people who suffer from disorders of desire? First, the therapists identify, evaluate, and, if appropriate, treat any underlying depression or marriage problems (as they do with any form of sexual problems). Couples who present themselves to a therapist and turn out not to care for their partner or wish they had married someone else are poor candidates for sex therapy. Once depression or marriage tensions are under control, the therapist can turn to the sexual problems. Kaplan has specific ideas about treating couples with desire disorders. She teaches such couples to use sensate focus in small steps and to discuss their feelings, sensations, and dreams at each step. Because people with desire disorders may fear sex or be angered by its demands, they may avoid or sabotage the execution of exercises like sensate focus. Therefore, much of the therapy is aimed at circumventing the sabotage of the sexual exercises. Couples with desire disorders do improve significantly, although not with the dramatic quality of couples with arousal and orgasmic dysfunctions. Generally, the problem diminishes during the course of therapy and couples report much greater sexual pleasure. Once therapy is over, however, some loss of pleasure occurs. Nevertheless, after termination, patients do report more desire than they felt when therapy started (Arentewicz and Schmidt, 1983; Schover and LoPiccolo, 1982). When small samples of couples treated for desire disorder (and other common sexual dysfunctions too) are followed up 3 years after therapy ends, some gains are maintained. Couples show increased sexual satisfaction and self-acceptance and less feeling of relationship dissatisfaction than they had when they started therapy. The sexual behaviors that brought them to therapy originally show more loss than gain. Despite the well-documented gains immediately after therapy, the therapy research team concludes that sex therapy may do more in the long term for people's feelings about their sexuality than for their presenting symptoms (DeAmicis, et al., 1985). How to hold on to therapy's behavioral gains is likely to be the next frontier of sex therapy.

SEX THERAPIES

Therapies: Past and Present

Classical Treatments   Before the 1970s, most people who sought help for sexual problems went to their family doctor. Some went to their clergyman or to their friends. The lucky ones found a receptive ear and helpful advice. The less lucky ones found a lack of sympathy and a lot of misinformation that only confirmed their worst fears: impotence is "inevitable" in middle age; pain during intercourse is "all in your head"; sexual indifference is part of aging, and so on. Until the 1970s, there were few experts on sexual function and dysfunction. These areas were routinely given short shrift by medical schools, so few doctors knew much about human sexuality. Psychotherapists were the only trained experts on sexual problems, and they used two types of therapy. One was **supportive therapy,** in which they tried to reassure or offer emotional support to dysfunctional people, to give them some sexual information, to enlarge their ideas of permissible fantasy and behavior, and to reduce their anxiety. Such permission to be lusty is often all that a dysfunctional couple needs. Supportive therapy was (and is) conducted in an open, relaxed atmosphere; the patient was accepted, reassured, and essentially given permission for his or her sexuality.

The second type of therapy was **psychoanalysis** and its close relative, **psychoanalytic psychotherapy.** Psychoanalytic theory holds that sexual attitudes and fantasies develop in early childhood and that psychological symptoms reflect deeper, unconscious problems. Psychoanalysts believe that if a patient can be made conscious of these hidden, unconscious wishes, sexual symptoms can disappear. The insights of psychoanalysis do help some patients. But these "talking cures" tend to be slow, expensive, and not always successful. In fact, attempts at deep insights into the meaning of sexual symptoms probably encourage watchfulness during sex, a disastrous course for overcoming sexual dysfunction. Today most psychoanalysts refer their patients with sexual dysfunctions to therapists who specialize in treating these disorders.

Sex Therapy Today

Sex therapists have found that a combination of education, specific exercises to change behavior, and brief psychotherapy help couples with sexual problems. Virtually all of Masters and Johnson's cases of premature ejaculation, which had been a disaster area for regular psychotherapy, improved. (In other words, the sexual problem did not recur for five years, as documented by telephone interview.) Seventy-eight percent of their cases of secondary dysfunction and 67 percent of the cases of primary erectile dysfunction improved. Although 10 percent of clients experience a repeat of their problems with erections within five years, repeated treatment works. Other treatment centers, which use techniques like those of Masters and Johnson, report roughly the same high rates of success (Kaplan, 1974). Some men with secondary erectile disorders are now being treated without partners, and with some success (Price, et al., 1981; Zilbergeld, 1975). Women therapists who tell such men about women's concerns with affection and caring rather than with sexual virtuosity seem to help such men relate sexually to women (Lobitz and Baker, 1979).

SEXUALITY IN PERSPECTIVE: HOW TO FIND A SEX THERAPIST

Professional sex therapists may be psychiatrists (M.D.s) or psychologists, social workers, or counselors. If you feel that you want to consult a professional sex therapist but do not know the name of a good one, you can take one of several routes. Colleges and universities usually have health services that can recommend a reputable sex therapist. Professors who teach sexuality courses probably can offer recommendations, too. A friend who has been treated and is happy with the results can be an excellent source for a recommendation. Your regular doctor can often make referrals.

A certificate on the wall is not adequate proof of a therapist's training. Some states license sex therapists, and it is a wise course to see a therapist who does have a license to practice as a psychologist, psychiatrist, or social worker. For a fee, you can get a list of certified, trained sex therapists in your area from:

American Association of Sex
Educators, Counselors, and Therapists
(AASECT)
11 Dupont Circle, Suite 220
Washington, D.C. 20036

The American Association for Marriage and Family Therapy (AAMFT), which certifies marital and family therapists, is located at:

924 W. 9th Street
Upland, California 91786

One way to start evaluating therapists is with a brief telephone call. You might explain your goal for therapy and ask enough questions (fees, treatment methods, rates of success, etc.) to get a feel for whether you would feel comfortable working with him or her. If you have a preference for a particular kind of therapy, make your preference known at the beginning. That way you won't get stuck with a practitioner of psychoanalysis when you really wanted behavior modification, or vice versa; and you won't find yourself with a therapist who considers monogamy hopelessly outdated when you wanted help with your live-in partner. You can choose your therapist after you've had an initial interview or a few interviews together. It's quite acceptable to tell the therapist that you are shopping around and have other interviews before you will be making your decision.

Once a thorough physical examination has ruled out organic causes of dysfunction, treatment begins. Couples receive sexual information and affirmation of each individual's right to sexual satisfaction. The bonds between partners are explored and lines of communication strengthened during interviews. Before any intervention begins, a couple's history and problem are explored. Only after all of this clinical work has been done and the couple's anxiety has abated are any behavioral exercises introduced. Each exercise provides the basis for more discussion of the couple's sexual feelings and problems. What doesn't work provides valuable material for further discussion. Sex therapists keep the couple communicating.

Helen Singer Kaplan (1974), for example, treated one couple's sexual and relationship problems. The husband had suffered from premature ejaculation since adolescence. The wife could achieve orgasm through clitoral stimulation, but she insisted that her husband bring her to climax during intercourse. Kaplan decided to treat the ejaculatory problem first and then to focus on the wife's orgasmic problem. The sensate focus sessions went well. As the husband gained enough control for the couple to proceed to intercourse with the wife on top, she grew upset about being "used." Further therapy uncovered the source of her upset: a childhood fear of abandonment. She had replaced her fear of abandonment by a beloved parent to a fear of abandonment by her husband. She was afraid that her handsome, and now sexually improved, husband would turn to other women. Therapist and couple discussed the wife's fears. She felt reassured by her husband's expressions of genuine love, and the couple's closeness increased. Feeling safer and closer, the wife could ask her husband for sexual stimulation during their "stop-start" exercises, and she had her first orgasm in intercourse. After eight sessions of treatment and follow-up sessions three and six months later, the husband still had good ejaculatory control. The wife often climaxed and felt less concerned that her climaxes occur during intercourse. Although the couple still was competitive and quarrelsome, the therapist believed that so long as these did not interfere with their sexual functioning, the goals of the therapy had been reached.

Many patients are still seen in individual sex therapy, but much sex therapy today takes place in group formats, and more people are treated at lower cost. All therapies, no matter the dysfunction, incorporate the important elements established by Masters and Johnson (1970): the right to be sexual, information about male and female sexual structure and function, and stress on communication within the pair. Exercises proceed gradually from the diffuse and general acceptance of bodily pleasure to the more anxiety-provoking sexual acts. Therapy ends when the acts that once aroused dysfunction and anxiety not only prove possible, but gratifying.

Behavior Therapy

In behavior therapy, also known as behavior modification, the disturbing sexual symptoms are taken as problems to be solved. These symptoms are considered to have their origin in dysfunctional learning, and behavior therapy offers the opportunity for learning new and functional responses. Modern sex therapy is much more akin to behavior therapy than to older, psychoanalytic therapy. Even in therapy for inhibited sexual desire, therapists do not try to illuminate deeply hidden, unconscious conflicts (Kaplan, 1979). Instead, they bring to light such problems as thinly veiled anger in sexual situations, and then they apply behavioral principles to treat them.

Behavior therapists have devised a number of specific techniques to help people overcome behavior problems, and many of these can be applied successfully to sexual problems. Behavior therapists have succeeded in treating phobias with systematic desensitization. As we mentioned earlier, some sexual dysfunctions can be seen as sexual phobias, and if so, they can be treated by systematic desensitization (Wolpe, 1958, 1969).

Systematic desensitization uses the treatment principle that graduated exposure to dosages of the problematic situation can lead to weakening and then extinction of the negative response. Thus if a particular sexual situation leads to anxiety, a dysfunctional response, and the wish to avoid the situation, then exposure to a graduated series of situations that are similar to, but less intense than, the feared situation may lead to weakening or extinction of the dysfunctional response. This exposure also may present the patient with an opportunity to substitute a desired, functional response. Although arranging a graduated series of sexual situations in reality may present a considerable tactical challenge, creating a series in fantasy is easier. Improvement then is transferred from the realm of fantasy to reality.

The behavior therapist's first task is to take a thorough sexual history and to rule out possible organic contributions to the patient's sexual dysfunction. Next, the therapist determines exactly which situations elicit dysfunctional responses. Once the critical situation is identified, and if the dysfunction seems amenable to treatment by desensitization, therapist and patient together create a hierarchy of fantasized sexual situations. Each fantasy in the hierarchy is related to the critical situation, but they range from small to strong in their ability to elicit anxiety. Hierarchies may extend along continua of time, distance, or magnitude. They usually consist of six to fourteen ordered steps, with approximately equal increments in anxiety provocation between them.

The therapist then begins to present the hierarchy to the patient, beginning with the least anxiety-provoking step. (The patient first may have been taught a relaxation technique.) Guided by the therapist, the patient creates each fantasy vividly. When the patient is reasonably comfortable with one fantasy, the therapist presents the next one. During each weekly session, the patient may go through two or three steps. The patient is assigned "homework," to practice the fantasy recreations at home every day. The therapist must carefully pace the treatment for the patient, because people being relieved of their sexual anxieties are usually delighted and ready to rush into more advanced steps, for which they may not be ready. Below is a case history of a systematic desensitization conducted by one of the authors. The complaint was situational erectile dysfunction:

Mr. E. was a 29-year-old single man who had problems getting and keeping erections strong enough for intercourse with partners he did not know well. Little in his history suggested an organic impairment. He had frequent nighttime erections and reliable erections with familiar partners. Because he reported anxious feelings that seemed to correspond to his erectile failure, the therapist chose systematic desensitization as the method of treatment.

The behavioral analysis showed that the imminence of vaginal penetration with a new partner was the critical situation. Therapist and patient together constructed a time-series of fantasy steps leading to a first sexual encounter with a woman to whom Mr. E. was attracted. The hierarchy had thirteen steps and was ordered as follows:

1 *Plan to talk to Ms. A.*

2 *Approach Ms. A. for a conversation.*

3 *Ask Ms. A. out for a drink.*

4 *Over the drink, suggest a dinner date to Ms. A. for the next day. She accepts.*

5 *Wake up the next morning, lie in bed, and anticipate the date with Ms. A.*

6 *Drive to Ms. A.'s house before the date.*

7 *Over dinner, suggest that they stop at his apartment. Ms. A. accepts.*

8 *Drive to Mr. E.'s apartment. Both sit on bed, talking about a shared, nonsexual experience.*

9 *Touch, kiss, pet with clothes on.*

10 *Mr. E. undresses Ms. A.; Ms. A. then undresses Mr. E.*

11 *Lie in bed unclothed.*

12 *Mutually fondle genitals.*

13 *Penetrate and continue to have intercourse.*

As Mr. E. relaxed, the therapist presented each step to him, guiding him to construct a vivid sensory image. The therapist told Mr. E. to bear with the anxiety at each step, to relax with the image as fully as possible, and to push away any anxious thoughts (such as "I'm going to lose my erection."). When Mr. E. signaled to the therapist that the anxiety was greatly diminished, the therapist presented the next step. Two or three steps were presented at each weekly session, and Mr. E. was asked to rehearse those already practiced every day at home. As he worked through the hierarchy, Mr. E. reported a decrease in anxiety. Near the end of the desensitization, Mr. E. approached the woman he was interested in, dated her, and had intercourse with few erectile problems. In time, he formed an enduring relationship with this woman. Although the relationship had not been the therapy's goal nor the target symptom of the desensitization, it was probably an outcome related to the treatment.

Anxiety interferes with relationships as well as sexual acts, and in Mr. E.'s case, diminished anxiety probably helped both. Behavior therapists often notice general improvements in clients whose specific dysfunctions are treated successfully.

As we have seen, people who have trouble getting aroused tend to engage in distracting internal comments: "I've done it again," or "Why am I so slow?" or "He's going to come, and where am I?" Comments like these turn people off and decrease sexual responses. Researchers also have found that dysfunctional men are less aroused than functional men when their partners are highly aroused (Beck, Barlow, and Sakheim, 1983). The dysfunctional men report feeling that the pressure to perform is much greater when their partner is highly aroused. People who get distracted by their own internal messages should focus on themselves and their own arousal. Sensate focus is one exercise designed to help people change their focus in this way. The relaxation techniques sometimes used in systematic desensitization can also reduce the internal messages.

SUMMARY

1   Repeated failure to enjoy sex or to share enjoyment with a partner may indicate sexual dysfunction. Common sexual problems for men are premature ejaculation and erectile dysfunctions. Among women, not to have an orgasm is a common dysfunction.

2   Many sexual problems are psychological in origin; some are physiological. Because psychological events can modify physiological responses, the distinction between them may be blurred. Although a therapist must carefully distinguish the source of a patient's dysfunction, in any case of sexual dysfunction, the patient's mind and body are affected.

3   The histories of many people who consult sex therapists include: ignorance about biological and sexual functioning; shame about sexual behavior; lack of communication about important (not necessarily sexual) issues; fear of failure in sexual encounters that leads to anxious watchfulness about performance.

4   Erectile dysfunction is a man's repeated inability to get or keep an erection of his penis. Diagnosing whether erectile dysfunction has a psychological or an organic cause is the therapist's job. Reliable nighttime erections usually rule out an organic cause. Treatment for erectile dysfunction is aimed at reducing anxiety about sexual performance.

5   Sensate focus is an important technique for teaching what gives each partner pleasure and for directing attention away from sources of sexual anxiety.

6   Premature ejaculation is a sexual dysfunction in which a man lacks voluntary control over ejaculation once he is highly aroused. Treatment consists of interrupting a man's feelings of intense arousal by having his partner stop stimulation and start again when he is less aroused. Repeated experience of intense arousal *without* ejaculation ends premature ejaculation.

7   The major sexual dysfunction women suffer is not reaching orgasm. Many women are trapped by our society's double standard, which shapes a population of resistant, controlled young women. They may have great trouble relearning that they may give in to sexual pleasure. Some women need to learn what gives their body pleasure or how to masturbate. Therapists first help women learn that they have a right to sexual pleasure. Sensate focus can be helpful in this regard. Once a couple has engaged in satisfying body and genital play, they may be instructed to engage in teasing, mounting, and dismounting. In many cases, women learn how to reach climax after such treatment.

8   Many of the sexual dysfunctions of aging couples can be treated successfully. Although aging may slow and mitigate certain reflex and other sexual reactions, healthy couples may have sex well into their 70s and 80s.

9 Clinicians have begun to see sexual problems whose roots lie close to sexual motivation. These disorders of desire and satisfaction, which may respond to therapy, often involve feelings of anger, anxiety, or aversion to sex. Infrequent or absent sex is not necessarily a sign of a failed relationship. Some people with low sexual desire do not wish for more sex. Others may be suffering from an organic problem that interferes with desire.

10 Many sex therapists today use specific exercises (such as sensate focus), principles from behavior modification, and guided insights in treating their patients.

KEY TERMS

sexual dysfunction
premature ejaculation
erectile dysfunction
anorgasmia
hymen
vaginismus
spectatoring
primary erectile dysfunction
secondary erectile dysfunction
transient erectile dysfunction
nocturnal penile tumescence (NPT)
infusion cavernosography
Xenon-washout blood flow test
sensate focus
stop-start technique
squeeze technique

plateau phase
basilar squeeze technique
phobic
systematic desensitization
primary orgasmic dysfunction
secondary orgasmic dysfunction
menopause
retarded ejaculation
hypoactive (low) sexual desire
satisfaction disorder
aversion disorder
secondary desire disorder
primary desire disorder
supportive therapy
psychoanalysis
psychoanalytic psychotherapy

SUGGESTED READINGS

Barbach, L. *For Each Other.* Garden City, NY: Doubleday, 1982. This popular book follows up Barbach's popular *For Yourself* (1975) and is a contribution both to women's positive sexual values and to the achievement of sexual fulfillment.

Kaplan, H. S. *Disorders of Sexual Desire.* New York: Brunner/Mazel, 1979. This is the best extended presentation on desire disorders. Not all therapists are agreed on details of Kaplan's treatment, but the clinical descriptions are typical of the new category of cases now coming to clinics.

Offit, A. K. *Night Thoughts: Reflections of a Sex Therapist.* New York: Congdon and Lattes, 1981. It's fun to read this informal overview of issues in sex therapy, presented as the musings of a sex therapist.

Zilbergeld, B. *Male Sexuality.* New York: Bantam Books, 1978. Some people will value this book for its exercises for men with sexual problems. Everyone should read it for its critique of our culture's irrational view of men as sexual battering rams.

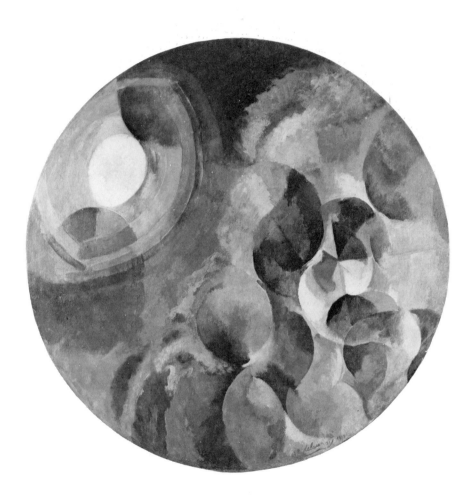

ROBERT DELAUNAY, "SIMULTANEOUS CONTRAST: SUN AND MOON." COLLECTION, THE MUSEUM OF MODERN ART, NEW YORK.

Chapter 17

Sexual Diseases and Infections

We human beings entertain a very pleasant illusion. We imagine that frequent baths, clean clothes, toothpaste, deodorant, and conscientious attention to medical problems will keep our bodies free from bacteria and harmful microorganisms. The reality is that even the squeaky cleanest among us is covered on the outside and filled on the inside with microscopic creatures, some harmful and some harmless.

Any number of factors can undermine the body's ability to fight disease: stress, fatigue, toxins, even a change in diet or surroundings. That is why people with some viral infections, for example, may notice that their symptoms flare up when they are under stress, menstruating, or out in the sun too long. It is also why women who take antibiotics for one problem may find themselves suddenly susceptible to another problem—vaginal infections, for example, when the antibiotics have disturbed the balance among the organisms normally in the vagina.

Some microorganisms fly through the air in sneezes and coughs. Some microorganisms die in the presence of oxygen; they need deep and airless wounds to multiply in. Some microorganisms jump ship during sexual encounters, moving from the warm, moist mucous membrane of one partner to another. **Sexually transmitted diseases (STDs)** are caused by microorganisms that spread from one human to another during intimate physical encounters. Many infections inhabit the warm, moist mucous membranes—mouth, vagina, urethra, anus—and avoid the parts of the human body that are exposed to light and air. Some cause changes in the skin, nerves, internal organs, or the immune system. Left untreated, STDs can do grave harm.

Many, but not all, STDs hit women harder than men.

Sexually transmitted diseases are intrinsically "sexist": not only are clinical manifestations more subtle and diagnosis more difficult in women than in men but complications are far more frequent and serious in women. Thus, pelvic inflammatory disease is more common than its male counterpart, epididymitis; genital herpes is generally more painful for women than for men; the diagnosis of vaginal discharge is more difficult than that of urethral discharge, and so on. . . . STDs pose special risks for pregnant women. Pelvic inflammatory disease increases the risk of ectopic pregnancy by a factor of 10 (Handsfield, 1982, pp.102–103).

Like other diseases, sexually transmitted diseases are part of the human—male and female both—heritage. Historically, they have afflicted virtually every human group except those who were physically isolated.

INCIDENCE OF STDs

Before we describe the common STDs, we should note their incidence (the incidence of a disease means the number of new cases each year). How many people have STDs? When it comes to collecting facts about the incidence of various STDs in the population, investigators have a hard time. Many people will not confide

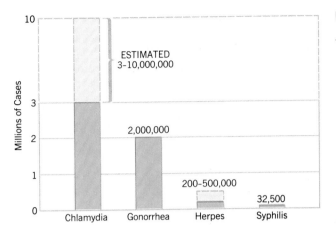

FIGURE 17.1

Annual incidence of STDs.

such potentially embarrassing information. Others fear damage to their current relationships. In cases where treatment depends on tracing a succession of sexual contacts, some people refuse to cite or do not know the names of their previous sexual contacts. Doctors are legally required to report all cases of syphilis and gonorrhea to public health authorities. But the authorities themselves estimate that many cases of legally reportable STDs are not reported. They believe that there are about 2 or 2.5 million cases a year of gonorrhea and about 30,000 cases a year of syphilis (Handsfield, 1982). (See Figure 17.1.) Recent estimates have put the incidence of genital herpes at between 200,000 and 500,000—more than syphilis and less than gonorrhea. Less well known, but still widespread, chlamydia is another STD that afflicts 3 to 10 million people a year. Chlamydia may soon join the group of STDs whose diagnosis is followed by the tracking of sexual contacts.

THE incidence of STDs rises and falls with each historical period, and it changes as well within certain population groups.

The incidence of STDs rises and falls with each historical period, and it changes as well within certain population groups. Politics affects STDs, and wars mix the STD microorganisms of many national groups. Thus the incidence of gonorrhea rose when soldiers met prostitutes during World War II. Today, AIDS is increasingly frequent in many parts of the world, among both homosexuals and heterosexuals. Sexual orientation influences the incidence of STDs. Some STDs are more common in homosexual than heterosexual communities, for example. Once diagnosis and treatment of an STD are possible, its incidence—in principle—should begin to decline. The incidence of gonorrhea has been stable since 1975, despite a worrisome climb between 1957 and 1975, but it has not disappeared, as some optimists predicted when antibiotic treatment was discovered. Syphilis has been decreasing steadily since 1982 (Handsfield, 1982). Both chlamydia and herpes have been increasing and, like all STDs, have been underreported.

But who actually has STDs? One way of finding out about a sample of people who consider themselves at risk is to survey the over 100,000 people every year who call the VD (for "Venereal Disease") National Hotline, a referral and information service for people who think they have STDs or who need to find treatment. Of the people who call the Hotline, one recent survey (Corey et al., 1982) showed:

1 Sixty percent are male and 40 percent female.
2 The mean age is 26.5 years, with 30 percent over 30 and 18 percent under 20.
3 Eighty-three percent are white.
4 Eighty-eight percent are heterosexual.
5 Twenty-six percent are married.
6 Thirty-five percent have a bachelor's degree, and the mean level of education is 14 years.
7 Income for 25 percent is at least $25,000 a year, and 30 percent earn between $15,000 and $25,000 a year.
8 About 70 percent report that they usually see a private physician for medical care.

We know even less about people who do not call for help or who do not know that they need help. Studies show that gonorrhea and syphilis remain serious public health problems. Part of the difficulty with gonorrhea is that half to three quarters of affected females and 10 percent of affected males show no symptoms (Sparling, 1982). Genital herpes and hepatitis B, two viral STDs, sometimes produce no symptoms. Some urinary tract infections show no overt symptoms. In all these asymptomatic cases, people often remain sexually active and contagious.

Why have so many STDs increased in incidence in the last 20 years or so? Proportionally more people are having sex outside of marriage. In part, this trend derives from the sexual maturity of the children who once were in the baby boom. In part, it derives from today's more permissive attitudes toward sex. And, again, in part it derives from the wider use of nonbarrier methods of birth control, that is, of methods like the pill and IUD that do not place any physical barrier between sexual partners, as diaphragms plus a spermicide or condoms do (Handsfield, 1982).

Information Can Help

Our purpose in writing this chapter is not to frighten or disgust. It is to describe the most common STDs so that you can do something about them. In this chapter, we are frankly directive: we want to advise on how to stay healthy and, failing that, how to get treatment.[1] We believe that everyone has a personal responsibility *not* to spread STDs to others. For more on how to prevent and treat STDs, see the section, "An Ounce of Prevention," and "Sexuality in Perspective: How Do

---

[1] Final decisions about diagnosis and treatment are from Centers for Disease Control *Morbidity and Mortality Weekly Report*, "STD Treatment Guidelines 1982," August 20, 1982, vol. 31, no. 25; Sparling (in Cecil) 1982; and Holmes (in Harrison), 1982.

You Tell Your Partner You May Have Passed on an STD?" We also include practical information in the discussions of specific STDs. If you have symptoms, or if you have been exposed to someone who has symptoms, see a doctor. Your school may have a clinic; your family doctor may be able to treat you readily; or you can get help from the VD National Hotline.[2]

People can sometimes contract STDs without sexual activity: infants, for example, can pick up microorganisms as they pass through the vagina during birth. STDs do not always require intercourse itself for transmission either: oral sex and genital petting are sometimes enough. Doctors are required by law to report to the Public Health Service cases of syphilis and gonorrhea for purposes of record-keeping, but the privacy of the patient and any sexual contacts is assured. Gynecologists are doctors who specialize in treating conditions of the female reproductive organs, and urologists specialize in treating conditions of the urinary tract, for both males and females. Both can treat STDs, and nearly all STDs are treatable. Even when no cures are available, physicians can help manage symptoms.

The STDs described below are the most common in the United States. In order of decreasing incidence, the most common STDs in the United States in 1984 were: chlamydia, gonorrhea, nongonococcal urethritis (especially in males), trichomoniasis, pelvic inflammatory disease, genital herpes, pubic lice, and syphilis. We begin with these. Then we proceed to certain other STDs. Our list, however, is not exhaustive.

CHLAMYDIA

A silent disease, **chlamydia** produces a range of dangerous, unseen symptoms. The chlamydia bacterium can infect and inflame the epididymis and the fallopian tubes. Left untreated, these infections can seal the route of sperm and egg, respectively, and thereby cause sterility. For women, the risk of ectopic pregnancy (an embryo that implants outside of the uterus, usually in the fallopian tubes) is added to the risk of infertility. Swedish research has shown that women who suffer one bout of chlamydia are three times likelier to be infertile than women who suffer one bout of gonorrhea. Urethral infections in men and cervical infection in women are part of the damage that *Chlamydia trachomatis* can cause. Chlamydia may also turn out to be the silent cause of many cases of pelvic inflammatory disease.

When chlamydia produces symptoms in men, it looks like gonorrhea. From one to three weeks after man and microorganism meet, the man produces a discharge from his penis and feels the need to urinate frequently and painfully. Women who are the sexual partners of chlamydia victims are more likely than not (70 percent) to have cervical infections from chlamydia. Symptoms in women include vaginal discharge, abdominal pain, and pain during urination. Because the symptoms often are mild, many people dismiss them as trivial.

Chlamydia has been diagnosed less often than other STDs because no fast and easy laboratory test had been available. Specialized laboratory tests, however, can be used in the diagnosis of chlamydia. Between 20 and 40 percent of those people diagnosed as having gonorrhea also have chlamydia infections. Both sexual part-

---

[2]The VD National Hotline number is 1-(800)-227-8922, or, in California, 1-(800)-982-5883. It is open from 8 to 8 on weekdays and from 10 to 6 on weekends. All calls are toll free and are treated confidentially.

ners should be treated at the same time so that they do not reinfect each other. Treatment consists of at least a week of antibiotics. (For pregnant women and infants, treatment is two weeks on the antibiotic erythromycin. Chlamydial conjunctivitis—inflammation of the eyes—in infants is treated with antibiotic ointment.)

GONORRHEA

Gonorrhea (in slang, "clap," "dose," "drip") is the second most common STD in the United States. It is spread by intimate contact and has been known all over the world since antiquity. In England it was called, accurately, the "running sore"; in France it was called *clap* and *chaudepisse, (chaude* meaning "hot") (Zinsser, 1935/1971). Gonorrhea is difficult to control because in its early stages, it may have no symptoms, especially in women. One strain, thought to have come from the Philippines to the United States, is resistant to penicillin, the usual treatment. Many people are unwitting carriers of gonorrhea. Many others, especially in Africa and in Third World nations, suffer the blindness and sterility that gonorrhea causes. The gonorrhea microorganism *Neisseria gonorrhea* thrives in warm, moist places and dies rapidly outside the human body. Penicillin used to be effective against all known strains, but it is no longer. In 1975, the first case of penicillin-resistant gonorrhea was documented. The Army is presently testing a vaccine against gonorrhea (Cooke, 1982). People spread gonorrhea only during vaginal, anal, or oral sex. Gonorrhea can infect the mouth and the anus as well as the genitals. Pregnant mothers can infect their newborns' eyes as they pass through the birth canal. To prevent blindness, silver nitrate or antibiotic drops are routinely administered to the eyes of newborns.

It takes one to seven days (although some people think up to 14 days) from contact to the development of symptoms, and males are more likely than females to show the symptoms of gonorrhea. Males first develop pain on urination or a discharge from their penis that is tinted white, yellow, or greenish. Then they may develop chills or fever. Untreated, the symptoms eventually subside, but the infection spreads to the internal reproductive organs. The testes may swell and feel sensitive to touch. Gonorrhea can cause sterility in males if it is not treated. Because it so rarely causes symptoms in females, any male who learns that he has gonorrhea should tell (or have a clinic tell) his sexual partners so that they can seek treatment.

Most women (50 to 80 percent) who contract gonorrhea do not have symptoms. Those who do have symptoms notice a change in their urine or a vaginal discharge or pain, but gonorrhea is usually diagnosed in women either by growing the microorganism in culture or, most often, by tracing the history of sexual contact. The microorganism first infects the cervix, at the base of the uterus. From there it may proceed into the other internal genitals, causing inflammation and scarring of the fallopian tubes, ovaries, or other organs. Untreated gonorrhea poses the threat not only of pelvic inflammatory disease and sterility, but arthritis-like inflammation if the microorganism moves along the bloodstream into the joints. The disease is treated with antibiotics, ideally with large doses of injected penicillin. Because some strains of the disease are resistant to penicillin, other antibiotics must be used instead. Oral tetracycline, for seven days, is also effective against gonorrhea (and any coexisting chlamydia infection as well). It is wise to

The "drip" of gonorrhea—a discharge from the penis. Men get symptoms of gonorrhea more often than women do.

follow up treatment to be certain of cure. Treatment does not prevent future infections, of course. Sexual partners of those with gonorrhea are assumed to be at risk for the disease and should be informed.

NONGONOCOCCAL URETHRITIS (NGU)

Nongonococcal urethritis (NGU) is very common among men and is classified as any inflammation of the urethra except gonorrhea. (Another name for NGU is *nonspecific urethritis,* or *NSU.*) NGU therefore is probably several diseases, each caused by its own microorganism, each transmitted during sexual intercourse. One such organism, implicated in some of the cases of NGU, is *Chlamydia trachomatis,* mentioned above. (Now that chlamydia is being diagnosed separately, the incidence of NGU will appear to drop.) Another organism implicated is *Ureaplasma urealyticum.* Physicians diagnose NGU when a complete bacteriologic evaluation is impossible or while they await the results of laboratory tests (CDC Report, August 20, 1982). Thus NGU typically is diagnosed by exclusion: when a test for gonorrhea is negative and when there is inflammation. Treatment for NGU includes the antibiotics tetracycline and erythromycin.

The symptoms of NGU are a thin, watery discharge from the penis and irritation during urination. Left untreated, NGU can cause infection and damage to the internal reproductive organs. Some NGU is self-limiting and disappears by itself, but some needs antibiotic treatment. Because a female who is the sexual partner of an infected male often harbors the NGU microorganism, some doctors advocate treating her as well so that she does not reinfect her partner. (Conversely, women who find themselves with stubborn cases of inflamed bladder, giving symptoms of burning on urination, or white cervical discharge, might suspect NGU microorganisms and check with their partners.)

TRICHOMONIASIS

Trichomonas vaginalis is a protozoan that can live in either sex but tends to cause symptoms in women. It thrives in a moist environment and is transmitted primarily during sexual contact. The parasite can be passed on by infected towels. The incubation period is from four days to a month. Some doctors urge that male partners of infected females be treated, so that the infection will not recur. Symptoms of **trichomoniasis** sometimes include a foul-smelling vaginal discharge that is white, greenish, or yellowish and a sore, itchy vagina and vulva. In a few cases, trichomoniasis invades the cervix or bladder. Trichomoniasis is the most common vaginal infection. Most people with trichomoniasis show no symptoms. Males show symptoms only rarely.

Treatment for trichomoniasis is by Flagyl, a prescription drug (metronidazole) that is taken for several weeks and that should not be combined with alcohol. Other than its symptoms, trichomoniasis is not known to cause serious consequences. In some cases (such as people with peptic ulcers and diseases of the central nervous system), trichomoniasis is preferable to treatment with Flagyl.

GENITAL HERPES

The earliest known account of **genital herpes** came from a French physician in 1736, a time when physicians monitored French prostitutes (Altman, 1982). But the disease received little media attention in this country until the mid-1970s, at which point it began to be spoken of as an epidemic. *Time* Magazine (August 2, 1982) even ran a cover story that sensationalized herpes as "Today's Scarlet Letter." Sensational publicity about this "new epidemic," dark hints about links between herpes and cervical cancer or other fatal complications, fears that it is incurable and painful, and the guilt, anguish, and even the hysteria of its victims, have blown people's perception of the disease out of all proportion to its severity.

Genital herpes is caused by a virus, *Herpes virus hominis* type 2, that is closely related to the type 1 virus that produces cold sores in the mouth. (To add confusion, herpes virus type 1 can cause genital sores, although in fewer than 5 percent of the cases of genital herpes [Holmes, 1980].) Genital herpes is an STD that causes painful blisters to spread (the name "herpes" derives from the Greek for "to creep") on the genitals from two to ten days after exposure to the virus. Headache, fever, and malaise may follow. Although the blisters usually clear up spontaneously in a few weeks, the virus may live on in a dormant state in the body, not infectious to others. (This, by the way, is a characteristic of many viruses.) New and usually less painful bouts may recur for years, although some people have few or no repeat bouts. About two-thirds of women have relapses; fewer men have relapses. Relapses tend to be milder than the first attack. Herpes in rare instances is accompanied by high fever and inflammation of membranes surrounding the spinal cord and brain. Stress, fatigue, and other factors that lower the body's resistance to disease can make people susceptible to herpes attacks, but doctors really do not know all the factors that make the disease recur. (The same holds true for the virus that causes cold sores.) Some women get flare-ups just before or after they menstruate. Some people feel such pain that they can barely walk; others feel a moderate soreness (Laskin, 1982).

Herpes is usually, but not always, spread by intimate contact, although only one member of a couple may contract an active case of the virus while in the other it remains dormant. People without herpes sores can transmit the disease, for they are contagious just before sores appear and until they heal. Even for active herpes, one in three sexual partners will contract the disease (Lerner, 1980). Mothers with herpes—those who are unaware that they harbor active herpes—can transmit it as the baby passes through the birth canal, causing permanent neurological damage or death. The incidence of newborns with herpes rose from 2.6 per 100,000 live births in 1966 to 11.9 per 100,000 during the period 1978 to 1981. During dormant periods, the virus remains in the dorsal, lumbar, or sacral ganglia of the spinal cord.

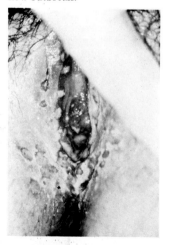

Herpes blisters on a female's genitals. Although the blisters usually clear up in a few days, the virus remains dormant—and not contagious—until there is a new outbreak.

PEOPLE WITH HERPES MAY THINK OF THEMSELVES MORE AS VICTIMS AND OUTCASTS THAN AS PATIENTS WITH A MEDICAL PROBLEM.

The Herpes Syndrome

Genital herpes sometimes causes psychological symptoms as painful as the blisters it raises. In what psychologists have come to call "the herpes syndrome," people may feel sexual guilt, fear rejection, avoid intimacy, abandon plans for bearing children, and watch their close relationships crumble. Part of the worry is in not knowing when or whether they are contagious. Herpes is most highly contagious just before and during outbreaks of blisters. Some people feel a warning or *prodromal* tingling or soreness just before an outbreak, and they know to avoid sexual contact for that time and for the duration of the visible attack. But others either receive no warning or misread their body's signals. Still others may have no apparent symptoms and still be contagious carriers (as, for example, happens when sores on a woman's cervix produce no symptoms). A husband or wife who "silently" (or otherwise) transmits herpes to his or her mate may jeopardize the marriage. People with herpes may think of themselves more as victims and outcasts than as patients with a medical problem.

Many herpes patients worry about how and whether to inform sexual partners about their problem. Many fear that people will desert them when they hear the news. Some avoid letting themselves get emotionally involved just to avoid the possibility of rejection. Others tell no one and just avoid all sexual contact. Herpes can play havoc with people's social lives. It can damage their self-esteem. Sufferers may feel tainted, depressed, and isolated. They may pass through a series of painful emotions: initial shock and denial, "through loneliness, anger, fear, self-imposed isolation and, finally, a deepening depression and a sense of entrapment similar to the hopelessness often felt by patients with chronic diseases like multiple sclerosis" (Laskin, 1982, p.94).

There are practical steps for reducing the chances of transmitting herpes and also for living with herpes (Gillespie, 1982; Laskin, 1982):

1 First, get medical treatment. The drug acyclovir, taken orally, can reduce symptoms and hasten healing of sores. Healed sores do not shed virus.

2 If you get a physical warning or know when your attacks are likely, get yourself treated, and avoid sexual contact. You are infectious only when you are shedding virus, that is, immediately before sores appear and until they heal.

3 The friction from masturbation or intercourse can make an active case feel even worse. Abstain while the infection is active.

4 During flare-ups, use a condom if you have sexual encounters. Some married couples have used this technique for years and have avoided passing on the virus.

5 Sores on the skin surface contain the virus, so avoid touching them and spreading the virus elsewhere on your body or someone else's. (Likewise for cold sores: don't kiss or have oral-genital sex when they're active.)

6 Use your own towels during any bout of infection. The virus can survive on a damp towel for several days. Many couples make this a general rule of hygiene, infection or not.

7 Find the situations that cause you stress, and try to avoid them or work out a way to diminish how upset you get. Herpes is a virus, and it is likelier

to flare up when your immune system is compromised. Stress, fatigue, or ill health in general can lower your resistance. Use the herpes as an excuse to take good care of yourself: eat well, exercise moderately, get enough sleep. Remember that no one knows how a herpes attack is produced, and so you can't be expected to figure it out by yourself.

8 To be responsible, you should tell a potential sexual partner about your herpes *before* you make love. But tell only after he or she knows you. A friend can usually handle the news if you break it tactfully. Bring it up *away from the bedroom,* give yourselves time to work it through if necessary, and try to remember that herpes is not deadly. Remember, people who don't have herpes get turned down sometimes, too.

9 Find a herpes self-help group where you can talk with others about the problem. The Herpes Resource Center is a support group located in Palo Alto, California.[3] It has branches across the country, publishes a quarterly journal with up-to-date information, and in confidential telephone conversations will provide information, referrals, and counseling.

10 The risk of cervical cancer in women with herpes is about 6 percent. These women should have semiannual Pap tests (painless smears of cervical cells examined for abnormality under a microscope). Cervical cancer is almost always curable if caught early.

11 If you are pregnant, tell your doctor that you have herpes. Most herpes is passed on to the newborn from the vagina. A Caesarean delivery *may* be needed to protect the baby.

12 Most important, keep yourself informed. Herpes is not fatal; it is not contagious all the time. Many people with herpes marry, have children, and live happily ever after.

To avoid getting herpes, take a few precautions: know your partner; look at your partner, and if there are any signs of infection, avoid sex. If that is impossible, take precautions (condom, no oral-genital sex, or whatever is necessary to avoid contact with the infection). It is perfectly reasonable to ask a new partner if he or she has herpes. You may actually be making it easier for someone to talk about it.

---

[3]The Herpes Resource Center's address is 260 Sheridan Avenue, Palo Alto, CA 94306. Telephone: [415] 328-7710. The New York branch is at 450 West 58th Street, New York, NY 10019.

SEXUALITY IN PERSPECTIVE: HOW DO YOU TELL YOUR PARTNER YOU MAY HAVE PASSED ON AN STD?

It is not easy for anyone to tell a partner that he or she may have passed on an STD. But the alternatives are worse: infecting a partner if it hasn't happened already; risking a partner's chance discovery of problems; or even reinfecting a partner. There are ways of managing the problem.

1 Tell the truth. "This is what happened. The doctor says that the treatment is thus-and-such. I think I can manage my own treatment. I never wanted to pass it on to you." Tell your partner that you didn't know you were infected, if in fact you did not. Tell your partner something like, "I want you to be all right, so please get checked. The doctor wants us both to be seen (or treated) so that we don't infect each other again." Focus on the task at hand.

2 Don't panic. Screams and recriminations will only complicate your life. Try to give your partner all the information you have. Good information can help people to cope with the anxiety that an illness can cause.

3 Postpone sexual intercourse until your doctor says that both of you are safe. Few couples find sexual activity easy when there is an STD lurking about them. *Sensate focus,* which is described in Chapter 16, may be your best bet for sexual activity for a while.

4 Don't wait until you have enough money to get treatment. Go now; pay later. Pool your resources if you have to. Public Health Service clinics provide free treatment. But don't delay. Early treatment minimizes the damage from STDs. Don't be fooled by symptoms that disappear. No hospital clinic will turn away a patient with an active STD.

5 Put aside for the time being any feelings of guilt or anger at your partner, and concentrate on treatment. Cure the disease first. Just as you would not feel ashamed of asking for treatment for a case of the flu, don't feel ashamed of asking for treatment for an STD.

6 Herpes and AIDS pose different problems from the other STDs. No known medication will cure them, but management is still very important. If you've passed on an infection, your partner needs to know.

In short then, realistically, the best ways for sexually active people of any age to cope with the STDs are: to know the signs of the most common STDs; to know how to get treatment for them; to check their sexual partners, especially new ones, for obvious signs of STDs and to ask about any not obvious conditions; to avoid sexual activity with infected and untreated partners; and to tell a partner or partners immediately if and when they find they have contracted an STD.

A crab louse.

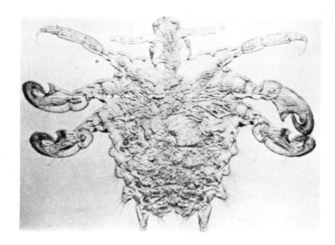

PUBIC LICE

Also called "crabs" because they look like little crabs under a microscope, **pubic lice** take up residence at the roots of human hair, usually pubic hair, where they breed and feed on human blood. They are transmitted during sexual contact as well as by other routes: on clothing, for example, and other personal articles. These tiny creatures do not cause infection, but they make their human hosts feel itchy and uncomfortable. Infested clothing and sheets should be thoroughly washed. Infested humans are treated with Kwell (gamma benzene hexachloride) cream, lotion, or shampoo. DDT is also effective against these lice. Crabs die if they spend 24 hours out of contact with their human host, but their eggs may hatch for several days thereafter.

SYPHILIS

In the world of microorganisms, there live thin, corkscrew-shaped forms called *Treponema pallidum*. They are part of a group of microorganisms called *spirochetes*, from two Greek words, one meaning spiral and the other meaning hair. If you look under a microscope, the spirochete is thin as a hair and spirals around. *Treponema pallidum* has been taking up residence in humans for some centuries, although no one actually knows where it first appeared. When this spirochete gains entrance to a human body and multiplies, that human has contracted a case of **syphilis.** A doctor diagnoses the symptoms, prescribes penicillin or another antibiotic, the spirochetes die, and the syphilis disappears. If in the meantime, the human has had sexual contact, the spirochetes probably have taken their chance to move into another, unsuspecting human host.

A Brief History of Syphilis

Although untreated syphilis can cripple and kill, today in developed nations, it is rare to find such advanced, untreated cases. Syphilis has only in this century been brought under control, however, first by arsenicals in an arduous course of injections, and later by penicillin. Just as today people dread cancer, they once felt the same dread of syphilis. It was a killer that spread not just during sexual activity, but during pregnancy and in the routine care of parent for child. Christopher Columbus died of it. Julius Caesar, Cleopatra, Henry VIII, Ivan the Terrible, Erasmus, Moliere, Casanova, Boswell, Catherine the Great, Napoleon, Keats, Schubert, Heine, Nietzsche, Mussolini, Hitler, Gaugin, Wilde, and Al Capone all had it (Offir, 1982). Syphilis thus may have changed the course of politics and history.

No one is really sure where syphilis originated. Even where historical records exist, their interpretation is subject to disagreement among scholars. They cannot be certain whether, for example, ancient manuscripts that describe symptoms that *sound like* syphilis in fact describe syphilis or some other disease. In Europe alone its name changed many times. It was called "the French disease" in Italy and "the disease of Naples" in France. We cannot know for sure whether syphilis began in the Old or the New World. Hans Zinsser's wonderful *Rats, Lice, and History* (1935/1971) suggests that syphilis probably existed for centuries in a relatively mild form all over the world. But when the troops of Charles VIII of France overpowered Naples in 1495, syphilis appeared in a new and far more virulent form than had existed in Europe before or than exists today:

The infection as it occurred in Naples was to all intents and purposes a new disease *in representing a completely altered relationship between*

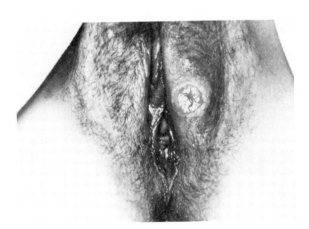

Chancres appear on the genitals during the primary—and contagious—stage of syphilis and then go away spontaneously. Secondary syphilis appears as a painless skin rash on hands, back, or other areas. Most people seek treatment during these two stages of the disease.

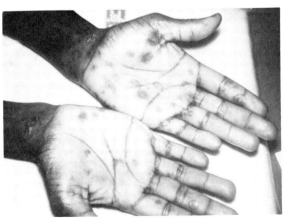

parasite and host, with consequent profound changes of symptoms. Something must have happened at that time, apart from war and promiscuity—both of which had been present to an equal degree many times before—which converted a relatively benign infection into a highly virulent one (p. 55).

In short, for half a century or so, syphilis was a violent, rapid killer. After passing through its human host enough times, however, the syphilis spirochete grew less virulent and became the slower killer that, without medical treatment, it remains today.

Syphilis Today

The syphilis spirochete, *Treponema pallidum,* follows predictable biological rules. After entering the human body during sexual activity, it forms a painless, hard open sore, called a *chancre,* on the host's skin, and usually on the skin of the genitals. The chancre appears where the spirochete first enters the host, but it goes away after five or six weeks, even without treatment. During this *primary stage,* the host is contagious. The spirochete migrates from the infected individual to the warm, moist, mucous membrane or the abraded skin of a sexual partner's vagina, cervix, labia, anus, mouth, urethra, penis, scrotum, or other body part. Expose the spirochete to light, air, or cleansing agents, and it dies. It can only be passed on through intimate sexual contact—vaginal or anal intercourse, oral-genital activity, or, rarely, kissing—or from a pregnant woman to her fetus.

The spirochete moves from the localized chancre into the host's bloodstream and spreads throughout the body. After a few weeks, the chancre heals. (The duration of all the stages of syphilis has a very wide range.) During the *secondary stage,* syphilis appears as a painless skin rash. Even if the host does not notice the rash or decides to do nothing about it, the rash will clear up by itself. Most people, however, do seek medical treatment during either the primary or secondary stages of syphilis. Then the spirochete burrows in for a *latent phase* that may last a few years, a few decades, or even a whole lifetime. During this stage, it multiplies in the host's internal organs. After a year of the latent phase, the host is no longer contagious to sexual partners (Cherniak and Feingold, 1977).

During the final, *tertiary stage,* the spirochete cripples and then may kill. The spirochete may cause blindness, heart failure, liver disease, or if it passes into the brain, paralysis or dementia. Left untreated, the spirochete can also kill its host. No one knows why the damage is limited in some patients but extreme in others or why some patients do not proceed to dementia but others do. In a study done in Oslo, Norway between 1891 and 1951, 2000 untreated cases of syphilis were followed. Untreated cases showed the natural course of the disease. Half the men, but only 18 percent of the women, died of the disease. The tertiary stage was also worse for men than for women, for reasons unknown. This study was undertaken well before antibiotic treatment for syphilis was developed. Penicillin is the antibiotic for treating syphilis, although it cannot reverse permanent damage. Other antibiotics are used for people who are allergic to penicillin.

AIDS
(ACQUIRED IMMUNE DEFICIENCY SYNDROME)

Acquired Immune Deficiency Syndrome, or AIDS, is an STD that first turned up in the late 1970s in communities of homosexual males but later was found in other groups as well. For epidemiologists, the medical people who specialize in tracking the cause and course of disease in various populations, AIDS presented a classic mystery. AIDS eluded investigators' efforts to learn its cause, how to save its victims, or how to prevent the disease altogether.

In 1984, two research teams discovered the virus AIDS. In laboratories in Paris and in The National Cancer Institute in Washington, DC, a human T-lymphotrophic retrovirus (HTLV-3) was isolated. It is likely that the virus traveled from Africa to Europe and from Africa to the Caribbean and from there to the United States. Antibodies in healthy people along this path suggest that the disease has been widespread.

AIDS begins, like many diseases, with a feeling of weakness, swollen glands, low fever, weight loss, symptoms that can be overlooked or misinterpreted. Blood tests of AIDS victims show a characteristic pattern among the blood cells responsible for fighting infection, a loss of part of the immune system called "T helper" cells. With their immune system weakened, AIDS victims cannot fight opportunistic infections. People who survive the first bout with some invading microorganism succumb within months or years to some other infection. Medicine still has no way to restore the functioning of the immune sytem. AIDS was first diagnosed when doctors grew suspicious at the large numbers of men in their 20s and 30s turning up with diseases previously rarely seen in young people. These diseases included a deadly form of pneumonia (*Pneumocystis carinii*) and Kaposi's sarcoma, a cancer that once was seen in older men of Mediterranean origin. Previously, cases of Kaposi's sarcoma had responded to treatment, many of the older men survived for 10 years with it, and they eventually died of other causes. Yet in the young men, Kaposi's sarcoma killed quickly. The pneumonia and Kaposi's sarcoma previously had been found also among people whose immune systems had been compromised by disease, immunosuppressive therapy (as in chemotherapy or transplantation treatment), or both. Working back from cases like these, doctors at the Centers for Disease Control found the young males whose immune systems were unable to protect them, males with what came to be called AIDS. They also found debilitated young men with other kinds of tumors, parasites, fungal and other severe infections (for instance, cytomegalovirus and Epstein-Barr virus). In short, often fatal infections had begun appearing in a whole new younger population.

AIDS is not a disease of homosexuals only. Most of the first American AIDS victims were gay males, but soon epidemiologists found AIDS within other groups as well: bisexual men; Haitian immigrants; intravenous-drug users and their sexual partners; hemophiliacs and other recipients of blood transfusions and their sexual partners. The early form of AIDS virus, which appeared widely in Central Africa, was nearly equally distributed among men and women. It was probably transmitted to Haiti in this form. Some men, women, and children who lived with AIDS victims began showing symptoms. A prostitute and drug user gave birth to a baby diagnosed as having AIDS (Sides, 1983). (She and the baby since have died, apparently from AIDS.) Epidemiologists hypothesized that the pattern

A sign in a San Francisco bath house for gay men warns against AIDS.

of victims suggested that the microorganism in question was a virus transmitted through blood, semen, or other body secretions. (This pattern appears in another viral STD found among gay men, hepatitis B.) Hospital experience with AIDS victims taught physicians that AIDS was not very infectious except through body fluids (CDC Task Force, 1982). It is likely to enter the body through small anal tears caused by fisting and anal sex.

AIDS unsettled gay communities in major cities. More than 4000 cases—72 percent of them gay men—had been diagnosed by early 1985. People felt frightened, helpless, and guilty. Said one gay man:

> *It used to be that I felt every act of gay sex was a political statement. It said, "I'm liberated." AIDS strikes at the heart of that. A lot of gays are demoralized and wondering whether the bad old days have returned.*

In response to widespread fear as the number of AIDS cases grew, both within the gay community and outside of it, some people panicked. Police in some cities insisted on wearing protective masks and clothing before transporting or helping

TABLE 17.1

AIDS: the Global Picture

The Americas	Cases Reported[a]
United States[b]	9,608
Haiti	340
Brazil	182
Canada	165
Trinidad	16
Mexico	12
Argentina	11

Europe, Asia, Africa	Cases Reported[c]
France	260
West Germany	135
United Kingdom	108
Belgium	65
Netherlands	42
Switzerland	41
Denmark	34
Spain	18
Sweden	16
Italy	14
Austria	13

Source: World Health Organization Centers for Disease Control.

[a]Cases reported through December, 1984.

[b]Cases reported as of April 15, 1985.

[c]Countries with ten or fewer reported cases eliminated.

AIDS spread originally from Africa and is now found in many parts of the world.

AIDS victims. Many blood donors feared getting AIDS from *giving* blood. (They cannot.) Landlords in San Francisco moved belongings of AIDS victims while the men were hospitalized. Prison guards demanded protection. Funeral home workers were told to handle AIDS victims with the precautions they take for meningitis (another contagious illness) victims. Techniques now have been developed for screening blood carrying the AIDS virus, and researchers are working to develop a vaccine. The problem of diagnosis largely has been solved. Treatment and cure of those already afflicted are problems still to be solved (Altman, New York *Times,* April 26, 1984). For the time being, AIDS victims must be treated vigorously for whatever diseases their weakened immune systems cannot fight.

One area of uncertainty is what may happen to the 1 million or so people who have been exposed to the AIDS virus and whose blood has antibodies in it. No large-scale longitudinal studies have been done on this population. Among a sample of 31 men exposed to AIDS before 1980, two thirds were symptom free in 1985. A second group is expected to develop a pre-AIDS syndrome. **Pre-AIDS, or lymphadenopathy syndrome,** causes swollen lymph nodes, fever, and malaise. A third group will develop AIDS itself (*Science,* November 29, 1985). Another complicating factor is that AIDS takes many different forms. It is a more

SEXUALITY IN PERSPECTIVE: HOW DOES STRESS AFFECT AIDS?

In one survey of 600 gay men in San Francisco, psychologists William Horstman, Leon McCusick, and Arthur Carfagni (APA *Monitor,* July 1983) asked whether the men had changed their frequency of engaging in four sexual acts. The investigators passed out questionnaires outside of gay bars and baths and mailed them to gay couples. Depending on the specific act, 25 to 32 percent of the respondents had reduced their participation, and 5 to 28 percent had stopped altogether. But 62 percent of the men continued to engage in risky acts with the same frequency as they had before they learned about AIDS. Most respondents said that a monogamous relationship would be the best protection against AIDS. But bar patrons were the least likely to have such a relationship. (It is in bars that gay leaders have distributed circulars on ways to protect against AIDS.) Bathhouse patrons were the most likely to acknowledge that they were engaging in possibly dangerous sex.

Two Boston investigators of the gay community, Rhonda Linde and Jim Fishman (APA *Monitor,* July 1983), have also noted changes in gay men's sexual habits in response to the threat of AIDS: "People are asking, 'Who am I going to have sex with, and what does it mean in my life?'" They believe that sex with many anonymous partners can bear several different interpretations. For some well-adjusted men, anonymous sex is recreation. For other men, anonymous sex represents an inability to maintain intimacy or an attempt to defend against feelings of anxiety and low self-esteem. The reaction to the prospect of AIDS may not be the same in the two groups.

Counselors find that men who do not moderate their risk of contracting AIDS tend toward one of two extreme reactions: panic or denial. Some men give up all sex. Some feel such stress that they may actually increase their chances of coming to harm with drugs or alcohol. Denial may lead men to bargain with a counselor (or with fate): "What's the point in giving up sex until they figure out what

complex disease than once was believed. For example, some patients who have died of AIDS have shown neurological symptoms of dementia, seizures, or loss of muscular control. Yet autopsies of the brain of some of these patients did not show the presence of the virus HTLV-3 (Shaw et al., 1985). Still other AIDS patients have shown neurological problems but no severe impairment of the immune system (*Science,* November 29, 1985). The fact that AIDS takes many forms has led some people to suggest that the very definition of AIDS be broadened.

For Help with AIDS

The Public Health Service has a toll-free hotline open daily and offers a free causes AIDS?" (The study was carried out before the virus was identified.) AIDS creates anxiety because people feel that they can do so little to protect themselves. Because the incubation period (the time between exposure and onset) is imprecise but may last for years, every day carries its small threat. Because the first signs are vague and variable, every sniffle is threatening. One bitter irony in the AIDS story: because so many men are getting sick so often—not all with AIDS—psychologists are beginning to study the precise mechanisms by which depression and stress can themselves interfere with the functioning of the immune system.

Based on "Onset and Progress of AIDS Shaped by Stress Factors," APA *Monitor,* July 1983, p. 1.

booklet, "Facts on AIDS."[4] Self-help groups have been meeting in gay communities across the country. Television stations in San Francisco, which has a large gay population, have shown programs on such groups with information on how to contact them. In New York and San Francisco, health alliances of gay men have publicized support services to all AIDS victims: transportation, meals, housekeeping, psychotherapy, and moral support. As people fall ill, they need both practical and emotional support. As they see their friends fall ill, they need support in dealing with their own fears as realistically as possible. All AIDS victims—men, women, and children—need to know to seek treatment at the first sign of infection.

[4]The Public Health Service, Office of Public Affairs, Room 721-H, 200 Independence Ave. SW, Washington, DC 20201. The toll-free number is 1-800-342-AIDS.

STDS AMONG HOMOSEXUAL MALES

Monogamous homosexual males do not have rates of STDs any higher than those found among monogamous heterosexual males, and homosexual women have lower rates of STDs than heterosexuals (Owen, 1980). But homosexual males who have a large variety of sexual partners increase their risk of contracting many STDs: syphilis, gonorrhea, AIDS, herpes, infections of the urinary tract, "gay bowel syndrome," hepatitis B, and others. Two factors can make treatment of STDs in homosexual males difficult. Anonymous sexual partners can make the tracing of sexual contacts for purposes of treatment nigh unto impossible. Syphilis, for example, can be controlled with penicillin, yet many gay men catch and pass on syphilis because they have no way of knowing that they have been infected. A second problem is that the social stigma attached to homosexuality can make a homosexual male hide his homosexuality or his symptoms from a doctor, especially a doctor who may seem judgmental. The prescription for this problem: homosexual males should find a nonjudgmental doctor who will treat them in confidence.

Anal and oral intercourse can transmit a number of diseases that do their work in the mucous membranes of the mouth or throat or anus. These infections occur among heterosexual couples as well as gay couples. Infectious diarrhea and anorectal gonorrhea can be transmitted by anal intercourse. Some of the infections found in homosexual populations are otherwise quite rare in this country; many are identified by specialists in tropical medicine (another reason why a good medical history can be important). Many are caused by exchanging organisms from anus to mouth and by organisms entering through small tears in the tissue of the anus. Homosexual males may also develop infections of the urinary tract. Viral illnesses like hepatitis B and herpes travel in body secretions such as saliva, urine, blood, and semen. Some carriers have no symptoms of infection. That makes control difficult—in any group. And one cure may be followed by reinfection, a sad truth for both heterosexuals and homosexuals with many partners.

For some of these STDs, the cure is already known and readily available. A vaccine effective against hepatitis B, for example, has been developed and is being distributed preferentially to gay men because they are at high risk. Many STD infections are susceptible to antibiotic treatment, although some are resistant to them. Amoebic infections of the bowel can, for instance, be difficult to eradicate.

Genital warts, here on the penis, afflict members of both sexes.

GENITAL WARTS

Genital warts are thought to be caused by sexual contact. Warts are caused by a virus and can occur anywhere on the skin, although they grow especially well on moist surfaces like the end of the penis or the labia. Warts may grow singly or in clusters. People tend to develop immunity to the virus that causes warts, and the warts therefore tend to clear up by themselves. But treatment with topical solutions and by washing and drying the area thoroughly are recommended so that the warts do not get infected or passed on to another person.

INFECTIONS OF THE FEMALE GENITALS

Any infection of the vagina is called **vaginitis;** any infection of the bladder is called *cystitis*. Either can be introduced or aggravated by sexual activity, although not all cases of either "itis" are sexual. The symptoms of vaginitis include itching or burning and often a discharge. The most common vaginal infection is trichomoniasis, already described. We will also describe yeast infections, and vaginal infections. Cystitis, which is just one form of many types of urinary tract infections (others include the urethral and kidney infections), tends to produce symptoms of frequent, burning urination, sometimes with fever and lower abdominal pain.

Cystitis

An infection of the bladder, **cystitis** is often caused in women by sexual intercourse that irritates the urethra, which leads from the outside of the body to the urinary bladder, or (more likely) that moves bacteria into the urinary tract. In many cases, *E. coli* bacteria, which normally live in the intestines and promote digestion, enter and inflame the bladder. Some women are prone to repeated urinary tract infections; others never suffer from them. (They are known to be rare among nuns.) Women suffer urinary tract infections more often than men do because a woman's urethra is about 1½ inches long compared to a man's 8 inches. Because the infection has to survive a longer journey in the male, the likelihood that urine will flush it out is greater. Organisms from the vagina or anus easily enter a woman's shorter urethra, where they cause infection. Urinary tract infections are thought to be caused in most instances by sexual intercourse (Harvard Medical School Health Letter, December 1982). One common syndrome afflicts women who have intercourse for the first time, or for the first time after long abstinence, or repeatedly over a short period of time. Symptoms of cystitis may include fever; blood in the urine; the need to urinate very often, even when the bladder is empty; and pain or burning on urination. Some urinary tract infections cause no symptoms, however.

Treatment is with antibiotics or sulfa drugs. Women can relieve some of the discomfort of cystitis by sitting in a tepid bath and by drinking large quantities of fluids to keep their urine diluted. Symptoms disappear soon after medication is started, and in some cases cystitis cures itself spontaneously. For women who repeatedly suffer urinary tract infections, the best course is to try to keep bacteria from the bladder: by wiping the anus from front to back after bowel movements; by washing the genitals of both partners before sexual intercourse; by emptying the bladder often, especially just before and after intercourse; and by keeping the urine diluted by routinely drinking lots of water. Drug treatment in all cases depends on how often a woman gets infections and on which bacteria cause them.

Yeast Infection

Some women are plagued with **yeast infections;** others go through life untouched by them. The acidic environment of the vagina ideally prevents infection by the many organisms that normally live there, but many factors can alter that acidity— pregnancy, birth control pills, menopause, douching, fatigue, and so forth—and allow microorganisms to multiply. *Candida albicans* is the microorganism that causes *moniliasis,* a yeast infection of the vagina. *Candida* is usually present in small numbers in the vagina and in the mouth and intestines of males and females. Although it is not always an STD, *Candida* can travel into the vagina during oral-genital sex, from the end of an uncircumcised penis, or from a woman's anus. When the fungus multiplies, a woman feels the symptoms typical of this kind of infection: a white, lumpy discharge and from mild to maddeningly intense itching of vagina and vulva. Intercourse becomes uncomfortable.

Yeast infections are treated locally with cream (Monistat or Mycostatin) or, in severe cases, with tablets. Symptoms usually abate within a day or two, but a woman should continue using the medication for as long as directed to make sure that the Candida organism has been controlled.

AN OUNCE OF PREVENTION

Celibacy eliminates the risk of STDs. But for sexually active people, only uninfected couples whose members never have sexual intercourse with others are *not* at risk for contracting certain STDs. But even they may come down with certain sexually transmitted infections such as yeast infections of the vagina, cystitis, or the like. One source of limited protection from STDs, besides the mutual fidelity of uninfected partners, is the condom. Because it covers the penis during sexual activity, it can block the transmission of certain STDs. (It cannot block STDs transmitted when the male is not wearing the condom or those transmitted from unprotected parts of the anatomy such as mouth or hand.) Some spermicides also kill organisms that cause certain sexually transmitted infections, but this sort of protection is even more limited than that afforded by condoms.

People who are at risk for STDs can significantly reduce that risk. Generally, prevention (also called *prophylaxis,* which explains why condoms sometimes are called "prophylactics" or "safes") means making sure one's sexual partner is healthy, taking necessary precautions, and blocking the bacteria that cause STDs from entering your body. You can block these bacteria, many of which thrive in the mucous membranes of vagina, urethra, anus, or mouth, in several ways. Some products sold for birth control and inserted in the vagina offer protection. Widely available over-the-counter products include: Certane Vaginal Jelly, Cooper Cream, Delfen Foam, Emko Foam, Koromex A-II Vaginal Jelly, Milex Crescent Jelly, Ortho Cream, Ortho-Gynol Jelly, and Preception Gel. These products can be used for anal as well as vaginal intercourse. Progonasyl, which is available only by prescription, and Lorphyn Vaginal Suppositories, which are available without prescription, are also protective (neither of these is a contraceptive). Using condoms during vaginal or anal intercourse and washing the genitals before and, especially, after sexual activity can help.

SUMMARY

1 Sexually transmitted diseases (STDs) are the many different infections and inflammations that people transmit during intimate contact. Only those who do not have sex or who have sex exclusively with an uninfected partner are not at risk for STDs. Some STDs are transmitted during sexual intercourse, some during oral sex, some during pregnancy or childbirth.

2 Chlamydia and gonorrhea are the most common STDs. Because they tend not to produce symptoms in many females, many people are unwitting carriers of both infections. In males, chlamydia and gonorrhea cause similar symptoms: discharge from the penis, possibly followed by fever and chills. In females, gonorrhea is usually diagnosed by tracing sexual contacts or by laboratory culture. Left untreated, gonorrhea can inflame and scar the internal genitals of males and females, causing sterility. In women, chlamydia may be asymptomatic or mild. Symptoms are vaginal discharge, abdominal pain, and pain on urination. Contacts of chlamydia cases should be traced, for left untreated, the disease can cause sterility.

3 Nongonococcal urethritis (NGU) is any inflammation of the urethra in males besides gonorrhea. NGU is probably caused by several different organisms, each of which causes discharge from the penis and irritation during urination. NGU can be treated with antibiotics. As chlamydia is diagnosed separately, the class of diseases called NGU will drop to half its previous incidence.

4 Trichomoniasis is a common vaginal infection that manifests itself with a discharge and soreness or itchiness of the vulva. Males rarely show symptoms, although they can carry the bacteria that cause trichomoniasis and reinfect their partner.

5 Genital herpes is caused by a virus. In its active phase, it causes painful blisters on the genitals. These can be treated. The virus may remain dormant for months or years, during which time the individual is not infectious. Active phases may occur periodically.

6 Pubic lice do not cause infection, but they do cause itching and discomfort. They are tiny crab-shaped organisms that live in human hair, especially pubic hair, and feed on blood. Topical treatments are effective against them.

7 Syphilis used to kill much more quickly than it does today. The disease goes through several stages of development. Left untreated, it can cripple and kill, but it is susceptible to treatment with penicillin.

8 AIDS, or Acquired Immune Deficiency Syndrome, is a serious STD that plagues gay males, intravenous drug users and their sexual partners, and recipients of repeated blood transfusions like hemophiliacs. Caused by a virus, AIDS affects the immune system and leaves victims vulnerable to opportunistic infections. Blood screening for the virus is possible; no cure has yet been found.

9 Genital warts are caused by a virus and appear on the moist surfaces of the genitals of both sexes. They should be treated so that they do not get infected or passed on to someone else.

10 Common genital infections that women get, often by sexual contact, are cystitis (an uncomfortable infection of the bladder that is treated with antibiotics or sulfa drugs) and yeast infections of the vagina and vulva that are treated with local creams.

KEY TERMS

sexually transmitted diseases (STDs)
chlamydia
gonorrhea
nongonococcal urethritis (NGU)
trichomoniasis
genital herpes
pubic lice
syphilis

Acquired Immune Deficiency Syndrome (AIDS)
pre-AIDS (lymphadenopathy syndrome)
genital warts
vaginitis
cystitis
yeast infection

SUGGESTED READINGS

Boston Women's Health Collective, *The New Our Bodies, Ourselves*. New York: Simon and Schuster, 1984. A generally excellent reference work about women's bodies with a helpful and forthright chapter on STDs.

Gillespie, Oscar, *Herpes: What to Do When You Have It*. New York: Grosset & Dunlap, 1982. This small book is full of sensible, reassuring, practical advice on herpes and how to deal with it.

Montreal Health Press, *VD Handbook*. Montreal: MHP, 1977. A bargain of a book ($2), available by mail from: VD Handbook, P.O. Box 1000, Station G, Montreal, Quebec H2W2N1, Canada. This is an informative, engaging, and easy-to-understand compendium of information on STDs.

Rosebury, Theodore. *Microbes and Morals*. New York: Viking, 1971. A very literate microbiologist actually makes STDs fun to read about.

Zinsser, Hans. *Rats, Lice, and History*. New York: Bantam, 1971. Another literate, witty bacteriologist whose story of disease and history is simply fascinating.

PART VI

SOCIAL AND CULTURAL ISSUES

Odilon Redon, "The Accused." Collection, The Museum of Modern Art, New York.

Chapter 18

Sex and the Law

Pʀobably most people in the United States have broken certain laws on sexual behavior.

THE RELATIONSHIP OF SEX AND LAW

Have you ever masturbated? Have you ever had intercourse with someone you were not married to? Have you ever had oral-genital sex? Have you ever cohabited? If you can answer yes to any of these questions, you have broken some state law. You are in good company. Probably most people in the United States have broken certain laws on sexual behavior. Although many people assume that laws governing sexual behavior are concerned only with dangerous, antisocial, or violent acts—rape, sexual murder, sexual abuse of children, and the like—the law actually prohibits many ordinary, everyday sexual experiences.

Laws do vary greatly from one state to another and from one time to another, but generally speaking, the only sexual acts universally considered legal across time and state are the kissing, caressing, and vaginal intercourse of two married adults. Alfred Kinsey in 1948, after surveying the sexual behavior of thousands of American men, concluded that 95 percent of them had broken the law. Eighty-five percent had had intercourse before they were married, a violation of fornication laws. Fifty-nine percent had had oral-genital sex, a violation of laws against "unnatural acts." Seventy percent had visited prostitutes, and about 45 percent had had intercourse with people who were not their lawful spouses, a violation of adultery laws.

Until recently, laws regulating sexual behavior in this society have been predicated on a basic ethic: sexual intercourse is for procreation. As a result, the law historically has restricted permissible sexual behavior to vaginal intercourse by married couples. All other forms of sexual activity—from masturbation to extramarital sex, prostitution to homosexual relations—violate this principle and therefore have at some time been considered illegal.

Because many sexual acts involve more than one participant, and because children may be born of such sexual acts, it has long seemed reasonable that the law would be concerned. But laws governing sex also uphold an old, revered, if inherently vague principle: that of a common or public good. Certain sexual acts are considered violations of this common good. Although most people would readily agree that laws against rape protect the rights of unwilling sexual victims and protect the social order, people may have more trouble deciding about the reasonableness of laws against, say, private sexual acts between consenting adults, whether those adults are unmarried or homosexual. After all, it can be argued, such acts do not violate the rights of the willing participants. Instead, laws against sexually active unmarried and homosexual people have been justified by courts as serving the greater good.

Changes in family law during the 1960s and 1970s do not directly concern us here. But the *direction* of the change in such law is important for our understanding of reforms in sex laws based on "the common good." Family law today is moving in the direction of increasing autonomy for members of families towards each other. The law is the meeting ground of conflicting forces, each of which exerts pressure to achieve its definition of what comprises the "common" good in the rights and responsibilities of family members. Sexual behavior has always been part of the rights and responsibilities of married people.

Although some sex laws may represent a *past* rather than a present consensus, all known societies regulate sexual behavior. But the aspects of behavior regulated by various societies themselves vary. Sexual activity that is legal in one sovereign nation may be illegal in others. Thus homosexual acts and abortion are illegal in Ireland but not in France. Of course, these laws do not develop randomly; they reflect a given society's ethical standards and values. (We talk about the relationship between social norms and sexuality in Chapter 1.) In the United States, sex laws often attempt to maintain some consensus on the common good and the rights of individuals. Besides ethical values, these laws also embody three views of sexuality that have their roots in our religious heritage: sex as sin; sex objects as personal property; and sex as punishable violence. Individual states differ on how closely to the biblical tradition their sex laws adhere, and they differ as well on the extent to which the law intervenes in private sexual matters. An activity that is legal in one state may be a misdemeanor or felony in another state. Prostitution, for example, is legal in Nevada but nowhere else. Laws are not static; they change in response to changing public opinion about the legitimacy of forms of sexual behavior.

SEX AS SIN

Laws in the United States traditionally have upheld the principle that sex is sinful. The idea is as old as the written tradition of humankind and may be much older. From the Old Testament comes the belief that human beings, sinful in having disobeyed God, may indulge their sexual passions only under strictly legislated circumstances. Within marriage, sexual relations are considered right and necessary, and the husband or wife who neglects these "conjugal duties" may be served with a bill of divorce.

The New Testament emphasized earthly life as a preparation for a spiritual afterlife, and so slightly different sexual principles emerged. Vaginal intercourse between married, Christian adults remained the only morally acceptable form of sexual activity. But abstinence from sex, in the service of spirituality, gradually became idealized. Whereas Jewish priests were expected to marry and procreate, by the sixth century after Christ, Christian priests had been ordered by the Pope to remain celibate. Although this rule was enforced strictly only after the Middle Ages, denial of the flesh was an enduring religious ideal, a concomitant of sex as sin. Passion was to be channeled into Christian service. The clergy was to channel

SEXUALITY IN PERSPECTIVE: SEXUAL MATTERS IN COURT

As cultural views on sexuality have shifted, matters that people once held to be private or secret are showing up in courts of law. There, for all the world to see, estranged spouses and unmarried sexual partners are suing for damages because they have been infected with genital herpes, or because they may have been infected with AIDS. In other lawsuits, people are suing for "wrongful" pregnancies. In one such case, a man promised his sexual partner that he was sterile, but he impregnated her nevertheless. He lost the lawsuit for damages that she brought after undergoing surgery for an abnormal pregnancy.

The lawsuits also demonstrate the flexibility of the common law, for traditional legal remedies like negligence, battery, and fraud are being applied to new areas of sexual behavior. In one California case, a nurse sued a doctor with whom she had had intercourse and from whom she claimed to have contracted herpes. She asked for damages for income lost, for medical expenses, and for physical and mental distress. The nurse claimed that the doctor lied when he told her that he did not have the disease. The doctor defended himself by claiming that the court had no right to intrude into so private a sexual matter. "The courts," said the doctor's lawyer, "should not intrude into areas of such intimacy and privacy." But the court ruled that its interest in the case was not improper. "The right of privacy," said the judge, "is not absolute and in some cases is subordinate to the state's fundamental right to enact laws which promote public health, welfare, and safety, even though such laws may invade the offender's right of privacy." Similar cases have been brought against herpes carriers in at least 10 other states. In California, the estate of Rock Hudson, the actor who died of AIDS in 1985, is being sued. Hudson's lover charges he was not told about the AIDS infection until well after Hudson knew he was ill and probably dying.

When sexual behavior is put on trial, the issue of privacy rights is never far from the surface. In such cases, courts must decide how far the government may intrude into what once had been considered purely private matters.

Based on Margolick, D. "Herpes and Similar Matters Get More Attention in Court," New York *Times,* February 26, 1984, p. 24.

sexual passion into spirituality. The laity was to channel sexual passion into marital, procreative sex. Because Christian sexual ethics are so austere, and because human sexual motivation is so powerful, many Christian societies have had problems trying to legislate morality. The results have been ambiguous, hypocritical, often unrealistic or unenforceable laws governing sexuality.

Virtually any sexual act that cannot lead to procreation has been considered sinful and, therefore, illegal. Kinsey once told of a wife who was angry at her husband for reasons unrelated to sex. She reported to the police that her husband had had anal intercourse with her. He was charged with "sodomy" (in this case, the legal term for anal intercourse) and sent to San Quentin prison. After some years, the wife wanted to withdraw the charges, but she could not. The prosecutors and courts insisted that the interest of the state was at stake in the case, as if the state itself had been sinned against (Wardell Pomeroy, personal communication).

SEX AS PROPERTY

Solidly founded on Judeo-Christian principles is the idea of the state and its microcosmic model, the family, as patriarchies. Just as God the Father rules the world, the patriarchal family is ruled by the male. He is served by a submissive female, who loves, honors, and obeys him. Together they create dependent, valuable children. Inherent in this patriarchal model is woman as a sex object. Western law traditionally has defined the wife as her husband's "chattel," or possession. Although a husband may have revered and cherished his wife, she was his property nonetheless, with few legal rights or legal recourse if she were sexually or otherwise brutalized.

The laws governing sexual behavior reinforce the male's interest in protecting his property. Legally, males traditionally have been owners of females and protectors of their virginity. Never has the opposite held: never have men been given to women as property. The traditional marriage ceremony talks about "man and wife," never about "woman and husband." A female who was not chaste—whether she were a young woman who was not virginal or an adulterous wife—threatened to ruin her value as property, a value that the law upheld. Thus wives were punished far more harshly than husbands for extramarital sex; girls were stigmatized far more severely than boys for premarital sex. For the same principle—to protect men's sexual property—laws once made it virtually impossible for wives to inherit their husbands' estates, for wives to accuse their husbands of rape, or even to sue for divorce. (See Chapter 19 for a discussion of rape law.) A clear **double standard**—that is, one standard for males and another, more restrictive one for females—prevailed in Western legal tradition for centuries. Only in the last hundred years or so have the assumptions of patriarchy been challenged strongly enough for the law in the United States to have begun to tilt in favor of women's rights.

One of the interesting questions raised by laws to guard sexual property has to do with prostitution and abortion (themselves areas of moral and legal ambiguity). Traditionally, a woman's body has been considered valuable sexual merchandise, but rarely has any society condoned the ownership of that body by anyone besides a male—father, husband, or pimp. Women have argued that their rights over their own bodies give them the right to decide whether to bear children

Many statutes reflect the Judeo-Christian tenets of family as patriarchy, women and children as chattel, sex only within marriage, and sex only for procreation.

or abort (an argument the courts have upheld so long as women exercise that right under medical care). Some women also have argued that they have the right to profit from their body's work, as in prostitution, just as men can profit from their physical labor.

SEX AS VIOLENCE

Sexual acts are intimate. They involve the exposure of otherwise private, vulnerable body parts to another person. During sexual intercourse, one person actually penetrates someone else's body. For this reason, sexual acts can be viewed as forms of violation of body boundaries. Some sexual acts are literal violence: forcible rape is literal violation against another person. Forced sexual acts often are intended to degrade—for example, rapists sometimes force their victims to perform fellatio to degrade them. Many victims find fellatio to be a more personal act than intercourse and, therefore, more upsetting when forced. Victims often feel deep and lasting emotional guilt at their failure to fight back when force is threatened but not used (McCahill et al., 1979). Virtually every culture ever studied has condemned rape (Brown, 1952). But the value of the raped woman as property played a role in the severity of the rapist's punishment. The rape of a slave since Babylonian days was treated by law as a far less serious transgression than the rape of a free woman. The rape of a virgin was treated more harshly than the rape of a virtuous married woman, which in turn was treated more harshly than the rape of a "promiscuous" woman. A "promiscuous" woman was assumed (by male judges) to be a consenting partner; her property value already had been lost. Sex as sin and sex as property often combined in history to determine how sex as violence was treated. Given the importance of rape, the act embodying sexual violence, we have devoted all of Chapter 19 to it.

SEX CRIMES WITHOUT VICTIMS

Do all sexual acts that violate (or once violated) the law in fact do damage, violate personal or property rights, or compromise the public good? The laws in many states once held anal intercourse, oral-genital contacts, mutual masturbation, and cohabitation—sexual activities that are far from rare—to be illegal. The laws in many states define sexual acts between two people of the same sex to be "unnatural." Who was the victim when two adults consented to homosexual or lesbian relations? Likewise, when a customer solicits a prostitute, who is the victim? Courts have viewed society as the victim. Prostitutes are still rounded up by police on "common nightwalker" charges despite the absence of any charges brought by victims. The wish to clear the streets is more often a property issue ("Whose street is this anyway?") than an attack on crime. Any sexual acts between consenting adults that are illegal have been called **victimless crimes.** Many people believe that so long as these acts hurt no one, they should not be illegal at all.

THE RELATIONSHIP OF SEXUALITY TO THE LAW IS NEITHER EXACT NOR SCIENTIFICALLY PRECISE.

HOMOSEXUALITY STATUTES: SEX AS SIN

The relationship of sexuality to the law is like the relationship of any other human activity to the law: it is neither exact nor scientifically precise. The laws of society are not like the laws of physics, which are expressions of unvarying regularities in nature. Laws are cultural expressions that balance many different interests: the welfare of the individual, the preservation of society, public opinion and belief. Ideally, sexual laws should discriminate between justifiable concerns and irrational prejudices. If they do not, the laws should change. Laws, of course, do change and generally in response to changes in social relations and shifts in public opinion. Below we will explore the issues that we have set forth—sex as sin, violence, and its relation to property—as we describe laws about homosexuality and prostitution.

The state of Virginia had a law that forbade private sexual acts between males. When this law was taken to the Supreme Court and challenged, the Supreme Court upheld the Virginia law. It held that Virginia's interest as a state was legitimate, because prohibitions of homosexuality were rooted in Judaic and Christian law. The Supreme Court ruling quoted Leviticus 18:22: "Thou shalt not be with mankind, as with womankind: it is abomination." It also quoted Leviticus 20:13: "If a man also be with mankind as he lieth with a women, both of them have committed an abomination: they shall surely be put to death; their blood shall be upon them."

Most modern American statutes once called homosexual acts "crimes against nature," a phrase that dates back to the sixteenth-century reign of Henry VIII of England and ultimately to Leviticus. "Buggery," as the English called anal sex, was the "abominable and detestable crime against nature with mankind or beast." Legal scholars argued about exactly which acts constituted buggery, acts considered so horrible that they could not be specified in the law. Until recently, many American laws used terms like "buggery" and "sodomy," without being precise about the acts in question. In the 1960s, more than half of all states with laws against **sodomy** (named after the biblical city of Sodom, so sinful that it was destroyed by God) used biblical terms to describe the act(s) as a "crime against nature," an 'infamous crime against nature," or an "abominable and detestable crime" (our analysis is based on state laws in the late 1960s. The language of the statutes sometimes was so vague that judges had to clarify whether the statutes referred to anal intercourse, oral-genital intercourse, or both. "Sodomy" generally

Nude show at a gay bar in New York City. Laws are cultural expressions, and some laws portray homosexual acts as sinful.

Group demonstrations press for equal rights for lesbians and gay men.

implies penetration of some body opening and therefore tends to include fellatio but to exclude cunnilingus (*State* v. *Forquer,* 74 Ohio App., 293 1944). Some sodomy statutes forbid mutual masturbation (*State* v. *Mortimer,* 105 Ariz., 472 1970). In some states, the maximum penalty for consenting sodomy has been 20 years in jail.

As public opinion in some places has shifted toward protecting the privacy rights of adults, old sex statutes like those against sodomy are left unenforced. In principle, such statutes can be used not only against gays, but also against heterosexuals who engage in oral or anal sex. In practice, today it is rare for sodomy to be prosecuted. Instead, charges of "lewd and lascivious" behavior are used.

But even unenforced statutes can do harm. Minorities of any sort fear the laws that *might* be used against them or seem to support their stigmatization. The chilling effect of any such laws increases the likelihood that gays will avoid any civic assertion of their sexual orientation. The tightrope that tennis star Billie Jean King had to walk after publicity revealed her affair with Marilyn Barnett reflected King's fears that her livelihood was threatened by a status as a bisexual. Her public position of the "errant wife" averted some of that stigma. Public antagonism toward gays is reflected in the King case and in the many court cases involving the firing, eviction, and harassment of gays. For these reasons, gay groups support legislation forbidding discrimination in housing, jobs, and other civil settings for reasons of sexual orientation.

Organizations of lesbians and homosexuals have adopted many tactics of the civil rights movement, from sit-ins and protest demonstrations to lobbying and getting out the vote. The aim has been to change the laws that discriminate against gay people, and to restore privacy rights.

LAWS AGAINST PROSTITUTION: SEX AS SIN AND PROPERTY

In the crime of solicitation of sex by prostitutes (heterosexual or homosexual) and by homosexual men, which also has been called a "crime without a victim," the prostitute or the homosexual sells or offers some sexual arrangement. If the solicitation is conducted in public, some people—who do not want the sexual services—are offended. The unwanted exposure to sexual negotiations constitutes the "harm" that the law sees in public soliciting. In addition to being a public nuisance, prostitution has also been criticized as a matter that should remain private and as a moral offense against society.

Police "sweeps" keep prostitutes off the streets for a short time and haul others into court. Street sweeps do not catch the callgirls, who deal by telephone appointments and who serve the solid middle class. Street sweeps mainly catch the poorer, rundown prostitutes, many of them addicted to drugs or alcohol. One court clerk remarked that a 44-year-old prostitute who had spent close to 13 years in jail in 10- to 90-day sentences, was "doing life on the installment plan." Many prostitutes consider arrests and jail normal hazards of their job. These hazards tie prostitutes to their **pimps,** men whom the women support in return for bail money and lawyers to represent them after street sweeps. Pimps are hustlers who specialize in keeping and living off prostitutes. They supply "their" prostitutes with housing, drugs, and other necessities (including love) in exchange for the women's earnings.

For the charge of soliciting to hold in court, the police must prove that a prostitute or a homosexual initiated the offer of sex in exchange for money, and not the client. That this is shadowboxing is proved by the rarity in most states of arrests of men who solicit prostitutes (Roby, 1969). (Southern California presents exceptions.) Male police decoys are sometimes used to entrap prostitutes or male homosexuals. Some people criticize the police for using public funds to entrap people, although the police do not admit to entrapment. Entrapment is a defense against prosecution. If a defendant can prove that the police or their agents implanted criminal ideas in the innocent mind of the defendant and thereby caused him or her to commit a crime, then the defendant will not be convicted. The police usually claim that they merely provide criminals with an opportunity to act.

A 1959 study by the U.N. Commission investigated whether prostitution should be considered a criminal offense. The arguments supporting punishment of adult prostitution were given as follows:

1   *It is the responsibility of the Government to regulate public morals in the interest of public good; hence, to declare prostitution a punishable offense.*
2   *If prostitution per se is not made a punishable offense, the abolition of the regulation of prostitution will merely replace controlled prostitution by clandestine prostitution.*
3   *It will be difficult strictly to enforce legal provisions proscribing the exploitation of the prostitution of others when prostitution itself is not considered a punishable offense.*
4   *Many women and girls on the borderline {of entering prostitution}*

may be encouraged to take up prostitution by the fact that the law does not proscribe such a calling.

5 *The absence of any legal provision against prostitution may be interpreted by the public as meaning that the Government tolerates commercialized vice because it is a "necessary evil."*

The arguments against criminalizing prostitution were:

1 *The prohibitionist legislation would necessitate the formulation of a definition of "prostitution." If the term "prostitute" were to be given wide scope, the fact of making prostitution a legal offense would entail unwarranted interference in private life which would be contrary to Article 12 of the Universal Declaration of Human Rights. [That article reads: "No one shall be subjected to arbitrary interference with his privacy, family, home, or correspondence, nor to attacks upon his honour and reputation. Everyone has the right to the protection of the law against such interference or attacks."] If, on the other hand, the term "prostitute" were to be given too restricted a legal connotation, then it would be difficult to establish the charge against the culprit.*

2 *Prostitution is an act which is committed by the prostitute and her client. Both are equally responsible. It would be a discrimination against the woman for the law to be directed only against her. Further, whenever the law inflicts penalties on the client as well as on the prostitute, experience shows that, in practice, the repressive measures are enforced on the prostitute alone.*

3 *Between prostitution and other sexual relations outside wedlock there is only a difference of degree and it would be unjust to limit the penalty only to persons who meet the arbitrary criteria set forth in a legal definition of prostitution.*

4 *The penal law should not take cognizance of every immoral act. To protect minors, and to maintain public order, prostitution with and of minors, as well as soliciting for the purpose of prostitution, may be proscribed. But adult prostitution should not be singled out from all other moral sins and be brought within the realm of the penal law.*

5 *In terms of the results achieved, experience teaches that prostitution cannot be eliminated by mere enactment and that making prostitution a criminal offense generally leads to clandestine prostitution and to a ruthless underworld organization for the exploitation of the prostitution of others. As long as a demand for prostitution exists on the part of men, there will undoubtedly be a corresponding supply on the part of women, despite the penalties inflicted on the latter.*

6 *The prohibitionist policy depends for its effectiveness upon a system of police espionage and entrapment which is itself detrimental to the common good.*

7 *By making prostitution per se a criminal offense, the prohibitionist system creates among persons engaged in prostitution a collective as*

*well as an individual antagonistic attitude which hamper the chances
of their rehabilitation (U.N. Study on Traffic in Persons and Prostitution, ST/SOA/SD/8, 1959, pp.10–11).*

The U.N. Commission concluded its report by saying that prohibiting prostitution does not work and suggesting that prevention might best be achieved by
educating and retraining women who were or might become prostitutes.

CHANGING THE LAWS ON PROSTITUTION

Prostitutes recently have organized to defend their right to sell sexual services.
Some feminist lawyers and criminologists agree with their arguments. These
feminist professionals see the issues as follows: the prostitute is neither the helpless
"whore with a heart of gold" nor the sex-crazed nymphomaniac. She is a woman
who has chosen an occupation from the choices available to her. As social worker
Jane Addams said, "[Lust] is a better paymaster than the mill owner or the tailor."
In this society, most women enter service occupations—nurse, teacher, secretary,
mother, and wife—that draw on their capacities as nurturers, servants, and sexual
providers. Despite the differences among these occupations, prostitution fits this
mold, according to the lawyers and feminists arguing the prostitutes' case.

Police sweeps, say feminists, interfere in the livelihood of women whose occupation is difficult and dangerous. Just as housekeeping and child care are considered easy because women do them, prostitution is also considered easy work.
Laws that penalize prostitutes and not their customers discriminate against women.
Prostitutes are double victims: first, the victim of certain customers' sexual aber-
rations and her pimp's violence; second, the victim of police harassment. A study

In Amsterdam's red light district, prostitutes openly solicit
customers.

in Washington, D.C., (Geis, 1972) showed that 64 percent of prostitutes who were injured had been injured by their customers, 20 percent by police, and 16 percent by pimps. If public opinion shifted to accept prostitution as an economic problem that grows out of women's inferior job opportunities, then laws might change. Prostitution laws would also be reformed if the public interpreted prostitution as part of a woman's right to possess her own body.

The double standard creates the moral conditions for prostitution. In our society and others, prostitutes are despised as "bad" women. According to one view, their redeeming value is in preventing men from seducing "good" women. The double standard helps to ensure that women, but not their customers, will be punished for prostitution—punished by police sweeps and by social stigma. Many feminist groups therefore endorse decriminalizing prostitution but not legalizing it (Women Endorsing Decriminalization, 1975).

Not everyone agrees that prostitution should be decriminalized or legalized. Some legal scholars, among others, believe that prostitution should remain a criminal offense. In fact, the majority position is probably in favor of criminal penalties for prostitution. Groups concerned with public soliciting defend morality and their own rights to use the neighborhood where prostitutes work. The law does not automatically give police the right to rid the streets of people just because their presence offends others.

Thus the streets sometimes become disputed territory. When business slows, pimps pressure their prostitutes to increase business. Passers-by who refuse the prostitutes' business may be beaten or robbed. Although laws against robbery, assault, and manslaughter exist to punish these offenders, irate citizens usually identify the crime in these cases as prostitution.

SOME SEXUAL ENCOUNTERS BETWEEN ADULTS AND CHILDREN ARE BRUTAL AND VIOLENT; OTHERS ARE LESS HARMFUL. BUT THEY ARE ALL ILLEGAL.

CHILDREN, SEX, AND THE LAW

Although sexual contacts between adults and children violate laws, social norms, and cultural taboos, they are not uncommon. Adults (usually adult males) may solicit sex from children of either sex, children to whom they are related by blood, marriage, or adoption as well as children to whom they are unrelated, close friends, or even barely known. It is important that in discussing sexual contacts between children and adults, people separate psychological from legal concerns, although that is not always an easy task. The motivation and psychological consequences of such sexual acts vary widely. Some sexual encounters between adults and children are brutal and violent; others are less harmful. But they all are illegal. By enacting laws against the sexual exploitation of children, society tries to protect those it sees as easily intimidated and vulnerable.

Children and Consent

An important concept in sex laws is that of **consent.** Legally, a sexual act is considered consensual when the participants agree or consent to an act. Consent requires that a person be free to accept or reject a sexual advance, with clear knowledge of the meaning of that advance. A woman may consent to sexual intercourse with a man she cares for, but the law will not see her as consenting to a man making advances as he wields a knife. Not everyone can legally give consent, and the person who cannot consent is considered a victim. The woman with a knife at her throat is a victim: if she is put in fear of her life, she is not consenting to sex. Similarly, the use of fraud or drugs makes consent highly questionable.

Someone who is too young cannot legally give consent. States usually define the age of consent, although the range varies across states from age 10 to 18. The intent of the law is to define an age at which a young person can understand what it means to consent to sexual acts. (See "Sexuality in Controversy: Statutory Rape—the Changing Age of Consent.") By extension, people who are severely mentally ill or retarded—and therefore unable to understand the nature of the sexual events—are usually considered unable to consent as well.

Despite evidence that first intercourse is occurring at younger ages on the average than it once did, consent laws have not routinely lowered the age of consent. It is likely that the consent laws have not followed because they reflect a cultural bias against legitimizing early sexual contact with adults. Instead, some states have adopted a varied set of punishments for having sex with females who are below the age of consent. The most severe punishment is reserved for adults who are much older than the girl, and the least severe punishment is meted out to those closer to the girl's age.

Children and adults usually have different frameworks for understanding sexual acts. Often a child's first awareness that a sexual act with an adult is unusual comes when the adult pledges the child to secrecy. Children may view sexual fondling, for example, as a form of affection. Because adults find it difficult to discuss with children other adults' sexual advances, it is not surprising that children may be confused by pressure for secrecy or threats connected with such "affection" (see "Sexuality in Perspective: Sexual Abuse of Children").

A recent case illustrates some of the difficulties adults face in dealing with children who engage—apparently willingly—in sexual acts with adults. In 1983, newspaper accounts of a group of Vermont children, mostly girls and a few boys, dramatized the problematic issue of children's consent to sexual acts (Kindelberger, 1983). In Brattleboro, Vermont, a 12-year-old girl had been paid by a man for sexual acts in his apartment. The girl told some friends, and they told other friends, until, ultimately, 10 children between the ages of 8 and 13 had been paid for sexual contact with two men. Police at first said that sexual intercourse was involved and that the acts were more extensive than fondling or touching, although they would not specify the sexual acts the children performed. The two men were arrested. One was charged with sexual assault; the other was charged with lewd and lascivious conduct with a child. None of the children was identified or charged. When reports first appeared, newspapers called the activity "prostitution." After all, children had been paid for their sexual services, services that apparently had been rendered willingly. Two days later, however, the Brattleboro,

SEXUALITY IN CONTROVERSY: STATUTORY RAPE— THE CHANGING AGE OF CONSENT

Statutory rape is the legal term for sexual intercourse with a young person who has not reached the legal age of consent. Although a young woman literally may consent to intercourse, the law may consider her too young to give truly informed consent. Age of consent is defined by each state, and the woman who has intercourse legally on one side of a border may be "jailbait" on the other. In the rural southern states of the nineteenth century, the age of consent was usually *ten*, lower than the age in most of the industrialized north. Since the nineteenth century, the legal age of consent has risen, and today many states consider it 16 or 18 or even 21 (Bienen, 1981).

Some illegal acts—intercourse among teenagers, smoking marijuana, and driving faster than the speed limit are three familiar examples—do become commonplace and impossible to punish reliably. When that happens, lawyers look for ways to reframe the laws to improve conformity. Instead of making any and all of a young woman's sexual partners statutory rapists, newly proposed laws would divide men into two categories. One category would consist of men who have intercourse with very young girls—under 10 or so—who are considered too young to understand the meanings or possible consequences of the act. The other category would consist of men who would be charged with corrupting a minor (a young woman between the ages of 10 and 18), if he is four or more years older than she. Penalties for men in the former group would be graver than those for the latter. Men in the former group would be classified statutory rapists, and they would not be allowed to plead ignorance of a girl's age. In sum, the new laws would dramatically decrease the age of consent, to 10 or so, and maintain the severity of the statutory rape charge if the girl is very young. But it would recognize that young women today just before and during adolescence cannot realistically be protected from consensual, nonviolent, sexual intercourse with a peer.

They may sound sensible, a good way to protect young girls who really are too young to consent to sex, but the proposed changes are not likely to happen very quickly. Sexual values and the laws that enshrine them change slowly, if at all. Interestingly enough, the same culture that uses young children in sexually suggestive advertisements is profoundly attached, in spirit, to protecting the young from sexual initiation.

SEXUALITY IN PERSPECTIVE: SEXUAL ABUSE OF CHILDREN

Adults find it very hard to talk to children about sexual abuse, even though many parents think that sexual abuse is not a rare occurrence. Researchers from the University of New Hampshire's Family Violence Research Program interviewed 521 Boston area parents on topics related to the sexual abuse of children. (From 4344 households randomly selected, 700 fit the study's requirements, and 521 parents agreed to interviews.) As sociologist David Finkelhor, the study's director, remarked, "Parents seem to be telling their children too little, too late. Kids need to know they can tell parents and other adults about it." Children may be confused when an adult insists that the sexual activity is proper, and they may not understand that they can refuse sex to an adult. They may also be afraid of getting punished if they tattle.

Many parents, it seems, tell their children about kidnaping and think that they are also warning them about sexual abuse. Because many parents believe that abusers are strangers, they may think a warning like, "Never go with a stranger" is enough protection. But in only one-third of the cases of sexual abuse parents reported were strangers involved. The other two-thirds of sexual abuse were relatives, acquaintances, and parents themselves.

Only 29 percent of the parents reported having spoken to their children about sexual abuse specifically. How can others broach the subject with their children? They can tell children that certain parts of their body are off limits to other people. They can also tell them that some kinds of touching feel good, but some kinds feel bad.

The study also turned up these findings:

1 Nine percent of parents said that their own children had been sexually abused. (Dr. Finkelhor believes that twice this number of children are actually victimized.)

Vermont, police chief and a state social worker insisted that the children had not engaged in "prostitution." Instead, they called it a case of "sexual child abuse." Many experts were quoted in the flurry of news articles that appeared on the case. Some said that the children must have been coerced; some said that the children must have been desperate for money or previously sexually victimized.

Although some of the psychological questions surrounding children's consent in the Vermont case are unsettled, the *law* on consent is clear. In Vermont, children 8 to 13 years old cannot legally give consent. In contrast, in some states, 10- to 13-year-olds may be treated as consenting adults.

2 Almost half of the parents (47 percent) personally knew a child who had been sexually abused. These children were family members, children of neighbors, or friends.

3 Fifteen percent of the mothers and 6 percent of the fathers reported that they themselves had been sexually abused as children.

4 Parents considered sexual abuse more harmful to children than divorce or a friend's death.

5 Half the parents believed that abusers usually are strangers to their child victims. As Dr. Finkelhor said, "None of the parents in our study revealed that they themselves had abused their children. Yet we believe that a considerable number of children are abused by their own parents."

6 Children from every social class, ethnic and racial group had suffered sexual abuse equally. But children whose parents remarry are more vulnerable to sexual abuse than others. (Dr. Finkelhor hypothesizes that dating mothers may bring "sexually opportunistic" men into the family and that because stepchildren are not blood relatives, their new relatives may abuse them.)

In short, the sexual abuse of children is not rare. Parents seem to know that it is widespread, but they mistakenly believe that strangers are the most frequent abusers. Relatives and friendly strangers, in fact, are the most common abusers, and it may be far more difficult for children to escape from them than from strangers.

Based on Glenn Collins, "Child Sexual Abuse Prevalent," New York *Times,* February 2, 1983, p. C 1.

Sexual Acts with Children

The sexual acts between children of both sexes and adults cover a wide range. Nearly all of the acts—98 percent—are initiated by the adult, and in roughly half the cases, the adult used force. Exhibitionism accounts for about 20 percent of the acts, touching and fondling for 38 percent. Completed intercourse accounts for only 4 percent of the sexual experiences girls report; simulated intercourse is about twice as common (Finkelhor, 1979).

In Chapter 15, "Sexual Variations," we drew a profile of the convicted **pedophile,**

In a survey of 119 girls and 23 boys who reported sexual contact with adults, David Finkelhor (1979, 1984) found a wide variety of reported sexual acts and reactions by children involved. Percentages may not add up to 100 because the respondents could cite more than one response.

TABLE 18.1

Girls' and Boys' Reported Sexual Experiences with Older People

	Girls	Boys
Nature of activity		
Invitation	3%	5%
Hugging in sexual way	6	—
Showing genitals	20	14
Fondling sexually	17	—
Touching genitals	38	55
Simulated intercourse	10	5
Intercourse	4	9
Other	3	14
Partner initiated	98	91
Partner used force	55	54
More than once	40	41
Longer than one week	39	41
Told someone	37	27
Average age of child	10.2	11.2
Average age of partner	31.7	26.9
Homosexual	6	84
Family member	44	17
Reaction of child		
Fear	58	41
Shock	26	14
Surprise	18	23
Interest	14	41
Pleasure	8	23
Negative reaction	66	38

Source: David Finkelhor, *Sexually Victimized Children,* New York: Free Press, 1979. *Child Sexual Abuse,* New York: Free Press, 1984.

the adult who makes sexual advances to a child. The profile described pedophiles as men who may know their victims and plan their sexual contact. Male homosexual pedophiles are attracted to young boys, but heterosexual pedophiles usually turn to children only after failing with adult sexual partners. For every homosexual pedophile picked up and charged by the police, four heterosexual pedophiles will be charged. Pedophiles may look, touch, and fondle their victims and show their own genitals. Many then masturbate. Pedophilia is sometimes, but not generally, physically aggressive (Gebhard et al., 1965; Groth and Burgess, 1978). Pedophiles are not always men without adult sexual contacts. In many cases, situational stress in a man's life precedes his turning to children for bodily solace and affection. Groth (1979) has suggested that such men have *regressed* (fallen into immature behavior) as a psychological defense against stress. He has suggested that other men, who never have had sexual contacts with adults, are *fixated* in their immature behavior. If his distinction is correct, the two groups of men would respond to different types of treatment.

One society, which takes the name of René Guyon, defends and endorses sexual contacts between adults and children. Guyon wrote *Ethics of Sexual Acts* (1933), in which he encouraged sexual contacts between adults and children as contributing to children's development. Guyon also believed that sexual experience in childhood decreased delinquency and divorce later in life. Such assertions are, of course, open to empirical test. What *are* the effects on children of sexual contacts with adults? In one survey (Finkelhor, 1979), 58 percent of the girls reported fear and 26 reported shock as their reactions; only 8 percent reported feeling pleasure. Of the boys, 41 percent reported reacting with fear, and 41 percent also reported reacting with interest. Twenty-three percent of the boys reported reacting with pleasure. Overall, 66 percent of the girls and 38 percent of the boys said that their reaction had been negative. Two other studies report predominantly negative results from sexual contact between adults and children (Finkelhor, 1983; Russell, 1983). When West Coast prostitutes were studied, a disproportionately high number of them had been forced to have intercourse with older men in their families, after which the girls ran away from home. Beyond prostitution, there are few means of support available to young runaways (James and Meyerding, 1977). Similar histories of sexual abuse appear in high proportions among drug abusers and adolescent runaways (Finkelhor, 1984). Clinicians who conduct therapy with patients who have reported childhood sexual experiences with adults say that the impact of those experiences is almost uniformly negative (Herman, 1981; Meiselman, 1978).

Two recent surveys (Finkelhor, 1979; Fritz et al., 1981) of college students—who certainly were not selected (like patients) on the basis of their childhood sexual experiences—help psychologists estimate the incidence among children of (admitted) exposure to sexual acts with adults as well as recall of the children's reactions to those acts. A 1979 study at the University of New Hampshire by sociologist David Finkelhor reveals that about 1 in 5 women students and 1 in 11 men students recall some sexual advance from an adult. The actual incidence is likely to be higher, because young children are less likely than adults to code many acts as sexual and because lower-class students are underrepresented at the university. When exhibitionists are excluded from the number making sexual advances, a range of studies find 15% of women recalling childhood sexual victimization (Finkelhor, 1979; Gagnon, 1965; Landis, 1956).

TABLE 18.2
Women's Recollections of Sexual Victimization during Childhood

Study	As Originally Reported	Under 13 Only	Column 1 Excluding Exhibitionists	N
Kinsey-Gagnon	28%	28%	14%	1200
Landis	35	19	16	—
Finkelhor	19	16	15	530

Source: Finkelhor, 1979.

When all reported sexual experiences during childhood are considered, children on whom force has been used and whose partner was at least five years older than they report the greatest amount of trauma. Older children suffer more, too, for older children are likelier to have a framework for interpreting the sexual events than are younger children (Finkelhor, 1979). In the New Hampshire survey, three out of five girls reported feeling frightened. Boys are more likely to express combinations of fear and pleasure. Not all children are traumatized by sexual contact with an adult. In a large-scale study of nearly 1000 college women, queried about their memories of unsolicited childhood sexual acts with others, force was not necessary for them to have experienced trauma (Fritz et al., 1981). Failure to resist when no physical force or threat of force had been used increased the trauma for girls. Failure to resist proved to be strongly guilt-inducing.

In the wake of sexual contacts with adults, clinicians encourage children of any age to talk about their experience. Clinicians encourage giving the children reassurance and realistic answers about the meaning of the events. Many children assume that they caused the events or that the adult was angry with them. Sometimes they have been sworn to secrecy and threatened. It is a rare child who can face such threats calmly. Clinicians try to help children to distinguish between the normality of sexual feelings—arousal, cuddling, touching—and the illegitimacy of an adult's sexual initiative toward children. Some sexual contacts take place in contexts that make the children feel beloved by their adult sexual partner. In these cases, clinicians try to work from the children's point of view and to recognize their legitimate needs for love and affection. But they also try to help these children develop new ways to fill those needs. In many cases of sexual contact between adults—relatives or not—and children, the psychological aftermath for the children depends largely on how parents, police, social workers, or other adults behave toward the children.

Incest

Almost all societies forbid sexual relations within the family (Ford and Beach, 1951), or **incest**. The degree of genetic relationship considered incestuous, and therefore taboo, varies across cultures. Some cultures include genetically unrelated people within the incest taboo, people like in-laws or godparents, who usually have a quasi-familial role or economic ties to a family or community. Some cultures use marriage outside of a village as a way of increasing family power, village influence, or community alliances. Marriage and sexual relations between members of this extended, nongenetically related family are regarded as a threat to the social order. Some anthropologists believe that cross-cultural incest taboos are more concerned with regulating reproduction—the consequences of sexual acts—than sexual acts themselves (Fox, 1980).

Genetic arguments against incest sometimes are based on the fear that offspring from incestuous unions may inherit genetic diseases or anomalies. It is true that first-degree relatives like parents and children share half their genes, and it is true that the expression of many diseases and anomalies requires two genes. First-degree relatives are more likely to share such genes than less closely related people are. But in practice, children born from incestuous unions and offspring of animals' incestuous unions do *not* show disproportionately high frequencies of genetic defects. In nature, for example, monkey and ape mothers sometimes mate with their male offspring, and in zoos, such unions are routine breeding practice. In cases where genetic defects already have shown themselves in a genetic line, however, higher frequencies of genetic defects can be expected from incestuous matings.

In common parlance, people often talk about "incest" as any sexual acts within the family. In fact, as we saw in the case of other sexual contacts between (unrelated) adults and children, most incestuous acts are *not* acts of intercourse. Most incestuous acts involve siblings exposing their genitals, touching, and fondling. Sex between siblings accounts for the largest proportion of these incestuous acts. As sisters approach puberty, the incidence of attempted intercourse rises. In one-quarter of these cases, brothers use force on their sisters. Cousins of both sexes account for the next greatest amount of sex in the family. (States do not typically include cousins in incest statutes.) Sexual contacts across generational lines account for about 10 percent of the cases of incest.

In David Finkelhor's survey (1979) at the University of New Hampshire, father-daughter incest accounted for slightly over 1 percent of the total student group sampled. From this admittedly small figure, Finkelhor extrapolates that 16,000 new cases of father-daughter incest will occur each year among girls between 15 and 17 in the United States. Among women 18 or older, about 750,000 are estimated to have had sexual contact with their fathers. Daughters seem to be at increased risk of sexual abuse when their father is a stepfather, not directly from him, but from men in his social network or from men whom their mother previously has dated. These men may not consider a stepfather's biologically unrelated daughter as out of sexual bounds (Finkelhor, 1982). Clinicians express concern about daughters with stepfathers and overwrought, ailing, or passive mothers in disorganized families. In contrast, adult women rarely make sexual advances toward children. This profound difference between the sexes, which has been noted repeatedly by virtually all researchers in the field, has led some feminist clinicians (Herman, 1981; Meiselman, 1978) to view adult men who commit incest as wielders of power over their children. Just as wives once were their husbands' property, so are children—according to these writers—the property of fathers. Fathers therefore may feel free to do what they will to children who "belong" to them.

Whether a child is traumatized or not, all incestuous acts are illegal. By law, no child can give consent to sexual acts. Adults are so powerful in children's eyes that it is naive to believe that they have freedom to choose *not* to comply with adults' sexual demands or requests. No doubt some children comply with adults' sexual invitations out of a combination of sexual interest, curiosity, even physical longing. But the law on consent is society's way of warning adults that they alone will be held accountable for sexual acts involving children. Society's goal is to prevent and deter the easy sexual exploitation of children.

In practice, most cases of incest probably go unreported, and only a minority are punished. Both psychologists and lawyers (Holzman, 1984) recommend a two-part course of action in cases of sex between children and adults. First, they urge that the acts be reported. Reporting is a necessary first step in delegitimizing such sexual acts. Second, they urge the repeal of state laws requiring corroboration of the sexual act by someone other than the young victim. (Only Nebraska in 1985 still had corroboration requirements.) In the aftermath of reported incest, a family needs help. The child and the offending adult must be separated at least temporarily, a wrenching process for which families need financial and social support. Children and adolescents need support as well in forming or renewing ties to peers that were disrupted or forbidden by the adult sexual partner. Many families that decide to stay together need help in establishing a new set of rules for living.

IN THE UNITED STATES, STATE LAWS FORBID INCEST BETWEEN PARENTS AND CHILDREN, BETWEEN BROTHERS AND SISTERS, AND BETWEEN ALL RELATIVES ABOVE THE LEVEL OF COUSINS.

STATE LAWS AGAINST INCEST

In the United States, state laws forbid incest between parents and children, between brothers and sisters, and between all **consanguinous,** or blood-related, relatives above the level of cousins. These laws forbid marriage and sexual intercourse (and sometimes "deviate" sexual intercourse, by which is meant fellatio and anal intercourse). The punishments for violating incest laws range from fines or some months in jail to as many as 21 years in jail (Bienen, 1981). The severity of the punishment depends on the state, the nature of the incestuous relation, the relative ages of the participants, and the degree of force, if any, involved. Many laws specifically forbid sexual acts between step- and adoptive relatives. In some statutes, the forbidden sexual acts are called "adultery" or "fornication," words that reflect the legal concern for protecting the integrity of the married pair. That integrity translates into: sex restricted to husband and wife.

In some cases, the legal punishment for incest involves removing a father or other adult from the home where he is a breadwinner. To many families, this sort of punishment feels like double jeopardy. Exposure is powerful punishment, the reasoning goes, but taking away economic support is double punishment. Families often prefer to see the offending man as "sick," "crazy," in need of mental health treatment rather than as a felon in need of jailing (Finkelhor, 1984). Because families often prefer to see a man who has committed incest as mentally ill, the courts often lean heavily towards sentences aimed at rehabilitation. The New Jersey Supreme Court in early 1984 sent back two sexual assault cases to Superior Court for reconsideration. In both cases, sentences had been low on punishment and high on probation. Both cases involved forced sexual assault, one with a 13-year-old stepdaughter and one with an unrelated 19-year-old woman. Both men were given five years probation; the stepfather was also given a 63-day jail term. The Supreme Court ordered the lower courts to consider the nature of the crime as primary and rehabilitation as secondary.

A new turn in the course of punishment for incest came in 1984 when the heir to the Upjohn drug fortune was ordered chemically "castrated." The 44-year-old stepfather had sexually assaulted his wife's child during a 7-year period when the child had been between 7 and 14. At 14, she ran away from home. The stepfather pleaded no contest to first-degree criminal sexual conduct. He was sentenced by a Michigan court to five years probation, with the first year of probation in the county jail. The chemical "castration" consisted of treatment with the drug Depo-Provera, the experimental drug produced by Upjohn that is reported by researchers at Johns Hopkins Medical School to diminish sexual drive.

Can rehabilitation reasonably be expected in cases of incest? Not all cases of incest are alike. When San Francisco's Adult Probation Program provided counseling groups to men who had committed incest with their daughters, one counselor described the men's self-justifications as falling into three categories. The men uniformly saw themselves as good, benign, and generous. One group considered their daughters to be seducers; this was the *Lolita* group. A second group considered their wives as *wicked witches* who provided grounds for their husbands' seeking sex with an appreciative daughter. A third group considered themselves generous fathers who were giving their children what they wanted; this was the *Santa Claus* group. When the children or the men's counselor challenged the men's justifications, the men grew coercive and abusive (Snowden, 1982). The "wicked witch" pattern has a long history. One historian at the University of Wisconsin, Linda Gordon, has found (1983) many stories of incest in the nineteenth century records of a Boston social agency serving mostly poor families. Then, as now, father-daughter incest was not unknown. Fathers who took their daughters to bed believed that they were entitled to do so. Housework, the reasoning went, is for mothers and daughters. Sex is for fathers, and when wives are too tired, they can be replaced with daughters.

Women who have experienced incest have begun to organize to make incest a more serious crime. Because law is always the compromise of the interests of conflicting groups, incest law is likely to change in the next few years. Yet the move away from probationary sentences without jail terms is likely to be slow, given the crowding in jails, the sizable pool of incest offenders, and the cost to families when adult male wage earners are removed. Making incest a more serious offense may translate into longer probationary periods and short jail terms. An increased probability of apprehension may be more of a deterrent than harsher punishment. As in the case of rape laws, the biggest change in incest or sexual abuse law may be better reporting and greater public awareness of children's rights to refuse adults' sexual advances. Students of all forms of violence in the family, incest included, look to more equal division of power—economic and familial—between husbands and wives to exert pressure against cross-generational sex in the family. Power in the family is not only privately arranged; it reflects the larger society.

SEXUAL HARASSMENT IN THE WORKPLACE

As more and more women have entered the paid work force since World War II, their problems with sexual harassment have increased. All people—male and female—who need their jobs are relatively powerless before those who employ them. But women occupy jobs in which they are more likely to be powerless. Because men customarily make most sexual advances, most sexual harassment besets women. Men are sexually harassed at work, but the incidence is much lower than it is among women. Workers who are harassed sometimes quit their jobs, lose their jobs, develop symptoms of stress, and lose their efficiency at work. They may have to contain their anger.

In 1979, Catherine McKinnon, a feminist lawyer, published a book analyzing sexual harassment in the workplace as a violation of a worker's civil rights. In 1980, the federal Equal Employment Opportunities Commission (EEOC) estab-

As more and more women have entered the paid work force, their problems with sexual harassment have increased.

lished guidelines defining sexual harassment and based them on the Civil Rights Act of 1964. Today employers can be held financially responsible by a court for failing to recognize and correct situations involving sexual harassment.

Apart from the fundamental discrepancy in power between many women and men on the job, there is another problem. Men and women do not have the same definitions of what constitutes harassment. Although both men and women in a Los Angeles survey agreed that requiring sexual acts from someone to keep a job is harassment, twice as many women as men considered recurrent comments—even positive ones—as well as unspoken sexual behavior as sexual harassment (Gutek et al., 1981). This discrepancy between what members of the two sexes consider sexual harassment is found not only in southern California. A survey at Harvard University showed the same discrepancy among students and professors (Verba et al., 1982).

The law today requires universities to have an office that handles harassment cases. These offices usually serve as centers for education on sexual harassment as well. Laws alone are not likely to stop sexual harassment, just as laws alone do not stop other frequent but forbidden acts. Laws simply increase the risk to the perpetrator. They also spell out how victims can document their complaints and thereby increase the likelihood that they will win their case.

THE CHANGING PICTURE OF SEX LAWS

Pressures for change of sex laws have succeeded in many areas. In 1965, the Supreme Court of the United States ruled, in *Griswold* v. *Connecticut,* that married people could buy and use contraceptives. The court's ruling was based on the married couple's right to privacy. Today, in every state, unmarried people have the same right to buy contraceptives as married people do (*Eisenstadt* v. *Baird,* 405 U.S. 438 1971). Today people take for granted the right to buy contraceptives, yet the law changed a mere 15 years ago.

Pressures to change other sex laws will continue to be felt by legislators. The growing numbers of sexually active *un*married people represent a force for change today. Cohabitation, age at first sexual intercourse, a high incidence of divorces, and the resulting high incidence of single women heading families all increase the pressure to change laws. Many of these never married (or once married) people expect to gratify their sexual needs. Their number is too great for anyone to suggest prosecuting them. Instead, they will pressure legislators to grant not only privacy rights but property and other rights after cohabitation. Already, handbooks explain the legal rights of the unmarried but sexually active. (On cohabitation, see Hirsch, 1976; Massey and Warner, 1975; Weitzman, 1981). The American Civil Liberties Union in 1980 updated a handbook called *The Rights of Gay People* that summarized all the state laws on gay rights. The handbook also explains how gays can use their rights to gain equal treatment before the law.

Recent changes in family law are likely to increase the rights of unmarried and divorced sexual minorities.

Recent changes in family law are likely to increase the rights of unmarried and divorced sexual minorities. The traditional family (formed by marriage) was embodied in law by: the husband as head and as economic supporter and the wife as housewife, mother, and sexual partner. From British law, American law inherited the view of marriage as a special status, with responsibilities set by the state. So it remains today. But contract law—whereby two people decide what their marital, sexual, and property relationship will be—now has gained legal support. The American Bar Association in 1983 published a guide, *Law and Marriage,* for the public. There, in lay terms, lawyers explain new laws that affect cohabitors and married people as well. They describe laws on money matters, children, rights in court, and breaking apart. *Law and Marriage* sends a message to sexual minorities about the new role of legally drawn contracts. Cohabitors and gay partners can spell out property divisions on death or separation as well as rights and responsibilities toward children and rights and responsibilities within the relationship. Contracts drawn up by two people served by two lawyers, one for each partner, have been found binding by the courts (*Law and Marriage,* 1983; Weitzman, 1981).

The law has responded to change. How much more change will there be? That is hard to predict. The law is always a compromise between current ideas of justice and prevailing social standards, and sexual behavior is a sensitive area for social standards.

SUMMARY

1 Laws regulate sexual behavior for the protection of individuals and the common good. Traditionally, laws have valued the family and life within it.

Family law today is moving in the direction of increasing autonomy of family members.

2 All known societies regulate sexual behavior, although the specific aspects of sexual behavior regulated vary from one society to another.

3 Many sex laws are attempts to enforce moral values. In the United States, many sex laws embody three views of sexuality with roots in religious tradition: sex as sin; sex objects as personal property; and sex as punishable violence.

4 Sexual acts between consenting adults that are illegal have been called "victimless crimes." Sodomy and prostitution have been called two such victimless crimes. In some places, public opinion has shifted toward protecting the privacy rights of adults, and so statutes against sodomy often go unenforced. It can be argued that these statutes exert a chilling effect just by being on the books.

5 Just as gays have organized to defend their rights to sexual freedom and to equality in hiring, housing, and other civil matters, some prostitutes have organized to defend their right to sell sexual services. But other social groups strongly resist such propositions, and sex laws tend to reflect this push-and-pull among competing interest groups.

6 The legal concept of consent is applied to cases of sexual contact between adults and children, because children are assumed *not* to be able to consent to sexual acts. The age of consent varies from one state to another, and it is often difficult for adults to know when and whether a child has reached the age of consent.

7 Adults are reported to commit a variety of sexual acts with children, and children later report reactions ranging from fear and shock to pleasure and interest. Clinicians believe that generally such sexual contacts have negative effects on the child.

8 Incest, which is sexual relations between family members, is forbidden in virtually every society. Societies do vary, however, in the specific categories of relatives who are forbidden to engage in sexual relations. Explanations of why incest is tabooed range from fear of genetic anomalies to the strengthening of social and family bonds. Behavioral mechanisms among nonhuman primates, including adolescents' lack of interest in long-familiar members of the other sex, have been claimed to render incest relatively rare.

9 Most cases of incest occur between brothers and sisters. About 1 percent of incest cases are between adult men and their daughters. Daughters of stepfathers seem to be at risk from sexual advances by older men, often acquaintances of the family. Although it is difficult for social scientists to estimate or report in uniform fashion the trauma that children experience from incest, it is likely that children who suffer most are those on whom force was used and whose partner was five or more years older than they. Older children suffer more trauma than younger children. Very probably, most cases of incest go unreported.

10 In the United States, state laws against incest forbid marriage and sexual relations between all blood relatives above the level of cousins. Punishments range from fines to long jail sentences. In practice, however, most men are given probationary sentences.

11 Sexual harassment in the workplace is now forbidden by federal guidelines. The problem grows out of women's relative powerlessness at work and sex differences in defining sexual harassment.

12 Sex laws are changing in many areas. A growing number of unmarried people—whether divorced or never married, heterosexual or homosexual— expect to gratify their sexual needs and to enjoy privacy and property rights after cohabitation. Contract law now assures such rights.

KEY TERMS

double standard
dowry
victimless crimes
sodomy
tearoom
pimp

sexually transmitted disease (STD)
consent
pedophile
incest
consanguinous relatives

SUGGESTED READINGS

Boggan, E. C., Haft, M. G., Lister, C., and Rupp, J. P. *The Rights of Gay People*. New York: Avon Books, 1980. This book was assembled by the American Civil Liberties Union so that gay people might have a current picture of laws that affect them.

De Rougemont, D. *Love in the Western World*. New York: Harcourt Brace Jovanovich, 1940. This classic makes clear to the contemporary reader why laws on sex and love have changed so much—and so little.

Finkelhor, D. *Child Sexual Abuse*. New York: Free Press, 1984. This book presents the facts and issues concerning values as well as laws.

Weitzman, L. *The Marriage Contract*. New York: Free Press, 1981. Common views about the rights of husbands and wives are reflected in the law. This lively book documents how the law changes.

Chapter 19

Rape and Sexual Violence

RAPE IS A PERVERSION OF SEXUAL INTIMACY.

FORCED SEX

Rape is not only a physical act, but also a symbolic act of violent power over another human being. Rape is a perversion of sexual intimacy. Most state laws today define rape as sexual assault. Both females and males can be—and are—sexually assaulted. A male may rape a stranger or an intimate; a husband may rape his wife, a father his daughter.

To the rapist, forced sex may be more exciting than consensual sex: the greater the resistance or degradation of his victim, the more aroused he may feel. In a study of rape within marriage, sociologist Diana E. H. Russell (1982) classified men as follows: some men equally enjoy consensual and forced sex; some prefer consensual sex but are willing to rape; some men would like to rape but do not; and some men have no wish to rape at all (Russell, 1982).

Although not all rapists use deadly weapons on their victims, by our definition, the man who rapes a woman uses force or the threat of force to have sex with her. **Rape** is sexual violence committed by one person—an aggressor—against another person—a victim. Although most of us probably think of rape as violent, forced intercourse, rape can be a sexual assault without vaginal penetration of the victim. Forced fellatio, anal penetration, or ejaculating before vaginal penetration are acts of rape (or attempted rape) that do not involve actual coitus. Acts that express cruelty and disgust are even more common in **gang rapes,** that is, rapes with three or more assailants. Interviews with rape victims admitted to a hospital emergency ward showed that the incidence of biting or burning the victim's breasts, of fellatio, of anal intercourse, of rapists urinating on their vicims, and other sadistic acts was proportionately higher in gang rapes than in rapes by a lone assailant (Holmstrom and Burgess, 1980). In gang rape, rapists are likely to perform largely for the approval of their male audience. As they watch each other having sex, the female becomes just the vehicle for the social ranking. They have no sexual *relationship* with her. They are playing out their fantasies in the presence of other men. One irony of gang rape is that the same men alone might be horrified to rape, but the social facilitation of a group of men increases the likelihood of rape.

Nearly all rapists are males, nearly all victims females. But a few cases are known in which women, usually in groups, have been sexual aggressors and men sexual victims (Sarrel and Masters, 1982). In prisons, males victimize weaker, smaller males. (See "Sexuality in Perspective: Homosexual Rape in Prison.") Under any circumstances, however, rape is a perversion of sexual intimacy and a violent assertion of power. Rape brings to the sexual encounter feelings that are the very opposites of those people usually feel: wishing to know one's partner intimately and to be known intimately in return, feelings of closeness, sharing, and affection. Whereas in shared sexual encounters people usually are aroused by their partner's arousal, in rape, the aggressor overpowers a weaker person and actually may feel aroused by the victim's resistance.

SEXUALITY IN PERSPECTIVE: HOMOSEXUAL RAPE IN PRISON —SEX THAT IS DEGRADING

In the late 1960s, a slightly built 19-year-old male and a slender 21-year-old male were both raped repeatedly by a gang of criminals in a Philadelphia sheriff's van and sexually assaulted minutes after entering the Philadelphia Detention Center for evaluation before sentencing. A complaint by the men's attorney led to an investigation of the Philadelphia prison system by the office of the Philadelphia District Attorney and the Police Department.

The report revealed that almost every young man of slight build sent to prison in Philadelphia had been sexually approached within the first two days of admission. These men were either repeatedly raped by gangs of prisoners or entered a protective homosexual relationship with a stronger, experienced aggressor. Raped men became marked as sexual victims within that prison and within any other prison to which they were later committed.

An 18-year-old man in prison in less than two weeks was accosted by a group of four prisoners, apparently because he owed them cigarettes and would have to repay somehow. The four raped him until he bled, cried, and shouted out. The next morning four other prisoners raped him after warning him of the consequences of reporting the rapes to the guard.

During the 26-month period of the study, the investigators documented and substantiated 156 sexual assaults. The actual numbers must be higher. The pattern of the assaults was clear. Victims were so fearful of retaliation by other prisoners that they told no one. Guards discouraged complaints. Victims feared the dishonor to themselves and their families from a rape. Moreover, victims believed the guards could not control the rapist prisoners. Victims who did complain were often isolated with no recreation, TV, or exercise (ostensibly for their own safety).

Both victims and aggressors were generally younger prisoners. Victims were younger and weighed less than the aggressors, but the age and size differences were not large. However, the victims were good-looking men who appeared young for their age, and who seemed less athletic and less well-coordinated than average. The aggressors were in prison for felonies like violent assault. The victims were in prison for less serious crimes. Racial tensions in the city of Philadelphia were also acted out inside the prisons. Black victims were unwilling to disclose information on black rapists. There were many white victims of black rapists.

The prison view defines the aggressor as male and the victim as homosexual. Sexual release is not the real goal of the rapes. The degradation of the victim is the goal: to "make a girl" of the victim or to "take his manhood." (Based on Davis, 1968).

RAPE'S SOCIAL ORIGINS

Cross-cultural studies find that rape is much more likely when societies have particular social arrangements between men and women. When societies separate the sexes, subscribe to values of male dominance, and sanction male violence for solving all sorts of personal problems, not only sexual ones, then rape is more frequent. Conversely, when men and women share experiences, when there is little or no male dominance, and when violence is not tolerated as a way to solve problems, societies have a low incidence of rape. This was the discovery made by an anthropologist after analyzing cross-cultural files at Yale University (Sanday, 1981). But how do these three factors foster rape? We can only make educated guesses. One such guess is represented by Susan Brownmiller's analysis of our society (1976), published well before Sanday's cross-cultural study. Brownmiller holds that our culture is a patriarchy that gives men dominance over women in all realms: work, family, and sex. Men learn early that they are entitled to what they want from mothers, sisters, and lovers. Because women in our society ordinarily assent to males' power, the domination is rarely nakedly visible. But in rape, the domination and assertion of power that are always present appear brutally and glaringly. Men know that they can assert their dominance by raping; women fear that power, and their fear keeps them docile and dependent. Brownmiller spells out how one of the factors found across cultures operates, but the addition of Peggy Sanday's discovery of the other two social factors, gender segregation and acceptance of violence to solve men's personal problems, helps us to understand how the rapist's thinking can be in tune with his society: if females are kept separate from males while they are growing up, then it is easier for men to stereotype them, to see them as objects or "others," to consider them not as individuals. Lack of experience with the other sex can make any contact across gender lines problematic, whether that contact is sexual or not. Male dominance may increase a culture's likelihood of accepting violence from males to "solve" their problems. When women become problems, men solve them with violence.

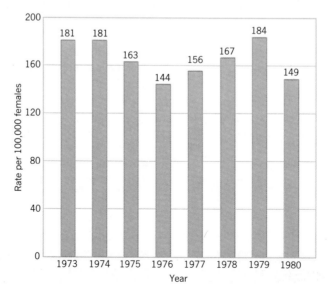

FIGURE 19.1

Estimated number of rapes of women over 12.

Battering and rage are outcomes of particular cultural arrangements, not simple derangements of individual men. As disturbing as that hypothesis may be, it contains the germ of a more hopeful conclusion: changed social relations could affect the incidence of rape. All men are not inherently rapists, any more than women are inherently victims.

Compared to other societies, the United States is part way between rape-free societies and rape-prone societies (but see "Sexuality in Research: How Good Are the Rape Statistics?" for problems with the estimates). The United States is, for example, part way between, the Arunta of Australia, in which all marriageable young women of 14 or 15 are gang raped and then presented to their husbands, and the Ashanti of West Africa, among whom men and women are considered the complementary parts of a whole and therefore among whom rape is unthinkable. The anthropologist Robert LeVine (1959) has studied a tribe in Kenya, the Gusii, among whom all sexual expression once was rape. Until the late 1950s, norms among the Gusii were such that wives resisted their husbands and taunted them about their sexual adequacy. Husbands proved themselves by overpowering their wives sexually. Gusii men had to work hard for sexual access to women: premarital sex was forbidden, and marriage required an expensive brideprice. Prospective husbands labored long and hard to earn the cost of a bride. The only way to avoid paying was to kidnap a woman from another clan and rape her, usually with the aid of other men. But social patterns among the Gusii have changed significantly, and sex as rape is far less common now. More boys and girls go to school and go together. Boys and girls are far less segregated than they were in the past, when a system of chaperones kept them apart. Women are no longer protected, they move about on their own, and they have access to men. Brideprice has been replaced in large part by premarital sex, prostitution, consensual unions (informal, not legalized marriages), and elopement. Marital rape has fallen victim to the greater mixing of the sexes and to the disappearance of the brideprice (Robert LeVine, 1982, personal communication). This gentler social arrangement testifies to the power of new gender relationships in shaping society's rules.

SEXUALITY IN RESEARCH:
HOW GOOD ARE THE RAPE STATISTICS?

TABLE 19.1

An Analysis of Reported Rapes

If reporting is this accurate:	100%	50%	40%	30%	20%
Then a female's chance of being raped is:	8%	17%	21%	28%	42%

Source: Based on A. G. Johnson, "On the Prevalence of Rape in the United States," *Signs,* 1980, 6, pp. 136–146. U.S. Bureau of the Census, "Marriage, Divorce, Widowhood, and Remarriage by Family Characteristics," *Current Population Reports,* Series P-20, #312, June 1975.

WHO RAPES?

In the United States, a sociological study (Amir, 1979) was conducted in Philadelphia among convicted rapists. The profile that emerged showed the rapist to be young, unmarried, to have worked as a skilled laborer or to have been unemployed, to have had a record of crimes other than rape, and to have raped someone of his own race. Among convicted criminals as a whole, rapists were most like men convicted of aggravated assault and of robbery. Rapists were men who took what they wanted: things as well as women. Earlier studies by social scientists at the Kinsey Institute (Gebhard et al., 1965) had found that almost 40 percent of convicted rapists had been drunk when they had raped. That finding still holds today: most rapists have been drinking when they assault their victims (Wolfe and Baker, 1980). These studies also found that one-fourth to one-third of the convicted rapists were **sadists,** that is, derived sexual pleasure from hurting others.

Rape is not merely an assault; it is an act of symbolic defilement. Rapists consider sex to be dirty and thereby a powerful means for degrading a victim. Not surprisingly, many rapists have themselves been sexually abused (Griffin, 1980). The director of Connecticut's Sex Offender Program, psychologist A. Nicholas Groth, points out (Griffin, 1980) the emotional and psychological violence of rape. Groth's interviews with over 500 convicted rapists led him to conclude that rapists often want to degrade and sully their victims. Husbands who had raped their wives told him, "Beating her up wasn't enough. I wanted to dirty her," and "Raping her seemed the worst thing I could do. This would really knock her down off her pedestal." One husband tied his wife's hands and anally raped her and "claimed that he did not have any interest in inflicting physical pain on his wife, but wanted instead to dominate and degrade her" (p.66).

Most convicted rapists who have been studied by psychologists turn out to have had childhoods characterized by large doses of violence, assault—some of it sexual—and neglect. By primary or secondary school, these boys had begun victimizing others, often sexually (Groth, 1979). Medical people have noted the high incidence—33 percent—of sexual dysfunctions among rapists. In one study, some (3 percent) were premature ejaculators, some (16 percent) had erectile dysfunctions, and some (15 percent) had retarded ejaculation, a disorder in which a man cannot ejaculate inside the vagina (Groth and Burgess, 1977).

A group of psychologists studied 100 convicted rapists at the Bridgewater treatment center in Massachusetts (Cohen et al., 1971). They divided the men into three categories: aggressive, inadequate, and psychopathic. Aggressive rapists think that *all* women, except one, are bad. Because they use their mothers as the model of the good, unattainable, pure madonna, they see all women who are potentially attainable as whores. These men use sex in the service of their aggression against these debased sexual objects. In contrast, rapists who feel inadequate force themselves on women to get sex. They are likely to be frightened off if a woman resists them. Psychopathic rapists are aroused by a victim's resistance and seem to need aggression to fuel their arousal. Psychopathic rapists (discussed more fully below) are the most dangerous, and they are the hardest group for psychologists to understand. A woman facing her attacker cannot know which category of rapist she has been dealt.

Studies of convicted rapists, of course, do not tell us about the rapists who escaped conviction. Rapists in the two groups may be different from one another.

A rapist with a prestigious job, fine education, or a substantial income may escape a long prison sentence for a variety of reasons. A victim may feel it is useless to accuse her educated date (or mate) of rape, for he may have the resources to hire a skillful attorney and psychiatrist to sidestep a conviction. Police may be less suspicious of well-educated men and not often arrest them; judges may think that warnings, short, or suspended sentences are sufficient deterrence for them. In one recent case, for example, three young Boston area doctors were convicted of gang raping a nurse after a hospital party. They were sentenced to 3 to 5 years of prison, with all but six months of the sentence suspended. Such respected professional men are rarely charged with rape and even more rarely imprisoned for it. In prison populations, rapists rarely have higher job status than skilled worker (Gebhard et al., 1965). But when a researcher put an advertisement in some Los Angeles newspapers, asking "Are you a rapist? If so, call me," 50 callers responded. Unlike the prison population, half the callers were college educated (Smithyman, 1978).

Myths about Rape

Psychologists and others who study rapists want to learn the individual psychological patterns that might explain rapes and that might lead to effective forms of individual therapy and prevention. Convicted rapists have been found to believe that women really want sex when they resist and protest. But they share with many other people this belief of women as instigators of rape. More than half of the respondents of a representative sample of Minnesotans, for example, agreed that "In the majority of rapes, the victim was promiscuous or had a bad reputation" and that a woman usually reports rape "to get back at the man she got angry with" or "to cover up an illegitimate pregnancy" (Burt, 1980). The Gallup Poll of American adults found similar results (Gallup, 1978).

Two out of three Americans believe that women provoke rapes by their appearance or actions (Feild and Bienen, 1980). Given scenarios of dates in which females *clearly* have refused males' invitations to sexual intercourse, teenagers still assign one-quarter of the responsibility for rape to the female (Zellman and Goodchild, 1983). Females are also more often assigned responsibility for rape if they are divorced, attractive, and in certain lines of work (topless dancer rather than social worker, for instance) (Calhoun et al., 1978; DeJong and Anabile, 1979; Feldman-Summers and Lidner, 1976; Seligman et al., 1977).

Blaming the rape victim, in fact, is endemic in our society. But why has it been so easy to blame the rape victim? Many people in our society accept the idea that males have a right to expect females' sexual compliance under many circumstances. If they do not comply, male peer group values condone pushing. Indeed, college men admitted that they would be most likely to rape a woman if they thought that other men in their situation would do so. Although that finding does not prove that most men actually would rape, it suggests that some men think their peers sanction rape. Female aggressors are rare in all forms of sexual abuse—assault on women and men, child molesting, incest (Finkelhor, 1979). When men push women to have sex, they are declaring their entitlement. For example, it has been found that when women resist—whether by refusing, crying, screaming, or the like—most high-school men consider them out of line if they have got a man sexually excited, if they have agreed to sex and then changed their minds, and if they've "led on" their partners. Most high-school women agree with these conditions (Giarusso et al., 1979).

A laboratory study has shown that rapists are aroused by film sequences of forced as well as (and sometimes more than) consensual sex. Nonrapists are more aroused by scenes of consensual sex and by scenes of women who consent. Rapists may use a woman's resistance plus their personal belief that women instigate rape to rationalize a sexual attack. Their reasoning may be something like this: women expect men to be sexual adversaries; a man who shows he can be violent is a real and desirable man; this attack is not a rape, because she likes it, no matter what she says (Malamuth, 1981). In this scenario, a woman's "no" is never believable.

Social psychologists have tested college men to learn more about public sexual attitudes that might fuel rape. One interesting study took a two-pronged approach. First, male college students watched videotaped seduction scenes, some of which showed women as consenting partners, others of which showed women as unwilling victims. The students were asked to rate whether they would "push" a woman into sex in each of a series of sexual encounters *if the men knew that they would not get caught*. From their ratings, the psychologists derived a score of a man's theoretical "likeliness to rape." Men with high (the "push" condition) and low (the "wouldn't push" condition) scores entered the second part of the study. They wore a rubber band-like apparatus to measure erections of the penis, as they watched videotaped sexual scenes. The findings? College men rated unlikely to rape were aroused most by scenes of willing sex; college men rated likely to rape were aroused by *both* willing and forced sex (Malamuth, 1981). Although it is important to realize that the college students were not rapists, their attitudes were like some rapists'.

Dating and Rape

Most date rapes, experts believe, are committed by acquaintances. They probably are reported more rarely than rapes by strangers. In one survey of 262 first-year college women, well over half had experienced offensive sexual aggression in the year before starting college. Fewer than one woman in six had reported the aggression to a parent or other authority (Kanin, 1957). In a more recent study of university students, the researchers compared the experience of sexual aggression from 1971 to 1972 and from 1978 to 1979 (Korman and Leslie, 1982). They found that of 543 women in the later sample, 18 percent reported attempted intercourse and 2 percent violently attempted intercourse. Comparable figures for the earlier period (1971–1972) were 12 percent and 0.5 percent, respectively. The researchers also found that women who paid their own way on a date were likelier to report sexual aggression than were women whose date paid for them. But they also pointed out that women who paid their way were likelier to be feminists and perhaps quicker to perceive aggression than the more traditional women.

Although women once could postpone unwanted intercourse by appealing to a double standard, today's relaxed attitudes about intercourse outside of marriage can make a woman's refusal seem like a personal rejection of her date. His humiliation may increase if he thinks that she has "nothing to lose." In that men often believe that women need "urging," sexual persuasion can easily turn ugly. Many men who push are afraid of the humiliation of "losing" an encounter. Many women have been raped by their dates, very much to their surprise and horror. One 21-year-old student described this incident:

A guy I met in class invited me to his apartment to draw up some posters. When I got there, it was clear that he wanted to have sex. He was so clumsy about it I thought he was joking at first. When he pinned me to the floor and kneeled over me, I got scared and then angry. I twisted out of his grip, ran to the door, and out to the street. He called after me, "Hey, what's the matter with you?" If I hadn't run, he would have raped me.

The Psychopathic Rapist

Psychiatrists call certain rapists "sociopaths" or "psychopaths." **Psychopaths** are people who repeatedly commit antisocial acts without a sense of guilt and without the inner controls necessary for stopping the acts. Psychopaths know that society considers their acts wrong. The Boston Strangler was one such psychopathic rapist. Between June of 1962 and March of 1963, he strangled 13 women, who ranged in age from 19 to 85. He strangled most of them with pieces of clothing tied in a characteristic knot, and evidence of intercourse or ejaculation was found on the women. He would bind his victims in a spread-eagle position before his sexual attack. Albert De Salvo, a 32-year-old father of two young children, was arrested for the crimes. He confessed to the 13 murders and to more than 300 other assaults. (He later insisted that his confession was false.) His childhood had been spent in a poor, disorganized family, with an abusive father. But he had a brother who had committed no sex crimes, although they shared their dreadful early life. People who knew De Salvo considered him polite, well meaning, and serious about his family responsibilities (Frank, 1966).

The violent rapist is in the minority of sex offenders. Albert De Salvo's sexual history was not typical, for few sex offenders—only 10 percent—move from less to more serious offenses, as De Salvo did. He reported that he began as a **voyeur,** that is, someone who derives sexual pleasure from secretly watching another person. Violent sex offenders represent only 5 percent of all sex offenders, although they command most of the public attention. Kenneth Bianchi, the California "Hillside Strangler," raped and killed across the western states, terrifying young women—his favored target—and eluding police. Like De Salvo, Bianchi had a regular sexual partner. Bianchi also feigned a multiple personality to avoid legal responsibility. A psychiatric expert in hypnosis disproved Bianchi's dodge, and Bianchi was convicted of the murders. Men like Bianchi are likely to repeat their offenses, and they are exceedingly difficult for professionals to understand or to treat. For these reasons, social pressure toward controlling violent sex offenders is strong.

Court Treatment of Sexual Psychopaths

Rape and sexual murder seem so irrational that people who commit them may be perceived not only as criminals but as sick. The laws of many states are aimed at finding out "who are sexually dangerous persons for the protection of society, and to cure and rehabilitate them as soon as possible," as the Massachusetts law on sexually dangerous people says. Such laws can promote two forms of treatment for sex offenders: criminal procedures and psychiatric treatment. Criminal procedures provide the accused with due process, but psychiatric procedures often

Kenneth Bianchi, California's "Hillside Strangler," in court. Psychopathic rapists like Bianchi are difficult for psychologists to treat successfully.

do not. Thus although a court may commit a person to psychiatric treatment, in which that person is expected to communicate deeply personal thoughts, the person is often denied the protection of due process. The criminal gets a sentence of a specific length, but the psychiatric patient may get compulsory treatment "until well" or until no longer a "sexually dangerous person." Commitment to psychiatric treatment is made in a civil proceeding, rather than a criminal one, on the decision of a judge who has listened to psychiatric testimony. This testimony is based on several weeks of psychological testing and observation in a treatment center and on a recommendation that the accused can benefit from psychotherapy and become "well." In practice, psychiatric treatment may last longer than a prison sentence for the same offense. Many states now have laws that limit the duration of treatment to that of a typical prison sentence for the crime.

Psychologists have no perfect way of knowing when a sex offender can be safely released. They decide on the basis of a man's behavior in a treatment center; his age (the older the man, the less likely to commit offenses); and their best guess about the likelihood of his committing another sexual crime. Psychologists and psychiatrists tend to predict more pessimistically than actual events would warrant (Dershowitz, 1969), but it is easy to understand why they err in the direction of caution: a prisoner who is kept in a treatment facility rapes no one during that time.

Psychological Treatment of Sexual Psychopaths

The sexual psychopath—like all psychopaths—is very difficult for a clinician to treat, for he tends not to admit to his feelings, has no conscience, and lacks a sense of responsibility. He also has only a flimsy lid on his impulses. Psycho-therapy is aimed at helping him to build and strengthen his conscience and to control his impulses. As one psychologist described the sexual psychopath, he is:

> *A person out of touch with his inner experience. He claims usually to think and feel "nothing." He has a low tolerance for frustration and a need for immediate gratification. He has a low level of object relations both socially and sexually, being restrained, inhibited, and immature in his relations with people. He handles conflicts through action rather than through fantasies. Lacking a sense of conscience, having no strong sense of rules governing behavior, his acting-out is likely to infringe on the rights of others. He is almost completely oriented toward the present; it's hard for him to remember the past (and when he does, he feels that he was a different person); and he doesn't plan for the future (and didn't so plan even before being sent to the Treatment Center). He lacks a sense of legal accountability, blaming his acts on others, or believing that they "just happened." An underlying conflict which is thought to be the root of his behavior can sometimes be discerned by the staff (R. Siegel, quoted in Beyer, 1973, pp.9–10).*

Psychotherapy may be conducted with individual or groups of violent sexual offenders. The emphasis is on active forms of therapy like role-playing. The goals of the therapy are, first, to teach a man the consequences of his actions and, second, the feelings of others in response to those actions. Sexual psychopaths often know the difference between right and wrong. (They produce very moralistic prison newspapers.) They strongly believe in the double standard and the impor-tance of virginity (Griffin, 1976).

Because drugs are reversible, courts have permitted the use of anti-androgens, presumably to cut down sexual appetite in men whose sexual behavior leads to illegal acts like rape or sex with children. It is too early to judge the long-term efficacy of such treatment. In the short term, the drug decreases men's erections, sexual fantasies, and sexual acts but not their sexual preferences or attitudes (Hermann and Beach, 1980). In some states, repeat violent offenders are given psychosurgery. Courts once gave shorter prison sentences in exchange for brain surgery, but pressure from civil liberties groups has made some courts judge brain surgery as inherently unfair. Prisoners, the argument has gone, are in no position to evaluate the long-range costs and benefits of irreversible psychosurgery.

PENALTIES FOR RAPE

Our legal system uses punishment not only to punish but to deter crimes. Im-prisoning a rapist is meant not only to punish him and to protect society, but to deter him from raping again and to deter others from raping. Rapists have high rates of repeat offenses: they need deterring. Studies have shown that the certainty of punishment following detection is a greater deterrent to crime than is the severity of the punishment.

Since 1975, when the state of Washington passed a law that prescribed graded punishments for rape according to degrees of force or threat, Seattle courts have handed out more but shorter sentences than they had done under harsher laws.

Fewer offenders have been released than under the older laws, and suspended sentences have decreased markedly. Commitment to treatment centers has more than doubled. Imprisonment is about as frequent as it had been before 1975, but juries now convict more often for rape than for surrogate charges like assault. One legal scholar has called this "truth in criminal labeling" (Loh, 1981). The outcome in Seattle has been more convictions, lesser but surer punishment, and more in-patient, psychological rehabilitation. Only time will tell if making the punishment fit the crime will work for rape.

Many states now have rape laws that define the extent of the offense, with rape 1 the most serious and rape 3 or 4 the least serious. Some states, like Michigan, have dropped the term "rape" completely and instead define the aggressor's behavior. Like laws on burglary or assault, they do not try to define the resistance of the victim (a knotty problem in rape law, as we will see). The new laws define these degrees of criminal sexual acts: sexual penetration with aggravation, elsewhere called rape 1); sexual contact with aggravation (assault); sexual penetration without aggravation (elsewhere rape 2 and 3); and sexual contacts without aggravation (indecent liberties). The last charge is hard to win in court, for it describes acts like fondling a woman's breast over her clothes or a man's buttock over his trousers. Most juries treat these acts as nuisances rather than as crimes.

THE POLITICS OF RAPE

For nearly two decades, the women's movement has considered the fight against rape one of its highest priorities. People in the women's movement identify rape as the most visible and most violent form of social control over women. When women are fearful of men, they must spend their energies protecting themselves or worrying about their safety. Psychologists have long known that all people must assure their needs for safety and survival first, before they can consider other needs. A woman who fears for her body or for her children necessarily leads a constricted life. Her fear keeps her imprisoned at home at night, out of "dangerous" places, but also from classes or jobs or simply taking a walk. She leads but half a life, a daytime existence. Most men are neither rapists nor would-be rapists. Not all men keep women down either. But the men who are rapists remind women that men have power and that pathological men have fearful power literally to destroy women.

The Fight Against Rape

For combating rape, people in the women's movement drew three targets. They had first to convince rape victims to report the crime, for only a minority of victims ever did so. Second, they had to get the police to change their behavior toward rape victims. The third goal was changing the rape laws, in order to remove the widespread, informal legitimacy of rape.

Since 1970, rape victims' reports have doubled, an increase that experts ascribe to better reporting rather than to more rapes. For 1982, the FBI's Uniform Crime Reports gave 77,800 as the number of reported rapes and attempted rapes in the United States, down from 81,500 in 1981. One-quarter of the rapes reported in 1982 were attempted rapes or assaults to commit forcible rape; three-quarters were forcible rapes. Conservative estimates are that the actual number of rapes is still two to three and one-half times that number, or 150,000 to 266,000 rapes

TABLE 19.2
Total Rape 1973–1982

Total Rape	Number of Victimizations	Yearly Rate of Victimizations per 1000 People
1,634,000		.93
male victims	123,000	.15
female victims	1,511,000	1.65
attempted rapes	1,032,000	1.13
completed rapes	479,000	.52

Source: Bureau of Justice Statistics Bulletin, March, 1985, "The Crime of Rape," Table 1.)

This table shows the numbers of all attempted and completed rapes of male and female victims between 1973 and 1982 that were reported to the police.

every year. Some sociologists use the studies on aggression against dates to estimate an even greater annual number of rapes—3,500,000 (Mahoney, 1983). The Bureau of Crime Statistics (April 1982) reported that between 1973 and 1979, a national average of 65 percent of all rapes were committed by strangers. All local studies do not reproduce this finding, a possible reflection of local biases in reporting by both female and male victims (see Table 19.2).

When women expect to be blamed for rape, they are unlikely to report it. Rape is punishment enough; humiliation by police or in court is more than many women can bear. When lawyers say that women "asked for it," juries are often convinced. Judges used to read the following *cautionary advice,* taken from British common law, to juries in rape cases:

> *A charge of rape such as that made against the defendant in this case is one which is easily made and, once made, difficult to defend against, even if the person accused is innocent. Therefore, the law requires that you (the jury) examine the testimony of the female person . . . with caution (our emphasis).*

In our society, many people still believe that "some girls rape awful easy." When researchers find four out of five rapes are premeditated and nearly nine out of ten involve force or the threat of force (Amir, 1971), blaming the victim is cruel and unjust.

RAPE LAWS

The central legal issue in rape cases traditionally has been consent: did the alleged rapist have the consent of the victim? The burden of proof was until recently on the victim; she had to prove that she had resisted. If she could not prove her resistance, if she had no telltale bruises or lacerations, she was assumed to have consented to her rape. A woman who had had many sexual partners, courts believed, could not even be raped, so complete was her sexual consent assumed to be. (By this logic, no prostitute could ever be raped.) A woman who had *ever* willingly had intercourse with a man could not charge him later with raping her. Thus women whose husbands or former lovers raped them were not protected by the law. Neither were women protected who had no noticeable bruises but who had been raped under a gun or threats of harm to their children. Many states required that a woman provide witnesses to prove that a rape had occurred. Witnesses, of course, are rare. When they are present, they may have participated in a gang rape. In any event, they are unlikely to testify against the friends they watched.

THE HISTORY OF RAPE LAW

Today's rape laws have roots at least as far back as ancient Babylonia and Assyria. In those societies, the severity of rape was judged by the victim's sexual and social status. If she had been a virgin and therefore considered to possess a magical power to do good, the penalties were severe. A married rapist was put to death. An unmarried rapist had to marry his victim and to pay her father three times her original brideprice. For good measure, a victim's father was allowed to rape the wife or sister of the rapist.

A rape for a rape was property exchange, and Biblical law ended the practice. The idea of a woman as her father's and then her husband's property lived on, however. The Bible thus prescribed as punishments for rape, marriage to the victim and the loss of the right to divorce one's wife. Biblical law punished most severely when the victim had been a virgin, when the rapist was of low status and the victim of high status, and when the victim's resistance could be proved or inferred. Punishments were attempts to restore part of a woman's lost property value (the "damaged goods" notion again) or to decrease a rapist's chance of acquiring property in the marriage market.

In ancient English law, status considerations were important—and would later move into American law. A man who raped a "maiden belonging to the King" was fined 50 shillings; rape of the king's "grinding slave" cost only 25 shillings. Rape of a nobleman's serving maid cost 12 shillings, a commoner's serving maid, 5 shillings. If a slave raped a commoner's serving maid, he was castrated; if he raped any women above the rank of serving maid, he was put to death (Horos, 1974). The same graded punishment was meted out in the mid-nineteenth-century laws of some states, condemning to death or life imprisonment any black or mulatto who raped a white female, with lesser punishments possible for other racial combinations (Bienen, 1979).

American family law, long based on English common law, has traditionally seen the wife's person and property subsumed and dominated by the husband. According to the great legal authority, Blackstone:

> *By marriage, the husband and wife are one person in law; that is, the very being or legal existence of the women is suspended during the marriage, or at least is incorporated and consolidated into that of the husband; under whose wing, protection, and cover, she performs everything (Blackstone, 1813, p.444).*

A woman whose very being is suspended and whose every act is under the "wing, protection, and cover" of her husband cannot bring a charge of rape against him, no matter how abusive he is. He owns her.

Marriage licenses long have been considered implicit permits for husbands to beat or rape their wives. So long as husband and wife are "one person in law," a wife has no legal recourse. Beating and raping can become everyday facts of marriage.

Rape in Marriage

Many people have trouble believing that rape in marriage exists. The closer the relationship between attacker and victim, the less likely is an incident to be defined as rape (Klemmack and Klemmack, 1976). Solid figures on the incidence of rape in marriage are hard to come by. Few wives complain of their husbands' sexual abuse. Marriage, after all, means consent to sex, does it not? Not only husbands but wives, too, are likely to believe that. Diana Russell (1982), a sociologist who has studied rape in marriage, has described how carefully her interviewers' questions had to be worded in order not to frighten women away from describing violence in their marriages. Perhaps more disturbing still, she found that many women did not recognize that they had been raped: over and over, the women interviewed described sex forced on them as *"like* rape," and many excused or rationalized away their husbands' violence. Similarly, when wives in South Australia were asked whether they had ever been raped by their husbands, they said no. But when the question was rephrased and they were asked, "Have you ever had sexual intercourse against your will with your husband?" many changed their answer to yes (Chappell and Willis, 1979, cited in Freeman, 1981). Russell found that San Francisco women who cohabit are likelier to be raped by their men than women who marry.

The history of the laws governing rape in marriage extends back to English law. Just as laws governing rape outside of marriage originally were designed in the interests of men, to protect their property, that property being women, the laws governing rape within marriage were also designed in the interests of propertied men. Because a wife was legally her husband's chattel, without separate existence, it was a legal impossibility and a logical absurdity for her to charge him with rape.

The English judge, Sir Matthew Hale (1609–1676), is usually cited as the originator of the *exclusionary rule,* which exempted husbands from the charge of rape by wives. Yet Hale was probably only stating the law as it had for centuries been believed:

> *But the husband cannot be guilty of rape committed by himself upon his lawful wife, for by their mutual matrimonial consent and contract, the wife hath given up herself in this kind unto her husband which she cannot retract (cited in Freeman, 1981, p.10).*

Hale's assertion has since been interpreted to mean that a husband is exempt because his wife has given her irrevocable consent to sexual relations. It has also been used to justify the accusation that rape in marriage is difficult to prove and, therefore, that no husband should be prosecuted for rape.

As attitudes about the proper place of women and the relationships between the sexes recently have changed, attitudes toward the law have also changed. Several lawyers have challenged the grounds for excluding husbands from prosecution for rape, arguing, "A woman enters marriage consenting to voluntary relations, not to rape" and

> *A new bride would be surprised indeed to find that she has agreed to give up her right to bodily privacy and will henceforth submit to any force, brutal or otherwise, her new spouse may use to enforce his desire. In*

addition, the proper remedy for breach of contract is damages, not forced performance (Griffin, 1980, p.65).

But reform of the state laws has come slowly, when it has come at all, and it is not unfair to say that laws still widely discriminate against wives. Only two states, New Jersey and Oregon, have abolished the exclusionary rule for husbands. Laws in other states vary: in six states, wives can charge rape if the mates live apart and have filed for divorce or separation; in ten states, wives must have obtained a separation order to charge rape; two states require the mates to have lived apart but do not require a judicial order of separation, and so on. Most wives still face daunting legal barriers to charging their husbands with rape.

Through the American Law Institute's Model Penal Code, new laws were drafted by academic lawyers incorporating changes urged by the women's movement and other pressure groups. Law-and-order groups who were lobbying for tougher sentencing for many sorts of crimes probably contributed to a political atmosphere in which rape laws could also be changed.

Recent Rape Laws

The old laws on rape did not give women justice in court or protect their rights. It took a social and political movement made up of women and their allies to change these laws and, in the process, to change people's attitudes toward rape. (One measure of this success is the appearance of a chapter on rape in textbooks of human sexuality.)

> The new rape laws that describe what the presumed *aggressor* does rather than what the victim does get around the problem of documenting resistance.

The new rape laws in many states prevent judges from reading the cautionary rule about a victim's testimony and dispense with the need for witnesses to corroborate a rape charge. The marital exclusion rule, by which husbands are excluded from the charge of rape by their wives, is also falling in one state after another; by the mid-1980s, the rule had fallen in about one-third of the states. Some lawyers predict (perhaps optimistically) that within a decade, husband-rapists will be subject to punishment in all of the states. Many state courts disallow any information on a woman's sexual history. Proofs of resistance to document nonconsent appear to be more readily accepted in some courts today. The new rape laws that describe what the presumed *aggressor* does rather than what the victim does get around the problem of documenting resistance.

Because they knew that certain punishment is an effective deterrent, lawyers wanted to draft laws that would increase the number of convictions for rape. Two factors had kept juries from convicting: rape myths and severe sentences. As we have seen, juries shared with rapists certain myths about how women really want to be raped, about how even if they say no, they mean yes. Statutes called for extreme sentences for rape, like life imprisonment or death. In 1977, the Supreme

Court struck down the death penalty for rape, a ruling that opened the way for more reasonable sentences and thus for more convictions. Juries had been reluctant to sentence a rapist to life imprisonment or to death if he had not killed or dismembered his victim. They routinely acquitted rapists rather than give them such severe mandatory sentences. In simple rape cases, judges sometimes choose to convict even when juries do not (Kalven and Zeisel, 1966). When rape laws began to classify rape and to tailor punishments to the severity of the crime, conviction rates began to rise.

The most modern rape laws are not sexist in language and omit any reference to gender. Older laws (still in effect in several states) were written as if only women are raped, but men, too, are sometimes raped (usually by other men).

HELP FOR THE RAPE VICTIM

A victim has much more than legalities to deal with after a rape. Most victims feel deeply fearful, anxious about everything connected with the rape and its aftermath. Many develop phobic feelings about lovers and spouses. They need prompt help. Many hospitals and clinics have developed rape crisis centers to help rape victims through the crisis. The crisis intervention is aimed at treating the social, psychological, legal, and medical needs of rape victims. It extends from something as simple as providing a female officer to lead a victim through uncomfortable police procedures to something as complex as long-term psychotherapy. Rape crisis centers help victims to decide whether and how to report a rape and how to put the trauma of rape behind them. Counselors in these centers often are former rape victims who well know how terrifying rape is and how

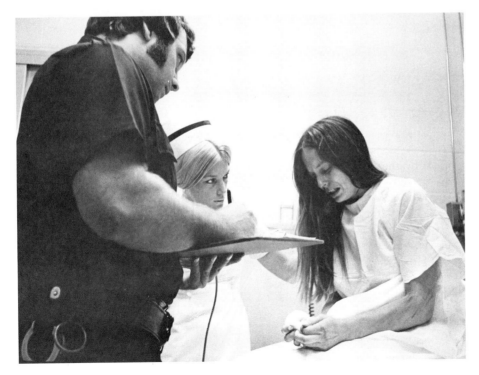

Many hospitals and clinics have rape crisis centers to help victims to cope with the shock and trauma of a sexual assault.

fearful its aftermath can be. Follow-up studies of rape victims who have had crisis treatment reveal that four to six years after treatment, 75 percent of women have returned to normal sexual functioning. Yet most of them report some sexual problems, and some women have flashbacks to the rape five years afterwards (Burgess and Holmstrom, 1979). The writer and poet, Maya Angelou, has said (1983) that she thinks every single day about the rape she underwent when she was seven. For four years, she could not speak to anyone except her brother. Men, too, may develop sexual dysfunction after a sexual assault. Eleven men who were raped by women turned up seeking help for erectile problems, sexual anxiety, and dysfunction brought on by the rapes (Sarrel and Masters, 1982).

When women are raped, they develop a cluster of symptoms in response. Called the **rape trauma syndrome (RTS),** this reaction includes: emotional responses like fear, anxiety, guilt, and shame; dysfunctions of appetite, sleep, sex, and sociability; and changed habits aimed at eluding a rapist such as repeatedly changing addresses, telephone numbers, or jobs. RTS is actually a kind of depression in response to a sudden and pervasive loss of safety, and many victims respond to treatment for depression. How long RTS lasts and how a victim deals with rape depend on her history and personality, the social supports in her environment, and her previous methods for coping. Not all women have all the symptoms, and some women manage very well soon after a rape, especially if they have solid social supports. Current clinical practice with rape victims does not blame the victim. It aims to alleviate pain and to return victims to their everyday lives as quickly as possible (Burgess and Holstrom, 1974).

Two sources of help and information about rape:

National Center for the Prevention and Control of Rape
Room 10C03
Parklawn Building
5600 Fishers Lane
Rockville, MD 20857

The National Center provides funds for police rape investigation units and hospital units for treating rape victims as well as literature, audiovisual aids, and research on rape.

Rape Crisis Center
917 15th Street, N.W.
Washington, D.C. 20009
(202) 333-RAPE

This Center helps rape victims and gives legal support to children victimized by sexual assault.

Despite increased support for rape victims, many—and probably most—do not come forward to report crimes or use the support available. They, their friends, and families may suffer in silence.

SEXUALITY IN PERSPECTIVE:
ADJUSTMENT PROBLEMS AFTER RAPE

TABLE 19.3

Adjustment Problem	Immediately after the Rape	One Year after the Rape
Increased fear of streets	65.9%	54.1%
Increased negative feelings toward unknown men	57.5	50.7
Decreased social activities	50.3	53.6
Change in sleeping patterns	49.9	43.0
Change in eating habits	47.3	43.0
Worsened sexual relations with partner[a]	46.6	39.1
Increased fear of being home alone	43.2	24.8
Worsened heterosexual relationships	40.2	26.2
Increased negative feelings toward known men	36.6	29.3
Increased nightmares	31.1	20.7
Worsened relations with husband or boyfriend[a]	26.9	26.0
Increased insecurities concerning sexual attractiveness	18.7	15.7
Worsened relations with family	17.0	15.2

Source: Based on Cahill et al., 1979, Table 6.1, p. 74.

[a]Computed only for appropriate ages.

Some Practical Advice about Rape

No one can act as if rape were always imminent, for life would become intolerable. No one can assure safety under every possible circumstance. But it is important for females and males, too, to use reasonable caution against rape. Useful advice to women on avoiding rape would include:

1 Alone in your home with an armed rapist, your choices are limited. See if you can get out, and if you can, run. Crying aloud, screaming, and acting hysterical sometimes work. Screaming *plus* physical resistance often abort rapes (Bart, 1981). Only you can tell whether resistance might frighten or arouse

FIGURE 19.2

How to defend yourself from a
sexual attacker.

the rapist. To prevent a rapist from entering your home, make sure your doors and windows are locked securely. Install a peephole in your door. Don't let in repairpeople or salespeople without checking to see that they are legitimate. (Ask for identification. Call their place of work to check on them. Better to be embarrassed than victimized.)

2   On your third date, he suddenly gets drunk and dangerous. He thinks he is seducing you; you think it is rape. Tell him *firmly* that you do not want to have intercourse. If you are in a car, get out and run. Cry to others for help. Utter some convincing curses; show that you are tough. Struggle physically. Make up a story about the incurable sexually transmitted disease you have. Liquor, isolation from others, and an almost unknown date are a common combination in acquaintance rape, probably the most common and underreported form of rape.

3 A man is following you down a dark street that you have to walk along to get to your class. Walk as if you mean business: attackers are known to prey on people who look like easy targets, people who are weak, laden with bundles, or otherwise not striding purposefully. Walk with a whistle around your neck or with your keys in your hand, ready to be used as a weapon. Try to avoid being alone; find people quickly. Call out. (In the future, see if you can get someone to accompany you. Some schools, offices, and other institutions offer escort services.) Cross the street. Run. Scream. Hail a passing car or taxi while you are screaming. If an attacker catches you, surprise him by crushing your heel into his instep (see Figure 19.2). Police recommend great care with an armed attacker.

4 Your husband rapes you. (In what may seem a surprising analogy, an older male prisoner rapes you, a younger male prisoner. These cases are analogous in that the law is reluctant to intervene in both situations, and practical solutions are not easy to provide.) A wife whose husband beats or rapes her can run from home, get neighbors to help calm her husband, seek refuge with friends or a shelter for battered women, go to the police (and the young prisoner can ask to transfer to a jail with fewer long-term prisoners and thus with more freedom and less violence). But many wives cannot leave a husband who is a rapist (or prisoners leave a violent prison), and they must spend years living with the threat of sexual violence. Laws are being passed that will affect this kind of rape.

AFTER A RAPE   After a rape, it is important that a victim know what to do. A telephone call to a friend or a rape crisis center can be a good first step toward getting social support. Then the police should be told of the rape (or attempted rape) and given a description of the rapist. The purpose of these reports is primarily to protect others who might be harmed. Bringing charges against a rapist is a separate issue. The charge, made with a lawyer's help, is aimed at bringing a rapist to justice. Rape crisis centers can help victims find lawyers with experience in rape cases.

A rape victim should not shower or bathe until she has had a medical examination, even though washing herself clean may be the one thing she most wishes for. But semen analysis, regardless of where the rapist has ejaculated, provides information about his blood type and can be critical as evidence. A victim also should be checked for any sexually transmitted disease and for possible pregnancy, although the latter examination is not done immediately after the rape.

SUMMARY

1 Rape is a perversion of sexual intimacy and an act of violent power over another person.

2 The double standard may create an atmosphere in which rape occurs, because men are seen as violent and sexual, women as passive and asexual. Both men and women are victims of rape.

3 A gang rape is a sexual assault by more than two assailants.

4   Rape is more common in some societies than others. In rape-prone societies, the sexes are separated, men are dominant, and men resort to violent solutions for personal problems. In societies with few or no rapes, the sexes share experiences, men are not dominant, and violence is not tolerated as a way to solve problems.

5   Many convicted rapists have childhood histories of neglect, abuse, and victimization. Many were drinking when they raped. Most have low-status jobs. They see sex as dirty and want to sully their victims. Many suffer from sexual dysfunctions. Rapists who are not convicted may present a different profile: better education, income, and job.

6   Peer group values and sexual myths serve to perpetuate rape. Many high-school students feel that men may legitimately push an unwilling partner into sex under certain conditions. College men were most likely to say that they would rape if they thought other men in their situation would do the same. Pushing for sex is an expression of widely shared views of male entitlement to sex.

7   Several attitudes tend to foster rape. Many rapists and others in society believe that women's dress or actions instigate men to rape; they "blame the victim." Some men are sexually aroused by watching violent sex. Some people feel that men are to "win" sexual encounters over their passive, resistant partners.

8   Psychopathic rapists repeatedly commit antisocial acts without feeling guilt and without the inner controls necessary for stopping the acts. They are very difficult for clinicians to treat.

9   New rape laws do not try to define the resistance of the victim. Instead, they define degrees of criminal sexual acts.

10 People in the women's movement drew three targets in their fight against rape and the sexual politics that feed it. They have tried to make rape victims report the crime; to change the behavior of police toward rape victims; and to change rape laws.

11 Rape laws for centuries have described women as the property of their husbands or fathers, and marriage long has offered legal protection to husband-rapists. Many women and men today still believe that a man cannot be said to rape his wife. Many women report being forced to have sex unwillingly with their husbands or live-in partners.

12 Clinicians aim at helping victims to cope with the fear and trauma of rape and its aftermath of depression and anxiety. Therapists try to help victims return as soon as possible to their everyday lives.

KEY TERMS

rape
gang rape
sadist
sexual scripts

psychopath
voyeur
rape trauma syndrome (RTS)

SUGGESTED READINGS

Groth, A. Nicholas. *Men Who Rape.* New York: Plenum, 1980. The head of Connecticut's program for convicted sex offenders has written a book in which he interviews many rapists and hypothesizes about their background and motives. Remember that these are imprisoned rapists.

Medea, Andrea and Thompson, Kathleen. *Against Rape.* New York: Farrar, Straus & Giroux, 1974. An excellent general historical source on rape.

Rape. Journal of Social Issues, 1981, 37 (#4). This collection of nine articles is thoughtful and up-to-date on knowledge about rape.

"Risks and Options in Sexual Assault Prevention." Available from Megha R. Ryzen, M.S.; c/o Department of Health Education; Southern Illinois University; Carbondale, IL 62901. Computer software on prevention of sexual assault.

Russell, Diana E. H. *Rape in Marriage.* New York: Macmillan, 1982. This report, on a San Francisco survey of rape within marriage, is an important contribution to our knowledge about marital rape. Clearly written, it raises disturbing questions about certain sexual values held by women as well as men.

Chapter 20

Pornography

PORNOGRAPHY IN A DEMOCRACY

Have you ever read Alex Comfort's *The Joy of Sex* or *More Joy of Sex?* Nine million copies of these books, which some consider pornographic, have been sold. Have you ever seen any frankly erotic material—perhaps a *Playboy* or a *Penthouse* magazine? Have you ever rented an "adult" videotape? If you said yes to any of these questions, you're far from alone. Eighty percent of men and 70 percent of women interviewed for the U.S. Commission on Obscenity and Pornography (1970) said that they'd seen erotic material before they turned 18. Among *Redbook* Magazine readers, 60 percent of married women had seen a pornographic movie. Among *Psychology Today* readers, a young group, 92 percent of men and 72 percent of women had used pornography for sexual arousal (Carrara, 1981). In our society, pornography is widespread—and controversial.

What *is* pornography? An abstract definition of pornography is simple enough to create. Deriving from the Greek words for writing (*graphy*) about harlots (*porne*), **pornography** is any written, spoken, or visual matter that is aimed primarily at sexually arousing a consumer. But this seemingly narrow definition may be the only simple thing about pornography. People rarely agree on where the border lies between the pornographic and the obscene. Obscenity is a subset of pornography, but the issue of their boundaries is not settled simply by calling pornography arousing and obscenity revolting. One person's arousal is another person's revulsion. Indeed, one person's pornography is another person's **erotica**. Although technically it is a synonym, "pornography" has a more negative connotation than "erotica" does.

The government suppression of sexually explicit materials has a long history. In 8 A.D., when the Roman Emperor Augustus wanted to rid the streets of vice, he banished the great classical poet Ovid to the Black Sea. Ovid's crime had been to write *Ars amatoria,* a tract on the art of love. In this century, literary master-pieces like James Joyce's *Ulysses* and D.H. Lawrence's *Lady Chatterley's Lover* were suppressed by the U.S. government and allowed into the country only after bitter court fights. Other works suppressed by the U.S. government have included John Cleland's *Fanny Hill* and Henry Miller's *Tropic of Cancer*. France once banned Flaubert's *Madame Bovary* and Vladimir Nabokov's *Lolita*. When governments suppress literature containing sexually explicit passages, they engage in censorship.

Censorship

For people who live in a democracy, any form of censorship is a serious issue, because it limits people's access to the marketplace of ideas. Some people argue against all censorship; others argue that censorship be restricted to cases in which the message presents a "clear and present danger." People may express their ideas freely, but they may not capriciously endanger others. Constitutional law guards freedom of expression in the absence of clear and present danger. Some people advocate censorship of some pornography, because they view it as potentially dangerous to some citizens (to children, for example, or to women). Because it is impossible to prove that pornography hurts no one, discussions about pornography often produce more heat than light.

The presumed effects of pornography, especially pornography that contains violence, deeply trouble many people. Some people feel that violent pornography must be banned. But those who abhor censorship in any form find themselves in a painful dilemma. Is it better to allow freedom of speech, even if that means allowing violent pornography? Or is the lesser evil to censor violent pornography?

SEXUALITY IN CONTROVERSY: DIAL-A-PORN

Pornography raises the issue of government intrusion into private lives. Governments act *as if* controlling people's sexual attitudes and feelings were important to national security—an assumption that is open to question. But what must citizens sacrifice for governing powers to feel secure? This dilemma poses itself regularly in the news. For example, Car-Bon Publishers, which publish *High Society* magazine, made available by telephone a recording of a woman making provocative, sexy sounds. The recording, later dubbed "Dial-a-Porn" by offended members of Congress, attracted up to a half-million calls a day and earned Car-Bon up to $10,000 a day ("FCC Opens Inquiry on 'Sex Talk' Phone Service," *New York Times,* September 11, 1983). But the television networks and the newspapers also reported that Defense Department employees spent $25,000 a month calling the "Dial-a-Porn" number (*New York Times,* Dec. 15, 1983). No one can argue seriously that those in-house, government department phone calls were warranted, and the Defense Department has since blocked such calls electronically—at a cost to taxpayers. A New York county official asked the Federal Communications Commission (FCC) to shut down the line because it was obscene and was being used by children.

But officials faced a dilemma. The law says that any phone service is illegal that uses "obscene or indecent" language and that is readily available to people younger than 18. But lawyers for the FCC were not even sure that the law covers the Dial-a-Porn service.

Can a law be framed—and should it be framed—that will protect dubious "innocent" victims from heavy breathing by women on the other end of a phone line? Do the businesspeople who profit from the telephone recordings have rights that should be protected by law? The editor of *High Society,* a woman, insists that the many calls are signs of the service that the magazine is providing. *High Society,* she insists, does not solicit minors. How *might* phone service be regulated such that no one's rights are violated? Parents, children, the people who dial, and the people who offer the recordings all have an interest in the matter. The FCC knows that it faces a complex and sensitive issue.

Opposition to Pornography

Opposition to pornography is deeply rooted in many American religious groups. Pornography's explicit rendition of sexual acts represents, for many church groups, the flaunting of immorality. Many Americans find explicit sex in films or magazines personally offensive because it makes sex public. In their view, private sexual acts deserve protection under the law, but public sexual acts do not. The Supreme Court has ruled that pornography is *not* covered by the constitutional guarantees of freedom of speech and publication. Official suppression of pornography is based on two assumptions. The first is psychological: pornography can significantly affect human behavior. The second is a value judgment: the effects of pornography are socially undesirable. These assumptions are another example of society's deep interest in regulating sexual behavior.

Opposition to pornography today derives from many different quarters of society. Roman Catholic and Eastern Orthodox bishops and members of the Moral Majority oppose pornography for publicly flouting sexuality and for violating sexual values about marriage and the family. Conservative religious and political groups have lobbied for government officials to prevent the broadcasting, importation, or transportation of obscene material across state lines (Austin, 1983). Some feminists oppose pornography for degrading women and for showing a model of unequal relations between the sexes, relations that feminists claim show women as passive sex objects who deserve and invite violence (Dworkin, 1981;

Many Americans are deeply offended by pornography. When it came to light that a former Miss America, Vanessa Williams, had posed for a series of nude photographs, the furor was such that she had to give up her title.

Griffin, 1982). Some feminists have argued that pornography deprives women of civil rights and increases the incidence of rape. They have marched and demonstrated to "Take Back the Night" from "adult areas" filled with pornographic bookstores, peep shows, and commercial sex. Some feminists, as we saw above, prefer boycotts of pornography to laws that prohibit it, for they fear that such laws ultimately could abridge freedom of the press. What government, asks feminist writer Susan Griffin (1983), can be trusted to distinguish between the obscene and the erotic?

If people do need government to act as a parent and save them from harm, then the sacrifice of some civil liberties is warranted. Most people agree that government is legitimately concerned with preventing violent antisocial acts. But whether government should intervene in **victimless crimes,** such as voluntary marijuana use, is more controversial. (A discussion of victimless crime appears in Chapter 18.) Is using pornography a victimless crime, and does pornography lead to antisocial behavior? To answer those questions, we need to examine how pornography actually affects people. We need to ask another set of questions about pornography as well, questions that are rarely posed. Does pornography have any *benefits?* Can it serve as an outlet for otherwise antisocial actions? Can it increase understanding between couples? Finally, we must ask whether pornography is perhaps neither harmful nor beneficial and thus unworthy of serious concern.

LAWS AGAINST PORNOGRAPHY

Laws against pornography in the West did not take shape until three historical events joined: the invention of the printing press, widespread literacy, and the combination of pornography and religious themes. Religious leaders were furious at depictions of supposedly celibate clergy frolicking through sexual adventures.

FIGURE 20.1

"Pornography" on a cave wall from Africa's Sahara-Atlas region.

Throughout the 1700s in England, pornography without religious themes was not banned. By the 1800s, however, English courts were banning obscenity even without religious themes. In *Queen* v. *Hicklin* (1868), the English courts defined obscenity as material that depraves and corrupts the minds of consumers.

English antiobscenity laws were favored by the Puritans, who exported them to America. In the mid-1800s, federal laws were passed banning the import and mailing of obscene literature. The early laws against obscenity went largely unused. But a man named Anthony Comstock successfully lobbied the federal and many state governments into passing and enforcing stricter laws. (The same Anthony Comstock pursued and arrested Margaret Sanger, the leader of the movement for birth control.) In 1957, growing unhappiness with the vague and untestable "tendency to deprave" criterion for obscenity led to a landmark Supreme Court case. In *Roth* v. *U.S.*, the court held that to be obscene, a work must meet three strict, but hard to identify, standards. *First, the dominant theme of the work as a whole must appeal to prurient (improperly sexual) interests. Second, the work must be offensive to community standards. Third, the work must be without redeeming social value.* These are the criteria that legally define obscenity today.

The court held that the constitutional guarantees of freedom of speech and the press do *not* apply to pornography. Until then, the only constitutionally supported reason for suspending such guarantees had been the presence of "clear and present danger"—which was not established. The court relaxed pornography standards a bit in 1959 when it ruled, in *Stanley* v. *Georgia*, that adults have the right to possess pornography although not to distribute it. In 1973, the court ruled that lower courts could assume, rather than prove, that pornography has negative effects. It also ruled that prosecution of obscenity was a local matter (*Miller* v. *California*). This ruling has significantly affected the conduct of pornography law. The court's rulings sometimes are vague and confusing indeed.

In practice, given the vagueness of the standards for obscenity, the Supreme Court often overturns such convictions. The exceptions are cases that involve minors, forced distribution, or forceful promotion.

Child Pornography

What about the children who appear in pornographic films and magazines? Not all of these children appear voluntarily. Some are the essentially helpless prey of unscrupulous adults. Even if children pose voluntarily, few people would deny that they are too young legally to give their "informed consent" to sexual activities. (For a discussion of consent, see Chapter 18.)

THE SUPREME COURT RULED THAT ANYONE WHO "PRODUCES, DIRECTS, OR PROMOTES ANY PERFORMANCE WHICH INCLUDES SEXUAL CONDUCT BY A CHILD LESS THAN 16 YEARS OF AGE" IS BREAKING THE LAW.

On June 2, 1982, the Supreme Court ruled that anyone who "produces, directs, or promotes any performance which includes sexual conduct by a child less than 16 years of age" is breaking the law. The court took the view that child pornography laws are aimed at protecting the children who engage in sexual acts and that children under 16 are harmed by sexual acts. Such laws differ from those aimed at protecting audiences from seeing obscene sexual acts (as defined by *Miller*).

Twenty states have laws against the distribution of any work that shows children performing sexual acts, and the Supreme Court decision upholds these laws (Mann, 1982). The law now *assumes* harm to children performing these acts; no proof of harm is required.

Will the law against "kiddie porn" have any effect? It probably will. Given the marginality of many adult bookstores, the relatively small size of the special market for child pornography, public outrage, and the risks the law creates for distributors, it is likely that producing child pornography will become more dangerous and thus more expensive and secretive.

THE COMMISSION ON OBSCENITY AND PORNOGRAPHY

Lacking information about pornography and its effects, Congress in 1967 authorized the creation of the Commission on Obscenity and Pornography. (A new Commission was formed in 1985.) In its final report, in 1970, the Commission recommended: the abolition of all antipornography laws for adults; and keeping restrictions on selling pornography to minors without their parents' consent and on forced soliciting of pornography. In 1983, a former chairman of the Commission reaffirmed its recommendations (Boston *Globe,* February 13, 1983). The Commission investigated a number of questions. First, it wanted to know who uses pornography. The answer: as of the late 1960s in the United States, about 85 percent of men and 70 percent of women had been exposed to erotica, mostly voluntarily. Highly educated people were likelier than less educated people to have seen erotica. The average pornographic movie patron was male, white, married, between the ages of 26 and 45, a white-collar worker or professional, college-educated, with an annual income above the national average.

The Commission wanted to know who profits from pornography. It found that few people did. The yearly gross dollar income as of about 1970 for all pornographic materials was $537 to $574 million, well below what people had estimated.

How concerned were Americans about pornography? The Commission found that only 2 percent of Americans cited pornography among the two or three most important problems in the country. Finally, and most important, the Commission investigated the effects of pornography on consumers. It found that:

1 Pornography stimulates slight and short-lived increases in sexual arousal—at most.

2 Pornography has limited effects on even socially sanctioned sexual behavior.

3 Pornography was not a factor in sex crimes or in the creation of sex offenders.

Commissioners in other countries, such as Great Britain, reached similar conclusions (Kutchinsky, 1985).

SEXUALITY IN PERSPECTIVE: AN ANTIPORNOGRAPHY LAW

A new model antipornography law, drafted by Andrea Dworkin and Catharine MacKinnon, has been and will continue to be tested around the country. Part of it appears here.

STATEMENT OF POLICY

Pornography is a systematic practice of exploitation and subordination based on sex that differentially harms women. The harm of pornography includes dehumanization, sexual exploitation, forced sex, and social and sexual terrorism and inferiority presented as entertainment. The bigotry and contempt it promotes, with the acts of aggression it fosters, diminish opportunities for equality of rights. . .

DEFINITIONS

1   *Pornography is the graphic sexually explicit subordination of women through pictures and/or words that also includes one or more of the following: (i) women are presented dehumanized as sexual objects, things, or commodities; or (ii) women are presented as sexual objects who enjoy pain or humiliation; or (iii) women are presented as sexual objects who experience sexual pleasure in being raped; or (iv) women are presented as sexual objects tied up or cut up or mutilated or bruised or physically hurt; or (v) women are presented in postures or positions of sexual submission, servility, or display; or (vi) women's body parts—including but not limited to vaginas, breasts, or buttocks—are exhibited such that women are reduced to those parts; or (vii) women are presented as whores by nature; or (viii) women are presented being penetrated by objects or animals; or (ix) women are presented in scenarios of degradation, injury, torture, shown as filthy or inferior, bleeding, bruised, or hurt in a context that makes these conditions sexual.*

2   *The use of men, children, or transsexuals in the place of women in (1) above is pornography for purposes of this law.*

The *subordination* referred to by the law means several things. Subordination means that:

1 There is a hierarchy in which some people are on top and some on the bottom.
2 People are objectified, made less than human than the person who is on top. The person on top becomes the standard for what a human being is.
3 There is submission, for when people on the bottom of the hierarchy have been turned into objects by those with power, they act submissively.
4 It means that violence exists and is widespread.

The antipornography law by 1985 had approached in several places. In Minneapolis, the mayor vetoed the City Council's passage of the law on the grounds that it was too vague. Another court test came in Suffolk County, New York, where there were few feminists but wide local support. A 1985 Cambridge, Massachusetts poll on the bill attracted feminist groups on both sides. The statute was turned down by the voters. A court overturned the law in Indianapolis. The Indiana judge, Sarah Evans Barker, ruled as follows:

> *It ought to be remembered by defendants and all others who would support such a legislative initiative that, in terms of altering sociological patterns, much as alteration may be necessary and desirable, free speech, rather than being the enemy, is a long-tested and worthy ally. To deny free speech in order to engineer social change in the name of accomplishing a greater good for one sector of our society erodes the freedoms of all and, as such, threatens tyranny and injustice for those subjected to the rule of such laws. The First Amendment protections presuppose the evil of such tyranny and prevent a finding by this Court upholding the Ordinance.*

Based on Mary Kay Blakely, "Is One Woman's Sexuality Another Woman's Pornography?" *Ms.*, April 1985, pp. 37ff.

SEXUALITY IN CROSS-CULTURAL PERSPECTIVE: PORNOGRAPHY IN CHINA

Like so many other aspects of sexuality, the pornographic materials that a culture produces give clues to its broader sexual values. In prerevolutionary China, for example, Confucianism, a philosophy of the proper relations among humans, had held sway for centuries. Within the Confucian system, loyalty was an ideal to be sought in human relationships. Virtue consisted in the loyalty of child to parent, subject to emperor, and wife to husband. Loyalty was the bond in a marriage, not romantic love. In Chinese novels, pornographic and otherwise, romantic love is not a central theme, as it is in so many Western novels.

Chinese pornography was a highly developed art, matched only recently in the West for its explicitness and detail. Before 1949, the beginning of Communist rule in China, a sixteenth-century novel by an unknown author, *The Golden Lotus,* was widely enjoyed. It recounts the personal lives of men and women (the latter for the first time in Chinese literature) and describes the relationships of a rich merchant, Hsi-men Ching, and his wives, lovers, neighbors, maids, and prostitutes. Western missionaries tried to suppress the novel, but the Chinese enjoyed descriptions of the heroine Golden Lotus and her lovers such as this one:

In the days when Golden Lotus had performed the act of darkness with Chan [an earlier lover], that miserable old man had never been able to offer any substantial contribution to the proceedings, and not once had she been satisfied. Then she married Wu Ta. You may imagine the prowess which might be expected from Master Tom Thumb. It could hardly be described as heroic. Now she met Hsi-men Ching, whose capability in such matters was unlimited and whose skill was exceptionally refined and cunning.

Soon they had drunk as much as they desired, and a fit of passion swept over them. Hsi-men Ching's desire could no longer be restrained; he disclosed the treasure which sprang from his loins, and made the woman touch it with her delicate fingers. Upstanding it was, and flushed with pride, the black hair strong and bristling. A mighty warrior in very truth.

Then Golden Blossom took off her clothes. Hsi-men Ching fondled the fragrant blossom. No down concealed it. It had all the fragrance and tenderness of fresh-made pastry, the softness and the appearance of a new-made pie. It was a thing so exquisite all the world would have desired it.

Based on Fox Butterfield, *China* (New York: Times Books), 1982, pp. 134–135. Quotation from *The Golden Lotus,* translated by Clement Egerton (London: Routledge & Kegan Paul, 1939), vol. 1, p.67.

PORNOGRAPHY TODAY

Pornography today is in flux. The producers and consumers who want it freely available push the limits forward, and opponents drive them back. Some cities, such as Boston, have institutionalized the erotica business: merchants are allowed to sell their wares and exhibit their products in certain prescribed areas of the city but are prosecuted if they violate those boundaries. In Boston, this area is colorfully called "The Combat Zone." In New York, it is Times Square; in San Francisco, it is North Beach.

How explicit pornography is varies from city to city and typically represents a compromise between conflicting groups. Thus while hard-core movies, which show completely uncensored sexual activities or live sex shows, are tolerated in large cities, a soft-core magazine like *Playboy* may violate community standards in smaller, rural areas. On average in this country, the East and West coasts are probably most liberal. Most pornography is manufactured on the West Coast. In Los Angeles, a special school trains aspiring porn actors (Boston *Globe,* February 13, 1983).

Law enforcement officials estimate that $4 to $6 billion a year is spent on all pornography: films, books, video cassettes, and all other forms of erotica. Whereas once hard-core films were available from adult bookstores in 8 mm or 16 mm versions or at theatres, today such explicit films are widely available at video stores. Videotape, in fact, has broadly expanded the outlets for pornography. A former commissioner estimates that total current income from hard-core pornography, with adjustments for inflation, is about the same as it was when the Commission reported: $100 million in 1970 and an estimated $200 to $300 million in 1982 (Lipton, 1983). Not only is pornography commercially available in thousands of retail outlets, but some people tape their own sexual activities and trade them through the mail (Boston *Globe,* February 13, 1983). The 1984

Pornography is found around the world. This is a "nonstop" movie theatre for pornographic films in Hamburg, West Germany.

SEXUALITY IN PERSPECTIVE:
A PORNOGRAPHY GLOSSARY

Have you ever wondered what "marital aids" were or the difference between soft- and **hard-core pornography?** Wonder no more. Here is a porn glossary.

hard-core—pornography depicting sexual acts and penetration, generally in close focus; *Deep Throat* is an example.

kiddie porn—pornography showing children in sexual acts; kiddie porn is now illegal.

live peeps—small booths around a stage on which a model gyrates to music. One dollar usually buys three minutes of viewing time.

marital aids—sexual devices such as fake penises, lotions, unusual condoms, straps and belts, vibrators, large rubber dolls, and other erotic materials meant to be arousing.

peep shows—small booths in "adult" bookstores that show a few minutes of 8 mm film of hard-core material. Customers choose films of heterosexual or homosexual acts. Films usually are silent.

pornography—any filmed, printed, or videotaped depiction of sexual acts or genitals appealing primarily to prurient interests.

rap booths—small booths where patrons view and talk to a model. Some patrons masturbate. One dollar usually buys three minutes.

soft-core—pornography depicting nudity or sex without showing penetration; for example, R-rated movies or *Playboy*.

Adapted from: "Glossary," *Boston Globe* Spotlight Team, February 13, 1983, p. 61.

Supreme Court ruling that videotape recording of television programs for personal use did not violate copyright laws will probably expand the number of videocassettes of sexual activities. The new interpretation of the law forbids sale of privately taped programs but not their private use.

Pornography is widely available on cable and subscription television stations—other phenomena the new Commission will report on. Industry estimates are that 500,000 people regularly watch pornographic material (Boston *Globe,* February 13, 1983), an audience that is solidly middle-class and middle-aged. Commercial broadcasters must adhere to a Federal Communications Commission decency code, or they risk losing their license. But pay TV broadcasters, who sell a product to individual consumers, are not bound by such a code. Opponents worry that children will not be protected from pornographic programs that appear regularly on television. Cable industry spokespeople insist, however, that pornography appears mainly after midnight, when most children are asleep, that films often are preceded by warnings to parents to put the children to bed, and that electronic locks can tune out offensive wavelengths.

EFFECTS OF PORNOGRAPHY

There are three basic theories of how pornography affects people. The first is the **modeling theory,** styled on the theory that observing highly arousing behavior increases the likelihood that related behavior will follow. A second theory, the **catharsis theory,** proposes the opposite of the modeling theory. According to the catharsis theory, pornography acts as a safety valve for pent-up sexual feelings and thereby makes some—presumably both socially acceptable and unacceptable—modeled sexual behavior *less* likely. The third theory is a **null theory.** According to the null theory, pornography neither stimulates nor depresses sexual behavior. We will evaluate these competing theories by examining some effects of pornography on ordinary people and then on convicted sex offenders.

Pornography and the Sexual Behavior of Ordinary People

In the 1960s, researchers began to investigate how pornography affects people's sexual behavior. They exposed a group of people to pornography and then compared their sexual behavior a day to several weeks before and after the exposure. (See the Commission on Obscenity and Pornography, 1970 for a review of these experiments.) To summarize the results: exposing ordinary people one time to pornography produces, at most, slight and temporary increases in sexual behavior and some exploration of new techniques (although not usually exotic techniques). Viewers' sexual behavior is not very different from their usual, previewing practice. Clearly, ordinary people do not turn into sex offenders from a single exposure to pornography.

Of course, these laboratory experiments fail to capture the essence of a real-life situation. What are the effects of repeated, long-term exposure to pornography? Although no one has yet measured the effects of years of viewing pornography, two groups of experiments have examined how several weeks' exposure to pornography affects sexual behavior. In the first experiment, 51 stably married couples filled in daily questionnaires about their sexual behavior for 12 weeks

(Mann et al., 1973). During the middle four weeks only, the couples were exposed to erotic films once a week. The results were interesting: the subjects' sexual behavior increased more *before* than once they began seeing the movies. The increases during the movie period usually were confined only to the nights of the film showings. Few couples tried new sexual acts, and unusual sexual acts did not increase in frequency. Control subjects, who were shown neutral films during the middle four weeks (but who were promised pornography at the study's end), did not show the relative decline in sexual behavior during the movie period. For couples like these, we can conclude that the *anticipation* of erotic events stimulates sexual behavior more than the erotica itself does.

In a second experiment, young adult males were exposed to several forms of erotica for 90 minutes each day, five days a week, for three weeks (Howard et al., 1973). The findings? The men's sexual behavior did not change. Although at first they thought more about sex, soon they were thinking *less* about sex than they had before the experiment began. Several measures showed the exposure to large "doses" of pornography steadily reduces interest; the men's appetites were ultimately sated. If the subjects had not been paid, many would have quit before the experiment ended. Thus some exposure to pornography and anticipating that exposure can be stimulating, but massive exposure turns out to be a turn-*off*. These and other research results support the null theory of pornography. University students in German showed moderate arousal to erotic slides, films, and stories. For the most part, men's and women's responses were alike. Both showed small increases in their usual sexual behavior (Schmidt, 1975; Sigusch and Schmidt, 1973; see Chapter 2 for full details.) In short, pornography may stimulate minimal amounts of sexual acts and ideas. It rarely stimulates people to act out new sexual behaviors.

Pornography and the Convicted Sex Offender

How do sex offenders—those who force themselves on unwilling or incompetent partners—react to pornography? Does pornography have its most damaging effects on a vulnerable, potential sex offender? Some clear answers come from the Kinsey Institute (Gebhard et al., 1965). Their study reached over 2700 men, all prisoners, some convicted of sex offenses and others, the controls, convicted of nonsexual crimes. Most were from poor or lower-class backgrounds. All of the men were interviewed in depth. The researchers assessed the men's interest in and arousal from pornography and found that fewer than 0.5 percent had *not* been exposed to pornography. But pornography proved rarely to be important in the men's lives or their criminal acts. A conviction for sex offenses went along with *low* interest in and response to pornography. Kinsey and his colleagues had previously found (1948) that fantasy and reverie play only a minor role in the sexual behavior of relatively uneducated, lower-class men.

Among the many categories of offenders interviewed, only two types showed marked interest in pornography. Homosexual offenders against adults were the first type. (This group was also the highest in socioeconomic status.) The second type, men who had sexually attacked minors, were

> *uninhibited young men who respond unthinkingly and violently to various stimuli. Their reaction to pornography is merely a part of their exaggerated reaction to almost everything (Gebhard et al., 1965).*

Interview studies of sex offenders aimed at documenting their experience with pornography confirm these findings (Goldstein and Kant, 1973). One new finding to emerge is that sex offenders generally had *less* early and current exposure to pornography than other prisoners. (Again, homosexual offenders were the exception.) Rapists especially have histories of sexual repression, both by their parents and themselves. This repression probably shaped their meager exposure to pornography. When rapists did view pornography, it seemed to inspire more guilt and disgust in them than in other offenders. They tended to oppose intercourse outside of marriage and to be ignorant of sexual matters. The rapists' daydreams seemed to be dominated by a wide variety of sexual wishes, and they were more likely than other sex offenders to daydream about homosexual, cross-dressing or oral-genital acts. Their dilemma was that they had lived repressed lives but fantasized actively. Goldstein and Kant proposed that in using pornography to try and resolve the conflict between their real and their imagined sexual experiences, rapists use pornography differently from other offenders. Thus most people use pornography *expressively*—to increase their sexual arousal. But rapists may use pornography *defensively*—to ward off unwelcome, insistent fantasies. Rapists choose strictly heterosexual pornography, perhaps to compensate for those fantasies. Goldstein and Kant also proposed that pornography neither heightens nor dampens rapists' sexual desire (the null theory), merely that it deflects anxiety.

But rapists are, of course, violent men. The combination of sexual and aggressive themes can be very stimulating to them, although it may not influence their crimes. Rapists were aroused by the sexually cruel writings of the Marquis de Sade, the story of the sadistic Boston Strangler, and motorcycle movies that showed gang rapes. One imprisoned rapist found a description of rape in the *Ladies' Home Journal* stimulating. Finally, just as some people have long—and wrongly—assumed that pornography is an important cause of sex crimes, some have asserted that pornography is an important cause of male homosexuality. That conclusion is also wrong. Homosexuals are often interested in pornography, but most homosexuals' patterns of behavior are set long before they see any homosexual pornography (Goldstein and Kant, 1973).

PORNOGRAPHY AND VIOLENCE

Some groups in the United States have asserted that pornography is increasingly violent (Eysenck and Nias, 1978) and that pornography—violent or not—increases sexual crimes like rape (Court, 1985). What is the evidence on these serious charges?

Between 1973 and 1977, soft-core pornography did show some increase in incidence of violence with sex. Although a fairly stable 10 percent of the cartoons in *Playboy* and *Penthouse* paired sex and violence, the number of such pictures (especially in *Penthouse*) increased from 1 to 5 percent (Malamuth and Spinner, 1980). *Hustler* ran cartoons about child molesting until 1978. When a sociologist surveyed 428 "adult" paperback novels, published between 1968 and 1974, 4588 explicit sexual scenes emerged, of which 195 were rapes. The later books had twice the incidence of violent sexual acts as the earlier books (Smith, 1976). Thus there does seem to be a somewhat higher incidence of violence in some forms of erotica today than there was in the early 1970s. A content analysis of all of the 430 soft- *and* hard-core magazines sold in one Times Square bookstore turned up

5% with bondage and submission themes and another 1.2% of S/M. Much of the violence was in stylized static pictures, i.e. whip in hand, not hitting. Men were submissive in 29% of the images (Winick, 1985). Given the inclusion of hardcore material, these figures seem quite low. The strongest feelings for banning pornography are in response to sexual violence. A *Newsweek* poll, taken by the Gallup Organization in 1985, showed that most Americans polled wanted no stricter restrictions on sexually explicit material, but most wanted restrictions on violent material. Fully 75% agreed with feminist charges that pornography may lead to loss of respect for women, acts of sexual violence, and rape (Garrido, 1985). (Some feminists argue that all pornography is violence against women. If so, the question we are investigating here becomes circular: if it is pornography, then it is, by definition, violent.) No one knows precisely the true rates of consumption of violent as opposed to nonviolent pornography, because no studies of borrowed or "hand-me-down" pornography have yet appeared. In contrast, soft-pornography publishers are likely to know a good deal about magazine sharing, because it affects their advertising rates.

The question is whether men who view violent pornography are thereby predisposed to act violently. Experimental psychologists have used laboratory models to answer this question, because they have wanted to control both the nature of the pornography and the instigation to aggression. Psychologists know that people imagine far more violence than they actually commit.

Psychologists have found in college laboratories that particular sequences of aggressive and sexual events—some in film, some in symbolic acts—increase the likelihood that men will say that they endorse statements and acts that are sexually aggressive. Soft-core photographs do not typically arouse men to aggression. But films of active coitus, oral and anal sex, and **sadomasochistic** sex seem to make some men willing to aggress against women, to endorse callous statements about women, and to express more leniency toward rapists (Donnerstein, Donnerstein, and Evans, 1975; Ramirez, 1982; Zillmann, 1979). Other experiments show that

Many people are concerned because they believe that pornography has become increasingly violent.

when men watch a film in which a woman looks sexually aroused during a rape, men are likely to misperceive her visible expressions of pain (Malamuth and Check, 1980).

An Experiment in Anger and Sexual Arousal

The details of an experiment show how psychologists can test hypotheses about sexual aggression against women. Psychologists doing this kind of work are testing modeling theory, the theory that says we learn to do what we see others do, especially if those others are powerful, rewarding, and like ourselves. In an experiment by Edward Donnerstein (1980), a group of men was angered by either a male or a female confederate of the experimenter and then shown one of three films. (The men didn't know that the confederates were in league with the experimenter.) A control group saw a neutral film, neither aggressive nor sexually arousing. The other two films were very (and equally) sexually arousing, but only one was aggressive, too. Donnerstein had three hypotheses: (1) that the angered men would act more aggressively than the never-angered men later in the experiment; (2) that men who saw the aggressive erotic film would be more aggressive than the men who saw the nonaggressive film; and (3) that men who had been both angered by a female confederate and also had seen the sexual-aggressive film would show the highest levels of aggression. Donnerstein measured the subjects' aggression somewhat indirectly, for no responsible psychologist provokes open-ended aggression in a laboratory. Donnerstein's subjects were given elaborate stories justifying each step in the research. The final measure of aggression was not face-to-face aggression but the decision by the subject on how much shock to give the hidden confederate. The shocks were meant to correspond to the confederate's score on a test. Subjects never actually saw shocks administered nor gave the shocks.

Donnerstein measured actual physiological arousal by taking each man's blood-pressure readings. (The experimenter concocted an elaborate story to get the subjects to cooperate without self-consciousness.) The blood-pressure readings told Donnerstein that the two erotic films were arousing but that the neutral film was not. The men's aggressive behavior turned out to vary according to the sex of the confederate. Thus while both erotic films (aggressive and nonaggressive) led subjects to "administer" equally intense shocks to male targets, only the aggressive film elicited the most intense shocks to female targets. The shocks administered to the women were significantly more intense than those administered to the men. Men who had not been angered administered mild shocks, regardless of the kind of film they had seen. Overall, both erotic films caused more intense shocks than the neutral film, and the aggressive erotic film caused the most intense shocks of all.

What *is* the relationship between experimentally produced aggression and real-life aggression against women? Experimental psychologists are careful not to extrapolate their findings wholesale into daily life, for the constrained environment of experiments is different from the varied, everyday environment. Even so, the impact of the laboratory work is clear: overdosing on viewing sexual violence may make some men think about such violence and judge as acceptable norms of behavior that encompass more violence. Heightening awareness of the make-believe, immoral, and punishable nature of sexual aggression makes overt behavior less likely after modeled acts. Donnerstein is careful to "debrief" his subjects after they see violent films. In the debriefings, the experimenters, reinforced by video-taped presentations, dispel certain myths about sexual violence and try to "resensitize" subjects to issues of violence, especially violence against women.

Of course, aggressive acts are not repeated by all men who view them in films or television. Many factors alter that likelihood. Some of the factors—like the film—are in the environment, and some are within the men. Their ideas about violence and its probable punishment, their views of the moral justification of the acts, their interpretations of the targets of possible aggression, and their view of the events as real or imaginary all play a role (Berkowitz, 1984).

A CROSS-CULTURAL VIEW OF LEGALIZED PORNOGRAPHY: THE DANISH EXPERIENCE

In the United States, the attack on pornography has been aimed largely at violent pornography. When Sweden debated pornography more than 10 years ago, it chose to decriminalize it. In 1982, the Swedish government voted to ban sex clubs and live sex shows, although violence is not usually an issue in such settings. The experience with pornography of another Scandinavian country, Denmark, serves to answer certain questions about the effects of pornography on people's behavior. During the early 1960s in Denmark, pornographic books grew ever more widely available. In the mid-1960s, a wave of hard-core pornographic magazines hit the country. In response, Denmark legalized pornographic literature in 1967. In 1969, it legalized the sale of pornographic pictures to people over 16. The Danish experience—a rapid increase in pornography followed by legalization—is a good case study for evaluating the effects of pornography on sex crimes.

When we chart the incidence of sex crimes in Denmark from 1948 to 1970 (see Figure 20.2), we see that there were fewer sex crimes after pornography was legalized. This pattern seems to support the catharsis theory of pornography's effects: freely available pornography may prevent the outbreak of antisocial sexual

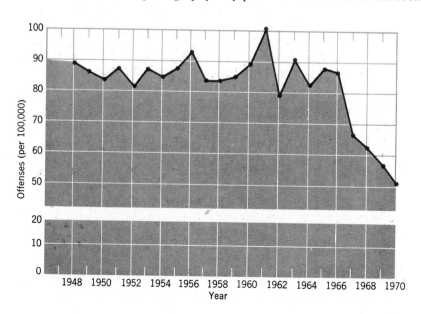

FIGURE 20.2

Sex offenses in Denmark.

TABLE 20.1

Sex Offenses against Females in Copenhagen[a]

Offenses	Year			Decrease in Percent 1959–1969
	1959	1964	1969	
Rape	32	20	27	16
Exhibitionism	249	225	104	58
Peeping	99	61	20	80
Coitus with minors	51	18	19	63
Verbal indecency	45	43	13	71
Other offenses against women	137	103	60	56
Other offenses against girls	282	204	87	69

Source: B. Kutchinsky, The effect of easy availability of pornography on the incidence of sex crimes: the Danish experience. *Journal of Social Issues,* 1973, *29,* 163–182.

[a]Based on police records.

acts. But other factors, such as a change in community standards on what constitutes a sex crime or relaxed vigilance by the police, may also have played a part. If we then look at the kinds of sexual crimes Danish men committed between 1959 and 1969 (see Table 20.1), we see that *exhibitionism* decreased about 60 percent. But at the same time, public and police attitudes relaxed. (However, one researcher who studied the change in Danish attitudes concluded that the change was more apparent than real [Kutchinsky, 1973].) The decrease in exhibitionism probably can be ascribed to greater social tolerance. But *voyeurism* dropped 80 percent, and people's views on this offense did not change much during the period under study. The conclusion: pornography seems an excellent way of satisfying potential voyeurs. Child molesting decreased 69 percent between 1959 and 1969, and research showed that this drop was certainly *not* due to relaxed standards. (If relaxed standards were the cause, there would have been more of a decrease than there actually was in the reporting of the less serious cases.) The biggest yearly decrease happened in 1965, the year when pornographic pictures became widely available. Child molesters usually desire adult sexual partners and molest children only when adults are absent or unapproachable. Pornography provided potential child molesters with a preferable alternative. Finally, rape decreased only slightly, as we might expect from knowing that most rapists tend not to be interested in pornography.

CONCLUSIONS: THE EFFECTS OF PORNOGRAPHY

Pornography does not seem to change people's lives significantly, and it certainly does not seem to be destroying Western civilization. The consumers of pornography tend to be relatively well educated and affluent men, and pornography probably meshes well with their sexual fantasies. It does not evoke exotic new fantasies or sexual acts. Pornography seems not to create sexual criminals either. Convicted sex offenders are ill-equipped to use the pornography they encounter. Like many men of low socioeconomic status, they prefer the "real thing." Knowing that rapists and other sex offenders have limited early exposure to pornography, plus histories of sexual repression and ignorance, suggests a sort of "immunization theory" of sexual development. People who are exposed as children to sexual stimuli—pornography, family nudity, formal sex education, and the like—may be "immunized" against antisocial sexual acts as adults (Commission on Obscenity and Pornography, 1970). The other side of the argument about immunization is that too much early exposure to pornography might bring on the "disease." There is some evidence that the first argument is true; there is none to support the second. Laboratory studies suggest that violent pornography leads some men to an increase in their expressed tolerance of sexual violence and a readiness to act violently. Such experimental studies need validating outside of the laboratory.

AN OVERVIEW

Pornography may well reflect social and psychological problems between men and women. Almost all pornography is created with the male sexual fantasy in mind (or what pornographers imagine is the male sexual fantasy). Women tend to be treated as sex objects in much pornography, sometimes brutally so. Women involved in pornography have been known to lose "straight" jobs—as stockbrokers and as reigning Miss America, for example. Pornography as we know it today may itself contribute to the perpetuation of harmful, unfortunate stereotypes of women and their roles. Some feminists propose that women produce their own forms of erotica to use in expanding the bounds of female sexuality (English, 1983).

In addition, pornography is very popular among and strongly affects young teenage boys who are beginning the transition to adult sexual life. Soft-core pornography often accompanies their masturbating. If pornography serves to cue them to sexual arousal, and if they are stimulated repeatedly by subservient, bosomy women or tall, robust, and booted women, those stereotypes might become the established stimuli for arousing a part of a generation of young men. Restricting pornography would have little effect, for in the more restrictive past, young boys managed to get their hands on pornography.

In sum, society must strike a balance between the freedom to experience sexually explicit material and the freedom to be protected from it. Probably it is impossible to respect everyone's sexual values precisely, but a democratic society strives to achieve the best balance among conflicting values.

SUMMARY

1 Pornography is material aimed primarily at sexual arousal. Governments and religious powers have a long tradition of censoring pornography, assuming (without proof) that it affects human behavior for the worse.

2 The Supreme Court has ruled (1957) that to be obscene, a work must: appeal to prurient interests; offend community standards; and have no redeeming social value. It has also ruled that the constitutional guarantees of freedom of speech and publication do not apply to pornography. The vague standards for pornography meant that until recently many obscenity convictions were overturned by the Supreme Court.

3 A Commission on Obscenity and Pornography concluded (1970) that pornography: at most stimulates slight, temporary increases in sexual arousal; has limited effects on even socially sanctioned sexual behavior; and is not a factor in sex crimes.

4 There are three basic theories of how pornography affects people. The modeling theory predicts that people enact forms of sexual behavior that they see modeled in pornography. The catharsis theory predicts that pornography acts as a safety valve for pent-up sexual feelings. The null theory predicts that pornography does not significantly affect sexual behavior. Laboratory experiments tend to support the null theory. Interviews with sex offenders have revealed that few are interested in or responsive to pornography. Only two types of offenders were found to be interested in pornography: homosexual offenders against adults and child molesters. In fact, sex offenders (excepting homosexual offenders) generally had less exposure to pornography than other prisoners.

5 Denmark, which legalized pornography in the 1960s, has seen certain categories of sex crimes—voyeurism and child molesting—decrease, probably as a result of legalization. In no category of sex crimes was there an increase for the 10-year period following legalization. The rate of rape seemed unaffected.

6 From the evidence (rather than from intuition), one can conclude that pornography does not significantly alter people's behavior. It does not evoke new fantasies or exotic forms of sexual behavior. Pornography seems to play no verifiable part in creating sex offenders.

7 Pornography is not always benign. It often treats women as sex objects, at times brutally so. In stereotyping sexual responses, it may provide a damaging model of the relationships of men to women. Pornography may hurt children, too. Because they cannot give informed consent on sexual matters, and because there is a possibility of psychological damage to them, children may not legally appear in sexual acts in pornographic films or magazines. Finally, people have a right to be protected from unwanted sexual advertising or products and a right to direct the sexual education of their children. For all of these reasons, society must try to balance the freedom to experience pornography and the freedom to be protected from it.

KEY TERMS

pornography
erotica
victimless crimes
hard-core pornography
modeling theory

catharsis theory
null theory
sadomasochism
exhibitionism
voyeurism

SUGGESTED READINGS

English, D. "The Politics of Porn: Can Feminists Walk the Line?" *Mother Jones,* April 1980. A graphic description of pornography by a feminist editor, this article challenges the politics behind pornography.

Griffin, S. *Pornography and Silence: Culture's Revenge Against Nature.* New York: Harper & Row, 1981. A feminist and poet addresses the pornographic fantasy that she views as obliterating women. This book is a literary and cultural analysis.

"Pornography: Attitudes, Use, and Effects." *Journal of Social Issues,* 1973, vol. 29, no. 3. A series of articles by various authors discussing, in nontechnical language, the research of the U.S. Commission on Obscenity and Pornography.

Schwartz, T. "The TV Pornography Boom." New York *Times Sunday Magazine,* September 13, 1981. This article describes how videocassettes and cable television change people's access to pornography.

Webb, P. *The Erotic Arts.* New York: Farrar, Straus, & Giroux, 1983. A comprehensive review of the erotic in all forms of art, throughout the ages.

Afterword

A book ends. But you go on learning and questioning about sexuality all your
lives. You will deal with personal matters as well as profuse information on sexual
topics. Sexuality is not esoteric. It marches across the TV screen and fills the
newspapers. In one week in May, 1985, a single newspaper (the *New York Times*)
carried the following stories:

- The latest Gallup Poll showed that in the United States, 52 percent of the
  people didn't think that premarital sex was wrong. (In 1969, 68 percent of
  just such a sample thought it was wrong.) Among people between 18 and 29
  years old, only 18 percent thought it wrong; among those 30 to 49, 35
  percent; and among those 50 and over, 56 percent thought it wrong. The
  sampling error was 3 percent; the Gallup organization is reliable on sampling.
  What else do you need to know? Did the *Times* say it all? Is there anything
  surprising in the results? What does it make you think about?

- "Symptomless Victims May Spread AIDS for Years" was another headline.
  How did they know that? Can the results be trusted? The article said that 22
  of 25 blood donors from groups usually cited as being at high risk for AIDS
  (even though symptom-free for up to 52 months) carried the virus continuously. What does that say about the incidence of AIDS? A blood test can
  detect the AIDS virus in blood, but what does that mean about the control
  of AIDS? A few days later, the *Times* said that AIDS is less contagious than
  measles. Out of more than 100 health workers who have stuck themselves
  with a needle previously used on an AIDS patient, only one got the virus.
  No classmate, housemate, or fellow worker of any AIDS victim came down
  with AIDS. The Centers for Disease Control, we read, estimate that perhaps
  1 million symptom-free people carry AIDS and perhaps 10 percent will become sick. How do these two stories fit together?

- In families with children under 18, more than one quarter have only one
  parent present. In 90 percent, that parent is the mother, and in 10 percent,
  the father. We might skim that story, but we know that pregnant teenagers

fill that pool of single-parent families as surely as divorces do. Just two days before, the *Times* ran a story on a one-year study, begun in 1980, on people 17 years old or younger who have not finished high school. The sample was taken largely from the poor and from minorities. Its goal was to reduce teenage pregnancy and to get teenagers to use social services. For a year, they did. But two years later, about as many in the program were pregnant as in the control group. How can one decide what went wrong? What went so right for that one year? What do the teenagers say? It's not in the story. How can you find out more?

- We read that an official of the Association of American Colleges has information on over 50 cases of fraternity house gang rapes. An elite university has revoked one house's recognition for a year after a woman was reportedly gang raped there. The rapes typically happen at parties where people are drinking alcohol. Sounds familiar, doesn't it? What were the Kinsey Institute findings about rape and alcohol?

- A storm may be brewing at the Justice Department's Office of Juvenile Justice and Delinquency Prevention. A lawyer there has $24 million in research money to distribute. He has given $750,000 to a researcher with little demonstrated skill to connect pornography with the involvement of children in commercial sex, although a Justice Department memo said the job could be done for $60,000. The researcher has stated publicly that the publisher of *Playboy* magazine is "every bit as dangerous as Hitler." (It's clear which theory of pornography she subscribes to.) Congress is up in arms about the size of the grant. In her grant proposal, the researcher said that she had information that "millions" of children are involved in commercial sex. If she's right, it is a significant problem, for the Supreme Court has ruled children's involvement in commercial sex to be illegal. But other experts question the numbers. In April, 1982, the government's General Accounting Office published a report on children in commercial sex called "Sexual Exploitation of Children— A Problem of Unknown Magnitude." The report is searching and tentative, but finds no "millions" of exploited children. Is this just an inter-office fight, or will there be some relation between the grant and the Attorney General's new Commission on Pornography? Stay tuned.

When one is very young, information about sexuality seems hard to find. But here, in one week, is a great deal of information. With the framework you now have for understanding issues of human sexuality, you can now see a larger sexual world.

GLOSSARY

abortifacient   Any substance that causes the pregnant uterus to rid itself of its contents.

absolutist ethic   A system of beliefs in which right and wrong are unchanging and absolute. Compare relativistic and hedonistic ethics.

Acquired Immune Deficiency Syndrome (AIDS)   An as yet incurable sexually transmitted disease, transmitted in some body fluids, and found among gay and bisexual men, Haitians, intravenous drug users, hemophiliacs, their sexual partners, and some heterosexuals. AIDS is characterized by a weakened immune system and opportunistic infection that can cause death.

actual failure rate (of contraceptives)   The failure rate of contraceptives in actual use. The actual failure rate is always higher than the theoretical failure rate. Compare theoretical failure rate.

adolescence   A sociological and psychological term for the mental and social growth of the child into a young adult. During adolescence, children mature sexually into young adults. See also puberty.

adrenogenital females   See pseudohermaphrodites.

adult gender identity   The developments at puberty that consolidate the core gender identity of childhood and integrate a new, adult body image, with new secondary sexual characteristics and sexual orientation. Compare core gender identity. See secondary sexual characteristics.

agents of socialization   People from whom one learns sexual and other values. See also sexual values.

agape   Selfless, charitable love.

amenorrhea   Absent menstruation. Primary amenorrhea is the failure to begin menstruating; secondary amenorrhea is the disappearance of menstruation once it has begun.

amniocentesis   A test of fetal cells, performed in the fifth month of pregnancy, for the detection of abnormalities in the fetus. Compare chorionic villus sampling.

amniotic fluid   A liquid contained within the uterine membranes that cushions the fetus.

anaphrodisiacs   Substances that detract from sexual performance and pleasure. Compare aphrodisiacs.

androgen insensitivity   A condition in which an individual's genes lack the full instruction for building androgen receptors, with the result that 46,XY fetuses develop normal testes but the external genitals of females. These androgen-insensitive women are sterile, but they have firm feminine gender identities. Compare partial androgen insensitivity.

androgens   A class of steroid hormones, the most powerful of which is testosterone. For the male internal reproductive tract to develop before birth, androgen must be present. See also steroid hormones.

androgyny   The quality of possessing both masculine and feminine traits.

anilingus   Mouth-to-anus stimulation.

anorgasmia   Sexual dysfunction in women consisting of not reaching orgasm.

anovulatory cycle   A menstrual cycle during which no ovulation occurs.

Apgar score   A rapid assessment of a newborn's condition made immediately after birth and again in five minutes. Named after Virginia Apgar, the pediatrician who devised the test.

aphrodisiacs   Substances that enhance sexual performance and pleasure. Compare anaphrodisiacs.

appetitive behavior   In motivation, the behavior that draws an animal or human closer to the thing that it wants or needs. Searching for food is an appetitive behavior. May be followed by consummatory behavior.

areola The pigmented area of the breast that surrounds the nipple. During sexual arousal, the areola swells with blood.

arterioles Parts of the blood vessels that open and close, within the autonomic nervous system. See also autonomic nervous system.

asexual reproduction The division of a single organism into two identical organisms; asexual reproduction is the way in which simple forms of life re-create themselves. See also sexual reproduction.

attraction The way that people positively or negatively evaluate others.

attribution The tendency that people have to ascribe causes to their subjective experiences. The attribution process itself can shape the subjective experience. Compare misattribution.

autonomic nervous system The part of the nervous system that controls blood flow, muscle tension, heart, internal organs, and endocrine glands.

autosome The 22 pairs of chromosomes that are the same in males and females. Compare sex chromosomes.

aversion disorder Sexual dysfunction in which people feel revolted by sex. A form of desire disorder. See also hypoactive sexual desire.

Bartholin's glands Glands in the female, located within the labia minora near the vaginal opening, that may secrete fluid to lubricate the vagina during sexual arousal.

basilar squeeze technique Treatment for erection dysfunction in which a man's penis is squeezed at the root (base). Compare squeeze technique.

bisexuality Romantic and sexual attraction to people of both sexes.

blastocyst The group of dividing cells that develops from a fertilized egg and implants in the uterine lining.

brain hemisphere The left or right half of the brain. Some theories about observed sex differences in cognitive abilities suggest that the cause lies in differential specialization of the two brain hemispheres.

Braxton-Hicks contractions During pregnancy, the painless tightening of the uterine muscles that prepare the uterus for the work of childbirth.

breech position The birth position of a fetus, in which feet or buttocks precede the head out of the uterus.

Caesarean section Birth of an infant through a cut in the mother's abdominal wall and into her uterus.

carpopedal spasm The involuntary contraction of the muscles of the hands and feet during sexual arousal.

catharsis theory A theory that holds that pornography acts as a safety valve for people's unexpressed sexual feelings. Compare modeling theory, null theory.

cervical os Opening of the cervix.

cervix The neck of the uterus; it projects downward into the vagina.

chlamydia The most common sexually transmitted disease in males, and females, caused by *Chlamydia trachomatis.* In females it may cause infertility.

chorionic villus sampling A test of fetal cells, performed as early as the eighth week of pregnancy, to allow for the detection of abnormalities in the embryo. A villus is a small protrusion from the chorionic membrane surrounding the embryo. Compare amniocentesis.

chromosomes   The physical structures that carry the chemical instructions for fetal reproduction and all later physical development. Through sexual reproduction, humans inherit 46 chromosomes, half from each parent. Two chromosomes are sex chromosomes and differentiate male from female. The other chromosomes are the same in members of both sexes. See also autosome, genes, sex chromosome.

cilia   Tiny, hair-like structures that line the fallopian tubes and move ova toward the uterus. See also fallopian tubes.

circumcision (male)   Surgical removal of the foreskin of the penis. See superincision. Compare excision.

climacteric   A period of great physical change during human development, such as menopause.

clinical method   A research technique, often used to generate hypotheses, that may describe how a particular course of treatment affects subjects. Compare observational method.

clitoris   An organ of female sexual anatomy, the sole function of which is to provide sexual pleasure. It consists of a covering, the *clitoral hood,* a head (*clitoral glans*), and a *clitoral shaft.*

close coupled   Stable, monogamous homosexual pairs.

cohabitation   An unmarried man and woman living together.

coitus interruptus   A male's interrupting vaginal intercourse by withdrawing his penis before he ejaculates.

colostrum   A thin fluid, rich in protein and antibodies, secreted by the breasts before breast milk comes in.

combination pill   A form of oral contraceptives containing progesterone and estrogen.

come out   To accept a homosexual identity.

companionate love   The friendship, caring, and deep attachment of established couples.

competence   Psychologists' term for what a child knows about a certain subject. Compare performance.

congenital microphallus   An unerect penis at birth less than ¾-inch long. The condition requires medical attention.

consanguinous relatives   Those related by blood as opposed to by marriage or adoption.

consent   In law, the free agreement or rejection by someone considered legally competent to agree or reject participation in an act.

consummatory behavior   In motivation, the acts performed on the object an animal or human seeks. Eating, for example, is the consummatory behavior that follows hunger. May follow appetitive behavior.

contact comfort   The warmth and comfort infants derive from touching their mothers or other caretakers. Contact comfort is an aspect of normal sexual development.

contraception   Any method of preventing pregnancy, from blocking union of sperm and egg, to preventing production of sex cells, to preventing sexual intercourse.

contraceptive sponge   Spermicide-filled, disposable sponge worn at the cervix to prevent pregnancy.

control condition   In research, the condition of subjects whose behavior is not manipulated. Used for purposes of comparison.

convergent validity   A description of identical results from more than a single method of inquiring into the same research question. Such results are considered very strong. See also replicability, validity.

Coolidge effect   The tendency for males' sexual motivation to increase in the presence of a new female partner.

core gender identity   The deeply held inner conviction of one's maleness or femaleness that develops in the first few years of life. The sex chromosomes and the gonads a child inherits, the apperance of the child's genitals, and how the child and others see his or her body all influence the formation of core gender identity. Compare adult gender identity. See also gender identity.

corona   The ridge at the bottom of the glans of the penis. Many males find the corona sensitive to stimulation.

corpora cavernosa   Tissue in the penis that fills with blood during sexual arousal.

corpus luteum   Latin for "yellow body," a hormone-producing organ that develops from an ovarian follicle. The corpus luteum secretes the hormone progesterone.

corpus spongiosum (spongy body)   Spongy tissue within the penis containing the urethra. The column of tissue fills with blood on sexual arousal.

cortex   The outer cells of the human embryo's indifferent gonad. These cells may develop into female ovaries. See also indifferent gonad.

covert desensitization   In psychotherapy, the linking of a previously anxiety-provoking stimulus with rewarding (non-anxious) outcomes in fantasy.

cortisone   A hormone produced by the adrenal glands.

covert sensitization   In psychotherapy, the linking of a previously rewarding stimulus with a fantasy of punishment.

Cowper's glands   In males, a pair of glands located just below the prostate gland. These glands secrete a few drops of fluid during sexual arousal that may contain live sperm.

critical period   A point during development when an event must happen or development is forever after altered. Compare sensitive period.

cross-cultural (ethnographic) research   A form of observational research by which investigators study the behavior, customs, and values of people in other cultures. See also observational method.

cross-dressing   Dressing in the clothes of the other sex for sexual arousal. Also known as transvestism.

crowning   The point during childbirth when the fetus's head is visible in the birth canal and does not recede with each uterine contraction.

culdoscopy   Surgery in which a woman's pelvis is entered through an incision in the upper vagina.

cultural evolution   The effects of human culture on human evolution, the changing pattern in humans that results from the transmission of learned behavior and acquired knowledge.

culture   Shared, relatively stable patterns of belief, thought, and action. Humans alone have culture, and it meshes with biology in the many human arrangements for mating, bearing, and rearing young. See also society.

culture-bound   The tendency to think that the customs prevailing in one's own culture are the "natural" way of doing things.

cunnilingus   Oral-genital sex performed on a female.

cystitis   An infection of the bladder. Cystitis often is sexually transmitted and afflicts more women than men.

dependent variable   In scientific research, behavior that results from the systematic variation of one or more independent variables. Compare independent variable.

descriptive statistics   Summaries of measurements of behavior within a given group of subjects, often including how often they have behaved in some way. Compare inferential statistics. See also frequency, incidence.

desire phase   A necessary first step in the sequence of human sexual responses. See also hypoactive sexual desire, satisfaction phase.

detumescence   The draining of blood from the erect (tumescent) penis. In the terminology of Havelock Ellis, detumescence was the second stage of sexual response. See also tumescence.

deviance   Behavior that differs from a statistical norm. See also primary deviance, secondary deviance.

diaphragm   Wire-rimmed rubber barrier worn over the cervix, ideally in combination with a spermicide, to prevent pregnancy.

diethylstilbestrol (DES)   A form of the hormone estrogen formerly used to treat pregnant women against spontaneous abortion. DES has been associated with an elevated incidence of genital cancers in the children of women so treated.

dilation and evacuation (D&E)   Procedure for abortion used in pregnancy, consisting of opening the cervix and removing the contents of the uterus.

dildo   Penis substitute.

disposable diaphragm   A form of contraceptive worn at the cervix and thrown away after an act of sexual intercourse.

distal urethra   A structure in women homologous to the male's prostate gland.

dominant gene   A gene that will dominate over another, recessive gene on a matching chromosome. See also recessive gene.

double standard   Within a particular culture, the application of different standards of behavior to members of the two sexes. Compare single standard.

douching   Rinsing the vagina with a solution. Ineffective when used as a means of birth control.

dowry   Goods or money given by a bride's family to the family of her intended.

drag queens   Homosexual men who habitually dress as women.

drones   Slang term for gay men who dress in leather and other very masculine fashions and who may favor sadomasochism.

dysmenorrhea   Painful menstruation.

ectopic pregnancy   A pregnancy in which the fertilized ovum implants not in the lining of the uterus but elsewhere in the pelvis, perhaps in a fallopian tube (a tubal pregnancy), on the exterior of an ovary or the uterus, or elsewhere. Compare tubal pregnancy.

ejaculatory duct   The pathway for sperm and seminal fluid once they have passed through the prostate gland. The ejaculatory duct opens into the urethra.

embryo   The human organism as it develops prenatally in its first 2 months. The embryonic period is when basic structures form; it is the period of the most concentrated differentiation of cells. Compare fetus.

embryonic period   The first 2 months of prenatal development.

endometriosis   A condition in which tissue from the uterine lining grows elsewhere in the pelvis. Endometriosis may be congenital or the result of surgery or pelvic infection. It can cause infertility.

endometrium   The lining of the uterus, part of which is shed at the end of every menstrual cycle during which no conception has taken place.

endorphins   Natural painkillers produced in the brain.

epididymus   A coiled tube in the testes in which sperm mature after leaving the seminiferous tubules and before entering the vas deferens. See also seminiferous tubules, vas deferens.

episiotomy   A surgical cut made during childbirth between a woman's vagina and rectum to prevent tearing as her infant emerges from the birth canal.

equity theory   The idea that in some human relationships people's exchanges, although unequal, may over time be deemed equitable.

erectile dysfunction   Repeated inability to keep or get an erection. Men who have never been able to have erections in intercourse have primary erectile dysfunction. Men who have lost the ability to have erections have secondary erectile dysfunction. Transient erectile dysfunction is temporary, due to fatigue, alcohol, distraction, or the like.

eros   Passionate love.

erotica   Material aimed primarily at sexually arousing a consumer. "Erotica" has a more positive connotation than "pornography."

estradiol   The most powerful of the estrogens, which are steroid hormones. See also steroid hormone.

estrus   Nonprimate female mammal's period of sexual readiness.

ethnographic studies   Anthropologists' data on the habits and conventions within other cultures.

exchange theory   The idea that marriage or other serious romantic relationships are exchanges of resources.

excision   Female circumcision, which varies in extent from the nicking of the clitoral hood to the removal of all external genitals. Compare to circumcision.

excitement phase   A stage early in the sexual response cycle during which, in males, the penis grows erect and, in females, the vagina gets wet and lengthens. See also plateau phase, sexual response cycle.

exhibitionism   Deriving sexual pleasure from exposing one's genitals to an unwilling audience.

experimental method   A research method in which investigators try to isolate biological or environmental factors that they think may determine a particular behavior and then test subjects to see if their behavior changes when such factors are present. Compare clinical method, observational method.

extragenital responses   The responses of the parts of the body other than the reproductive organs to sexual arousal.

fallopian tubes   The two narrow ducts that extend from ovaries to uterus. Fertilization of ova usually occurs in the fallopian tube. See also fimbriae.

fellatio   Oral-genital sex performed on a male.

fetal alcohol syndrome Mental retardation, widely spaced eyes, and other facial abnormalities found in children of pregnant women who have consumed large quantities of alcohol. See also teratogen.

fetishism Using an object or body part for sexual arousal. Fetishes often are used for solitary sex. Some are incorporated into social sex. See also partialism.

fetus The human organism as it develops from the third prenatal month until birth. The fetal period is the phase of growth and maturation. Compare embryo.

field study A form of observation in which a researcher studies people in natural situations (rather than in a laboratory or other contrived situation). See also observational method.

fimbriae The fringed ends of the fallopian tubes that are nearest to the ovaries. The fimbriae wave ova from the ovaries into the fallopian tubes. See also fallopian tubes.

fimbrial hood Experimental form of contraception that operates by covering the fimbriae of the ovaries, thereby preventing eggs from entering the fallopian tubes.

fisting Penetration of the anus with hand or fist.

follicle A structure produced by the ovaries that surrounds a mature ovum and when ripened releases the ovum from the ovary for fertilization. From the follicle develops the corpus luteum. See also corpus luteum, ovulation.

follicle-stimulating hormone (FSH) A hormone released by the pituitary gland. In females, FSH along with luteinizing hormone cyclically stimulate the ovaries to release an ovum. In males, the two hormones stimulate the testes to manufacture sperm. See luteinizing hormone.

follicular (proliferative) phase That part of the menstrual cycle when hormonal signals prepare an ovum to ripen and the endometrium to receive it. See also endometrium.

foreskin The covering of the glans of the penis, removed at circumcision.

formal standard Within a particular culture, an idealization of how people ought to act sexually. Compare informal standard.

fraternal twins Siblings born when two mature ova are released from the ovaries and fertilized. Fraternal twins are no more alike than any other two siblings. Compare identical twins.

frenum Triangular spot on the underside of the penis where the foreskin attaches.

frequency The statistical measure of how often a behavior occurs in a sample during some unit of time.

frottage Rubbing up against women for sexual pleasure.

fundus Top of the uterus.

gamete A sex cell such as a spermatozoon or ovum.

gang rape A rape committed by three or more assailants.

gay A male or female who voluntarily engages in homosexual acts.

gender Masculinity and femininity. See also gender identity, sex.

gender identity A person's inner conviction of maleness or femaleness that develops in the first three years of life (the core gender identity) and that consolidates at puberty (into the adult gender identity). Compare sexual identity.

gender role   The pattern of behavior considered usual for one's sex and the public expression of one's maleness or femaleness.

gender script   See scripts (sexual).

genes   Chemical units, arranged linearly on chromosomes, that carry the instructions for reproducing cells. Genes are the physical units that one generation inherits from another. See also chromosome.

genital herpes   A sexually transmitted disease generally caused by *herpes virus hominis* type 2.

genital responses   The responses of the reproductive organs to sexual arousal.

genitals   Internal and external sexual and reproductive structures.

genital sexuality   The adult sexual behavior that comes with the hormonal changes of puberty, according to Freud.

genital tubercle   Part of the rudimentary genitals common to male and female human embryos that will develop into either penis or clitoris. The other parts are the urogenital slit, urethral folds, and labio-scrotal swellings. The presence or absence of the hormone androgen will determine whether the genitals develop into, respectively, male or female form.

genital warts   Warts on genitals of either sex, caused by sexually transmitted viruses.

gentle birth   As advocated by French obstetrician Leboyer, childbirth in which the alert and responsive infant is born into a dimly lit, quiet room, allowed to lie on its mother's stomach until the umbilical cord stops pulsing, and then is bathed calmly in a warm bath. Gentle birth was thought to make infants calmer and more alert than traditional childbirth.

glans   The tip of the penis. In uncircumcised males, the glans is covered by the foreskin.

gonadal hormones   Hormones secreted by the gonads. See also gonadotropins, gonads.

gonadotropins   Hormones produced in the pituitary that stimulate the gonads to secrete their own hormones. See also gonads.

gonads   Reproductive glands. In males, the gonads are the testes. In females, they are the ovaries. See also gonadal hormones.

gonorrhea   The second most common sexually transmitted disease in the United States. Caused by the bacterium *Neisseria gonorrhea*, it may cause no symptoms, especially in females, yet it may cause infertility.

gossypol   An experimental contraceptive for men that inhibits sperm production.

G-spot   A spot on the anterior vaginal wall of some women that increases in size during sexual arousal. In some women stimulation of the spot has been reported to lead to orgasm.

guevodoces   In Spanish, literally "penis at twelve." A group of 46,XY individuals in the Dominican Republic who, because of an inherited disorder in the production of androgen, are born with female-looking external genitals but become masculinized at puberty.

gynecologist   Physician who specializes in treating female anatomy and reproductive functions.

hard-core pornography   Materials aimed at sexually arousing a consumer, often depicting sexual acts including penetration in close focus. Compare soft-core pornography.

hedonistic ethic   A system of values in which maximizing pleasure minimizing pain to all are the highest goods. Compare absolutist ethic and relativistic ethic.

historical (archival) method   A technique for researching behavior in times past.

homologous organs   Structures in males and females that develop prenatally from similar tissue. Penis and clitoris, scrotum and labia majora are examples of homologous organs.

homophobia   Intense irrational dislike of homosexual people and practices.

homosexual   Man or woman who voluntarily has sex with members of his or her own sex. See also gay, lesbian.

homosexual act   Erotic practice or feeling directed toward a member of the same sex. Compare homosexual identity.

homosexual identity   Incorporation into one's self-definition the acceptance of an erotic or romantic attraction to a person of one's sex. Compare gender identity, homosexual act.

hormones   Chemicals secreted by endocrine glands that turn on and off activities in various parts of the body. Before birth and at puberty, hormones provide environments that determine crucial steps in the creation of observable sex differences.

human chorionic gonadotropin (HCG)   A hormone secreted by the cells of a developing embryo that is detected in a pregnancy test.

hustlers (gay)   Male prostitutes who cater to gay men.

hymen   A thin membrane that may cover the opening to the vagina.

hypoactive (low) sexual desire   A condition in which people who once cared about sex have lost their sexual appetites. See also desire.

hypophallus   A markedly small penis. See also congenital microphallus.

hypospadias   In males, a condition in which the urethral opening is not at the tip of the penis but at or near the root of the penis.

hypothalamus   Part of the brain that in females signals for the cyclical production of hormones and in males signals for the noncyclic production of hormones at puberty.

hysterectomy   Surgical removal of the uterus.

hysterotomy   Surgical removal of the uterine contents, a late abortion procedure.

identical twins   Children born after a single fertilized ovum has divided into two identical cells. Identical twins are always of the same sex. Compare fraternal twins.

inbreeding   The mating of close relatives.

incentive motivation   Motivation inspired by external stimuli rather than internal states of need. Sexual motivation is largely motivated by incentives.

incest   Sex by closely related family members.

incidence   A statistical measure of how many people *ever* have behaved in a particular way. Compare frequency.

independent variable   In scientific research, some factor that researchers systematically vary in order to gauge its possible effects on a dependent measure. Compare dependent variable.

indifferent gonads   The sexual glands of human embryos of both sexes during the fifth week of prenatal development. These gonads consist of outer cells, the cortex, which can develop into female ovaries and inner cells, the medulla, which can develop into male testes.

inferential statistics Comparisons of behavior between different groups of subjects aimed at testing the probability that a difference could be replicated reliably. Compare descriptive statistics.

infertility Diagnosed when a couple has not conceived a child after one year of unprotected intercourse. Infertility may result from conditions in both males and females, many of which are curable. Compare sterility.

informal standard Within a particular culture, the expectation for how people should behave sexually that fairly closely approximates their actual behavior. Compare formal standard.

infusion cavernosography Injecting male genitals with radioactive substance to monitor blood flow. Used in diagnosing erectile dysfunction.

interview A research technique in which subjects are personally asked survey questions.

intrauterine device (IUD) Plastic or metal devices that are inserted into the uterus and that prevent pregnancy. Properly inserted, IUDs are effective forms of birth control, although some have undesirable side effects.

introitus The opening to the vagina.

inverted nipple A normal physical condition of the breasts in which the nipple turns inward rather than outward from the areola. Inverted nipples almost never interfere with functioning. See also areola, nipple.

in vitro fertilization Literally "in glass' fertilization. A technique for treating infertility in which human ova are fertilized in a laboratory dish and then reintroduced into a human female's uterus for the duration of prenatal development.

Kallmann's syndrome A disorder of males in which the hypothalamus at puberty fails to trigger the release of male hormones, preventing the development of adult male sexual characteristics.

Kegel An exercise for toning vaginal and perineal muscles. It is performed by tightening the muscles that stop the flow of urine.

kiddie porn Slang for pornography depicting children engaged in sexual acts.

labia majora (outer lips) In females, large skin folds surrounding clitoris, urethra, and vagina. Compare labia minora.

labia minora (inner lips) In females, small, inner folds of skin around the opening of the vagina. Compare labia majora.

labio-scrotal swellings Part of the rudimentary genitals common to male and female human embryos that develop into either scrotum or labia majora. The other parts are the genital tubercle, urethral folds, and urogenital slit. The presence or absence of the hormone androgen will determine whether the genitals develop into, respectively, male or female form.

lactational amenorrhea The tendency for women's fertility to be reduced when they are lactating (breast feeding). An ineffective form of birth control, however, for ovulation and pregnancy can occur during lactation.

laparoscopy   Pelvic surgery through small incisions performed to inspect—via a lighted laparoscope—and treat conditions that prevent women from conceiving or to sterilize them and prevent future pregnancies. See also tubal ligation.

laparotomy   Major abdominal surgery, previously used for tubal ligations and now replaced by laparoscopy. See also laparoscopy.

latency   A stage in late childhood when sexual development lies dormant, as postulated by Freud. Most psychologists today believe that evidence on childhood sexuality disproves the existence of latency.

lesbian   Female homosexual.

Leydig's cells   In males, the cells within the testes that produce the sex hormone testosterone. See also testosterone.

libido   Sexual energy.

lithotomy position   A position in which a woman lies on her back, with her legs spread and her feet up in stirrups, often used during childbirth and pelvic examinations.

live peeps   Slang for small booths in which customers watch a model pantomime sexual acts.

lobotomy   Surgery that cuts connections to the brain's frontal lobe, once performed on men considered sexually deviant.

lochia   A vaginal discharge of endometrial tissue and blood that follows childbirth. See also endometrium.

longitudinal study   An investigation into the behavior of a group of subjects, called a *panel,* over a long period of time.

lumbar region   The upper part of the spinal cord, which controls the ejaculation reflex. Compare sacral region.

luteal phase   The part of the menstrual cycle following ovulation, during which a fertilized egg implants in the uterine lining. If conception does not occur, the luteal phase gives way to menstruation.

luteinizing hormone (LH)   A hormone released by the pituitary gland. In females, LH along with follicle-stimulating hormone (FSH) cyclically stimulate the ovaries to release an ovum. In males, the two hormones stimulate the testes to manufacture sperm. See also follicle-stimulating hormone.

macropapular flush   See sex flush.

mammals   Warm-blooded creatures who bear live young.

mammary (milk) glands   Structures in the female breasts, made up of 15 to 20 lobes, that produce milk in response to hormones secreted after childbirth.

marital aids   Slang for sexual devices and erotic materials such as dildoes, vibrators, straps and belts, etc.

masochism   Acceptance of physical or mental pain for sexual pleasure.

median age   The age at which half of a particular group has experienced a particular behavior.

medulla   The central cells of the human embryo's indifferent gonad. These cells may develop into male testes. See also indifferent gonad.

menarche   A young woman's first menstrual period.

menopause   The end of menstrual cycling in a female.

menstruation   (menstrual phase) The part of the menstrual cycle when lowered hormone levels cause the endometrium, blood, and fluid to be shed.

menstrual phase   See menstruation.

menstrual regulation (extraction)   A vacuum aspiration of the uterus, performed up to six weeks after the beginning of the last menstrual period.

milk duct   The connection between the mammary glands and the nipple of the female's breast. See also mammary glands.

mini pill   Progestin birth-control pills.

misattribution (mislabeling)   The erroneous subjective interpretation of physical changes. For example, people may interpret nonsexual responses as sexual arousal. Compare attribution.

miscarriage   Spontaneous abortion of an embryo or fetus. Many miscarriages result from abnormalities of the embryo.

missionary position   Named after the missionaries who introduced it to the "heathens," a front-to-front (ventral-ventral) position in sexual intercourse with the male above the female.

Mittelschmerz   German for "middle pain," the discomfort some women feel when an ovum and follicle burst from an ovary at ovulation. See also ovulation.

modeling theory   A theory of pornography's effects holding that people who observe sexual acts are likely to engage in sexual acts themselves. Compare catharsis theory, null theory.

mons veneris (mound of Venus)   The triangular area at the base of a female's abdomen, covered with pubic hair after puberty, and sensitive to pressure and touch.

motility   The ability of mature sperm to swim on their own.

Mullerian ducts   Tissue that may differentiate into female uterus, fallopian tubes, and innermost vagina. The ducts are present in the human embryo during the seventh through twelfth weeks of prenatal development. Compare Wolffian ducts.

Mullerian inhibiting substance (MIS)   A hormone that stops the development of the Mullerian, or female, duct system. See also Mullerian ducts.

myotonia   Muscle tension. Myotonia increases during sexual arousal.

natural childbirth   Childbirth during which the mother is awake and alert, unmedicated, and can cooperate with her body to deliver her infant. Infants born through natural childbirth have a good chance themselves of being alert and responsive.

natural selection   According to Charles Darwin, the natural force by which individuals and species are tested for fit with their environment by their ability to reproduce and leave copies of their genes.

navel   Bellybutton; the spot where the fetus is attached to the umbilical cord and placenta. See also placenta.

necrophilia   Sex with a corpse.

neurosis   Psychological difficulty created when a significant conflict and its associated emotions are unresolved and repressed from consciousness.

neurotransmitters   Chemicals that carry signals among neurons and that may be discovered to play roles in sexual response and behavior.

nipple   The central pigmented area, made of smooth muscle, of the breasts in both males and females. Nipples have many nerve endings and may therefore be sources of pleasurable sensations. The nipple grows erect during sexual arousal. See also inverted nipple.

nocturnal penile tumescence (NPT) Erections of the penis during sleep. Used to diagnose erectile dysfunction.

nongonococcal urethritis (NGU) Inflammations of the urethra (other than gonorrhea), common in men. Some NGU is caused by *Ureaplasma urealyticum*. Also called nonspecific urethritis (NSU).

norm Social standard or rule.

null theory A theory of pornography's effects holding that pornography neither stimulates nor depresses sexual behavior. Compare catharsis theory, modeling theory.

object fetish Sexually arousing inanimate object.

observational method A technique for conducting research in which people observe and describe subjects' behavior. See also participant observation. Compare clinical method, experimental method.

Oedipal conflicts According to Freud, the central problem for individuals to resolve in the course of psychosexual development. They must resolve their hostility toward their same-sex parent for "usurping" the sexual love of their opposite-sex parent.

onanism Ejaculation outside of a woman's vagina.

orgasm The climactic, satisfying response to sexual stimulation found in males and females. In the sexual response cycle, orgasm is a reflex that follows the earlier stages of excitement and precedes the stage of resolution. See also resolution phase, sexual response cycle.

orgasmic dysfunction Sexual dysfunction in which a woman does not reach orgasm. If she has never experienced orgasm, the condition is primary orgasmic dysfunction. If she has lost the ability, the condition is secondary orgasmic dysfunction.

orgasmic platform The expansion of the outer vaginal walls during sexual arousal as they fill with blood.

osteoporosis Loss of calcium from the bones, resulting in brittle, fragile bones. Osteoporosis is most common in women following menopause and is best counteracted by weight-bearing exercise and calcium in the diet.

ovarian follicle. See follicle.

ovaries Ovum-producing glands in females. Each ovary contains up to 200,000 immature ova at a female infant's birth. The ovaries also produce sex hormones necessary for reproduction.

ovatestis An organ that contains both ovarian and testicular tissue, found in some true hermaphrodites. See also true hermaphrodites.

ovulation The process by which a ripened follicle moves to the surface of an ovary and bursts open, releasing a mature ovum. See also follicle.

oxytocin A hormone secreted by the pituitary gland that causes lactation and uterine contractions.

Pap test A painless sampling of cervical cells that detects cancerous or precancerous conditions. Pap tests are performed during a female's pelvic examination. See also pelvic examination.

panel A group of research subjects followed during a longitudinal study. See also longitudinal study.

partial androgen insensitivity A genetic disorder of 46,XY individuals, in which their bodies have only a partial ability to use androgen. At birth, their genitals are ambiguous-looking. Compare androgen insensitivity.

partialism   Fetish for small part of an animate object. See also fetishism.

participant observation   A research method in which a researcher joins the group of people under study. Some participant observers reveal their true purpose ahead of time to the group; others do not. See also observational method.

passionate love   Strong attachment and physical desire.

pedophilia   Sexual attraction to children.

peep shows   Small booths in pornographic bookstores or similar establishments where customers watch short films of hard-core pornography.

pelvic (internal) examination   An examination of a female's vagina, cervix, uterus, and rectum, performed by a medical professional.

pelvic inflammatory disease (PID)   An infection of the pelvic organs in women, due to chlamydia, gonorrhea, or other STDs. PID may cause pain, scarring, and infertility.

penis   The male organ that eliminates urine, ejaculates, and is sensitive to sexual stimulation. The penis consists of the root, at the abdominal wall, shaft, and glans. The glans contains the urinary opening and in uncircumcised males is covered by the foreskin.

performance   Psychologists' terms for that part of what a child knows offered in response to a direct question. Compare competence.

pheromones   Chemicals that act as olfactory stimuli to convey specific messages between members of the same species.

philia   The love between good friends.

phobia   An unwarranted fear that leads to the wish to avoid particular situations or objects.

pimp   A man supported by a prostitute in exchange for bail money, lawyers, and emotional support.

pituitary gland   Part of the brain that releases luteinizing hormones or follicle-stimulating hormone. At puberty, females begin releasing these hormones cyclically; males begin releasing them rather continuously.

placebo effect   The tendency for psychological beliefs to cause physical effects.

placenta   An organ that develops from fetal cells and connects the circulatory systems of mother and fetus during prenatal development. Many substances ingested by the mother cross the placental barrier.

plateau phase   A stage in the sexual response cycle during which many of the changes that began during the earlier excitement phase intensify. Plateau is a preparation for sexual climax. See excitement phase, sexual response cycle.

pleasure principle   A drive behind human behavior, hypothesized by Freud, to maximize sensual pleasure and minimize pain.

population   In research, all subjects within a given group of people. Compare sample.

pornography   Filmed, printed, or videotaped depictions of material, aimed at arousing sexual feelings. See hard-core and soft-core pornography.

positive feedback system   The enhancement of one erotic stimulus by another.

positive signs (of pregnancy)   Heartbeat, movement, and sonograms of the fetal skeleton. Compare presumptive signs, probable signs.

postpartum period   The time following childbirth when a woman undergoes the many physical and psychological changes that mark the end of pregnancy and the start of parenthood.

pre-AIDS (lymphadenopathy) syndrome   A sexually transmitted syndrome that resembles AIDS but is less severe. See also AIDS.

premature ejaculation   Sexual dysfunction in which a man ejaculates before he would like to.

premenstrual syndrome (PMS)   A mixture of uncomfortable physiological and psychological symptoms preceding menstruation.

prenatal   Before birth.

presumptive signs (of pregnancy)   Absence of menstruation, breast tenderness, frequent urination, or other early signs that lead a woman to suspect pregnancy. Compare positive signs, probable signs.

priapism   A state of chronic erection caused by irritation of the sacral region of the spinal cord. See also sacral region.

primary desire disorder   See hypoactive sexual desire.

primary deviance   A sociological term for behavior that deviates from a norm but that is not used as a basis for self-definition. Compare secondary deviance.

primary erectile dysfunction   See erectile dysfunction.

primary erotic stimuli   Stimuli that may lead to sexual arousal in the absence of prior learning or experience. Light touches are primary erotic stimuli. Compare secondary erotic stimuli.

primary orgasmic dysfunction   See orgasmic dysfunction.

primary sexual characteristics   The internal and external genitals, which develop before birth. Compare secondary sexual characteristics.

primates   The order of animals including humans, apes, and monkeys.

probability sample   Sample that matches the characteristics of a population by matching the proportion of subgroups in the sample to that of the population.

probable signs (of pregnancy)   A positive pregnancy test plus characteristic changes in the uterus and cervix. Compare positive signs, presumptive signs.

prolactin   A hormone secreted by the pituitary gland that causes lactation.

prostaglandins   Hormones contained in seminal fluid, which, when ejaculated into the vagina, make the uterus and fallopian tubes contract. Prostaglandins also have been implicated in severe menstrual cramps and in the uterine contractions of childbirth. Prostaglandins sometimes are used to induce abortion. See also dysmenorrhea, seminal fluid.

prostate gland   In males, the gland that secretes fluid that can make sperm motile. See also motility, seminal fluid.

pseudohermaphrodites   Individuals with gonads of one sex and genitals that appear to be that of the other sex. Compare adrenogenital females, true hermaphrodite.

psychoanalysis   Psychotherapy aimed at making conscious unconscious conflicts and feelings, in order to improve sexual (and other kinds of) functioning.

psychoanalytic psychotherapy   Psychotherapy modeled on the tenets of psychoanalysis.

psychopath   A person who commits antisocial acts without a sense of guilt or the inner controls to stop the acts.

puberty   Maturation of the reproductive system and secondary sexual characteristics at adolescence.

pubic lice   Tiny sexually transmitted organisms that cause itching and discomfort. They live at the roots of human hair, usually pubic hair.

questionnaire   Survey questions in written form.

quickening   The pregnant woman's earliest feelings of the fetus moving within her.

random (representative) sample   A randomly chosen subset of a population. Compare stratified sample.

rap booths   Small booths in which customers watch and talk to a person modeling sexual acts or nudity.

rape   Sexual violence committed by one (or more) person(s) against another.

rape trauma syndrome (RTS)   A cluster of symptoms found among rape victims, including fear, anxiety, guilt, shame; eating, sleeping, and sexual disorders; and changes in daily habits.

recessive gene   A gene that will not express itself if a dominant gene is present on a matching chromosome. Sex-linked disorders like colorblindness and hemophilia are carried in recessive genes. See also dominant gene.

reference group   People against whom a person judges him- or herself.

reflex   Unlearned physical response. Orgasms depend on reflexes: vasocongestion, orgasm, and (in males) ejaculation. See also orgasm, vasocongestion.

refractory phase   A stage that in males follows orgasm. Females do not necessarily have a refractory phase after orgasm. See sexual response cycle.

relativistic ethic   A system of values in which right and wrong are considered to vary with circumstances. Compare absolutist and hedonistic ethics.

releasing hormones   Hormones produced by the hypothalamus and directed to the pituitary gland.

replicability (reliability)   In scientific research, the ability of one researcher to duplicate the findings of another. Replicability is an important criterion for studies of behavior. See also validity.

resolution phase   In the sexual response cycle, the stage after orgasm when the changes begun in response to sexual excitement reverse themselves. See sexual response cycle.

retarded ejaculation   Sexual dysfunction in which a man is aroused but does not ejaculate.

Rh factor   A substance found in human blood cells. Most people have this substance and are therefore Rh positive. Those who do not have it are Rh negative. When a pregnant woman is Rh negative and her fetus is Rh positive, her blood may develop antibodies to the fetus's blood.

rhythm method   A form of birth control in which couples note on a calendar and abstain from sexual intercourse during women's cyclical fertile periods.

rite of passage   A ritualized transition from one social status to another.

role model   A person who is used as a source of learning about some social role.

root   The end of the penis at the abdominal wall.

sacral region (sacrum)   The lower part of the spinal cord, which communicates with the genital area and controls the erection reflex. Compare lumbar region.

sadism   Infliction of physical or mental pain for sexual gratification.

sadomasochism   The composite variation made up of sadism and masochism, often enacted through elaborate fantasies. See also masochism, sadism.

saline infusion   An abortion procedure used after the sixteenth week of pregnancy, in which a strong salt solution is injected into the amniotic fluid surrounding the fetus.

sample   In research, a representation of a population. The sample may be representative; chosen at random; or it may match the demographic characteristics of the total population in question. See also random sample. Compare population.

Sapphic love   Lesbianism.

satisfaction disorder   Sexual dysfunction in which people do not feel pleasure as a result of their sexual acts.

satisfaction phase   The feeling of pleasure associated with and following sexual responses. Compare desire phase.

scaled behavior   The given sequence of incrementally more intimate sexual acts that most people within a particular culture follow during social sex.

scientific method   The asking of questions and objective obtaining of data so that others can repeat the methods and reach comparable results—or refute them. The scientific method is aimed at generating new knowledge and refuting findings that cannot be reproduced. See also convergent validity, replicability.

scripts (sexual)   Proposed by Gagnon and Simon, the differing cultural rules for sexual beliefs and acts used by males and females in the course of sexual development.

scrotum   In males, the loose pouch of skin that attaches to the abdominal wall and lies behind the penis. The scrotum contains the testes. See also tunica dartos.

secondary desire disorder   See hypoactive sexual desire.

secondary deviance   Sociological term for behavior that deviates from a norm and that is used as a basis for self-definition. Compare primary deviance.

secondary erectile dysfunction   See erectile dysfunction.

secondary erotic stimuli   Learned or conditioned stimuli that strongly influence sexual motivation in adulthood. Compare primary erotic stimuli.

secondary orgasmic dysfunction   See orgasmic dysfunction.

secondary sexual characteristics   Sexual features such as pubic hair, breasts (in females), enlarged penis and scrotum (in males), that develop at puberty. Hormones cause the sexual organs to grow larger and to mature. Compare primary sexual characteristics.

self-disclosure   The revelation of oneself to another.

seminal fluid   Secretions from the seminal vesicles and prostate gland that provide medium to make sperm motile. Seminal fluid contains prostaglandins, which are hormones that make the female's uterus and fallopian tubes contract. See also prostate gland, seminal vesicles.

seminal vesicles   Structures in the male that secrete seminal fluid before ejaculation. See seminal fluid.

seminiferous tubules Tiny ducts coiled within the testes where sperm are manufactured and stored. See also epididymus, sperm.

sensate focus An exercise in focusing on the sensual pleasures afforded by all parts of the body.

sensitive period A period of development when a form of behavior occurs most readily. Compare critical period.

sensory threshold The least physical stimulus to which an individual responds.

sex Biological maleness and femaleness. See also gender.

sex chromosome See chromosome.

sex (macropapular) flush A measles-like rash that spreads across the skin during sexual arousal as blood flow increases.

sex hormones See hormone.

sex-linked disorders Inherited physical problems such as colorblindness and hemophilia that are carried on sex chromosomes.

sex stereotype A highly standardized and distorted view of gender roles. See also gender role, stereotyping.

sexual dimorphism The structural and functional differences between the sexes.

sexual dysfunction Repeated failure to enjoy sex or to share sexual enjoyment with a partner.

sexual identity A person's commitment to heterosexual, homosexual, or bisexual behavior. Compare gender identity.

sexuality All of the human feelings, attitudes, and actions that people attach to their own and others' biological sex. Sexuality partakes of psychology, biology, and sociology, in contrast to sex, which partakes only of biology. See also sex.

sexually transmitted diseases (STDs) Diseases such as gonorrhea, chlamydia, syphilis, AIDS, cystitis, nongonoccocal urethritis, trichomoniasis, and yeast infections caused by microorganisms spread from one person to another through intimate physical encounters.

sexual motivation The arrangement of one's environment so that one can approach erotic stimuli or create them in fantasy.

sexual reproduction The process by which half of the genes of two parent organisms combine to create a new organism. Sexual reproduction offers a species new genetic types that may give it a survival advantage. Human beings and higher animals and plants reproduce sexually. See also asexual reproduction, sexual selection.

sexual response cycle The sequence of physical and psychological changes that males and females undergo when they are sexually aroused. These phases include (and see separate entries for): desire, excitement, orgasm, plateau, refractory period, resolution, and satisfaction.

sexual scripts Frameworks or contexts within which people interpret sexual events. The sexual script for childhood differs from that for adolescence, and that for adolescent girls differs from that of adolescent boys.

sexual selection The nonrandom choice of a mate among animals that reproduce sexually. See also natural selection, sexual reproduction.

sexual values Social rules about sexuality that people internalize.

sexual variation Any sexual activity that a person prefers to or compulsively

substitutes for heterosexual intercourse or a sexual activity that involves unusual methods of arousal.

shaft   The part of the penis between the root and the glans. See also glans,
root.

single standard   Within a particular culture, the application of one standard
of behavior to members of both sexes. Compare double standard.

situational homosexuality   Homosexual behavior that takes place in sex-seg-
regated situations like prisons, the military, boarding schools, and the like.

69   Colloquial term for two partners engaging in oral sex at the same time.

skewing   In research, the displacing of frequencies up or down, usually from
a normal curve.

smegma   A whitish, pungent substance secreted by the clitoral hood (in females) or the glans of the penis (in males).

society   A cooperative, relatively stable, reproducing group of individuals
with organized patterns of relationships. Humans, most nonhuman primates,
and other social animals form societies. See also culture.

sodomy   Named after the sinful Biblical city of Sodom, the practice of anal
intercourse.

soft-core pornography   Depictions of nudity or sexual acts without penetration. Compare hard-core pornography.

somatotropin   A growth hormone produced by the pituitary gland of both
sexes. Somatotropin triggers the growth spurt of adolescence.

sonogram   Image derived from bouncing sound waves off an object (such as a
fetus in the womb) and used for medical diagnoses.

Spanish fly   A supposed aphrodisiac, the powdered skeleton of blister beetles.
It irritates the urogenital system. See also aphrodisiac.

spectatoring   Self-consciously watching and judging one's own sexual performance. A form of sexual dysfunction because it inhibits pleasure and sexual responsiveness.

speculum   An instrument that separates the vaginal walls and allows for examination of the vagina, cervix, and bottom of the uterus.

sperm   The male reproductive cells, which carry half of the chromosomes
necessary for reproduction.

spermatic cord   The tube within the scrotum that contains the vas deferens.
See also vas deferens.

spermatogenesis   The 18 stages of development of sperm cells, a process that
takes 70 or more days to complete.

spermicide   Chemicals that kill sperm, used to protect against pregnancy.

squeeze technique   Method for treating premature ejaculation, in which the
man's penis is squeezed under the rim of the glans just before he feels he
will ejaculate. Compare basilar squeeze technique, stop-start technique.

status orgasmus   An intense orgasm in females, lasting 20 to 60 seconds.

stereotyping   The quality of possessing an oversimplified, preconceived idea
about all individuals within a given group of people. See also sex stereotype.

sterility   The absolute inability to reproduce. Compare infertility.

steroid hormones   Hormones secreted by the gonads and the adrenal glands,
some of which influence sexual behavior. See also estradiol, gonadal hormones, testosterone.

stop-start technique   Treatment for premature ejaculation in which partner brings male to full erection. As he feels about to ejaculate, partner stops arousing him, and erection subsides. Compare squeeze technique.

storgé   The love between children, parents, and grandparents.

stratified (quota) sample   A subset of people whose demographic characteristics match those of a larger population. Compare random sample.

Sturm und Drang   German for "storm and stress," describes a view of adolescence now largely discredited in favor of one that views adolescence as a series of smoother, more gradual changes.

suction curettage   See vacuum aspiration.

superincision   Removal of the foreskin from the penis plus cutting of the shaft of the penis. See also circumcision.

supportive therapy   Psychotherapy consisting of emotional support and reassurance for people with sexual dysfunction.

survey   A research technique in which subjects are asked questions about their behavior such as whether and how often they engage in certain acts.

syphilis   A three-stage sexually transmitted disease, caused by *Treponema pallidum,* that may be fatal if untreated. Syphilis responds to treatment with penicillin and some other antibiotics.

systematic desensitization   Therapeutic technique by which people are gradually exposed to increasing amounts of an anxiety-producing situation.

taboo   A powerful prohibition within a culture. Incest, for example, is a taboo.

tearoom   (slang) A men's public toilet where men meet for fast, impersonal sex, usually fellatio.

teratogens   Substances that cause malformations of the embryo.

testes   Sperm-producing glands in males; the male gonads.

testosterone   The most powerful androgen; a steroid hormone. See also steroid hormone.

theoretical failure rate (of contraceptives)   The failure rate of a form of contraception under ideal conditions. Compare actual failure rate.

toxemia   A serious disease of pregnancy, characterized by high blood pressure, protein in the urine, and swelling.

toxic shock syndrome (TSS)   A massive infection of *Staphylococcus aureus* that can be brought on (among other ways) by wearing tampons. Children and men can also contract TSS.

transient erectile dysfunction   See erectile dysfunction.

transsexual   A person who feels trapped in the body of the wrong sex. Some transsexuals have reversed core gender identities. Transsexualism probably has more than a single cause. See also core gender identity.

transvestite   A person who dresses in the clothes of the other sex for sexual pleasure. Also known as cross-dressing.

trichomoniasis   Sexually transmitted disease, caused by the protozoan *Trichomonas vaginalis,* that afflicts more women than men.

true hermaphrodites   Individuals born with the gonads of both sexes. Compare pseudohermaphrodite.

tubal ligation   Surgery that severs the fallopian tubes and thereby sterilizes a woman. See also fallopian tubes.

tubal pregnancies   Pregnancies in which the fertilized ovum implants not in the lining of the uterus but in the fallopian tubes. Tubal pregnancies do not proceed to maturity, and often the affected fallopian tube must be surgically removed. Compare ectopic pregnancy.

tumescence Engorgement with blood. In the terminology of Havelock Ellis, tumescence was the first stage of sexual response. See also detumescence.

tunica dartos In the scrotum, the inner layer of smooth muscle that contracts during arousal, strenuous exercise, and exposure to cold. See scrotum.

Turner's syndrome A chromosome error that results in the development of a 45,XO female. External genitals look female, but the internal reproductive tract is partly or entirely missing.

undescended testicles An error of development in which the male's testes do not descend from the abdomen into the scrotum during the prenatal period.

urethra (meatus) In males and females, the pathway for urine to leave the body. In males, the ejaculatory duct, containing sperm and seminal fluid, opens into the urethra.

urethral folds Part of the rudimentary genitals common to male and female human embryos. The other parts are the genital tubercle, urogenital slit, and labio-scrotal swellings. The presence or absence of the hormone androgen will determine whether the genitals develop into, respectively, male or female form.

urogenital slit Part of the rudimentary genitals common to male and female human embryos. The other parts are the genital tubercle, urethral folds, and labio-scrotal swellings. The presence or absence of the hormone androgen will determine whether the genitals develop into, respectively, male (tissue around penile shaft) or female (labia minora) form.

urologist A doctor who specializes in treating urinary and genital tracts.

uterus The womb, a muscular organ found in females, in which a fertilized ovum matures into a fully developed infant.

vacuum aspiration A brief, simple form of abortion used early in a pregnancy. It is the most common type of abortion in the United States. Also called suction curettage.

vagina In females, a thin muscular tube that leads from the internal organs of reproduction to the outside of the body. The vaginal walls are elastic and accommodate an erect penis during intercourse and a fully developed infant during childbirth.

vaginal ring A form of contraception, worn at the cervix and containing the hormones progestin and natural estrogen. Vaginal rings may help women to avoid some of the side effects of hormones taken orally to prevent conception.

vaginismus Sexual dysfunction that consists of the reflexive tightening of vaginal muscles, preventing penetration.

vaginitis Any infection of the vagina, many of them sexually transmitted.

validity The quality of research that tests what it purports to test and a measure of objectivity. See also convergent validity.

varicocele A varicose vein in a male's spermatic vein(s) that can cause infertility. See also infertility.

vas deferens   A tube into which mature sperm move before being ejaculated. See also prostate gland, vasectomy.

vasectomy   The surgical cutting of the vasa deferentia to render a male sterile.

vasocongestion   During arousal, the reflexively increased blood flow to various parts of the body.

vernix   A whitish, pasty covering on the newborn infant made up of shed fetal cells. Vernix protects the newborn's skin in the fluid environment of the uterus.

victimless crimes   Illegal acts that hurt no one.

voyeurism   Watching people undressing or having sex, without their permission or knowledge, for the purpose of sexual pleasure.

vulva   A collective term for the external female genitals, including the mons, labia majora and minora, vaginal and urethral openings.

wet dreams   Ejaculations of seminal fluid that begin during adolescence, as androgen levels mount.

Wolffian ducts   Tissue that may differentiate into male semen-producing and delivering pathways. The ducts are present in the human embryo during the seventh through twelfth weeks of prenatal development. Compare Mullerian ducts.

Xenon-washout blood flow test   Test of blood flow to male genitals, used to diagnose erectile dysfunction. See also infusion cavernosography.

yeast infection   Vaginal infection caused by *Candida albicans*, sometimes sexually transmitted.

yohimbine   An alkaloid substance from plants that is an aphrodisiac in male rats. Its role in human sexual motivation is under investigation. See also aphrodisiac.

zona pellucida   The coating of the human ovum.

zygote   A one-celled organism that results when a sperm cell and an ovum merge.

REFERENCES

REFERENCES

Abbot, S., and Love, B. *Sappho was a right-on woman*. New York: Stein and Day, 1972.

Abel, G. G.; Blanchard, E. B.; and Becker, J. V. An integrated treatment program for rapists. In R. T. Rada (ed.), *Clinical Aspects of the Rapist*. New York: Grune and Stratton, 1978.

Abel, C. G.; Murphy, W. D.; Becker, J. V.; and Bitar, A. Women's vaginal responses during REM sleep. *Journal of Sex and Marital Therapy*, 1979, 5, 5–14.

Aberle, D. F., and Naegele, K. D. Middle class fathers' occupational role and attitudes toward children. *American Journal of Orthopsychiatry*, 1952, 22, 366–378.

Adams, D. B.; Gold, A. R.; and Burt, A. D. Rise in female-initiated sexual activity at ovulation and its suppression by oral contraceptives. *New England Journal of Medicine*, 1978, 299, 1145–1150.

Addiego, F.; Belzer, E. G., Jr.; Comolli, J.; Moger, W.; Perry, J. D.; and Whipple, B. Female ejaculation: A case study. *Journal of Sex Research*, 1981, 17, 13–21.

Ainsworth, M. D. S. The development of infant-mother interaction among the Ganda. In B. M. Foss (ed.), *Determinants of infant behavior*, Vol. 2, New York: Wiley, 1963.

Ainsworth, M. D. S.; Blehar, M.; Waters, E.; and Wall, S. *Patterns of attachment: Observations in the strange situation and at home*. Hillsdale, NJ: Erlbaum, 1978.

Alan Guttmacher Institute. *Teenage pregnancy: The problem hasn't gone away*. New York: Alan Guttmacher Institute, 1981.

Alston, J. P., and Tucker, F. The myth of sexual permissiveness. *Journal of Sex Research*, 1973, 9, 34–40.

Althers, L. *Kinflicks*. New York: New American Library, 1977.

Altman, L. K. Is the alarm over herpes excessive? New York *Times*, November 2, 1982, p. C3.

————. Clues to toxic syndrome found. *New York Times*, June 6, 1985, p. 1.

Alvarez, A. *Life after marriage: Love in an age of divorce*. New York: Simon & Schuster, 1981.

American Civil Liberties Union, *Rights of gay people*. (See E. C. Boggan, et al.)

Amir, M. *Patterns of forcible rape*. Chicago: University of Chicago Press, 1971.

Anderson, T. P., and Cole, T. M. Sexual counseling of the physically disabled. *Postgraduate Medicine*, 1975, 58, 117–123.

Angelou, M. *The heart of a woman*. New York: Random House, 1981.

Angrist, S. The study of sex roles, *Journal of Social Issues*, 1969, 25, 215–232.

————, and Almquest, C. M. *Careers and contingencies: How college women juggle with change*. New York: Dunellen, 1975.

Annon, J. S. *The behavioral treatment of sexual problems*, Vol. 1, Honolulu: Kapiolani Health Services, 1974.

APA Monitor. Onset and progress of AIDS shaped by stress factors, July 1983, 1.

Arafat, I., and Yorburg, B. On living together without marriage. *Journal of Sex Research*, 1973, 11, 997–1006.

Ard, B. N., Jr. Sex in lasting marriages: A longitudinal study. *Journal of Sex Research*, 1977, 13, 274–285.

A Reluctant Judge Concurs in Smut Ruling. New York *Times*, May 23, 1983.

Arentewicz, G., and Schmidt, G. *The treatment of sexual disorders: Concepts and techniques of couple therapy*. New York: Basic Books, 1983.

A Sexual Rite on Trial, *Newsweek*, November 1, 1982, p. 5.

Assaad, M. B. Female circumcision in Egypt: Social implications, current research, and prospects for change. *Studies in Family Planning*, January 1980, 3–16.

Athanasiou, R.; Oppel, W.; Michelson, L.; Unger, T.; and Yager, M. Psychiatric sequelae to term birth and induced early and late abortion: A longitudinal study. *Family Planning Perspectives*, 1973, 5, 227–231.

Austin, C. Bishops ask Reagan for a monitor of antipornography laws. New York *Times*. May 25, 1983.

Austin, C. R., and Short, R. V. (eds.). *Reproduction in Mammals* (5 Volumes). London: Cambridge University Press, 1972.

Ayoub, D. M.: Greenough, W. T.; and Juraska, J. M., Sex differences in dendritic structure in the preoptic area of the juvenile macaque monkey brain. *Science*, 1983, 219, 197–198.

Babcock, B. A.; Freedman, A. E.; Norton, E. H.; and Ross, S. C. *Sex discrimination and the law: Causes and remedies*. Boston: Little, Brown, 1975.

Baker, S. W. Biological influences on human sex and gender. *Signs*, 1980, 6, 80–96.

Baldwin, W., and Cain, V. S., The children of teenage parents. *Family Planning Perspectives*, 1980, 12, 34–43.

Bamberger, J. The myth of matriarchy: Why men rule in primitive society. In M. Z. Rosaldo and L. L. Lamphere (eds.), *Woman, Culture and Society*. Stanford: Stanford University Press, 1974.

Bancroft, J. *Deviant sexual behavior*. Oxford: Clarendon Press, 1974.

Bane, M. J. *Here to stay*. New York: Basic Books, 1976.

Barbach, L. *For yourself: The fulfillment of female sexuality*. Garden City: Doubleday, 1975.

Bardin, C. W., and Catterall, J. F. Testosterone: A major determinant of extragenital sexual dimorphism. *Science*, 1981, 211, 1285–1294.

Barlow, D.; Abel, G. G.; and Blanchard, E. B. Gender identity change in a transsexual: An exorcism. *Archives of Sexual Behavior*, 1977, 6, 387–395.

Barlow, D. H.; Reynolds, E. J.; and Agras, W. J. Gender identity change in a transsexual. *Archives of General Psychiatry*, 1973, 28, 569–579.

————; Sakheim, D. K.; and Beck, J. G., Anxiety increases sexual arousal, *Journal of Abnormal Psychology*, 1983, 92, 49–54.

————, and Wincze, J. P., Treatment of sexual deviations. In S. Lieblum and L. Pervin (eds.), *Principles and practice of sex therapy*. New York: Guilford Press, 1980.

Bart, P. B. A study of women who both were raped and avoided rape. *Journal of Social Issues*, 1981, 37, 123–137.

————, and O'Brien, P. H. Stopping rape: Effective avoidance strategies. *Signs*, 1984, 10, 83–101.

Bartell, G. *Group sex*. New York: Wyden, 1971.

Baruch, G.; Barnett, R.; and Rivers, C. *Lifeprints: New patterns of love and work for today's women*. New York: McGraw-Hill, 1983.

Bates, J. E.; Skilbeck, W. M.; Smith, K. U. R.; and Bentler, P. M. Intervention with families of gender-disturbed boys. *Amer-*

ican Journal of Orthopsychiatry, 1975, *45,* 150–157.

Baum, M. J.; Koos, S. A.; DeJong, F. H.; and Westbrock, D. C. Persistence of sexual behavior in ovariectomized stumptail macaques following dexamethasone treatment or adrenalectomy. *Hormones and Behavior,* 1978, *11,* 323–347.

Bauman, K. Volunteer bias in a study of sexual knowledge, attitudes, and behavior. *Journal of Marriage and the Family,* 1973, *35,* 27–31.

Bauman, K. E., and Wilson, R. R. Sexual behavior of unmarried university students in 1968 and 1972. *Journal of Sex Research,* 1974, *10,* 327–333.

Bayer, R. *Homosexuality and American psychiatry: The politics of diagnosis,* New York: Basic Books, 1981.

Beach, F. A. Characteristics of masculine "sex drive." In M. Jones (ed.), *Nebraska Symposium on Motivation.* Lincoln: University of Nebraska Press, 1956.

——— (ed.). *Sex and behavior.* New York: Wiley, 1965.

———. Human sexuality and evolution. In W. Montagna and W. A. Sadler (eds.), *Reproductive Behavior.* New York: Plenum Press, 1974.

———. Cross-species comparisons and the human heritage. *Archives of Sexual Behavior,* 1976, *5,* 469–486.

———. Cross-species comparisons and human heritage. In F. A. Beach (ed.) *Human Sexuality in Four Perspectives,* Baltimore: Johns Hopkins University Press, 1977.

———. Editorial preface to Chapter 7. In F. A. Beach (Ed.), *Human Sexuality in Four Perspectives.* Baltimore: Johns Hopkins Press, 1977a.

——— (ed.). *Human Sexuality in Four Perspectives.* Baltimore: Johns Hopkins Press, 1977b.

Beck, J. G., and Barlow, D. H., Current conceptualizations of sexual dysfunction: A review and an alternative perspective. *Clinical Psychology Reviews,* 1984, *4,* 363–378.

Becker, D., Creutzfeldt, O. D.; Schwibbe, M., and Wuttke, W., Changes in physiological, EEG and psychological parameters in women during the spontaneous menstrual cycle and following oral contraceptives. *Psychoneuroendocrinology,* 1982, *7,* 75–90.

Bell, A. P. Homosexualities: Their range and character. In J. K. Cole and R. Dienstbier (eds.), *Nebraska Symposium on Motivation, 1973.* Lincoln: University of Nebraska Press, 1974.

———; **Weinberg, M. S.; and Hammersmith, S. K.,** *Sexual preference: Its development in men and women.* Bloomington: Indiana University Press, 1981.

———, ———. *Homosexualities: A study of diversity among men and women.* New York: Simon & Schuster, 1978.

Bell, R., et al. *Changing bodies, changing lives: A book for teens on sexual relationships.* New York: Random House, 1980.

Bell, R. R. Changing aspects of marital sexuality. In S. Gordon and R. W. Libby (eds.), *Sexuality Today and Tomorrow.* North Scituate, MA: Duxbury, 1976.

———, **and Bell, P. C.** Sexual satisfaction among married women. *Medical Aspects of Human Sexuality,* December 1972, *6,* 136–144.

———, **and Chaskes, J. B.** Premarital sexual experience among coeds, 1958 and 1968. *Journal of Marriage and the Family,* 1970, *32,* 81–84.

———, **and Peltz, D.** Extramarital sex among women. *Medical Aspects of Human Sexuality.* March 1974, *8,* 10ff.

———; **Turner, S.; and Rosen, L.** A multivariate analysis of female extramarital coitus. *Journal of Marriage and the Family,* 1975, *37,* 375–384.

Bellinger, D. C., and Gleason, J. B. Sex differences in parental directives to young children. *Sex Roles,* 1982, *8,* 1123–1140.

Belliveau, F., and Richter, L. *Understanding Human Sexual Inadequacy.* Boston: Little, Brown, 1970 (paperbound ed., New York: Bantam, 1970).

Belzer, E. G. Jr.; Whipple, B.; and Moger, W. On female ejaculation. *Journal of Sex Research,* 1984, *20,* 403–406.

Bem, S. L. Androgeny and gender schema theory: Conceptual and empirical integration. In T. B. Sondereggery (ed.), *Nebraska Symposium on Motivation: Psychology and Gender.* Lincoln: University of Nebraska Press, 1984.

———, Gender schema theory: A cognitive account of sex typing. *Psychological Review,* 1981, *88,* 354–364.

Benkert, O. Clinical studies on the effects of neurohormones on sexual behavior. In M. Sandler and G. L. Gessa (eds.), *Sexual Behavior: Pharmacology and Biochemistry.* New York: Raven Press, 1975.

Bennets, L. Teen-age pregnancies: Profiles in ignorance. New York *Times,* December 20, 1981, p. 57.

Bentler, P. M. Heterosexual behavior assessment—I. Males. *Behavior Research and Therapy,* 1968, *6,* 21–25. (a).

———. Heterosexual behavior assessment—II. Females. *Behavior Research and Therapy,* 1968, *6,* 27–30. (b).

———. A note on the treatment of adolescent sex problems. *Journal of Child Psychology and Psychiatry,* 1968, *9,* 125–129. (c)

———. A typology of transsexualism: Gender identity theory and data. *Archives of Sexual Behavior,* 1976, *5,* 567–584.

Berger, C.; Gold, D.; Andeir, D.; Gillet, P.; and Kinch, R. Repeat abortion: Is it a problem? *Family Planning Perspectives,* 1984, *16,* 70–75.

Berger, R. M. *Gay and gray: The older homosexual man.* Urbana, Ill.: University of Illinois Press, 1982.

Bergquist, D. C.; Nillius, S. J.; and Wide, L., Endometrial patterns in women on chronic LHRL agonist treatment for contraception. *Fertility and Sterility,* 1981, *36,* 339–343.

———. Long-term intranasal luteinizing hormone-releasing hormone (LHRH) agonist treatment for contraception in women. *Fertility and Sterility,* 1982, *38,* 190–198.

Berkowitz, L. Some effects of thoughts on anti- and prosocial influences of media events: A cognitive-neoassociation analysis. *Psychological Bulletin,* 1984, *95,* 410–427.

Berlin, F. S., and Meinicke, C. F. Treatment of sex offenders with antiandrogenic medication, conceptualizations, review of treatment modalities and preliminary findings. *American Journal of Psychiatry,* 1981, *138,* 601–607.

Bermant, G., and Davidson, J. *Biological bases of sexual behavior.* New York: Harper & Row, 1974.

Bernstein, A. C. *The flight of the stork.* New York: Delacorte, 1978.

———, **and Cowan, P. A.,** Children's concepts of how people get babies. *Child Development,* 1975, *46,* 77–91.

Berscheid, E., and Walster, E. A little bit about love. In T. L. Huston (ed.), *Foundations of interpersonal attraction.* New York: Academic Press, 1974.

———, ———; **and Bohrnstedt, G.** The

body image report. *Psychology Today,* 1973, 7, 119–131.

Bieber, I. Sexual arousal mechanisms in male homosexuals. In M. Sandler and G. L. Gessa (eds.), *Sexual behavior: Pharmacology and biochemistry.* New York: Raven Press, 1975.

———. A discussion of "Homosexuality: The ethical challenge." *Journal of Consulting and Clinical Psychology,* 1976, 44, 163–166.

Bieber, I.; Dain, H. J.; Dince, P. R.; Drellich, M. G.; Grand, H. G.; Gundlach, R. H.; Kremer, M. W.; Rifkin, A. H.; Wilbur, C. B.; and Bieber, T. B. *Homosexuality.* New York: Vintage Books, 1962.

Bienen, L. Rape IV, *Women's Rights Law Reporter Supplement,* Summer, 1980, 6, #3.

Bischof, N. The biological foundations of the incest taboo. *Social Science Information,* 1972, 11, 7–36.

———. The comparative ethology of incest avoidance. In R. Fox (ed.), *Biosocial anthropology.* New York: Halsted, 1975.

Bixler, R. H. Sibling incest in the royal families of Egypt, Peru, and Hawaii. *Journal of Sex Research,* 1982, 18, 264–281.

Black, K. N. and Stevenson, M. R. The relationship of self-reported sex role characteristics and attitudes toward homosexuality. *Journal of Homosexuality,* 1984, 10, 83–93.

Blackstone, Sir W. *Commentaries on the laws of England.* Boston: Beacon, 1962 (original: 1813).

Blackwood, E. Sexuality and gender in certain native American tribes: The case of cross-gender females. *Signs,* 1984, 10, 27–42.

Blaine, W. L., and Bishop, J. *Practical guide for the unmarried couple.* New York: Sun River Press, 1976.

Blake, J. Can we believe recent data on birth expectations in the United States? *Demography,* 1974, 11, 25–44.

Blakely, M. K. Is one woman's sexuality another woman's pornography? *Ms.,* April 1985, 37ff.

Block, J. H. Issues, problems, and pitfalls in assessing sex differences: A critical review of *The Psychology of Sex Differences. Merrill-Palmer Quarterly,* 1976, 22, 283–308.

Blumstein, P. W., and Schwartz, P. Bisexuality in women. *Archives of Sexual Behavior,* 1976, 5, 171–181.

———. *American couples: Money, work, sex.* New York: Morrow, 1983.

Blurton-Jones, N. (ed.). Comparative Aspects of Mother-Child Contact. *Ethological*

studies of child behavior. Cambridge, England: Cambridge University Press, 1972.

Boggan, E. C.; Haft, M. G.; Lister, C.; and Rupp, J. P. *The rights of gay people.* New York: Avon, 1983.

Bohlen, J. G. "Female ejaculation" and urinary stress incontinence. *Journal of Sex Research,* 1982, 18, 360–368.

———; Held, J. P.; and Sanderson, M. O. The male orgasm: Pelvic contractions measured by anal probe. *Archives of Sexual Behavior,* 1980, 9, 503–521.

———; ———; and Sanderson, M. O. Response of the circumvaginal musculature during masturbation: In B. Graber (ed.), *The circumvaginal musculature and sexual function.* Basel: Karger, 1982. (a)

———; ———; ———; and Abigreu, A., The female orgasm: Pelvic contractions. *Archives of Sexual Behavior,* 1982, 5, 367–386.

———; ———; ———; and Boyer, C. M., Development of a woman's multiple orgasm: A research case report. *Journal of Sex Research,* 1982, 18, 130–145.

Bolles, R. C., Endorphins and behavior. *Annual Review of Psychology.* 1982, 33, 87–101.

Bongaarts, J. Building a family: Unplanned events. *Studies in Family Planning,* 1984, 15, 14–19.

Borgaonkar, D. S., and Shah, S. A. The XYY Chromosome Male Syndrome? In A. G. Steinberg and A. G. Bearn (eds.), *Progress in Medical Genetics. (vol. 10),* New York: Grune and Stratton, 1974.

Bossard, J. H. S. Residential propinquity as a factor in mate selection. *American Journal of Sociology,* 1932, 38, 219–224.

Boswell, J. *Christianity, social tolerance and homosexuality.* Chicago: University of Chicago Press, 1980.

Bosworth, P. Let's call it suicide. *Vanity Fair,* March, 1985, 52ff.

Bouhoutsos, J. Sexual intimacy between therapists and patients. Paper at American Psychological Association, Los Angeles, CA, August 1981.

Bowlby, J. *Maternal care and mental health.* World Health Organization Monograph 2. Geneva: World Health Organization, 1951.

Brecher, E. M. *The sex researchers.* Boston: Little, Brown, 1969 (paperbound ed., New York: Signet, 1971).

———. Prevention of sexually transmitted diseases. *Journal of Sex Research,* 1975, 11, 318–328.

———, and the editors of *Consumer Reports. Love, sex, and aging.* Boston: Little, Brown, 1984.

Bretschneider, J., and McCoy, N. Sexual attitudes and behavior among healthy 80-102-year olds. Paper read at Sixth World Congress of Sexology, Washington, D.C., May 22–27, 1983.

Brim, O. G., Jr., and Ryff, C. D. On the properties of life events. In P. B. Baltes and O. G. Brim, Jr., *Life-span development and behavior.* Vol. 3. New York: Academic Press, 1980.

Brockner, J., and Swap, W. C. Effects of repeated exposure and attitudinal similarity on self-disclosure and interpersonal attraction. *Journal of Personality and Social Psychology,* 1976, 33, 531–540.

Brody, J. How drugs can cause decreased sexuality. New York *Times,* September 28, 1983, p. C1.ff.

———. Major study dispels fears of possible harm in vasectomy. New York *Times,* November 15, 1983, C1.

———. "Autoerotic" death of youths causes widening concern. New York *Times,* March 27, 1984, C1, 3.

———. Infection linked to sex surpasses gonorrhea. New York *Times,* June 5, 1984, p. C1.

Bronowski, J. *The ascent of man.* Boston: Little, Brown. 1974.

Broude, G. J., and Green, S. J. Cross cultural codes on twenty sexual attitudes and practices. *Ethology,* 1976, 15, 409–429.

Brown, H. *Familiar faces: Hidden lives: The story of homosexual men in America today.* New York: Harcourt Brace Jovanovich, 1976.

Brown, J. A comparative study of deviations from sexual mores. *American Sociological Review,* 1952, 17, 135–146.

Brown, R. *Social Psychology.* New York: Free Press, 1965.

Brown, W. A.; Bholchain, M.; and Harris, T., Social class and psychiatric disturbances among women in an urban population. *Sociology,* 1975, 9, 225–254.

Brown, W. A.; Monti, P. M.; and Corriveau, D. P. Serum testosterone and sexual activity and interest in men. *Archives of Sexual Behavior.* 1978, 7, 97–103.

Brownmiller, S. *Against our will: Men, women and rape.* New York: Simon and Schuster, 1975 (paperbound ed., New York: Bantam Books, 1976).

————. *Femininity.* New York: Simon and Schuster (Linden Press), 1984.

Broznan, N. Sexuality of the disabled. New York *Times,* May 6, 1980, p. B18.

Bryan, J. H., Occupational ideologies and individual attitudes of callgirls, *Social Problems,* 1966, *13,* 441–450.

Bryden, M. P. Evidence for sex-related differences in cerebral organization. In M. A. Wittig and A. C. Petersen, *Sex-related differences in cognitive functioning.* New York: Academic Press, 1979.

Buffery, A. and Gray, J. Sex differences in the development of perceptual and linguistic skills. In C. Ounsted and D. Taylor (Eds.). *Gender differences: their autogeny and significance.* London: Churchill, 1972.

Buhrich, N.; Armstrong, M. S., and McConaghy, N., Bisexual feelings and opposite-sex behavior in male Malaysian medical students. *Archives of Sexual Behavior.* 1982, *5,* 387–392.

Burgess, A. W.; Groth, A. N.; Holmstrom, L. L.; and Sgroi, S. M. *Sexual assault of children and adolescents.* Lexington, MA: Lexington Books, 1978.

————, and Hazelwood, R. R. Autoerotic asphyxial deaths: A social network response. *American Journal of Orthopsychiatry,* 1983, *53,* 166–170.

————, and Holmstrom, L. L. Rape trauma syndrome. *American Journal* of Psychiatry, 1974, *131,* 981–986(a).

————. *Rape: Victims of crisis.* Bowie, MD: R. J. Brady Co., 1974.(b)

Burnell, G., and Norfleet, M. Women who place their infant for adoption: A field study. *Parent Counseling and Health Education,* 1979, *1,* 169–172.

Burt, M. R. Cultural myths and supports for rape. *Journal of Personality and Social Psychology,* 1980, *38,* 17–230.

Bush, D. Fertility-related state laws enacted in 1982. *Family Planning Perspectives,* 1983, *15,* 111–116.

Bussey, K., and Perry, D. G., Same-sex imitation: The avoidance of cross-sex models or the acceptance of same-sex models? *Sex Roles,* 1982, *8,* 773–784.

Butterfield, Fox, *China,* New York Times Books, 1982.

Byerly, G., and Rubin, R. *Pornography: The conflict over sexually explicit materials in the U.S.,* New York: Garland, 1980.

Byrne, D. *The attraction paradigm.* New York: Academic Press, 1971.

————. Social psychology and the study of sexual behavior. *Personality and Social Psychology Bulletin,* 1977, *3,* 3–30.

————. Sex without contraception. In D. Byrne and W. A. Fisher (eds.), *Adolescents, sex and contraception.* Hillsdale, NJ: Erlbaum, 1983.

————, and Baron, R. A., *Social psychology: Understanding human interaction.* 4th ed. Boston: Allyn and Bacon, 1984.

————, and Fisher, W. A. (eds.) *Adolescents, sex, and contraception.* Hillsdale, NJ: Erlbaum, 1983.

Cairns, D. E. Talking about sex: Notes on first coitus and the double sexual standard. *Journal of Marriage and the Family,* 1973, *35,* 677–688.

Cairns, R. B. *Social development: The origins and plasticity of interchanges.* San Francisco: Freeman, 1979.

Calderone, M. S., and Johnson, E. W. *The family book about sexuality,* New York: Harper & Row, 1981.

Calderwood, D. *About your sexuality. Course materials for a sex education curriculum for junior high schoolers.* Boston: Unitarian Universalist Association, 1971.

Caldwell, M. A., and Peplau, L. A. Sex differences in same-sex friendship. *Sex Roles,* 1982, *8,* 721–732.

Calhoun, L.; Selby, J.; Cann, A.; and Keller, G. T. The effects of victim's physical attractiveness and sex of respondents on social reactions to victims of rape. *British Journal of Social and Clinical Psychology,* 1978, *17,* 191–192.

————; ————; and King, H. E. The influence of pregnancy on sexuality: A review of the current literature. *Journal of Sex Research,* 1981, *17,* 139–151.

Califia, P. Feminism and sado-masochism. *Heresies,* 1981, *3,* 30–34.

Callahan, S., and Callahan, D. (eds.). *Abortion: Understanding Differences.* New York: Plenum, 1984.

Caplan, P. J.; MacPherson, J. M.; and Tobin, P. Do sex-related differences in spatial abilities exist? *American Psychologist,* 1985, *40,* 786–799.

Carrera, M. *Sex: The facts, the acts, and your feelings.* New York: Crown, 1981.

Carrera, M. A., and Calderone, M. S. Training of health professionals in education for sex health. *SIECUS Report,* March 1976, *4,* 1–2.

Carrier, J. M. Sex-role preference as an explanatory variable in homosexual behavior. *Archives of Sexual Behavior.* 1977, *6,* 53–66.

Casper, R. F.; Yen, S. S. C.; and Wilkes, M. M. Menopausal flushes and the pulsatile release of luteinizing hormone. *Science,* 1979, *205,* 823–825.

Cates, W. Jr. Legal abortion: The public health record. *Science,* 1982, *215,* 1586–1590.

Catholics, protestants agree: Make abortion, contraception widely available. *Family Planning Perspectives,* 1980, *12,* 53.

Catterall, R. D. Biological effects of sexual freedom. *The Lancet,* February 7, 1981, 351A.

Centers, R. The completion hypothesis and the compensatory dynamic of intersexual attraction and love. *Journal of Psychology,* 1972, *82,* 111–126.

Chaiken, S. Heuristic versus systematic information processing and the use of source versus message cues in persuasion. *Journal of Personality and Social Psychology,* 1980, *39,* 752–766.

Chalker, R. Your body, your sex life. *Playgirl.* June 1982, 95–98.

Chambers, K. C., and Phoenix, C. H. Sexual behavior in old male rhesus monkeys: Influence of familiarity and age of female partners. *Archives of Sexual Behavior,* 1982, *11,* 299–308.

Chambless, D. L.; Stern, T.; Sultan, F. E.; Williams, A. J.; Goldstein, A. J.; Lineberger, M. H.; Lifshetz, J. L.; and Kelly, L. The pubococcygeus and female orgasm: A correlational study with normal subjects. *Archives of Sexual Behavior,* 1982, *11,* 479–490.

Chandler, P. T. Neurogenic impotence. *Medical Aspects of Human Sexuality,* June 1983, *17,* 142ff.

Chappell, D.; Geis, R.; and Geis, G. *Forcible rape.* New York: Columbia University Press, 1977.

Chevalier-Skolnikoff, S. Male-female, female-female, and male-male sexual behavior in the stumptail monkey, with special attention to the female orgasm. *Archives of Sexual Behavior,* 1974, *3,* 95–116.

Chilman, C. S. *Adolescent sexuality in a changing American society: Psychological perspectives for the human service professions.* New York: Wiley Interscience, 1983.

Christenson, H. T., and Gregg, C. F. Changing sex norms in America and Scandinavia. *Journal of Marriage and the Family*, 1970, *32*, 616–627.

Christenson, L. W., and Gorski, R. A. Independent masculinization of neuroendocrine systems by intercerebral implants of testosterone or estradiol in the neonatal female rat. *Brain Research*, 1978, *146*, 325–340.

Claiborne, C. *A feast made for laughter: A memoir with recipes*. Garden City, NY: Doubleday, 1982.

Clark, A. L., and Wallin, P. Women's sexual responsiveness and the duration and quality of their marriages. In W. W. Wagner (ed.), *Perspectives on human sexuality*. New York: Behavior Publications, Inc. 1974.

Clark, J. T.; Smith, E. R.; and Davidson, J. M. Enhancement of sexual motivation in male rats, *Science*, 1984, *224*, 847–849.

Clark, M. S., and Mills, J. Interpersonal attraction in exchange and communal relationships. *Journal of Personality and Social Psychology*, 1979, *37*, 12–24.

Clarke, A. M., and Clarke, A. D. B. *Early experience: Myth and evidence*. New York: Free Press, 1977.

Clarke-Stewart, K. A. Observation and experiment: Complementary strategies for studying day care and social development. In S. Kilwer (ed.), *Advances in early education and day care*, (Vol. 2). Greenwich, CT: JAI Press, 1981.

Clarkson, T. B., and Alexander, N. J. Long-term vasectomy: Effects on the occurrence and extent of atherosclerosis in rhesus monkeys. *Journal of Clinical Investigation*, 1980, *65*, 15.

Clement, U., and Pfafflin, F. Changes in personality scores among couples subsequent to sex therapy. *Archives of Sexual Behavior*, 1980, *9*, 235–244.

Clement, U.; Schmidt, G.; and Kruse, M. Changes in sex differences in sexual behavior: A replication of a study on West German students (1966–1981). *Archives of Sexual Behavior*, 1984, *13*, 99–120.

Clifford, R. Development of masturbation in college women. *Archives of Sexual Behavior*, 1978, 7, 559–573.(a)

———. Subjective sexual experience in college women. *Archives of Sexual Behavior*. 1978, 7, 183–197.(b)

Coburn, J. S & M. *New Times*, February 4, 1977, 42.

Cohen, H. D.; Rosen, R. C.; and Goldstein, L. Electro-encephalographic lateral-ity changes during human sexual orgasm. *Archives of Sexual Behavior*, 1976, 5, 189–199.

Cohen, M. L.; Garofalo, R.; Boucher, R.; and Seghorn, T. The psychology of rapists. *Seminars in Psychiatry*, 1971, *3*, 307–327.

Coleman, E. M.; Hoon, P. W.; and Hoon, E. F. Arousability and sexual satisfaction in lesbian and heterosexual women. *Journal for Sex Research*, 1983, *19*, 58–73.

Coleman, R. P., and Rainwater, L. *Social Standing in America*. New York: Basic Books, 1978.

Collins, G. Child sexual abuse prevalent. New York *Times*, February 2, 1983, C1.

———. New Studies on "Girl Toys and Boy Toys," New York *Times*, February 13, 1984.

Comfort, A. *The anxiety makers*. New York: Dell, 1969.

———. *The joy of sex*. New York: Simon and Schuster, 1972.

———. *More Joy*. New York: Crown Publishers, 1973.

Commission on Obscenity and Pornography. *The Report of the Commission on Obscenity and Pornography*. New York: Random House, 1970 (paperbound ed., New York: Bantam Books, 1970).

Condry, J., and Condry, S. Sex differences: A study of the eye of the beholder. *Child Development*, 1976, *47*, 812–819.

Conn, J. H. Children's reactions to the discovery of genital differences. *American Journal of Orthopsychiatry*, 1940, *10*, 747–755.

Conn, J. H., and Kanner, L. Children's awareness of sex differences. *Journal of Child Psychiatry*, 1947, *1*, 3–57.

Constantine, L., and Constantine, J. *Group Marriage*. New York: Macmillan, 1973.

———, and Martinson, F. M. *Children and sex: New findings, new perspectives*. Boston: Little, Brown, 1981.

Consumer Reports, Condoms, 1979, *44*, 538–539.

Cook, M., and Howells, D. (eds.) *Adult sexual interest in children*. New York: Academic Press, 1981.

Cook, M., and McHenry, R. *Sexual attraction*, New York: Pergamon, 1978.

Cooke, R. Gonorrhea vaccine being tested. Boston *Globe*, August 12, 1982, p. 3.

Coombs, R. H., and Kenkel, W. F. Sex differences in dating aspirations and satisfaction with computer-selected partners. *Journal of Marriage and the Family*. 1966, *28*, 62–66.

Cooper, P. J. (ed.) Better Homes and Garden's woman's health and medical guide. Meredith Corp., 1981.

Corey, L.; Knox, S. R.; Perkins, R. L.; Boble, R. C.; Lee, R. Y.; and Dans, P. E. Countering the epidemic of sexually transmitted diseases: A call to action. *Journal of Infectious Diseases*, March 1982, *145*, 422–426.

Corzine, J. and Kirby, R. Cruising the truckers: Sexual encounters in a highway rest area. *Urban Life*, July 1977, *6*, 171–192.

Court, J. H. Contemporary pornography as a contributor to sexual offenses against women. In M. P. Safer, M. S. Mednick, D. Izraeli, and J. Bernard, *Women's worlds: The new scholarship*. New York: Praeger, 1985.

Cowell, C. A., M.D. The gynecologic examination of infants, children, and young adolescents. In A. Cowell (Ed.), *The pediatric clinics of North America, Symposium on pediatric and adolescent gynecology, Vol. 28*, No. 2, May 1981. Philadelphia: W. B. Saunders, 1981, 247–266.

Cozby, D. C. Self-disclosure, reciprocity, and liking, *Sociometry*, 1972, *35*, 151–160.

Cramer, D. W.; Schiff, I.; Schoenbaum, S. C.; Gibson, M.; Belisle, S.; Albrecht, B.; Stillman, R. J.; Berger, M. J.; Wilson, E.; Stadel, B. V.; Seibel, M. Tubal infertility and the intrauterine device. *New England Journal of Medicine*, 1985, *312*, 941–947.

Crepault, C., and Couture, M. Men's erotic fantasies. *Archives of Sexual Behavior*, 1980, *9*, 565–581.

Croughan, J. L.; Saghir, M.; Cohen, R.; and Robins, E. A comparison of treated and untreated male cross-dressers. *Archives of Sexual Behavior*, 1981, *10*, 15–528.

Curran, J. P. Convergence toward a single sexual standard? *Social Behavior and Personality*, 1975, *3*, 89–195.

———. The social psychology of sexual behavior. In K. Deaux and L. Wrightsman, *Social psychology in the 1980's*, 4th ed. Belmont, CA: Brooks, Coole, 1984.

———; Neff, S.; and Lippold, S. Correlates of sexual experience among college students. *Journal of Sex Research*, 1973, *9*, 124–131.

Daley, B. S., and Koppenaal, G. S. The treatment of women in short-term women's groups. In S. H. Budman (ed.), *Forms of brief therapy*, New York: Guilford, 1981.

Daling, J. R.; Weiss, N. S.; Metch, B. J.;

Chow, W. H.; Saderstrom, R. M.; Moore, D. E.; Spadoni, L. R.; and Stadel, B. V. Primary tubal infertility in relation to the use of an intrauterine device. *New England Journal of Medicine,* 1985, *312,* 937–941.

Dan, A. J.; Graham, E. A.; Beecher, C. P. (eds.). *The menstruation cycle, Vols. 1 and 2,* New York: Springer, 1980; 1981.

D'Andrade, R. G. Sex differences and cultural institutions. In E. E. Maccoby (ed.), *The development of sex differences.* Stanford, CA: Stanford University Press, 1966.

Daniels, P., and Weingarten, K. *Sooner or later: The timing of parenthood in adult lives.* New York: Norton, 1983.

Davenport, W. Sexual patterns and their regulation in a society of the Southwest Pacific. In F. A. Beach (ed.), *Sex and behavior.* New York: Wiley, 1965.

———. Sex in cross-cultural perspective. In F. A. Beach (ed.), *Human sexuality in four perspectives.* Baltimore: Johns Hopkins Press, 1977.

David, H. P., and Matejeck, Z. Children born to women denied abortion. *Family Planning Perspectives,* 1981, *13,* 32–34.

Davidson, J. M. The psychology of sexual experience. In J. M. Davidson and R. J. Davidson (eds.), *The psychobiology of consciousness.* New York: Plenum, 1980.

———; Camargo, C. A.; and Smith, E. R. Effects of androgen on sexual behavior in hypogonadal men. *Journal of Clinical Endocrinology and Metabolism.* 1979, *48,* 955–958.

———; Chen, J. J.; Crapo, L.; Gray, G. D.; Greenleaf, W. J.; and Catania, J.A., Hormonal changes and sexual function in aging men. *Journal of Clinical Endocrinology and Metabolism,* 1983, *57,* 71–77.

Davis, A. J. Sexual assault in the Philadelphia prisons and sheriff's vans. *Trans-action,* 1968, *6,* 8–17.

Davis, J. A. General social surveys, 1972–1980; *Cumulative Data.* Chicago: NORC, 1980. New Haven, Conn.: Yale University, Roper Public Opinion Research Center.

Davis, J. D. Self-disclosure in an acquaintance exercise: Responsibility for level of intimacy. *Journal of Personality and Social Psychology,* 1976, *33,* 87–792.

Davis, M. S. *Smut: Erotic reality/obscene ideology.* Chicago: University of Chicago Press, 1983.

Davison, G. C. Homosexuality: The ethi-cal challenge. *Journal of Consulting and Clinical Psychology,* 1976, *44,* 157–162.

Degler, C. What ought to be and what was: Women's sexuality in the nineteenth century. *American Historical Review,* 1974, *79,* 1467–1490.

———. *At odds: Women and the family in America from the revolution to the present,* New York: Oxford University Press, 1980.

De Jong, W., and Anabile, T. M. Rape and physical attractiveness: Judgments concerning the likelihood of victimization. Paper presented at the American Psychological Association, New York, September 1979.

De Lamater, J., and Mac Corquodale, P. *Premarital sexuality.* Madison: University of Wisconsin Press. 1979.

Delaney, J.; Lupton, M. J.; and Toth, E. *The curse: A cultural history of menstruation.* New York: Dutton, 1976.

Delph, E. W. *The silent community: Public homosexual encounters.* Beverly Hills, CA: Sage. 1978.

Denney, N. W.; Field, J. K.; and Quadagno, D. Sex differences in sexual needs and desires. *Archives of Sexual Behavior.* 1984, *13,* 233–246.

'Depo-Provera' Inquiry, *The Lancet,* 1983, #8328, 833–834.

Derlega, V. J., and Chaikin, A. L. Norms affecting self-disclosure in men and women. *Journal of Consulting and Clinical Psychology,* 1976, *44,* 376–380.

Derogatis, L., and Meyer, J. K. A psychological profile of the sexual dysfunctions. *Archives of Sexual Behavior,* 1979, *8,* 201–224.

Dershowitz, A. The psychiatrist's power in civil commitment: A knife that cuts both ways. *Psychology Today,* February, 1969, *43,* 47.

———. *The best defense.* New York: Random House, 1982.

DeRougemont, D. *Love in the western world.* New York: Harcourt Brace Jovanovich, 1940.

Dewolfe, D. J., and Livingston, C. A. Sexual therapy for a woman with cerebral palsy: A case analysis, *Journal of Sex Research,* 1982, *18,* 253–263.

Deykin, E. G.; Campbell, L.; and Patti, P. The post-adoption experience of surrendering parents. *American Journal of Orthopsychiatry.* 1984, *54,* 271–280.

Diamond, J. Pornography and repression: A reconsideration. *Signs,* 1980, *5,*(4), 686–701.

Diamond, M. Monozygotic twins reared in discordant sex roles and the BBC follow up. *Archives of Sexual Behavior.* 1982, *11,* 181–186.

———; Diamond, A. P.; and Mast, M. Visual sensitivity and sexual arousal levels during the menstrual cycle. *Journal of Nervous and Mental Diseases,* 1972, *155,* 170–176.

Dion, K.; Berscheid, E.; and Walster, E. What is beautiful is good. *Journal of Personality and Social Psychology,* 1972, *24,* 285–290.

Dixon, J. K. The commencement of bisexual activity in swinging married women over age thirty. *Journal of Sex Research.* 1984, *20,* 71–90.

Djerassi, C. *The politics of contraception,* New York: W. W. Norton, 1979.

Doering, C. H.; Brodie, H. K. H.; Kraemer, H.; Becker, H.; and Hamburg, D. A. Plasma testosterone levels and psychologic measures in men over a 2-month period. In R. C. Friedman, R. M. Richart, and R. Van de Wiele, *Sex differences in behavior.* New York: Wiley, 1974.

Donnerstein, E., and Berkowitz, L. Victim reaction in aggressive erotic films as a factor in violence against women. *Journal of Personality and Social Psychology.* 1981, *41,* 710–724.

———; Donnerstein, M.; and Evans, R. Erotic stimuli and aggression: Facilitation or inhibition. *Journal of Personality and Social Psychology,* 1975, *32,* 237–244.

———, and Linz, D. Sexual violence in the media: A warning. *Psychology Today,* January 1984, 14ff.

Donovan, J. Empowering the victims of impotence. *San Francisco Chronicle,* March 14, 1985, 21ff.

Dörner, G.; Rohde, W.; Stahl, F.; Krell, L.; and Masius, W. G. A neuroendocrine predisposition for homosexuality in men. *Archives of Sexual Behavior,* 1975, *90,* 1316–1318.

Doty, R. L.; Ford, M.; Preti, G.; and Huggins, G. R. Changes in the intensity and pleasantness of human vaginal odors during the menstrual cycle. *Science,* 1975, *190,* 1316–1318.

Douvan, E., and Adelson, J. *The adolescent experience.* New York: Wiley, 1966.

Downs, A. C., and Langlois, J. H. Differential sex-typed socialization by mothers, fathers, and peers: Impact on young children's subsequent sex-typed behaviors. Biannual Meeting of the Society for Research in Child Development, Boston, April 1981.

Driscoll, R.; Davis, K. E.; and Lipetz, M. E. Parental interference and romantic love: The Romeo and Juliet effect. *Journal of Personality and Social Psychology*, 1974, *30*, 510–517.

Dutton, D. G., and Aron, A. P. Some evidence for heightened sexual attraction under conditions of high anxiety. *Journal of Personality and Social Psychology*, 1974, *30*, 510–517.

Dweck, C. S., and Bush, E. S. Sex differences in learned helplessness: I. Differential debilitation with peer and adult evaluation. *Developmental Psychology*, 1976, *12*, 147–156.

———, and Goetz, F. E. Attributions and learned helplessness. In J. H. Harvey, W. Ickes, and R. F. Kidd (eds.), *New directions in attribution research*, vol. 2. Hillsdale, NJ: Erlbaum, 1977.

Dworkin, A. *Pornography: Men possessing women.* New York: Perigee Books, 1981.

Dye, N. S. History of childbirth in America. *Signs*, 1980, *6*, 97–108.

Eagly, A. H. Analysis of social roles and social influences: The Case of gender roles. Division 8 Presidential address, American Psychological Association, Los Angeles, August 1981.

Edwards, J. N., and Booth, A. Sexual behavior in and out of marriage: An assessment of correlates. *Journal of Marriage and Family*, 1976, *38*, 73–81.

Ehrhardt, A. A., and Baker, S. W. Fetal androgens, human central nervous system differentiation, and behavioral sex differences. In R. C. Friedman, R. M. Richart, and R. Van de Wiele (eds.), *Sex Differences in Behavior.* New York: Wiley, 1974.

———; Evers, K.; and Money, J. Influence of androgen on some aspects of sexually dimorphic behavior in women with the late-treated adrenogenital syndrome. *Johns Hopkins Medical Journal*, 1968, *123*, 115–122.

———; Ince, S. E.; and Meyer-Bahlburg, H. F. L. Career aspiration and gender role development in young girls. *Archives of Sexual Behavior.* 1981, *10*, 279–297.

———; Meyer-Bahlburg, H. F. L.; Feldman, J. F.; and Ince, S. E. Sex-dimorphic behavior in childhood subsequent to prenatal exposure to exogenous progestogens and estrogens. *Archives of Sexual Behavior.* 1984, *13*, 457–477.

Ehrmann, W. *Premarital dating behavior.* New York: Holt, 1959.

Eisenberg, C., and Eisenberg, L. On making it at college. Annual meeting of the American Academy of Pediatrics, New York, November 9, 1977.

Elder, G. Appearance and education in marriage mobility. *American Sociological Review.* 1969, *34*, 519–533.

Elias, J., and Gebhard, P. Sexuality and sexual learning in childhood. *Phi Delta Kappa*, 1969, *50*, 401–405.

Ellis, H. *Studies in the psychology of sex.* New York: Random House, 1906.

Engelhardt, H. T. Jr. The disease of masturbation: Values and concept of disease. *Bulletin of the History of Medicine*, 1974, *48*, 234–248.

Englehardt, L. S. II, *Living together: What's the law?* New York: Crown/Herbert Michelman, 1981.

English, D. The politics of porn: Can feminists walk the line? *Mother Jones*, April 1980.

———. Feminism and pornography. Speech sponsored by the Center for Research on Women, Stanford University, Stanford, CA: April 1983.

———; Hollibaugh, A.; and Rubin, G. Talking sex: A conversation on sexuality and feminism. *Socialist Review*, 1981, *58*, 43–62.

Epidemiologic Aspects of the Current Outbreak of Kaposi's Sarcoma and Opportunistic Infections. Special Report, Centers for Disease Control Task Force in Kaposi's Sarcoma and Opportunistic Infections. *New England Journal of Medicine*, 1982, *306*, 248–252.

Erikson, E. H. *Identity and the life cycle.* New ed. New York: Norton, 1980.

Erikson, K. T. *Wayward puritans.* New York: Wiley, 1966.

Evans, M. C., and Wilson, M. Friendship choices of university women students. *Educational and Psychological Measurements*, 1949, *9*, 307–312.

Evans, R. B. Childhood parental relationships of homosexual men. *Journal of Counseling and Clinical Psychology*, 1969, *33*, 129–135.

Everaerd, W.; Dekker, J.; Dronkers, J.; Van der Rhee, K.; Staffelen, J.; and Wiselius, G. Treatment of homosexual and heterosexual sexual dysfunction in male-only groups of mixed sexual orientation. *Archives of Sexual Behavior.* 1982, *11*, 1–10.

Everitt, B. J., and Herbert, J. Adrenal glands and sexual receptivity in female rhesus monkeys. *Nature*, 1969, *222*, 1065–1066.

Eysenck, H. J., and Nias, D. K. *Sex, violence and the media.* New York: Harper, 1978.

Ezekiel, E. Harping on herpes. *New Republic.* Sept. 13, 1982, 14–15.

Falik, M. *Ideology and abortion policy politics.* New York: Praeger, 1983.

Farkas, G. M.; Sine, L. F.; and Evans, J. M. Personality, sexuality and demographic differences between volunteers and non-volunteers for a laboratory study of male sexual behavior. *Archives of Sexual Behavior.* 1978, *7*, 513–520.

Farnsworth, N. R.; Bingel, A. S.; Cordell, G. A.; Crane, F. A.; and Fong, H. H. S. Potential value of plants as sources of new antifertility agents I. *Journal of Pharmaceutical Sciences*, 1975, *64*, 535–598. (a)

———. Potential value of plants as sources of new antifertility agents II. *Journal of Pharmaceutical Sciences*, 1975, *64*, 717–754. (b)

Farrell, W. *The liberated man.* New York: Random House, 1975.

Fast, J., and Wells, H. *Bisexual living.* Philadelphia: Lippincott, 1975.

Fasteau, M. *The male machine.* New York: McGraw-Hill, 1974.

Faust, M. S. Developmental maturity as a determinant in prestige of adolescent girls. *Child Development*, 1960, *31*, 173–184.

F. C. C. opens inquiry on "Sex Talk" phone service. *New York Times*, September 11, 1983.

F. C. C. takes a look at an issue of sex. *New York Times*, December 15, 1983, p. A25.

Federman, D. D. *Abnormal sexual development: A genetic and endocrine approach to differential diagnosis.* Philadelphia: Saunders, 1967.

Feild, H. S., and Bienen, L. B. *Jurors and rape,* Lexington, MA: D.C. Heath, 1980.

Fein, G.; Johnson, D.; Kosson, N.; Stork, L.; and Wasserman, L. Sex stereotypes and preferences in the toy choices of 20-month-old boys and girls. *Developmental Psychology*, 1975, *11*, 527–528.

Feinbloom, D. H. *Transvestites and transsexuals: Mixed views.* New York: Delacorte Press/Seymour Lawrence, 1976.

Feldman-Summers, S., and Lidner, K. Perceptions of victims and defendants in criminal assault cases. *Criminal Justice and Behavior*, 1976, *3*, 135–149.

Felman, Y. F. Risk of gonorrhea. *Medical Aspects of Human Sexuality*, November 1982.

Fenton, J. A., and Lifchez, A. S. *The*

fertility handbook. New York: Clarkson N. Potter, Inc. 1980.

Ferber, A. S.; Tietze, C.; and Lewit, S. Men with vasectomies: A study of medical, sexual, and psychosocial changes. *Psychosomatic Medicine,* 1967, *29,* 354–365.

Festinger, L.; Schachter, S.; and Back, K. *Social pressures in informal groups: A study of human factors in housing.* New York: Harper, 1950.

Filene, P. G. *Him/Her/Self: Sex roles in modern America.* New York: Harcourt Brace Jovanovich, 1974.

Fimmara, N. J. Unusual Sites for Venereal Infections. *Medical Aspects of Human Sexuality,* February 1984.

Finch, B. E., and Green, H. *Contraception through the ages.* London: Peter Owen, 1963.

Finger, F. W. Changes in sex practices and beliefs of male college students over 30 years. *Journal of Sex Research,* 1975, *11,* 304–317.

Finkelhor, D. *Sexually victimized children.* New York: Free Press, 1979.

———. Sex among siblings: A survey on prevalence, variety, and effects. *Archives of Sexual Behavior,* 1980, *9,* 171–197.

———. Child sexual abuse in a sample of Boston families. Paper presented to the Symposium on Family and Sexuality. Minneapolis, MN: April 1982.

———. What parents tell their children about child sexual abuse. Paper presented to the American Psychological Association. Anaheim, CA: August, 1983.

———. *Child sexual abuse.* New York: Free Press, 1984.

Fisher, C.; Cohen, H. D.; Schiair, R. C.; Davis, D.; Furman, G.; Ward, K.; Edwards, A.; and Cunningham, J. Patterns of female sexual arousal during sleep and waking: Vaginal thermo-conductance studies. *Archives of Sexual Behavior.* 1983, *12,* 97–122.

Fisher, S. *The female orgasm.* New York: Basic Books, 1973.

Fisher, W. A.; Branscomb, N. R.; and Lemery, C. R. The bigger the better? Arousal and attributional responses to erotic stimuli that depict different size penises. *Journal of Sex Research,* 1983, *19,* 377–396.

Fiske, M. Changing hierarchies of commitment in adulthood. In N.J. Smelser and E.H. Erikson (eds.) *Themes of work and love in adulthood.* Cambridge, MA: Harvard University Press, 1980.

Fisk, M. Gender dysphoria syndrome (The how, what, and why of a disease). In D. R. Laub and P. Gandy (eds.), *Proceedings of the Second Interdisciplinary Symposium on Gender Dysphoria Syndrome,* Stanford, CA: Stanford University Press, 1973.

Fitzgerald, R., and Fuller, L. I hear you knocking but you can't come in! The effects of reluctant respondents and refusers on a sample survey estimates. *Sociological Methods and Research,* 1982, 11, 3–32.

Fleming, K., and Fleming, A. T. *The first time.* New York: Simon & Schuster, 1975 (paperbound ed., New York: Berkeley Medallion, 1976).

Fletcher, J. *Situation ethics: The new morality.* Philadelphia: Westminster (paperback). 1966.

Ford, C. S., and Beach, F. A. *Patterns of sexual behavior.* New York: Harper & Row, 1951 (paperbound ed., New York: Harper Colophon, 1972).

Forrest, J. D., and Henshaw, S. K. Contraception in America, *Family Planning Perspectives,* 1983, *15,* 154–156. (a)

———. "What U.S. women think and do about contraception." *Family Planning Perspectives,* 1983, *15,* 157–166. (b)

Forest, M. G.; Saez, J. M.; and Bertrand, J. Assessment of gonadal function in childhood. *Paediatrician,* 1973, *2,* 102–128.

Foucault, M. *The history of sexuality, Vol. I, An introduction.* New York: Vintage, 1980.

Fox, R. *The red lamp of incest.* New York: Dutton, 1980.

Fox, C. A.; Ismail, A. A. A.; Love, D. N.; Kirkham, K. E.; and Loraine, J. Studies on the relationship between plasma testosterone levels and human sexual activity. *Journal of Endocrinology,* 1972, *52,* 51–58.

Fraiberg, S. *Every child's birthright: In defense of mothering.* New York: Basic Books, 1977.

Frank, E.; Anderson, C.; and Rubenstein, D. Frequency of sexual dysfunction in normal couples. *New England Journal of Medicine,* 1978, *299,* 111–115.

Frank, G. *The Boston strangler.* New York: New American Library, 1966.

Freeman, D. *Margaret Mead and Samoa: The making and unmaking of an anthropological myth.* Cambridge, MA: Harvard University Press, 1983.

Freeman, E. W. Abortion—subjective attitudes and feelings. *Family Planning Perspectives,* 1978, *10,* 150–155.

Freeman, Michael D. A. "But if you can't rape your wife, who[m] can you rape?": The Marital Rape Exemption Re-examined. *Family Law Quarterly,* 1981, *15,* 1–29.

Freese, M. P., and Levitt, E. E. Relationships among intra-vaginal pressure, orgasmic function, parity factors, and urinary leakage. *Archives of Sexual Behavior.* 1984, *13,* 261–268.

Freud, S. *Three essays on the theory of sexuality.* (J. Strachey, Ed.). New York: Avon Books, 1972. (Originally published, 1905.)

———. *Totem und Tabu.* Vienna: Hugo Heller, 1913 (Translated by J. Strachey, *Totem and taboo).* New York: Norton, 1952.

———. *Civilization and its discontents.* In Standard Edition, Vol. 21. London: Hogarth Press, 1927, 1961. (First German edition, 1930.)

Freund, D.; Scher, H.; and Hucher, S. The courtship disorders: A further investigation. *Archives of Sexual Behavior.* 1984, *13,* 133–140.

Fried, J. J. *Vasectomy.* New York: Pyramid Books, 1974.

Friedman, R. C.; Richart, R. M.; and Van de Wiele, R. (Eds.). *Sex differences in behavior.* New York: Wiley, 1974.

Friendly, J. New Bedford gang rape case. New York *Times,* April 25, 1984.

Fritz, G. S.; Skoll, K.; and Wagner, N. A. Comparison of males and females who were sexually molested as children. *Journal of Sex and Marital Therapy,* 1981, *7,* 54–59.

Gager, N., and Schurr, C. *Sexual assault: Confronting rape in America.* New York: Grossett and Dunlap, 1976.

Gagnon, J. H. Female child victims of sex offenses. *Social Problems,* 1965, *13,* 176–192.

———. Scripts and the coordination of sexual conduct. In J. K. Cole and R. Dienstbier (eds.), *Nebraska Symposium on Motivation 1973.* Lincoln: University of Nebraska Press, 1974.

——— (Ed.). *Human sexuality in today's world.* Boston: Little, Brown, 1977.

———; Keller, S.; Lawson, B.; Miller, P.; Simon, W.; and Huter, J. Report on the American Sociological Association's task group on homosexuality. *American Sociological Review,* 1982, *17,* 164–180.

———, and Simon, W. (Eds.). *The sexual scene.* Chicago: Transaction, 1970.

———. *Sexual conduct: The social sources of human sexuality.* Chicago: Aldine, 1973 (a).

———. Youth, sex, and the future. In A.

Gottlieb (Ed.) *Youth in contemporary society.* Beverly Hills, CA: Sage, 1973 (b).

Gajdusek, C. The Muniri and Simbari (Kuku Kuku People) of New Guinea. Abstracts of the American Pediatric Society Seventh Annual Meeting, 1964.

Ganong, W. F. *Review of medical physiology* (5th ed.). Los Altos, CA: Lange, 1971.

Gantt, P. A., and McDonough, P. G. Adolescent dysmenorrhea. In A. Karen Kreutner (ed.), *The Pediatric clinics of North America, Symposium on pediatric and adolescent gynecology.* Vol. 28, No. 2. Philadelphia: W. B. Saunders, May 1981, 389ff.

Garrison, H. H. Gender differences in the career aspirations of recent cohorts of high school seniors. *Social Problems,* 1979, 27, 170–185.

Gebhard, P. H. Factors in marital orgasm. *Journal of Social Issues,* 1966, 22, 88–95.

————. Post-marital coitus among widows and divorcees. In Bohannan, P. (ed.), *Divorce and after.* Garden City, NY: Doubleday, 1970.

————. Human sexual behavior: A summary statement. In D. S. Marshall and R. C. Suggs (eds.), *Human sexual behavior.* Englewood Cliffs, NJ: Prentice Hall, 1971.

————. Sex differences in sexual response. *Archives of Sexual Behavior,* 1973, 2, 201–203.

————; Gagnon, J. H.; Pomeroy, W. B.; and Christenson, C. V. *Sex offenders.* New York: Harper & Row, 1965 (paperbound ed., New York: Bantam Books, 1967).

————, and Johnson, A. B. *The Kinsey data: Marginal tabulations of the 1938–1963 interviews conducted by the Institute for Sex Research.* Philadelphia: Saunders, 1979.

Geer, J.; Morokoff, P.; and Greenwood, P. Sexual arousal in women: The development of a measurement device for vaginal blood volume. *Archives of Sexual Behavior,* 1974, 3, 559–564.

Geis, G. *Not the law's business? An examination of homosexuality, abortion, prostitution, narcotics, and gambling in the United States.* National Institute of Mental Health, 1972. Government Publications Office Publication 72–9132.

Gelman, R., and Gallistel, C. R. *The child's understanding of number.* Cambridge, MA: Harvard University Press, 1978.

Gemme, R., and Wheeler, C. C. (Eds.) *Progress in sexology.* New York: Plenum, 1976.

Gerbner, G., and Signorielli, N. The world according to television. *American Demographics,* 1982, 4, 15–17.

Giambra, L. M., and Martin, C. E. Sexual daydreams and quantitative aspects of sexual activity: Some relations for males across adulthood. *Archives of Sexual Behavior.* 1977, 6, 497–505.

Giarrusso, R.; Johnson, P.; Goodchilds, J.; and Zellman, G. Adolescents' cues and signals: Sex and assault. Paper read at Western Psychological Association, San Diego, CA, April 1979.

Gibson, G. G. *By her own admission: A lesbian mother's fight to keep her son.* Garden City, NY: Doubleday, 1977.

Gillespie, Oscar, *Herpes: What to do when you have it.* New York: Grosset and Dunlap, 1982.

Gilmartin, B. G., and Kusisto, D. V. Some personal and social characteristics of matesharing swingers. In R. W. Libby and R. N. Whitehurst (eds.), *Renovating marriage: Toward new sexual life styles.* Danville, CA: Consensus, 1973.

Gittelson, N. Sexual delight: How to keep it alive in your marriage, *McCall's,* August 1980, 20ff.

Gittelson, N. L.; Eacott, S. E.; and Mehta, B. M. Victims of indecent exposure. *British Journal of Psychiatry,* 1978, 132, 61–66.

Gladue, B. A.; Green, R.; and Hellman, R. E. Neuroendocrine response to estrogen and sexual orientation. *Science,* 1985, 225, 1496–1499.

Glass, S. P., and Wright, T. L. The relationship of extramarital sex, length of marriage, and sex differences on marital satisfaction and romanticism: Athanasiou's data reanalyzed. *Journal of Marriage and the Family,* 1977, 32, 3–41.

Glassman, M. B., and Ross, J. A. Two determinants of fertility decline: A test of competing models. *Studies in Family Planning,* 1978, 9, 193–197.

Glenn, N. D. The contribution of marriage to psychological well-being of males and females and the family. *Journal of Marriage and the Family,* 1975, 37, 594–601.

Glick, I. D., and Bennett, S. E. Psychiatric effects of progesterone and oral contraceptives. In R. I. Shader (ed.), *Psychiatric complications of medical drugs.* New York: Raven Press, 1972.

Globe Spotlight Team, The pornography industry, Boston *Globe,* February 13, 1983.

Gloger-Tippelt, G. A process model of the pregnancy course. *Human Development,* 1983, 26, 134–148.

Goldberg, D. C.; Whipple, G.; Fishkin, R. D.; Waxman, H.; Fink, P. J.; and Weisberg, M. The Grafenberg spot and female ejaculation: A review of initial hypotheses. *Journal of Sex and Marital Therapy.* 1983, 9, 27–37.

Goldman, R., and Goldman, J. *Children's sexual thinking: A comparative study of children aged 5 to 15 Years in Australia, North America, Britain, and Sweden.* London: Routledge and Kegan Paul, 1982.

Goldstein, M. J., and Kant, H. S. *Pornography and sexual deviance,* Berkeley: University of California Press, 1973.

Goleman, D. Sexual fantasies: What are their hidden meanings? *New York Times,* February 28, 1984, p.C1, 7.

Gondonneau, J.; Nironer, L.; Dourlin-Rollier, A. M.; and Simon, P. *Rapport Sur le Comportement Sexuel des Français.* Paris: Pierre Charronet Rene Juillard, 1972.

Gonsiorek, J. C. Review of *Homosexuality in Perspective. Journal of Homosexuality,* 1981, 6, 81–88.

Goode, E. *Deviant behavior.* Englewood Cliffs, NJ: Prentice-Hall, 1978.

————, and Troiden, R. R. Correlates and accompaniments of promiscuous sex among male homosexuals. *Psychiatry,* 1980, 43, 51–59.

Goode, W. J. A theory of role strain. *American Sociological Review.* 1960, 25, 483–496.

————. *The family,* 2nd. ed. Englewood Cliffs, NJ: Prentice-Hall, 1982.

Goodman, E. Gays fighting a new stigma. *Boston Globe.* July 7, 1983.

————. The turmoil of teenage sexuality. *Ms,* July 1983, 37ff.

Gordon, J. W., and Ruddle, F. H. Mammalian gonadal determination and gametogenesis. *Science,* 1981, 24, 1265–1271.

Gordon, L. *Woman's body, Woman's right,* New York: Penguin, 1977.

————. When good girls become bad girls. Incest and sexual delinquency: Notes from an historical study of family violence. Bunting Colloquium, Radcliffe College, Cambridge, MA: December 13, 1983.

————, and DuBois, E. Seeking ecstacy on the battlefield: Danger and pleasure in nineteenth-century feminist sexual thought, *Feminist Studies,* 1983, 9, 7–26.

Gordon, S., and Scales, P. Preparing to-day's youth for tomorrow's family, Address at Conference for Youth, University of Vermont, Summer 1977.

Gorzynski, G., and Katz, J. L. The polycystic ovary syndrome: Psychosexual correlates. *Archives of Sexual Behavior,* 1977, *6,* 215–222.

Gouax, C. Induced affective states and interpersonal attraction. *Journal of Personality and Social Psychology.* 1972, *24,* 53–58.

Gould, R. E. What we don't know about homosexuality. *New York Times Magazine,* February 24, 1974.

Goy, R. W., and Goldfoot, D. A. Neuroerdocrinology: Animal models and problems of human sexuality. *Archives of Sexual Behavior.* 1975, *4,* 405–420.

————, and McEwen, B. S. *Sexual differentiation of the brain.* Cambridge, MA: MIT Press, 1980.

————, and Phoenix, C. H. The effects of testosterone propionate administered before birth on the development of behavior in genetic female rhesus monkeys. In C. Sawyer and R. Gorski (eds.), *Steroid hormones and brain function.* Berkeley: University of California Press, 1971.

Graber, B. *The circumvaginal musculature and sexual function.* New York: S. Karger, 1982.

Grady, W. R.; Hersh, M. B.; Keen, N.; and Vaughan, B. Contraceptive failure and continuation among married women in the United States, 1970–1975. *Studies in Family Planning,* 1983, *14,* no. 1.

Grafenberg, C. C. The role of urethra in female orgasm. *International Journal of Sexology,* 1950, *3,* 145–148.

Grass, G. *Cat and mouse.* New York: New American Library, 1964.

Gray, S. H. Exposure to pornography and aggression toward women. *Social Problems,* 1982, *29,* 387–389.

Green, R. (ed.) *Human sexuality: A health practitioner's text,* Baltimore: Williams & Wilkins, 1974.

————. *Sexual identity conflict in children.* New York: Basic Books, 1974 (paperbound ed., Baltimore: Penguin Books, 1975).

————. The behaviorally feminine male child: Pretranssexual? Pretransvestic? Prehomosexual? Preheterosexual? In R. C. Friedman, R. M. Richart, and R. Van de Wiele (eds.), *Sex differences in behavior.* New York: Wiley, 1974.

————. The significance of feminine behavior in boys. *Journal of Child Psychology and Psychiatry,* 1975, *16,* 341–344.

————. One hundred ten feminine and masculine boys: Behavioral contrasts and demographic similarities. *Archives of Sexual Behavior,* 1976, *5,* 425–446.

————. "The sissy boy syndrome" and the development of homosexuality: A 15-year prospective study. New Haven, CT.: Yale University Press, 1986.

————, and Fuller, M. Family doll play and female identity in preadolescent males. *American Journal of Orthopsychiatry,* 1973, *43,* 123–127.

————, and Money, J. (Eds.). *Transsexualism and sex reassignment.* Baltimore: Johns Hopkins Press, 1969.

————; Williams, K.; and Goodman, M. Ninety-nine "tomboys" and "non-tomboys": Behavioral contrasts and demographic similarities. *Archives of Sexual Behavior,* 1982, *11,* 247–266.

Greif, E. B. A study of role-playing in preschool children. Ph.D. Thesis, Johns Hopkins University. 1973, #73–28, 401, Dissertation Abstracts.

————. Sex differences in parent-child conversations. *Women's Studies International Quarterly,* 1980, *3,* 253–258.

————; Alvarez, M.; and Ulman, K. Recognizing emotions in other people: Sex differences in socialization. Society for Research in Child Development. Boston, April 1981.

————, and Ulman, K. J. The psychological impact of menarche on early adolescent females: A review of the literature. *Child Development,* 1982, *53,* 1413–1430.

Grellert, E. A.; Newcomb, M. D.; and Bentler, P. M. Childhood play activities of male and female homosexuals and heterosexuals. *Archives of Sexual Behavior,* 1982, *11,* 451–478.

Griffin, S. Feminism and pornography. Speech sponsored by the Center for Research on Women, Stanford University, Stanford, CA, April, 1983.

————. Rape: The all American crime. *Ramparts,* September 26, 1971, 35ff.

————. *Pornography and silence.* New York: Harper Colophon, 1982.

Griffith, P. D.; Merry, J.; Browning, M.; Eisingerr, A. J.; Huntsman, R. G.; Lord, E. J. A.; Polani, P. E.; Tanner, J. M.; and Whitehouse, R. H. Homosexual women: An endocrine and psychological study. *Journal of Endocrinology,* 1974, *63,* 549–556.

Griffitt, W. Environmental effects on interpersonal affective behavior: Ambient effective temperature and attraction. *Journal of Personality and Social Psychology,* 1970, *15,* 240–244.

Grimes, D. A., and Cates, W. Jr. Deaths from paracervical anesthesia used for first-trimester abortion, 1972–1975. *New England Journal of Medicine,* 1976, *295,* or 1397 397–1399.

————. *Second-trimester abortion.* In G. S. Berger, W. E. Brenner, and L. Keith (eds.), *Second Trimester Abortion: Perspectives After a Decade of Experience.* Littleton, MA: PSG, 1981.

————; Schulz, K. F.; Cates, W. Jr.; and Tyler, C. W. Jr., Mid-trimester abortion by dilation and evacuation: A safe and practical alternative. *New England Journal of Medicine,* 1977, *296,* 1141–1145.

Grossman, A.; Moult, P. J. A.; McIntyre, H.; Evans, J.; Silverstone, T.; Reese, L. H.; and Besser, G. M. Opiate mediation of amenorrhoea in hyperprolactinaemia and in weight-loss related amenorrhoea. *Clinical Endocrinology,* 1982, *17,* 379–388.

Groth, A. N. *Men who rape: The psychology of the offender.* New York: Plenum, 1979.

————, and Burgess, *Sexual assault of children and adolescents.* Lexington: Lexington Books, 1978.

Grubb, G. Centers for Disease Control, DHHS, Personal Communication, 1983. Cited in J. Forrest and S. Henshaw, Contraception in America, *Family Planning Perspectives,* 1983, *15,* 156.

Grudzinskas, J. G., and Atkinson, L. Sexual function during the puerperium. *Archives of Sexual Behavior,* 1984, *13,* 85–91.

Gully, K. J.; Pepping, M.; Dengerink, H. A. Gender differences in third-party reports of violence. *Journal of Marriage and Family,* 1982, *44,* 497–498.

Gurland, B. J., and Gurland, R. V. Methods of research with sex and aging. In R. Green and J. Wiener (eds.), *Methodology in sex research.* National Institute of Mental Health. 1980.

Gutek, B. A., and Nakamura, C. G. Gender roles and sexuality in the world of work. In E. R. Allgeier and M. B. Mc-

Cormick (eds.), *Changing boundaries: Gender roles and sexual behavior.* Palo Alto, CA: Mayfield, 1983.

Guttentag, M., and Bray, H. *Undoing sex stereotypes: Research and resources for education.* New York: McGraw Hill, 1976.

———, and Longfellow, C. Children's social attributions: Development and change. In *Nebraska Symposium of Motivation, Vol. 25.* Lincoln: University of Nebraska Press, 1977.

Guyon, R. Sex life and sex ethics. London: John Lane, 1933.

Gysler, M. Toxic shock syndrome—a synopsis. In C. A. Crowell (ed.), *The Pediatric Clinics of North America, Vol. 28,* no. 2, (May). Philadelphia: W. B. Saunders, 1981.

Hall, J. A. Gender differences in nonverbal communication skills. *New Directions for Methodology of Social and Behavioral Science,* 1980, *5,* 63–77.

Hallström, T. Sexuality of women in middle age: The Göteborg study. *Journal of Biosocial Science Supplement,* 1979, *6,* 165–175.

Halverson, H. Genital and sphincter behavior of the male infant. *Journal of Genetic Psychology,* 1940, *56,* 5–136.

Hamburg, B. A.; Kraemer, H. C.; and Jahnke, W. A hierarchy of drug use in adolescence: Behavioral and attitudinal correlates of substantial drug use. *American Journal of Psychiatry,* 1975, *132,* 1155–1163.

Handsfield, H. H. Sexually transmitted diseases:. *Hospital Practice,* January 1982, 99–116.

Hardy, K. R. An appetational theory of sexual motivation. *Psychological Review,* 1964, *71,* 1–18.

Hariton, E. B. The sexual fantasies of women. *Psychology Today,* 1976, *6,* 39–44.

———, and Singer, J. Women's fantasies during sexual intercourse. *Journal of Comparative and Physiological Psychology,* 1974, *42,* 313–322.

Harlow, H. F. The development of the affectional patterns in infant monkeys. In B. M. Foss (ed.), *Determinants of infant behavior,* Vol. 1. New York: Wiley, 1961.

———. *Learning to love.* New York: Ballantine, 1971.

Harrison's Principles of Internal Medicine, 10th ed. K. J. Isselbacher, R. D. Adams, E.

Braunwald, R. G. Petersdorf, and J. D. Wilson, eds. New York: McGraw-Hill, 1983.

Hart, B. L. Gonadal androgen and sociosexual behavior of male mammals: A comparative analysis. *Psychological Bulletin,* 1974, *81,* 383–400. (a)

———. The medial preoptic anterior hypothalamic area and sociosexual behavior of male dogs: A comparative neuropsychological analysis. *Journal of Comparative Physiology and Psychology,* 1974, *68,* 328–249. (b)

Hart, B. L., and Haugen, C. M. Activation of sexual reflexes in male rats by spinal implantation of testosterone. *Physiology and Behavior,* 1968, *3,* 735–738.

Haseltine, F. P., and Ohns, S. Mechanisms of gonadal deafferentiation, *Science,* 1981, *211,* 1272–1277.

Hass, A. *Teen-age sexuality: A survey of teenage sexual behavior.* New York: Macmillan, 1979.

Hatcher, R. A.; Stewart, G. K.; Stewart, F.; Guest, F.; Josephs, N.; Dale, J. *Contraceptive technology 1912–1983* (Eleventh revised ed.) New York: Irvington Publishing, 1982.

Hatfield, E.; Greenberger, D.; Traumann, J.; and Lamber, P. Equity and sexual satisfaction in recently married couples. *Journal of Sex Research,* 1982, *18,* 18–32.

Hawthorne, Nathaniel, *The scarlet letter, and other tales of the puritans.* Boston: Houghton-Mifflin. 1961.

Heath, D. An investigation into the origins of a copious vaginal discharge during intercourse: "Enough to Wet the Bed." *Journal of Sex Research,* 1984, *20,* 194–215.

Heath, R. G. Pleasure and brain activity in man. *Journal of Nervous and Mental Disease,* 1972, *154,* 3–18.

Heider, K. G. *The Dugum Dani: A Papuan culture in the highlands of West New Guinea.* Chicago: Aldine, 1970.

———. Dani sexuality: A low energy system. *Man,* 1976, *11,* 188–201.

Heim, N., and Hursch, C. J. Castration for sex offenders: Treatment or punishment?: A review and critique of recent European literature. *Archives of Sexual Behavior,* 1979, *8,* 281–303.

Heiman, J. R. Uses of psycho-physiology in the assessment and treatment of sexual dysfunction. In J. Lo Piccolo, and L. Lo Piccolo (eds.), *Handbook of sex therapy.* New York: Plenum Press, 1978.

Heise, D. R. Cultural patterning of sexual socialization. *American Sociological Review,* 1967, *32,* 726–739.

Heise, D. R., and Roberts, E. P. The development of role knowledge. *Genetic Psychology Monographs,* 1970, *82,* 83–115.

Hellman, R.; Green, R.; Gray, J.; and Williams, K. Childhood sexual identity, childhood religiosity and homophobia as influences in the development of transsexualism, homosexuality, and heterosexuality. *Archives of General Psychiatry,* 1981, *38,* 910–915.

Hendrick, C.; Bixenstine, V. E.; and Hawkins, G. Race versus belief similarity as determinants of attraction: A search for a fair test. *Journal of Personality and Social Psychology,* 1971, *17,* 250–258.

Hendrick, C., and Hendrick, S. S. *Liking, loving and relating.* Monterey, CA.: Brooks/Cole, 1984.

Hendrick, S. S. Rehabilitation from spinal cord injury and neuromuscular disorders. In. N. Schneiderman and J. Tapp (eds.), *Behavioral medicine: The biopsychosocial approach.* Hillsdale, NJ: Erlbaum, 1983.

Henig, R. M. AIDS: A new disease's deadly odyssey. **New York** *Times Magazine,* February 6, 1983, 28ff.

Henley, N. M. *Body politics.* Englewood Cliffs, NJ: Prentice-Hall, 1977.

Henson, C.; Rubin, H. B.; and Henson, D. E. Women's sexual arousal concurrently assessed by three genital measures. *Archives of Sexual Behavior,* 1979, *8,* 459–469.

Herdt, G. *Guardians of the flutes: Idioms of masculinity.* New York: McGraw-Hill, 1981.

Herman, J. L. *Father-daughter incest.* Cambridge, MA: Harvard University Press, 1981.

Herold, E. S., and McNamee, J. E. An explanatory model of contraceptive use among young single women. *Journal of Sex Research,* 1982, *18,* 289–304.

———, and Way, L. Oral-genital sexual behavior in a sample of university females. *Journal of Sex Research,* 1983, *19,* 327–338.

Herrmann, W. M., and Beach, R. C. Pharmacotherapy for sexual offenders. *Modern Problems in Pharmacopsychology,* 1980, *15,* 182–194.

Herzog, A. R., and Bachman, J. G. Sex role attitudes among high school seniors: Views about work and family roles. Institute for Social Research. Ann Arbor: University of Michigan, 1982.

High rates of pregnancy and dissatisfaction

mark first cervical cap trial. *Family Planning Perspectives,* 1981, *13,* 48.

Hill, C. T.; Rubin, Z.; and Peplau, L. A. Breakups before marriage: The end of 103 affairs. *Journal of Social Issues,* 1976, *32,* 147–168.

Himes, N. E. *Medical history of contraception.* Baltimore: Williams & Wilkins, 1936 (paperbound ed., New York: Schocken, 1970).

Himmelweit, H. T., and Bell, N. Television as a sphere of influence on the child's learning about sexuality. In E. J. Roberts (ed.) *Childhood sexual learning: The unwritten curriculum.* Cambridge: Ballinger, 1980.

Hirsch, B. B. *Living together: A Guide to the law for unmarried couples.* Boston: Houghton Mifflin, 1976.

Hite, S. *The Hite report.* New York: Macmillan, 1976.

————. *The Hite report on male sexuality.* New York: Macmillan, 1981.

Hochschild, A. R. Emotion work, feeling rules and social structure. *American Journal of Sociology,* 1979, *85,* 551–575.

Hoeffer, B. Children's acquisition of sex-role behavior in lesbian-mother families. *American Journal of Orthopsychiatry,* 1981, *51,* 536–544.

Hohmann, G. W. Some effects of spinal cord lesions on experienced emotional feelings. *Psychophysiology,* 1966, *3,* 143–156.

Hoffman, M. *The gay world.* New York: Basic Books, 1968 (paperbound ed., New York: Bantam Books, 1969).

Hollerorth, B. *The haunting house: Building and living in houses.* Boston: Unitarian Universalist Association, 1974.

Holmes, K. K. Syphilis. In K. J. Isselbacher, R. B. Adams, E. Braunwald, R. G. Petersdorf, and J. D. Wilson (eds.), *Principles of Internal Medicine* (Ninth ed.). New York: McGraw-Hill, 1980.

Holmstrom, L. L., and Burgess, A. W. *The victim of rape: Institutional reactions.* New York: Wiley, 1978.

————. Sexual behavior during reported rapes. *Archives of Sexual Behavior,* 1980, *9,* 427–439.

Hooker, E. The adjustment of the male overt homosexual. *Journal of Projective Techniques,* 1957, *21,* 18–26.

————. Male homosexuality in the Rorschach. *Journal of Projective Techniques,* 1958, *25,* 22–54.

————. An empirical study of some rela-

tions between sexual patterns and gender identity in male homosexuals. In J. Money (ed.), *Sex research: New developments.* New York: Holt, Rinehart and Winston, 1965 (a).

————. Male homosexuals and their "worlds." In J. Marmor (ed.), *Sexual inversion.* New York: Basic Books, 1965 (b).

————. Parental relations and male homosexuality in patient and non-patient samples. *Journal of Counseling and Clinical Psychology,* 1969, *33,* 140–142.

Hoon, P. W.; Wincze, J. P.; and Hoon, E. F. Physiological assessment of sexual arousal in women. *Psychophysiology,* 1976, *13,* 196–204.

————. The effects of biofeedback and cognitive mediation upon vaginal blood volume. *Behavior Therapy,* 1977, *8,* 694–702.

Hope, C. *A separate development.* New York: Scribner, 1981.

Horn, J. C. Vasectomy: The unpopular choice. *Psychology Today,* June 1984, 17.

Horos, C. V. *Rape: The private crime, a social horror.* New Canaan, CT: Tobey Publishing Co., 1974.

Horstman, W.; McCusick, L.; and Carfagni, A. Onset and progress of AIDS shaped by stress factors. American Psychological Association, *Monitor,* July 1983.

Hotvedt, M.; Green, R.; and Mandel, J. The lesbian parent: Comparison of heterosexual and homosexual mothers and children. *Archives of Sexual Behavior,* 1985, in press.

Howard, J. L.; Liptzin, M. B.; and Reifler, C. B. Is pornography a problem? *Journal of Social Issues,* 1973, *29,* 133–146.

Howes, C.; Rubenstein, J.; and Eldredge, C. Sex differences in peer interaction in a naturalistic setting. Symposium on *Gender Segregation in the Peer Group.* Society for Research in Child Development. Detroit: April 1983.

Hughes, Douglas (Ed.) *Perspectives on pornography.* New York: St. Martin's, 1970.

Humphries, R. A. L. *Tearoom trade.* Chicago: Aldine, 1970.

Hunt, M., *The affair.* New York: World, 1962.

————. *Sexual behavior in the 1970's.* Chicago: Playboy Press, 1974.

————. *The young person's guide to love.* New York: Farrar, Straus, Giroux, 1975.

————. *Gay: What you should know about homosexuality.* New York: Farrar, Straus and Giroux, 1977. (a)

————. Why "open marriage" failed. *Family Circle,* January 1977 (b).

————, and Hunt, B. *The divorce experience.* New York: New American Library, 1977.

Hyyppa, M. T.; Falck, S. C.; and Rinne, U. K. Is L-DOPA an aphrodisiac in patients with Parkinson's disease? In M. Sandler and G. L. Gessa (eds.), *Sexual behavior: Pharmacology and biochemistry.* New York: Raven Press, 1975.

Imperato-McGinley, J.; Guerrero, L.; Gautier, T.; and Peterson, R. Steroid 5-alphareductase deficiency in man: An inherited form of male pseudohermaphroditism. *Science,* 1974, *186,* 1213–1215.

————; Peterson, R. E.; Gautier, T.; and Sturla, E. The impact of androgens on the evolution of male gender identity. In S. J. Kogan and E. S. E. Hafez (eds.), *Pediatric andrology.* The Hague, Netherlands: Martinus Nyhoff, 1981.

Instone, D.; Major, B.; and Bunker, B. B. Gender, self confidence, and social influence strategies: An organizational simulation. *Journal of Personality and Social Psychology,* 1983, *44,* 322–333.

Irwin, P., and Thomson, M. L. Acceptance of the rights of homosexuals: A social profile. *Journal of Homosexuality.* 1977, *3,* 107–121.

Izard, C. E. *Human emotions.* New York: Plenum, 1977.

Jacklin, C. N.; DiPietro, J. A.; and Maccoby, E. E. Sex-typing behavior and sex-typing pressure in child/parent interaction. *Archives of Sexual Behavior.* 1984, *13,* 413–425.

————, and Maccoby, E. E. Social behavior at thirty-three months in same-sex and mixed-sex dyads. *Child Development,* 1978, *49,* 557–569.

Jackson, E. D., and Potkay, C. R. Precollege influences on sexual experiences of coeds. *Journal of Sex Research,* 1973, *90,* 143–149.

Jacobs, P. A.; Brenton, M.; Melville, M. M.; Brittain, R. P.; and McClemont, W. F. Aggressive behavior, mental subnormality and the XYY male. *Nature,* 1965, *208,* 1351–1352.

Jacobs, R. H. *Life after youth: Female, forty-what next?* Boston: Beacon, 1979.

James, J. Prostitutes and prostitution. In E. Sagrin, and F. Montanino (eds.), *Deviants.*

Morristown, NJ: General Learning Press, 1977.

————, and Meyerding, J.   Early sexual experience and prostitution. *American Journal of Psychiatry*, 1977, *134*, 1381–1385.

James, W. H.   The distribution of coitus within the human intermenstrum. *Journal of Biosocial Science*, 1971, *3*, 159–171.

————.   The honeymoon effect on marital coitus. *Journal of Sex Research.* 1981, *17*, 114–123.

Jay, K., and Young, A.   *The gay report.* New York: Simon & Schuster, 1979.

Jedlicka, D.   Sequential analysis of perceived commitment to partners in premarital coitus. *Journal of Marriage and the Family*, 1975, *37*, 385–390.

Jessor, S. L., and Jessor, R.   Transition from virginity to nonvirginity among youth: A social psychological study over time. *Developmental Psychology*, 1975, *11*, 473–484.

Jones, E. E., and McGillis, D.   Correspondent inferences and the attribution cube: A comparative reappraisal. In J. H. Harvey, W. J. Ickes, and R. F. Kidd (eds.), *New Directions in Attribution Research, Vol. 1.* Hillsdale, NJ: Erlbaum, 1976.

Jong, E.   *Fear of flying.* New York: Holt, Rinehart & Winston, 1973 (paperbound ed., New York: Signet, 1974).

Julty, S.   *Men's bodies, men's selves.* New York: Dell (Delta), 1979.

Kaats, G., and Davis, K.   Effects of volunteer biases in studies of sexual behavior and attitudes. *Journal of Sex Research*, 1971, *7*, 219–227.

Kagan, J., and Moss, H. A.   *Birth to maturity: A study in psychological development.* New York: Wiley, 1962.

Kalmuss, D. S., and Straus, M. A.   Wife's marital dependency and wife abuse. *Journal of Marriage and Family*, 1982, *44*, 277–286.

Kalven, H. J., and Zeisel, H.   *The American jury.* Boston: Little, Brown, 1966 (paperbound ed., Chicago: University of Chicago, 1971).

Kandel, D. B.   Similarity in real-life adolescent friendship pairs. *Journal of Personality and Social Psychology*, 1978, *36*, 306–312.

Kanin, E. J.   Male aggression in dating-courtship relations. *American Journal of Sociology*, 1957, *63*, 197–204.

————.   Selected dyadic aspects of male sexual aggression. *Journal of Sex Research*, 1969, *5*, 12–28.

Kanin, E. J., and Parcell, S. R.   Sexual aggression: A second look at the offended female. *Archives of Sexual Behavior*, 1977, *66*, 67–76.

Kantner, J. F., and Zelnik, M.   Sexual experience of young unmarried women in the United States. *Family Planning Perspectives*, 1972, *4*, 1–25.

————.   Contraception and pregnancy: Experience of young unmarried women in the United States. *Family Planning Perspectives*, 1973, *5*, 21–35.

Kaplan, H. S.   *The new sex therapy, Vol. 1.* New York: Brunner/Mazel, 1974.

————.   *The illustrated manual of sex therapy.* New York: Quadrangle/New York *Times*, 1975.

————.   *Disorders of sexual desire.* New York: Simon & Schuster, 1978.

————.   *Disorders of sexual desire: The new sex therapy,* Vol. 2. New York: Brunner/Mazel, 1979.

————.   *The Evaluation of Sexual Disorders: Psychological and Medical Aspects.* New York: Brunner/Mazel, 1983.

————; Kohl, R. N.; Pomeroy, W. B.; Offit, A. K.; and Hogan, B.   Group treatment of premature ejaculation. *Archives of Sexual Behavior*, 1974, *3*, 443–452.

————, and Sager, C. J.   Sexual patterns at different ages. *Medical Aspects of Human Sexuality*, June 1971, *5*, 10ff.

Karacan, I.   Nocturnal penile tumescence as a biologic marker in assessing erectile dysfunction. *Psychosomatics*, 1982, *23*, #4.

————; Aslan, C.; and Hershkowitz, M. Erectile mechanisms in man. *Science*, 1983, *220*, 1080–1082.

————; Gozukirmizi, E.; Derman, S.; Hartse, K. M.; Hanusa, T.; Hershkowitz, M.; and Williams, R. L.   Peripheral autonomic system disturbances in impotent patients. *Sleep Research*, 1981, *10*, 250–252.

————; Ware, S. C.; Dervent, B.; Altinel, A.; Thornby, J. L.; Williams, R. L.; Kaya, N.; and Scott, F. B.   Impotence and blood pressure in the flaccid penis: Relationship to nocturnal penile tumescence. *Sleep*, 1978, *1*, 125–132.

Karczmar, A. G.   Drugs, transmitters and hormones and mating behavior. *Modern Problems in Pharmacopsychology*, 1980, *15*, 1–76.

Katcher, A.   The discrimination of sex differences by young children. *Journal of Genetic Psychology*, 1955, *87*, 131–143.

Katz, J.   (ed.). *Gay American history: Lesbians and gay men in the U. S. A.* New York: Crowell, 1976.

Kawai, M.   Newly acquired precultural behavior of the mature troop of Japanese monkeys on Koshima Island. *Primates*, 1965, *6*, 1–30.

Kegel, A. H.   Sexual functions of the pubococcygeus muscle. *Western Journal of Obstetrics and Gynecology*, 1952, *60*, 521.

Kelly, R.   *Etoro social structure.* Ann Arbor: University of Michigan Press, 1974.

————.   Witchcraft and sexual relations: An exploration in the social and semantic implications of the structure of belief. In P. Brown and G. Buchbinder (eds.), *Man and woman in the New Guinea Highlands.* Washington, D.C.: American Anthropological Association, 1976.

Kemmann, E., and Jones, J. R.   The female climacteric. *American Family Physician*, November 1979, *20*, 140–151.

Kephart, W.   Some correlates of romantic love. *Journal of Marriage and the Family.* 1967, *29*, 470–479.

Kesey, K.   *One flew over the cuckoo's nest.* New York: Viking, 1970 (paperbound ed., New York: New American Library, 1972).

Kester, P. A.   Effects of prenatally administered 17 alpha hydroxyprogesterone caproate on adolescent males. *Archives of Sexual Behavior*, 1984, *13*, 447–455.

————; Green, R.; Finch, S.; and Williams, K.   Prenatal "female hormone" administration and psychosexual development in human males. *Psychoneuroendocrinology*, 1980, *5*, 269–285.

Kilmann, P. R.; Sabalis, R. F.; Gearing, M. L. II; Bukstel, L. H.; and Scovern, A. W.   The treatment of sexual paraphilias: A review of the outcome research. *Journal of Sex Research.* 1982, *18*, 193–252.

Kimura, D.   Functional asymmetry of the brain. *Cortex*, 1967, *3*, 163–178.

————.   Spatial localization in left and right visual fields, *Canadian Journal of Psychology*, 1969, *23*, 445–458.

————.   The asymmetry of the human brain. *Scientific American*, 1973, *228*, 70–78.

Kindleberger, R. S.   The difficulty of discussing sex and children. Boston *Globe*, September 15, 1983, 27ff.

King, M., and Sobel, D.   Sex on the college

campus: Current attitudes and behavior. *Journal of College Student Personnel.* 1975, *16,* 205–209.

Kinsey, A. C.; Pomeroy, W. B.; Martin, C. E.; and Gebhard, P. H. *Sexual behavior in the human male.* Philadelphia: W. B. Saunders, 1948.

———. *Sexual behavior in the human female.* Philadelphia: W. B. Saunders, 1953.

Kirby, D.; Alter, J.; and Scales, P. An analysis of U.S. sex education programs and evaluation methods. Bethesda, MD: Mathtech, Inc. (for Department of HEW), 1979.

Kirkpatrick, C., and Kanin, K. Male sex aggression on a university campus. *American Sociological Review,* 1957, *22,* 52–58.

Kirpatrick, M.; Smith, K.; Roy, R. Lesbian mothers and their children: A comparative study. *American Journal of Orthopsychiatry.* 1981, *51,* 545–551.

Kirsch, J., and Rodman, J. The natural history of homosexuality, *Yale Scientific Magazine.* 1977, *51,* no. 3, 7–13.

Klaus, M., and Kennell, J. *Maternal and infant bonding.* St. Louis: C. V. Mosby Co., 1976.

Kleiman, D. When abortion becomes birth. New York *Times,* February 15, 1984, B1ff.

Klemmack, S. H., and Klemmack, D. L. The social definition of rape. In M. J. Walker and S. L. Brodsky (eds.), *Sexual assault,* Lexington, MA.: D.C. Heath, 1976.

Klerman, L. V., and Jekel, J. F. Unwanted pregnancy. In M. B. Bracken (ed.), *Perinatal Epidemiology,* New York: Oxford University Press, 1984.

Kline-Graber, G., and Graber, B. *Women's orgasm.* New York: Bobbs Merrill, 1975.

Klitsch, M. Sterilization without surgery. *Family Planning Perspectives.* 1982, *14,* 324–327.

Knapp, J. J. An exploratory study of seventeen sexually open marriages. *Journal of Sex Research,* 1976, *12,* 206–219.

Knox, W. E., and Kupferer, H. F. A discontinuity in the socialization of males in the United States. *Merrill-Palmer Quarterly,* 1972, *17,* 251–262.

Koch, H. L. A study of some factors conditioning the social distance between the sexes. *Journal of Social Psychology,* 1944, *20,* 79–107.

Kockott, G.; Dittman, F.; and Nusselt, L. Systematic desensitization of erectile impotence: A controlled study. *Archives of Sexual Behavior,* 1975, *4,* 493–499.

Kohlberg, L. A cognitive-developmental analysis of children's sex-role concepts and attitudes. In E. E. Maccoby (ed.), *The development of sex differences.* Stanford, CA: Stanford University Press, 1966.

Kohlenberg, R. J. Directed masturbation and the treatment of primary orgasmic dysfunction. *Archives of Sexual Behavior,* 1974, *3,* 349–356.

Kohn, M. L. Social class and parental values. *American Journal of Sociology,* 1959, *44,* 337–351.

Kolarsky, A., and Madlafousek, J. The inverse role of preparatory stimulation in exhibitionists: Phallometric studies. *Archives of Sexual Behavior,* 1983, *12,* 123–148.

Kolodny, R. C. Evaluating sex therapy: Process and outcome at the Masters and Johnson Institute. *Journal of Sex Research,* 1981, *17,* 301–318.

———, and Bauman, J. E. Female sexual activity at ovulation: Letter to the editor of the *New England Journal of Medicine,* 1979, *300,* 626.

———; Masters, W. H.; Kolodny, R. M.; and Toro, G. Depression of plasma testosterone levels after chronic intensive marijuana use. *New England Journal of Medicine,* 1974, *290,* 872–874.

Komarovsky, M. Patterns of self-disclosure of male undergraduates. *Journal of Marriage and the Family,* 1974, *36,* 677–686.

———. *Dilemmas of masculinity.* New York: Norton, 1976.

Komisaruk, B. R.; Adler, N. T.; and Hutchinson, J. Genital sensory field: Enlargement by estrogen treatment in female rats. *Science,* 1972, *178,* 1295–1297.

Kopay, D., and Young, P. D. *The David Kopay story.* New York: Arbor House (Division of Hearst), 1980.

Korman, S. K., and Leslie, G. R. The relationship of feminist ideology and date expense sharing and perceptions of sexual aggression in dating. *Journal of Sex Research,* 1982, *18,* 114–129.

Kraemer, H. C.; Becker, H. B.; Brodie, H. K. H.; Doering, C. H.; Moos, R. H.; and Hamburg, D. A. Orgasmic frequency and plasma testosterone levels in normal human males. *Archives of Sexual Behavior,* 1976, *5,* 125–132.

Krafft-Ebing, R. V. *Psychopathia sexualis.* New York: Pioneer Publications, 1939.

Kramer, M. J. Legal abortion among New York City residents: An analysis according to socioeconomic and demographic characteristics. *Family Planning Perspectives,* 1975, *7,* 128–137.

Kreutner, A. K. (ed.). *The pediatric clinics of North America: Symposium on pediatric and adolescent gynecology,* Vol. 28, no. 2, Philadelphia: W. B. Saunders, 1981. (a)

———. Sexuality, fertility, and the problems of menstruation in mentally retarded adolescents. In A. K. Kreutner (ed.), *The Pediatric Clinics of North America,* Vol. 28, no. 2, Philadelphia: W. B. Saunders, 1981. (b)

———. Adolescent contraception in A. K. Kreutner (ed.), *The Pediatric Clinics of North America.* Philadelphia: W. B. Saunders, 1981. (c)

Kreuz, L. E.; Rose, R. M.; and Jennings, J. R. Suppression of plasma testosterone levels and psychological stress. *Archives of General Psychiatry,* 1972, *26,* 479–482.

Kronhausen, E., and Kronhausen, P. K. *Pornography and the law.* New York: Ballantine, 1964.

Kronhausen, P., and Kronhausen, E. *Erotic art.* New York: Bell, 1968.

Kuhn, D.; Nash, S.; and Brucken, L. Sex role concepts of two- and three-year olds. *Child Development,* 1978, *49,* 445–451.

Kutchinsky, B. The effect of easy availability of pornography on the incidence of sex crimes: The Danish experience. *Journal of Social Issues,* 1973, *29,* 163–182.

Ladas, A. K.; Whipple, B.; and Perry, J. D. *The G spot and other recent discoveries about human sexuality.* New York: Holt, Rinehart & Winston, 1982.

La Free, G. D. Official reactions to social problems: Police decisions in sexual assault cases. *Social Problems,* 1981, *28,* 582–594.

Lamb, M. *The role of the father in child development.* New York: Wiley-Interscience, 1976.

Lancaster, J. B. Sex and gender in evolutionary perspective. In H. A. Katchedourian (ed.), *Human sexuality: A comparative and developmental perspective.* Berkeley: University of California, 1979.

Lancaster, J. B., and Whitten, P. Family matters. *The Sciences,* January 1980, 10–15.

Landers, A. Cross-dressing father. Boston *Globe,* December 8, 1978.

Landis, J. Experiences of 500 children with adult sexual deviation. *Psychiatry Quarterly,* (Supplement), 1956, *30,* 91–109.

Landy, D., and Sigall, H. Beauty is talent: Task evolution as a function of the performer's physical attractiveness. *Journal of Personality and Social Psychology*, 1974, *29*, 299–304.

Langevin, R.; Paitich, D.; Ramsay, G.; Anderson, C.; Kamrad, S.; Pope, S.; Geller, G.; Pearl, L.; and Newman, S. Experimental studies of the etiology of genital exhibitionism. *Archives of Sexual Behavior*, 1979, *8*, 307–331.

Langlois, J., and Downs, C. Mothers, fathers and peers as socialization agents of sex-typed play behaviors in young children, *Child Development*, 1980, *51*, 1217–1247.

Larsen, K. S.; Reed, M.; and Hoffman, S. Attitudes of heterosexuals toward homosexuality: A Likert-type scale and construct validity. *Journal of Sex Research*, 1980, *16*, 245–257.

Laskin, D. The herpes syndrome, New York *Times Magazine*, February 21, 1982, 94ff.

Laub, D. R., and Gandy, P. *Proceedings of the second interdisciplinary symposium on gender dysphoria syndrome*. Stanford, CA: Stanford University Press, 1973.

Lauritsen, J. G. Research review: The cytogenetics of spontaneous abortion. *Research in Reproduction*, 1982, *14*, 3ff.

———; Pagel, J. D.; Vangsted, P.; and Storup, J. Results of repeated tuboplasties. *Fertility and Sterility*, 1982, *37*, 68–723.

Lavori, N. *Living together, married or single: Your legal rights*. New York: Harper & Row/Perennial, 1976.

Lawrence, D. H. *Lady Chatterley's lover*. New York: Bantam Books, 1968 (originally published, 1928).

Laws, J. L. *The Second X: Sex role and social role*. New York: Elsevier, 1979.

———. Female sexuality through the life span. In P. B. Baltes and Brim, O. G. Jr. (eds.), *Life span development and behavior, Vol. 3*. New York: Academic Press, 1980.

———, and Schwartz, P. *Sexual scripts: The social construction of female sexuality*. Hinsdale, IL: Dryden Press, 1977.

Lear, M. W. *Heartsounds: The story of a love and loss*. New York: Simon & Schuster. 1980.

Lebovitz, P. Feminine behavior in boys: Aspects of its outcome. *American Journal of Psychiatry*, 1972, *128*, 1283–1289.

Leboyer, F. *Birth without violence*. New York: Knopf, 1975.

Lederer, L. (ed.). *Take back the night*. New York: W. Morrow, 1980.

Lee, P. A.; Jaffe, R. B.; and Midgley, Jr., A. R. Lack of alteration of serum gonadotrophins in men and women following sexual intercourse. *American Journal of Obstetrics and Gynecology*, 1974, *120*, 985–987.

Leon Rosenberg on the 'Human Life' bill. *Science*, 1981, *212*, 907.

Lerner, A. M. Infections with herpes simplex virus. In K. J. Isselbacher; R. D. Adams; E. Braunwald; R. G. Petersdorf; and J. D. Wilson (eds.) *Harrison's principles of internal medicine, Ninth ed*. New York: McGraw-Hill, 1980.

Le Shan, E. Virginity clinics. *Woman's Day*, May 18, 1982, 52.

Lester, D. *Unusual sexual behaviors*. Springfield, IL: Charles C. Thomas, 1975.

Lever, J. Sex differences in the games children play. *Social Problems*, 1976, *23*, 478–487.

———. Sex differences in the complexity of children's play and games. *American Sociological Review*, 1978, *43*, 471–483.

Levin, S. M.; Balistrieri, J.; and Schukit, M. The development of sexual discrimination in children. *Journal of Child Psychology and Psychiatry*, 1972, *13*, 47–53.

LeVine, E. M.; Shaiova, C. H.; and Mihailovic, M. Male to female: The role transformation of transsexuals. *Archives of Sexual Behavior*, 1975, *4*, 173–185.

LeVine, R. Gusii sex offenses: A study in social control. *American Anthropologist*, 1959, *61*, 965–990.

Levine, S. Stress and behavior. *Scientific American*, 1971, *224*, 26–31.

Levine, S. B. Marital sexual dysfunction: Introductory concepts. *Annals of Internal Medicine*, 1976, *84*, 448–453.

———, and Yosh, M. A. Jr. Frequency of sexual dysfunction in a general gynecological clinic: An epidemiological approach. *Archives of Sexual Behavior*, 1976, *5*, 229–238.

Levinger, G. Husbands' and wives' estimates of coital frequency. *Medical Aspects of Human Sexuality*, 1970, *4*, 45–57.

Lev-Ran, A. Gender role differentiation in hermaphrodites. *Archives of Sexual Behavior*, 1974, *3*, 391–424.

Levy, D. M. Finger sucking and accessory movements in early infancy. *American Journal of Psychiatry*, 1928, *7*, 881–918.

Levy-Agresti, J., and Sperry, R. W. Differential perceptual capacities in major and minor hemispheres. Paper read at National Academy of Sciences meeting, California Institute of Technology, Pasadena, CA. *Proceedings of the National Academy of Science, 1968, 61*.

Lewin, B. The adolescent boy and girl: First and other early experiences with intercourse from a representative sample of Swedish school adolescents. *Archives of Sexual Behavior*. 1982, *5*, 417–428. (a)

———. Unmarried cohabitation: A marriage form in a changing society. *Journal of Marriage and the Family*, 1982, *44*, 763–773. (b)

Lewis, R. A., and Burr, W. R. Premarital coitus and commitment among college students. *Archives of Sexual Behavior*, 1975, *4*, 73–79.

LHRL found to inhibit ovulation successfully with few side effects. *Family Planning Perspective*, 1983, *15*, 32–35.

Liebert, R. M.; Neale, J. M.; and Davidson, E. S. *The early window*. New York: Pergamon Press, 1973.

Libby, R. W., and Carlson, J. E. A theoretical framework for premarital sexual decisions in the dyad. *Archives of Sexual Behavior*, 1973, *2*, 365–378.

———, and Whitehurst, R. N. (eds.). *Renovating marriage: Toward new sexual life styles*. Danville, CA: Consensus, 1973.

Lincoln, R. Institute of Medicine reports on legalized abortion and public health. *Family Planning Perspectives*, 1975, *7*, 185–188.

———. The pill, breast and cervical cancer, and the role of progestogens with arterial disease, *Family Planning Perspectives*, 1984, *16*, 55–63.

Linde, R.; Doelle, G. C.; Alexander, N.; Kirchner, F.; Vale, W.; Rivier, J.; and Rabin, D. Reversible inhibition of testicular steroidogenesis and spermatogenesis by a potent gonadotropin-releasing hormone agonist in normal men. *New England Journal of Medicine*, 1981, *305*,663ff.

———, and Fishman, J. Response to threat of AIDS. American Psychological Association. *Monitor,* July, 1983.

Lindenbaum, S. The mystification of female labours. Paper presented at the conference on *Feminism and kinship theory*, Bellagio, Italy, August 1–6, 1982.

Linner, B. The new handbook on instruction in sex and personal relationships in the Swedish schools. *Current Sweden*, February 1978, *5*, #183, 1–10.

Linnet, L.; Moller, N. P. H.; Bernth-

Petersen, P.; Ehlers, N.; Brandslund, L.; and Svehag, S. E. No increase in arteriosclerotic retinopathy or activity in tests for circulating immune complexes five years after vasectomy. *Fertility and Sterility*, 1982, *37*, 798–800.

Lipton, M. A. The problem of pornography. In W. E. Fann, I. Karacan, A. D. Pokorny, and R. L. Williams, *Phenomenology and treatment of psychosexual disorders*. New York: SP Medical and Scientific Books (Spectrum), 1983.

Litman, R. E., and Swearington, C. Bondage and suicide. *Archives of General Psychiatry*, 1972, *27*, 80–85.

Littman, I. The play preferences of nursery school children. Ph. D. Thesis, University of Oregon, 1971, *Dissertation Abstracts*, #72–946.

Lobel, T. E. Parental antecedents of need for approval: A longitudinal study. *Journal of Research in Personality*, 1982, *16*, 502–510.

Lobitz, W. C., and Baker, E. Group treatment of single males with erectile dysfunction. *Archives of Sexual Behavior*, 1979, *9*, 127–138.

Loh, W. D. What has reform of rape legislation wrought? *Journal of Social Issues*, 1981, *37*, 28–52.

LoPiccolo, J. Mothers and daughters: Perceived and real differences in sexual values. *Journal of Sex Research*, 1973, *7*, 171–177.

———, and Lobitz, W. C. The role of masturbation in the treatment of orgasmic dysfunction. *Archives of Sexual Behavior*, 1972, *2*, 163–171.

———, and LoPiccolo, L. *Handbook of sex therapy*. New York: Plenum Press, 1978.

Loraine, J. A.; Adamopoulos, D. A.; Kirkham, K. E.; Ismail, A. A. A.; and Dove, G. A. Patterns of hormone excretion in male and female homosexuals. *Nature*, 1971, *234*, 552–554.

Lothstein, L. M. Sex reassignment surgery: Historical, bioethical, and theoretical issues. *American Journal of Psychiatry*. 1982, *139*, 417–426.

Louis Harris and Associates, *The Playboy Report on American Men*. Chicago: Playboy, 1979.

Lowenstein, S. F.; Block, N. E.; Campion, J.; Epstein, J. S.; Gale, P.; and Salvatore, M. A study of satisfactions and stresses of single women in midlife. *Sex Roles*, 1981, *11*, 1127–1141.

Luckey, E. B.; and Nass, G. D. A comparison of sexual attitudes and behavior in an international sample. *Journal of Marriage and the Family*, 1969, *31*, 364–379.

Luker, K. Contraceptive risk taking and abortion: Results and implications of a San Francisco Bay area study. *Family Planning Perspectives*, 1977, *8*, 190–196.

———. *Abortion and the politics of motherhood*. Berkeley: University of California Press, 1984.

Luria, Z. Recent women college graduates: A study of rising expectations. *American Journal of Orthopsychiatry*, 1974, *44*, 312–326.

———. Psychosocial determinants of gender identity, role, and orientation. In H. A. Katchedourian (ed.), *Human sexuality: A comparative and developmental perspective*. Berkeley: University of California Press, 1979.

———. Sexual fantasy and pornography: Two cases of girls brought up with pornography. *Archives of Sexual Behavior*, 1982, *11*, 395–404.

Luria, Z., and Herzog, E. W. Gender segregation in play groups: A matter of where and when. Symposium on gender segregation in the peer group. Society for Research in Child Development. Detroit, MI: April 1983.

———, ———. Gender segregation across and within settings. Society for Research in Child Development. Toronto, Ont., Canada: April 1985.

———, and Meade, R. Sexuality and the middle-aged woman. In G. Baruch and J. Brooks-Gunn, *Women in Midlife*, New York: Plenum, 1984.

———, and Rose, M. D. *The Psychology of Human Sexuality*. New York: Wiley, 1979.

Maccoby, E. E., and Jacklin, C. N. *The psychology of sex differences*. Stanford, CA: Stanford University Press, 1974.

MacKinnon, C. A. *Sexual harassment of working women*. New Haven, CT: Yale University Press, 1979.

Macklin, E. D. Nonmarital heterosexual cohabitation. *Marriage and Family Review*, 1978, *1*, 1–12.

———. Unmarried heterosexual cohabitation on the university campus. In J. P. Wiseman (ed.), *The social psychology of sex*. New York: Harper & Row, 1976.

MacLusky, M. J., and Naftolin, T. Sexual differentiation of the central nervous system. *Science*, 1981, *211*, 1294–1303.

Mahoney, E. R. Patterns of sexual behavior among college students. Unpublished research report, Department of Sociology, Western Washington University, 1979. Cited in G. R. Mahoney's *Human Sexuality*. New York: McGraw-Hill, 1983.

———. Religiosity and sexual behavior among heterosexual college students, *Journal of Sex Research*, 1980, *16*, 97–113.

Mailer, N. *The prisoner of sex*. Boston: Little, Brown, 1971.

Makinson, C. The health consequences of teenage fertility. *Family Planning Perspectives*, 1985, *17*, 132–139.

Malamuth, N. M. Rape fantasies as a function of response to violent sexual stimuli. *Archives of Sexual Behavior*, 1981, *10*, 33–48.

———, and Chan, J. U. P. The effects of mass media exposure on acceptance of violence against women: A field experiment. *Journal of Research in Personality*, 1981, *15*, 436–446.

———, and Check, J. V. P. The effects of mass media exposure on acceptance of violence against women: A field experiment. *Journal of Research in Personality*, 1981, *15*, 436–446.

———, and Donnerstein, E. (eds.). *Pornography and sexual aggression*. New York: Academic Press, 1982.

———, and Spinner, B. A longitudinal content analysis of sexual violence in the best-selling erotic magazines. *Journal of Sex Research*, 1980, *16*, 226–237.

Malinowski, B. *The sexual life of savages in North-Western Melanesia* (Trobriand Islands, British New Guinea). New York: Halcyon House, 1929.

Mann, J. Court bans child porn. *Boston Globe*. June 3, 1982. 1.

Mann, J.; Sidman, J.; and Starr, S. Evaluating social consequences of erotic films: An experimental approach. *Journal of Social Issues*, 1973, *29*, 113–132.

Manning, A. *An introduction to animal behavior*. New York: Addison-Wesley, 1979.

Marcia, J. E. Identity in adolescence. In J. Adelson (ed.), *Handbook of adolescent psychology*. New York: Wiley, 1980.

Marcus, S. *The other Victorians: A study of sexuality and pornography in mid-nineteenth-century England*. New York: Basic Books, 1966 (paperbound ed., New York: Bantam Books, 1967).

Margolese, M. S., and Janiger, O. Androsterone/etiocholanolone ratios in male homosexuals. *British Medical Journal,* 1973, *3,* 207–210.

Margolick, D. Herpes and similar matters get more attention in court. New York *Times,* February 26, 1984, 24.

Margolis, A.; Rindfuss, R.; Coghlan, P.; and Rochat, R. Contraception after abortion. *Family Planning Perspectives,* 1974, *6,* 56–60.

Marmor, J. (Ed.). *Sexual inversion.* New York: Basic Books, 1965.

———. *Homosexual behavior: A modern reappraisal.* New York: Basic Books, 1980.

Marshall, D. S. Sexual behavior in Mangaia. In D. S. Marshall and R. C. Suggs (eds.), *Human sexual behavior,* Englewood Cliffs, NJ: Prentice-Hall, 1971.

———, and Suggs, R. C. (Eds.). *Human sexual behavior.* Englewood Cliffs, NJ: Prentice-Hall, 1971.

Martin, D., and Lyon , P. *Lesbian/woman.* San Francisco: Glide Publications, 1972.

Marx, J. L. Contraception: An antipregnancy vaccine. *Science,* 1978, *200,* 1258.

Mason, A. S. The events of the menopause. *Royal Society of Health Journal,* 1976, 96, 70–85.

Massey, C., and Warner, R. *Sex, living together, and the law,* Berkeley, CA: Nolo Press, 1974.

Masters, W. H., and Johnson, V. E. *Human Sexual Response.* Boston: Little, Brown, 1966.

———. *Human Sexual Inadequacy.* Boston: Little, Brown, 1970.

———. *The Pleasure Bond.* Boston: Little, Brown, 1975 (paperback ed., New York: Bantam Books, 1976).

———. *Homosexuality in perspective.* Boston: Little, Brown, 1979.

Mastroianni, L. Rhythm: Systematized chance-taking. *Family Planning Perspectives,* 1974, *6,* 209–212.

Mathes, E. W. The effects of physical attractiveness and anxiety on heterosexual attraction over a series of five encounters. *Journal of Marriage and the Family,* 1975, *37,* 769–773.

May, J. L., and Hamilton, P. A. Females' evaluations of males as a function of affect arousing musical stimuli. Midwestern Psychological Association, Chicago, May 1977.

Mayo, C., and Henley, N. M. (eds.). *Gender and nonverbal behavior.* Secaucus, NJ: Springer-Verlag, 1981.

McCabe, M. P., and Collins, J. K. The sexual and affectional attitudes and experiences of Australian adolescents during dating: The effects of age, church attendance, type of school, and socioeconomic class. *Archives of Sexual Behavior,* 1983, *12,* 525–539.

McCahill, T. W.; Meyer, L. C.; and Fischman, A. M. *The aftermath of rape,* Lexington, MA: Lexington Books, 1979.

McCann, M. F., and Cole, L. P. Laparoscopy and minilaparotomy: Two major advances in female sterilization. *Studies in Family Planning,* 1980, *11,* 119–127.

McCarthy, B. W.; Ryan, M. G.; and Johnson, F. A. *Sexual awareness: A practical book.* San Francisco: Boyd and Fraser, 1975.

McCarthy, J., and Menken, J. Marriage, remarriage, marital disruption and age at first birth. *Family Planning Perspectives,* 1979, *11,* 21–30.

McCarthy, J., and Radish, E. S. Research note: Education and childbearing among teenagers. *Family Planning Perspectives,* 1982, *14,* 154–155.

McCarthy, P. In New Haven, a sculpture sparks debate on esthetics, New York *Times,* November 13, 1983, C1.

McClintock, M. K. Menstrual synchrony and suppression. *Nature,* 1971, *229,* 244–245.

McCormack, T. Pornography and the mass media. Lecture series on the mass media, Tufts University. Medford, MA, February 21, 1985.

McDermott, S. *Female sexuality: Its nature and complicity.* New York: Simon & Schuster, 1970.

McDonald, A. P., and Gomes, G. M. Some characteristics of those who hold positive and negative attitudes toward homosexuality. *Journal of Homosexuality,* 1974, *1,* 9–27.

McEwen, B. S. Neural gonadal steroid actions. *Science,* 1981, *211,* 1303–1311.

McGlone, J. Sex differences in cerebral organization of verbal functions in patients with unilateral brain lesions. *Brain,* 1977, *100,* 775–793.

———. Sex differences in functional brain asymmetry. *Cortex,* 1978, *14,* 122–128.

———. Sex differences in human brain asymmetry. *Behavioral and Brain Sciences,* 1980, *3,* 215–263.

McGovern, K. B.; Stewart, R. C.; and LoPiccolo, J. Secondary orgasmic dysfunction. I. Analysis and strategies for treatment. *Archives of Sexual Behavior,* 1975, *4,* 265–275.

McGuire, R. J.; Carlisle, J. M.; and Young, B. G. Sexual deviation as conditioned behavior: A hypothesis. *Behavior Research and Therapy,* 1965, *2,* 185–190.

McNeilly, A. S. Paradoxical prolactin. *Nature,* 1980, *284,* 212–214.

McWhirter, D. P., and Mattison, A. M. *The male couple.* Englewood Cliffs, NJ: Prentice-Hall, 1981.

Mead, B. T. What impact does adultery generally have on a marriage? *Medical Aspects of Human Sexuality,* 1975, *9,* 122ff.

Mead, M. *Sex and temperament in three primitive societies.* New York: Morrow, 1935 (paperback ed., New York: Laurel, 1968).

Medical aspects of homosexuality, editorial. *New England Journal of Medicine,* 1980, *311,* 463–464.

Mehl, M. C. Transsexualism: A perspective. In D. R. Laub and P. Gandy (eds.), *Proceedings of the second interdisciplinary symposium on gender dysphoria syndrome.* Stanford, CA: Stanford University Press, 1973.

Meiselman, K. C. *Incest: A psychological study of causes and effects with treatment recommendations.* San Francisco: Jossey-Bass, 1978.

Merriam, A. P. Aspects of sexual behavior among the Bala (Basongye). In D. S. Marshall and R. C. Suggs (eds.), *Human Sexual Behavior.* Englewood Cliffs, NJ: Prentice-Hall, 1971.

Merrick, F. Personal communication to Jean Sorrells-Jones, 1978.

Messenger, J. Sex and repression in an Irish folk community. In D. S. Marshall and R. C. Suggs (eds.), *Human Sexual Behavior.* Englewood Cliffs, NJ: Prentice-Hall, 1971.

Meyer, J. (ed). *Clinical management of sexual disorders.* Baltimore: Williams and Wilkins, 1976.

Meyer, J., and Reter, C. Sex assignment: Follow up. *Archives of General Psychiatry,* 1979, *36,* 1010–1015.

Meyer, J. K. Some thoughts on nosology and motivation among "transsexuals." In D. P. Laub and P. Gandy (eds.), *Proceedings of the Second Interdisciplinary Symposium on Gender Dysphoria Syndrome.* Stanford, CA: Stanford University Press, 1973.

Meyer, J. P., and Pepper, S. Need compatibility and marital adjustment in young married couples. *Journal of Personality and Social Psychology,* 1977, *35,* 331–342.

Meyer-Bahlburg, H. F. L. Sex hormones and male homosexuality in comparative perspective. *Archives of Sexual Behavior*, 1977, *6*, 297–325.

————. Sex hormones and female homosexuality: A critical examination. *Archives of Sexual Behavior*, 1979, *8*, 101–119.

————. Sex chromosomes and aggression in humans. In P. F. Brain and D. Benton (eds.), *The biology of aggression*. The Netherlands: Sythoff and Noordhoff International, 1981.

————, and Ehrhardt, A. A. Prenatal sex hormones and human aggression: A review and new data on progestogen effects. *Aggressive Behavior*, 1982, *8*, 39–62.

————; Grisanti, G. C.; and Ehrhardt, A. A. Prenatal effects of sex hormones on human male behavior: Medroxyprogesterone acetate (MPD). *Psychoneuroendocrinology*, 1977, *2*, 383–390.

Michael, R. P.; Bonsall, R. W.; and Warner, P. Human vaginal secretions: Volatile fatty acid content. *Science*, 1974, *186*, 1217–1219.

————, and Keverne, E. B. Pheromones in the communication of sexual status in primates. *Nature*, 1968, *218*, 746–749.

————, and Zumpe, D. Potency in male rhesus monkeys: Effects of continuously receptive females, *Science*, 1978, *200*, 451–453.

Mill, J. S. *On Liberty*. Boston: Ticknor and Fields, 1863 (paperbound ed., New York: Norton, 1975).

Miller, P. Y., and Simon, W. Adolescent sexual behavior: Context and change. *Social Problems*. 1974, *22*, 58–76.

————. The development of sexuality in adolescence. In J. Adelson (ed.), *Handbook of Adolescent Psychology*, New York: Wiley-Interscience, 1980.

Miller, W. R., and Lief, H. I. Masturbatory attitudes, knowledge and experience: Data from the Sex Knowledge and Attitude Test (SKAT). *Archives of Sexual Behavior*, 1976, *5*, 447–468.

Mischel, W. A social-learning view of sex differences in behavior. In E. E. Maccoby (ed.), *The Development of Sex Differences*. Stanford, CA: Stanford University Press, 1966.

Mitchell, G. *Behavioral sex differences in nonhuman primates*. New York: Van Nostrand Reinhold, 1979.

Mohr, J. C. *Abortion in America: The origins and evolutions of national policy*. New York: Oxford University Press, 1978.

Money, J. Sex hormones and their variables in human eroticism. In W. C. Young (ed.), *Sex and internal secretions, Third ed.* Baltimore: Williams and Wilkins, 1961.

————. *Sex errors of the body*. Baltimore: Johns Hopkins Press, 1968.

————. Sexual dimorphism and homosexual gender identity. *Psychological Bulletin*, 1970, *74*, 425–440.

————. Ablatio penis: Normal male infant sex-reassigned as a girl. *Archives of Sexual Behavior*, 1975, *4*, 65–72.

————, and Ehrhardt, A. A. *Man and woman: Boy and girl*. Baltimore: Johns Hopkins Press, 1972.

————, and Green, R. Prepubertal morphologically normal boys demonstrating signs of cross-gender identity: A five-year follow-up. *American Journal of Orthopsychiatry*, 1964, *34*, 365–366.

————; Hampson, J. G.; and Hampson, J. L. Imprinting and the establishment of gender role. *Archives of Neurology and Psychiatry*, 1957, *77*, 333–336.

————, and Mathews, D. Prenatal exposure to virilising progestens: An adult follow-up study of 12 women. *Archives of Sexual Behavior*, 1982, *11*, 73–78.

————, and Ogunro, C. Behavioral sexology: Ten cases of genetic male intersexuality with impaired prenatal and pubertal androgenization. *Archives of Sexual Behavior*, 1974, *3*, 181–205.

————, and Primrose, C. Sexual dimorphism and dissociation in the psychology of male transsexuals. *Journal of Nervous and Mental Disease*, 1968, *147*, 472–486.

————, and Sollod, R. Body image, plastic surgery (prosthetic testes) and Kallmann's Syndrome. *British Journal of Medical Psychology*, 1978, *51*, 91–94.

————, and Tucker, P. *Sexual signatures*. Boston: Little, Brown, 1975.

Montagna, W., and Sadler, W. A. *Reproductive Behavior*, New York: Plenum, 1974.

Moran, A. F. Video contraception. New York *Times*, December 8, 1982, A31.

Morgan, M. *The total woman*. New York: Pocket Books, 1975.

Morris, D. *The naked ape*. New York: McGraw-Hill, 1967 (paperbound ed., New York: Dell, 1969).

Morris, J. *Conundrum*. New York: Harcourt

Brace Jovanovich, 1974 (paperback ed., New York: Signet, 1975).

Morris, N. M. The frequency of sexual intercourse during pregnancy. *Archives of Sexual Behavior*, 1975, *4*, 501—508.

Morrison, T. *The bluest eye*, New York: Simon & Schuster, 1970.

Morse, S. J. Family law in transition: From traditional families to individual liberty. In V. Tufte and B. Myerhoff (eds.), *Changing images of the family*. New Haven, CT: Yale University Press, 1979.

Mosher, C. D. *The Mosher survey: Sexual attitudes of 45 Victorian women*. New York: Arno, 1980.

Mosher, D. L. Sex differences, sex experience, sex guilt, and explicitly sexual films. *Journal of Social Issues*, 1973, *29*, 95–112.

————, and Cross, H. J. Sex guilt and premarital sexual experiences of college students. *Journal of Consulting and Clinical Psychology*, 1971, *36*, 27–32.

Mosher, W. D. Fertility and family planning in the 1970's: The national survey of family growth. *Family Planning Perspectives*. 1982, *14*, 314–320.

Moss, H. A. Early sex differences and mother-infant interaction. In R. C. Friedman, R. M. Richart, and R. Van de Wiele (eds.), *Sex differences in behavior*. New York: Wiley, 1974.

Mould, D. E. Women's orgasm and the muscle spindle. In B. Graber (ed.), *The circumvaginal musculature and sexual function*. Basel, Switzerland: Karger, 1982.

Mumford, S. D. The vasectomy decision-making process. *Studies in Family Planning*, 1983, *14*, 83–88.

Munger, M. B. T. Sex-differentiation in preschool children: Sex-typical toy preferences and knowledge of peers' sex-typical toy preferences. Ph.D. Thesis, University of Nebraska, 1970. Dissertation Abstracts #72-170.

Murstein, B. I. *Who will marry whom*. New York: Springer, 1976.

Mussen, P. H., and Jones, M. D. Self conceptions, motivations, and interpersonal attitudes of later and early maturing boys. *Child Development*, 1957, *28*, 243–256.

Naftolin, F., and Butz, E. (eds.) Sexual dimorphism. *Science*, 1981, *211*, (entire issue).

————; Ryan, K. J.; and Petro, Z. Aromatization of androstenedione by the anterior hypothalamus of adult male and female rats. *Endocrinology*, 1972, 90, 295–298.

Nahemow, L., and Lawton, M. Similarity and propinquity in friendship formation. *Journal of Personality and Social Psychology*, 1975, 32, 205–213.

Nance, D. M.; Shryne, J.; and Gorski, R. A. Septal lesions: Effects on lordosis behavior and pattern of gonadotropin release. *Hormones and Behavior*, 1974, 5, 73–81.

Nawy, H. In the pursuit of happiness?: Consumers of erotica in San Francisco. *Journal of Social Issues*, 1973, 29, 147–162.

Nedoma, K.; Mellan, J.; and Podelickoua, J. Sexual behavior and its development in pedophilic men. *Archives of Sexual Behavior*, 1971, 1, 267–271.

Negri, G. Holbrook defendants. Boston *Globe*, June 18 and 19, 1983.

Neugarten, B. Education and the life cycle. *School Review*, 1972, 80, 209–218.

Neugarten, B. L. Women's attitudes towards the menopause. *Vita Humana*, 1963, 6, 140–153.

Newcomb, M. D., and Bentler, P. M. Cohabitation before marriage. *Alternative Lifestyles*, 1980, 3, 65–85.

Newcomb, T. M. *The acquaintance process.* New York: Holt, Rinehart & Winston, 1961.

Newcomer, S. F., and Udry, J. R. Oral sex in an adolescent population. *Archives of Sexual Behavior*, 1985, 14, 41–46.

Newman, G., and Nichols, C. R. Sexual activities and attitudes in older persons. *Journal of the American Medical Association*, 1960, 173, 33–35.

————. Sexual activities and attitudes in older persons. In N. W. Wagner (ed.), *Perspectives on human sexuality.* New York: Behavioral Sciences, 1974.

The new scarlet letter, *Time*, Aug. 2, 1982. 61–69.

Newson, J., and Newson, E. *Four years old in an urban community.* London: Allen and Unwin, 1968.

Newton, N. Interrelations between sexual responsiveness, birth, and breast feeding. In J. Zubin and J. Money (eds.), *Contemporary sexual behavior.* Baltimore: Johns Hopkins Press, 1973.

No atherosclerosis risk in vasectomized men,

preliminary studies find. *Family Planning Perspectives.* 1981, 13, 276–277.

Norplant: Subdermal implants approved in Finland. *Studies in Family Planning*, 1984, 15, no. 1, 48.

Notman, M. T. Changing roles for women at mid-life. In W. H. Norman and T. J. Scarawella (Eds.), *Mid-life: Developmental and clinical issues.* New York: Brunner/Mazel, 1980.

O'Brien, D. P.; Walton, K. N.; and Wheatley, J. K. Some common urologic causes of sexual problems. *Medical Aspects of Human Sexuality*, 1983, 17, 203–209.

Offer, D. *The psychological world of the teenager: A study of normal adolescent boys.* New York: Basic Books, 1969.

————, and Offer, J. B. *From teenage to young manhood.* New York: Basic Books, 1975.

————; Ostrov, E.; and Howard, K. I. *The adolescent: A psychological self-portrait,* New York: Basic Books, 1981.

Office of Technology Assessment, *World population and fertility planning technologies: The next 20 years.* Congress of the United States, 1983.

Offir, C. W. *Human sexuality.* New York: Harcourt Brace Jovanovich, 1982.

Offit, A. K. *Night thoughts of a sex therapist.* New York: Congdon and Weed, 1982.

Ololski, M. Abortion and contraception in Poland, *Studies in Family Planning*, 1983, 14, 263–274.

O'Neill, N. *The marriage premise.* New York: M. Evans, 1977.

O'Neill, N., and O'Neill, G. *Open marriage.* New York: Avon, 1972.

O'Neill, S.; Fein, D.; Velit, K. M.; and Frank, C. Sex differences in preadolescent self-disclosure. *Sex Roles*, 1976, 2, 85–88.

Orr, M. T. Sex education and contraceptive education within U.S. public high schools, *Family Planning Perspectives*, 1982, 14, 304–313.

Osborn, C. A., and Pollack, R. H. The effects of two types of erotic literature on physiological and verbal measures of female sexual arousal. *Journal of Sex Research*, 1977, 13, 250–256.

Osofsky, J., and Osofsky, H. The psychological reaction of patients to legalized abortion. *American Journal of Orthopsychiatry*, 1972, 42, 48–60.

Owen, W. F. Jr. Sexually transmitted diseases and traumatic problems in homosexual men. *Annals of Internal Medicine*, 1980, 92, 805–808.

Parker, J.; Nelson, F.; and Svigin, M. Legal abortion: A half-decade experience. *Family Planning Perspectives*, 1975, 7, 248–255.

Parlee, M. Menstrual rhythms in sensory processes: A review of fluctuations in vision, olfaction, audition, taste, and touch. *Psychological Bulletin*, 1983, 93, 539–548.

Paul, W.; Weinrich, J. D.; Gonsiorek, J. C.; and Hotvedt, M. E. (eds.) *Homosexuality: Social, psychological and biological issues.* Beverly Hills, CA: Sage Publications, 1982.

Pauly, I. Adult manifestations of male transsexualism. In R. Green and J. Money (eds.), *Transsexualism and sex reassignment.* Baltimore: Johns Hopkins Press, 1969.

Pauly, I. B. Female transsexualism: Parts I and II. *Archives of Sexual Behavior*, 1974, 3, 487–526.

Pear, R. FDA approves new sponge contraceptive. New York *Times*, April 7, 1983, A1.

Peplau, L. A. Sex, love and the double standard. Paper presented at the convention of the American Psychological Association, San Francisco, September 1976.

————, and Cochran, S. D. Value orientations in the intimate relationships of gay men. *Journal of Homosexuality*, 1981, 3, 1–20.

————; Cochran, S.; Rook, K.; and Padesky, C. Loving women: Attachment and autonomy in gay relationships. *Journal of Social Issues*, 1978, 34, 7–27.

————; Rubin, Z.; and Hill, C. T. Sexual intimacy in dating relationships. *Journal of Social Issues*, 1977, 33, 86–109.

Perry, J. D., and Whipple, B. Pelvic muscle strength of female ejaculators: Evidence in support of a new theory of orgasm. *Journal of Sex Research*, 1981, 17, 22–39.

————. Multiple components of female orgasm. In B. Graber (ed.), *Circumvaginal musculature and sexual function.* New York: S. Korger, 1982.

Persky, H.; Charney, N.; Lief, H. I.; O'Brien, C. P.; Miller, W. R.; and Strauss, D. The relationship of plasma estradiol level to sexual behavior in young women. *Psychosomatic Medicine*, 1978, 40, 523–535.

———; Lief, H. I.; Strauss, D.; Miller, W. R.; and O'Brien, C. P. Plasma testosterone level and sexual behavior of couples. *Archives of Sexual Behavior.* 1978, *7,* 157–173.

———; O'Brien, C. P.; Lief, H. I.; Strauss, D.; and Miller, W. R. Female sexual activity at ovulation. Letter to the editor of the *New England Journal of Medicine,* 1979, *300,* 626.

Peterman, D. J.; Ridley, C. A.; and Anderson, S. M. A comparison of cohabiting and non-cohabitating college students. *Journal of Marriage and the Family,* 1974, *36,* 344–354.

Pfaff, D. W., and McEwen, B. S. Actions of estrogens and progestins on nerve cells. *Science,* 1983, *219,* 808–813.

Pfeiffer, E., and Davis, G. C. Determinants of sexual behavior in middle and old age. *Journal of the American Geriatrics Society,* 1972, *20,* 151–158.

———; Verwoerdt, H.; and Davis, G. C. Sexual behavior in middle life. *American Journal of Psychiatry,* 1972, *128,* 1282–1287.

———; ———; and Wang, H. S. Sexual behavior in aged men and women. *Archives of General Psychiatry,* 1968, *19,* 753–758.

———; ———; ———. The natural history of sexual behavior in a biologically advantaged group of aged individuals. *Journal of Gerontology,* 1969, *24,* 193–198.

Philliber, S. G., and Philliber, W. W. Social and psychological perspectives on voluntary sterilization: A review. *Studies in Family Planning,* 1985, *16,* 1–29.

Pickles, V. R. A plain-muscle stimulant in the menstrum. *Nature,* 1957, *180,* 1198.

Pietropinto, A., and Simenauer, J. *Beyond the male myth.* New York: New York Times Books, 1977.

Pirke, K. M.; Kockott, G. M.; and Dittmar, F. Psychosexual stimulation and plasma testosterone in man. *Archives of Sexual Behavior,* 1974, *3,* 577–583.

Playboy report on American men: A study of values, attitudes and goals of U.S. males 18 to 49 years old. Louis Harris and Associates poll 1976–1977. Analysis and interpretation by W. Simon and P. Y. Miller, Playboy Enterprises, Inc., 1979.

Pleck, J. H. Male sex role behaviors in a representative national sample, 1973. In D. McGuigan (ed.), *New research on women and sex roles.* Ann Arbor: Center for Continuing Education of Women, 1976.

———. *The myth of masculinity.* Cambridge, MA: MIT Press, 1981.

———, and Sawyer, J. (eds.) *Men and masculinity.* Englewood Cliffs, NJ: Prentice-Hall, 1974.

Polivy, J.; Hackett, R.; and Bycio, P. The effect of perceived smoking status on attractiveness. *Personality and Social Psychology Bulletin,* 1979, *5,* 401–404, 420–422.

Pomeroy, W. B. *Dr. Kinsey and the Institute for Sex Research,* New York: Harper & Row, 1972.

Pornography: Attitudes, use, and effects. *Journal of Social Issues,* 1973, *29.*

Pregnant runner won't ease pace. New York *Times,* A18.

Price, S. C. Counseling adolescents who have sexual problems. In R. O. Passau (ed.), *Psychological aspects of medical practice: Children and adolescents.* Menlo Park, CA: Addison-Wesley, 1982.

Price, S. C.; Reynolds, B. S.; Cohen, B. D.; Anderson, A. J.; and Schochet, B. V. P. Group treatment of erectile dysfunction for men without partners: A controlled evaluation. *Archives of Sexual Behavior,* 1981, *10,* 253–268.

Prince, V., and Bentler, P. M. Survey of 504 cases of transvestism. *Psychological Reports,* 1972, *32,* 902–917.

Project reduction results in better method use, few second pregnancy among teenage parents. *Family Planning Perspectives,* 1982, *14,* 335–336.

Purnick, J. School board updated sex-education course. New York *Times,* December 4, 1983.

Rachman, S. Sexual fetishism: An experimental analogue. *Psychological Record,* 1966, *16,* 293–296.

Rada, R. T. Psychological factors in rapist behavior. In R. T. Rada (ed.), *Clinical aspects of the rapist.* New York: Grune and Stratton, 1978.

Radke-Yarrow, M.; Campbell, J. D.; and Burton, R. V. Recollections of childhood: A study of the retrospective method. *Monograph of the Society for Research in Child Development,* 1970, *35,* no. 5.

Rainwater, L. Marital sexuality in four cultures of poverty. *Journal of Marriage and the Family,* 1964, *26,* 457–466.

———. *Behind ghetto walls.* Chicago: Aldine, 1970.

Raisman, G., and Field, P. M. Sexual development in the preoptic area of the rat. *Science,* 1971, *173,* 731–733.

———. Sexual dimorphism in the neuropil of the preoptic area of the rat and its dependence on neonatal androgen. *Brain Research,* 1973, *54,* 1–29.

Ramirez, J.; Bryant, J.; and Zillmann, D. Effects of erotica on retaliatory behavior as a function of level of prior provocation. *Journal of Personality and Social Psychology,* 1982, *43,* 971–978.

Ramsey, G. V. The sex information of younger boys. *American Journal of Orthopsychiatry,* 1943, *13,* 347–352.

Rapoport, R., and Rapoport, R. *Dual-career families.* Baltimore: Penguin, 1971.

Ratcliffe, S. G., and Field, M. A. S. Emotional disorder in XXY children: Four case reports. *Journal of Child Psychology and Psychiatry,* 1982, *23,* 401–406.

Ravicz, T. Boston's crumbling combat zone. *Harvard Independent Commencement,* 1981, *12,* 14–15.

Rawson, P. (Ed.). *Primitive erotic art.* New York: Putnam, 1973.

Raymond, J. G. *The transsexual empire: The making of the she-male.* Boston: Beacon, 1979.

Read, K. E. *Other voices: The style of a male homosexual tavern.* Novato, CA: Chandler and Sharp, 1980.

Rechy, J. *City of night.* New York: Grove Press, 1963 (paperbound ed., New York: Grove Press, 1964).

Reevy, W. R. Premarital petting behavior and marital happiness prediction. *Marriage and Family Living,* 1959, *21,* 349–355.

Reichelt, P. A. Coital and contraceptive behavior of female adolescents. *Archives of Sexual Behavior,* 1979, *8,* 159–172.

Reinisch, J. M. Prenatal exposure of human foetuses to synthetic progestin and oestrogen affects personality. *Nature,* 1977, *266,* 561–562.

———. Prenatal exposure to synthetic progestins increases potential for aggression in humans. *Science,* 1981, *211,* 1171–1173.

Reis, H. T.; Nezlek, J.; and Wheeler, L. Physical attractiveness in social interaction.

Journal of Personality and Social Psychology, 1980, *38,* 604–617.

Reis, H. T., and Wright, S. Knowledge of sex-role stereotypes in children ages 3 to 5. *Sex Roles,* 1982, *8,* 1049–1056.

Reiss, I. L. Premarital sexual permissiveness among Negroes and whites. *American Sociological Review,* 1964, *29,* 688–698. (a)

————. The scaling of premarital sexual permissiveness. *Journal of Marriage and the Family,* 1964, *26,* 188–198. (b)

————. *The social context of premarital sexual permissiveness.* New York: Holt, Rinehart & Winston, 1967.

————. How and why America's sex standards are changing. In J. H. Gagnon and W. Simon (eds.), *The Sexual Scene.* Chicago: Transaction, 1970.

————. Premarital sexuality: past, present, and future. In I. L. Reiss (ed.), *Readings on the Family System.* New York: Holt, 1972.

————. Trouble in paradise: The current status of sexual science. *Journal of Sex Research,* 1982, *18,* 97–113.

Rekers, G. A. Stimulus control over sex-typed play in cross-gender identified boys. *Journal of Experimental Child Psychology,* 1975, *20,* 136–148.

Resnik, H. Eroticized repetitive hanging: A form of self-destructive behavior. *American Journal of Psychotherapy.* 1972, *26,* 4–21.

Resnik, H. L. P., and Wolfgang, M. E. *Treatment of the sex offender.* Boston: Little, Brown, 1972.,

————. New directions in the treatment of sex deviance. In H. L. P. Resnik and M. E. Wolfgang (eds.), *Treatment of the Sex Offender.* Boston: Little, Brown, 1972.

Rheingold, H. L., and Cook, K. V. The contents of boys' and girls' rooms as an index of parents' behavior. *Child Development,* 1975, *46,* 459–463.

Rich, B. R. Anti-pornography: Soft issue, hard world. *Village Voice,* July 20, 1982, 1ff.

Richards, R., and Ames, J. *Second serve,* New York: Stein & Day, 1983.

Richards, R. N. *Venereal diseases and their avoidance.* New York: Holt, Rinehart & Winston, 1974.

Richardson, L. W. *The dynamics of sex and gender,* Second ed. Boston: Houghton-Mifflin, 1981.

Rist, R.C. *The pornography controversy.* New Brunswick, NJ: Transaction, 1974.

Robbins, M. B., and Jensen, G. D. Multiple orgasm in males, *Journal of Sex Research,* 1978, *14,* 21–26.

Roberts, E. J.; Kline, R.; and Gagnon, J. *Family life and sexual learning: A study of the role of parents in the sexual learning of children.* Vol. 1. Cambridge, MA: Population Education, 1978.

Robinson, I.E., and Jedlicka, D. Change in sexual attitudes and behavior of college students from 1965 to 1980: A research note. *Journal of Marriage and the Family,* 1982, 237–240.

Robinson, P. *The modernization of sex.* New York: Harper & Row, 1976.

Robson, K. S. The role of eye-to-eye contact in maternal-infant attachment. *Journal of Child Psychology and Psychiatry,* 1967, *8,* 13–25.

Roebuck, J., and McGee, M. G. Attitudes toward premarital sex and sexual behavior among black high school girls. *Journal of Sex Research,* 1977, *13,* 104–114.

Rooth, G. Exhibitionism, sexual violence and paedophilia. *British Journal of Psychiatry.* 1973, *122,* 705–710.

Rose, R. M. The psychological effects of androgens and estrogens: A review. In R. I. Shader (ed.), *Psychiatric complications of medical drugs.* New York: Raven Press, 1972.

————. Psychoendocrinology of the menstrual cycle. *New England Journal of Medicine,* 1978, *299,* 1186–1187.

————; Holaday, J. W.; and Bernstein, I. S. Plasma testosterone levels in the male rhesus: Influences of sexual and social stimuli. *Science,* 1972, *178,* 643–645.

Rosenberg, C. Sexuality, class and role. *American Quarterly,* 1973, *25,* 131–153.

Rosenberg, F. R., and Simmons, R. G. Sex difference in the self-concept in adolescence. *Sex Roles,* 1975, *1,* 147–159.

Rosenfeld, A. A. Incidence of a history of incest among eighteen female psychiatric patients. *American Journal of Psychiatry,* 1979, *13,* 791–795.

Ross, M. W. Retrospective distortion in homosexual research. *Archives of Sexual Behavior,* 1980, *9,* 523–531.

Rossi, A. S. Aging and parenthood in the middle years. In P. B. Baltes and O.G. Brim, Jr., *Life span development and behavior.* Vol. 3. New York: Academic Press, 1980. (a)

————. Life-span theories and women's lives. *Signs,* 1980, *6,* 4–32. (b)

Rubenstein, C. The modern art of courtly love, *Psychology Today,* July 1983.

Rubin, E. R. *Abortion, politics, and the courts: Roe v. Wade and its aftermath.* Westport, CT: Greenwood, 1982. (Contributions in American Studies, No. 57.)

Rubin, J. Z.; Provenzano, F.; and Luria, Z. The eye of the beholder: Parents' view of sex of newborns. *American Journal of Orthopsychiatry,* 1974, *44,* 512–519.

Rubin, L. B. *Worlds of pain,* New York: Basic, 1976.

————. *Women of a certain age.* New York: Harper & Row, 1979.

Rubin, Z. *Liking and loving: An invitation to social psychology.* New York: Holt, Rinehart & Winston, 1973.

Russell, D. E. H. *The politics of rape,* New York: Stein & Day, 1975.

————. *Rape in marriage.* New York: Macmillan, 1982.

Rutter, M. *Maternal deprivation reassessed,* Second ed. New York: Penguin, 1981.

Ryan, W. *Blaming the victim,* New York: Pantheon, 1974.

Ryder, N. B. Contraceptive failure in the United States. *Family Planning Perspectives,* 1973, *5,* 133–142.

Rynearson, E. Relinquishment and its maternal complications: A preliminary study. *American Journal of Psychiatry,* 1982, *139,* 338–340.

Saario, T. N.; Jacklin, C. N.; and Tittle, C. K. Sex role stereotyping in the public schools. *Harvard Educational Review,* 1973, *43,* 386–416.

Sack, A. R.; Keiller, J. F.; and Hinkle, D. E. Premarital sexual intercourse: A test of the effects of peer group, religiosity, and sexual guilt. *Journal of Sex Research,* 1984, *20,* 168–185.

Sade, D. S. Some aspects of parent-offspring and sibling relations in a group of rhesus monkeys. *American Journal of Physical Anthropology,* 1965, *23,* 1–118.

————. A longitudinal study of social behavior of rhesus monkeys. In R. Tuttle (ed.), *The functional and evolutionary biology of primates,* Chicago: Aldine Atherton, 1972.

Safran, C. What men do to women on the job: A shocking look at sexual harassment. *Redbook,* November, 1976, 148ff.

Sagarin, E. Prison homosexuality and its effect on postprison sexual behavior. *Psychiatry*, 1976, *39*, 245–257.

Saghir, M., and Robins, E. *Male and female homosexuality*. Baltimore: Williams & Wilkins, 1973.

Salminies, P.; Kockott, G.; Pirke, K. M.; Vogt, H. J.; and Schill, W. B. Effects of testosterone replacement on sexual behavior in hypogonadal men. *Archives of Sexual Behavior*, 1982, *11*, 345–354.

SAMOIS. *Coming to Power*. Palo Alto, CA: UP Press, 1981.

Sanday, P. R. The socio-cultural context of rape: A cross cultural study. *Journal of Social Issues*, 1981, *37*, 5–27.

Sanders, W. B. *Rape and women's identity*, Beverly Hills, CA: Sage, 1980.

Sandler, M., and Gessa, G. L. (Eds.). *Sexual behavior: Pharmacology and biochemistry*. New York: Raven Press, 1975.

San Francisco Committee on Crime: *A report on non-victim crime in San Francisco. Part II: Sexual conduct, gambling, prostitution, 1971*.

Sanger, M. *Margaret Sanger: An autobiography*. New York: W. W. Norton, 1938.

Sapolsky, B. S., and Zillmann, D. The effect of soft-core and hard-core erotica on provoked and unprovoked hostile behavior. *Journal of Sex Research*. 1981, *71*, 319–343.

Sarrel, L. J., and Sarrel, P. M. *Sexual unfolding: Sexual development and sex therapies in late adolescence*. Boston: Little, Brown, 1979.

Sarrel, P. M., and Masters, W. H. Sexual molestation of men by women. *Archives of Sexual Behavior*, 1982, *2*, 117–131.

Scacco, A. *Rape in prison*. Springfield, IL: Charles C Thomas, 1975.

Scanzoni, J. *Sexual bargaining: Power politics in the American marriage*. Englewood Cliffs, NJ: Prentice-Hall, 1972.

Scarr, S. *Mother care/Other care*. New York: Basic Books, 1984.

Schachter, S. The interaction of cognitive and physiological determinants of emotional state. In L. Berkowitz (ed.), *Advances in experimental social psychology*, Vol. 1. New York: Academic Press, 1964.

———, and Singer, J. E. Cognitive, social and physiological determinants of emotional state. *Psychological Review*, 1962, *69*, 379–399.

Schäfer, S. Sexual and social problems of lesbians. *Journal of Sex Research*, 1976, *12*, 50–69.

———. Sociosexual behavior in male and female homosexuals. A study in sex differences. *Archives of Sexual Behavior*, 1977, *6*, 355–364.

Schaffer, H. R. *The growth of sociability*. Baltimore: Penguin, 1971.

Schearer, S. B. Current efforts and development of male hormonal contraception. *Studies in Family Planning*, 1978, *9*, 229–231.

Schearer, S. B.; Alvarez-Sanchez, F.; Anselmo, J.; Brenner, P.; Continho, E.; Latham-Faundes, A.; Frich, J.; Heinild, B.; and Johannson, E. D. B. Hormonal contraception for men. *International Journal of Andrology*, 1978, Supplement, 2, 680–712.

Schell, R. E., and Silber, J. W. Sex-role discrimination among young children. *Perceptual and Motor Skills*, 1968, *27*, 379–389.

Schiff, A. F. Rape in foreign countries. *Medical Trial Technique Quarterly*, 1973, *20*, 66–74.

Schlissel, L. *Women's diaries of the westward journey*. New York: Schocken Books, 1982.

Schlassman, S., and Wallach, S. The crime of precocious sexuality: Female juvenile delinquency in the progressive era. *Harvard Educational Review*, 1978, *48*, 65–94.

Schmeck, H. M., Jr. Fetal defects discovered early by new method. New York *Times*, October 18, 1983, C1.

Schmidt, G. Male-female differences in sexual arousal and behavior during and after exposure to sexually explicit stimuli. *Archives of Sexual Behavior*, 1975, *4*, 353–365.

———. Letter to the Editor on H. Geise and G. Schmidt, 1968, *Archives of Sexual Behavior*, 1978, *7*, 73–74.

———, and Sigusch, V. Sex differences in response to psychosexual stimulation by films and slides. *Journal of Sex Research*, 1970, *6*, 268–283.

———, and ———. Patterns of sexual behavior in West German workers and students. *Journal of Sex Research*, 1971, *7*, 89–106.

———, and ———. Changes in sexual behavior among young males and females between 1960–1970. *Archives of Sexual Behavior*, 1972, *2*, 27–45.

———, and ———. The effects of pornography. *International Journal of Sex Medicine*, September 1980, 3–6.

Schmidt, S. S. Vasectomy: Indications, technique, and reversibility. *Fertility and Sterility*, 1968, *19*, 192–196.

Schneider, H. K. Romantic love among the Turu. In D. S. Marshall and R. C. Suggs (eds.), *Human Sexual Behavior*. Englewood Cliffs, NJ: Prentice-Hall, 1971.

Schofield, M. *The sexual behavior of young people*. Boston: Little, Brown, 1965.

Schoof-Jams, K.; Schlaegel, J.; and Walczak, L. Differentiation of sexual morality between 11 and 16 years. *Archives of Sexual Behavior*, 1976, *5*, 353–370.

Schover, R., and LoPiccolo, J. Treatment effectiveness for dysfunctions of sexual desire. *Journal of Sex and Marital Therapy*, 1982, *8*, 179–197.

Schrome, S. H.; Lief, H. I.; and Wein, A. J. Clinical profile of experience of 130 consecutive cases of impotent men. *Urology*, 1979, *13*, 511–515.

Schumacher, S., and Lloyd, C. W. Physiological and psychological factors in impotency. *Journal of Sex Research*, 1981, *17*, 40–53.

Schur, E. M. *Labeling deviant behavior*. New York: Harper & Row, 1971.

Schwartz, M. F., and Masters, W. H. The Masters and Johnson treatment program for dissatisfied homosexual men. *American Journal of Psychiatry*, 1984, *141*, 173–181.

Schwartz, S. Effects of sex guilt and sexual arousal on the retention of birth control information. *Journal of Consulting and Clinical Psychology*, 1973, *41*, 61–64.

Schwyhart, W. R., and Kutner, S. J. A reanalysis of female reactions to contraceptive sterilization. *Journal of Nervous and Mental Disease*, 1973, *156*, 354–370.

Sears, R.; Maccoby, E. E.; and Levin, H. *Patterns of child rearing*. Evanston, IL: Row, Peterson, 1957.

Sears, R. R., and Wise, G. W. Relation of cup feeding in infancy to thumb-sucking and the oral drive. *American Journal of Orthopsychiatry*, 1950, *20*, 123–138.

Seay, B.; Alexander, B. K.; and Harlow, H. Maternal behavior of socially deprived rhesus monkeys. *Journal of Abnormal and Social Psychology*, 1964, *69*, 45–354.

Segraves, R. T.; Schoenberg, H. W.; Zarims, C. K.; Knopf, J.; and Cameo, P. Referral of impotent patients to a sexual dysfunction clinic. *Archives of Sexual Behavior*, 1982, *11*, 521–528.

Seligman, C.; Brickman, J.; and Koulack,

D. Rape and physical attractiveness: Assigning responsibility to victims. *Journal of Personality,* 1977, *45,* 554–563.

Semans, J. Premature ejaculation: A new approach. *Southern Medical Journal,* 1956, *49,* 353–358.

Sex and Herpes, *Medical Aspects of Human Sexuality,* October, 1982, 34ff.

Sexually Transmitted Diseases. *Harvard Medical School Health Letter,* April 1981, 1ff.

Seyler, L. E., Jr.; Canalis, E.; Spare, S.; and Reichlin, S. Abnormal gonadotropin secretory responses to LRH in transsexual women after diethylstilbesterol priming. *Journal of Clinical Endocrinology and Metabolism,* 1978, *47,* 176–183.

Sgroi, S. M. *Handbook of clinical intervention in child sexual abuse.* Lexington, MA: Lexington Books, 1982.

Shah, F.; Zelnik, M.; and Kantner, J. F. Unprotected intercourse among unwed teenagers. *Family Planning Perspectives,* 1975, *7,* 39–44.

Sharpe, L. How various illnesses affect sexual functioning. *Medical Aspects of Human Sexuality,* 1983, *17,* 148–159.

Sheehy, G. *Passages: Predictable crises of adult life,* New York: Dutton, 1977.

Shephard, B. D., and Shephard, C. A. *The complete guide to women's health.* Tampa, FL.: Mariner Publishing, 1982.

Sherfey, M. J. *The nature and evolution of female sexuality.* New York: Random House, 1972 (paperbound ed., New York: Vintage, 1973).

Sherman, J. A. *On the psychology of women.* Springfield, IL: Charles C Thomas, 1971.

Shipp, E. R. More married women choosing sterilization, New York *Times,* July 5, 1985, A 1ff.

Sholty, M. J.; Ephross, P. H.; Plant, S. M.; Fischman, S. H.; Charnas, J. F.; and Cody, C. A. Female orgasmic experience: A subjective study. *Archives of Sexual Behavior,* 1984, *13,* 155–164.

Short, R. V. Reproduction and human society. In C. R. Austin and R. V. Short (eds.), *Artificial Control of Reproduction.* London: Cambridge University Press, 1972.

Shostak, M. *Nisa: The life and words of a Kung woman,* Cambridge, MA: Harvard University Press, 1981.

Sicuteri, F. Serotonin and sex in man. *Pharmacological Research Communications,* 1974, *6,* 403–411.

Sides, W. Lana: A story of scarlet letters and public risks, *New Journal,* December 9, 1983, *16,* 16–20.

SIECUS. *Sexuality and Man.* New York: Scribner, 1970.

Siegel, J. S. Some demographic aspects of aging in the United States. In U.S. Department of HEW, National Institute of Aging, *Epidemiology of Aging,* (GP01746-0027).

Siegelman, M. Adjustment of homosexual and heterosexual women. A cross-national replication. *Archives of Sexual Behavior,* 1979, *8,* 121–125.

Signorielli, N. The demography of the television world. In O. H. Gaudy, Jr.; P. Espinosa; and K. Ordover (eds.) *Proceedings of the tenth annual telecommunications policy research conference.* Norwood, NY: Ablex, 1983.

Sigusch, V., and Schmidt, B. Lower class sexuality: Some emotional and social aspects in West German males and females. *Archives of Sexual Behavior,* 1971, *1,* 29–44.

————, and ————. Teenage boys and girls in West Germany. *Journal of Sex Research,* 1973, *9,* 107–123.

————; Schorsch, E.; Dannecker, N.; Schmidt, G. Official statement by the German Society for Sex Research (Deutsche Gesellschaft für Sexual-forschung e.v.) on the research of Professor Dr. Gunter Dörner on the subject of homosexuality. *Archives of Sexual Behavior,* 1982, *11,* 445–449.

Silka, L., and Kiesler, S. Couples who choose to remain childless. *Family Planning Perspectives,* 1977, *9,* 16–25.

Silver, D. S. The normative development of psychological variables in gender identification in 3 to 8 year old children. Ph.D. Thesis, Wayne State University, 1972.

Simenauer, J., and Carroll, D. *Singles: The new Americans.* New York: Simon & Schuster, 1982.

Simmer, H.; Pion, R.; and Dignam, W. *Testicular feminization.* Springfield, IL: Charles C Thomas, 1965.

Simmons, R. G.; Blyth, D. A.; Van Cleave, E. F.; and Bush, D. M. Entry into early adolescence: The impact of school structure, puberty, and early dating on self-esteem. *American Sociological Review,* 1979, *44,* 948–967.

Simon, K. *Bronx primitive,* New York: Viking, 1982.

Simon, W., and Gagnon, J. H. Homosexuality: The formulation of a sociological per-spective. In R. Weltge (ed.), *The same sex.* Philadelphia: Pilgrim Press, 1969.

————, and Miller, P. Y. *The Playboy report on American men,* Chicago: Playboy, 1979.

Singer, J. J. Control of male and female sexual behavior in the female rat. *Journal of Comparative Physiology and Psychology,* 1968, *66,* 738–742.

Sisson, W. H. III. The self perception of male and female homosexuals. *Criminal Justice Monograph,* 1975, *6,* 4–17.

Sivin, I. IUD's and ectopic pregnancy. *Studies in Family Planning,* 1983, *14,* 57–63.

————; Alvarez-Sanchez, F.; Diaz, S.; McDonald, O.; Holma, P.; Continho, E.; and Robertson, D. N. The Norplant contraceptive method: A report on three years of use. *Studies in Family Planning,* 1982, *1,* 258–261.

————; Diaz, S.; Holma, P.; Alvarez-Sanchez, F.; and Robertson, D. N. A four-year clinical study of Norplant implants. *Studies in Family Planning,* 1983, *14,* 184–191.

————; Robertson, D. N.; Stein, J.; Groxatto, E.; da Silva, A .R.; Sanchez, F. A.; Faunders, A.; McDonald, O.; Holma, P.; Melsen, N. C.; Osler, M.; and Nash, H. A. Norplant: Reversible implant contraception. *Studies in Family Planning,* 1980, *11,* 227–235.

Skeels, H. M. Adult status of children with contrasting early life experiences: A follow-up study. *Monographs of the Society for Research in Child Development,* 1966, *31,* No. 3, Serial #105.

————, and Dye, H. B. A study of the effects of differential stimulation on mentally retarded children. *Proceedings of the American Association on Mental Deficiency,* 1939, *44,* 114–136.

Skodak, M. Adult status of individuals who experienced early intervention. In B. W. Richards (ed.), *Proceedings of the First Congress of the International Association for the Scientific Study of Mental Deficiency.* Reigate: Michael Jackson, 1968.

Skolnick, A. Early attachment and personal relations across the life course. In D. Featherman and R. Lerner (eds.), *Life span development and behavior,* Vol. 7. Hillsdale, NJ: Erlbaum, 1986.

Slimp, J. C.; Hart, B. C.; and Goy, R. W. Heterosexual autosexual, and social sexual behavior of adult male rhesus monkeys with medial preoptic-anterior hypothalamic lesions. *Brain Research,* 1978, *142,* 105–122.

Sloane, E. *Biology of women.* New York: Wiley, 1980.

Smelser, N. J., and Erikson, E. H. (eds.). *Themes of work and love in adulthood.* Cambridge, MA: Harvard University Press, 1980.

Smith, D. D. The social content of pornography. *Journal of Communication,* 1976, *26,* 16–33.

Smith, H., and Cox, C. Dialogue with a dominatrix. *Village Voice,* January 29, 1979, 19.

Smith, J., and Smith, L. (eds.). *Beyond monogamy.* Baltimore: Johns Hopkins Press, 1974.

Smith, R. E. (ed.). *The subtle revolution: Women at work.* Washington, D.C.: Urban Institute, 1979.

Smith-Rosenberg, C. The female world of love and ritual. *Signs,* 1975, *1,* 1–29.

————. Sex as symbol in Victorian purity: An ethnohistorical analysis of Jacksonian America. In J. Demos and S. S. Boocock (eds.), *Turning points: Historical and sociological essays on the family,* Chicago: University of Chicago Press, 1978.

Smithyman, S. D. The undetected rapist. Ph.D. dissertation, Claremont Graduate School, 1978. *Dissertation Abstracts International, 39,* #6, 3058-B.

Snapper, C. M. When a judge orders "chemical castration": Letters to the Editor, New York *Times,* February 8, 1984.

Snowdon, R. Working with incest offenders: Excuses, excuses, excuses. *Aegis,* Summer, *35,* 56–63.

Snyder, A.; LoPiccolo, L.; and LoPiccolo, J. Secondary orgasmic dysfunction II. Case study. *Archives of Sexual Behavior,* 1975, *4,* 277–283.

Sokolov, J. J.; Harris, R. T.; and Hecker, M. R. Isolation of substances from human vaginal secretions previously shown to be sex attractant pheromones in higher primates. *Archives of Sexual Behavior,* 1976, *5,* 269–274.

Solnick, R. L., and Birren, J. D. Male erectile responsiveness. *Archives of Sexual Behavior,* 1977, *6,* 1–9.

Solomon, S., and Saxe, L. What is intelligent, as well as attractive, is good. *Personality and Social Psychology Bulletin,* 1977, *3,* 670–673.

Sommer, B. The effect of menstruation on cognitive and perceptual-motor behavior: A review. *Psychosomatic Medicine,* 1973, *35,* 515–534.

Sorenson, R. C. *Adolescent sexuality in contemporary America.* New York: World, 1973.

Sorrells-Jones, J. A comparison of the effects of Leboyer delivery and modern "routine" childbirth in a randomized sample. Unpublished Ph.D. dissertation, University of Chicago, 1983.

Spark, R. F. A new approach to impotence. *Medical Aspects of Human Sexuality.* 1983, *17,* 228–244.

Spence, J. T., and Helmreich, R. L. *Masculinity and femininity.* Austin: University of Texas Press, 1978.

Spengler, A. Manifest sadomasochism of males: Results of an empirical study. *Archives of Sexual Behavior,* 1977, *6,* 441–456.

Spitz, C. J.; Gold, A. R.; and Adams, D. B. Cognitive and hormonal factors affecting coital frequency. *Archives of Sexual Behavior,* 1975, *4,* 249–263.

Srole, L., and Fischer, A. K. The midtown Manhattan longitudinal study vs. "The mental Paradise lost" doctrine. *Archives of General Psychiatry,* 1980, *37,* 209–221.

Staines, G. L., and Pleck, J. H. *The impact of work schedules on the family.* Ann Arbor: Institute for Social Research, University of Michigan Survey Research Center, 1983.

Starr, B. D., and Weiner, M. B. *The Starr-Weiner report on sex and sexuality in the later years.* New York: Stein & Day, 1981.

Stearns, C. L.; Winter, J. S. D.; and Faiman, C. Effects of coitus on gonadotropin, prolactin and sex steroid levels in man. *Journal of Clinical Endocrinology and Metabolism,* 1973, *37,* 687–691.

Stein, L., and Belluzzi, J. D. Brain endorphins: Possible role in reward and memory formation. *Federation Proceedings.* 1979, *38,* 2468–2472.

Steinman, D. L.; Wincze, J. P.; Sakheim, D. K.; Barlow, D. H.; and Mairssakalian, M. A comparison of male and female patterns of sexual arousal. *Archives of Sexual Behavior,* 1981, *10,* 529–549.

Stephan, W.; Berscheid, E.; and Walster, C. Sexual arousal and heterosexual perception. *Journal of Personality and Social Psychology,* 1977, *20,* 93–101.

Sterilizations off sharply in 1982; Drop due mostly to Vasectomy Decline. *Family Planning Perspectives,* 1984, *16,* 40–41.

Stern, D. *The first relationship: Infant and mother.* Cambridge, MA: Harvard University Press, 1977.

Stevens, V. C. Potential control of fertility in women by immunization with HCG. *Research in Reproduction,* May 1975, *7,* 1.

Stewart, A. J., and Rubin, Z. The power motive in dating couples. *Journal of Personality and Social Psychology,* 1976, *34,* 305–309.

Stock, W. E., and Geer, J. H. A study of fantasy-based sexual arousal in women. *Archives of Sexual Behavior,* 1982, *11,* 33–47.

Stoller, R. *Sex and gender.* New York: Science House, 1968.

————. *Perversion: The erotic form of hatred.* New York: Dell (Delta Books) 1975.

————. Sexual deviations. In F. A. Beach (ed.), *Human sexuality in four perspectives.* Baltimore: Johns Hopkins Press, 1977.

————. Tranvestism in women. *Archives of Sexual Behavior,* 1982, *2,* 99–115.

Storms, M. D. A theory of erotic orientation development. *Psychological Review,* 1981, *88,* 340–353.

Storms, M. D. Theories of sexual orientation. *Journal of Personality and Social Psychology,* 1980, *38,* 783–792.

Strasser, S. *Never done: A history of American housework.* New York: Pantheon, 1982.

Strickler, R. C.; Borth, R.; Cecutti, A.; Cookson, B. A.; Harper, J. A.; Potom, R.; Riffel, P.; Sarbara, V. J.; and Woolever, C. A. The role of estrogen replacement in the climacteric syndrome. *Psychological Medicine,* 1977, *7,* 631–639.

Stubblefield, P. G.; Monson, R. R.; Schoenba, S. C.; Wolfson, C. E.; Cookson, D. J.; and Ryan, K. J. Fertility after induced abortion: A prospective follow-up study. *Obstetrics and Gynecology,* 1984, *63,* 186–193.

Student Committee on Human Sexuality, Yale University. *The student guide to sex on campus.* New York: Signet, 1971.

Study finds no rise in atherosclerosis symptoms in men vasectomized an average of 15 years ago. *Family Planning Perspectives,* 1983, *15,* 30–31.

Sturrup, G. K. Castration: The total treatment. In H. L. P. Resnick and M. E. Wolfgang (eds.), *Treatment of the sex offender.* Boston: Little, Brown, 1972.

Suggs, R. C., and Marshall, D. S. Anthropological perspectives on human sexual behavior. In R. C. Marshall and D. S. Suggs (eds.), *Human Sexual Behavior.* Englewood Cliffs, NJ: Prentice-Hall, 1971.

Sundstrom, K. Young people's sexual habits in today's Swedish society. *Current Sweden,* July 1976, *125,* 1–8.

Symposium on homosexuality and the ethics of behavioral intervention. *Journal of Homosexuality,* 1977, *2,* 195–259.

Symposium on homosexual couples, *Journal of Homosexuality,* Winter 1982, 8, (#2).

Szasz, T. S. *Sex by prescription.* New York: Penguin, 1980.

Tannahill, R. *Sex in history.* New York: Stein & Day, 1980.

Tanner, J. M. *Growth at adolescence,* Second ed. Oxford: Blackwell Scientific Publications, 1962.

Tavris, C., and Sadd, S. *The Redbook report on female sexuality.* New York: Delacorte, 1975.

Taylor, D. A.; Gould, R. K.; and Brounstein, P. J. Effects of personalistic self-disclosure. *Personality and Social Psychology Bulletin,* 1981, *7,* 487–492.

Taylor, G. R. *Sex in history.* New York: Vanguard Press, 1954 (paperbound ed., New York: Vanguard, 1970).

———. *The angel-makers.* London: Heinemann, 1958.

Teevan, J. G., Jr. Reference groups and premarital sexual behavior. *Journal of Marriage and the Family,* 1972, *34,* 283–291.

Tennent, B. J.; Smith, E. R.; and Davidson, J. M. The effects of estrogen and progesterone on female rat proceptive behavior. *Hormones and Behavior,* 1980, *14,* 65–75.

Terlecky, N. E., and Levy, D. M. *U.S. Economic Growth Outlook, 1980–2000.* Center for Socio-Economic Analysis, Washington, D.C., 1981.

Thoman, E. B.; Liederman, P. H.; and Olson, J. P. Neonate-mother interaction during breast feeding. *Developmental Psychology,* 1972, *6,* 110–118.

Thompson, A. P. Extramarital sex: A review of the research literature. *Journal of Sex Research,* 1983, *19,* 1–22.

Thompson, C. *On women.* New York: Mentor, 1964.

Thompson, L., and Spanier, G. B. Influence of parents, peers and partners on the contraceptive use of college men and women. *Journal of Marriage and Family,* 1978, *40,* 481–492.

Thompson, S. K. Gender labels and early sex role development. *Child Development,* 1975, *46,* 339–347.

———, and Bentler, P. M. The priority of cues in sex discrimination by children and adults. *Developmental Psychology,* 1971, *5,* 181–185.

———. A developmental study of gender constancy and parent preference. *Archives of Sexual Behavior,* 1973, *2,* 379–385.

Thorne, B., and Luria, Z. Sexuality and gender in children's daily worlds. Paper read at American Sociological Assn. August 1985. Washington, D.C.

Thorton, A.; Feedman, D. S.; and Camburn, D. Obtaining respondent cooperation in family panel studies. *Sociological Methods and Research,* 1982, *11,* 35–45.

Tietze, C. *Induced Abortion,* First ed. New York: Population Council, 1973.

———. The "problem" of repeat abortions. *Family Planning Perspectives,* 1974, *6,* 148–150.

———. *Induced Abortion: 1979,* Third ed. New York: Population Council, 1979.

———. *Induced Abortion: A World Review, 1981,* Fourth ed, New York: Population Council, 1981.

———. Legal abortions in the United States: Rates and ratios by race and age, 1972–1974. *Family Planning Perspectives,* 1977, *9,* 12–15.

———, and Bongaarts, J. Repeat abortions in the United States: New insights. *Studies in Family Planning,* 1982, *13,* 373–379.

———, and Jain, A. K. The mathematics of repeat abortion: Explaining the increase. *Studies in Family Planning,* December 1978, *9,* 294–299.

Tittle, C. K. *Careers and family: Sex roles and adolescent life plans.* Beverly Hills, CA: Sage, 1981.

Trilling, L. The Kinsey report. *Partisan Review,* April 1948. Reprinted in Trilling, L. *The Liberal Imagination.* New York: Viking, 1950 (paperbound ed., New York: Anchor, 1953).

Tripp, C. A. *The homosexual matrix.* New York: McGraw-Hill, 1975 (paperbound ed., New York: New American Library, 1976).

Trivers, R. E. Parental investment and sexual selection. In B. Campbell (ed.), *Sexual selection and the descent of man.* Chicago: Aldine, 1972.

Troiden, R. R., and Goods, E. Variables related to the acquisition of a gay identity. *Journal of Homosexuality,* 1980, *5,* 383–392.

Trost, J. Married and unmarried cohabitation: The case of Sweden, with some comparisons. *Journal of Marriage and the Family,* 1975, *3,* 677–682.

Tsai, M., and Wagner, N. N. Therapy groups for women sexually molested as children. *Archives of Sexual Behavior,* 1978, *7,* 417–427.

Turkington, C. Parents found to ignore sex stereotypes. *APA Monitor,* April 1984, 12.

Turner, C. B., and Dairty, W. A. Black organizations and population policy. Paper presented at the annual meeting of the American Public Health Association, Chicago, November 15–20, 1975. Cited in *Family Planning Perspectives,* 1976, *8,* 27.

Udry, J. R. *The social context of marriage.* Philadelphia: Lippincott, 1974.

———. Changes in the frequency of marital intercourse from panel data. *Archives of Sexual Behavior,* 1980, *9,* 319–325.

Udry, J. R.; Bauman, K. E.; and Morris, N. M. Changes in premarital coital experience of recent decade-of-birth cohorts of urban American women. *Journal of Marriage and the Family,* 1975, *37,* 783–787.

Udry, J. R., and Morris, N. M. Effect of contraceptive pills on the distribution of sexual activity in the menstrual cycle. *Nature,* 1970, *227,* 502–503.

———. The distribution of events in the human menstrual cycle. *Journal of Reproduction and Fertility,* 1977, *51,* 419–425.

———. Relative contribution of male and female age to the frequency of marital intercourse. *Social Biology,* 1978, *25,* 128–134.

Uhlenberg, P. Cohort variations in family life cycle experiences of U.S. females. *Journal of Marriage and the Family,* 1974, *36,* 284–292.

Ullerstam, L. *The erotic minorities: A sexual bill of rights.* New York: Grove, 1966.

United Nations Commission. Study on traffic in persons and prostitution. ST/SOA/5D/8, 1959. (Cited in Geis, G., 1972.)

United Nations Report, *The status of women in Sweden,* 1968.

United States House of Representatives, Select Committee on Aging. *Women in midlife: Security and fulfillment, Vol. 1.* Washington, D.C.: Government Printing Office, 1979.

United States Senate, 94th Congress. 1976. School-age Mother and Child Health Act, 1975. Hearings before the Subcommittee on Labor and Public Welfare: November 4, 1975.

Updike, J. *Rabbit is rich,* New York: Knopf, 1981.

Up to 16 weeks of gestation, abortions performed as safely in nonhospital facilities as in hospitals. *Family Planning Perspectives,* 1981, *13,* 181–182.

Urinary tract infections in women. *Harvard Medical School Health Letter,* December 1982.

Using local anesthesia for first-trimester abortion cuts mortality sharply. *Family Planning Perspectives,* 1982, *14,* 332–333.

Using an IUD for five or more years may lead to an increased risk of severe pelvic infection. *Family Planning Perspectives,* 1984, *16,* 93–94.

Utian, W. H. Estrogen replacement in the menopause. *Obstetric and Gynecology Annual,* 1979, *8,* 369–391.

Van Buren, A. *The best of dear abby.* New York: Andrews and McNeel, 1981.

Vance, E. B., and **Wagner, N. N.** Written description of orgasm: A study of sex differences. *Archives of Sexual Behavior,* 1976, *5,* 87–98.

Vance, C. S. (Ed.). Pleasure and danger: Exploring female sexuality. London: Routledge and Kegan Paul, 1985.

Van Lawick-Goodall, J. Behavior of free-living chimpanzees of the Gombe stream area. *Animal Behavior Monographs,* 1968, #3.

Van Wyk, P. H. A critique of Dörner's analysis of hormonal data from bisexual males. *Journal of Sex Research,* 1984, *20,* 412–414.

Varied causes of impotence. *Harvard Medical School Health Letter,* November 1983, 1ff.

Veitch, R., and **Griffitt, W.** Good news, bad news: Affective and interpersonal effects. *Journal of Applied Social Psychology,* 1976, *6,* 69–75.

Vener, A. M., and **Stewart, C. S.** Adolescent sexual behavior in middle America revisited: 1970–1973. *Journal of Marriage and the Family,* 1974, *36,* 728–735.

Venereal transmission of uterine disease. *Medical Aspects of Human Sexuality,* November 1982, 168ff.

Verba, S., with J. DiNunzio and C. Spalding. *Unwanted attention.* Unpublished paper, Faculty of Arts and Sciences, Harvard University, 1982.

Veroff, J.; Douvan, E.; and **Kulka, R. A.** *The inner American: A self-portrait from 1957 to 1976.* New York: Basic Books, 1981.

———, and **Feld, S. C.** *Marriage and work in America.* New York: Van Nostrand Reinhold, 1970.

Vessey, M.; Wiggins, P.; Doll, R.; Petro, R.; Johnson, B. A long-term follow-up study of women using different methods of contraception: An interim report. *Journal of Biosocial Science,* 1976, *8,* 373–427.

Village Voice survey. The "Scenes" survey of sexual semantics. *Village Voice,* New York: July 14 and July 21, 1976. (In J. H. Gagnon (ed.), *Human Sexuality in Today's World.* Boston: Little, Brown, 1977.)

Vorenberg, E., and **Vorenberg, J.** The biggest pimp of all. *Atlantic Monthly,* January 1977, 27–38.

Waber, D. P. Sex differences in cognition: A function of maturation rate? *Science,* 1976, *192,* 572–574.

———. Sex differences in mental abilities, hemispheric lateralization, and rate of physical growth at adolescence. *Developmental Psychology,* 1977, *13,* 29–38.

Wachtel, S. S. H-Y antigen and the genetics of sex determination. *Science,* 1977, *198,* 797–799.

———; **Koo, G. C.; Breg, W. R.; Thaler, H. T.; Dillard, G. M.; Rosenthal, I. W.; Dosik, H.; Gerald, P. S.; Saenger, P.; New, M.; Lieber, E.;** and **Miller, O. J.** Serologic detection of a Y-linked gene in XX males and XX true hermaphrodites. *New England Journal of Medicine,* 1976, *295,* 750–751.

Walker, M. J., and **Brodsky, S. L. (Eds.).** *Sexual assault.* Lexington, MA: D.C. Heath, 1976.

Waller, W. The rating and dating complex. *American Sociological Review,* 1937, *2,* 727–734.

Walsh, P. C.; Madden, J. D.; Harrod, M. J.; Goldstein, J. L.; MacDonald, P. C.; and **Wilson, J. D.** Familial incomplete male pseudohermaphroditism, type 2: Decreased dihydrotestosterone formation in pseudovaginal perineoscrotal hypospadias. *New England Journal of Medicine,* 1974, *290,* 944–949.

Walster, E. Passionate love. In B. I. Murstein (ed.), *Theories of attraction and love.* New York: Springer, 1971.

———; **Aronson, V.; Abrahams, D.;** and **Rottmann, L.** Importance of physical attractiveness in dating behavior. *Journal of Personality and Social Psychology,* 1966, *4,* 508–516.

———; **Walster, G. W.;** and **Berscheid, E.** *Equity: Theory and research.* Boston: Allyn and Bacon, 1978.

Ward, I. L.; Crowley, W. R.; and **Zemlan, F. P.** Monaminergic mediation of female sexual behavior. *Journal of Comparative and Physiological Psychology,* 1975, *88,* 53–61.

Waterman, C. K., and **Chiarezzi, E. J.** The role of orgasm in male and female sexual enjoyment. *Journal of Sex Research.* 1982, *18,* 146–159.

Waters, E. The reliability and stability of individual differences in infant-mother attachment. *Child Development,* 1978, *49,* 483–494.

———; **Wippman, J.;** and **Sroufe, L.** Attachment, positive affect, and competence in the peer group: Two studies in construct validation. *Child Development,* 1979, *50,* 821–829.

Waxenberg, S. E.; Drellich, M. G.; and **Sutherland, A. M.** The role of hormones in human behavior. I. Changes in female sexuality after adrenalectomy. *Journal of Endocrinology,* 1959, *19,* 193–202.

Weinberg, M. S. (Ed.). *Sex research.* New York: Oxford University Press, 1976.

Weinberg, M. S., and **Williams, C. J.** *Male homosexuals.* New York: Oxford University Press, 1974.

Weinberg, T., and **Leir Kamel, G. W. (Eds.).** *S and M: Studies in sadomasochism.* Buffalo, NY: Prometheus Books, 1983.

Weis, D. L. Affective reactions of women and their initial experience of coitus. *Journal of Sex Research,* 1983, *19,* 209–237.

Weis, K., and **Borges, S. S.** Victimology and rape: The case of the legitimate victim. *Issues in Criminology,* 1973, *8,* 71–115.

Weisz, J. Critical periods of CNS masculinization in relation to testicular androgen secretion: The critical period. MIT workshop on sexual differentiation of the brain, 1978, Cambridge, MA.

Weitzman, L. J. *The marriage contract: A guide to living with lovers and spouses.* New York: Free Press, 1981.

———, and **Rizzo, D.** Images of males and females in elementary school textbooks in five subject areas. In E. H. Weiner (ed.), *Sex* *role stereotyping in the schools*, Washington, D.C.: National Education Association, 1980.

West, D. J. *Homosexuality*. Chicago: Aldine, 1967.

Westoff, C. F. Coital frequency and contraception. *Family Planning Perspectives*, 1974, *6*, 136–141.

Westoff, C. F. Marriage and fertility in the developed countries. *Scientific American*, 1978, *239*, 51–57.

————, and Bumpass, L. The revolution in birth control practices in U.S. Roman Catholics. *Science*, 1973, *179*, 41–44.

————; DeLung, J. S.; Goldman, N.; and Forrest, J. D. Abortions preventable by contraceptive practice. *Family Planning Perspectives*, 1981, *13*, 218–223.

————, and Jones, E. F. The secularization of U.S. Catholic birth control practices. *Family Planning Perspectives*, 1977, *9*, 203–207.

Whalen, R. E. Sexual motivation. *Psychological Review*, 1966, *73*, 151–163.

————. Sexual differentiation: Models, methods, and mechanisms. In R. C. Friedman, R. M. Richart, and R. Van de Wiele (eds.), *Sex Differences in Behavior*. New York: Wiley, 1974.

Whitam, F. L. The homosexual role: A reconsideration. *Journal of Sex Research*, 1977, *13*, 1–11.

————. The prehomosexual male child in three societies: The United States, Guatemala, Brazil. *Archives of Sexual Behavior*, 1980, *9*, 87–99.

————, and Zeut, M. A cross-cultural assessment of early cross-gender behavior and familial factors in male homosexuality. *Archives of Sexual Behavior*. 1984, *13*, 427–439.

White, E. *A boy's own story*, New York: Dutton, New American Library, 1982.

White, G. L. Physical attractiveness and courtship progress. *Journal of Personality and Social Psychology*, 1980, *39*, 660–668.

————. A model of romantic jealousy. *Motivation and Education*, 1981, *5*, 295–310(a).

————. Some correlates of romantic jealousy. *Journal of Personality*, 1981, *49*, 129–146(b).

White, S. E., and Reamy, K. Sexuality and pregnancy: A review. *Archives of Sexual Behavior*, 1982, *5*, 429–444.

Whitehead, H. The bow and the burden strap: A new look at institutionalized homosexuality in native North America. In S. Ort-

ner and H. Whitehead, *Sexual Meanings*. New York: Cambridge University Press, 1981.

————. The sexual substance symbolism of New Guinea. Paper presented at the Conference "Feminism and Kinship theory," Bellagio, Italy, August 1–6, 1982.

Whiting, B., and Edwards, C. P. A cross-cultural analysis of sex differences in the behavior of children aged three to eleven. *Journal of Social Psychology*, 1973, *91*, 171–188.

Whitley, M. P., and Poulsey, S. B. Assertiveness and sexual satisfaction in employed professional women. *Journal of Marriage and the Family*, 1975, *37*, 573–581.

Wickler, W. *Sexual code: Social behavior of animals and men*. New York: Doubleday, 1972.

Williams, J. E.; Bennett, S. M.; and Best, D. C. Awareness and expression of sex stereotypes in young children. *Developmental Psychology*, 1975, *11*, 635–642.

Williams, K.; Green, R.; and Goodman, M. Patterns of sexual identity development: A preliminary report on the "tomboy." *Research in Communities and Mental Health*, 1979, *1*, 103–123.

Wilson, E. O. *Sociobiology: The new synthesis*. Cambridge, MA: Harvard University Press, 1975.

Wilson, J.; George, F. W.; and Griffin, J. E. The hormonal control of sexual development. *Science*, 1981, *211*, 1278–1284.

Wilson, J. D. Sex hormones and sexual behavior. *New England Journal of Medicine*, 1979, *300*, 1269–1270.

Wilson, J. D.; Harrod, M. J.; and Goldstein, J. L. Familial incomplete male pseudohermaphroditism, type 1: Evidence for androgen resistance and variable clinical manifestations in a family with the Reifenstein syndrome. *New England Journal of Medicine*, 1974, *290*, 1097–1103.

Wilson, W. C. The distribution of selected sexual attitudes and behaviors among the adult population of the United States. *Journal of Sex Research*, 1975, *11*, 46–64.

Wincze, J. P.; Hoon, E. F.; and Hoon, P. W. A comparison of physiological responsivity of normal and sexually dysfunctional women during exposure to erotic stimuli. *Journal of Psychosomatic Research*, 1976, *20*, 44–50.

————; Venditti, E.; Barlow, D.; and Mavessakalian, M. The effects of a subjective

monitoring task in physiological measurement of genital response to erotic stimulation. *Archives of Sexual Behavior*, 1980, *9*, 533–545.

Winick, C., and Kinsie, P. M. *The lively commerce: Prostitution in the United States*. Chicago: Quadrangle, 1971.

Witkin, H. A. Sex after mastectomy. *Medical Aspects of Human Sexuality*, February 1982, 50ff.

Witkin, H. A.; Mednick, S. A.; Schulsinger, F.; Bakkestrom, E.; Christiansen, K. O.; Goodenough, D. R.; Hirschhorn, K.; Lundsteen, C.; Owen, D. R.; Phillip, J.; Rubin, D. B.; and Storking, M. Criminality in XYY and XXY Men. *Science*, 1976, *193*, 547–555.

Wolchik, S. A.; Beggs, V. E.; Wincze, J. P.; Sakheim, D. K.; Barlow, D. H.; and Mavissakalian, M. The effect of emotional arousal in men. *Journal of Abnormal Psychology*, 1980, *89*, 595–598.

Wolfe, J., and Baker, V. Characteristics of imprisoned rapists and circumstances of the rape. In E. G. Warner (ed.), *Rape and sexual assault*. Germantown, MD: Aspen Systems Co., 1980.

Wolfe, L. Playing around: Women and extramarital sex. New York: New American Library, 1975.

Wolfenden, J. *Report of the Committee on homosexual offenses and prostitution*. London: Her Majesty's Stationery Office, 1957, New York: Stein and Day, 1963.

Wollheim, Richard, *Sigmund Freud*, New York: Viking, 1971 (Modern Masters Series).

Wolpe, J. *Psychotherapy by reciprocal inhibition*. Stanford, CA: Stanford University Press, 1958.

————. *The practice of behavior therapy*. New York: Pergamon, 1969.

Women Endorsing Decriminalization of Prostitution. A nonvictim crime? *Issues in Criminology*, 1973, *8*, 137–162.

Women on Words and Images. *Channeling children*. P.O. Box 2163, Princeton, NJ, 1975.

Women on Words and Images. *Dick and Jane as victims*, Revised ed. P.O. Box 2163, Princeton, NJ, 1976.

Women who use the barrier methods are less likely to be hospitalized for PID. *Family Planning Perspectives*, 1982, *14*, 331–332.

World Health Organization Task Force on

Psychosocial Research in Family Planning, Hormonal contraception for men: Acceptability and effects on sexuality. *Studies in Family Planning*, 1982, *13*, 328–342.

Wright, J.; Perreault, R.; and Matheirn, M. The treatment of sexual dysfunction: A review. *Archives of General Psychiatry*, 1977, *34*, 881–890.

Yalom, I. D.; Green, R.; and Fisk, N. Prenatal exposure to female hormones. *Archives of General Psychiatry*, 1973, *28*, 554–561.

Young, W. C.; Goy, R. W.; and Phoenix, C. H. Hormones and sexual behavior. *Science*, 1964, *143*, 212–217.

Zeiss, K. A.; Christensen, A.; and Levine, A. G. Treatment for premature ejaculation through male-only groups. *Journal of Sex and Marital Therapy*, 1978, *4*, 139–143.

Zellman, G. L., and Goodchild, J. O. Becoming sexual in adolescence. In E. R. Allgeier and N. B. McCormick (eds.), *Changing boundaries: Gender roles and sexual behavior*. Palo Alto: Mayfield, 1983.

Zelnik, M., and Kantner, J. F. Sexual and contraceptive experience of young unmarried women in the United States, 1976 and 1971. *Family Planning Perspectives*, 1977, *9*, 55–71.

————. First pregnancies to women aged 15–19: 1976 and 1971. *Family Planning Perspectives*, 1978, *10*, 11–20. (a)

————. Contraceptive patterns and premarital pregnancy among women aged 15–19 in 1976. *Family Planning Perspectives*, 1978, *10*, 135–142. (b)

————. Reasons for nonuse of contraception by sexually active women aged 15–19. *Family Planning Perspectives*, 1979, *11*, 289–296.

————. Sexual activity, contraceptive use and pregnancy among metropolitan-area teenagers: 1971–1979. *Family Planning Perspectives*, 1980, *12*, 230–237.

Zelnik, M., and Kim, Y. J. Sex education and its association with teenage sexual activity, pregnancy, and contraceptive use. *Family Planning Perspectives*, 1982, *14*, 117–119; 123–126.

Ziegler, F. J.; Rodgers, D. A.; and Kriegsman, S. A. Effects of vasectomy on psychological functioning. *Psychosomatic Medicine*, 1966, *28*, 50–63.

Ziegler, F. J.; Rodgers, D. A.; and Prentiss, R. J. Psychosocial response to vasectomy. *Archives of General Psychiatry*, 1969, *21*, 46–54.

Zilbergeld, B. Group treatment. *Journal of Sex Marital Therapy*, 1975, *1*, 204–214.

————. *Male sexuality: A guide to sexual fulfillment*. Boston: Little, Brown, 1978.

————, and Ellison, C. R. Desire discrepancies and arousal problems in sex therapy. In S. R. Leiblum and L. A. Pervin, *Principles and practice of sex therapy*. New York: Guilford, 1980.

————, and Evans, M. The inadequacy of Masters and Johnson. *Psychology Today*, 1980, *14*, 29–43.

Zillmann, D. *Hostility and aggression*. Hillsdale, NJ: Erlbaum, 1979.

————; Bryant, J.; and Carveth, R. A. The effect of erotica featuring sadomasochism and bestiality on motivated intermale aggression. *Personality and Social Psychology Bulletin*, 1981, *7* 153–159.

————, and Sapolsky, B. S. What mediated the effect of mild erotica on annoyance and hostile behavior in males? *Journal of Personality and Social Psychology*, 1977, *35*, 587–596.

Zinsser, Hans. *Rats, lice, and history*. New York: Bantam, 1971. (First pub. Boston: Little, Brown, 1935.)

Zubin, J., and Money, J. *Contemporary sexual behavior*. Baltimore: John Hopkins Press, 1973.

Zuger, B. Feminine-like behavior in boys present from early childhood. *Journal of Pediatrics*, 1966, *69*, 1098–1107.

————. The role of familial factors in persistent effeminate behavior in boys. *American Journal of Psychiatry*, 1970, *126*, 151–154.

Zumpe, D., and Michael, R. P. The clutching reaction and orgasm in the female rhesus monkey (*Macaca Mulatta*). *Journal of Endocrinology*, 1968, *40*, 117–123.

Zussman, J. V.; Zussman, P. P.; and Dalton, K. Post-pubertal effects of prenatal administration of progesterone. Paper presented at the meeting of the Society for Research in Child Development, Denver, CO, April 1975.

Photo Credits

CHAPTER 9   OPENER: KENNETH NOLAND, "BEGINNING," (1958). 90 × 96" SYNTHETIC POLYMER ON CANVAS. HIRSHORN MUSEUM AND SCULPTURE GARDEN SMITHSONIAN INSTITUTION.

Page 257: David Scharf/Peter Arnold. Page 258: R. Yanagimachi/Biological Photo Service. Page 261: Omikron/Photo Researchers. Page 272: Hella Hammid/Photo Researchers. Page 273: Suzanne Arms/Jeroboam. Page 274: Mariette Pathy Allen/Peter Arnold. Page 276: Suzanne Wu/Jeroboam. Page 278: Nancy Durrell McKenna/Photo Researchers.

CHAPTER 10   OPENER: M.C. ESCHER, "BOND OF UNION." © M.C. ESCHER HEIRS c/o CORDON ART—BAARN—HOLLAND.

Page 291: Paolo Koch/Photo Researchers. Page 318: Martin A. Levick/Black Star. Page 331: Patricia Agre/Photo Researchers.

CHAPTER 11   OPENER: PABLO PICASSO. "FIRST STEPS," (1943). 51¼ × 30¼" OIL ON CANVAS. YALE UNIVERSITY ART GALLERY. GIFT OF STEPHEN CLARK.

Page 341: Bettmann Archive. Page 343: Erika Stone/Peter Arnold. Page 345, 347 and 350: Hella Hammid/Photo Researchers. Page 352: Courtesy of Harlow Primate Laboratory, University of Wisconsin. Page 353: A. Harcourt/Anthro Photo. Page 355: Hella Hammid/Photo Researchers.

CHAPTER 12   OPENER: OSKAR SCHLEMMER. "BAUHAUS STAIRWAY," (1932). 65⅞ × 45" OIL ON CANVAS. COLLECTION, MUSEUM OF MODERN ART. GIFT OF PHILIP JOHNSON.

Page 374: Joseph Szabo/Photo Researchers. Page 375: News World/FPG. Page 381: Hella Hammid/Photo Researchers. Page 388: Joseph Szabo/Photo Researchers. Page 399: Nancy J. Pierce/Photo Researchers.

CHAPTER 13   OPENER: MAN RAY. "RAYOGRAPH," (1922). 8¹⁵⁄₁₆ × 6¾", GELATIN-SILVER PRINT. COLLECTION, MUSEUM OF MODERN ART, NEW YORK.

Page 404: Chester Higgins, Jr./Photo Researchers. Page 405: Suzanne Szasz/Photo Researchers. Page 407: Chester Higgins, Jr./Photo Researchers. Fig. 13.1: Sam Presser/Black Star. Fig. 13.2: D. Carleton Gajdusek. Page 416: Richard Laird/FPG. Page 417: Peter Vandermark/Stock Boston.

CHAPTER 13   OPENER: FERNAND LEGER. "TWO MEN," HIRSHORN MUSEUM & SCULPTURE GARDEN. SCALA/ART RESOURCE.

Page 434: Bettye Lane/Photo Researchers. Page 437: Metropolitan Museum of Art, Fletcher Fund, 1928. Page 441: Mariette Pathy Allen/Peter Arnold. Page 444: Bob Combs/Rapho-Photo Researchers. Page 445, 449, and 450: Bettye Lane/Photo Researchers. Page 452: Peter Keegan/FPG. Page 457: Rose Skytta/Jeroboam. Page 463: Bettye Lane/Photo Researchers.

CHAPTER 15   OPENER: LYNBOV SERGEIEVNA POPOVA. "ARCHETECTONIC PAINTING," (1917). 31½ × 38⅝" OIL ON CANVAS. COLLECTION, THE MUSEUM OF MODERN ART. PHILIP JOHNSON FUND.

Page 479: © 1976 Esaias Baitel/Photo Researchers. Page 480: Laurie Cameron/Jeroboam. Page 382: Art Stein/Photo Researchers. Page 487: David Cain/Photo Researchers.

CHAPTER 16   OPENER: VICTOR VASARELY. "GOTHA," FROM A PORTFOLIO OF 12 SERIGRAPHS PRINTED IN COLOR, (1959). 19¾ × 13³⁄₁₆". COLLECTION, THE MUSEUM OF MODERN ART, NEW YORK. TRANSFERRED FROM THE MUSEUM LIBRARY.

CHAPTER 17   OPENER: ROBERT DELAUNAY. "SIMULTANEOUS CONTRAST: SUN & MOON" 53" DIAMETER, OIL ON CANVAS. COLLECTION, THE MUSEUM OF MODERN ART, NEW YORK. MRS. SIMON GUGGENHEIM FUND.

Pages 542, 544, 548 and 549: Center for Disease Control, Atlanta. Page 552: Rick Browne/Picture Group. Page 555: Bettye Lane/Photo Researchers. Page 556: Center for Disease Control.

CHAPTER 18   OPENER: Odilon Redon. "The Accused," (1886). 21 × 14⅝" Charcoal, sheet. Collection, The Museum of Modern Art, New York. Acquired through the Little P. Bliss Bequest.

Page 568: Michael Hayman/Photo Researchers. Page 570: James H. Karales/Peter Arnold. Page 571: Bettye Lane/Photo Researchers. Page 574: Richard Falco/Photo Researchers. Page 586: Hella Hammid/Photo Researchers.

CHAPTER 19   OPENER: Pablo Picasso. "Weeping Woman" (1937). Collection Sir Roland Penrose, London. Bridgeman Art Library/Art Resource.

Page 600: S. Ragan/UPI/Bettmann News Photos. Page 607: Robert Goldstein/Photo Researchers.

CHAPTER 20   OPENER: Fernand Leger. "The City," (1919) 6'6¾" × 9'9¼". Oil on canvas. Philadelphia Museum of Art. A.E. Gallatin Collection.

Page 618: UPI/Bettmann News Photos. Page 619: Frobenius Institut. Page 625: Christa Armstrong/Photo Researchers. Page 630: Bernard Pierre Wolff/Photo Researchers.

Index